- Front Page
• Chapter Outline
with just titles of chapters
and sections
- Then full outline

3 copies

www.wadsworth.com

wadsworth.com is the World Wide Web site for Wadsworth and is your direct source to dozens of online resources.

At wadsworth.com you can find out about supplements, demonstration software, and student resources. You can also send email to many of our authors and preview new publications and exciting new technologies.

wadsworth.com
Changing the way the world learns®

Engineering Ethics: Concepts and Cases

Second Edition

With a new CD-ROM prepared by Donald Searing,
Taknosys Software Corporation

Engineering Ethics:
Concepts and Cases
Second Edition

Charles E. Harris, Jr.
Texas A&M University

Michael S. Pritchard
Western Michigan University

Michael J. Rabins
Texas A&M University

Wadsworth
Thomson Learning

Australia • Canada • Denmark • Japan • Mexico • New Zealand • Philippines
Puerto Rico • Singapore • South Africa • Spain • United Kingdom • United States

Philosophy Editor: Peter Adams
Assistant Editor: Kerri Abdinoor
Editorial Assistant: Mindy Newfarmer
Marketing Manager: Dave Garrison
Print Buyer: Stacey Weinberger
Permissions Editor: Robert Kauser

Production Service: Ruth Cottrell
Copy Editor: Lura Harrison
Cover Designer: William Reuter Design
Cover Image: © Corbis Digital Stock
Compositor: Ruth Cottrell Books
Printer/Binder: Webcom

Printed in Canada
5 6 03 02

For permission to use material from this text,
contact us by
  web: www.thomsonrights.com
  fax: 1-800-730-2215
  phone: 1-800-730-2214

 *This book is printed on
acid-free recycled paper.*

**For more information, contact
Wadsworth/Thomson Learning
10 Davis Drive
Belmont, California 94002
USA
www.wadsworth.com**

International Headquarters
Thomson Learning
290 Harbor Drive, 2nd Floor
Stamford, CT 06902-7477
USA

UK/Europe/Middle East
Thomson Learning
Berkshire House
168-173 High Holborn
London, WC1V 7AA,
United Kingdom

Asia
Thomson Learning
60 Albert Street #15-01
Albert Complex
Singapore 189969

Canada
Nelson/Thomson Learning
1120 Birchmount Road
Scarborough, Ontario M1K 5G4
Canada

Library of Congress Cataloging-in-Publication Data
Harris, Charles E.
    Engineering ethics: concepts and cases/ Charles E. Harris, Michael S. Pritchard,
  Michael J. Rabins.—2nd ed.
        p. cm.
    ISBN 0-534-53397-3
    1. Engineering ethics. 2. Engineering ethics—Case studies.
  I. Pritchard, Michael S. II. Rabins, Michael J. III. Title.
  TA157.H357 1999
  174'.962—DC21
                                                    99-32022

To:
Charles E. Harris, PE retired
R. William Eddy, the family engineer, retired
Herman Rabins

Our families, who put us on the right road, and our engineering students who continue to illuminate the way

And, finally, to all those engineers whose "good works" protect and enhance public safety, health, and welfare

Contents

Preface   xv

PART ONE   **CRITICAL APPROACHES**   **1**
Chapter 1   **Engineering Ethics: Making the Case**   **3**
  1.1   Introduction   7
  1.2   Role Morality   9
  1.3   What Is a Profession?   11
  1.4   Professional Ethics   13
  1.5   The NSPE Board of Ethical Review   16
  1.6   Engineering Ethics as Preventive Ethics   17
                  The Importance of Thinking Ahead   18
                  Education in Preventive Ethics   19
  1.7   Cases, Cases, Cases!   22
  1.8   Chapter Summary   26
                Cases to Consider   27

Chapter 2   **Framing the Problem**   **30**
  2.1   Introduction   31
  2.2   Common Morality   32
  2.3   Moral Justification   35
                  An Illustration: Research Involving Humans   35
                  Two Key Concepts: Universalizability and Reversibility 37
  2.4   Analyzing a Case   37
                  A Sample Case   38
  2.5   Factual Issues   41
                  Discerning Relevant Facts   44
                  Known and Unknown Facts   44
  2.6   Conceptual Issues   45
                  Defining Concepts   46
                  Applying Concepts   49
  2.7   General and Specific Moral Problems   52
  2.8   Chapter Summary   55
                Cases to Consider   57

Chapter 3   **Methods for Moral Problem Solving**   **59**
  3.1   Introduction   59
  3.2   Line-Drawing   60
  3.3   Conflicting Values: Creative Middle Way Solutions   64
                  Gilbane Gold   69
  3.4   Standpoints of the Judge and the Agent   72
  3.5   Chapter Summary   73
                Cases to Consider   73

Chapter 4	**Organizing Principles**	**75**
4.1	Introduction	75
4.2	Utilitarian Thinking	77
4.3	Three Utilitarian Approaches	78
	The Cost/Benefit Approach	79
	The Act Utilitarian Approach	81
	The Rule Utilitarian Approach	82
4.4	The Ethics of Respect for Persons	84
4.5	Three Respect for Persons Approaches	85
	The Golden Rule	85
	The Self-Defeating Criterion	88
	Rights	89
4.6	Convergence, Divergence, and Creative Middle Ways	93
4.7	Chapter Summary	94
	Cases to Consider	95
PART TWO	**GENERIC CONCERNS**	**97**
Chapter 5	**Responsible Engineers**	**99**
5.1	Introduction	99
5.2	Concepts of Responsibility	100
5.3	The Minimalist View	101
5.4	Reasonable Care	103
5.5	Good Works	104
5.6	Do Engineers Need Virtues?	107
5.7	Impediments to Responsibility	108
	Self-Interest	108
	Fear	109
	Self-Deception	109
	Ignorance	110
	Egocentric Tendencies	110
	Microscopic Vision	110
	Uncritical Acceptance of Authority	111
	Groupthink	112
5.8	Chapter Summary	113
	Cases to Consider	114
Chapter 6	**Honesty, Integrity, and Reliability**	**117**
6.1	Introduction	117
6.2	Ways of Misusing the Truth	119
	(1) Lying	119
	(2) Deliberate Deception	120
	(3) Withholding Information	120
	(4) Failing to Adequately Promote the Dissemination of Information	120
	(5) Failure to Seek Out the Truth	120
	(6) Revealing Confidential or Proprietary Information	121
	(7) Allowing One's Judgment to Be Corrupted	121
6.3	Why Is Dishonesty Wrong?	121

6.4	Honesty on Campus	123
6.5	Integrity in Engineering Research and Testing	125
6.6	Integrity in the Use of Intellectual Property	128
6.7	Integrity and Client-Professional Confidentiality	132
6.8	Integrity and Expert Testimony	134
6.9	Integrity and Failure to Inform the Public	135
6.10	Conflicts of Interest	137
	What Is a Conflict of Interest?	138
	Conflicts of Interest and Accepting Gifts	139
6.11	Chapter Summary	142
	Cases to Consider	143

Chapter 7 **Risk, Safety, and Liability in Engineering**   **145**
7.1	Introduction	146
7.2	The Codes and Engineering Practice Regarding Risk and Safety	147
7.3	Difficulties in Estimating Risk	148
	Detecting Failure Modes	148
	Are There "Normal Accidents"?	150
7.4	Normalizing Deviance	153
7.5	The Expert's Approach to Acceptable Risk: Identifying and Defining Acceptable Risk	154
	Identifying Risk	154
	Utilitarianism and Acceptable Risk	155
	Risk as Maximizing Benefit	156
7.6	The Layperson's Approach to Acceptable Risk	157
	Expert and Layperson	157
	Informed Consent and Justice	158
7.7	The Government Regulator's Approach to Risk	161
7.8	The Engineer's Liability for Risk	163
	The Standards of Tort Law	163
	Protecting Engineers from Liability	165
7.9	Becoming a Responsible Engineer Regarding Risk	166
7.10	Chapter Summary	168
	Cases to Consider	169

PART THREE **SPECIAL TOPICS**   **173**
Chapter 8 **Engineers as Employees**   **175**
8.1	Introduction	176
8.2	The Codes and Employer-Employee Relationships	176
8.3	The Changing Legal Status of Employee Rights	178
	The Public-Policy Exception	178
	Statutory Protection	179
8.4	The Manager-Engineer Relationship	180
	Differences in Perspective Between Managers and Engineers	180
	Two Empirical Studies	181

8.5	Paradigmatic Engineering and Management Decisions	183
	Functions of Engineers and Managers	183
	Paradigmatic and Nonparadigmatic Examples	185
8.6	The Challenger Case	188
8.7	Loyalty: Uncritical and Critical	191
8.8	Responsible Organizational Disobedience	194
	Disobedience by Contrary Action	194
	Disobedience by Nonparticipation	196
	Disobedience by Protest	197
8.9	Implementing Professional Employee Rights	199
8.10	Chapter Summary	202
	Cases to Consider	203
Chapter 9	**Engineers and the Environment**	**206**
9.1	Introduction	207
9.2	Engineering Codes and the Environment	208
	Code References to the Environment	208
	Sustainable Development	209
9.3	Controversy over the Environment	210
	Two Important Distinctions	210
	Why the Reluctance to Be Concerned with the Environment?	212
	Searching for a Criterion for "Clean"	213
9.4	What Does the Law Say?	215
	Federal Laws on the Environment	215
	The Courts on the Environment	217
	So, How Clean Is Clean?	218
9.5	Balancing Wealth and Health: A Criterion for "Clean"	219
	A Degree-of-Harm Criterion	219
9.6	The Anthropocentric Approach to Environmental Ethics	221
	Animal Liberation and Engineering Ethics	222
	The Environmental Movement and Engineering Ethics	223
9.7	The Scope of Professional Engineering Obligations to the Environment	225
9.8	Two Modest Proposals	227
9.9	Chapter Summary	230
	Cases to Consider	231
Chapter 10	**International Engineering Professionalism**	**233**
10.1	Introduction	234
10.2	Problems in International Professionalism	235
	Values and Practices	236
	Economic Conditions	237
	Background Institutions	237
	Corruption	238
	Noncitizen Status	238
	Vulnerability	238

10.3	Problems in Interpreting and Applying the Codes	
	in the International Context	239
	The Welfare Requirement	240
	Bribery and Conflicts of Interest	241
	The Environment	242
	Nondiscrimination	242
	The Reputation of the Profession	243
	Promoting Knowledge and Avoiding Deception	243
10.4	Striking a Balance	244
10.5	Guidelines for Interpreting the Codes: (1) Human Rights	246
	The Internationalization of Rights	246
	Are Rights a Western Invention?	248
10.6	Guidelines for Interpreting the Codes:	
	(2) Avoiding Paternalism and Exploitation	250
10.7	Guidelines for Interpreting the Codes:	
	(3) Applying the Golden Rule	253
10.8	Bribery, Extortion, Grease Payments, and Gifts	256
	Bribery	256
	Extortion	257
	Grease Payments	258
	Gifts	259
10.9	Sweatshops in Asia	259
10.10	Chapter Summary	262
	Cases to Consider	263
Chapter 11	**Engineering Professionalism and Ethics:**	
	Issues Old and New	**265**
11.1	Introduction	265
11.2	Professional Engineering Societies:	
	Promoting Rather Than Enforcing Ethics	266
	Limitations in Enforcing Ethics	266
	Promoting Ethics	268
11.3	American Engineering Societies	270
11.4	State Registration Boards	272
11.5	The National Council of Examiners	
	for Engineering and Surveying (NCEES)	273
11.6	Universal Engineering Licensure	
	and the Industry Exemption	275
11.7	Gender and Minority Issues	277
11.8	Chapter Summary	278
	Cases to Consider	279
Cases		**281**
Bibliography		**359**
Videotapes for Use in Engineering Ethics		**367**
Index		**371**

List of Cases

Case 1   Aftermath of Chernobyl 287
Case 2   Air Bags 287
Case 3   Auditory Visual Tracker
           (AVIT)* 288
Case 4   Borrowed Tools 289
Case 5   Cadillac Chips 289
Case 6   Catalyst* 290
Case 7   Containers 294
Case 8   The Co-Op Student* 295
Case 9   Cost-Cutting 297
Case 10 The Deadline 297
Case 11 To Dissent or Not to Dissent?* 298
Case 12 Drinking in the Workplace 302
Case 13 Disaster Relief 303
Case 14 Employment Opportunity* 306
Case 15 An Excess? 309
Case 16 Failure 310
Case 17 Faulty Valves 310
Case 18 Fire Detectors 311
Case 19 Forced-Sex Accusation 312
Case 20 Ghost of an Executed
           Engineer 313
Case 21 Gilbane Gold 313
Case 22 Glass Ceiling 315
Case 23 Golfing 316
Case 24 Highway Safety
           Improvements 317
Case 25 Hydrolevel 318
Case 26 Innocent Comment? 321
Case 27 Inside Tool & Die 321
Case 28 Last Resort 322

Case 29 Mere "Technicality"? 323
Case 30 Microwaves 324
Case 31 Moral Beliefs in the
           Workplace 325
Case 32 Oil Spill? 325
Case 33 Parkville* 326
Case 34 Pinto 330
Case 35 Price Is Right? 331
Case 36 Promotion 332
Case 37 Pulverizer 332
Case 38 Recommendation for a Friend 333
Case 39 Renewable Energy 335
Case 40 Side-Saddle Gas Tanks 335
Case 41 "Smoking System" 339
Case 42 Sunnyvale 340
Case 43 Training Firefighters 342
Case 44 Trees 342
Case 45 TV Antenna 343
Case 46 "Underground" Project 344
Case 47 Unlicensed Engineer 345
Case 48 USAWAY 346
Case 49 Vacation 346
Case 50 Walkway Disaster 347
Case 51 Waste Disposal 348
Case 52 Whose Property? 349
Case 53 Why Won't They Read? 350
Case 54 Window Safety 351
Case 55 Wonderful Development? 352
Case 56 Working Overtime 353
Case 57 XYZ Hose Co. 354

* Includes an analysis of the case.

Preface to the Second Edition

We have been pleased with the favorable comments on the first edition of *Engineering Ethics: Concepts and Cases*. Nevertheless, the second edition incorporates extensive changes, and we believe it is substantially improved. The major changes are as follows:

• The book has a clearer overall organization, with three major sections: Critical Approaches, Generic Concerns, and Special Topics.

• Many new cases have been added, and the placement of cases has been changed so that they can more easily be located.

• We have introduced more cases that illustrate engineers acting in a professionally responsible manner, in contrast to cases that emphasize failure to act responsibly. This includes many examples of what we call "good works," going well beyond meeting what is minimally required as a matter of professional obligation. The three cases that introduce the first chapter, as well as several cases in the back of the book encourage students to reflect on this more positive side of professional ethics. The montage of photographs on this edition's cover symbolize the broad range of responsibilities engineers accept, many of which provide opportunities for "good works."

• The chapters on methods of analysis have been thoroughly revised with a view to improving the clarity of the basic concepts and methods for ethical problem solving. This material has also been moved forward in the book; chapters 4 through 6 of the first edition are now chapters 2 through 4 in this edition.

• There is an entirely new chapter on international engineering ethics.

• A CD-ROM now comes with the book. It contains the professional society codes and many additional cases and materials, including those resulting from National Science Foundation grants undertaken by the authors to develop cases in engineering ethics.

• The photographs at the beginning of each major section of the text are new, and we have revised a number of the figures from the first edition and added new ones for this edition. Given the visual orientation of most engineers, we believe these additions will enhance the book's appeal to students.

As we outline the main features of this edition, we will discuss these changes in more detail.

Organization

A number of students commented that the first edition did not provide them with a clear, overall organization of our engineering ethics courses. In response, we have divided the text into the three sections already noted. Also, we and other instructors have found that it is useful to present ethical problem-solving strategies early in the course so that students are encouraged to discuss issues and cases with more precision and insight from the outset rather than waiting until completing three chapters of the book. So, the first part of the book, Critical Approaches, emphasizes methods of analysis. The second part, Generic Concerns, emphasizes topics of concern that are likely to arise in virtually all aspects of engineering practice: basic concepts of responsibility, honesty, integrity, reliability, risk, and safety. The third part, Special Topics, focuses on more particular areas of concern, such as employer/employee relations, environmental concerns, engineering in an international context, and the role of professional engineering societies.

The Importance of Cases

Our experience with the first edition confirms our original belief that using cases should be central in the teaching of engineering ethics. Engineers love cases! Engineers, like most professionals, are interested in real-world problems—in the specific, the concrete, and the practical. Theory is important insofar as it is useful in problem solving, but the way to get the attention of engineering students is to focus on cases.

As in the first edition, chapters begin with cases that introduce main topics to be discussed, and we use short illustrative cases throughout the chapters as often as possible. In the first edition each chapter was followed by a case that is analyzed and a set of cases for students to analyze. In this edition some case analyses are presented within chapters, but all other cases are now in a special section at the back of the book. We found the first edition arrangement to be cumbersome. A case located at the end of one chapter might have been equally appropriate for use with another chapter. But the first edition did not provide a convenient way of locating cases easily and quickly. In this edition, at the end of each chapter we provide only a list of cases that might be appropriate for that chapter, but the cases themselves are presented by title in the cases section at the back of the book. Readers should feel free to select any cases that seem appropriate to them for a given chapter. Locating all cases in a single section should make it easier to survey different possibilities and find the desired cases.

The cases we include are intended to enable readers to apply concepts developed in the various chapters of the book. Some of the cases are what might be called the "media splash" issues that hit the front pages of newspapers, but most are more mundane—representing the kinds of circumstances engineers are most likely to encounter in their own careers. We do provide analyses of a few cases in the special section at the back of the book, but we leave most of the cases for readers to analyze.

An Analytical Frame of Mind

Exposing students to cases has another value: It helps them appreciate the importance and value of ethical methodology in thinking about ethical issues. The first task is to understand what is going on in a case. What are the known facts and what factual questions remain unanswered? Are there some future events whose outcome is important in evaluating the case? Are there concepts (for example, "safe" or "clean") that are especially important to define in trying to resolve the issues?

This book helps engineering students carry their natural analytical talents into a new area: moral deliberation. It shows them the importance of being analytical in addressing moral problems. It stresses the fact that many apparent moral disagreements are really disagreements about the facts or the meanings of crucial terms, and that the locus of moral disagreement can be discovered only by analysis.

Engineering ethics is a branch of practical ethics. So, it is a problem-solving discipline. Engineers are professional problem solvers, but they are usually not trained in moral problem solving. A textbook in engineering ethics should build on the problem-solving orientation of engineers and provide techniques that will help them carefully think through moral problems. At the same time, we emphasize that no technique can make moral problem solving easy or painless. The techniques show students that there can be method and structure in moral deliberation, but that there are no algorithms.

In the first edition we presented several methods for analyzing moral problems. In this edition we try to improve their clarity. For example, although in our teaching we emphasize line-drawing as one of the most useful methods, we have found that students often use it incorrectly. Our own conception of the proper use of the method has also evolved since writing the first edition. In Chapter 3 we attempt to give a clearer account; and we use the line-drawing method extensively in Chapter 6. We hope the tables help clarify the use of the method.

Engineering Codes of Ethics

We take engineering codes of ethics seriously. Professional codes represent the consensus of a professional community about the standards that should govern their conduct. This does not mean that the codes are complete or above criticism, or that there can be no questions as to how the codes apply in particular situations. Far from it! But the codes are a reasonable starting point for discussion of most issues in engineering ethics.

We attempt to meet a need for a code-oriented text (not a code-dominated text!) by discussing what the codes say about a topic and, when appropriate, suggesting where the codes may be inconsistent, unclear, or in need of modification. This provides a way for students to engage themselves realistically and productively with the engineering community as a whole.

The Responsible Engineer

One of the functions of a course in engineering ethics is to help students assume intelligently the mantle of professional responsibility. The best way to do this is to help them see that their actions as engineers will affect the lives and well-being of others; and the best way to do this is to focus on cases. This is another reason for the case orientation of the book.

In addition, however, we have written a whole chapter on professional responsibility. What does it mean to be a responsible engineer? Is it simply to avoid malpractice and perform one's assigned tasks, or is there a more positive component? What possibilities for "good works" are there? What are some of the impediments to professional responsibility, and how can they be overcome? We attempt to help students understand professional responsibility intellectually, but exposure to case studies helps them feel it on a more visceral level as well.

International Ethics

Increasing numbers of engineers are finding employment overseas or designing for an international market. The engineering profession is also becoming internationalized, with similar professional and ethical standards being adopted by countries other than those in North America and Western Europe. For several semesters our Texas A&M course has included a section on international ethics. We have included some of this material in a new chapter. We are anxious to hear the reactions of instructors and students to this chapter.

The CD-ROM

The addition of a CD-ROM has enabled us to increase vastly the number of cases in the text and to incorporate some useful software. A few of the cases have pictures and films and even animation. We believe this addition will increase the usefulness and enjoyment of the text for both instructors and students.

The CD-ROM is organized into four sections: Cases, Codes, Links, and Software. There are more than 200 cases on the CD-ROM, originating from National Science Foundation sponsored projects, the Board of Ethical Review of the National Society of Professional Engineers, and the experiences of many engineers. The cases can be used as practice or extra exercises for students, as well as a source for reports and projects. The Codes section contains seven codes of ethics from engineering societies. The Links section contains links to some of the major on-line ethics sites. These sites provide additional cases, methodologies, discussion groups, and news that should be useful to readers.

The CD-ROM contains two software packages. Ethos System from Taknosys Software provides a framework for ethical decision making. This software, developed by Donald Searing, leads the reader through a case analysis, utilizing the ideas and concepts presented in the text. The second software system, developed by John Dilworth, allows the reader to interact while reading through a set of cases developed in one of Michael Pritchard's NSF projects.

The CD-ROM requires Windows 95 or higher and an Internet browser. Navigating the CD is as easy as navigating a website. The insert on the packet with the CD has further instructions, including installation instructions.

Use of the Text

This text is suitable for a full semester course in engineering ethics. In our courses we are able to cover all the chapters as well as devote several sessions to videotapes and/or outside speakers. For shorter courses in the quarter system, we recommend using the first five chapters, and selecting from the remaining six.

Ethics and Morality

Readers may notice, both in the text and in this preface, that we move easily back and forth in our use of words like *ethics* and *morality*. This may seem confusing. However, neither textbooks nor ordinary language show any clear, consistent differences in meaning between these terms. In this book we follow the common practice of treating them as roughly synonymous.

Acknowledgments

Just as with the first edition, our students have been a continual source of encouragement in writing this edition. Their responses have helped us to know when the ideas we have been developing are plausible and clearly presented and when they need further work. They still tell us that the subject of engineering ethics is important and that a course in it is long overdue. Our students should not, however, be held responsible for anything we say in this book.

For help in preparing the second edition we want especially to thank Peter Adams, Kerri Abdinoor, and Jerry Holloway of Wadsworth. We appreciate Lura Harrison's helpful editing and Ruth Cottrell's assistance with production. We owe special thanks to Mark Holtzapple, Lee Lowery, Linda Radzik, and Donald Searing for their many helpful suggestions while teaching our class with us at Texas A&M University. Thanks also to the reviewers for the second edition: Ronald Hirschbein, California State University, Chico; Finley R. Shapiro, Ph.D., P.E.; P. Aarne Vesilind, Duke University; and Laurie Anne Whitt, Michigan Technological University. Others who sent us many helpful and encouraging suggestions include Rosana Martinez-Cruzado of the University of Puerto Rico at Mayaguez, Moshe Kam of Drexel University, Kevin Passino of Ohio State University, John Reizes of the Sydney Institute of Technology, Wade Robison of the Rochester Institute of Technology, and Joseph Wujek of the University of California at Berkeley. Special thanks go to Donald Searing, President of Taknosys Software, for preparing the CD-ROM for this edition, and to John Dilworth of Western Michigan University for allowing us to use his software program in the CD-ROM. Once again we thank Joan Rabins for her fine work in preparing the index.

We repeat our thanks to those who helped us with the first edition. Most especially we thank the readers of our manuscript: Michael Davis of the Illinois Institute of Technology; P. Aarne Vesilind of Duke University; Donald Gotterbarn of East Tennessee State University; L. S. Fletcher of Texas A&M; and Kevin Passino of Ohio State. Jimmy Smith, Penny Vann, and Dave Dorchester, all associated with the Murdough Center for Engineering Professionalism and Ethics, have encouraged us since we first entered the field of engineering ethics. W. Gale Cutler, James A. Jaksa, and David Zacker were early sources of encouragement, and of cases in engineering ethics. Rachelle Hollander at the National Science Foundation has been a constant source of encouragement and support. In fact, she is responsible for initially bringing the three of us together. Engineering faculty on many campuses have encouraged our work, as did Ken King and Tammy Goldfeld at Wadsworth when we wrote our first edition.

Part One

Critical Approaches

With permission of St. Peter's Lutheran Church

1 *Engineering Ethics: Making the Case*
2 *Framing the Problem*
3 *Methods for Moral Problem Solving*
4 *Organizing Principles*

Chapter 1

Engineering Ethics: Making the Case

This book focuses on the ethical dimensions of engineering practice. We begin with three widely discussed cases that illustrate how ethics can come into play in engineering practice.

The Citicorp Building

William LeMessurier was understandably proud of his structural design of the 1977 Citicorp building in downtown Manhattan. He had resolved a perplexing problem in a very innovative way. A church had property rights to a corner of the block on which the 59-story building was to be constructed. LeMessurier proposed constructing the building *over* the church, with four supporting columns located at the center of each side of the building rather than in the four corners. The first floor began the equivalent of 9 stories above ground, thus allowing ample space for the church. LeMessurier used a diagonal bracing design that transferred weight to the columns, and he added a tuned mass damper with a 400-ton concrete block floating on oil bearings to reduce wind sway.

In June 1978, LeMessurier received a call from a student at a nearby university who said his professor claimed the Citicorp building's supporting columns should be on the corners instead of midway between them. LeMessurier replied that the professor did not understand the design problem, adding that the innovative design made it even more resistant to quartering, or diagonal, winds. However, because the New York City building codes required calculating the effects of only 90-degree winds, no one actually had worked out calculations for quartering winds. LeMessurier decided that it would be instructive for his own students to wrestle with this design problem.

This may have been prompted by not only the student's call, but also by a discovery LeMessurier had made just a month earlier. While consulting on a building project in Pittsburgh, he called his home office to find out what it would cost to weld the joints of diagonal girders similar to those in the Citicorp building. To his surprise, he learned that the original specification for full penetration welds had not been followed. Instead, the joints had been bolted. But, this still more than adequately satisfied the New York building code requirements, so LeMessurier was not concerned.

However, as he began to work on calculations for his class, LeMessurier recalled his Pittsburgh discovery. He wondered what difference bolted joints might make to the building's ability to withstand quartering winds. To his dismay, LeMessurier determined that a 40 percent stress increase in some areas of the structure would result in a 160 percent increase in stress on some of the building's joints. This meant that the building was vulnerable to total collapse if certain areas were subjected to a "sixteen year storm" (that is, the sort of storm that could strike Manhattan once every sixteen years). Meanwhile, hurricane season was not far away.

LeMessurier realized that reporting what he had learned could place both his engineering reputation and the financial status of his firm at substantial risk. Nevertheless, he acted quickly and decisively. He drew up a plan for correcting the problem, estimated the cost and time needed for rectifying it, and immediately informed Citicorp owners of what he had learned. Citicorp's response was equally decisive. LeMessurier's proposed course of action was accepted and corrective steps were immediately undertaken.

As the repairs neared completion in early September, a hurricane was reportedly moving up the coast in the direction of New York. Fortunately, it moved harmlessly out over the Atlantic, but not without first causing considerable anxiety among those working on the building, as well as those responsible for implementing plans to evacuate the area should matters take a turn for the worse.

Although correcting the problem cost several million dollars, all parties responded promptly and responsibly. Faced with the threat of increased liability insurance rates, LeMessurier's firm convinced its insurers that, because of his responsible handling of the situation, a much more costly disaster may have been prevented. As a result, the rates were actually reduced. A *New Yorker Magazine* account of LeMessurier's story brought a flood of supportive responses from other engineers, including several who asked whether faced with a similar situation, "Would I be this good?"[1]

 ## The *Challenger* Disaster

On the night of January 27, 1986, the pre-launch teleconference involving Morton Thiokol and the Marshall Space Center was filled with tension. Morton Thiokol engineers conveyed their recommendation against launching the *Challenger* space shuttle the next morning. This recommendation was based on their worries about the ability of the O-rings to seal at low temperatures.

Chief O-ring engineer Roger Boisjoly knew the problems with the O-rings all too well. More than a year earlier he had warned his colleagues of potentially serious problems. The O-rings were part of the sealing mechanism between the segments of the booster rockets. If they lost too much of their resiliency, they could fail to seal altogether. The result would be the escape of hot gases, ignition of the fuel in the storage tanks, and a fatal explosion.

The technical evidence was incomplete but ominous: there appeared to be a correlation between temperature and resiliency. Although there was some leaking around the seal even at relatively high temperatures, the worst leakage was at 53 degrees. With a predicted ambient temperature of 26 degrees at launch, the O-rings were estimated to be at 29 degrees. This was much lower than the launch temperatures of any previous flight.

The teleconference was temporarily suspended. The Space Center had questioned Morton Thiokol's no-launch recommendation, and Morton Thiokol had requested the suspension to allow their engineers and management time to reassess their recommendation. The Space Center would not fly without approval from Morton Thiokol, and Morton Thiokol management would not recommend launching without approval from their managers.

Jerald Mason, senior vice president at Morton Thiokol, knew that NASA badly needed a successful flight. He also knew that Morton Thiokol needed a new contract with NASA, and a recommendation against launch was probably not perceived as enhancing the prospects of obtaining the contract. Finally, Mason was aware that the engineering data were inconclusive. The engineers could not give any firm figures as to the precise temperature at which it would be unsafe to fly. They were relying on the apparent correlation between temperature and resiliency and their tendency to be conservative on serious safety O-ring issues.

The teleconference with the Space Center would resume shortly and a decision had to be made. Turning to Robert Lund, the supervising engineer, Mason directed him to "take off your engineering hat and put on your management hat."[2] The earlier no-launch recommendation was reversed.

Roger Boisjoly was deeply upset by this reversal of the engineers' recommendation. As a human being, he no doubt felt concern for the well-being of the astronauts. He did not want to be a part of something that could lead to death and destruction. But, Boisjoly was not just a concerned citizen—*he was an engineer*. It was his *professional* engineering judgment that the O-rings were not trustworthy. He also had a *professional* obligation to protect the health and safety of the public, and he evidently believed that this obligation extended to the astronauts. Now his *professional* judgment was being overridden.

Boisjoly also did not believe it was appropriate to take off one's engineering hat in such circumstances. His engineering hat was a source of pride, and it also carried with it certain obligations. He believed that *as an engineer* he had an obligation to render his best technical judgment and to protect the safety of the public, including the astronauts. So he made one last attempt to protest the decision to reverse the no-launch recommendation, pointing out the low-temperature problems to Thiokol management. He frantically attempted to persuade management to stick to the original no-launch recommendation, but his protests were not heeded. Thiokol managers reversed the original no-launch decision.

The next day, just 73 seconds into the launch, the *Challenger* exploded, taking the lives of the six astronauts and schoolteacher Christa McAuliffe. In addition to the tragic loss of human life, the disaster destroyed millions of dollars' worth of equipment and severely tarnished NASA's reputation. Boisjoly had failed to prevent the disaster, but he had exercised his professional responsibilities as he saw them.[3]

Water Restoration in Sarajevo

In 1993, engineer Frederick Cuny, founder of Dallas's INTERTECT Relief and Reconstruction Corporation, led a team of associates to Sarajevo to try to help restore heat and safe water for besieged residents of that war-torn city. When they arrived they found that, for many, their only source of water was from a polluted river. Those who took their pails to the edge of the river exposed themselves to sniper fire, which had already killed hundreds of residents.

Preliminary investigation of the scene led the Cuny team to conclude that there must be an inactivated water system somewhere in Old Town Sarajevo. Fortunately, they discovered a network of old cisterns and channels that could be put back into good working order if a new water filtration system could be designed and installed. Unfortunately, materials for constructing the filtration system would have to be brought in from outside.

Modules for the system were designed to fit into a C-130 airplane that was flown from Zagreb, the Croatian capital, into Sarajevo. The storage area was packed with only 3 inches to spare on each side. To sneak the modules by Serbian checkpoints, the team had to unload the modules in less than 10 minutes. As a result of the Cuny team's efforts, more than 20,000 residents of Sarajevo were provided with a clean, safe source of water.[4]

Fred Cuny founded INTERTECT in 1969, at age 27. Since then he and associates have provided disaster relief assistance in many countries around the world, including Bangladesh, Sri Lanka, Lebanon, Guatemala, Armenia, Cambodia, the Sudan, Ethiopia, Somalia, Kurdistan, and Chechnya. Asked about his basic approach to disaster relief, Cuny commented, "In any large-scale disaster, if you can isolate a part that you can understand you will usually end up understanding the whole system."[5] In Sarajevo the main problems seemed to center around water and heat. So, this is what Cuny and his associates focused on.

In preparing for disaster relief work, Cuny was struck at the outset by the fact that medical professionals and materials are routinely flown into international disasters, but engineers and engineering equipment and supplies are not. His recurrent thought was, "Why don't you officials give first priority to, say, fixing the sewage system, instead of merely stanching the inevitable results of a breakdown in sanitary conditions?"[6]

1.1   Introduction

Each of these three cases illustrates both the importance of engineering knowledge to the lives and well-being of the public and the consequent responsibilities that engineers bear. It is unfortunate that, despite Roger Boisjoly's best efforts, the *Challenger* saga had a tragic ending. However, it is reassuring to hear stories with happier endings, like those of Citicorp and Sarajevo.

In any case, it is clear that engineers play a vital role in protecting and assisting the public, and that this requires not only basic engineering competence and technical skills but also imagination, persistence, and a strong sense of responsibility. Also, as these three cases illustrate, sometimes this may require great courage.

Although most engineers will never face situations involving the high drama of the Citicorp, *Challenger*, and Sarajevo stories, all engineers will encounter challenging situations that require careful ethical reflection and decision making. Consider the following examples:

• Tom is designing a new chemical plant. One of his responsibilities is to specify the valves to be used in a certain portion of the plant. Before he makes his final decision, a salesperson for one of the firms that manufactures valves invites Tom to a golf game at the local country club. Should Tom accept the offer?

• Mary discovers that her plant is discharging a substance into the river that is not regulated by the government. She decides to do some reading about the substance and finds that some of the studies suggest that it is a carcinogen. As an engineer, she believes she has an obligation to protect the public, but she also wants to be a loyal employee. The substance will probably be very expensive to remove, and her boss advises, "Forget about it until the government makes us do something. Then all the other plants will have to spend money too, and we will not be at a competitive disadvantage." What should Mary do?

• Jim's company has an in-house tool and die department that would like to bid on a contract that has been submitted to outside vendors. The in-house department manager asks Jim for the quotes from the other vendors, so he can underbid them. "After all," the department manager argues, "we are both on the same team. It's better to keep the money inside if we can. You don't have to tell the outsiders what you have done." What should Jim do?[7]

Issues such as these arise in the professional experience of most engineers. This book should help students and professional engineers to handle such issues more effectively. We believe that a study of professional ethics promises to help engineers be better professionals and that such study should be a part of their professional education.

The major emphasis of this book is on professional ethics, not simply personal ethics. The two cannot, of course, be totally separated. In one respect it is appropriate to say that personal ethics is a foundation for professional ethics— one's desire to be an ethical engineer is part of one's desire to be an ethical person. Nevertheless, there are important differences, as the ensuing discussion will show.

The most obvious difference is that professional ethics has to do with the ethical standards accepted by a professional community. Becoming a professional means joining a community of other professionals. The Model Rules of Professional Conduct adopted by the National Council of Examiners for Engineering and Surveying (NCEES) articulate standards that it recommends state boards of registration use in developing their own codes.[8] These standards emphasize obligations engineers have to the public, clients, employers, and customers. Although most engineers are not formally registered to practice, it seems reasonable to expect all engineers to acknowledge these responsibilities.

Other sources where standards of engineering responsibility can be found are the codes of ethics of engineering societies. Several codes are included in the CD-ROM accompanying this book. The basic principles of these codes are very similar to one another, suggesting a high degree of consensus among these societies concerning the professional responsibilities of engineers.

 In this book we shall often cite provisions in the **code of the National Society of Professional Engineers (NSPE)**. The NSPE is especially concerned with professional development and all engineers are invited to join, regardless of their engineering specialty. The NSPE code is also used by the NSPE Board of Ethical Review, to which we shall occasionally refer.

Although we take the NSPE code and other engineering codes very seriously, we do not find them above criticism. Engineering codes have undergone considerable evolution in the past and no doubt will continue to evolve in the future. One of the marks of a living and vital moral community is that it can grow as a result of changed circumstances and intelligent self-criticism. We shall make some suggestions for code modifications ourselves. Therefore, we take the codes seriously as formal expressions of the ethical norms of the professional engineering community, but we do not adhere to them slavishly, nor do we think they are always adequate or complete.

Many practicing engineers are not members of any professional society. This raises the question of whether the provisions of the codes apply beyond the official membership of the professional societies they represent. Still, the codes seem to reflect ideas that are inculcated into the minds of engineering students in their professional training and later confirmed by the practice of many (we hope most) practicing engineers. The codes, to a great extent, simply state formally a set of ideas that engineers learn both in their education and in their professional practice.

1.2   Role Morality

All of us occupy many roles: We are students, professors, children, parents, members of clubs and organizations of various types, employees, members of religious and professional communities, and citizens of countries. Many of these roles carry with them special obligations and prerogatives. We can refer to the obligations and prerogatives associated with a specific role as *role morality*. Parents, for example, have obligations to their children that they would not have if they were not the children's parents. They must provide food, clothes, and shelter for them and take care of them when they are sick. They must also keep them out of danger, give them emotional support and comfort, and provide for their education. Parents also have certain prerogatives with regard to their children that they would not have if they were not parents. They can have a considerable say as to how their children are educated. They can even educate their children at home if they do not like public or private education. Parents can also deeply influence the religious and political views of their children.

Sometimes the obligations associated with the various roles one occupies may conflict. On the one hand, a parent whose child has committed a crime may feel an obligation as a parent to protect the child from prosecution. As a law-abiding citizen, on the other hand, the same parent may feel obligated to cooperate with the law in prosecuting his or her own child. Employees whose company is polluting the waters in the community may experience a conflict between their obligations to the company and their obligations as citizens of the community. Persons whose religious views commit them to pacifism may feel a conflict between their roles as religious believers to be faithful to their beliefs and their roles as citizens to defend their country.

It is also possible to separate one's role as a human being from that as a professional. In their professional roles, lawyers may be obligated to defend clients whom they believe to be guilty. In one widely discussed case, lawyers found themselves defending a decision not to tell a grieving father where his murdered daughter was buried, even though their client had told them where he had buried the bodies of his victims.[9] They argued that this information had been conveyed to them confidentially and that, as lawyers, they could not break this confidentiality. They emphasized that as individual human beings they deeply sympathized with the father, but as lawyers they felt compelled to protect lawyer-client confidentiality.

Similar conflicts between personal morality and professional morality can arise in medicine. A physician may believe that medical confidentiality compels her to refrain from telling a woman that her future husband has a serious disease that can be transmitted through sexual intercourse, and that he could only have contracted it from someone else. However, in her role as a human being, she may believe she should tell the patient about the danger.

How professionals should resolve such conflicts is often a matter of controversy, even among professionals themselves. Nevertheless, decisions about what one should do in these difficult circumstances must be made. Like lawyers and physicians, engineers sometimes experience conflicts between their professional ethics and their personal moral convictions. This can be seen by raising two basic questions about engineering codes of ethics.

First, *What should the codes say?* The engineering community already has ethical standards, but they are subject to change. This is also true in other professions as well. Some believe that the standards governing legal and medical confidentiality should be modified, especially in areas having to do with the defense of guilty clients and professional confidentiality. Similarly, some engineers believe that engineering codes should include stronger statements about the engineer's obligations to the environment. At present, only a few engineering codes of ethics explicitly mention environmental responsibilities. But environmental issues can raise difficult and important questions for engineers. Should engineers impose on themselves responsibilities for the environment that go beyond the law? Should professional engineering ethics protect the right of engineers to refuse to participate in projects (such as designing dams that flood farmlands or tame "wild" rivers) to which they object, much as medical ethics protects the right of physicians not to participate in medical procedures (such as abortions) to which they object? Should engineers have professional obligations to protect virgin forests or endangered species?

Second, *What direction do the codes give in particular circumstances?* How are the standards to be applied in particular circumstances? Consider the following examples.

1. Section 4.a of the NSPE code requires engineers to avoid "conflicts of interest," but the code does not define conflicts of interest or give directions as to how potential conflicts of interest should be handled. Suppose that Scott, a design engineer, has a brother who owns a small company that manufactures a device for shutting off the fuel supply to boilers when the pressure gets too high. Scott believes that his brother's product is superior to anything else on the market. Should he avoid specifying his brother's valve in his designs, even though he believes it is the best available? How could he handle this situation to avoid a conflict of interest?

2. Section 10.a of the NSPE code requires engineers to "recognize the proprietary interests of others." Suppose Andrea, a chemical engineer, recognizes that some of the ideas she developed for her former employer provide the basis for a solution to a problem faced by her new employer. The two companies are not competitors, and the applications of the ideas are so different that very few people

would even recognize them as having a common origin. Is it ethical for her to employ her old ideas in this new and creative way?

3. The first canon of the NSPE code requires engineers to "hold paramount the safety, health and welfare of the public in the performance of their professional duties." John, a chemical engineer, notices that workers in his section of the plant are complaining of noxious fumes from hot metals. "They give me headaches every day," one worker complains. Are workers part of the "public" for whom John has a professional responsibility? Does he have an obligation as an engineer to try to remedy the problem?

4. The fourth canon of the NSPE code directs engineers to "act in professional matters for each employer or client as faithful agents or trustees." Lisa knows that the code gives priority to protecting the public, but this knowledge does not seem sufficient to resolve her problem. Her company manufactures a product that appears to have a slightly greater likelihood of harming users than similar products of the competition. Her employer does not want to change the design, and she wonders whether in this case her obligation to protect the public outweighs her obligation to be a loyal and obedient employee.

This book will contain many other cases in which the codes do not give sufficient direction. No code, in fact, could supply an algorithm that would give an automatic solution to all ethical problems faced by engineers. Furthermore, codes of ethics should not be expected to cover all areas of professional concern. Rather, they address only those matters about which there is a current consensus among members of the profession, and their contents often undergo changes over time. They are best understood within the larger framework of the professions themselves. So, we will now discuss that framework in greater detail.

1.3   What Is a Profession?

The early meaning of the term *profession* and its cognates referred to a free act of commitment to a way of life. The *Oxford Shorter Dictionary* says that the earliest meaning of the adjective *professed* referred to the activity of a person who had taken the monastic vows of a religious order. We might think of a person who had made a public promise to enter a distinct way of life with allegiance to high moral ideals. One "professed" to be a certain type of person and to occupy a special social role, which carried with it stringent moral requirements. By the late seventeenth century, the word had become secularized to refer to anyone who professed to be duly qualified.

Thus "profession" originally meant, according to the *Oxford Shorter Dictionary*, the act or fact of "professing." It has come to mean: "The occupation which one professes to be skilled in and to follow. . . . A vocation in which professed knowledge of some branch of learning is used in its application to the affairs of others, or in the practice of an art based upon it."

This brief historical account, however, is not sufficient for our purposes; we need to discuss the *characteristics* of professions in more detail. In particular, we need an account of the characteristics of professions that will enable us to distinguish professions from other occupations. There is no universally accepted account. It is unwise to claim that the characteristics of professions constitute a true definition—that is, a statement of the necessary and sufficient conditions for having the status of a profession. Rather, we will consider a set of characteristics that at least usually holds true of professions. A genuine profession might not have a given characteristic (so the characteristic would not be necessary for being a profession), or an occupation might have a characteristic without being a genuine profession (so the characteristic would not be sufficient for being a profession). Nevertheless, the following five characteristics will be useful in distinguishing professions from nonprofessional occupations.[10]

1. Entrance into a profession typically requires an extensive period of training, and this training is of an intellectual character. Many occupations require extensive apprenticeship and training, and they often require practical skills, but the training typically required of professionals focuses more on intellectual content than on practical skills. Professionals' knowledge and skills are grounded in a body of theory.

This theoretical base is obtained through formal education, usually in an academic institution. Today, most professionals have at least a bachelor's degree from a college or university, and many professions require more advanced degrees, often conferred by a professional school. Thus, the professions are usually closely allied in our society with universities, especially the larger and more prestigious ones.

2. Professionals' knowledge and skills are vital to the well-being of the larger society. A society that has a sophisticated scientific and technological base is especially dependent on its professional elite. We rely on the knowledge possessed by physicians to protect us from disease and restore us to health. The lawyer has knowledge vital to our welfare if we have been sued or accused of a crime, if our business has been forced into bankruptcy, or if we want to get a divorce or buy a house. The accountant's knowledge is also important for our business success or when we have to file our tax return. Likewise, we are dependent on the knowledge and research of scientists and engineers for our safety in an airplane, for many of the technological advances upon which our material civilization rests, and for national defense.

3. Professions usually have a monopoly or near monopoly on the provision of professional services. This control is achieved in two ways. One way is that the profession convinces the community that only those who have graduated from a professional school should be allowed to hold the professional title. The profession usually also gains considerable control over professional schools by establishing accreditation standards that regulate the quality, curriculum content, and number of such schools. A second way is to persuade the community that there should be a licensing system for those who want to enter the profession. Those who practice without a license are subject to legal penalties.

4. Professionals often have an unusual degree of autonomy in the workplace. Professionals in private practice have considerable freedom in choosing their clients or patients. But even professionals who work in large organizations may exercise a large degree of individual judgment and creativity in carrying out their professional responsibilities. Whether in private practice or an organizational setting, physicians must determine the most appropriate type of medical treatment for their patients and lawyers must decide the most successful type of defense for their clients. This is one of the most satisfying aspects of professional work. The justification for this unusual degree of autonomy is that only the professional has sufficient knowledge to determine the proper professional service. The possession of specialized knowledge is thus a powerful defense of professional autonomy.

5. Professionals claim to be regulated by ethical standards, usually embodied in a code of ethics. The degree of control that professions possess over the services vital to the well-being of the rest of the community provides an obvious temptation for abuse. Therefore, most professions attempt to limit these abuses by regulating themselves for the public benefit. Professional codes are ordinarily promulgated by professional societies, and there is occasionally some attempt to punish members who fail to abide by the provisions of the code.

Holding these five characteristics in mind, it is easy to see that occupations form a continuum, extending from those that are unquestionably professions to those that are unquestionably not. The occupations that hold a clear title to professional status include medicine, law, veterinary medicine, architecture, accounting (at least certified public accountants), and dentistry. Engineering could be regarded as more borderline. Engineers who work in large organizations may have less autonomy in their work than those who work as independent consultants. Furthermore, much engineering work can be performed without being professionally registered or licensed as a professional. Nevertheless, given the critical role formal education and special expertise ordinarily play in engineering practice, it seems entirely reasonable to regard engineering as a profession.[11]

1.4   Professional Ethics

Let us return to the fifth common characteristic of a profession: regulation by ethical standards, usually embodied in a code of ethics. We have already noted that professional ethics should be distinguished from personal ethics and common morality. (We use the terms *ethics* and *morality,* interchangeably, to refer to standards of proper conduct.) *Professional ethics* is the set of standards adopted by professionals insofar as they see themselves acting *as professionals*. *Personal ethics* is the set of one's own ethical commitments, usually given in early home or religious training and often modified by later reflection. *Common morality* is the set of moral ideals shared by most members of a culture or society.

The relationships of these three types of morality can be complex. Often they overlap, even though they have different origins. Sometimes it is not easy to tell whether a given activity is required or prohibited by one or more of the three types of morality. Many moral ideals, such as honesty and fairness, are a part of personal, professional, and common morality. Nevertheless, there are situations in which professional standards may differ from those of personal morality and even the usual standards of common morality.

The following examples illustrate some of the possible relationships between professional, personal, and common morality:

• An engineer refuses to design military hardware because she believes war is immoral. This refusal is based on personal moral convictions, not on professional or common morality.

 • A civil engineer refuses to design a project he believes will be contrary to the principles of sustainable development. This refusal could be based on **provisions regarding sustainable development in the ASCE (American Society of Civil Engineers)** professional code of ethics. It might also be based on personal moral commitments.

• An engineer insists on complete honesty in the reporting of technical information to his client or employer. This insistence could be based on personal, professional, or common morality.

Professional codes of ethics articulate shared standards of professional ethics. Virtually every occupational group that claims to have professional status has a code of ethics. In engineering, there are many such codes, and they serve several important functions.[12]

First, professional codes furnish common, agreed-upon standards for professional conduct. The existence of such standards is of benefit both to professionals and to the public.

For professionals, the codes state what is expected of them in the way of professional conduct. The individual professional is not left on her own to try to figure out what conduct is proper; the codes tell her, at least in general terms. Furthermore, the professional can assume that, by and large, other professionals in her field will act by the same standards. Engineer Jane can assume that other ethically conscientious professionals will not attempt to underbid her by specifying clearly inferior equipment or attempt to gain a competitive advantage by obtaining confidential information from her firm.

For the public, the existence of professional standards embodied in codes of ethics enables a potential client or customer to make certain assumptions about professional conduct, even if the client or customer has no knowledge of the personal ethics of the professional. When we enter a physician's office, we can assume that what we tell our physicians will be kept in confidence, even if we have never met them. We can also assume that they will inform us of options so that we can make free and informed decisions, and that they will be up to date on the latest medical procedures. An employer or client can make similar assumptions about ethically conscientious engineers.

All of this is to say that the codes of ethics can be understood as expressing an implicit *agreement* among professionals and between professionals and the public. Professionals agree among themselves to abide by uniform standards. They agree with the public that these uniform standards will (1) promote the well-being of the general public as this relates to the profession's area of expertise and (2) ensure the competence (and continued competence) of professionals in their area of expertise.

Second, professional codes of ethics provide a focus for debate on how professional ethics should be modified. Professional codes have not always been the same. They have been modified in a number of areas as a result of changing perceptions of professional obligations.

One area of change has been in regard to acknowledging professional obligations to the public. The earliest American codes typically held: "The engineer should consider the protection of a client's or employer's interests his first professional obligation, and therefore should avoid every act contrary to this duty."[13] The only stated responsibility to the public was that an engineer "should endeavor to assist the public to a fair and correct general understanding of engineering matters, to extend the general knowledge of engineering, and to discourage the appearance of untrue, unfair, or exaggerated statements on engineering subjects in the press or elsewhere."[14]

Not until mid-century was greater responsibility to the public acknowledged in the major codes. In 1947, the Engineers' Council for Professional Development (ECPD) endorsed the idea that engineers have not only duties of fidelity to their employers and clients but also duties to the public. The ECPD code specified that engineers "will have due regard for the safety and health of the public." In 1974 the ECPD code was revised to say that "engineers shall hold paramount the safety, health and welfare of the public in the performance of their professional duties." This statement or a similar one now occurs in the codes of all of the major engineering societies.

Another area of change has to do with professional obligations regarding the environment. As we shall see in Chapter 9, very few of the major engineering societies currently mention the environment. However, we believe that in the future most engineering codes will contain references to the environment. They may also include statements about the rights and responsibilities of engineers in the international arena, the topic of Chapter 10.

Third, professional codes of ethics can provide a rationale for professionals to adhere to professional standards even when pressured by others to violate them, as illustrated in the following hypothetical but not unrealistic situations:

• James has a client who is considering building a shopping mall in River City. The client wants to know something about the financial affairs of the other shopping mall in town, and the client knows that James regularly does engineering work for the mall. He asks James to reveal confidential information about the finances of the potentially competing shopping mall. James refuses on the grounds that it would violate his professional code of ethics.

• Mary is serving as an expert witness for Company X, and the lawyer for Company X asks her to omit certain facts from her testimony that might damage their case. Mary replies that her professional code requires her to include all relevant information in reports, statements, and testimony and that she cannot comply with the lawyer's request.

• Frances is a major stockholder in a small company that manufactures fasteners that she often specifies in her designs, because she believes they are the best on the market. Her fellow stockholders ask her to stop her practice of informing clients of her financial interest in the company when she specifies her company's fasteners. As one stockholder put it, "Why raise suspicions unnecessarily? Everyone knows our product is the best." Frances responds that her professional code requires her to disclose known or potential conflicts of interest.

• John's firm is in competition with another firm for a large construction contract. His supervisor asks him to make some public statements suggesting that the engineers in the competing firm are not as competent as the engineers in John's firm. He knows that this implied claim would be false and refuses to honor his superior's request, citing professional code requirements that he not untruthfully criticize other engineers.

A defense based on standards that apply to all professionals is likely to be more successful than one that merely expresses the ideas of an individual about what constitutes proper professional conduct.

1.5   The NSPE Board of Ethical Review

One example of a professional engineering society's promotion of ethics deserves special mention. The National Society of Professional Engineers established its **Board of Ethical Review (BER)** in 1958. The board considers questions submitted by state societies or members, rendering opinions on the ethical and professional propriety of the actions described in the cases. It bases its judgments on the NSPE Code of Ethics; and its judgments do not attempt to criticize the code or suggest modifications to it. The board emphasizes that its judgments are to have educational value only. It does not engage in any independent attempt to investigate and confirm the facts presented to it, and it has no legal power to enforce its judgments. Nevertheless, the activities of the board stimulate discussion of ethical issues. The opinions of the board, which are clear and well reasoned, usually provide helpful guidance for engineers.

Unlike the media, the BER commentaries concentrate more on the everyday ethical concerns of engineers rather than on disaster stories such as the *Challenger* accident. Although the BER case studies are based on actual situations, few are newsworthy enough to attract the attention of the media. Their importance for most engineers and engineering students lies precisely in their ordinariness. These are problems that *any* engineer might have to deal with.[15]

Despite the value of the BER's opinions, exclusive focus on them has several shortcomings. First, because the case studies are designed to aid understanding of the NSPE's Code of Ethics, they are essentially code-driven. Analyses by the BER are quasi legalistic in tone, mirroring the specific provisions of the NSPE code, with little analytical discussion of the underlying ethical principles and concepts. But codes themselves need to be evaluated.[16]

Second, BER commentaries give few minority dissenting opinions. They are almost always consensus reports. Of course, it is important that engineers be aware of the extent to which consensus (and shared commitment) on ethical issues in engineering exists. However, more complex ethical issues do not necessarily command consensus, and examples of reasoned disagreement are needed.[17]

Third, the BER's cases and commentaries tend to focus on issues faced by independent consulting engineers. Most of the cases have to do with problems arising in the private practice of engineering. Most of the firms involved are civil engineering firms, where most of the private practice of engineering takes place. The cases involving engineering in the corporate setting are less numerous. There are only two whistle-blowing cases. Few cases discuss the potential conflict between managers and engineers in decision making. There is little discussion of the potential conflict between the code provision requiring engineers to "act in professional matters for each employer or client as faithful agents or trustees" and the requirement to "hold paramount the safety, health and welfare of the public in the performance of their professional duties."

Fourth, relatively few cases deal with such professional issues as negligence and incompetence.[18]

Finally, BER cases seldom require a consideration of the likely implications of initial decisions for subsequent decision making. However, decisions that seem to resolve matters for the moment do have consequences that often set the stage for even greater ethical problems later. Codes of ethics can remind us of the sorts of ethical concerns we need to be ready to deal with, but they cannot tell us which ones are likely to come next—and they cannot replace the need for careful and imaginative thinking, the topic we turn to next.

1.6   Engineering Ethics as Preventive Ethics

Much of what we will be discussing in this book is what can be called *preventive ethics*, analogous to the concept of preventive medicine. By attending carefully to our health needs before we become seriously ill, we may prevent such illnesses from occurring. Similarly, by anticipating the sorts of ethical problems that, left unattended, could become ethical crises, we may prevent such crises from occurring. We will explain how this can work in engineering.

The Importance of Thinking Ahead

In their professional capacity, engineers can be faced with significant ethical choices. Some would argue that moral character is already well in place by the time a young engineer might be faced with significant ethical choices. If we haven't learned the difference between right and wrong long ago, a skeptic might say, it's really too late. But engineer Samuel Florman answers:

> Skeptics—both within academe and without—argue that moral character is formed in the home, the church, and the community, and cannot be modified in a college classroom or professional symposium. I cannot agree with the skeptics on this count. Most evil acts are committed not by villains but rather by decent human beings—in desperation, momentary weakness, or an inability to discern what is morally right amid the discordant claims of circumstances. The determination to be good may be molded at an early age, but we grapple all our lives with the definition of what is good, or at least acceptable.[19]

At the very least, responsible engineering requires familiarity with the kinds of circumstances in engineering practice that call for ethical sensitivity and reflection. It also requires opportunities to gain a clearer understanding of the concepts and principles that are essential to ethical reflection in engineering.

Until quite recently, engineering education has not emphasized the importance of including ethics as a part of the engineering curriculum. However, the 1985 Accreditation Board for Engineering and Technology (ABET) requirements for accredited engineering programs in the United States include making serious efforts to foster in their students "an understanding of the ethical characteristics of the engineering profession and practice."[20] ABET 2000 is more specific. It requires that engineering programs demonstrate that their graduates also understand the impact of engineering in a global and societal context and have a knowledge of contemporary issues related to engineering. It also directs that students are to have a "major design experience" that includes a consideration of ethical factors in addition to economic, environmental, social, and political factors.[21]

As many professional engineers can testify, ethical lessons are often learned only after something has been overlooked or has gone wrong. By requiring engineering programs to introduce students to ethical concerns, ABET is taking the position that students need to begin to think about ethical issues in engineering before things go wrong. In essence, ABET is advocating a kind of preventive ethics. Preventive ethics contains two dimensions: (1) engineers must be able to think ahead to anticipate possible consequences of their actions as professionals, especially consequences that may have an important ethical dimension; (2) engineers must be able to think effectively about those consequences and decide what is ethically right. Let us look at some of the aspects of ethics education that are important in achieving these two aspects of preventive ethics.

Education in Preventive Ethics

After a two-year study of ethics programs in higher education sponsored by the Hastings Center, an interdisciplinary group of educators agreed on five main objectives of such programs.[22] These objectives are an excellent summary of training in preventive ethics. Engineering was one of the areas explicitly considered by this team of educators, and this makes their conclusions all the more relevant to training in preventive ethics. Taking our cue from the Hastings study, we can isolate the following elements involved in training in preventive ethics.[23]

1. *Stimulating the moral imagination.* For engineers, as for anyone else, imagination is necessary in anticipating the consequences of actions as professionals and in coming up with solutions to ethical problems encountered in professional life. William LeMessurier's handling of the Citicorp situation is a good illustration of effective moral imagination. Once he realized there might be a problem, he carefully weighed the available options. But this case also illustrates the difficulty of anticipating problems. In the initial planning, calculations of wind resistance were made only from a 90-degree angle, which is all that the regulations required. However, LeMessurier did not anticipate a possible change from deep welds to bolts in the joints.

To minimize the chances of being taken by surprise, engineers must exercise great imagination in considering possible alternatives and their likely consequences. One of the managers interviewed in Barbara Toffler's *Tough Choices* explains how he tries to deal with difficult situations:

> I first play out the scenario of what would happen if I did it one way and what would happen if I did it the other way. What would be the follow-up? What would be the next move? What would be the response back and what would be the consequences? That's the only way you can tell if you're going to make the right move or not because I think something that instinctively may feel right or wrong, if you analyze it, may not pan out that way.[24]

2. *Recognizing ethical issues.* It is not difficult to recognize that suppressing data raises ethical questions, even if deciding what to do about it is difficult. However, as the Citicorp story shows, the ethical dimensions of situations are not always so apparent. Consider this illustration.[25] At a meeting of engineering educators and professional philosophers an engineer briefly described a housing project. The property adjacent to the housing development was a large, heavily treed, hilly area. The engineer then asked his audience what size drainage pipe should be recommended for the sewer system. Crude estimates were made by engineers and philosophers alike, with little consensus and much amusement. Finally, someone asked the question that no doubt was on the minds of many: What did this problem have to do with ethics?

The engineer replied by asking the audience to consider what the surrounding environment might be like shortly after the completion of the housing project. Perhaps a shopping mall would replace the heavily treed, higher adjacent area—resulting in a much greater rain water run-off problem. Should an engineer recommend a pipe size that takes into consideration such future contingencies? What if the housing developer wants to get by with minimal costs and shows no concern for who might have to bear the expense of replacing the inadequate draining system in the near future? Who should bear the expense, and to what extent, if at all, should an engineer be concerned about such questions when making recommendations?

However these background questions are answered, they make clear that the question of what should be recommended is not just a technical one. In addition, although an engineering code of ethics might address issues like this in a very general way, it will not necessarily guide engineers to a consensus.

3. *Developing analytical skills.* In one sense engineering students obviously have well-developed analytical skills. However, the technical and analytical skills essential to good engineering practice must be used with some caution in analyzing moral issues. Sometimes they may even impede moral analysis, which requires clear thinking about concepts such as utility, justice, rights, duties, and respect for persons. These concepts are not necessarily amenable to quantitative analysis.

Suppose David Weber, a highway safety engineer, has to assign priorities to projects in a county with diverse traffic patterns.[26] After considering a number of options, he concentrates on two intersections that need safety improvements. One is an urban intersection that handles about 2400 cars per day. The other is a rural intersection that handles about 600 cars per day. The annual number of fatal accidents at each intersection is virtually identical (approximately 2), but the number of property damage and minor injury accidents at the urban intersection is substantially greater. There is just enough money left in this year's budget to improve one of the intersections. The expected result of the improvement at either intersection will be to cut the number of annual fatalities roughly in half. There will be a greater reduction in property damage and minor injury accidents if the improvement is made at the urban intersection. Which improvement should David Weber give higher priority?

Versions of this fictional case been have presented to engineering students for more than fifteen years. The overwhelming initial response is always that the urban intersection should take priority. Why? As the numbers clearly reveal, more people will be served at the urban intersection. Invariably someone will say, "It's the greatest good for the greatest number."

If students are asked if anyone favors the rural intersection, one or two may volunteer that, in fact, the rural intersection is more dangerous. Individual drivers are at higher risk of having a serious or fatal accident. This, too, can readily be demonstrated mathematically.

So, what do the numbers settle in this case? By themselves, nothing. From the standpoint of maximizing the overall good, the numbers do seem to favor the urban intersection. But the utilitarian assumption that we should promote the greatest good for the greatest number is not itself based on numerical analysis. It requires philosophical support. In fact, the utilitarian perspective is not the only one that might be brought to bear on the situation. For example, considerations of fairness or respect for individual rights strengthen the case for the rural intersection. Again, although numerical analysis can be joined with considerations of fairness or individual rights, those considerations require philosophical support. However the numbers in this case are used, we need to ask what ethical assumptions we are making about their relevance. The temptation to take comfort in numbers may be there, but ethical analysis reveals the value assumptions that underlie giving in to this temptation.

4. *Eliciting a sense of responsibility.* Preventive ethics can be practiced most effectively by people who have a sense of themselves as moral agents. Even though we give codes a central place in our conception of professional ethics, they cannot be relied upon uncritically. Codes may need to be modified in certain areas, and how they should be applied to particular moral problems is not always evident. Practice in preventive ethics is thus not indoctrination but practice in independent thought. Also, many codes of ethics make a distinction between ethical requirements and ethical ideals. Ethical requirements are basic obligations and duties. Ethical ideals go beyond basic obligations and duties, and engineers are encouraged rather than required to aspire to fulfill these ideals. However, having such aspirations is also a part of having a sense of oneself as a moral agent.

5. *Tolerating disagreement and ambiguity.* Discussions of problems like David Weber's are often frustrating to engineering students. Sorting out the nuances of ethical concepts reveals a certain amount of vagueness, ambiguity, and, above all, disagreement. Lack of consensus on such cases may prove frustrating for those accustomed to technical solutions to problems. Some may be tempted to turn to a code of ethics for bringing matters to an authoritative resolution, but we have already pointed out that the codes do not provide ready-made solutions to all moral problems. No code of ethics is self-interpreting. Its principles and rules are stated in general terms and need to be applied thoughtfully to particular circumstances; and some parts of a code might potentially conflict with one another. For example, protecting public safety and being faithful to one's employer may, on the face of it, pull an engineer in opposite directions. We have already pointed out how even the fact that the codes give priority to protecting the public may not resolve all of these conflicts. Only careful reflection and discerning judgment can adequately resolve such potential conflicts. Even then, engineers might find themselves reasonably disagreeing to some extent among themselves.

The willingness to persevere in our reflections even to the point of such disagreement is itself a mark of responsibility. However, it is also a mark of responsibility to continue to search for possible points of agreement and further clarity when confronted with difficult and challenging problems.

Figure 1.1 on page 22 summarizes these five aims in studying ethics. Studying ethics aims at stimulating our moral imagination; helping us recognize moral issues; helping us analyze key ethical concepts; engaging our sense of responsi-

Figure 1.1 Aims in Studying Ethics

bility; and helping us address unclarity, uncertainty, and disagreement about moral issues.

1.7   Cases, Cases, Cases!

Throughout this chapter we have referred frequently to cases in engineering ethics. Their importance cannot be overemphasized. It is by studying cases that we can most easily develop the abilities necessary to engage in constructive ethical analysis. Cases stimulate the moral imagination by challenging us to anticipate the possible alternatives in resolving them and the consequences of those alternatives. Through cases we learn to recognize the presence of ethical problems and to develop the analytical skills necessary to resolving them. A study of cases is the most effective way to see that the codes cannot provide ready-made answers to all moral questions that professional engineering practice generates and that the individual must become a responsible moral agent. Finally, the study of cases convinces us that there may be some unresolvable uncertainties in ethical analysis and that in some situations rational and responsible professionals may disagree about what is right.

Cases will appear throughout the text. Each chapter is introduced with a case, which is usually referred to in the chapter. In many chapters we shall present our own attempts to resolve ethical problems. We often use brief cases to illustrate various points in our argument, and we present a large number of cases at the end of this book and on the accompanying CD-ROM for further discussion and analysis. Also, Chapters 2, 3, and 4 are devoted to methods for analyzing and resolving the ethical issues presented in cases.

Cases are of several types. Some cases are fictional but realistic. Some cases focus on highly publicized events, such as the *Challenger* disaster or the Ford Pinto gas tank controversy, whereas others concern more ordinary events and issues in the professional experience of engineers. Some cases are simplified to better focus on a particular issue; others are more complex and multifaceted. Every case furthers the study and understanding of professional engineering ethics. Two final points are important with regard to the use of cases.

First, the use of cases is especially appropriate in a text in professional ethics. A medical school dean known to one of the authors once said, "Physicians are tied to the post of use." By this he presumably meant that physicians do not have the luxury of thinking indefinitely about moral problems. They must make decisions about what treatment to administer or what advice to give. Physicians feel tethered or constrained by the necessity of making these decisions that vitally affect the lives of others.

Engineers, like other professionals, are also tied to the post of use. They must make decisions about designs that will affect the lives and financial well-being of many people, give professional advice to managers and clients, make decisions about purchases, decide whether to protest decisions by managers and others that affect the well-being of the public, and take other actions that have important consequences for themselves and others. Engineers, like other professionals, are case-oriented. In the study of cases they see that professional ethics is not simply a gloss on professional education but is intimately related to what it means to be a professional.

Second, the study of cases is especially valuable for engineers who aspire to management positions. Cases have long been at the center of management education. Many if not most of the issues faced by managers have ethical dimensions. Some of the methods for resolving ethical problems discussed in Chapters 2 through 4—especially finding a "creative middle way"—have much in common with the methods employed by managers. Managers must make decisions within constraints, and they usually try to make decisions satisfy as many of these constraints as possible. The kind of creative problem solving necessary to make such decisions is very similar to the brainstorming that is helpful in resolving many ethical problems.[27]

The use of preventive ethics is also a worthwhile tool for managers. If they can avoid serious ethical problems before they appear, managers can avoid many difficult and painful decisions that might otherwise arise. Some large health-care firms now employ medical ethicists on the corporate level to assist in establishing corporate policy regarding health care. Presumably the thinking of corporate executives is that if corporate policy is ethically sound, it will avoid liability lawsuits and public relations problems that often result from unethical actions. (If these are the sole motives of such executives, we may have questions about them from an ethical standpoint.) Nevertheless, we cannot deny the importance of ethics in sound health-care management. The importance of ethics in sound engineering management is equally obvious.

A Sample Case and Analysis

To preview the kind of ethical analysis we are urging, we will close this chapter with an analysis of a fictional case study. Although fictional, this case study is realistic. The analysis we offer here does not presuppose familiarity with ideas discussed in subsequent chapters. Readers might want to return to this example to see if the analysis might be improved in light of what is presented in later chapters.

 ## The Forklifter[28]

Engineering student Bryan Springer has a high-paying summer job as a forklift operator. This job enables him to attend college without having to take out any student loans. He is now staring at a 50-gallon drum filled with used machine coolant, wondering what he should do.

Just moments ago, Bryan's supervisor, Max Morrison, told him to dump half of the used coolant down the drain. Knowing the coolant was toxic, Bryan noted this to Max. But Max was not swayed.

Max: The toxins settle at the bottom of the drum. If you pour out half and dilute it with tap water while you're pouring it, there's no problem.

Bryan: I don't think that's going to work. Besides, isn't it against the law?

Max: Look, kid, I don't have time for chitchat about a bunch of silly laws. If I spent my time worrying about every little regulation that comes along, I'd never get anything done—and neither will you. Common sense is my rule. I just told you—toxins settle at the bottom, and most of them will stay there. We've been doing this for years, and nothing's happened.

Bryan: You mean no one's *said* anything about it? That doesn't mean the environment isn't being harmed.

Max: You aren't one of those "environmentalists," are you? You college guys spend too much of your time in the "ivory tower." It's time to get real—and get on with the job. You know, you're very lucky to have a good-paying job like this, kid. In three months you'll be back in your cozy college. Meanwhile, how many other college kids do you think there are out there wondering if they'll be able to afford to go back—kids who'd give their eyetooth to be where you are right now.

Max then left, fully expecting Bryan to dump the used coolant. As Bryan stared at the drum, he pondered his options. What options do you think he has? What do you think he should do?

Analysis

Bryan is in a difficult situation. He seems to believe that complying with Max's order is both illegal and wrong. Yet he has little if any power in the company and is in danger of losing a valuable job if he disobeys. Furthermore, he is faced with the necessity of making an immediate decision. He might decide that he just does not want to do something that he considers wrong and that he has already earned as much as most students earn in a summer. If need be, he can take out a student loan. He might also believe that his example of refusing to dump the coolant could have an effect on company policy.

However, he might decide to dump the coolant down the drain. He might try to convince himself that one more dumping will not make that much difference, and it will give him a little more time to make a decision. He might also believe that staying on will have more effect on company policy than merely quitting or being summarily fired. This is a factual issue, having to do with the likely consequences of various courses of action.

Bryan also must be aware of what laws he may be violating if he decides to follow Max's orders. He must be prepared personally to deal with the consequences of those laws (fine and/or imprisonment) if he is indicted for the felony of toxic waste dumping under the terms of the U.S. Resource Conservation and Recovery Act (RCRA). Equally important, he must be conscious of what he personally would be doing to the environment.

As a budding engineer Bryan should be aware of the first Fundamental Canon in the NSPE Code of Ethics that engineers "hold paramount the safety, health, and welfare of the public in the performance of their professional duties." Maybe driving a forklift is not yet one of his professional duties, but it is a means for his eventually becoming a professional engineer. Also, the company he is working for is ostensibly involved in engineering-related work; it is machine coolant he was asked to dump. So, NSPE's Fundamental Canon concerning public safety, health, and welfare clearly is addressed to the setting within which Bryan is working.

It looks as though, if Bryan wants to convince Max to stop dumping toxins, he will need to gather information on the toxicity of the specific chemicals he is dumping and what medical evidence is available about the effects of that toxic waste on the public. This is most effective if put in numerical terms such as the probability of whatever serious consequence is possible per unit level of exposure (for example, probability of the number of serious illnesses per 100,000 people exposed to one part per million in their drinking water). Next, he will need to gather information on current applicable laws, and particularly what fines and penalties are at risk. Finally, he will need to present the cost of alternatives available to Max's company other than just outright dumping. That is a lot of work, but if Bryan is really disturbed about the situation and still wants to keep his summer job, he may have no other alternative to spending some significant research time in the local library.

Suppose Bryan discovers that Max's theory about how to reduce the toxic effect has no validity at all. He also confirms his suspicion that repeated dumping of the toxins into the drain is not only illegal, but a considerable source of environmental pollution and a potential health hazard. If Bryan wants to persuade Max that they should not dump the toxins, he will have to proceed with great tact and diplomacy. He will likely have to convince Max that seriously considering alternatives to dumping may be in Max's and the company's best interests. He must somehow convince Max to be his ally in this.

What if Bryan concludes that Max will never take his advice seriously? If the company is large enough to have an "ethics hotline," an ombudsman, or an officer in charge of corporate responsibility, he should certainly make use of the opportunities that these resources afford. If not, he should consider laying his case before Max's superior or the personnel officer.

If this is done in a way that is both sincere and nonconfrontational and if Bryan manages to find a receptive person, he may have a good chance of both protecting the environment and protecting his job. If this fails, he will have to face an unpleasant choice. Bryan could take his case outside the company. There are those who argue that this course of action makes sense only after one has resigned from the company, in other words after there is no longer anything personal (job and income) at stake. This may be a moot point because once he goes public, it is highly likely that Bryan will no longer be employed by the company.

Nevertheless, Bryan may console himself with the thought that he has done what he thinks is right rather than keeping his job at the cost of his conscience—and perhaps at the cost of the surrounding environment. And he may take some satisfaction from the thought that he is preparing himself for professional life by determining that lines may have to be drawn even in the face of serious opposition and at the risk of personal sacrifice.

1.8   Chapter Summary

Engineering ethics is a type of professional ethics and as such must be distinguished from personal ethics and from the ethical obligations that one may have as an occupant of other social roles. Engineering ethics is concerned with the question of what the standards in engineering ethics should be and how to apply these standards to particular situations. One of the values of studying engineering ethics is that it can serve the function of helping to promote responsible engineering practice.

Part of responsible engineering practice is the exercise of preventive ethics: the practice of sound ethical decision making to avoid more serious problems later.

Practice in preventive ethics involves stimulating the moral imagination, developing the ability to recognize ethical issues when they arise, developing analytical skills in dealing with ethical problems, eliciting in engineers a sense of responsibility for their actions, and helping engineers to tolerate and also to resist disagreement and ambiguity.

The use of cases is an important aspect of developing skills in the practice of preventive ethics because professionals must always make decisions. Additionally, the study of cases in professional ethics is valuable practice for engineers who aspire to management, for many ethical problems are also management problems, and sound ethics usually makes for sound management.

 CASES TO CONSIDER

There are fifty-seven cases included in the section entitled "Cases" in the back of this book. Seven of these cases are accompanied by analyses. The remaining fifty are for you to analyze, making use of concepts, principles, and methods of analysis discussed in the various chapters. You should feel free to browse through any of the cases at this point. However, here are several cases you might want to try your hand at now. Cases followed by an asterisk are analyzed.

Case 9	Cost-Cutting
Case 23	Golfing
Case 24	Highway Safety
Case 47	Unlicensed Engineer
Case 52	Whose Property?
Case 53	Why Won't They Read?

Sample cases of NSPE's Board of Ethical Review (BER) can be found on the CD-ROM accompanying this text. Other BER cases can be found under "Cases" at the WWW Ethics Center for Engineering and Science: http://ethics.cwru.edu.

NOTES

1. This account is based on Joe Morgenstern, "The Fifty-nine Story Crisis," *The New Yorker Magazine* (May 29, 1995), 45–53. Also, see Caroline Whitbeck, *Ethics in Engineering Practice and Research* (New York: Cambridge University Press, 1998), pp. 146–154. Further details, as well as illustrations, can be found at the WWW Ethics Center for Engineering and Science at http://ethics.cwru.edu in the section on Moral Leaders.

2. Rogers Commission, *Report to the President by the Presidential Commission on the Space Shuttle Challenger Accident* (Washington, D.C.: June 6, 1986), pp. 772–773.

3. For Roger Boisjoly's own account of the *Challenger* disaster, see his "The *Challenger* Disaster: Moral Responsibility and the Working Engineer," in Deborah Johnson, ed., *Ethical Issues in Engineering* (Englewood Cliffs, N.J.: Prentice Hall, 1991), pp. 6–14. Much more on Roger Boisjoly can be found at the WWW Ethics Center for Engineering and Science at http://ethics.cwru.edu in the section on Moral Leaders.

4. This account is based on C. Sudetic, "Small Miracle in a Siege: Safe Water for Sarajevo," *New York Times* (January 10), A1 and A7. Chapter 5 includes a fuller account of Frederick Cuny's work. The Moral Leader section of the WWW Ethics Center for

Engineering and Science at http://ethics.cwru.edu provides a detailed account of many other disaster relief projects organized by Cuny.

5. This account is based on "The Talk of the Town," *The New Yorker*, 69, no. 39 (Nov. 22, 1993), 45–46.

6. Ibid.

7. Michael S. Pritchard, ed., *Teaching Engineering Ethics: A Case Study Approach*, National Science Foundation, Grant No. DIR-8820837 (June 1992), pp. 199–200.

8. The NCEES, as well as professional engineering societies, will be discussed in greater detail in Chapter 11.

9. Reported in several sources, including *The New York Times* (June 20, 1974).

10. These five characteristics are described in Ernest Greenwood, "Attributes of a Profession," *Social Work* (July 1957), 45–55.

11. Notice that we are not saying that engineering is a profession simply because it is so vital to our health, safety, and welfare. Many nonprofessional occupations share this feature.

12. There is a controversy in professional ethics as to whether it is even appropriate to have a code of ethics. Some of the most important articles in this debate are in Deborah Johnson, ed., *Ethical Issues in Engineering* (Englewood Cliffs, N.J.: Prentice Hall, 1991). See particularly Heinz Luegenbiehl, "Codes of Ethics and the Moral Education of Engineers"(pp. 137–138); and John Ladd, "The Quest for a Code of Professional Ethics: An Intellectual and Moral Confusion" (pp. 130–136). Judith Lichtenberg has a reply to Ladd's argument in "What Are Codes of Ethics For?" in Margaret Coady and Sidney Bloch, *Codes of Ethics and the Professions* (Melbourne, Australia: Melbourne University Press, 1996), pp. 13–27. Particularly strong arguments for the importance of engineering codes of ethics can be found in Stephen H. Unger, *Controlling Technology*, 2nd ed. (New York: John Wiley & Sons, Inc., 1994), Ch. 4, pp. 106–135 and Michael Davis, *Thinking Like an Engineer* (New York: Oxford University Press, 1998), Ch. 4, pp. 43–60.

13. This was a principle of the 1912 code of the American Institute of Electrical Engineers, the first American code, and one that served as the model for most of the other engineering societies. For a brief summary of the history of engineering codes, see Robert Baum, *Ethics and the Engineering Curriculum* (Hastings-on-Hudson, N.Y.: The Hastings Center, 1980), pp. 7–10.

14. Baum, p. 8. However, sometime prior to 1926 the American Association of Engineers (AAE) advanced the four-part "Compilation of Specific Principles of Good Professional Conduct for Engineers." According to some accounts, the first principle states: "The engineer should regard his duty to the public welfare as paramount to all other obliga-tions." This is cited in Carl F. Taeusch, *Professional and Business Ethics* (New York: Henry Holt & Co., 1926), p. 102. However, according to Michael Davis and Heinz Luegenbiehl, the 1920 version of the AAE code has no such provision. (See Appendix C of their *Engineering Codes of Ethics: Analysis and Applications*, Center for the Study of Ethics in the Professions, Illinois Institute of Technology, 1986.) What accounts for this difference is not clear. Nor is it clear why no other engineering societies adopted the AAE provision at that time. AAE itself soon dissolved, and emphasis on the primacy of the engineer's obligation to the public was not to reappear until much later.

15. For examples of BER cases, see our CD-ROM. Also see the WWW Ethics Center for Engineering and Science: http://ethics.cwru.edu.

16. See, for example, Juhn Kultgen, "Evaluating Codes of Professional Ethics," in Wade L. Robison, Michael S. Pritchard, and Joseph Ellin, Eds., *Profits and Professions* (Clifton, N.J.: Humana Press, 1983), pp. 225–264.

17. For good examples of constructive departures from BER consensus opinions, see Paula Wells, Hardy Jones, and Michael Davis, *Conflicts of Interest in Engineering* (Chicago: Center for the Study of Ethics in the Professions, Illinois Institute of Technology, 1986). Unfortunately, none of the case studies they present deal with engineers working in large organizations.

18. For a discussion of these limitations, see Donald Baker, "Social Mechanisms for Controlling Engineers' Performance," in Albert Flores, ed., *Designing for Safety: Engineering Ethics in Organizational Contexts* (Troy, N.Y.: Rensselaer Polytechnic Institute, 1982), especially p. 96.

19. Samuel Florman, "Moral Blueprints," *Harper's* (October 1978), 31.

20. Accreditation Board for Engineering and Technology, *Fifty-third Annual Report* (1985), p. 98.

21. For the precise ABET 2000 wording, see http://www.abet.org/EAC/each2000.html.

22. These goals are discussed in detail in Daniel Callahan, "Goals in the Teaching of Ethics," in Daniel Callahan and Sissela Bok, *Ethics Teaching in Higher Education* (New York: Plenum, 1980), pp. 61–74.

23. For good discussion of this see Robert Baum, *Ethics in Engineering* (Hastings-on-the-Hudson, N.Y.: The Hastings Center, 1980). Baum was an original member of the Hastings Center team of educators. His monograph is one of many prepared for use in the different disciplines.

24. Barbara Toffler, *Tough Choices: Managers Talk Ethics* (New York: John Wiley, 1986), p. 288.

25. This case was presented by engineer J. Kent Roberts (University of Missouri–Rolla) at the Illinois Institute of Technology's 1980 Summer Workshop on Engineering Ethics.

26. This case was developed by civil engineer James Taylor (University of Notre Dame).

27. For a discussion of brainstorming, see the CD-ROM.

28. From NSF Grant No. DIR-8820837, in Michael S. Pritchard, ed., *Teaching Engineering Ethics: A Case Study Approach* (June 1992). The case and accompanying commentaries are on pp. 162–171.

Chapter 2

Framing the Problem

In 1977, the Occupational Safety and Health Administration (OSHA) issued an emergency temporary standard requiring that the level of air exposure to benzene in the workplace not exceed 1 part per million (ppm).[1] This was a departure from the then current standard of 10 ppm. OSHA wanted to make this change permanent because of a recent report to the National Institutes of Health of links between leukemia deaths and exposure to benzene. However, the reported deaths were in workplaces with benzene exposure levels of above 10 ppm, and there were no animal or human test data for lower levels of exposure. Nevertheless, because of evidence that benzene is carcinogenic, OSHA advocated changing the standard to the lowest level that can be easily monitored (1 ppm).

OSHA's authority seemed clear in the Occupational Safety and Health Act, which provides that "no employee will suffer material impairment of health or functional capacity even if such employee has regular exposure to the hazard dealt with by such standard for the period of his working life."[2] The law went on to say that "other considerations shall be the latest available scientific data in the field, the feasibility of the standards, and experience gained under this and other health and safety laws."[3]

On July 2, 1980 the U.S. Supreme Court ruled that OSHA's proposed 1 ppm standard was too strict. The law, said the Court, does not "give OSHA the unbridled discretion to adopt standards designed to create absolutely risk-free workplaces regardless of the costs."[4] It said that although the current limit is 10 ppm, the actual exposures are often considerably lower. It pointed out that a study by the petrochemical industry reported that, out of a total of 496 employees exposed to benzene, only 53 percent were exposed to levels between 1 and 5 ppm, and only 7 employees were exposed to between 5 and 10 ppm.[5] But most of the scientific evidence involved exposure well above 10 ppm.

The Court held that a safe work environment need not be risk-free. OSHA, it ruled, bears the burden of proof that reducing the exposure level to 1 ppm will result in substantial health benefits. OSHA, however, believed that in the face of scientific uncertainty and when lives are at risk, it should be able to enforce stricter standards. OSHA officials objected to shifting to them the burden of proof that chemicals like benzene are dangerous, when it seemed to them that formerly, with support of the law, the burden lay with those who were willing to expose workers to possibly dangerous chemicals.

2.1   Introduction

The conflicting approaches of OSHA and the Supreme Court illustrate legal and probably also moral disagreement. OSHA officials were concerned about protecting workers, regardless of the cost. The Supreme Court justices apparently believed that OSHA officials had not sufficiently taken into account the small number of workers affected, the technological problems involved in implementing the new regulations, and the impact of regulations on employers and the economy. OSHA officials seemed to be concerned almost exclusively with protecting the rights of individuals, whereas the justices were also concerned with promoting the overall good of society.

Despite this disagreement, OSHA officials and the justices probably agreed on many of their basic moral beliefs: that it is wrong to murder, that it is wrong to fail to meet obligations and responsibilities that one has accepted, that it is in general wrong to endanger the well-being and safety of others, and that one should not impose responsibilities on others that are greater than they can legitimately be expected to bear.

These observations point out the important fact that *we usually experience moral disagreement and controversy within a context of agreement.* Prior to our disagreement as to what ought to be done, we usually agree about many general moral precepts and factual beliefs. When we disagree, this often is because we still are not clear enough about important matters that bear on the issue. But even then we often agree about what the unclear areas are and why they are important in the disagreement.

When we think about moral issues, we must keep in mind the wide areas of agreement, including agreement on what is unclear or simply unknown. The focus on moral problem solving in this book and in most discussions of morality tends to obscure the wide areas of moral agreement that most of us share. In this chapter, we consider some of the concepts and distinctions that are useful in understanding both the areas in which we agree about morality and the areas in which we disagree. We begin with a discussion of *common morality*, the basic moral beliefs most of us share. Then, we turn to the basic elements of ethical analysis: determining the relevant facts, determining the relevant ethical considerations, determining whether there are any ethical issues in need of further clarification, and drawing an appropriate ethical conclusion about what should or should not be done. Sometimes this is quite straightforward and uncontroversial. However, frequently there are complications. We also will introduce two special kinds of problems of *relevance*: first, there are factual issues (problems in determining what facts need to be taken into account); second, there are conceptual issues (problems in determining definitions, or meanings, of concepts and how they apply to particular cases).[6] The chapter closes with a discussion of the distinction between two kinds of problems: general moral problems and specific moral problems.

2.2   Common Morality

We can call the stock of common moral beliefs *common morality*. The term is used by analogy with the term *common sense*. Just as most of us share a common body of beliefs about the world and about what we must do to survive—a body of beliefs that we call *common sense*—so we share a common stock of basic beliefs about moral standards, rules, and principles we believe should guide our lives. If asked, we may offer different grounds for holding these beliefs. Many will appeal to their religious commitments, others to more secular commitments. Nevertheless, there is a surprising degree of agreement about the content of common morality.

We also agree in many specific moral judgments, both general and particular. We not only agree with the general idea that murder is wrong, but we also commonly agree in particular instances that a murder has occurred, and that this is wrong. We not only agree with the general idea that for engineers not to disclose conflicts of interest is wrong, but we also commonly agree in particular instances that an engineer has failed to disclose a conflict of interest, and that this is wrong.

Despite this shared body of moral beliefs and judgments about particular cases, however, moral disagreement often occurs. Can we isolate the major factors that account for this? In the succeeding sections of this chapter we will do this, but first we will say more about common morality.

We have said that there is a body of general moral beliefs that most of us hold in common. Of course, people do differ in their moral beliefs, due to such factors as family background and religious upbringing, but most of these differences appear at a less general level. The differences occur with respect to beliefs about specific practices, such as abortion, euthanasia, sexual morality, and capital punishment, or with respect to specific moral judgments, such as the judgment that a particular person should or should not have an abortion. The differences are not as prevalent at the level on which we are now focusing, our more general moral beliefs.

To examine these general moral beliefs more closely, we must formulate them—no easy matter. We will begin by listing some common features of human life that suggest the sorts of general moral beliefs we share.

• *Vulnerability:* We are susceptible to pain, suffering, unhappiness, disability, and ultimately death.

• *Autonomy:* We are, to at least some degree, capable of thinking for ourselves and making our own decisions.

- *Interdependency:* We depend on others helping us to get what we want, through cooperative endeavor and the division of labor; and our well-being also depends on others refraining from harming us.

- *Shared expectations and goals:* Beyond wanting things for ourselves as individuals, we may want things together, as groups working toward shared ends; these groups may range from caring relationships between two or more individuals to larger groups, such as a particular profession, religious institution, nation, or even an international organization such as the United Nations or the World Heath Organization.

- *Common moral traits:* Fair-mindedness, self-respect, respect for others, compassion, and benevolence toward others are common traits; despite individual differences in their strength, scope, and constancy, these traits can be found to some degree in virtually all human beings.

Without suggesting that this list is complete, it does seem to provide a reasonable basis for understanding why common morality would include general moral rules or principles about duties not to harm others; to make reparations for harms done to others, not to lie or cheat, to keep our promises, not to interfere with the freedom of others, to respect others' capacity to make rational decisions about matters affecting their basic values, to treat others fairly, to help those in need, and so on.[7]

Although these rules or principles are quite general, this does not mean that they have no exceptions. Usually it is wrong to lie; but if the only way to save an innocent person from being murdered is to lie to the assailant about that person's whereabouts, most would agree that lying is justified. The main point is not that moral rules and principles have no exceptions; it is that taking exception to them requires having a *justification*, or *good reason*, for doing so. This contrasts with, for example, deciding whether to take a walk, go to the movies, or read a book. Breaking a promise, however, always calls for a justification, as does injuring others.[8]

It is likely that engineers share these general moral beliefs, and many engineering codes of ethics reflect them. Most codes enjoin engineers to be faithful agents of their employers, and this injunction can be seen to follow from the duty to keep one's promises (here, those made when accepting employment). Most codes oblige engineers to act in a way that protects the health, safety, and welfare of the public, and this duty has a special connection with common morality duties not to injure others and to prevent harm, especially because engineers often are in privileged positions of trust and responsibility to provide such protection.

To understand our reference to common morality, we should keep the following points in mind. First, we should distinguish common morality from both personal morality and professional morality. As we have said, common morality refers to those moral standards, rules, and principles that are shared by virtually everyone, regardless of other differences we might have. Personal morality includes those moral standards, rules, and principles we accept as individuals but which are not necessarily accepted by others. Professional morality includes those moral standards and principles that apply especially to one's role as a professional. Although it is rare that common morality, personal morality, and professional morality will give three different answers to the same moral question, sometimes differences do arise. Taking a bribe is contrary to both common and professional morality, but it might not be contrary to the personal morality of some people. Likewise, an engineer's decision to refuse to design military hardware might be contrary to her personal morality, but it is not necessarily contrary to either professional engineering ethics or to common morality.

Second, many of the standard provisions of engineering codes are simply specific applications of common morality to the engineering profession. In this regard, there is no "special" engineering ethics, even though, given their professional roles, engineers have special responsibilities and opportunities to apply the rules and principles of common morality in their work. Common morality recognizes the place of special duties and prerogatives attached to special roles. Many of the provisions of engineering codes embody the special role obligations of engineers. Even such provisions as the prohibition of dishonesty can be related to the role of engineers: scientific and technical information cannot be used for the good of clients and the public if engineers are dishonest. The duty of engineers to hold paramount the health and safety of the public embodies role morality, because these go beyond the duties of nonengineers. Because of their special technical knowledge and their important role in creating the technology that can endanger the health and safety of the public, engineers have a special duty to protect the public from the harm that technological innovation can cause and to use their technical knowledge to benefit the public.

Third, in common morality priority is usually given to negative duties—duties not to cause harm, not to break promises, not to be dishonest, and so on. This enables us to understand some of the perplexing and troubling questions that engineers often encounter. Few engineers doubt that they should not design products that cause harm, but they differ on how much responsibility they have to prevent harm caused by others. For example, does an engineer have a duty to blow the whistle on wrongdoing committed by other engineers?

Fourth, the relationship of common morality to professional morality is complex. On the one hand, we have pointed out that many of the provisions of engineering codes simply transpose the provisions of common morality into the professional setting. Therefore, much of professional ethics is based on or derived from common morality. On the other hand, common morality and professional morality are both subject to criticism and change, but they may or may not change at the same time or in the same way. Whereas, the prohibitions of dishonesty in common morality are unlikely to change, beliefs about our obligations to the environment are in the process of modification. Future generations may take certain types of obligations to the environment as uncontroversial, even though today they are the subject of considerable debate. This modification may, in turn, lead to changes in the codes, but it is also possible for professional societies to take the lead by making changes in their codes that will contribute to changes in common morality.[9]

2.3   Moral Justification

Acknowledging that common morality is subject to criticism and change raises the question of its reliability. If we are to use common morality as an aid for formulating professional codes of ethics and in making moral judgments about engineering practice, don't we have to justify this? After all, the fact that something is commonly believed does not necessarily mean that it is right. So, we might feel the need to move to a more fundamental level, one that will provide us with the "ultimate" foundation of morality (and which, we might hope, will vindicate common morality).

However, much as we might want to "get to the bottom of things" in morality, we may find that attempting to do so actually makes it harder to see what we have in common morally. Although philosophical and religious traditions around the world have long sought to articulate the ultimate foundations of morality, thus far no consensus has been reached.[10] Thoughtful, reasonable people can be expected to have different views at this level. More promising is the idea that consensus might be found if we concentrate on moral values that have had to be worked out by all human societies and that are held in common by nearly all human beings.[11]

This more modest approach seems especially appropriate for professional ethics, and engineering ethics in particular. Professional ethics seeks a body of moral beliefs that should be accepted by all members of the profession in question. Such a body of beliefs will have to cut across religious differences and include those who have no particular religious commitments as well. Trying to identify moral values that have had to be worked out by all human societies and that are held in common by nearly all human beings should yield a *minimalist* set of values; these would include positive duties of mutual support, loyalty, and reciprocity; negative duties to refrain from harming others; and norms for determining just procedures in resolving issues of justice.[12] In a minimalist set of common moral values room is left for personal differences, including deeply religious ones. At the same time, the points of agreement provide a reasonable basis for framing codes of professional ethics and for exploring areas in need of further understanding and clarification.

An Illustration: Research Involving Humans

A good illustration of the wisdom of this approach is the experience of the National Commission for the Protection of Human Subjects of Biomedical and Behavioral Research, established by the U.S. Congress in 1974. In 1978 the commission issued what is known as the *Belmont Report*, which contains the guidelines used by institutional review boards (IRBs) at colleges, universities, and other institutions that receive federal funding for research involving human subjects. It is the responsibility of IRBs to examine research proposals to make certain that the rights and welfare of human subjects are protected.

In setting up the commission, Congress selected a broadly representative group of commissioners:

The eleven commissioners had varied backgrounds and interests. They included men and women; blacks and whites; Catholics and Protestants, Jews, and atheists; medical scientists and behavioral psychologists; philosophers; lawyers; theologians; and public representatives. In all, five commissioners had scientific interests and six did not.[13]

The commission began by trying to "get to the bottom of things." However, their deep religious and philosophical differences brought them to a stalemate. So, they decided to talk about specific examples rather than their more foundational concerns. They discussed many of the kinds of disturbing experiments that had caused Congress to convene the commission in the first place: the infamous Tuskegee study, in which poor, illiterate black men in rural Alabama were denied treatment for syphilis (without being informed about the nature of their disease) so that its natural course of development could be studied; the injection of cancer cells into elderly persons without their knowledge or consent; experiments on children and prisoners; and so on.

Members of the commission found that they basically agreed on what was objectionable in these experiments. Eventually, they formulated a set of guidelines that emphasizes three basic areas of concern: respect for persons, beneficence, and justice. *Respect for persons*, the commission agreed, includes acquiring the informed consent of subjects to participate in an experiment. *Beneficence* involves attempting to maximize benefits and minimize harm to the subjects. *Justice* requires avoiding the use of discrimination in the selection of research subjects, with special attention given to particularly vulnerable groups such as prisoners, children, and the elderly. Commissioners might have disagreed about the ultimate foundations of the principles of respect for persons, beneficence, and justice, but they agreed that these principles are basic in addressing areas of concern in research involving humans.

So, despite their differences, the commissioners discovered that they had much in common morally, and they were able to put this to good use in formulating a national policy. At the same time, they realized that they had not come up with a set of guidelines that eliminate the need for good judgment, or that eliminate controversy:

> Three principles, or general prescriptive judgments, that are relevant to research involving human subjects are identified in this statement. Other principles may also be relevant. These three are comprehensive, however, and are stated at a level of generalization that should assist scientists, subjects, reviewers and interested citizens to understand the ethical issues inherent in research involving human subjects. These principles cannot always be applied so as to resolve beyond dispute particular ethical problems. The objective is to provide an analytical framework that will guide the resolution of ethical problems arising from research involving human subjects.[14]

Notice that the *Belmont Report's* analytical framework resulted from the joint deliberation of the commissioners. They were willing to listen to, and reason with, each other in their search for common ground, not only among themselves but also with the general public. These are the marks of *reasonableness* among thoughtful, but diverse, people. To the extent that we try to justify our moral judgments, rather than simply assert them, we are striving to be reasonable with others. The process of justification is essentially public, not private. This is true in morality as well as in science and engineering.

Two Key Concepts: Universalizability and Reversibility

There are two basic moral concepts that are especially important to keep in mind in all efforts to justify our moral judgments. The first concept is *universalizability*: Whatever is right (or wrong) in one situation is right (or wrong) in any relevantly similar situation.[15] Although this does not by itself specify what is right or wrong, it requires us to be consistent in our thinking. For example, in considering whether or not it would be morally acceptable to falsify data in a particular project, a scientist or engineer needs to think about not just this particular situation but all situations relevantly like it. Falsifying data is, essentially, a form of lying or cheating. When we broaden our focus to consider what *kind* of act is involved, the question of whether it is all right to falsify data is bound to look quite different from focusing only on the immediate situation.

The second, related, concept is *reversibility*. We find this concept expressed in the Golden Rule, a principle found in the religious and ethical writings of virtually all cultures: Treat others as you would have them treat you.[16] In thinking about treating others as I would have them treat me, I need to ask what I would think if the roles were reversed. If I am tempted to tell a lie to escape a particular difficulty, I need to ask what I would think if I were the one to whom the lie is told.

The idea of reversibility can be viewed as a special application of the idea of universalizability. Accepting the idea that whatever is right (or wrong) is right (or wrong) in any relevantly similar situation implies that, from a moral point of view, it should not matter whether one is on the giving or receiving end of what is done. The idea of universalizability implies that my judgment should not change simply because the roles are reversed.

2.4 ✳ Analyzing a Case

A primary task in ethically analyzing any situation is to assemble information relevant to the resolution of the ethical problem(s) it presents. An ethics case study describes a set of circumstances that calls for ethical reflection. It is helpful to begin an analysis with two questions: (1) What are the relevant facts? (2) What are the relevant kinds of ethical considerations? These two questions are interconnected; they cannot be answered independently of one another. Let's see why.

What are the relevant facts? Note the key term here is *relevant*. Relevant to what? To the ethical questions in need of attention. That is, we need to have our eye on what is ethically important to know which of the many facts available to us we should be considering. On the one hand, it may be a fact that engineer Joe

Smith was wearing a suit and tie on the day he was deciding whether or not to blow the whistle on his employer. But it is not obvious that this fact is relevant to the question of whether he should blow the whistle. On the other hand, the fact that blowing the whistle might prevent serious injuries is relevant.

What are the relevant kinds of ethical considerations in any given case? Note, again, the key term *relevant*. Relevant to what? To the facts of the case. For example, conflicts of interest are ethically important to consider—but only when the facts of a case suggest that there might actually be a conflict of interest.

What are some of the resources we might use in framing the ethical considerations that could apply to a given case? These are the ideas of common morality discussed; professional codes of ethics; more general, comprehensive principles of ethics; and our personal morality. All of these may be helpful in determining what facts are relevant in any given case. To this we should add our ability to *critically evaluate* all of these resources, including our personal morality.

A Sample Case

As we shall see, taking these resources into account can be very complicated and often quite controversial. However, it is not always this way, and it is important not to lose sight of this, as the following fictional case illustrates:

> Thirty-four-year-old Steven Severson was in his last semester of the graduate program in mechanical engineering. Father of three small children, he was anxious to get his degree so that he could spend more time with his family. Going to school and holding down a full-time job not only kept him from his family, it shifted more parental responsibility to his wife Sarah than he felt was fair. But the end was in sight, and he could look forward both to a better job and to being a better father and husband.
>
> Steven was following in the footsteps of his father, who had received a graduate degree in mechanical engineering just months before tragically dying in an automobile accident. Sarah understood how important getting a graduate degree was to Steven, and she never complained about the long hours he spent studying. But she, too, was anxious for this chapter in their lives to end.
>
> As part of his requirement to complete his graduate research and obtain his advanced degree, Steven was required to develop a research report. Most of the data strongly supported Steven's conclusion as well as prior conclusions developed by others. However, a few aspects of the data were at variance and not fully consistent with the conclusions contained in his report. Convinced of the soundness of his report and concerned that inclusion of the ambiguous data would detract from and distort the essential thrust of the report, Steven decided to omit references to the ambiguous data. Was it unethical for Steven to fail to include reference to the unsubstantiated data in his report?

We should notice first that there is a great deal of information in this scenario that is not relevant to the ethical question. In fact, despite their human interest, the first two paragraphs have no real bearing on the ethical question. Even though they explain why Steven is doing the research, and why he is anxious to bring it to a successful close, none of this is relevant to the question of whether it is right to omit possibly important data from his report. No doubt there is also a great deal of irrelevant, unmentioned information—like the size and color of the paper on which he prepared the report, whether or not Steven wears eyeglasses, how tall he is, what he ate for breakfast on the day he completed the report, and so on.

In short, what we must do in resolving an ethical question is focus only on those facts that are relevant. Sometimes this may be an easy task, and sometimes the facts make the resolution seem obvious. But in these cases ethical criteria guide the sorting out of relevant from irrelevant facts. These criteria may come from our common morality, professional codes, or even our personal morality. Hence, we must remind ourselves of all three.

Common morality should have reminded Steven Severson of the importance of honesty. His examiners had a right to expect him not to distort his data, and Steven's misrepresentation is a breach of the trust they had in him that he would do honest work and not interfere with their responsibility to assess his qualifications for an advanced degree. But the harm does not necessarily stop there. If Steven thought he was justified in leaving out the data in this case, he might also think this will be acceptable in the workplace as well. There the stakes will be much higher, risking not only economic costs to his employer but also product quality and possibly the health, safety, or welfare of the public. Steven may have thought that the pressure to graduate was unusually great and that he would not repeat this behavior in the workplace. However, this is more a rationalization of his action than a realistic assessment of the challenges that will face him as a practicing engineer. For example, one of the most common challenges practicing engineers face is meeting the pressure of deadlines.

We can also apply the concepts of universalizability and reversibility to Steven's situation. If Steven is justified in leaving out data when he is convinced that it doesn't really discredit his conclusion, so are others who feel the same way about their research data. What would be the consequences of such a general practice? Notice that Steven cannot simply assume that his case is different because he knows he is right, whereas others do not. He should realize that the strong pressure he feels to finish his work successfully could compromise his judgment. So, he is really not in a good position to determine this for himself. Subjective certainty in his own case is not a defensible criterion; and he should be wary of generalizing this criterion to others who might be similarly tempted. A sounder position would be for him to concede that, if he actually is right, a full presentation of the data should convince others as well. By withholding the data from his examiners, Steven seems to be saying that he is more capable than they of assessing the significance of his data. Here the concept of reversibility is especially relevant. What would Steven think if the roles were reversed—if he were one of the examiners and he learned that one of his students omitted data in this way?

From the standpoint of engineering codes of ethics this case is also quite straightforward. Actually, the Steven Severson case is simply an embellishment of a fictional case prepared and discussed by the Board of Ethical Review (BER) of the National Society for Professional Engineers (NSPE).[17] The BER case consists basically only of the last paragraph of the Steven Severson case; that is, the BER streamlined its presentation to include only relevant facts. In any actual case, however, much other information will be present and must be sifted through. In the original BER case, the presentation of the scenario is followed by several relevant provisions in NSPE's Code of Ethics. These provisions—calling for objectivity, truthfulness, and cooperative exchange of information—seem to settle the matter decisively. Steven should not have omitted the data.

In regard to Steven's personal morality, we can only speculate, of course. But it is quite possible that, had he thought through his situation more thoroughly, Steven would have realized that his personal integrity was on the line. However, he was convinced of the overall soundness of his report and was not trying to convince his examiners of something he thought was untrue or unsupportable. This suggests that he valued truthfulness but underestimated what it requires.

Our ability to analyze a case depends on our experience with problems of the sort under consideration. Our understanding of common morality, relevant codes of ethics, and our own personal morality can assist us. These constitute our initial ethical sensitivities as we examine the scenario presented to us. Then we need to sort relevant from irrelevant facts and ethical considerations. This will lead us to revise the scenario somewhat. As we analyze the key elements in the revised scenario we may go directly to a resolution, as the Steven Severson case illustrates; or we may want to revisit earlier phases of the process. This reiterative process is represented by the feedback loop in Figure 2.1.

Initial perceptions of a given case are likely to vary somewhat from individual to individual, so discussing a case with others is likely to result in revisiting earlier phases. Although this may seem to slow down the task of analysis, it often results in a much better understanding and resolution of the case; in ethical analysis two (or more) heads are often much better than one. Sometimes, as the Steven Severson case shows, matters are fairly uncomplicated and uncontroversial.

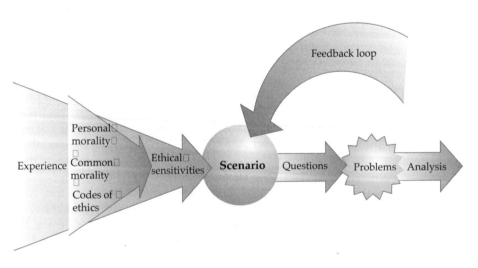

Figure 2.1
The First Phase of Moral Thinking

However, as we shall see in the next sections, sorting out matters is often not so easy. When we try to determine what facts and ethical considerations are relevant to a given case, two kinds of issues often underlie apparent disagreement among those considering the case. The first kind of issue pivots around difficulties in determining just what the relevant facts are; we will call these *factual issues*. The second kind of issue pivots around the definitions, or meanings, of key concepts (such as *bribery, safety,* and *public*) and how to apply these concepts to the case in question: we will call these *conceptual issues*.

2.5   Factual Issues

We have seen that we cannot discuss moral issues intelligently apart from a knowledge of the relevant facts. So, we must begin with a consideration of what those facts are. In any given case, many facts will be obvious to all, and they should be taken into account. However, if people disagree about some facts, or if they are not all aware of the same facts, they may well make different moral judgments. Then we have a *factual issue*.

To see the importance of facts in a moral controversy, we propose three theses about factual issues.

1. *Disagreements that appear to be about moral issues often turn out to be about the relevant facts.* Imagine a conversation between two engineers, Tom and Jim, that might have taken place shortly before OSHA issued its directive in May 1977 that worker exposure to benzene emissions be reduced from 10 ppm to 1 ppm. Their conversation might proceed like this:

Tom: I hear OSHA is about to issue stricter regulations regarding worker exposure to benzene. Oh, boy, here we go again! Complying with the new regulations is going to cost our company several million dollars. It's all well and good for the bureaucrats in Washington to make rules, as long as they don't have to pay the bills. I think OSHA is just irresponsible!

Jim: But Tom, human life is at stake! You know the dangers of benzene. Would you want to be out in the area where benzene exposure is an issue? Would you want your son or your daughter to be subjected to exposures higher than 1 ppm?

Tom: I wouldn't have any problem with that at all. There is just no scientific evidence that exposure to benzene below 10 ppm has any harmful effect. In fact, the scientific literature I've read and the data I've seen from our own studies indicate that exposure to benzene below 10 ppm is not harmful.

Tom shows Jim some of the evidence he has collected, inviting him to revisit his earlier understanding of the relevant facts (and, as a result, the relevant ethical considerations). The next day the conversation continues:

Jim: Well, Tom, maybe I was wrong. The data you've shown me look more convincing than anything I've seen before.

In this scenario, Jim and Tom agree when they see eye to eye on the facts. What looked like a moral disagreement was a lack of common agreement about the facts of the situation. But all along they agreed that, if it can be shown that lower levels of exposure to benzene are harmful, stronger regulations are needed. Thus, all along they agreed with the general moral rule against harming others. What they disagreed about was whether this rule had any relevant application in the circumstances under consideration; and they could not agree about this until they agreed about the facts.

Here is another example. Suppose two engineers, Judy and Jane, disagree about whether the government should enforce affirmative action policies in the workplace. They may think their disagreement is about the moral issue of the permissibility of affirmative action policies. Further discussion may reveal, however, that their real disagreement is about the factual question of how discrimination can be eliminated. On the one hand, Judy may think that, without affirmative action policies, women and minorities will continue to experience gross discrimination in the workplace. Jane, on the other hand, may believe that fair treatment in the workplace can be achieved without governmental intervention. Jane may admit that if governmental intervention is the only way to eliminate injustice in the hiring system, she would be in favor of it, too. Thus, the real difference between Judy and Jane is not over basic moral beliefs, but over a factual belief about what it takes to eliminate unjust hiring practices. If they could agree on the factual question as to how injustice to women and minorities could be eliminated, they could agree on their moral evaluation of the permissibility of government intervention.

2. *Factual issues are sometimes very difficult to resolve.* It is particularly important for engineering students to understand that many apparent moral disagreements are reducible to disagreements about factual (in many cases technical) matters. The dispute between Tom and Jim was very easy to resolve. Tom simply shared information that Jim had not seen before. Often, however, the factual issues are not easily resolved. Sometimes engineers and engineering students, after a debate about professional ethics issues, come away with an attitude that might be stated like this: "Well, here was another dispute about ethics in which nobody could agree. I'm glad that I'm in engineering, where everything depends on the facts that everybody can agree on. Ethics is just too subjective." But the dispute may pivot more around the difficulty of determining factual matters than any disagreement about ethical values as such. Sometimes the information is not available, and sometimes it is difficult to imagine how it could be available.

In the dispute about affirmative action, for example, it would be very difficult to resolve the factual issue over whether affirmative action is the only method for eliminating discrimination in the workplace. We would like to try each option for 100 years and compare the two, but such social experiments are impossible. Many technical and scientific issues are also in dispute and are not capable of decisive resolution at a given time. When moral judgments depend on the resolution of these issues, the moral judgments are going to be controversial. Here it is especially important to revisit the scenario as initially described, this time taking into account the uncertainty of the factual assumptions and, in light of that uncertainty, exploring possible alternative courses of action and their likelihood of success.

3. *Once the factual issues are clearly isolated, moral disagreement can reemerge on another and often more clearly defined level.* Suppose Judy and Jane finally agree that their dispute over whether affirmative action policies are necessary to eliminate injustice in hiring policies cannot be resolved on the basis of known facts. Then they might have the following conversation:

Judy: So we both agree that if we knew affirmative action policies were the only way to eliminate injustice in hiring practices, we would say affirmative action was a good thing. You say you are convinced affirmative action is not the only way to eliminate injustice, and I believe it is. But I still think you are wrong in what you conclude from this. I believe we should promote affirmative action in the face of this factual uncertainty, because it is better to err on the side of promoting justice for women and minorities.

Jane: I think we still disagree, Judy. I believe we should give the benefit of the doubt to employers. If we don't know that affirmative action policies are really necessary to promote justice, we ought to let employers exercise their own judgment. This is more likely to promote economic efficiency.

Judy: But surely justice is more important than economic efficiency! If we don't know what the facts are, I believe we should give the benefit of the doubt to the employees. We ought to give more weight to considerations of justice.

Jane: Remember that if we enforce affirmative action we are only *possibly* preventing injustice, while we are very likely to diminish economic efficiency, because we might not be hiring the most appropriate person for the job. Besides, economic efficiency is not the only consideration. We also have to consider the freedom of the employer to do what he wants with his own company. Again, we are trading off almost certain losses in economic efficiency and certain losses in employer freedom against a possible increase in justice. I don't think this is a good trade-off.

Judy: But Jane, depriving people of equal opportunity in the workplace is very serious business. It strikes at the heart of people's self-esteem and their ability to pursue their own goals in life. Surely even the chance of injuring people in this way is more important than the kinds of considerations you bring up. And with respect to your argument about employer freedom, I don't think affirmative action programs limit employer freedom in a very serious way.

Here a value disagreement reemerges, but now it is more precisely formulated. Now Judy and Jane understand that they are disagreeing about what should be done in the light of the factual uncertainty about whether affirmative action is the only way to end discrimination. Jane thinks that in the light of this uncertainty the benefit of the doubt should go to the employers, and Judy thinks it should go to women and minorities. The considerations necessary to resolve this disagreement are different from the considerations necessary to resolve the original disagreement—which turned out to be about the facts. Now the disagreement is about what is the best policy in the face of factual uncertainty. This is more clearly a matter of moral disagreement.

Discerning Relevant Facts

We have seen that in many cases uncertainty and disagreement about moral issues can be traced to uncertainty and disagreement about facts. As the Steven Severson case shows, not all facts are relevant to a moral issue. However, sorting out relevant from irrelevant facts must be done with care, and sometimes how this is done can be quite controversial.

Recall the previous conversation between Tom and Jim about worker exposure to benzene. Whether the workers were male or female would not ordinarily be relevant to whether they deserve to be protected from exposure to benzene. It might be relevant under certain conditions, however. If research shows that males are more susceptible than females to the effects of benzene, then males might deserve special protection. This would be the result of their special vulnerability, however, not simply their gender. If research shows that fetuses are even more likely to be harmed by exposure to benzene than adult males, then pregnant women would deserve more consideration than either men or nonpregnant women.

In both of these cases, the moral relevance of these facts will probably not be disputed by most people. The issue under consideration is protection from harm. If men are more likely to be harmed than women and fetuses still more likely to be harmed than men, then the degree of protection should correspond to the degree of vulnerability to harm. But matters can be more complicated. For example, because of concerns about potential harm to fetuses, it might be recommended that more research on harmful effects of benzene be done with women subjects than men. If the fetus is shown to be vulnerable, then efforts might be made to exclude pregnant women from work that exposes them to benzene. Further, this might be extended to women who *could* become pregnant, as well. However, it is also quite possible that sperm is affected in ways harmful to fetuses, too.[18] So, if there is more research on women than men for possible adverse affects on the fetus, charges of bias may be leveled. One possible solution to this sort of occupational discrimination is to improve workplace conditions by lowering the level of exposure to benzene to a level that poses no risk to fetuses.

Known and Unknown Facts

Many of the facts relevant to the resolution of moral disputes are known; but sometimes the facts are not known, and therefore moral disagreements cannot be firmly resolved. Thus, it is important to distinguish not only between relevant and irrelevant facts, but between known relevant facts and unknown relevant facts. The relationship is illustrated by Figure 2.2.

As this figure illustrates, we are concerned with the facts that are relevant to the resolution of a moral issue; some are known and some are unknown. The

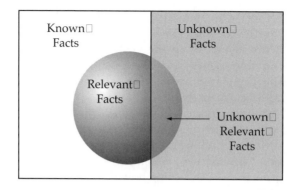

Figure 2.2
Analyzing the Facts

known relevant facts are only some of the relevant facts about a moral issue. In this figure, more of the relevant facts are known than unknown. However, the number of relevant facts is less important than the degree of their relevance. Even a single unknown relevant fact might make a crucial difference to what should be done. So, we have a special responsibility to seek answers to unanswered factual questions.

2.6 ✳ Conceptual Issues

Good moral thinking requires not only attending carefully to relevant facts but also having a good grasp of the key concepts we need to use; that is, we need to get as clear as we can about the meanings of key terms. For example, *public health, safety, and welfare, conflict of interest, bribery, extortion, confidentiality, trade secret,* and *loyalty* are key terms for ethics in engineering.

It would be nice to have precise definitions of all these terms; but like most terms in ethics, their meanings are somewhat open-ended. In many cases it is sufficient to clarify our meaning by thinking of paradigms, or clear-cut examples, of what we have in mind. In less straightforward cases it is often useful to compare and contrast the case in question with paradigms.[19] Suppose a firm signs a contract with a customer that specifies that all parts of the product will be made in the United States, but the product has a special 1/4-inch staple hidden from view that was made in England. Is the firm *dishonest* if it does not tell its customer about this staple?

A clear-cut case of dishonesty would be if Mark, the firm's representative, answers "No" to the customer asking, "Is there *anything* in this product that wasn't made in the U.S.A.?" Suppose, instead, the customer asks, "Does this product have any parts not made in the U.S.A.?" and Mark replies, "No," silently thinking, "After all, that little staple isn't a *part*; it simply holds parts together." Of course, this raises the question of what is meant by "part." But given the contract's specifications, honesty in this case would seem to call for full disclosure. Then the customer can decide whether the English staple is acceptable. Better yet would be for the firm to contact the customer before using the staple, explaining why it is needed and asking whether using it would be acceptable.

Although in this case we may question the firm's motives (and therefore its honesty), sometimes apparent moral disagreement turns out to rest on conceptual differences where no one's motives are in question. These are issues about the general *definitions*, or *meanings*, of concepts. (Shortly we will discuss related conceptual issues concerning how they *apply* to the case in question.) In the benzene case, the most obvious conceptual issue of meaning has to do with the proper definition of "safe." Closely related to this is the definition of what constitutes a "substantial" health risk, or what constitutes a "material impairment" of health. Finally, the definition of "burden of proof" can be a point of controversy, especially if we are considering the issue from a moral and not merely a legal standpoint, where the term may be more clearly defined.

Defining Concepts

We can imagine a continuation of the conversation between Tom and Jim that illustrates the importance of some of the conceptual issues that can arise in the context of apparent moral disagreement.

Jim: Tom, I've conceded that you are right about the facts. The evidence that exposures to benzene between 1 and 10 ppm is harmful is weak at best, but I think I was too hasty in concluding that this is the end of the matter. I'll go back to one of my original points: human life is involved. I just don't believe we should take a chance on harming people when we aren't certain about the facts. I think we ought to provide a safe environment for our workers, and I wouldn't call an environment "safe" when there is even a chance that the disputed benzene levels are harmful.

Tom: Here we go again on that old saw, "How safe is safe?" How can you say that something is not safe when you don't have any evidence to back up your claim?

Jim: I think something is unsafe when there is any kind of substantial health risk.

Tom: But how can you say there is any substantial health risk when, in fact, the evidence that is available seems to point in the other direction?

Jim: Well, I would say that there is a substantial health risk when there is any reason to suspect that there is a problem, at least when something like carcinogens are involved. The burden of proof should rest on anyone who wants to expose a worker to even a possible danger.

Tom: I'll agree with you that workers should not be exposed to substantial health risks, but I think this is a strange definition of "substantial." Let me put the question another way. Suppose the risk of dying from cancer due to benzene exposure in the plant over a period of thirty years is no greater than the risk over the same period of time of dying from an automobile accident while driving home from the plant. Would you consider the health risk from benzene exposure in this case to be "substantial"?

Jim: Yes, I would. The conditions are different. I believe we have made highways about as safe as we can. We have not made health conditions for workers in plants as safe as we can. We can lower the level of benzene exposure in the plant, and with a relatively moderate expenditure. Furthermore, everyone accepts the risks involved in auto travel. Many of the workers don't understand the risk from benzene exposure. They aren't acting as free agents with informed consent.

Tom: Wow! I don't think we are going to get anywhere on this one. Let's try another approach. Suppose at the lower levels of benzene exposure—I mean under 10 ppm—the risk of cancer is virtually nil, but some workers find that the exposure causes the skin on their faces, hands, and arms to be drier than usual. They can treat this with skin lotion. Would you consider this a health problem?

Jim: Yes, I would. I think it would be what some people would call a "material impairment" of health, and I would agree. Workers should not have to endure *any* change in their health or bodily well-being as a result of working at our plant. People are selling their time to the company, but not their bodies and their health. And dry skin is certainly unhealthy.

Tom: Well, this just seems too strict. I guess we really do disagree. We don't even seem to be able to agree on what we mean by the words we use.

Here genuine disagreement about moral issues has reappeared, but this time in the form of disagreement about the definitions of crucial terms. Many concepts, such as "safe," "substantial," "health," and "material impairment," are a blend of factual elements and value elements. Tom and Jim might agree on the effects of exposure to benzene at various levels and still disagree on what is "safe" or "healthy" and what is not. To know whether benzene is safe, we have to have some notion of what the risks are at various exposure levels, but we also have to have a notion of what we consider "acceptable risk." The use of the term *acceptable* should be sufficient to alert us that there is a value element here that cannot be determined by the facts alone.

When disagreements about the meanings of words arise, it may be tempting to say "We're just quibbling about words," or "It's just a semantic question." Insofar as the choice of meanings we make affects our chosen course of action, this understates the significance of the disagreement. Tom and Jim, for example, would choose different regulatory standards based on their different understandings of "safe." The different meanings they give safe also reflect different levels of risk to which they are willing to give their approval. Although Tom and Jim might never resolve their differences, it is desirable for them to try. At this point they at least can see more clearly what these differences are. If they can agree that safe is best understood in terms of acceptable risk rather than "absolutely risk-free" (a standard that is virtually unattainable), they can then proceed to discuss reasonable standards of acceptability.

Here is another example. Suppose Bill is an engineer who represents his U.S. company in the foreign country of Morotavia. One day he is told by a Morotavian official that his company's warehouses may catch fire and the firefighters may not arrive in time to extinguish the fire unless Bill's company contributes $100,000 to the official's reelection campaign. What should Bill do?

The Federal Foreign Corrupt Practices Act of 1977 distinguishes between *bribery* and *extortion*. It allows American companies to pay extortion in some cases, but not bribes; so it is important to know whether the payment would be a bribe or an extortion—that is, the set of conditions both necessary and sufficient for something to qualify as one or the other. It is easier to give a characterization, a condition that, if met, is sufficient for something to count as either bribery or extortion. The following characterizations will be adequate for our purposes:[20]

Bribery—voluntary offering of goods, services, or money to secure an unjustified privilege to the briber

Extortion—nonvoluntary provision of goods, services, or money to the extortioner to secure treatment, to which the one being extorted is already lawfully and morally entitled, from the extortioner

According to these characterizations, Bill's company is being asked to pay extortion, not bribery.

Not only do these characterizations involve value terms, such as *unjustified privilege* and *morally entitled,* but the question of moral permissibility raises ethical questions as well. In general, paying bribery, which is voluntary, seems more morally serious than paying extortion, which is nonvoluntary. Furthermore, extortion merely allows one to obtain what she is entitled to anyway, whereas bribery enables one to obtain something she does not deserve—at least not as a result of bribery. Although paying extortion may be unjustifiable in many situations (and extracting extortion is always unjustifiable), there are morally relevant differences between bribery and extortion. Regardless of how one resolves the question of what Bill should do, it is important to know whether he is dealing with bribery or extortion. And if one were to define these terms differently, their moral evaluation might be quite different.

The definitions or characterizations of some terms do not involve such obvious value issues. In thinking about the benzene case, we want to be sure that we agree on the meanings of such terms as *cancer* or *leukemia*. Although scientists might well dispute the precise definitions of these diseases, no obvious value terms are present here. In debating what caused the leukemia, there could well be disagreements about what constitutes a "cause." Again, no obvious value terms are here. Whereas some conceptual issues involve important value questions, some do not.

Usually the question of the meaning of a concept arises because we do not know how the concept applies to a particular situation. Sometimes such a question can be most appropriately resolved by a reexamination and further definition of the concept itself. Michael Davis provides an example of this tactic.[21] Most engineering codes require engineers to give priority to the health, safety, and welfare of the "public." How should we understand the scope of the term *public*? For example, how should this term have been interpreted by engineers when, on the night before the fateful launch of the *Challenger* space shuttle, they were considering their obligations as engineers? Are the astronauts part of the "public" and thus proper objects of the engineer's professional concern? Davis considers three ways in which we might interpret the term public.

First, the public might include everyone. In this case, the astronauts are clearly a part of the public. Davis believes, however, that this is an unrealistic definition because few dangers are likely to threaten everyone, and the obligation would demand too little. The engineer's work might often threaten some of the public without threatening everyone.

A second possible definition takes this observation into account by defining public as "anyone" who might be threatened by the engineer's professional activities. This definition might imply that engineers should not do anything that threatens anyone who stands to be affected. If so, it is still too broad, for it would make engineering impossible. For example, it is difficult to imagine how we could have electric power stations or manufacturing plants that would pose no threat to anyone.

A third and more plausible definition of public begins with the claim that what makes people part of the public is that they are liable to be affected by engineering products and services without being in a position to give free or informed consent to these effects. The "public" is characterized by their relative innocence, helplessness, and passivity. On this interpretation, "public" would refer to those persons whose lack of information, technical knowledge, or time for deliberation renders them more or less vulnerable to the powers an engineer wields on behalf of his client or employer.[22]

As Davis points out, this interpretation implies that someone might be part of the public in one respect and not in another. For example, the astronauts would be part of the public with respect to the danger of explosion due to the faulty O-rings, because they had no knowledge of the danger. They would not be a part of the public with respect to the ice formation on the booster rockets, for they were aware of this danger and evidently gave their informed consent to the risk involved. They could have chosen to abort the launch if they had been unwilling to accept that risk.

Given this definition of public, the moral principle that engineers should look after the health, safety, and welfare of the public does apply to the astronauts. Roger Boisjoly did have an obligation as an engineer to try to protect the astronauts from dangers to which they had not given their informed consent.[23] We can, of course, question this definition of public and offer alternative definitions. However, if we accept it, Boisjoly's obligation to object to the launch of the *Challenger* seems to be settled. In this way, the resolution of a conceptual issue can help to resolve a moral question.

Applying Concepts

We were able to trace part of Tom and Jim's disagreement to their different definitions of such terms as *safe* and *material impairment* of health. Sometimes, however, people appear to have the same definitions of terms, but disagree on their application in particular situations. There are several reasons why this might happen. First, because they may be operating from different factual premises, people who agree on meanings or definitions of key terms may apply them differently. Second, people may agree on the facts and the meanings or definitions of key terms but disagree about the relevance or importance of certain laws, policies, or ethical principles or rules. All of these are, in some sense, application issues.

However, in this section we emphasize a special kind of application issue, one that rests on a common feature of concepts. Attempts to specify the meanings of terms ahead of time can never anticipate all of the cases to which they do and do not apply. No matter how precisely one attempts to define a concept, it will always remain open-ended; that is, it will always remain insufficiently specified, so that some of its applications to particular circumstances will remain problematic.

We can clarify this further in a somewhat more formal way. If we let "X" refer to a concept, such as "keeping confidentiality" or "proprietary information," a conceptual issue concerning the *definition* of a concept has to do with what X is— that is, with what characteristics it has. A conceptual issue concerning its *application* has to do with whether a given situation *counts* as an instance of X. It is one thing to determine what we *mean* by "safe" and another to determine whether a given situation should *count* as safe, considering the definition. In many situations a clear definition of a term can make its application unproblematic. Many times the concept either clearly does or does not apply to a situation. Sometimes, however, this is not the case. As we have said, this is because definitions cannot possibly be so clear and complete that every possible situation clearly does or clearly does not count as an instance of the concept. This inherent limitation of all definitions and explanations of concepts gives rise to problems in applying concepts.

Although definitions of concepts are open-ended in the ways we have described, this does not mean that every application of a concept is problematic. In fact, it is usually quite easy to find clear-cut, unproblematic instances. We can refer to these as *paradigm* cases. For example, here is a paradigm case of bribery: A vendor offers an engineer a large sum of money to get the engineer to recommend the vendor's product to the engineer's company. The engineer accepts the offer, and then decides in favor of the vendor. The engineer accepts the offer for personal gain, rather than because of the superior quality of the vendor's product (which actually is one of the worst in industry). Furthermore, the engineer's recommendation will be accepted by the company because only this engineer makes recommendations concerning this sort of product. As Figure 2.3 illustrates, in such a case we can easily identify *features* that contribute heavily in favor of this being a clear-cut instance of bribery.

The advantage of listing major features of clear-cut applications of a concept is that these features can help us decide less clear-cut cases as well. Consider this case, which we will call the *test case* (the case to be compared with clear-cut cases):

> Victor is an engineer at a large construction firm. It is his job to specify rivets for the construction of a large apartment building. After some research and testing, he decides to use ACME rivets for the job. On the day after Victor's order, an ACME representative visits him and gives him a voucher for an all-expense paid trip to

Features of Bribery	Paradigm Instances of Features of Bribery
Gift size	Large (>$10,000)
Timing	Before recommendation
Reason	Personal gain
Responsibility for decision	Sole
Product quality	Worst in industry
Product cost	Highest in market

Figure 2.3
Paradigm Case of Bribery with Features

the ACME Forum meeting in Jamaica. Paid expenses include day trips to the beach and the rum factories. If Victor accepts, is this a bribe?

For this case we can modify Figure 2.3 by constructing a horizontal scale, with common features of paradigm cases of bribery at one end of the scale and cases that clearly are not bribery at the other end. For each listed feature, an X can be placed for the test case in an appropriate place on the scale, as in Figure 2.4. This figure represents a useful method of analysis, which we will call *line-drawing*, a method we will explain more fully in Chapter 3. (We have listed the same features here as in Figure 2.3. However, as we look at other cases, additional features might be added.)

Although Victor's case is not a paradigm instance of bribery, Figure 2.4 suggests that it comes close enough to the paradigmatic case to raise a real worry about whether he would be accepting a bribe. Of course, assessing the bribe requires more than determining where on the spectrum the various factors fall. The importance of each factor in particular cases must be weighed.

Feature	Paradigm (Bribery)	Test Case	Paradigm (*Not* bribery)
Gift size	Large	——X——————	Small (<$1.00)
Timing	Before decision	—————————X——	After decision
Reason	Personal gain	—————X————	Educational
Responsibility	Sole	—X—————————	None
Product quality	Worst	—————————X——	Best
Product cost	Highest	—X—————————	Lowest

Figure 2.4
Line-Drawing Test of Concepts

It is sometimes difficult to know whether two people disagree on the definition of concepts or on their application to a particular situation. There are at least two reasons for this. First, as we have seen, all definitions are open-ended; they cannot cover all of the situations that one might find in his or her experience. That is, the definitions cannot be specified in enough detail so that in every possible situation it is clear whether the concept in question describes the situation. Second, we often may want to change or modify our definitions of crucial terms in the face of experience. Sometimes an experience may not appear to exemplify the concept as we have defined it, but we believe it should count as an instance of the concept. In this case the experience prompts us to modify the definition. When this happens in analyzing a case, it is a good idea to revisit the initial depiction of the case and reassess the relevant facts and ethical considerations before attempting a final resolution of the case. Figure 2.5 depicts the various tasks of conceptual analysis we have discussed in this section.

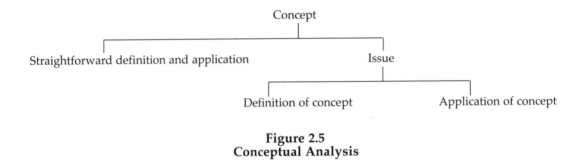

Figure 2.5
Conceptual Analysis

2.7   General and Specific Moral Problems

Most moral disagreements occur on one of two levels of generality. Many of the moral problems or issues we have dealt with so far have to do with what should be done in a specific situation. We shall call these *specific moral problems*. Bill's question about whether he should pay the $100,000 to a Morotavian official's reelection campaign was a specific moral problem.

Some moral problems are more general in nature. Rather than having to do with what should be done in a particular situation, they raise more general questions about policy—about what should be done in situations of a certain general type. We shall refer to these as *general moral problems*. Tom and Jim are more concerned with what regulations ought to apply to benzene levels in the workplace rather than what either of them should do about the problem. This is a question of general policy and, therefore, a general moral problem. If Judy and Jane disagree about the moral acceptability of an affirmative action policy, they are disagreeing about the merits of a general policy rather than about what should be done in any particular case.

Most of the moral problems that engineers face are specific, but sometimes more general issues arise, such as issues about the policies that should be adopted by the engineering community. When we consider how the professional engineering community should respond to such issues as the environment or the rights of professional employees, for example, we are dealing with general moral problems. As with specific moral problems, these disagreements often turn out to be about facts and concepts, including the applications of concepts to a general *type* of action rather than a specific action.

An example is the controversy about advertising and competitive pricing. Engineers in private practice constitute only a small percentage of the membership of the engineering profession. For them, however, advertising and competitive bidding are vital issues. Prior to the 1980s, most engineering codes contained provisions severely limiting advertising and price competition by engineers in private practice. Section 5 in the 1974 code of the Engineers' Council for Professional Development (ECPD), which has been superseded by the Accreditation Board for Engineering and Technology (ABET), reads:

> 5. Engineers shall build their professional reputation on the merit of their services and shall not compete unfairly with others.

As the following subsections reveal, "unfair" competition includes virtually all advertising and price competition:

> 5.c. Engineers should negotiate a method and rate of compensation commensurate with the agreed upon scope of services. A meeting of the minds of the parties to the contract is essential to mutual confidence. The public interest requires that the cost of engineering services be fair and reasonable, but not the controlling consideration in selection of individuals or firms to provide these services.
>
> 5.g. Engineers may advertise professional services only as a means of identification and limited to the following:
>
> (g.1) Professional cards and listings in recognized and dignified publications regularly devoted to such professional cards and listings. The information displayed must be restricted to firm name, address, telephone number, appropriate symbol, names of principal participants and the fields of practice in which the firm is qualified....
>
> (g.4) Listings in the classified section of telephone directories, limited to name, address, telephone number and specialties in which the firm is qualified without resorting to special or bold type.
>
> 5.l. Engineers shall not enter competitions for designs for the purpose of obtaining commissions for specific projects, unless provision is made for reasonable compensations for all designs submitted.

These guidelines prohibited engineers from submitting bids without compensation and from advertising, except in highly restricted forms. In the 1970s, however, the U.S. Supreme Court issued some important decisions that have fundamentally changed professional practice in the areas of advertising and price competition. In the 1977 decision *Bates v. State Bar of Arizona*, the Supreme Court declared that it was a violation of the Sherman Antitrust Act for the Arizona state bar to forbid two lawyers, Bates and O'Steen, from advertising the services and prices at their legal clinic in the Phoenix newspaper.[24] The Court did place some restrictions on professional advertisements: (1) they should only be for routine services, (2) they should not be misleading or deceptive, and (3) they should be restrained as to claims for the quality of professional services.

In 1975, the Court ruled in *Goldfarb v. Virginia State Bar* that the state bar may not prohibit deviations from set fees for title insurance.[25] The Court suggested, however, that state legislatures could prohibit competitive pricing of professional services in a given profession if they (1) created a mechanism (such as a state board of registration) to regulate the profession, (2) promulgated a specific policy against competitive pricing in the profession, and (3) compelled professionals to comply with this policy. On April 25, 1978, the Court applied this doctrine directly to the engineering profession, ruling that the National Society of Professional Engineers' (NSPE) ban on competitive bidding was not permissible under the Sherman Antitrust Act.

These decisions resulted in changes in the codes of most engineering societies. They did not, however, put to rest the controversy about the desirability of advertising and competitive bidding by professionals, or about how the professional societies and state registration boards should regulate these two activities within the guidelines set out by the Court.

To illustrate some of the controversies, let us imagine a conversation between two consulting engineers, Caroline and Bill, which might have occurred in the late 1970s, at the time of the two Supreme Court decisions.

Caroline: I guess our world is about to change, Bill. It looks like we're going to be right in there with roofing contractors and pest exterminators as far as advertising and competitive bidding go. The Supreme Court has really knocked the wind out of our professional status with its decision that professional societies must not forbid advertising and competitive bidding for professional services.

Bill: Well, Caroline, maybe things aren't as bad as you think. After all, the Court's rulings against prohibitions of advertising and competitive bidding apply to all professions, not just engineering; so our professional status won't change relative to the other professions. Besides, some limitations on these activities are still allowed.

Caroline: I know, but things are going to change. I really think it's disgraceful. It's bad for our self-image as professionals, and if we think less of ourselves, we'll produce lower quality work. You know all the codes in engineering and every other profession have traditionally said that professionals may not advertise or engage in competitive bidding, except in special circumstances and within strict limitations.

Bill: I'm not so sure it's bad for either engineers or the public. As far as harming our self-image is concerned, I think it's a matter of what you get used to. When everybody gets used to professionals' advertising, it won't harm our self-image. And allowing advertising and competitive bidding may benefit the public. Advertising may give a client knowledge about other engineers, and competitive pricing might result in lower costs for professional services.

Caroline: I can't believe you said that! Sure, the changes might result in lower prices for professional services, but it's going to lead to cost-cutting measures that will lower quality as well. As for the value of advertising, it will just lead potential clients to select an engineering firm on the basis of the firm's expertise in advertising and public relations, rather than its expertise in engineering. Besides, the cost of advertising must be added into the engineer's expenses; so it could even increase the cost of engineering services.

Bill: I admit that this could be true, but I suspect it will not work out that way. Studies have been done that compare the price and quality of eyeglasses and prescription medicines in states where price competition is allowed with price and quality in states where it's not allowed. The results seem to show that price competition doesn't lower quality, although it does lower price.

This conversation represents a disagreement about a general, rather than a specific, moral problem. The real disagreement between Caroline and Bill is not about the moral principle that "engineers should practice their profession in accordance with policies that promote the public welfare," but rather about the factual question of whether allowing advertising and competitive bidding in the professions (and engineering in particular) promotes the public welfare.[26]

2.8   Chapter Summary

Most of us agree on what is right or wrong in many particular situations, as well as on many moral rules or principles. Nevertheless, we are all familiar with moral disagreement, whether it occurs with respect to general rules or principles or with respect to what ought to be done in a particular situation.

It is possible to isolate several sources of moral disagreement. We can disagree about the factual issues relevant to an ethical problem. If two people disagree about the relevant facts, they may disagree about what ought to be done in a particular situation, even though they have the same basic moral beliefs. We can also disagree about conceptual issues, about either the definitions of crucial terms or their application to a given situation.

Moral problems usually exist at various levels of generality; it is useful to divide them into two groups, however. Specific moral problems have to do with what should be done in a particular situation, such as whether John should correctly report the data on tests he conducted. General moral problems apply to a class of issues, such as whether engineers should engage in advertising and competitive bidding or whether certain regulations are desirable.

Good moral thinking requires applying relevant facts (including laws and regulations), concepts, and moral rules or principles to the case in question. Carefully organizing one's thinking around these requirements often yields straightforward moral conclusions. However, sometimes it causes us to rethink matters, especially when we discover that there are unknown facts that might affect our conclusions. In any given case, we should:

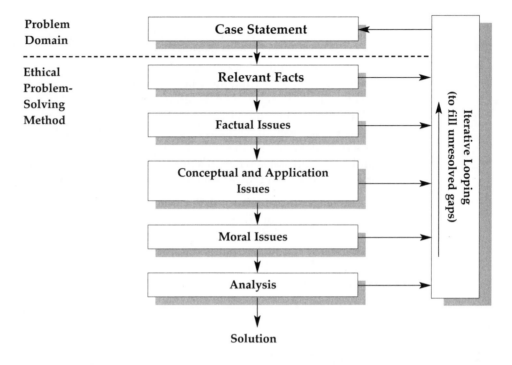

Figure 2.6
Analyzing a Moral Problem

• Identify the relevant known facts, including relevant laws and regulations (the factual considerations), bearing in mind that this cannot be done independently of ethical considerations.

• Identify the relevant moral concepts, rules, or principles (the ethical considerations), bearing in mind that this cannot be done independently of factual considerations.

• Identify and attempt to clarify and resolve factual issues, and consider how different unknown facts might affect the case.

• Identify and attempt to clarify and resolve conceptual issues about either the definitions or application of key concepts when presenting factual and ethical considerations.

• Revisit earlier phases in the process of analysis when bringing in new facts that may have been discovered when considering factual and conceptual issues, or when considering the possible implications of unknown relevant facts.

• Identify any additional relevant moral rules, principles, or concepts when rethinking the case.

• Suggest plausible resolutions of the case, with supporting reasons.

Figure 2.6 summarizes this process of analysis.

 Cases to Consider

Although you should feel free to try any of the cases in the back of the book, the following are especially well suited for Chapter 2:

Case 4	Borrowed Tools
Case 8	Co-op*
Case 12	Drinking Problem
Case 29	Mere Technicality?
Case 32	Oil Spill?
Case 52	Whose Property?

Notes

1. This case presentation is based on a much more extensive presentation by Tom L. Beauchamp, Jonanne L. Jurmu, and Anna Pinodo. See "The OSHA-Benzene Case," in Tom L. Beauchamp, *Case Studies in Business, Society, and Ethics*, 2nd ed. (Englewood Cliffs, N.J.: Prentice-Hall, 1989), pp. 203–211.

2. 29 U.S.C. §655(b)(5).

3. Ibid.

4. *Industrial Union Department, AFL-CIO v. American Petroleum Institute et al.*, 100 Sup. Ct. 2884 (1980).

5. Ibid.

6. In this chapter, our main concern is to clarify what kinds of relevance problems arise and why it is important to identify them with as much care and precision as possible. In Chapter 3, we will discuss methods of resolving relevance problems, as well as methods for resolving problems that arise when conflicting values are at stake.

7. For two interesting attempts to describe our common morality in the form of moral rules or principles, see W. D. Ross, *The Right and the Good* (New York: Oxford University Press, 1930), pp. 20–22 and Bernard Gert, *Morality* (New York: Oxford University Press, 1988), ch. 6 and 7. Neither Ross nor Gert attempts to organize his rules or principles around an even more general, single principle from which they can be derived. In Chapter 4, we will discuss two influential kinds of attempts to do this, utilitarianism and the ethics of respect for persons.

8. We will discuss the idea of moral justification more fully shortly.

9. We will discuss issues concerning the environment in Chapter 9.

10. It is worth pointing out that morality is not unusual in this regard. Specifying the ultimate philosophical foundations of virtually all disciplines (for example, mathematics, the sciences, history, and even philosophy itself) is highly controversial. Yet, this only rarely interferes with disciplines operating successfully at less "foundational" levels.

11. This suggestion is spelled out in some detail by Sissela Bok in her *Common Values* (Columbia, Mo.: University of Missouri Press, 1995). See, especially, p. 70.

12. Ibid.

13. Albert R. Jonsen and Stephen Toulmin, *The Abuse of Casuistry: A History of Moral Reasoning* (Berkeley: University of California Press, 1988), p. 17.

14. *The Belmont Report: Ethical Principles and Guidelines for Protection of Human Subjects of Biomedical and Behavioral Research*, pub. No. OS 78-0012 (Washington, D.C.: DHEW, 1978), pp. 1–2.

15. Universalizability is widely discussed among moral philosophers. See, for example, Kurt Baier, *The Moral Point of View* (Ithaca, N.Y.: Cornell University Press, 1958), Ch. 8

---

* Includes an analysis of the case.

Marcus G. Singer, *Generalization in Ethics* (New York: Knopf, 1961), Ch. 2; and any of the writings of R. M. Hare. Universalizability plays a particularly prominent role in discussions of respect for persons, a notion we will discuss in some detail in Chapter 6.

16. This is but one of several variations of the same basic idea. The Golden Rule will be discussed in greater detail in Chapter 4.

17. This is BER case no. 85-5 in NSPE's *Opinions of the Board of Ethical Review*, Vol. VI (Alexandria, Va.: National Society of Professional Engineers, 1989). The BER discussion is on pp. 67–69.

18. For a discussion of this and related issues, see Tom L. Beauchamp, "DuPont's Policy of Exclusion from the Workplace," in his *Case Studies in Business, Society, and Ethics*, 2nd ed. (Englewood Cliffs, N.J.: Prentice-Hall, 1989), pp. 33–39.

19. We will discuss this as a general strategy for resolving complex cases in Chapter 3.

20. We will discuss bribery and extortion in greater detail in Chapter 8.

21. Michael Davis, "Thinking Like an Engineer: The Place of a Code of Ethics in the Practice of a Profession," *Philosophy and Public Affairs*, 20, no. 2 (Spring 1991), pp. 150–167.

22. Ibid., 164–165.

23. In fact, during the discussions between Morton Thiokol and the Marshall Space Flight Center on the night before the launch Boisjoly did vigorously oppose the launch. Whether he should have done more (for example, notify NASA headquarters, or even attempt directly to inform the astronauts of the flight risks) is another matter, one which we are not addressing here.

24. *Bates v. State Bar of Arizona*, 433 U.S. 350, 53C, Ed. 2d 810.

25. *Goldfarb v. Virginia State Bar*, 421 U.S. 773, 44L, Ed. 2d 572.

26. For further discussion of whether advertising and competitive bidding affect quality or cost, see Milton F. Lunch, "Supreme Court Rules on Advertising for Professions," *Professional Engineer* (August 1977), reprinted in Robert Baum and Albert Flores, *Ethical Problems in Engineering*, 2nd ed., vol. 1 (Troy, N.Y.: Center for the Study of the Human Dimensions of Science and Technology, 1980), p. 123; Lee Benham, "The Effect of Advertising on the Price of Eyeglasses," *Journal of Law and Economics*, 15 (1972), 337–352; and John F. Cady, *Restricted Advertising and Competition: The Case of Retail Drugs* (Washington, D.C.: American Enterprise Institute, 1976).

Chapter 3

Methods for Moral Problem Solving

Ben is assigned by his employer, Cartex, to work on an improvement to an ultrasonic range-finding device. While working on the improvement, he gets an idea for a modification of the equipment that might be applicable to military submarines. If this is successful, it could be worth a lot of money to his company. However, Ben is a pacifist and does not want to contribute in any way to the development of military hardware. So Ben neither develops the idea himself nor mentions it to anybody else in the company. Ben has signed an agreement that all inventions he produces on the job are the property of the company, but he does not believe the agreement applies to his situation. For one thing, his idea is not developed. For another, his superiors know of his antimilitary sentiments. Yet he wonders if he is ethically right in concealing his idea from his employer.

3.1   Introduction

Difficult ethical issues like the one Ben faces call for techniques for resolving them. In the last chapter, we considered some ways of sorting out the factual and conceptual components of moral problems. Sometimes this sorting out process resolves moral problems. This is not always the case, however. Sometimes when all of the factual and conceptual issues are settled, there is still uncertainty about what ought to be done or decided. In this case, there is a moral problem in the fullest sense of the term; that is, there is disagreement or uncertainty about the moral evaluation of the person or action. In this chapter, we focus more directly on these kinds of moral problems and consider some techniques for resolving them.

Two common kinds of techniques are line-drawing and seeking a creative middle way. *Line-drawing* was introduced in Chapter 2 as a technique for determining the meanings and applications of concepts (such as *bribery* or *safety*). In this chapter, we will apply this technique to deciding whether a course of action is right or wrong. Line-drawing involves viewing a moral problem as located on a spectrum, with the action at one end being clearly right and the action at the other end being clearly wrong. The task is to determine whether the situation in question is more like the one in which the action is clearly right or more like the one in which the action is clearly wrong. Seeking a *creative middle way* involves looking for a way to resolve conflicting values that comes as close as possible to satisfying all relevant obligations.

Line-drawing and creative middle way techniques require a kind of practical, problem-solving ability that is in some ways analogous to the skills developed by experienced design engineers.[1] Judgment and creativity are at a premium in this kind of activity, and there is no wholly adequate substitute for experience. But even without experience, it can be helpful to study a range of hypothetical and actual cases to practice line-drawing and creative middle way techniques and to develop understanding. In any case, there are no easy formulae for resolving problems using these techniques.

3.2 ❋ Line-Drawing

An appropriate metaphor for line-drawing is a surveyor deciding where to set the boundary between two pieces of property: We know the hill to the right belongs to Jones and the hill to the left belongs to Brown, but who owns this particular tree? Where, precisely, should we draw the line?

Consider this example. The NSPE code says about disclosure of business and trade secrets: "Engineers shall not disclose confidential information concerning the business affairs or technical processes of any present or former client or employer without his consent (III.4). "Suppose Amanda signs an agreement with Company A (with no time limit) that obligates her not to reveal its trade secrets. Amanda later moves to Company B, where she finds a use for some ideas that she conceived while at Company A. She never developed the ideas into an industrial process at Company A, and Company B is not in competition with Company A; but she still wonders whether using those ideas at Company B is a violation of the agreement she had with Company A. She has an uneasy feeling that she is in a gray area and wonders where to draw the line between the legitimate and illegitimate use of knowledge. How should she proceed?

Once again it will be helpful to consider the experiences of the National Commission for the Protection of Human Subjects of Biomedical and Behavioral Research.[2] As we noted in Chapter 2, the members of the commission were from very different backgrounds, representing various disciplines and ideologies. They found themselves in hopeless disagreement when they appealed to their most fundamental philosophical and theological principles in addressing issues involving human experimentation. However, when they focused on actual cases and principles such as justice and beneficence, they came to a remarkable degree of consensus.

They considered cases that everyone believed to be examples of morally wrong actions and other cases that everyone considered to be examples of morally acceptable actions. Finding that they could agree on such cases, they proceeded to examine cases on which they disagreed, pointing out the similarities and dissimilarities with the cases on which they agreed. The members of the commission found this to be a much more useful and profitable method for resolving moral problems than beginning with general principles and arguing about their ultimate foundations.[3]

A useful way of employing this method is to arrange cases in a spectrum or series, with the clearest cases at the ends of the spectrum. Cases at one end depict actions that are unquestionably right, and cases at the other end depict actions that are unquestionably wrong. We can also list those features of these cases that make clear why they are unquestionably right or wrong. These features can then be compared with the features of cases that fall between the two ends of the spectrum.

It is helpful to develop some terminology for using this method. We shall call the cases on which there is agreement and that occupy the extreme ends of the spectrum *paradigm* cases. Cases that are uncontroversially wrong we shall call *negative paradigm* cases, and cases that are uncontroversially acceptable are *positive paradigm* cases. We shall call related, but controversial, cases that are in dispute (and that are clustered near the middle of the spectrum) *problematic* cases. We shall designate as the *test* case the one on which the analysis is to focus.

To illustrate, let us return to the case of Amanda wondering whether it is morally acceptable to use ideas at Company B she developed while working at Company A. She feels she is in a gray area, so it may be useful for her to compare her circumstance with a negative and a positive paradigm in regard to taking one's ideas to a new place of employment. In determining what these paradigms might be, she should try to construct a list of key features that themselves can be placed on a spectrum ranging from negative to positive. For example, violating a trade secret policy would be a negative feature, counting strongly against the appropriateness of taking her ideas to Company B. Acquiring permission from Company A would be a positive feature, counting strongly in favor of the appropriateness of taking her ideas to Company B. Schematically, Figure 3.1 on page 62 represents this part of Amanda's strategy.

A case dominated by negative features would be a negative paradigm, a clear instance of wrongdoing. A case dominated by positive features would be a positive paradigm, a clear instance of acceptable behavior. Amanda's situation is the test case. Once Amanda identifies the key features of her negative and positive paradigms, she can begin comparing the features of her situation with those of the paradigms. For example, a negative feature of her situation is that she signed a trade secret agreement that may include her ideas, and apparently she has not sought permission from Company A to use her ideas at Company B. A positive feature is that Company A and B are not competitors.

As Amanda engages in this comparative analysis, she may find that she has not thought thoroughly enough about certain features. For example, she may not

Negative Paradigm (Clearly wrong)	Positive Paradigm (Clearly acceptable)
Negative feature 1 (Vs. signed agreement)	Positive feature 1 (Permission granted)
Negative feature 2 (A and B competitors)	Positive feature 2 (A and B not competitors)
Negative feature 3 (Ideas jointly developed)	Positive feature 3 (Amanda's ideas only)
Negative feature 4 (All ideas developed on job)	Positive feature 4 (All ideas developed off job)
Negative feature 5 (Heavy use of A's lab/equipment)	Positive feature 5 (A's lab/equipment not used)
Negative feature n (Etc.)	Positive feature n (Etc.)

Figure 3.1
Features of Paradigms for Taking Ideas to the Next Job

have thought much about the extent to which others at Company A might also have helped develop her ideas. Or, although she developed her ideas on her own time, she might realize that Company A's lab and equipment played a crucial role in their development. Or, although Company A and B were not competitors when Amanda worked at A, they might become competitors in the area in which she developed her ideas, especially if those ideas were jointly developed with others at A. Figure 3.2 represents some of these possible complexities.

At this point, although Amanda may feel she has a clearer understanding of her situation, she may still be unsure of what to conclude. Some features of her case lean in the direction of features of the negative paradigm, whereas others lean in the direction of the positive paradigm. Furthermore, in this particular case some of the negative and positive features may be more important than others and should be more heavily weighted. Figure 3.2 does not represent the weighting of features. So, Amanda still has to assess the importance of the various negative and positive features she is considering. She may think of other possible scenarios that fall somewhere between the negative and positive paradigms; and she can compare the features of her case with those of the intermediate cases.

Although line-drawing techniques are often useful, we do not want to underestimate the complexities that might be involved. Several general points need to be made. First, the more ambiguous the case, the more we must know about its particular circumstances to determine whether it is morally acceptable or morally wrong. In everyday affairs, whether failing to return money borrowed for a

Negative Paradigm (Clearly wrong)	Test Case	Positive Paradigm (Clearly acceptable)
Negative feature 1 (Vs. signed agreement)	—X———————	Positive feature 1 (Permission granted)
Negative feature 2 (A and B competitors)	———X—————	Positive feature 2 (A and B not competitors)
Negative feature 3 (Ideas jointly developed)	—————X———	Positive feature 3 (Amanda's ideas only)
Negative feature 4 (Ideas developed on job)	——————X——	Positive feature 4 (Ideas developed off job)
Negative feature 5 (Used A's lab/equipment)	———X—————	Positive feature 5 (A's equipment not used)
Negative feature n (Etc.)	–?—?—?—?—?—?—?–	Positive feature n (Etc.)

Figure 3.2
Paradigm and Test Case Features for Amanda's Ideas

soda is wrong may be decided only by reference to the particular lender and his or her relationship to the borrower. Similarly, whether it is acceptable to use some ideas you developed at Company A for a very different chemical process at Company B may be decided only by knowing the nature of the ideas and the policies of Company A and Company B. Similarly, whether to consider a payment of money as a bribe will depend on the amount and timing of the payment, the influence it exerts on the person who accepts the payment, the appearance and taking of the action, and other factors.

Second, imposing a line of demarcation between some of the cases in a series involves an element of arbitrariness. It is erroneous to conclude from this, however, that there is no real moral difference between *any* of the cases in a series. The precise line between night and day may be arbitrary, but this does not mean there is no difference between night and day. Nevertheless, sometimes arbitrary conventions to separate acceptable from wrong actions are in order. Companies, and in some cases professional societies, should have policies that, for example, specify in some detail just what kinds of transfers of proprietary information from one job to the other are legitimate. Despite the rules, however, there will be many instances in which we cannot avoid an exercise of judgment. And, of course, judgment is called for in making rules.

Third, in using the method of line-drawing it is important to keep in mind that concentrating on only one feature will usually be insufficient to determine where on the continuum to place a given case. Line-drawing is based on the identification of analogies and disanalogies between various examples in a series of cases.

Unfortunately, we cannot depend on any single analogy or disanalogy to carry through all the examples.

Fourth, we need to bear in mind that the method of line-drawing resembles "a kind of common-law ethics" in which, as in law, what one decides in one case serves as a precedent for similar cases.[4] So, although one begins with the particular case and tries to determine relevant paradigms with which to compare and contrast it, eventually one links the case in question with relevant moral rules or principles, paying special attention to the importance of consistency—treating similar cases similarly (the universalizability criterion discussed in Chapter 2).

3.3 ❅ Conflicting Values: Creative Middle Way Solutions

We have already pointed out that values of common morality (for example, being honest and preventing harm) can conflict with one another. There are situations when two or more moral rules or duties seem to apply and when they appear to imply different and incompatible moral judgments. This situation arises often in engineering ethics, as in other areas.

When we take a closer look at such a situation we may find that one value clearly has a higher priority than the other. From a moral point of view, we then have what we can call an *easy choice*. Suppose you are driving along a freeway on your way to a dinner engagement. You have promised to meet a friend at 6 P.M. and are almost late. You see a person waving for help and realize there has been an accident. If you stop to assist, you will not be on time for your dinner. In a situation like this, you might well stop even though you have promised to meet your friend at 6 o'clock because the need to render assistance has a higher priority than keeping the date on time.

Examples occur in engineering ethics also. James is an engineer in private practice. He is approached by a client who asks him to design a project that both know clearly involves illegal activity. Engineer Susan is asked to design a product that will require the use of outmoded technology that, although less expensive and still legal, poses substantially greater risk to human life. James and Susan should simply reject such requests out of hand, even though they could dramatically increase the profits of their firms. The obligations to obey the law and to protect human life so clearly outweigh any obligation to maximize profits that James and Susan should have no difficulty in deciding what it is right to do.

In such situations, it may sometimes be difficult to *do* what is right, but it is not difficult to *know* what is right. We might not even want to refer to this as a serious moral conflict at all, for the obligations involved have very different weights. In many real-life situations, however, the values are more evenly matched, and no hierarchy of values can give an easy answer. For example, the value of human life normally overrides other considerations, but this is often not the choice we face. Usually, the trade-off is between a slightly increased *risk* to human life, as opposed to some other value. And we make trade-offs like this all the time.

Automobile manufacturers could make their products much safer if they could sell them for $100,000, but then few people could afford automobiles.

Sometimes we may be forced to make some *hard choices*, choices in which we are not able to honor some real and important values in a way that we consider desirable. However, before concluding this, it is best to look for a *creative middle way* between conflicting values, a resolution in which all the conflicting demands are at least partially met. In many situations all of the values make legitimate claims on us, so that the ideal resolution of the conflict is to find some way to honor each of them. This approach might suggest new possibilities for Amanda's situation (discussed in section 3.2). After employing line-drawing techniques, Amanda may still be unsure whether it would be all right for her to make use of ideas at Company B that she developed while working for Company A. She could explain her concerns to Company A and see what response it has. If Company A does not object, Amanda has successfully resolved her problem. If Company A objects, Amanda has a strong indication that, had she gone ahead without consulting A and A discovered this, she and Company B could have run into serious problems.

The remainder of this section will explore techniques for finding morally acceptable, creative middle way resolutions to problems involving conflicting values. The philosophy of protest against racial discrimination developed by Martin Luther King Jr. is an example of a creative middle way.[5] Dr. King felt deeply the moral imperative to protest the racial injustice in this country. At the same time, he respected the rule of law, and he did not want to take the stance of a revolutionary. His solution to this conflict was the theory of nonviolent resistance, according to which one violates laws that he or she believes to be immoral but does not use violence and is willing to take the consequences of illegal activity. In many cases this may mean that a person must go to jail, as Dr. King did. Although this philosophy may not have always been followed by all protesters of racial injustice, it was an attempt to find a creative middle way between two conflicting moral values, so that each of the values is given due consideration.

Notice that in this example neither of the moral values were honored in what we might call their original or "pure" form. Dr. King did disobey the law; so the obligation to obey the law was partially violated. At the same time, the obligation to oppose immoral laws was not followed in an unrestrained fashion, for Dr. King refused to use violence and was willing to take the consequences of disobeying laws that he considered immoral. In an important sense, he respected the law even while breaking it. Dr. King found a middle position that incorporated some features of both of the conflicting moral demands.

One of our students provided us with an example of a creative middle way solution to a moral challenge he faced as a co-op student. His supervisor did not have adequate funds to pay the student for his work on a particular project, but he had an excess of funds for another project. So the supervisor asked the student to fill out his time sheets, saying that he had worked on a project that had excessive funding—even though the student had not worked on that project at all. The student really needed the money to continue his college education, and he knew his supervisor had a short temper and would probably fire him if he did not do as requested. However, the student also abhorred lying.

The student came up with the following creative middle way solution. He told his supervisor, "I know you don't have money budgeted from the project I worked on to pay me. But my conscience will not permit me to sign a false statement on my time sheet. How about if I just don't put in a time sheet for my work last week; and if you can, in the future please assign me to projects with budgets sufficient to pay me." His supervisor was so embarrassed and moved by this response that, not only did he never again put the student in this kind of situation, but he paid the student's salary for the previous week out of his own pocket.

To take another example, suppose an engineer, John, is representing his company in a foreign country where bribery is common.[6] If John does not pay a bribe, valuable business opportunities may be lost. If he makes payments, he may be doing something illegal under the Foreign Corrupt Practices Act, or he may at the very least be violating his own conscience. Instead of yielding to either of these unattractive alternatives, one writer has proposed a "donation strategy," according to which donations are given to a community rather than to individuals. A corporation might construct a hospital or dig new wells. In the 1970s, for example, Coca-Cola hired hundreds of Egyptians to plant orange trees on thousands of acres of desert, creating more goodwill than it would have generated by giving bribes to individuals. In 1983, the British gained goodwill for themselves in Tanzania by assembling thousands of dollars worth of tools and vehicle parts. They also trained the Tanzanians to service the vehicles, enabling the Tanzanians to continue patrolling their wild game preserves, which they had almost stopped doing due to the weakened economy. This gift was given in place of a cash donation, which might well have been interpreted as a bribe.

We can, of course, object to this solution. Not all creative middle ways are satisfactory, or at least equally satisfactory. We might argue that such gifts are still really bribes and are morally wrong. The evidence for this is that the effect of the gift is the same as the effect of an outright bribe: the person giving the gift gets the desired business contract. Furthermore, the motivation of the gift-giver is the same as the motivation of the briber—securing the business. There are also certain disanalogies, such as the gift-giving not being done in secret and its satisfying something more than the self-interest of an individual. We shall not attempt to resolve the problems raised by this solution, which depend heavily on the details of particular circumstances. We simply point out that it is an example of an attempted creative middle way solution (and that line-drawing techniques can be useful in bringing it to a final resolution). Here is another example. Suppose Barbara, a young engineer on her first job, finds that a chemical process at her plant is both dangerous and polluting. She knows from her college training that another process would be less dangerous and polluting and would even save the plant money in the long run. By suggesting this new process to her superior, she honors her obligation both to be a "faithful agent or trustee" of her employer and to look out for the safety of the public.

Consider the study of Florida's solution to the problem of competitive pricing some years ago. The Consultants' Competitive Negotiation Act of 1973 gives directions for negotiation for "professional services" for state agencies in Florida. According to the act, the negotiation procedure should consist of the following steps:

1. By reviewing qualifications, the state agency selects "no less than three firms deemed to be most highly qualified to perform the required services."

2. The agency will then "negotiate a contract with the most qualified firm for professional services at compensation which the agency determines is fair, competitive and reasonable."

3. "Should the agency be unable to negotiate a satisfactory contract with the firm considered to be the most qualified at a price the agency determines to be fair, competitive and reasonable, negotiations with that firm shall be formally terminated. The agency shall then undertake negotiations with the second most qualified firm. Failing accord with the second most qualified firm, the agency shall terminate negotiations. The agency shall then undertake negotiations with the third most qualified firm."

4. "Should the agency be unable to negotiate a satisfactory contract with any of the selected firms, the agency shall select additional firms in order of their competence and qualifications and continue negotiations in accordance with this subsection until an agreement is reached."[7]

Advocates of this procedure might well argue that it is a middle way between prohibiting all competitive bidding and allowing unrestricted competitive bidding. Or they might argue that it fulfills two obligations that engineers have to the public: to allow the operation of market forces to reduce prices and to uphold high standards of quality. Engineering firms are originally selected on the basis of the reputation of the firm for quality and the appropriateness of the firm for the task. Only after a selection on the basis of quality do cost considerations play a role in the negotiation.

In thinking about creative middle way solutions to conflicts, it is often helpful to consider a *range* of solutions, rather than a single one. We can then evaluate them in terms of their moral acceptability. For example, in the following case, Brad is in the second year of his first full-time job after graduating from Engineering Tech.[8] He enjoys design, but he is becoming increasingly concerned that his work is not being adequately checked by more experienced engineers. He has been assigned to assist in the design of a number of projects that involve issues of public safety, such as schools and overhead walkways between buildings. He has already spoken to his supervisor, whose engineering competence he respects, and he has been told that more experienced engineers check his work. Later, he discovers that his work is often not adequately checked. Instead, his drawings are stamped and passed on to the contractor. Sometimes the smaller projects he designs are under construction within a few weeks after the designs are completed.

At this point Brad calls one of his former professors at Engineering Tech for advice. "I'm really scared that I'm going to make a mistake that will kill someone," Brad says. "I try to over-design, but the projects I'm being assigned to are becoming increasingly difficult. What should I do?" Brad's professor tells him that he cannot ethically continue on his present course, for he is engaging in engineering work that surpasses his qualifications and may endanger the public. What should Brad do?

Brad's case illustrates one of the most common conflicts faced by engineers, one in which an engineer's obligations to employers seem to conflict with obligations to the public. These dual obligations are stated in engineering codes. Canons 1 and 4 of the NSPE code illustrate this conflict:

Engineers, in the fulfillment of their professional duties, shall:

Canon 1: Hold paramount the safety, health and welfare of the public in the performance of their professional duties.

Canon 4: Act in professional matters for each employer or client as faithful agents or trustees.

Although the obligation to the public is paramount, Brad should also honor his obligation to his employer if possible. A range of options is open to him:

1. Brad could go to his supervisor again and suggest in the most tactful way he can that he is uncomfortable about the fact that his designs are not being properly checked, pointing out that it is not in the firm's interests to produce designs that may be flawed.

2. He might talk to others in the organization with whom he has a good working relationship and ask them to help him persuade his supervisor that he (Brad) should be given more supervision.

3. He might tell his supervisor that he does not believe that he can continue to engage in design work that is beyond his abilities and experience and that he might have to consider changing jobs.

4. He could find another job and then, after his employment is secure, reveal the information to the state registration board for engineers or others who could stop the practice.

5. He could go to the press or his professional society and blow the whistle immediately.

6. He could simply find another job and keep the information about his employer's conduct to himself, allowing the practice to continue with another young engineer.

7. He could continue in his present course without protest.

To be ethically and professionally responsible, Brad should spend a considerable amount of time thinking about his options. He should attempt to find a course of action that honors both his obligation to protect the public and his obligation to his employer. It is also completely legitimate for Brad to try to protect and promote his own career, insofar as he can while still protecting the public.

With these guidelines in mind, we can see that the first option is probably the one he should try first. The second is also a good choice if the first one is ineffective. The third option is less desirable, because it places him in a position of opposition to his employer, but he may have to choose it if the first two are unsuccessful. The fourth option produces a break in the relationship with his employer, but it does protect the public and Brad's career. The fifth also causes a break with his employer and threatens his career. The sixth and seventh are clearly unjustifiable, because they do not protect the public.

There are, of course, still other options Brad can consider. The important point is that Brad should exercise his imagination to its fullest extent before he takes any action. He must "brainstorm" to find a number of creative middle way solutions to his problem. Then he should attempt to rate the solutions and begin with the most satisfactory one. Only after this has failed is he justified in proceeding to a less satisfactory solution.

Figure 3.4 illustrates the procedure we are recommending in dealing with conflicting ethical concerns.

If the resolution of factual and conceptual issues is insufficient to resolve a moral conflict, we can begin by enumerating the conflicting values that are morally relevant. Then we must determine whether we have an easy choice, a hard choice, or an opportunity for a creative middle way solution. In this further analysis, we may need more facts and encounter further conceptual issues.

Gilbane Gold

Here is a final example involving moral problem solving where resolving conflicting moral values is required. This is the fictional case study presented in the

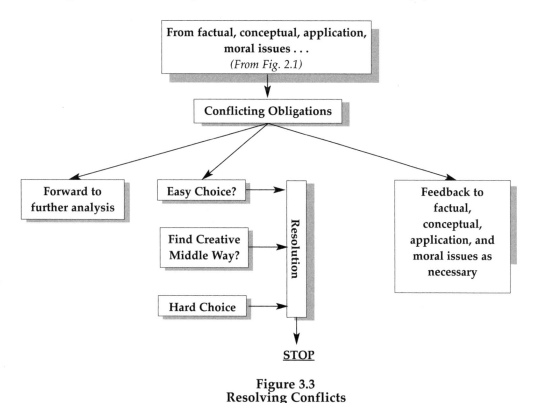

**Figure 3.3
Resolving Conflicts**

popular videotape *Gilbane Gold*.[9] The tape focuses on David Jackson, a young engineer in the environmental affairs department of ZCORP, located in the city of Gilbane. The firm, which manufactures computer parts, discharges lead and arsenic into the sanitary sewer of the city. The city has a lucrative business in processing the sludge into fertilizer, which is used by farmers in the area.

To protect its valuable product, Gilbane Gold, from contamination by toxic discharges from the new high-tech industries, the city has imposed highly restrictive regulations on the amount of arsenic and lead that can be discharged into the sanitary sewer system. However, recent tests indicate that ZCORP may be violating the standards. David believes that ZCORP must invest more money in pollution control equipment, but management believes the costs will be prohibitive. What should David do?

David faces a conflict situation that can be characterized by the convergence of four important moral claims. First, David has an obligation as a good employee to promote the interests of his company. He should not take actions that unnecessarily cost the company money or damage its reputation. Second, David has an obligation, based on his personal integrity, his professional integrity as an engineer, and his special role as an environmental engineer, to be honest with the city in reporting data on the discharge of the heavy metals. Third, David has an obligation as an engineer to protect the health of the public. Fourth, David has a right, if not an obligation, to protect and promote his own career.

The problem David faces is this: How can he do justice to all of these claims? If they are all morally legitimate, he should try to honor all of them, and yet they appear to conflict in the situation. David's first option should be to attempt to find a creative middle way solution, despite the fact that the claims appear to be incompatible in the situation. What are some of the creative middle way possibilities?

1. One would be to find a cheap technical way to eliminate the heavy metals.[10] If David could do this, he would provide a way out of a difficult situation for ZCORP. He would also enhance his professional career. He would keep trust with the city, because he would be able to report honestly that the city's regulations have been met. Finally, he would be upholding his professional obligation to protect the health of the public by finding a way to reduce the discharge of heavy metals.

2. Another possibility would be to suggest that the city, ZCORP, and other industries in the area form a consortium that would fund an upgrading of the city's water treatment facilities. Again, trust with the city would be sustained; and if the suggestion were accepted, other companies would join in a joint effort to protect environmental health in a way affordable by all.

3. If a technical solution is impossible, David might suggest a management solution to Diane, the manager of the plant. She could approach the city about the problem, perhaps in consort with other managers of high-tech plants in the area. If, indeed, product lines are in danger of becoming unprofitable and perhaps removed, with the consequent loss of jobs, managers could present these facts to the city. Positive suggestions could be made for a compromise whereby the city would grant additional tax incentives or other advantages to the plants, in exchange for further purification of their effluent. This approach, like the first one, would satisfy

all of David's obligations and protect, if not promote, his career. It would provide a service to ZCORP, by suggesting a way to avoid an almost inevitable public relations disaster. It would, like the first alternative, enhance David's stature within the firm. It would manifest good faith with the city. Finally, it would again provide a means for David to fulfill his obligation to protect the public's health.

If David cannot find a way to honor all of his obligations, he must make some hard choices, deciding which obligation(s) have priority. His conclusion should almost certainly be that, as the engineering codes stipulate, his first obligation is to protect the health of the public. He might think of several ways in which he could do this.

4. David could alert corporate headquarters to the problems at the Gilbane plant, informing Diane of his action. He could argue that Diane is following a course of action that can only lead to a public relations disaster. The problems of the plant are already public knowledge and David has been summoned to appear before city officials, which means that the issue of toxic waste is not going to disappear. He could argue that he wants to be a loyal employee and that he has thought long and hard about circumventing his superiors. He could also say that alerting corporate headquarters is the most reasonable course of action, because the first two options are not available or have failed. He could point out that he is attempting to protect the company from bad publicity and possible lawsuits, and to protect his professional integrity. He could also make some of the same suggestions to corporate management that were made to Diane (in 2).

This option would precipitate a break with the management of the local plant, but it would show a larger loyalty to the company. This is another way of manifesting David's obligation to the public, because one of his aims in alerting corporate management is to encourage a more rational response to the problem of toxic waste. Finally, it would be an attempt to preserve good faith with the city and to preserve his own career.

5. According to the videotape, David has been summoned to appear before city authorities; so another option would be to tell Diane that, if asked by city officials about the discharge of heavy metals, he will be completely truthful. As a conscientious employee, he will attempt to present ZCORP in a favorable light, but he will not misrepresent the situation or withhold knowledge.

This alternative would be at least a step in the direction of protecting the public. It would also satisfy David's obligation to the city. Although it would not manifest loyalty to the company in the sense of unqualified promotion of the company's interests, it would offer the possibility of an honest resolution of the issue. This poses risks for David's career, but management might view it as an honest attempt to be loyal to the company while preserving his own integrity.

6. David might announce to his supervisor that he can no longer in good conscience sign the documents that state that ZCORP is in compliance with city regulations on the discharge of toxic substances. He could emphasize that he wants to be a loyal employee, but that his professional career is at stake. In the light of the new tests, he cannot misrepresent the situation.

By taking this option, David has clearly placed the health of the public above loyalty to the firm or protecting his career, which might well be jeopardized by his action. If the previous options are not possible or are not successful, however, he may be forced to take it.

7. David could talk to the reporter about the problems ZCORP is having with the emission of heavy metals. This option would give a clear priority to protecting the health of the public and keeping good faith with the city and give a lower priority to being loyal to the company and promoting his own career. As a whistle-blower, this would endanger his career with ZCORP, if not elsewhere as well.

8. David could resign from ZCORP and then talk to the reporter about the problems with the emission of heavy metals. This would of course constitute a break with ZCORP and (as in 7) would endanger his own career by labeling him a whistle-blower. It would again acknowledge the higher priority of keeping faith with the city and protecting public health.

There are many other possible options that David could examine, but these are sufficient to show a gradual progression from creative middle way solutions in which all of the competing obligations can be honored to courses of action in which some of the obligations are given priority over others.

3.4   Standpoints of the Judge and the Agent

A person can take one of two different standpoints in resolving moral problems.[11] The first is that of a *judge* who evaluates how someone else has handled a moral problem. This external evaluator, or judge, usually has the benefit of knowing the consequences of the choices made and the success of the person's choice.

Many well-known cases in engineering ethics are often approached in this fashion. Examinations of the *Challenger* case often raise certain questions. Should Roger Boisjoly have protested the launch decision even more strenuously? In light of the consequences, what do you think about Robert Lund's decision to agree to the decision to launch? How could Robert Lund have responded differently to Gerald Mason's directive to take off his engineering hat and put on his management hat? Should Roger Boisjoly have refused to continue to work on the field joints once he concluded that their design was seriously flawed?

These are all important questions, and it is often instructive to ask and attempt to answer them. Engineers spend a great deal of time learning from past mistakes; and they can learn from past ethical as well as technical mistakes. But this approach is not the only way—and perhaps not the best way—to learn how to be a successful ethical problem solver.

A second standpoint one can take in resolving moral problems is that of the *agent*, the person actually facing a moral problem. We believe that this perspective is the best way to learn how to be a successful problem solver. This involves looking at the issue with the information that is available or could be available to the person facing the necessity of a decision; analyzing the moral, factual, and conceptual issues; and coming up with a conclusion about what we would do if we were in that situation. We invite readers, as much as possible, to approach cases in this text imaginatively as if they were themselves agents in the situations described.

The most appropriate cases for doing this may not be the highly publicized ones whose outcomes we already know. In the *Challenger* case, for example, we all know that the decision to launch led to a terrible disaster. This fact so influences our thinking that it is difficult to look at the situation from the perspective of those who were making the decisions, people who did not know the consequences of their choices ahead of time. Rather, the most appropriate cases are often ones with which we are not familiar, whether fictional or actual. Here we can realistically test our skills at anticipating outcomes, analyzing conceptual issues, and resolving conflict and line-drawing problems.

3.5   Chapter Summary

Line-drawing techniques can be used in cases in which we are unsure how to distinguish between acceptable and unacceptable actions. By comparing problematic cases with those where it is clear what we should do, we can often decide what we should do in the problematic cases.

Often we face two or more conflicting morally important values. Sometimes one value seems to be so much more important than the others that we must choose to honor the more important and, at least for the moment, neglect the others. Morally speaking, this is an easy choice. At other times, however, we may be able to come up with a solution to the conflicting values that enables us to honor all of the relevant values. However, sometimes we must make hard choices between competing values. Often it is useful to think of a range of solutions to the conflict. We should first attempt to act in accordance with the solution that most satisfactorily honors the competing values. If the optimum solution is not possible or does not work, we should continue to the next most desirable solution, and so on until the issue has been resolved.

In evaluating a moral problem, we can take either the standpoint of an external judge or of an agent actually immersed in the situation who does not know the outcome ahead of time. Usually the latter is a better way to develop the art of moral problem solving.

 CASES TO CONSIDER

Case 6	Catalyst*
Case 10	Deadline
Case 27	Inside Tool & Die
Case 44	Trees
Case 48	USAWAY
Case 49	Vacation

* Includes an analysis of the case.

NOTES

1. For a detailed discussion of similarities between moral reasoning and the engineering design practices, see Caroline Whitbeck, "Ethics as Design: Doing Justice to Moral Problems," *Hastings Center Report*, 26, no. 3 (May/June 1996), 9–16. This is also presented in Ch. 1 of her book, *Ethics in Engineering Practice and Research* (New York: Cambridge University Press, 1998), pp. 53–73.

2. See Albert R. Jonsen and Stephen Toulmin, *The Abuse of Casuistry* (Berkeley: University of California Press, 1988), pp. 1–20 for an account of the commission's procedures. Jonsen and Toulmin also defend casuistry against seventeenth-century philosopher Blaise Pascal's scathing critique of it as a sophistical and equivocal method of reasoning used to buy religious favors. Such abuses did occur, they concede, but this is not a defining feature of casuistic reasoning; rather, it is an abuse. To avoid this, they argue, the good judgment (discernment) of those with good character is necessary.

3. At least one person on the committee recognized this approach as embodying the essentials of a very old method of moral analysis. It is called *casuistry*, a method for determining the proper moral evaluation of actions in a given case or cases by comparison with reference cases. This method of comparison employs the sort of line-drawing technique we describe.

4. This point is made by David Boeyink in his "Casuistry: A Case-based Method for Journalists," *Journal of Mass Media Ethics* (Summer 1992), 112–113.

5. This example is taken from Henry A. Richardson, "Specifying Norms," *Philosophy and Public Affairs*, 19, no. 4 (1990), 279–310.

6. For this example, see Jeffrey A. Fadiman, "A Traveler's Guide to Gifts and Bribes," *Harvard Business Review* (July/August 1986), 122–126, 130–136.

7. James H. Schaub and Karl Pavlovic, *Engineering Professionalism and Ethics* (New York: Wiley-Interscience, 1983), pp. 122–126.

8. This case is suggested by the experience of a former engineering student at Texas A&M University.

9. This video was produced by the National Society for Professional Ethics (Alexandria, Va., 1989).

10. Unfortunately, the video does not directly address this possibility. It begins in the midst of a crisis at ZCORP and focuses almost exclusively on the question of whether David Jackson should blow the whistle on his reluctant company. For a detailed exploration of some creative middle way alternatives, see Michael Pritchard and Mark Holtzapple, "Responsible Engineering: *Gilbane Gold* Revisited," *Science and Engineering*, 3, no. 2 (April 1997), 217–231.

11. We are indebted to Caroline Whitbeck for pointing out the importance of this distinction. See Ch. 1 of her *Ethics in Engineering Practice and Research*.

Chapter 4

Organizing Principles

Engineer David Parkinson is a member of the Madison County Solid Waste Management Planning Committee (SWPC). State law requires that one of the committee members be a solid waste expert, David's area of specialization. SWPC has proposed a specific plot of land in a sparsely populated area of Madison County as the site for a needed public landfill. However, next to the proposed landfill site is a large tract of land that a small group of wealthy Madison County residents want to purchase to develop a private golf course surrounded by luxurious homes. This small group is very well organized, and it has managed to gather support from other wealthy residents in Madison County, including many who wield considerable political power.

Informally recognized as the Fairway Coalition, this influential group has bombarded the local media with expensive ads in its public campaign against the proposed landfill site, advocating instead a site that borders on one of the least affluent areas of Madison City. The basic argument is that a landfill (unlike the golf course and housing development) will destroy one of Madison County's most beautiful areas. Although as many as 8,000 of Madison City's 100,000 residents live within walking distance of the site favored by the Fairway Coalition, they lack the political organization and financial means to mount significant opposition.

SWPC is now meeting to discuss the respective merits of the two landfill sites. Members of the committee turn to David Parkinson for his views on the controversy. What basic kinds of ethical considerations should he take into account?

4.1   Introduction

The line-drawing and creative middle way methods we have proposed for resolving moral problems assume that we have a strong resource in common morality. For example, we have taken it for granted that there is no reason to doubt many of the paradigms of unquestionably right or unquestionably wrong actions to which we appeal in resolving problems by the line-drawing method. Likewise, we have not questioned the validity of the competing obligations in conflict situations. But we have not considered the question of whether there might be ways of organizing our moral concerns under some more general principle or principles that can be useful in analyzing moral problems.

In this chapter, we will discuss two basic kinds of principles that David Parkinson might be attracted to in thinking about the landfill issue. First, it might occur to him that locating the landfill in the more heavily populated area will benefit a relatively small number of wealthy people at the expense of risking the health and well-being of a much larger number of people. Although there may be many other factors to consider, this is a *utilitarian* concern to promote, or at least protect, the greatest good for the greatest number of people. Second, it might occur to David that favoring the urban site over the rural site would be basically unfair, in that it would fail to respect the rights of the poor to a reasonably healthy environment, while providing even more privilege to a wealthy minority. This is basically an appeal to the notion of equal *respect for persons.*

In this case utilitarian and respect for persons considerations seem to lead to the same conclusion. It is important to realize that different moral principles often do converge in this way, thereby strengthening our conclusions by providing support from more than one direction. However, as we have seen in the benzene case in Chapter 2, sometimes it seems that utilitarian and respect for persons principles point in different directions, making it necessary to try to determine which, if either, should take priority in a given case.

In the benzene case OSHA took the standpoint of the workers, arguing that their rights would be unduly infringed by being exposed to benzene, even if the concentrations are below those proven to be a health hazard. Protecting the rights of workers, OSHA officials assumed, requires that the burden of proof be placed on those who want to expose workers to any level of a carcinogen. Industry must prove that the exposure level is not harmful.

The Supreme Court justices, while not unmindful of the rights of workers, were also concerned about the economic welfare of industry and of the nation at large. If firms are forced to reduce toxic substance exposure to levels far below those proven to be harmful, the economy may be unduly harmed, possibly without any corresponding benefit to the workers themselves. In this case, at least, the Court believed that overall human welfare must override a possible (and in their view unlikely) risk to workers.

The conflict in this case indicates that, although they may often reach the same conclusions, two rather distinct approaches to moral thinking are involved—one taking the maximization of overall well-being as the primary concern, the other taking the preservation of the rights of each individual as the primary concern. These two approaches provide the basis for a number of tests for the rightness of actions and policies that are useful in practical moral problem solving. The utilitarian and respect for persons approaches are related to two important traditions in ethics that can be usefully applied to many problems in engineering ethics. We will explore several ways in which these traditions provide tests of rightness, beginning with the utilitarian approach.[1]

4.2   Utilitarian Thinking

Utilitarian thinking favors bringing about the greatest total amount of good that we can. A utilitarian moral standard expresses this basic idea. As we shall see, however, there is more than one way to formulate this standard. In any case, utilitarian values play an important part in the professional ethics of engineers.

Let us begin with a general statement of the utilitarian standard: Those individual actions or rules that produce the greatest total amount of utility to those affected are right. The codes enjoin engineers to promote the safety, health, and welfare of the public, and this principle seems to have a utilitarian flavor. The term *welfare* could even be interpreted as synonymous with *utility*.

There is a problem, however, in defining "utility" more precisely. The most common definition is "happiness," but happiness for one individual may not be happiness for another. John Stuart Mill, one of the most important proponents of utilitarian thinking in the nineteenth century, argued that human beings have capacities that nonhuman animals do not have and that the fulfillment of these unique human capacities is the basis of human happiness. He went on to say that we must give "pleasures of the intellect, of the feeling and imagination, and of the moral sentiments a much higher value as pleasures than those of mere sensation."[2] Others might not agree with Mill, however, finding the pleasures of the senses or the pleasures of earning money or the pleasures of fame or power more satisfying.

Utilitarians have responded to this problem by proposing *preference utilitarianism:* we should promote those general conditions that allow each individual to pursue happiness as he or she conceives it.

Utilitarian theorists generally agree that at least two conditions are necessary for most people to pursue happiness effectively: freedom and well-being. *Freedom* is the ability to make unforced choices in following our preferences. It refers primarily to noninterference by others in making fundamental decisions about life. *Well-being* is the set of conditions necessary to make effective use of freedom. It includes such factors as health, a certain degree of material well-being, food, shelter, and education. If a person is poor, sick, and uneducated, for example, mere noninterference from others will be of little value in achieving happiness.

Some utilitarians advocate the use of cost/benefit analysis in evaluating specific courses of action They maintain that the course of action that produces the greatest benefit relative to cost is the one that should be chosen. *Benefit* is usually defined in some relatively specific way, such as producing jobs or something else of value to society, but the utilitarian insists that these benefits be justified in terms of the more general conceptions of utility as providing the conditions of freedom and well-being.

There are several difficulties confronting the utilitarian perspective, but we shall consider only three of them here. First, sometimes it is difficult to come up with a directive for action from the utilitarian standpoint. We have seen that to know what we should do from the utilitarian perspective, we must know which course of action will produce the most utility for those affected, not only in the short run but also in the long run. Unfortunately, this knowledge is sometimes impossible to obtain. For example, we do not yet know whether permitting advertising and competitive pricing for professional services will lead to some of the problems suggested by those who oppose it. So we cannot say whether these are good practices from the utilitarian perspective. Sometimes all we can do is try a certain course of action and see what happens. This may be very risky in some circumstances.

Utilitarians reply that if we do not know the consequences of an action, we should not be sure of its moral status. The problem is not with the utilitarian standard but with the limitations of human knowledge. Nevertheless, this difficulty does mean that in some situations the utilitarian perspective cannot provide clear practical guidance.

A second problem with the utilitarian standard is closely related to the first. Utilitarians want to bring about the greatest amount of good that they can. We shall refer to the population over which the good is maximized as the *audience*. The problem for utilitarians is determining the scope of this audience. There may appear to be a dilemma over this issue. The audience should include all human beings, or at least all human beings who might be affected by the action to be evaluated. Perhaps the audience should even include all beings capable of experiencing pleasure or pain. But then it becomes virtually impossible to calculate which actions actually produce the most good for so large an audience. If we limit the audience, so that it includes only our country, or our company, or our community, then we face the criticism that others have been arbitrarily excluded.

A third difficulty with the utilitarian standard is that it seems sometimes to justify perpetrating injustice on individuals. Suppose a plant discharges a pollutant into the local river, where it is ingested by fish. If humans eat the fish, they experience significant health problems. Eliminating the pollutant will be so expensive that the plant will become unprofitable and will be closed. Allowing the discharge to continue will save jobs and even permit the local community to remain economically viable. The pollutant will adversely affect only a relatively small proportion of the population, the most economically deprived members of the community who fish in the river and eat the fish.

Under these conditions, allowing the plant to continue to discharge the pollutant might be justifiable from a utilitarian perspective, even though it would be unjust to the poorer members of the community. Thus, there is a problem of justly distributing benefits and burdens. Many would say that the utilitarian solution should be rejected for this reason. Thus, utilitarian reasoning seems sometimes to lead to implausible moral judgments, as measured by our understanding of common morality.[3]

4.3 ❋ Three Utilitarian Approaches

Despite the limitations discussed, the utilitarian perspective is often very useful in moral problem solving. Now let us consider three approaches suggested by the utilitarian moral standard.

✳ *The Cost/Benefit Approach*

Cost/benefit analysis is often used in engineering. This approach attempts to apply the utilitarian standard in as quantifiable a manner as possible. An effort is made to translate negative and positive utilities into monetary terms. However, this is a very complicated process. Cost/benefit analysis is sometimes referred to as *risk*/benefit analysis because much of the analysis requires estimating the probability of certain harms and benefits. It is possible to determine the actual cost of installing equipment to reduce the likelihood of certain health problems arising in the workplace. However, this does not guarantee that these health problems (or others) will not arise anyway, either from other sources or from the failure of the equipment to accomplish what it is designed to do. In addition, we do not know for sure what will happen if the equipment is not installed; perhaps money will be saved because the equipment will turn out not to have been necessary, or perhaps the actual consequences will turn out to be much worse than predicted. So, factoring in probabilities greatly complicates cost/benefit analysis. We will discuss some of these complications in greater detail in Chapter 7.

Cost/benefit analysis involves three steps:

1. Assess the available options.
2. Assess the costs and the benefits (each measured in monetary terms) of each option for the entire audience of the action, or all of those affected by the decision.
3. Make the decision that is likely to result in the greatest benefit relative to cost; that is, the course of action chosen must *not* be one in which the cost of implementing the option could produce greater benefit if spent on another option.

We can illustrate this method with an example of pollution from a chemical plant. Suppose a large chemical plant is near a residential area. The plant emits a number of noxious odors, some of them posing mild risks to health. How do we determine what level of pollution the plant should be allowed to contribute to the environment?

First, we must assess the options. The plant is emitting pollution into the air, which is a part of the commons. (The *commons* are those areas, such as the air, rivers, and oceans, that are not owned by anyone in particular.) Economists say that the plant is externalizing the cost of pollution by forcing others, such as the surrounding residents, to pay the cost of the pollution, in the sense of living with the odors, suffering the health effects, and perhaps expending funds to counteract these effects. We have the option of either allowing the plant to continue its present course of action or of forcing it to bear the total cost of its pollution, even if this means the plant must be closed.

Second, we must calculate the costs and benefits of the pollution. To measure the cost of the obnoxious smells, we consider several factors. We compare the costs of homes near the plant with costs of homes in locations that are equivalent, except that the pollutants are not present. This differential gives us one cost. Then we obtain some measure of the effect of pollution on health. We estimate the lost earnings from days missed at work, the cost in suffering, and any other costs attributed to poorer health. We also assign a monetary value to the negative aesthetic effects of the odors, if these were not adequately accounted for by the other costs. These and perhaps other costs, added together, give us the full cost of the odors.

There are also benefits of the pollution, because the plant confers benefits on the community, providing jobs and a substantial tax base. Some measure of the decrease in jobs or tax base due to the cost of eliminating the pollution must be made, a form of disutility.

Third, we must compare the costs and benefits of eliminating the pollution. The plant can be forced to eliminate the pollution itself, or to pay a "pollution tax" to the government, which will enable the government to eliminate the pollution, or to compensate the residents for the ill effects of the pollution. Then the pollution must be eliminated up to that point at which the costs of elimination outweigh the benefits, when an optimal state of cleanness will have been reached. An optimal state is not a "perfectly" clean environment, but an environment that is as clean as a cost/benefit analysis will allow. This state may be one in which the plant is forced to close, but it may not be. It all depends on the results of the cost/benefit analysis.

There are serious problems with using cost/benefit analysis as a sole guide for protecting the public from pollution that endangers health. One problem is that the cost/benefit analysis assumes that economic measures of cost and benefit override all other considerations. Cost/benefit analysis encourages the elimination of a pollutant only when it can be done in an economically efficient manner. However, suppose the chemical plant we have been considering is near a wilderness area that is damaged by one of the plant's emissions. It might not be economically efficient to eliminate the pollutant from the cost/benefit standpoint. Of course, the damage to the wilderness area must be included in the cost of the pollution, but this cost might still not justify the elimination—or even the reduction—of the pollution from the cost/benefit standpoint. Yet it is not necessarily irrational to hold that the pollutant should be eliminated, even if the elimination is not justified by the analysis. The economic value that anyone would place on saving the wilderness is not a true measure of its value.

Another problem is that it is often very difficult to ascertain the costs and benefits of the many factors that should enter into a cost/benefit analysis. The most controversial issue is how to assess in cost/benefit terms the loss of human life, or even serious injury. How, many ask, can a dollar value be placed on a human life (an issue we will discuss in Chapter 7)? Aside from the difficulty of determining the costs and benefits of known factors (such as immediate death or injury), it is also difficult to predict what factors will be relevant in the future. If the threat to human health posed by a substance is not known, it is impossible to execute a competent cost/benefit analysis. This problem becomes especially acute if we consider long-term costs and benefits, most of which are impossible to predict or measure.

In addition, cost/benefit analysis often does not take into account the unequal distribution of costs and benefits. Using an earlier example, suppose a plant dumps a pollutant into a river where many of the poorer members of the community fish, using the fish to supplement their diet. Suppose further that, after all of the costs and benefits are calculated, continued pollution of the river is justified; that is, the costs of eliminating it outweigh all of the health costs to the poor.

Still, if the costs are paid by the poor and the benefits are enjoyed by the rich, the costs and benefits are not equally shared. Even if the poor are compensated for the damage to their health, many would say that an injustice has still been done. After all, the wealthy members of the community do not have to suffer the same threat to their health.

Finally, cost/benefit analysis might well have justified many practices in the past that we have good reason to believe are morally wrong. In the nineteenth century, many people opposed child labor laws, arguing that they would lead to economic inefficiencies. They pointed out, for example, that tunnels and shafts in coal mines were too small to accommodate adults. Many arguments in favor of slavery were also based on considerations of economic efficiency. When our society did decide to eliminate child labor and slavery, it was not simply because they became economically inefficient, but rather that they came to be considered unjust. As we shall see in Chapter 9, most environmental legislation is based on values that transcend cost/benefit analysis.

Despite these problems, cost/benefit analysis can make an important contribution to moral problem solving. We can hardly imagine constructing a large engineering project, such as the Aswan High Dam in Egypt, for example, without performing an elaborate cost/benefit analysis. Cost/benefit analysis may not always succeed in quantifying values in ways that do justice to them, but it can play an important role in utilitarian analysis. Its ability to evaluate many conflicting considerations in terms of a single measure, monetary value, makes it invaluable in certain circumstances. As with all other tools for moral analysis, however, we must keep its limitations in mind.

 The Act Utilitarian Approach

Although the act utilitarian approach does not require that values always be rendered in strictly quantitative terms, it does require trying to determine what will maximize good consequences. It focuses on the consequences of particular actions, raising the basic question: "Will this course of action produce more good than any alternative course of action that I could take?" To answer this question, the following procedure is useful:

1. Enumerate the available options open to you.
2. Determine the appropriate audience for the options, keeping in mind the problems in determining the audience.
3. Whatever course of action you select, remember that you must be willing to approve of a similar course of action for others in relevantly similar circumstances; this is an application of the universalizability requirement of consistency discussed in Chapter 2.
4. Decide which available option is likely to bring about the greatest good for the appropriate audience, taking into account harms as well as benefits.

The act utilitarian test is often a useful mode of analysis of options in moral problem solving. For example, assuming the economic costs are roughly equal, the choice between two safety devices in an automotive design could be decided by determining which is more likely to reduce the most injuries and fatalities.

Or road improvements might be decided on the basis of the greater number of people served. Of course, in either case matters could be complicated by considerations of fairness to those who are *not* benefited by the improvements, or who might be put at even greater risk. Nevertheless, the utilitarian determinations seem to carry considerable moral weight even if, in some particular cases, they turn out not to be decisive; and how much weight these determinations should be given cannot be decided without first making careful utilitarian calculations.

❋ *The Rule Utilitarian Approach*

As we have noted, a utilitarian must be willing to universalize whatever course of action is recommended in a particular situation; it is a requirement of consistency that whatever is right (or wrong) in one situation is also right (or wrong) in relevantly similar situations. Thus, it is important to ask a question such as, "Would utility be maximized if everyone did the same thing in the same circumstances?" From a practical point of view, we know that what we do will often be emulated by others. Also, not everyone is especially good at estimating the likely consequences of the options before them. Furthermore, in many areas there are coordination problems that are best resolved by having commonly accepted rules that enable us to predict reliably what others will do. A clear example is rules of the road. Traffic lights, stop signs, yield signs, and other conventions of the road promote both safe and efficient travel. In general, it is better for all that we guide our driving by simply conforming to these rules and conventions rather than trying in each circumstance to determine whether, say, it is safe to go through a red light.

Admittedly, there are times when it would be safe for a driver to go through a red light or stop sign; but this may be only because others can be counted on to comply with the rules. If everyone, or even very many, decided for themselves whether to stop or go through the red light, the result would very likely be a sharp increase in accidents, as well as less efficient travel. The rule utilitarian approach holds that, in such circumstances, we should promote rules that are justified by their utility. When such rules are reasonably well understood and generally accepted, we should use the rules as a guide to action rather than attempt directly to calculate the likely consequences of the various alternative courses of actions in situations covered by the rules.

Traffic rules are an interesting case, and they should be of special interest to engineers. Useful traffic rules need to allow for exceptions that are not stated in the rules. For example, the rule that one come to full stop at a stop sign allows for exceptional circumstances, such as when a large van is running out of control and will crash into your car if you come to a full stop and you can see that there is no crossing traffic approaching the intersection. Stating all the possible exceptions in the rule would be impossible and, in any case, make for a very cumbersome rule.

Still, some kinds of exceptions are understood to be disallowed. For example, treating a stop sign as if it were a yield sign is disallowed (otherwise, it would be replaced by a yield sign); that is, individual discretion as a general rule is ruled out when there is a stop sign (or red light). Estimates of the overall utility of traffic rules sometimes change, thereby leading to changes in the rules. For example, some years ago it was determined, in most states, that using individual discretion in turning right on a red light (after coming to a full stop) is reasonably safe and efficient (except when a "No turn on red light" sign is posted).

From a rule utilitarian point of view, then, in situations covered by well-understood, generally observed rules or practices that serve utilitarian ends, one should justify one's actions by appealing to the relevant rules or practices. The rules or practices, in turn, are justified by their utility when generally observed.

However, there are complications. If there are widespread departures from rules or practices, it is less clear whether overall utility is still promoted by some individuals conforming to the rules or practices anyway. To preserve the beauty of a grassy campus quad, a "Please use sidewalks" sign may be posted. Even if everyone values the unmarked, grassy expanse, some may decide that, as long as only a few people take shortcuts when they find it convenient, it will retain its unmarked beauty. Although this is true, some people making themselves exceptions to the rule can work only if most do not. But when traces of a path begin to appear, a critical point is on the horizon. Eventually, the utilitarian must try to determine whether to continue observing the practice of staying on the sidewalks to discourage further damage or join others in cutting across the quad because it is too late to prevent the damage and the utilitarian point of observing the practice is lost.

In situations where the rule utilitarian mode of analysis is useful, we should use the following procedure. Suppose engineer Karen is facing a decision about whether unilaterally to substitute cheaper parts for those specified in a contract. In deciding what she should do from a rule utilitarian standpoint, she must first ask whether there are well-understood, generally observed rules that serve utilitarian ends that cover such situations. In thinking this through, she might consider the following two possibilities:

Rule 1: Engineers may unilaterally substitute cheaper parts for those specified in the contract.

Rule 2: Engineers may not unilaterally substitute cheaper parts for those specified in the contract.

(Note that the rules chosen to analyze the case must be directly relevant to the case circumstances and must not trivialize the case. For example, Karen should not use a rule like "It is always desirable to maximize company profits," because this ignores the specific issues of the case being tested.)

Next, Karen must determine the audience, which in this case is the producers and purchasers of such products and the general public. She should then ask which of these two rules comes closest to representing the audience's common expectations and whether meeting these expectations generally serves overall utility. If she decides (as she surely will) on Rule 2, then she should follow this rule in her own action and not substitute the cheaper parts.

Notice that the rule utilitarian approach does not consider directly the utility of a particular action unless no generally observed rules or practices that serve utilitarian ends are available.[4] Unlike the act utilitarian approach, the rule utilitarian approach judges the moral acceptability of particular actions by whether they conform to certain rules: those whose general observance promotes utilitarian ends. Notice also that the rules that may be subjected to a rule utilitarian analysis can be of very different types. The rules we examined in the arguments about advertising and competitive bidding in engineering are very general in nature and have to do with guidelines for a professional community. The rules we examined in Karen's case are much more specific, having to do with the permissibility of substituting inferior parts. Both are legitimate objects of rule utilitarian analysis.

The rule utilitarian approach is often used by utilitarians to respond to critics who say that utilitarians fail to accord individual rights their due. Utilitarian thinking, critics say, can approve violating the rights of some groups of individuals to promote the greater good of the majority. A rule utilitarian response might argue that there is greater utility in following a rule that disallows this than one that permits it. After all, if it is understood that the rights of some groups of individuals may be violated for the sake of the greater good of the majority, this will engender fear and insecurity throughout society, for we can never be certain that we will not end up in an unfortunate minority whose rights are violated. In general, a utilitarian might reply, more good overall is served by providing people with assurances that they will be treated in accordance with rules and practices that treat them justly and with respect for individual rights.

However, in addition to worrying about possible utilitarian exceptions to these rules and practices (recall that they are not necessarily exceptionless), many think the utilitarian account of rights is inadequate. People, they counter, have rights because, as individuals, they are entitled to respect, not simply because treating them as if they have rights maximizes overall utility. We will explain this view of rights more thoroughly in the next section, which presents the second major ethical tradition to be considered in this chapter, that of respect for persons.

4.4   The Ethics of Respect for Persons

The moral standard of the ethics of respect for persons is, Those actions or rules are right that, if followed, would accord equal respect to each person as a moral agent.

For the purposes of this theory, we can say that moral agents are those capable of formulating or pursuing goals and purposes of their own. They are autonomous. *Autonomy* comes from two Greek terms: *autos* meaning "self" and *nomos* meaning "rule" or "law." Thus, a moral agent is autonomous in the sense of being self-governing. In the terminology of the respect for persons theorist Immanuel Kant, moral agents are "ends in themselves," persons who are not to be treated as mere means to fulfilling the ends or goals of others.[5] An autonomous action has three aspects: (1) it is intentional—done with a certain aim or end in mind; (2) it is performed without external controlling influences that rule out real choice; and (3) it is made with understanding.

A moral agent must be distinguished from inanimate objects, such as knives or airplanes, which can only fulfill goals or purposes that are imposed externally. Inanimate objects certainly cannot evaluate actions from a moral standpoint. A paradigm of a moral agent is a normal adult human being who, in contrast to inanimate objects, can formulate and pursue goals or purposes of his or her own. Because this moral view has as its basic idea the requirement to respect the moral agency of persons, we refer to it as the *theory of respect for persons*, or respect for persons morality.

The respect for persons explanation of common morality is that its precepts protect the moral agency of individual human beings. Maximizing the welfare of the majority must take second place to this goal. People cannot be killed, deceived, denied their freedom, or otherwise violated simply to bring about a greater total amount of utility. Whereas utilitarianism has a positive, forward-looking orientation, respect for persons morality has a more defensive orientation. It has as its primary function the protection of individuals; so they can pursue their own aims within the parameters set by morality.

There are two principal difficulties with respect for persons morality. First, it is sometimes hard to apply. In some cases, any alternative open to one individual involves interference with the moral agency of someone else. Suppose engineer Harry makes a promise to deliver a new product to a customer by a certain date. He finds that he can keep this promise only by delivering an inferior product. He must therefore infringe on the moral agency of the customer, no matter what he does. As a moral agent, the customer has purposes he or she is pursuing. These purposes will be hindered if Harry breaks a promise, but they will also be hindered if he delivers an inferior product that will not perform as expected. We shall consider shortly some of the ways in which those who support the moral standard of respect for persons might respond to this problem.

A second problem with the moral standard of respect for persons is that sometimes it does seem justifiable to limit the moral agency of individuals for the sake of greater overall utility. Suppose engineer Jane owns a small engineering firm that is facing severe financial difficulties. She decides that the only way to save the firm is to institute a compulsory early retirement program. Although this may infringe on the moral agency of those forced to retire, it may be the right thing to do under the circumstances. Utilitarians, however, can account for the rightness of this action more straightforwardly than proponents of respect for persons morality.

4.5 Three Respect for Persons Approaches

The Golden Rule

The respect for persons moral standard requires us to treat everyone equally as a moral agent. This suggests a way of evaluating the resolution of moral issues, the *universalizability* principle (introduced in Chapter 2), which holds that the resolution of a moral issue must be one that would be universally acceptable if others resolved similar issues in similar ways. As we have seen, utilitarian thinking also employs the universalizability principle. Although to be consistent, both utilitarian and respect for persons approaches must employ this principle, their fundamental aims are different. One aims at maximizing overall utility; the other aims at equal respect for persons.

The universalizability principle is grounded in an idea that is familiar to all of us. Most of us would acknowledge that if we act in a morally praiseworthy fashion, we find it acceptable for others to do similar kinds of things in similar circumstances. This same insight can lead us to ask questions about fairness and equal treatment, such as, "What if everyone did that?" and "Why should you make an exception for yourself?" Such questions highlight the fundamental point of the universalizability principle, but it can be formulated in more than one way.

The best known version is the Golden Rule. A variant of the Golden Rule appears in the religious and ethical writings of most cultures, as the following list shows:

• *Christian version:* "Treat others as you would like them to treat you" (Luke 6:31, *New English Bible*).

• *Hindu version:* "Let not any man do unto another any act that he wisheth not done to himself by others, knowing it to be painful to himself" (*Mahabharata, Shanti Parva*, cclx.21).

• *Confucian version:* "Do not do to others what you would not want them to do to you" (*Analects*, Book xii, #2).

• *Buddhist version:* "Hurt not others with that which pains yourself" (*Udanavarga*, v. 18).

• *Jewish version:* "What is hateful to yourself do not do to your fellow man. That is the whole of the Torah" (*Babylonian Talmud*, Shabbath 31a).

• *Muslim version:* "No man is a true believer unless he desires for his brother that which he desires for himself" (*Hadith, Muslim, imam* 71-72).[6]

The Golden Rule requires us to evaluate the effects of our actions on others by asking whether we (the actors) would be willing to exchange places with those affected by our actions (the recipients). This is the *reversibility* requirement we introduced in Chapter 2.

To apply the Golden Rule, I must take three steps:

1. I must analyze the situation to determine the alternative actions available.
2. I must determine the consequences of the alternative actions.
3. I must place myself in the position of those who would be affected by the consequences of each alternative and ask whether I would be willing to accept those consequences. An action is morally unacceptable if I would not be willing to accept those consequences.

We can informally consider some examples, without proceeding through all the steps. Suppose I am an engineer trying to decide how to resolve the line-drawing issue of whether to accept a gift of a Thanksgiving turkey from a supplier. If I decide to reject the turkey because I believe it is a bribe, I must be willing to have the turkey returned to me if I were the supplier and the supplier were in my position.

Suppose again that I am a manager who orders a young engineer to remain silent about the discovery of an emission from the plant that might cause minor health problems for some people who live near the plant. For this order to be acceptable by the Golden Rule test, I must be willing to have my supervisor give a similar order to me if I were the young engineer. I must also be willing to place myself in the position of the people who live near the plant and would experience the health problem if the emission were not eliminated.

This last example highlights a problem in using the Golden Rule as a test for whether the resolution of a moral problem is acceptable. On the one hand, am I the kind of manager who believes that employees should obey their supervisors without question, especially if their supervisors are also professionals who have many years of experience? Then, I would not object to remaining silent in accordance with my supervisor's orders if I were in the young engineer's position. Am I a member of the public whose health might be affected by the emission? Am I also very concerned with economic efficiency and skeptical of environmental regulations? Then, I might even be willing to endure minor health problems to keep the plant from having to buy expensive new pollution control equipment. Thus, it seems that the Golden Rule could be satisfied. On the other hand, if I do not have these beliefs, I cannot justify my action by the Golden Rule. The results of using the Golden Rule as a test of morally permissible action seem to vary, then, depending on the values and beliefs of the actor.

One way of trying to avoid some of these problems is to interpret the Golden Rule as requiring not only that I place myself in the position of the recipient, but that I adopt the recipient's values and individual circumstances as well. Thus, I would not only have to put myself in the young engineer's place but also to assume her values and her station in life. Given that she was evidently troubled by my order to remain silent and probably is in a low position in the firm's hierarchy, I have to assume that I would find the order contrary to my own adopted wishes and values as well and that I believe a professional has the right to question her supervisor's judgment. Thus, I would not want to be ordered to remain silent, and my action as a manager in ordering the young engineer to remain silent would fail the requirements of the Golden Rule. I also have to assume the position of the people who would experience the minor health problems. Many of them—especially those whose health would be directly affected—would be as concerned for economic considerations as I am and would object to the emissions.

Unfortunately, this tactic does not resolve all the problems. In other situations, placing myself in the position of the other people and assuming their values creates a new set of problems. Suppose I am an engineer who supervises other engineers and I find that I must dismiss one of my supervisees because he is lazy and unproductive. The engineer whom I want to dismiss, however, believes that "the world owes me a living" and does not want to be punished for his irresponsibility. Now if I place myself in the position of the recipient of my own action, namely, the unproductive engineer, but retain my own values, I might use the Golden Rule to justify dismissing him. This is because I might believe that irresponsible employees should be dismissed and even be willing to be dismissed myself if I am lazy and unproductive. If I place myself in my supervisee's position and assume his values, however, I must admit that I would not want to be dismissed. Thus, dismissing the young engineer fails this interpretation of the Golden Rule requirement, even though most of us probably believe that this is the right thing to do.

We have identified two kinds of problems with the Golden Rule: (1) those that result from exclusive attention to what the agent is willing to accept and (2) those that result from exclusive attention to what the recipient is willing to accept.

However, both perspectives (agent and recipient) seem important for an appropriate interpretation of the Golden Rule.

Rather than focus simply on what a particular individual (agent or recipient) wants, prefers, or is willing to accept, we need to consider matters from a more general perspective, one in which we strive to treat others in accordance with standards that we can *share*.[7] What must be kept in mind is that whatever standards are adopted, they must respect *all* affected parties. Viewing oneself as, potentially, *both* agent and recipient is what is required. This process certainly requires attempting to understand the perspectives of agents and recipients; and the Golden Rule provides the useful function of reminding us of this. But understanding these perspectives does not require us to find them acceptable. At some point these perspectives must be evaluated in terms of the standard of respect for persons. Is the manager respecting the young engineer's professional autonomy when attempting to silence her? Understanding what the manager might be willing to accept if put in the position of the engineer does not necessarily answer this question.

The Golden Rule does not, by itself, provide all the criteria that must be met to satisfy the standard of respect for persons. But its requirements of universalizability and reversibility are vital steps in satisfying that standard. Next, we will consider some additional features of universalizability.

 ## *The Self-Defeating Criterion*

Another way of applying the fundamental idea of the universalizability principle is to ask whether I would be able to perform the action in question if everyone else performed the same action in the same or similar circumstances: If everyone else did what I am doing, would this undermine my own ability to do the same thing?[8] If we must say yes to this question, we cannot approve others doing the same kind of thing we have done, and thus universalizing one's action would be self-defeating.

Here are three steps that should be taken to determine if the universalization of a certain course of action would be self-defeating:

1. I must analyze the situation and determine the options.
2. I must determine the consequences of the options.
3. I must determine whether the options, if universally adopted, are self-defeating. If they are, the action is impermissible.

Unlike the Golden Rule, the self-defeating criterion does not refer to the values or the particular circumstances of either the agent or the recipient. The question is more general—whether everyone's performing the action would be self-defeating.

A universalized action can be self-defeating in either of two ways. First, sometimes the action itself cannot be performed if it is universalized. To use a famous example from Immanuel Kant, if I borrow money on the promise to return it and do not keep the promise, my action would be self-defeating if universalized. If everyone borrowed money on the promise to return it and did not keep the promise, promises would not be taken seriously, and no one would loan money on the basis of a promise. Second, sometimes the purpose I have in performing the action is undermined if everyone else does what I do, even if I can perform the action itself. If I cheat on an exam and everyone else cheats too, their cheating does not prevent me from cheating. My purpose, however, may be defeated. If my purpose is to make better grades than other students, it will be undermined if everyone else cheats, for I will no longer have an advantage over them.

When I imagine an action to be universalized, I imagine others not only doing the same sort of thing that I do but also their knowing that others will act the same way. Suppose engineer John decides to substitute an inferior and cheaper part in a product he is designing for one of his firm's large customers. He assumes that the customer will not check the product closely enough to detect the inferior part or will not have enough technical knowledge to know that the part is inferior. But if everyone practiced this sort of deception and expected others to practice it as well, customers would be far more inclined to have products very carefully checked by experts before they were purchased. This would make it much less likely that John's deception would be successful.

As with other approaches, the self-defeating test also has limitations. Some unethical actions might avoid being morally self-defeating. Engineer Bill is by nature an aggressive person who genuinely loves a highly competitive, even brutal, business climate. He enjoys an atmosphere in which everyone attempts to cheat the other person and to get away with as much deception as they can, and he conducts his business in this way. If everyone follows his example, his ability to be ruthless in a ruthless business is not undermined. His action is not self-defeating, even though most of us would consider his practice immoral.

Engineer John, who has no concern for preserving the environment, could design projects that were highly destructive to the environment without his action's being self-defeating. The fact that other engineers knew what John was doing and even designed environmentally destructive projects themselves would not keep him from doing so or destroy the point he had in designing such projects, namely, to maximize his profit.

However, as with the Golden Rule, we need to remember that the universalizability principle was introduced to help us apply the respect for persons standard. If it can be argued that Bill's ruthlessness fails to respect others as persons, it can hardly be universalized; in fact, Bill would have to approve of being disrespected by others (by the same standard, others could treat him with disrespect). Still, the idea of universalizability by itself does not generate the idea of respect for persons; it says only that *if* some persons are to be respected, this must be extended to all. We will turn to a consideration of rights to see if this can give further support to the idea of respect for persons.

 ## Rights

The respect for persons moral standard requires not only that we treat people equally but that we respect them as moral agents. Many theorists in the respect for persons tradition have concluded that respecting the moral agency of others requires that we accord others the rights necessary to exercise their agency. A *right* may be understood as an entitlement to act or to have another individual act in a certain way. Minimally, rights serve as a protective barrier, shielding individuals from unjustified infringements of their moral agency by others. Beyond this, rights are sometimes asserted more positively as requiring the provision of food, clothing, and education. In this section, we will focus primarily on rights as requiring only noninterference with another person, not active support of that person's interests. In Chapter 10, we will consider the significance of more positive rights, especially in an international context.

When we think of rights as forming a protective barrier, they can be regarded as prohibiting certain infringements of our moral agency by others. Some jurists use the expression "penumbra of rights" to refer to this protective barrier that gives individuals immunity from interference from others. Thinking of rights in this way implies that, for every right we have, others have corresponding duties of noninterference. Figure 4.1 provides a list of some important rights, with their corresponding duties of noninterference.

Rights	Corresponding Duties
Kelly has a right to life.	Others have a duty not to kill Kelly.
Kelly has a right to bodily integrity.	Others have a duty not to cause bodily harm to Kelly.
Kelly has a right to mental integrity.	Others have a duty not to cause debilitating mental harm to Kelly.
Kelly has a right to free action.	Others have a duty not to coerce Kelly.
Kelly has a right to free speech.	Others have a duty not to prevent Kelly from speaking freely.
Kelly has a right not to be deceived.	Others have a duty not to deceive Kelly.
Kelly has a right not to be cheated.	Others have a duty not to cheat Kelly.
Kelly has a right not to be stolen from.	Others have a duty not to steal from Kelly.
Kelly has a right not to be disrespected	Others have a duty not to disrespect Kelly.
Kelly has a right to kept promises.	Others have a duty not to break their promises to Kelly.
Kelly has a right to privacy.	Others have a duty not to invade Kelly's privacy.
Kelly has a right to nondiscrimination.	Others have a duty not to deny Kelly opportunities based on race, gender, creed, or sexual preference.
Kelly has a right to property.	Others have a duty not to bar Kelly opportunities for free and fair competition for property and its use.

Figure 4.1
Rights and Corresponding Duties

Just what rights people have, and exactly what they require from others, can be controversial. However, the general principle underlying the list in Figure 4.1 is that an individual should not be deprived of certain things if this deprivation interferes seriously with one's moral agency. If someone takes your life, you cannot exercise your moral agency at all. If someone harms your body or your mental capacities, that person has interfered with your capacity to act as a moral agent. In the case of other rights on the list, interference with them is perhaps not wholly negating your moral agency, but it is diminishing your power to exercise it effectively.

One problem any account of rights must face is how to deal with conflicting rights. Suppose a plant manager wants to save money by emitting a pollutant from his plant that is carcinogenic. The manager, acting on behalf of the firm, has a right to free action and to use the plant (the firm's property) for the economic benefit of the firm. But the pollutant threatens the right to life of the surrounding inhabitants. Notice that the pollutants do not directly and in every case kill surrounding inhabitants, but they do increase the risk of the inhabitants' getting cancer.

So we can say that the pollutant infringes on the right to life of the inhabitants, rather than violates those rights. In a rights violation, one's ability to exercise a right in a certain situation is essentially wholly denied; whereas in a rights infringement, one's ability to exercise a right is only diminished. This diminishment can come about in one of two ways. Sometimes the infringement is a potential violation of that right, as in the case of a pollutant that increases the chance of death. Sometimes the infringement is a partial violation, as when some of a person's property is taken, but not all.

The problem of conflicting rights requires that we prioritize rights, giving greater importance to some than to others. A useful way of doing this is offered by philosopher Alan Gewirth.[9] He suggests a three-tiered hierarchy of rights, ranging from more basic to less basic ones. The first tier includes the most basic rights, the essential preconditions of action: life, physical integrity, and mental health. The second tier includes rights to maintain the level of purpose-fulfillment an individual has already achieved. This category includes such rights as the right not to be deceived or cheated, the right to informed consent in medical practice and experimentation, the right not to have possessions stolen, the right not to be defamed, and the right not to suffer broken promises. The third tier includes those rights necessary to increase one's level of purpose-fulfillment, including the right to try to acquire property.

Using this hierarchy, it would be wrong for the plant manager to attempt to save money by emitting a pollutant that is highly carcinogenic because the right to life is a first-tier right and the right to acquire and use property for one's benefit is a third-tier right. Sometimes, however, the hierarchy is more difficult to apply. How shall we balance a slight infringement of a first-tier right against a much more serious infringement or outright violation of a second-tier or third-tier right? Recall the benzene case in Chapter 2, where the U.S. Supreme Court had to balance a possible decrease in the risk of leukemia against the considerable expenses involved in mandating a reduction in exposure to benzene. The hierarchy of rights provides no automatic answer to such questions. The Court apparently believed that the introduction of utilitarian considerations was necessary to resolve the issue.

We can apply the standard of respect for rights both to the evaluation of general moral rules or laws (as in the benzene case) or to the evaluation of particular courses of action (as in a decision whether to reveal information about criminal activity to one's employer). In either case, we can apply the standard in five different stages:

1. Identify the basic obligations, values, and interests at stake, noting any conflicts.

2. Analyze the action to determine what options are available and what rights are at stake.

3. Determine the audience of the action (those whose rights would be affected).

4. Evaluate the seriousness of the rights infringements that would occur with each option, taking into account both the tier level of rights and the number of violations or infringements involved.

5. Choose the principle or course of action that produces the least serious rights infringements.

Let us apply this analysis of rights to the following case. Karen is a junior engineer at a big oil company. She has been working under Andy's supervision for the past three years. Karen knows that Andy is a good manager, but she has noticed that he frequently has liquor on his breath at work and that sometimes his speech is slurred. One day Karen learns that Andy is about to be offered a new and better paying position. She is happy for Andy until she learns that his new job will be the chief safety inspector for all the oil rigs that the company owns in the region. Karen worries that Andy's drinking will interfere with his work as a safety inspector much more seriously than it interferes with his present job. She tells Andy her concerns and urges him not to accept the job. Andy agrees that he will have to cut back on his drinking, but he tries to assure Karen that he has things under control. He says that he is going to take the job, and he asks Karen not to tell anyone about his drinking.

Should Karen take her concerns to higher management? Let us go through the five recommended steps:

1. The conflicting obligations, values, and interests include worker safety, loyalty to the employer and to fellow employees, Andy's career, and loyalty to Andy.

2. Assuming that there is no way to convince Andy to reject the offer or to refuse it until he clearly has his drinking under control, Karen's options seem to be two: inform management or do not inform management.

3. The audience is Karen, Andy, the employees of the company, and the employer.

4. If Karen informs management, the rights violated are Andy's right to free action, to try to acquire property, to privacy, and perhaps his right to self-respect. If she does not inform management, the employees who operate the oil rigs may have their right to life or bodily integrity violated or seriously infringed.

5. Assuming that Andy really does have a drinking problem that might interfere with his job performance, it seems that Karen's not informing management would result in the most serious rights violations or infringements. The employees' first-tier rights are at stake. Andy's rights here are also first tier, but his life and physical well-being are not being jeopardized. So, it seems that Karen would be morally justified, if not obligated, to inform management.[10]

4.6 ❄ Convergence, Divergence, and Creative Middle Ways

As we have noted, although utilitarian and respect for persons standards are different, they often lead to the same conclusions about what should be done in particular cases. This convergence strengthens those conclusions, because more than one kind of basic reason supports those conclusions. However, occasionally these standards seem to lead to conflicting conclusions. This divergence may leave us in some doubt about what we should do in those cases. Sometimes a creative middle way solution can be worked out that makes it unnecessary to make a hard choice between the two standards. We offer the following case to illustrate this possibility.

In 1993 it was publicly revealed that Germany's Heidelberg University used more than 200 corpses, including those of 8 children, in automobile crash tests.[11] This revelation drew immediate protests in Germany. Rudolph Hammerschmidt, spokesperson for the Roman Catholic German Bishops' Conference objected, "Even the dead possess human dignity. This research should be done with mannequins." ADAC, Germany's largest automobile club, issued a statement saying, "In an age when experiments on animals are being put into question, such tests must be carried out on dummies and not on children's cadavers."

In reply, the university claimed that, in every case, relatives granted permission, as required by German law. It added that, although it had used children in the past, this practice had been stopped in 1989. The rationale for using corpses is that data from crash tests are "vital for constructing more than 120 types of instrumented dummies, ranging in size from infants to adults, that can simulate dozens of human reactions in a crash." These data, it claimed, have been used to save many lives, including those of children.

Similar testing has also been conducted in the United States at Wayne State University's Bioengineering Center. Robert Wartner, a Wayne State spokesperson, indicated that this has been done as a part of a study by the federal government's Centers for Disease Control. However, he added, "Cadavers are used only when alternatives could not produce useful safety research."

Clarence Ditlow, head of the Center for Auto Safety, a Washington, D.C. public advocacy group, said that the center advocates three criteria for using cadavers in crash testing: (1) assurance that the data sought by the tests cannot be gained from using dummies, (2) prior consent by the deceased person, and (3) informed consent of the family.

These three criteria for using cadavers in crash testing combine utilitarian and respect for persons concerns. Criterion (1) is essentially utilitarian. It implies that benefits (saving lives and reducing injuries) can result from the use of cadavers that are not obtainable from using dummies alone. Criteria (2) and (3) acknowledge the importance of respect for persons—both the deceased person and his or her family. If we focus only on adults, assuming that enough cadavers are available, it seems that the consent requirement incurs no utilitarian loss. Criterion (2) rules out the use of the cadavers of children too young to have given their informed consent. This may come at some utilitarian expense, because data on adults may not provide a reliable enough basis for determining how children fare in crashes. (An important illustration is the recent concern about the special vulnerability of small children in cars equipped with air bags.) However, another utilitarian consideration is the level of public concern about the use of children's cadavers.

Does this creative middle way solution satisfactorily resolve the issues? For most, it may. For others (for example, those who would deny the right to volunteer one's own body), perhaps nothing short of a total cessation of the practice will suffice. However, from both utilitarian and respect for persons perspectives, it is not clear how the imposition of the protesters' desire for further restrictions can be justified. Without consent restrictions, the utilitarian and respect for persons standards seem to conflict. With consent restrictions a high degree of convergence seems obtainable.

4.7   Chapter Summary

We have seen in this chapter that utilitarian and respect for persons approaches to moral problems sometimes assist us in attempting to resolve moral problems. At the same time we have been alerted to possible shortcomings of these approaches.

The utilitarian standard says, That which is likely to bring about the greatest overall utility to those affected determines what is morally right. We have presented three utilitarian approaches to problems: cost/benefit, act utilitarian, and rule utilitarian.

The moral standard of respect for persons says, Those actions or rules are right that accord equal respect to each person as a moral agent. We have presented three respect for persons approaches as well: Golden Rule reasoning, determining whether universalizing a course of action would be self-defeating, and respect for rights.

Utilitarian and respect for persons approaches can be combined in various ways with the methods for resolving line-drawing and conflict problems. The person who is skilled in moral thinking must determine which approaches to moral problem solving are the most appropriate in a given situation.

Often the utilitarian and respect for persons approaches lead to the same conclusions. Both approaches have initial plausibility, so this convergence should strengthen our conviction that those conclusions are defensible, even though the two approaches proceed differently. Sometimes, however, these two approaches lead to different conclusions, and this divergence can lead to particularly difficult problems.

Several suggestions may aid in resolving divergence problems. First, when the violation of individual rights is minimal or questionable (as when there may be a small or uncertain threat to human health), utilitarian considerations may sometimes prevail. Second, in cases of divergence, it may be useful to employ line-drawing or creative middle way techniques. Third, when the violation of individual rights is serious, respect for persons considerations take on greater weight, and utilitarian considerations are harder to sustain.

However, it is not our task in this book to provide algorithms for determining which, if either, approach should prevail in any given case. Those skilled in ethical thinking will have their own views on how best to resolve problems of divergence; and, for better or worse, they must bear the responsibility of deciding for themselves.

✳ CASES TO CONSIDER

Case 18	Fire Detectors
Case 24	Highway Safety
Case 34	Pinto
Case 37	Pulverizer
Case 40	Side-Saddle Gas Tanks
Case 42	Sunnyvale

NOTES

1. These are by no means the only important traditions in ethics. For a more comprehensive treatment of these and other philosophical traditions in ethics see, for example, C. E. Harris, *Applying Moral Theories*, 3rd ed. (Belmont, Calif.: Wadsworth, 1997) and James Rachels, *Elements of Moral Philosophy*, 2nd ed. (New York: Random House, 1996).

2. John Stuart Mill, *Utilitarianism* (New York: Liberal Arts Press, 1957), p. 10. For a fuller exposition of utilitarianism, see Harris, *Applying Moral Theories*.

3. A thoroughgoing utilitarian might say at this point, "So much the worse for common morality." We will not attempt to resolve this conflict here. However, we will point out that there are other moral theories that stand behind common morality on this point, one of them being the respect for persons perspective to be discussed later.

4. What if there are such rules or practices but one can think of other rules or practices, which if generally observed, would promote even greater utility? This might provide a utilitarian with a good reason for advocating changes in existing rules or practices, but it would not necessarily justify treating these merely ideal rules or practices as one's guide to action. This is because the utility of observing those ideal rules or practices depends on others doing likewise. In general, acting unilaterally is unlikely to bring about the desired changes; in fact, it may have the opposite effect.

5. Immanuel Kant, *Foundations of the Metaphysics of Morals* (New York: Liberal Arts Press, Bobbs-Merrill, 1959).

6. These quotations, with the exception of the one from Luke, are taken from John Hick, *Disputed Questions in Theology and the Philosophy of Religion* (New Haven, Conn.: Yale University Press, 1993), p. 93.

7. For a defense of this possibility, see Marcus G. Singer, "Defense of the Golden Rule," in Singer, ed., *Morals and Values* (New York: Scribners, 1977).

8. This version of the universalizability criterion is suggested by Immanuel Kant. For another exposition of it, see C. E. Harris, *Applying Moral Theories*, 3rd ed., pp. 158–162.

9. Alan Gewirth, *Reason and Morality* (Chicago: University of Chicago Press, 1978), especially pp. 199–271 and 338–354.

10. If she were Andy's supervisor, rather than the other way around, there would be a stronger case for saying that Karen is obligated, for she would likely have had some direct responsibility to pass a recommendation on to management. However, given that Andy is her supervisor, she might not have been asked to evaluate his qualifications for the new position. Her question, then, would be whether she should step forward even though not asked.

11. The following account is based on Terrence Petty, "Use of Corpses in Auto-Crash Tests Outrages Germans," *Kalamazoo Gazette* (November 24, 1993), A3, and *Time* (December 6, 1993), 70.

Part Two

Generic Concerns

With permission of the Johnson Space Center, NASA

5 *Responsible Engineers*
6 *Honesty, Integrity, and Reliability*
7 *Risk, Safety, and Liability in Engineering*

Chapter 5

Responsible Engineers

Carl Lawrence was alarmed by Kevin Rourke's urgent early afternoon message: "All supervisors immediately check for open caustic valves. Supply tank is empty. Pump still running—either an open valve or a leak. Emergency order of caustic supply on the way." In only the first year of his work as a supervisor of one of Emerson Chemical's acid and caustic distribution systems, Carl had never had to deal with anything like this before. He knew he should move quickly to see if his unit was the source of the problem.

Much to his dismay, Carl found that the problem had originated in his unit. One of his lead operators discovered that a seldom-used caustic valve was open. Although the valve was immediately closed, Carl knew the cleanup remedy would be costly. Minimally, several hundred gallons of caustic would have to be replaced, and as many as thirty drums of hydrochloric acid might need to be used to reduce the pH level of effluent rushing out of the plant toward the local publicly owned wastewater treatment works. Beyond this, Carl knew that eventually he would need to determine who was responsible for the accident. But, for now, he knew his primary responsibility was to help get the problem under control.

5.1 Introduction

Although it is fictional, this is an instructive case. First, it makes clear that what engineers do matters a great deal. Accidents like this are costly, both to our environment (and perhaps public health) and to those who have to pay for the cleanup. Carl Lawrence's engineering responsibilities include much more than preventing and responding to accidents. But this is an important part of his job.

This chapter explores different ways in which engineers might understand and act on their responsibilities. Some engineers are independent consultants or members of consulting firms. Consulting engineers provide services to clients. However, most engineers are corporate employees. Whether they work for clients or corporate employers, engineers have basic job responsibilities. Canon 4 of NSPE's Code of Ethics emphasizes this by insisting that "engineers shall act in professional matters for each employer or client as faithful agents or trustees." We will discuss this in some detail in Chapter 8, "Engineers as Employees." In this chapter, we concentrate on some broader issues of responsibility, especially those concerning possible harms and benefits to society that are associated with engineering practice. We also discuss a variety of impediments to acting responsibly.

We begin with a conception of responsibility that relies heavily on minimal standards. Then, we consider conceptions that require more than meeting minimal standards. Next, we explore the idea that engineers might accept responsibilities that go "above and beyond the call of duty." We show that which of these conceptions best describes engineers can have very important consequences for others. Finally, we explore several impediments to responsibility, especially a variety of obstacles that stand in the way of taking fully into consideration all the factors relevant to responsible engineering practice.

5.2   Concepts of Responsibility

Although legal and moral responsibility are distinct, they are related to each other. Responsibility is attributed to *persons* in both law and morality. However, in law corporations and institutions can be given legal standing as persons, whereas in morality it is highly debatable whether corporations and institutions can be persons.[1] These two areas aside, notions of legal and moral responsibility have much in common.

For example, in regard to responsibility for causing harm, in both law and morality we distinguish:[2]

• *Intentionally* causing harm (knowingly and deliberately causing harm)

• *Negligently* causing harm (not knowingly causing harm but failing to exercise "due care")

• *Recklessly* causing harm (not aiming to cause harm but acting in conscious awareness that harm is likely to result)

It is plausible to say that the legal distinctions rest on their parallel distinctions in morality. We attach the legal importance we do to each because of their parallel moral importance.

In some areas of law there is *strict liability*, where there is no attribution of fault or blame, but there is a legal responsibility to provide compensation, make repairs, or the like. Whether there should be a parallel notion in morality is controversial. However, insofar as there is a moral responsibility to meet one's legal responsibilities, strict liability in law does have moral implications.[3]

All of these conceptions of responsibility come into play in engineering practice. From a moral point of view, engineers are morally responsible for harms they intentionally, negligently, or recklessly cause, regardless of whom, if anyone, is held legally responsible (those who cause the harms, their supervisors, or the company itself). In some instances, they may also be morally responsible for failing to report, or even prevent, such behavior on the part of others. More positively, engineers have a responsibility to serve their employers and the public in ways that reduce the likelihood of harms to others for which either they, their supervisors, or their companies can be held legally liable.

However, the way in which engineers understand and act on this responsibility can vary quite widely. We will discuss three basic attitudes toward responsibility. They can best be viewed as falling within a continuum ranging from a minimalist view of responsibility to one that goes "above and beyond the call of duty." These are not intended as rigid categories, and there are many possible nuances we will not discuss, but they do usefully depict some basic attitudes toward responsibility. We will call these the *minimalist, reasonable care,* and *good works* views of responsibility.[4]

5.3   The Minimalist View

The minimalist view of responsibility holds that engineers have a duty to conform to the standard operating procedures of their profession and to fulfill the basic duties of their job as defined by the terms of their employment. They are accountable for harms caused by their failure to fulfill these responsibilities. Although this approach works well in many instances, standard operating procedures tend to be minimalist, stipulating only minimally acceptable standards. Furthermore, although these standards are based on past experience and the expected outcomes of present practice, unexpected problems can arise that standard operating procedures are not well equipped to handle.

The minimalist view also emphasizes a negative approach to responsibility. It tends to define responsibility in terms of a kind of exclusivity: "It's my job, not his," or "It's his job, not mine."[5] Responsibility is linked with the idea of individual fault, or blame; and it is interpreted in narrow, legalistic terms. Avoidance of blame, or "staying out of trouble," tends to be the dominant concern.

To see the shortcomings of this view, let us return to the case with which we began this chapter. Eventually, Carl Lawrence will have to try to determine what was responsible for the accident. What should he look for? No doubt he should look for the cause of the accident. But, beyond this, he needs to ask if anyone should be held accountable for it. Clearly, not just any possible cause can be connected with the idea of accountability. If the cause is not traceable to a responsible agent, legal or moral accountability seemingly does not apply. But, given that the valve was opened, it is likely that a responsible agent was involved.

This does not mean that someone intentionally left the valve open. It could be a case of negligence. But whose negligence? Carl discovers, let us suppose, that Rick Duffy, a lead operator from the early shift, forgot to close the valve before leaving. That particular valve is in a remote and seldom-used section of Carl's unit, so no one noticed it was open until Kevin Rourke sent out his emergency notice. Does this settle the question of responsibility? It might seem so. As lead operator, Rick Duffy has the responsibility to open and close valves in his area at the appropriate times. He failed to remember to close the seldom-opened valve.

However, let us suppose that Carl reflects further. He recalls his first day on the job. After taking Carl around the facilities, Kevin Rourke asked Rick Duffy to show Carl how the distribution systems work. As Carl and Rick moved from the acid to the caustic distribution system, Carl noted a striking difference. The acid distribution piping had spring-loaded valves that close automatically when not in use. To pump acid into a remote receiving tank, a pump switch must be activated at the remote location. The operator has to hold the pump switch on when the tank is filling. Rick mentioned that the penalty for propping the switch on by other means is immediate dismissal. In contrast, no similar precautions apply to the caustic system. The caustic valves have to be manually opened and closed.

Carl remembers asking Rick why the caustic system was so different. Rick shrugged, "I don't really know. It's been this way at least as long as I've been here. I suppose it's because the acid distribution system is used so much more." Carl also asked Rick if the lead operators have written procedures for filling the caustic tanks. Rick answered that he had never seen any—nor did he recall any review of the practice during the four years he had been an operator. Carl then asked Rick if he was satisfied with this. Rick replied, "Well, I don't have any problems with it. Anyway, that's someone else's concern, not mine. I suppose they don't want to put out the money to change it. 'Don't fix the wheel if it's not broken' seems to be their attitude."

Carl remembers not being very impressed with this line of reasoning and wondering if he should ask his supervisor, Kevin Rourke, about it. However, not wanting to make a stir at the very beginning of his work for Emerson, Carl simply dropped the matter. He now wonders if he bears some of the responsibility for the caustic overflow. Perhaps he should have persisted. Further, he begins to wonder about Kevin's responsibility. Shouldn't people in Kevin's position be looking out for potential problem areas and encouraging others, including Carl and Rick, to do likewise?

We can ask these questions as part of the query about who is to blame, or at fault, for the accident. But we need not. We might ask, instead, what virtues, or qualities of character, it is important for engineers, technicians, and others to have, especially those who work in environments in which accidents can occur. This involves shifting to a more positive model of responsibility. In reflecting on why the accident occurred, Carl Lawrence is thinking of a variety of factors that, taken together, increased the likelihood that such an accident would occur. His conclusion seems to be that the responsibility is *shared*. There are constructive things that several people could have done. More important, there are lessons to be learned for the future. Carl might have taken on the responsibility of discussing his concerns about the caustic system with Kevin Rourke. His reason for doing this should have been to determine if the system needed to be improved, not simply to avoid blame later.

Using only the minimalist view of responsibility is unlikely to lead us to this conclusion. Rick Duffy failed to follow standard operating procedures at Emerson. Shutting off the valve was his responsibility. He, then, is to be faulted. It is not clear that anyone else, including Carl Lawrence, failed to follow standard operating procedures at Emerson, or any externally imposed regulations. However, given human fallibility and standard practices at Emerson, the caustic spill was, we might say, an accident waiting to happen.

5.4   Reasonable Care

The reasonable care view moves beyond the minimalist view's concern to "stay out of trouble." We might say that the minimalist view is most directly concerned with what will happen to those who cause harm (those who will be held liable either legally or morally). However, the reasonable care view is more directly concerned with the perspective of those who are at risk of being harmed and trying to prevent that harm. This appeals to "a standard of reasonableness as seen by a normal, prudent nonprofessional."[6]

Tort law, which addresses legal injuries or wrongs, employs a standard of reasonable care that relies on, but is not necessarily restricted to, the standard operating procedures of a profession and ordinary job responsibilities. The generally accepted standard of reasonable care the courts apply to professionals, including engineers, was stated in *Coombs v. Beede*:

> The responsibility resting on an architect is essentially the same as that which rests upon the lawyer to his client, or upon the physician to his patient, or which rests upon anyone to another where such person pretends to possess some special skill and ability in some special employment, and offers his services to the public on account of his fitness to act in the line of business for which he may be employed. The undertaking of an architect implies that he possesses skill and ability, including taste, sufficient enough to enable him to perform the required services at least ordinarily and reasonably well; and that he will exercise and apply, in the given case, his skill and ability, his judgment and taste reasonably and without neglect. [7]

Notice that this statement does not say that professionals need only conform to the established standards and practices of their field of expertise. Those standards and practices may be in a state of change, and they may not be able to keep pace with advancing knowledge of risks in particular areas. Furthermore, as many liability cases have shown, reasonable people often disagree about precisely what those standards and practices should be taken to be.

In any case, suits in tort law proceed from complaints by those who allege they have been injured or wronged by another party who should be held liable. If the complaint is against individual professionals, the claim is that there was a lack of reasonable care (a case of intentionally, negligently, or recklessly causing harm). However, companies are sometimes held strictly liable (without regard to fault).

A common complaint is that court determinations, particularly those involving juries, are often excessive. However valid this complaint may be, two points should not be lost. First, the fact that these determinations are made, however fair or unfair they may be, has important implications for engineers. As consultants who are themselves subject to liability, they have self-interested reasons for striving to take the reasonable care standard seriously. As corporate employees, they have a responsibility to be concerned about areas of corporate liability that involve their expertise.

Second, the idea of reasonable care has a moral basis, regardless of how it gets played out in courts of law. From a moral point of view, intentionally, negligently, or recklessly causing harm to others is to fail to exercise reasonable care. What, if any, legal redress is due is another matter.

Even strict liability as applied to companies has a moral basis.[8] Companies have both the opportunity and responsibility to test their products for safety. Consumers are not well positioned to determine where in the manufacturing process fault might lie. Economically, companies are in a much better position than consumers to afford compensation should harms result, and assuming this burden can be considered a known risk of those who take up the responsibility of providing reasonably safe products to consumers. As section 402A of the *Restatement (Second) of Torts* puts it:

> [T]he seller, by marketing his product for use and consumption, has undertaken and assumed a special responsibility toward any member of the consuming public who may be injured by it; that the public has the right to and does expect, in the case of products which it needs and for which it is forced to rely upon the seller, that reputable sellers will stand behind their goods. [9]

The minimalist view of responsibility can accommodate much of what is included in the reasonable care model. This can be done by attempting to determine the range of individual and corporate legal liability that has implications for one's role as an engineer. The aim would be to do whatever one can to keep oneself or one's company "out of trouble."

However, there are two reasons for thinking the minimalist view will not adequately cover the full range of reasonable care from a moral point of view. First, liability insurance provides another way to deal with questions of liability. In calculating the case for or against making a full effort to meet standards of reasonable care, the cost of doing so can be weighed against the chances of facing a tort claim. This involves estimating the likelihood that harm will actually occur—and, if it does, that anyone will take it to court (and that they will be successful). Liability insurance is already an expense, and those whose aim is simply to minimize overall costs might calculate that a less than full commitment to standards of reasonable care is worth the risk.

Second, there is little reason to assume that the courts, for all of their alleged excesses in some cases, are likely to address all wrongs that a "standard of reasonableness as seen by a normal, prudent nonprofessional" would include.[10] Thus, while mindful of liability issues, those engineers who fully embrace the reasonable care view commit themselves to doing their best to satisfy the public expectation that they will exercise reasonable care in their work.

5.5   Good Works

We call the third conception of responsibility *good works*. This is captured in the expression "above and beyond the call of duty."[11]

A simple example outside the engineering context illustrates what we mean by the concept of good works. Ralph wakes up at his usual time and prepares to go to work. When he looks out the window, he is shocked to see his long driveway drifted over with snow; this was not in last night's weather forecast. He has only a snow shovel, not a plow. He realizes he will be very late to work—and very tired. As he bundles up to go out and shovel, Ralph is surprised to see his driveway being cleared by a neighbor with a snowplow. Although they are neighbors, they have never met before.

No doubt Ralph appreciates what his neighbor is doing. What would he think if his neighbor had done nothing to help? Would he fault him, think he had failed to do his duty, or think his neighbor had some sort of moral deficiency? These responses are unlikely. His neighbor has gone "above and beyond the call of duty." His is not a saintly or heroic act, but it is an admirable one.

Such things happen in professional life as well, and on a more extended basis. Here are two examples.

• A statistician agrees to help analyze data to determine whether it is safe for residents in Love Canal to return to their homes after being ordered to leave because of a fear that toxic wastes in the area posed a health risk. Although modestly compensated for his services, he realizes there are many, much more lucrative consulting opportunities. Asked why he has accepted this task instead, he says: "Analyzing data just for the money doesn't mean anything to me. I want it to do some good."[12]

• A design engineer devotes a great deal of time after regular working hours to see if the features of a safety rope for those who wash windows of high rises can be improved—even though the current design more than satisfies legal requirements. Asked why he is not satisfied with the current design, he comments, "You have to do the best you can—and that's usually inadequate."[13]

Here we have two examples of professionals who take on responsibilities that no one has a right to expect from them. If they did not do these things, no one would fault them. Most of us would not think that their not taking on these responsibilities would indicate a moral shortcoming. In short, although they might say to themselves, "This is what I *ought* to do," it is unlikely that we would feel it is appropriate for us to tell them that they ought to do what they are doing. Instead, we praise them for their good works.[14]

Professional codes of ethics focus primarily on duties or obligations deemed so fundamental that failure to fulfill them warrants reproach or even formal sanctions. We will refer to these as *basic duties*. Although codes may commend ideals that go beyond basic duties, these commendations are stated quite abstractly, and they are often addressed to the profession as a whole, leaving it unclear how this applies to individual members of the profession.

Interpretations of codes typically focus on basic duties and their violations rather than on behavior that is ethically commendable. For example, the regularly issued *Opinions of the Board of Ethical Review* of the National Society for Professional Engineers (NSPE) offers very helpful interpretations of NSPE's code. Its opinions, however, deal almost exclusively with whether certain courses of action under consideration are ethically required, prohibited, or permitted by the code. Left undiscussed are examples of engineers whose behavior is ethically commendable but not required by the code.

Let us consider another example in more detail. This involves the collaborative efforts of engineers, rather than just one individual. In the late 1930s a group of General Electric engineers worked together to develop the sealed beam headlight, which promised to reduce sharply the number of fatalities caused by night driving.[15] To accomplish this it was necessary to involve engineers in research, design, production, economic analysis, and governmental regulation. Although the need for headlight improvement was widely acknowledged, there was also widespread skepticism about its technical and economic feasibility. By 1937 the General Electric team had proved the technical feasibility of the sealed beam headlight. However, the remaining task was to persuade car builders and designers to cooperate with each other in support of the innovation, and to convince regulators of its merits.

There is little reason to suppose that the General Electric engineers were simply doing what they were told—namely, to come up with a more adequate headlamp. Apparently, the virtual consensus was that this could not be done; so, the engineers had to overcome considerable resistance. That this was no ordinary task is evidenced by the remarks of another engineer of that era:

> The reaching of the consensus embodied in the specifications of the Sealed Beam Headlamp is an achievement which commands the admiration of all who have any knowledge of the difficulties that were overcome. It is an achievement not only in illuminating engineering, but even more in safety engineering, in human engineering, in the art of cooperation.[16]

The difficulties this group of engineers faced remind us that enthusiasm for good works needs to be tempered with realism. Other demands and constraints may discourage undertaking such projects. Nevertheless, looking for opportunities to do good works, as well as taking advantage of these opportunities when they arise, is a desirable trait in an engineer.

How should we understand good works within the context of engineering responsibility? Whereas we *hold* each other responsible for certain things, it is also possible for us to *assume*, or *take on*, certain responsibilities. The design engineer who has taken on the task of improving the quality of the safety rope is assuming additional responsibilities. These are self-imposed. The statistician, otherwise fully employed, agrees to additional consulting responsibilities only when convinced they will "do some good"—a commendable but self-imposed requirement. Finally, as the Sealed Beam Headlamp project illustrates, such efforts need not be solitary; engineers can undertake good works together.

It is easy to fail to notice that what we are calling good works commonly occur in professional life. Those who perform them may view themselves as simply doing what needs to be done. They may see important tasks that we fail to notice, and they quietly do them. Or we may grow accustomed to what they do and simply take their good works for granted. Furthermore, once they take on a responsibility and the work is under way, it often is appropriate to hold them accountable for completing the work. What we may overlook is that taking on the responsibility in the first place was fully optional.

We might ask if it really is important to emphasize good works in professional life. Why not assume that, if only professionals would meet their basic duties they would fulfill the basic needs of those whom the professions acknowledge they should serve? To see why not, consider the implications of the absence of good works. Disasters are averted not only by professionals fulfilling their duties but also by their doing more than this requires—so are less severe, but nevertheless unwelcome, consequences. Also, the fact that not all professionals do meet their basic duties creates needs that will be unmet unless others occasionally do more than their basic duties call for.[17]

However, as we have noted, good works are not always welcome. In fact, sometimes they are discouraged, intentionally or not. We need to ask to what extent the organizations within which professionals work present obstacles to doing good works. For example, organizations may define professional tasks and responsibilities too narrowly, actively discouraging "do-gooders," or rewarding only those who do not "rock the boat." Good works may also be discouraged by the need to meet tight time schedules, by limited budgets, and by the press of other matters at hand. Some of these obstacles are simply realistic and justifiable limitations (particularly if good works can be accomplished only by neglecting basic duties). Others seem, in principle, alterable. When this is so, it is important to examine the extent to which changes might be desirable and feasible.

5.6   Do Engineers Need Virtues?

We have suggested that professional responsibility can include virtues that go beyond fulfilling the basic duties typically found in a professional code of ethics. Virtues are normally understood to include attitudes and dispositions, not just conduct. They reflect our moral character. William F. May suggests that professional ethics should pay more attention to matters of character and virtue:

> Important to professional ethics is the moral disposition the professional brings to the structure in which he operates, and that shapes his or her approach to problems. . . . At the same time, his moral commitments, or lack of them, and the general ethos in which he and his colleagues function can frustrate the most well-intentioned structural reforms.[18]

May is talking about not just what professionals actually do, but also what they are ready, or disposed, to do—and to see. Those who care about public safety and welfare and who are actively looking for ways to improve it, for example, are more likely to see what needs doing and how to go about it.

May argues that attention to character and virtue is especially important because of the institutional settings within which most professionals work. He gives two reasons for saying this. First, large organizations have the ability rather easily to cover the mistakes of their employees. It is difficult to determine just where things went wrong and who bears responsibility. Second, large organizations are marked by highly specialized functions performed by professionals whose expertise is not shared by many other professionals, let alone laypersons.

May says of the expert: "He had better be virtuous. Few may be in a position to discredit him. The knowledge explosion is also an ignorance explosion; if knowledge is power, then ignorance is powerlessness."[19] May offers a test of professional character and virtue: "One test of character and virtue is what a person does when no one else is watching. A society that rests on expertise needs more people who can pass that test."[20]

What counts as passing this test? There are virtues that are associated with basic duties: honesty, fair-mindedness, reliability, and a kind of integrity that goes with them. But we must add other elements if we are to go beyond basic duty. May's list includes benevolence, perseverance, and public-spiritedness. Similarly, compassion, kindness, generosity, and many other character traits and virtues invite us to consider more than basic duties.

One of the attractions of restricting the idea of the moral responsibility of professionals to basic duties is that this makes responsibility seem more precisely stateable and thereby manageable. However, moral responsibility is more open-ended and admits of varying degrees of stringency. Although there are limits to what we can reasonably be expected to do, our work is never really done;—recalling the words of the designer of the safety rope, "You have to do the best you can—and that's usually inadequate."

5.7   Impediments to Responsibility

It is one thing to have a general understanding of engineering responsibility. It is quite another to apply this understanding in actual engineering practice. Unfortunately, many obstacles need to be confronted. We will discuss several of the more significant ones.

Self-Interest

Engineering codes of ethics, like the codes of other professions, articulate standards of conduct for engineers as engineers. However, engineers are not simply engineers. They are, like everyone else, people with personal hopes and ambitions not restricted to professional ideals. Sometimes concern for our own interests tempts us to act contrary to the interests of others, perhaps even contrary to what others expect from us as professionals. Sometimes concern for self-interest blocks us from seeing or fully understanding our professional responsibilities.

Taken to an extreme, concern for self-interest is a form of *egoism*—an exclusive concern to satisfy one's own interests, even at the possible expense of others. This is popularly characterized as "looking out for number one."

Whether a thoroughgoing egoist would act at the expense of others very much depends on the circumstances. All of us depend to some extent on others to get what we want; some degree of mutual support is necessary. But opportunities for personal gain at the expense of others do arise—or so it seems to most of us. Egoists are prepared to take advantage of this, unless they believe it is likely to work to their long-term disadvantage. But it is not just egoists who are tempted by such opportunities. All of us are, at least occasionally.

Fear

Even when we are not tempted to take advantage of others for personal gain, we may be moved by various fears—fear of acknowledging our mistakes, fear of losing one's job, or fear of some sort of sort of punishment or other bad consequences. Fears of these sorts can make it very difficult for us to act responsibly. William LeMessurier knew what was at stake when he faced the decision about what to do when he discovered that the Citicorp building was not constructed as he thought it had been. Fortunately, he had enough self-assurance that he was willing to risk finding out that the structure he had designed was flawed. When he discovered the flaw, he had the courage to step forward, even at the possible expense of his reputation and career. However, the fact that so many lauded him for his persistence and courage in behaving so responsibly is evidence that doing what one ought to do is, for most of us, not always easy.

LeMessurier blew the whistle on himself. However, most well-known whistle-blowing cases are instances in which it is alleged that others have made serious mistakes or engaged in wrongdoing.[21] It is also well-known that whistle-blowers commonly endure considerable hardship and suffering as a result of their open opposition. This may involve being shunned by colleagues and others, demotion or the loss of one's job, or serious difficulties in finding new employment (especially in one's profession). Although the circumstances that call for whistle-blowing are extreme, they do occur sometimes. Given the typical fate of whistle-blowers, it takes considerable courage to step forward even when it is evident that this is the morally responsible thing to do.

Here there is strength in numbers. Group resistance within an organization is more likely to bring about changes without the need for going outside; and when this fails, a group of whistle-blowers may be less likely than one to be perceived as simply disloyal or trying to get back at the organization for some grievance. However, the difficulty of finding others with whom to join a cause can itself increase one's fears. So, there seems to be no substitute for courage and determination in such circumstances.

Self-Deception

One way of resisting the temptations of self-interest is to confront ourselves honestly and ask if we would approve of others treating us in the same way we are contemplating treating them. This, as we have seen, is Golden Rule reasoning; and it can have a powerful psychological effect on us. However, for it to work, we must recognize what we are contemplating doing for what it is. *Rationalization* often gets in the way of this recognition. Some rationalizations show greater self-awareness than others, particularly those that exhibit self-defensiveness or excuse-making. ("I'm not really doing this just for myself." "Everyone takes shortcuts once in a while—it's the only way one can survive.") Other rationalizations seem to betray a willful lack of self-understanding. This is called *self-deception*, an intentional avoidance of truths we would find it painful to confront self-consciously.[22] Because of the nature of self-deception, it is particularly difficult to discover it in oneself. However, open communication with colleagues can help correct biases to which we are susceptible—unless, of course, our colleagues share the same biases (an illustration of "groupthink," to be discussed later).

Ignorance

An obvious barrier to responsible action is ignorance of vital information. If an engineer does not realize that, for example, a design poses a safety problem, he or she will not be in a position to do anything about it. Sometimes such a lack of awareness is willful avoidance—a turning away from information to avoid having to deal with the challenges it may pose. But often it is due to a lack of imagination, not looking in the right places for necessary information, a failure to persist, or the pressure of deadlines. Although there are limits to what engineers can be expected to know, these examples suggest that ignorance is not always a good excuse.

Egocentric Tendencies

A common feature of human experience is that we tend to interpret situations from very limited perspectives and that it takes special efforts to acquire a more objective viewpoint. This is what psychologists call *egocentricity*. It is especially prevalent in us as young children, and it never completely leaves us. Although egocentric thinking is sometimes egoistic (self-interested), it need not be. It is actually a special form of ignorance.

It is not just self-interest that interferes with our ability to understand things from other perspectives. We may have good intentions for others but fail to realize that their perspectives are different from ours in important ways. For example, some people may not want to hear bad news about their health. They may also assume that others are like them in this respect. So, if they withhold bad news from others, this is done with the best of intentions—even if others would prefer hearing the bad news. Similarly, an engineer may want to design a useful product but fail to realize how different the average consumer's understanding of how to use it is from those who design it. This is why test runs with typical consumers are needed.

Microscopic Vision

Like egocentric thinking, *microscopic vision*[23] embraces a limited perspective. However, whereas egocentric thinking tends to be inaccurate (failing to understand the perspectives of others), microscopic vision may be very accurate and precise. When we look into a microscope, we see things that we could not see before—but only in the narrow field of resolution on which the microscope focuses. We gain accurate, detailed knowledge—at a microscopic level. At the same time, we cease to see things at the more ordinary level. This is the price of seeing things microscopically. Only when we lift our eyes from the microscope will we see what is obvious at the everyday level.

Every skill, says Michael Davis, involves microscopic vision to some extent: "A shoemaker, for example, can tell more about a shoe in a few seconds than I could tell if I had a week to examine it. He can see that the shoe is well or poorly made, that the materials are good or bad, and so on. I can't see any of that. But the shoemaker's insight has its price. While he is paying attention to people's shoes, he may be missing what the people in them are saying or doing."[24] Just as shoemakers need to raise their eyes and listen to their customers, engineers sometimes need to raise their eyes from their world of scientific and technical expertise and look around them to understand the larger implications of what they are doing.

Uncritical Acceptance of Authority

Engineering codes of ethics emphasize the importance of engineers exercising independent, objective judgment in performing their functions. This is sometimes called professional *autonomy*. At the same time, the codes of ethics insist that engineers have a duty of fidelity to their employers and clients. Independent consulting engineers may have an easier time maintaining professional autonomy than the vast majority of engineers, who work in large, hierarchical organizations. Most engineers are not their own bosses, and they are expected to defer to authority in their organizations.

An important finding of the research of social psychologist Stanley Milgram is that a surprisingly high percentage of people are inclined to defer uncritically to authority.[25] In his famous obedience experiments during the 1960s, Milgram asked volunteers to administer electric shocks to "learners" whenever they made a mistake in repeating word pairs (for example, nice/day, rich/food) that volunteers had presented to them earlier. He told volunteers that this was an experiment designed to determine the effects of punishment on learning. No shocks were actually administered, however. Milgram was really testing to see the extent to which volunteers would continue to follow the orders of the experimenter to administer what they believed were increasingly painful shocks. Surprisingly (even to Milgram), nearly two-thirds of the volunteers continued to follow orders all the way up to what they thought were 450-volt shocks—even when shouts and screams of agony were heard from the adjacent room of the learner. The experiment was replicated many times to make sure that the original volunteers were a good representation of ordinary people, rather than especially cruel or insensitive people.

There is little reason to think that engineers are different from others in regard to obeying authority. In the Milgram experiments, the volunteers were told that the learners would experience pain but no permanent harm or injury. Perhaps engineers would have had doubts about this as the apparent shock level moved toward the 450-volt level. This would mean only that the numbers would need to be altered for engineers, not that they would be unwilling to administer what they thought were extremely painful shocks.

One of the interesting variables in the Milgram experiments was the respective locations of volunteers and learners. The greatest compliance occurred when learners were not in the same room with the volunteers. Volunteers tended to accept the authority figure's reassurances that he would take all the responsibility for any unfortunate consequences. However, when volunteers and learners were in the same room and in full view of one another, volunteers found it much more difficult to divest themselves of responsibility.

Milgram's studies seem to have special implications for engineers. As we have already noted, engineers tend to work in large organizations in which the division of labor often makes it difficult to trace responsibility to specific individuals. The combination of the hierarchical structure of large organizations and the division of work into specialized tasks contributes to the sort of "distancing" of an engineer's work from its consequences for the public. This tends to decrease the engineer's sense of personal accountability for those consequences. However, even though such distancing might make it easier psychologically to be indifferent to the ultimate consequences of one's work, this does not really relieve one from at least partial responsibility for those consequences.

One further interesting feature of Milgram's experiments is that volunteers were less likely to continue to administer what they took to be shocks when they were in the presence of other volunteers. Apparently, they reinforced each other's discomfort at continuing, and this made it easier to disobey the experiment. However, as we shall see in the next section, group dynamics does not always support critical response. Often quite the opposite occurs, and only concerted effort can overcome the kind of uncritical conformity that so often characterizes cohesive groups.

Groupthink

A noteworthy feature of the organizational settings within which engineers work is that individuals tend to work and deliberate in groups. This means that an engineer will often participate in group decision making, rather than function as an individual decision maker. Although this may contribute to better decisions ("two heads are better than one"), it also creates well-known, but commonly overlooked tendencies to engage in what Irving Janis calls *groupthink*—a situation in which groups come to agreement at the expense of critical thinking.[26] Janis documents instances of groupthink in a variety of settings, including a number of historical fiascos (for example, the bombing of Pearl Harbor, the Bay of Pigs invasion, the decision to cross the 38th parallel in the Korean War).

Concentrating on groups that are characterized by high cohesiveness, solidarity, and loyalty (all of which are prized in organizations), Janis identifies eight symptoms of groupthink:[27]

1. An *illusion of invulnerability* of the group to failure
2. A strong "we feeling" that views outsiders as adversaries or enemies and encourages *shared stereotypes* of others
3. *Rationalizations* that tend to shift responsibility to others

4. An *illusion of morality* that assumes the inherent morality of the group and thereby discourages careful examination of the moral implications of what the group is doing

5. A tendency of individual members toward *self-censorship*, resulting from a desire not to "rock the boat"

6. An *illusion of unanimity*, construing silence of a group member as consent

7. An application of *direct pressure* on those who show signs of disagreement, often exercised by the group leader who intervenes in an effort to keep the group unified

8. *Mindguarding*, protecting the group from dissenting views by preventing their introduction (by, for example, outsiders who want to present their views to the group)

Traditionally, engineers have prided themselves on being good team players, which compounds the potential difficulties with groupthink. How can the problem of groupthink be minimized for engineers? Much depends on the attitudes of group leaders, whether they are managers or engineers (or both). Janis suggests that leaders need to be aware of the tendency of groups toward groupthink and take constructive steps to resist it. Janis notes that, after the ill-advised Bay of Pigs invasion of Cuba, President John F. Kennedy began to assign each member of his advisory group the role of critic. He also invited outsiders to some of the meetings, and he often absented himself from meetings to avoid influencing unduly its deliberations.

5.8   Chapter Summary

In this chapter, we have explored different conceptions of the responsibilities of engineers. These conceptions range from a minimalist view that is primarily concerned with staying out of trouble to a reasonable care view to the idea of taking on responsibilities that go "above and beyond the call of duty"—what we call good works.

Although each of these conceptions has something positive to contribute to our understanding of engineering responsibility, each also has some difficulties. The minimalist view rightly points to the importance of complying with the law, adhering to standard norms and practices, and avoiding wrongful behavior. But strict adherence to these minimal standards can also contribute to avoidable harms and an overemphasis on attributing blame instead of seeking constructive alternatives. The reasonable care view insists that minimal standards may not be enough, but it is not clear that what prudent nonprofessionals expect is always attainable. The notion of good works reminds us that, in an important sense, one's work is never done, especially in professions like engineering, where the safety, health, and welfare of others is so clearly at stake. Yet, there are limitations of time and money, and other responsibilities. One may sometimes even meet with active resistance from employers, supervisors, and colleagues.

We might wish for some sort of algorithm for determining what our responsibilities are in particular circumstances. But this is an idle wish. Even the most detailed codes of ethics of professional engineering societies can provide only general guidance. The determination of responsibilities in particular circumstances depends on discernment and judgment on the part of engineers.

We have noted several possible impediments to the kind of discernment and judgment that responsible engineering practice requires. Self-interest, fear, self-deception, ignorance, egocentric tendencies, microscopic vision, uncritical acceptance of authority, and groupthink are commonplace and require special vigilance if engineers are to resist them.

 CASES TO CONSIDER

Case 1	Aftermath of Chernobyl
Case 2	Air Bags
Case 3	AVIT
Case 4	Disaster Relief*
Case 20	Ghost of an Executed Engineer
Case 21	Gilbane Gold
Case 31	Moral Beliefs in the Workplace
Case 39	Renewable Energy
Case 43	Training Firefighters
Case 45	TV Antenna
Case 54	Window Safety

NOTES

1. For discussions of this issue see, for example, Peter French, *Collective and Corporate Responsibility* (New York: Columbia University Press, 1984); Kenneth E. Goodpaster and John B. Matthews Jr., "Can a Corporation Have a Conscience?" *Harvard Business Review*, 60 (January/February 1982), 132–141; and Manuel Velasquez, "Why Corporations Are not Morally Responsible for Anything They Do," *Business and Professional Ethics Journal*, 2, no. 3 (Spring 1983), 1–18.

2. We are indebted to Martin Curd and Larry May for outlining these two models and showing how they can be applied to engineering. See Martin Curd and Larry May, *Professional Responsibility for Harmful Actions*, Module Series in Applied Ethics, Center for the Study of Ethics in the Professions, Illinois Institute of Technology (Dubuque, Iowa: Kendall/Hunt, 1984).

3. For an instructive discussion of the various forms of legal liability of consulting scientists and engineers, see Margaret N. Strand and Kevin C. Golden, "Consulting Scientist and Engineer Liability: A Survey of Relevant Law," *Science and Engineering Ethics*, 3, no. 4, (October 1997), 357–394. The authors explore liability in tort, contract, and statutory law. Although they concentrate on consulting engineers, the same areas of law apply to corporations, thereby affecting the responsibilities of engineers as corporate employees.

---

* Includes an analysis of the case.

4. The minimalist and reasonable care models are presented in Curd and May. The good works model is presented in Michael S. Pritchard, "Good Works," *Professional Ethics, 1,* no. 1, (Fall 1992), 155–177. Closely related views of responsibility are discussed in John Ladd, "Bhopal: An Essay on Moral Responsibility and Civic Virtue," *Journal of Social Philosophy,* XXII, no. 1 (Spring 1991), 73–91.

5. This is what John Ladd calls *negative,* or *task,* responsibility. Ladd, p. 81.

6. Curd and May, p. 15.

7. *Coombs v. Beede,* 89 Me. 187, 188, 36 A. 104 (1896). This is cited and discussed in Strand and Golden, pp. 362–363.

8. Strand and Golden, p. 371.

9. Cited in Strand and Golden, p. 372.

10. Curd and May, p. 15. One of the cases at the end of this chapter, The TV Antenna Tower, will confirm the point being made here.

11. Philosophers and theologians commonly refer to this as the *supererogatory.* However, because this is typically associated with the saintly and heroic, we use a more mundane expression, "good works." Philosopher J. O. Urmson captures what we have in mind by reminding us that there is a "vast array of actions, having moral significance, which frequently are performed by persons who are far from being moral saints or heroes but which are neither duties nor obligations. . . ." J. O. Urmson, "Hare on Intuitive Moral Thinking," in Douglas Seanor and N. Fotion, Eds., *Hare and Critics* (Oxford, England: Clarendon Press, 1988), p. 168.

12. Personal communication with statistician Michael Stoline at Western Michigan University.

13. The engineer's analysis of the problem is that when actually used by window washers the safety rope performs very well. But he worries that, even though wearing belts is mandatory, some workers will not use the mechanism because it does not permit them to lower themselves as quickly as they like. His primary concern, he says, is that, like those who refuse to wear seat belts in their cars, some will die or be seriously injured unnecessarily. Neither the engineer nor his company bears any risk of liability if accidents result from not wearing the belts. Nevertheless, the engineer is not satisfied.

14. This paragraph and the following two are based on Michael S. Pritchard, "Good Works."

15. This account is based on G. P. E. Meese, "The Sealed Beam Case," *Business & Professional Ethics, 1,* no. 3 (Spring 1982), 1–20.

16. H. H. Magsdick, "Some Engineering Aspects of Headlighting," *Illuminating Engineering* (June 1940), 533, cited in Meese, p. 17.

17. Of course, this may encourage laxity on the part of some. If Adam knows that someone else will pick up the slack when he neglects his responsibilities, this may encourage him all the more to neglect his duties. Eventually, this may backfire; but it may not, thus perpetuating a basic unfairness to those who pick up the slack he creates. But there are reasons other than deliberate neglect for falling short of one's duties (for example, illness). In any case, more than unfairness may be at stake. In some circumstances, if someone does not try to make up for Adam's shortcomings, others, too, may be seriously shortchanged or harmed.

18. William F. May, "Professional Virtue and Self-Regulation," in *Ethical Issues in Professional Life* (Oxford, England: Oxford University Press, 1988), p. 408.

19. Ibid.

20. Ibid.

21. We will discuss whistle-blowing in greater detail in Chapter 9.

22. This is Mike Martin's characterization of self-deception. See his *Self-Deception and Morality* (Lawrence, Kans.: University Press of Kansas, 1986) for his extended analysis of self-deception and its significance for morality.

23. This expression was introduced into engineering ethics literature by Michael Davis. See his "Explaining Wrongdoing," *Journal of Social Philosophy,* XX, nos. 1&2 (Spring/Fall

1989), 74–90. Davis applies this notion to the *Challenger* disaster, especially when Robert Lund was asked to take off his engineer's hat and put on his manager's hat.

24. Ibid., p. 74.

25. Stanley Milgram, *Obedience to Authority* (New York: Harper & Row, 1974).

26. Irving Janis, *Groupthink*, 2nd ed. (Boston: Houghton Mifflin, 1982).

27. Ibid., pp. 174–175.

Chapter 6

Honesty, Integrity, and Reliability

John is a co-op student who has a summer job with Oil Exploration, Inc., a company that does exploratory contract work for large oil firms.[1] The company drills, tests, and writes advisory reports to clients based on the test results. John, as an upper-level undergraduate student in petroleum engineering, is placed in charge of a field team of roustabouts and technicians who test-drill at various sites specified by the customer. John has the responsibility of transforming rough field data into succinct reports for the customer. Paul, an old high school friend of John's, is the foreperson of John's team. In fact, Paul was instrumental in getting this well-paying summer job for John.

While reviewing the field data for the last drilling report, John notices that a crucial step was omitted, one that would be impossible to correct without returning to the site and repeating the entire test, at great expense to the company. The omitted step involves the foreperson's adding a certain test chemical to the lubricant being pumped into the test-drill site. The test is important because it provides the data for deciding whether the drill site is worth developing for natural gas production. Unfortunately, Paul forgot to add the test chemical at the last drill site.

John knows that Paul is likely to lose his job if his mistake comes to light. Paul cannot afford to lose his job at a time when the oil business is slow and his wife is expecting a child. John learns from past company data files that the chemical additive indicates the presence of natural gas in approximately 1 percent of the tests.

Should John withhold the information that the test for natural gas was not performed from his superiors? Should the information be withheld from the customer?

6.1 Introduction

The concern with truth telling extends far beyond the boundaries of the engineering profession. Religious and secular literature contains many injunctions to tell the truth. One of the Ten Commandments forbids bearing false witness against one's neighbor. In Shakespeare's *Hamlet*, Polonius gives some advice regarding honesty to his son, Laertes, just before the son's first trip abroad from Denmark: "This above all: to thine own self be true, And it must follow, as the night the day, Thou canst not then be false to any man." John Bartlett's *Familiar Quotations* lists in the index two columns of entries on the word *true*, another four on *truth*, and a half column on *honesty*. Miguel de Cervantes is the author of the famous aphorism, "Honesty's the best policy," which was used by George Washington in his 1796 Farewell Address. In 1381 John Wycliffe told the Duke of Lancaster, "I believe that in the end the truth will conquer."

In light of the long emphasis on honesty in our moral tradition, it is not surprising that engineering codes contain many references to honesty. In section I.d, the **NCEES Model Rules of Professional Conduct** require registrants to be "objective and truthful in professional reports, statements, or testimony." The third canon of the IEEE Code of Ethics encourages all members "to be honest and realistic in stating claims or estimates based on available data." Canon 7 requires engineers "to seek, accept, and offer honest criticism of technical work."

The **ASME Code of Ethics** is equally straightforward. Fundamental Principle II states that engineers must practice the profession by "being honest and impartial." The seventh Fundamental Canon states, "Engineers shall issue public statements only in an objective and truthful manner." A subsection enjoins engineers not to "participate in the dissemination of untrue, unfair or exaggerated statements regarding engineering."

The more detailed **NSPE** code admonishes engineers "to participate in none but honest enterprise." The preamble states that "the services provided by engineers require honesty, impartiality, fairness, and equity." The third Fundamental Canon (I.3) requires engineers to avoid deceptive acts in the solicitation of professional employment." In the Rules of Practice there are several references to honesty. In item II.1.d, the code states: "Engineers shall not permit the use of their name or firm name nor associate in business ventures with any person or firm which they have reason to believe is engaging in fraudulent or dishonest business or professional practices." Items II.2.a through II.2.c and II.3.a through II.3.c in the Rules of Practice give more detailed direction for the practice of the profession. Item II.3 states that "Engineers shall issue public statements only in an objective and truthful manner." Item II.5 states that "Engineers shall avoid deceptive acts in the solicitation of professional employment." Items II.5.a and II.5.b give more detailed explanations as to how to implement this statement. In section III, "Professional Obligations," the code refers to the obligation for engineers to be honest and truthful and not to misrepresent facts in no less than six different locations (III.1.a, III.1.d, III.2.c, III.3.a, III.7, and III.8). In a statement that speaks directly to John's situation, part (a) of the third Rule of Practice states, "Engineers shall be objective and truthful in professional reports, statements or testimony. They shall include all relevant and pertinent information in such reports, statements or testimony."

In addition to the more explicit references to honesty, several of the codes require engineers to be responsible in other aspects of professional communica-

tion. The second canon of the **IEEE code** requires members to avoid conflicts of interest; conflicts of interest can distort professional judgment. A subsection of canon 3 of the **ASCE code** requires members not to issue statements on engineering matters "which are inspired or paid for by interested parties, unless they indicate on whose behalf the statements are made." Here again the emphasis is on full disclosure. A subsection of canon 4 of the same code speaks to the matter of confidentiality, an area where withholding information is justified. It enjoins engineers to avoid conflicts of interest and forbids them from using "confidential information coming to them in the course of their assignments as a means of making personal profit if such action is adverse to the interests of their clients, employers or the public."

We can easily state the primary reason for the importance of honesty. If we consider the engineering profession to be like a building, honesty is its foundation. Without honesty, the value of engineering services is undermined. Unreliable engineering judgment is worse than none at all. We shall now look more closely at some of the issues related to this topic.

6.2   Ways of Misusing the Truth

Engineers can misuse the truth in many different ways. These can include failing to communicate the truth (sections 1–5 below), communicating the truth when they should not (section 6), and allowing their judgment with regard to the truth to be corrupted (section 7).

(1) Lying

When we think of dishonesty, we usually think of lying. Ethicists have long struggled over the definition of lying. One of the reasons for the difficulty is that not every falsehood is a lie. If an engineer mistakenly conveys some test results on soil samples, she is not lying, even though she may not be telling the truth. To lie, a person must intentionally or at least knowingly convey false or misleading information. But even here complications arise. A person may give information that she believes to be false, even though it is actually true. In this case we may be perplexed as to whether we should describe her action as lying. Her intention is to lie, but what she says is actually true.

To make matters still more complicated, a person may give others false information by means other than making false statements. Gestures and nods, as well as indirect statements, can give a false impression in a conversation, even though the person has not told an outright lie.

Despite these complications, most people believe that lies—or at least paradigm cases of lies—have three elements: First, a lie ordinarily involves something that is believed to be false or seriously misleading. Second, a lie is ordinarily stated in words. Third, a lie is made with the intention to deceive. So perhaps we can offer the following working definition: "A lie is a statement believed to be false or seriously misleading, made with the intention to deceive." Of course, this definition leaves the phrase *seriously misleading* open for interpretation, but the open-ended nature of this working definition is deliberate. We call some misleading statements lies and others not.

(2) Deliberate Deception

If an engineer discusses technical matters in a manner implying knowledge that he in fact does not have to impress an employer or potential customer he is certainly engaging in deliberate deception, even if he is not lying. In addition to misrepresenting one's own expertise, one can misrepresent the value of certain products or designs by praising their advantages inordinately. Such deception can sometimes have more disastrous consequences than outright lying.

(3) Withholding Information

Omitting or withholding information is another type of deceptive behavior. If Jane deliberately fails to bring up some of the negative aspects of a project she is promoting to her superior, she engages in serious deception, even though she is not lying. Failing to report that you own stock in a company whose product you are recommending is a form of dishonesty. Perhaps we can say in more general terms that one is practicing a form of dishonesty by omission (1) if he fails to convey information that the audience would reasonably expect would not be omitted and (2) if the intent of the omission is to deceive.

(4) Failing to Adequately Promote the Dissemination of Information

The paramount ethical obligation of engineers is to protect the health and safety of the public. This may require engineers not only to disclose information but to do what they can to see to it that this information is properly disseminated. Those affected must receive the information, especially if the information can avoid a disaster. Roger Boisjoly's attempts to inform his superiors of the dangers inherent in the O-ring design exemplify one engineer's recognition of this obligation.

(5) Failure to Seek Out the Truth

Reliable judgment may include more than avoiding dishonesty in its various forms. The honest engineer is one who is committed to finding the truth, not simply avoiding dishonesty. Suppose engineer Mary suspects that some of the data she has received from the test lab are inaccurate. In using the results as they are, she is not lying, nor is she concealing the truth. But she may be irresponsible in using the results without inquiring further into their accuracy. Honesty in this positive sense is part of what is involved in being a responsible engineer.

It would not be correct to assume that lying is always more serious than deliberate deception, withholding information, failing to adequately promote the dissemination of information, or failing to seek out the truth. Sometimes the consequences of lying may not be as serious as the consequences of some of these other actions. The order of these first five types of misusing the truth reflects primarily the degree to which one is actively distorting the truth rather than the seriousness of the consequences of the actions.

(6) Revealing Confidential or Proprietary Information

One can misuse the truth not only by lying or otherwise distorting or withholding it but also by disclosing it in inappropriate circumstances. Engineers in private practice might be tempted to disclose confidential information without the consent of the client. Information may be confidential if it is either (1) given to the engineer by the client or (2) discovered by the engineer in the process of work done for the client.

Given that most engineers are employees, a more common problem involving the improper disclosure of information is the violation of proprietary information. Using designs and other proprietary information of a former employer can be dishonest and may even result in litigation. Even using ideas one developed while working for a former employer can be questionable, particularly if those ideas involve trade secrets, patents, or licensing arrangements.

(7) Allowing One's Judgment to Be Corrupted

An important part of any professional service is professional judgment. Allowing this to be corrupted or unduly influenced by conflicts of interest or other extraneous considerations can lead to another type of misusing the truth. Suppose engineer Joe is designing a chemical plant and specifies several large pieces of equipment manufactured by a company whose salesperson he has known for many years. The equipment is of good quality, but some newer and more innovative lines may actually be better. In specifying his friend's equipment, Joe is not giving his employer or client the benefit of his best and most unbiased professional judgment. In some cases this may be a form of dishonesty, but in any case Joe's judgment is unreliable.

6.3   Why Is Dishonesty Wrong?

The term *honest* has such a positive connotation and the term *dishonest* such a negative one that we forget that telling the full truth may sometimes be wrong and concealing the truth may sometimes be the right thing to do. A society in which people are totally honest with each other would be difficult to tolerate. The requirement of total honesty would mean that people would be brutally frank about their opinions of each other and unable to exercise the sort of tact and reticence that we associate with polite and civilized society. With regard to professionals, the requirement never to conceal truth would mean that engineers, physicians, lawyers, and other professionals could not exercise confidentiality or protect proprietary information. Doctors could never misrepresent the truth to their patients, even when there is strong evidence that this is what the patients prefer and that the truth could be devastating.

Despite possible exceptions, however, dishonesty and the various other ways of misusing the truth are generally wrong. A helpful way to see this is to consider dishonesty from the standpoints of the ethics of respect for persons and utilitarianism; each can provide valuable suggestions for thinking about moral issues. Here is a good example of their usefulness.

Let us review some of the major components of the respect for persons perspective. As we said in Chapter 4, actions are wrong if they violate the moral agency of individuals. Moral agents are human beings capable of formulating and pursuing goals and purposes of their own—they are autonomous. *Autonomy* comes from two Greek terms: *autos* meaning "self" and *nomos* meaning "rule" or "law." Thus, a moral agent is autonomous in the sense of being self-governing. In the terminology of the respect for persons theorist Immanuel Kant, moral agents are "ends in themselves," persons who are not to be treated as mere means to fulfilling the ends or goals of others. An autonomous action has three aspects:[2] (1) it is intentional, "willed in accordance with a plan";[3] (2) it is performed without external controlling influences; and (3) it is made with understanding.

This means that an autonomous action is made with informed consent. Thus, to respect the moral agency of other patients, physicians must ensure that their patients make decisions about their medical treatment with informed consent. They must see to it that their patients understand the consequences of their decisions and rationally make decisions that have some relationship to their life plans. They also have some responsibility to ensure that patients make decisions without undue coercive influences, such as stress, illness, and family pressures. Finally, physicians must see to it that patients are sufficiently informed about options for treatment and the consequences of the options.

Engineers have some degree of responsibility to see to it that employers, clients, and the general public make autonomous decisions, but their responsibilities are more limited than those of physicians. Their responsibilities probably extend only to the third of these three conditions of autonomy, ensuring that employers, clients, and the general public make decisions regarding technology with understanding, particularly understanding of their consequences. We have seen, for example, that the IEEE code requires members to "disclose promptly factors that might endanger the public or the environment" and that when the safety, health, and welfare of the public are endangered ASCE members must "inform their clients or employers of the possible consequences."

In engineering this applies to such issues as product safety and the provision of professional advice and information. If customers do not know that a car has an unusual safety problem, they cannot make an informed decision as to whether to purchase it. If a customer is paying for professional engineering advice and is given misinformation, he again cannot make a free and informed decision.

The astronauts on the *Challenger* were informed on the morning of the flight about the ice buildup on the launching pad and were given the option of postponing the launch. They chose not to exercise that option. However, no one presented them with the information about the O-ring behavior at low temperatures. Therefore, they did not give their fully informed consent to launch despite the O-ring risk, because they were unaware of the risk. The *Challenger* incident is a tragic example of the violation of the engineer's obligation to protect informed consent.

The fault, however, was not primarily with the engineers but with the managers who supported the launch and did not inform the astronauts of the danger.

Many situations are more complex. To be informed, decision makers must not only have the relevant information but also understand it. Furthermore, nobody has all of the relevant information or has complete understanding of it, so that being informed in both of these senses is a matter of degree. Therefore, the extent of the engineer's obligation regarding informed consent will sometimes be controversial, and whether or not the obligation has been fulfilled will also sometimes be controversial. We shall return to these considerations later, but what we have said here is enough to show that even withholding information or failing to adequately disseminate it can be serious violations of professional responsibilities.

Now let us turn to the utilitarian perspective on honesty. Utilitarianism requires that our actions promote human happiness and well-being. The profession of engineering contributes to this utilitarian goal by providing designs for the creation of buildings, bridges, chemicals, electronic devices, automobiles, and many other things on which our society depends. It also provides information about technology that is important in decision making on individual, corporate, and public-policy levels.

Dishonesty in engineering research can undermine these functions. If engineers report data falsely or omit crucial data, other researchers cannot depend on their results. This can undermine the relations of trust on which a scientific community is founded. Just as a designer who is untruthful about the strength of materials she specifies for a building threatens the collapse of the building, so a researcher who falsifies the data reported in a professional journal threatens the collapse of the infrastructure of engineering.

Dishonesty can also undermine informed decision making. Managers in both business and government, as well as legislators, depend on the knowledge and judgments provided by engineers in making decisions. If these are unreliable, the ability of those who depend on engineers to make good decisions regarding technology is undermined. To the extent that this happens, engineers have failed in their obligation to promote the public welfare.

From both a respect for persons and a utilitarian perspective, then, outright dishonesty as well as other forms of misusing the truth with regard to technical information and judgment are usually wrong. These actions undermine the moral agency of individuals by preventing them from making decisions with free and informed consent. They also prevent engineers from promoting the public welfare. In the following sections we shall consider some areas in which this irresponsibility can occur.

6.4   Honesty on Campus

Three students were working on a senior capstone engineering design project.[4] The project was to design, build, and test an inexpensive meter that would be mounted on the dashboard of automobiles and would measure the distance the car could travel on a gallon of gasoline. Even though personal computers, microchip calculators, and "smart instruments" were not available at the time, the students came up with a very clever approach that had a good chance of success. They devised a scheme to instantaneously measure voltage equivalents of both gasoline flow to the engine and speedometer readings on the odometer, while keeping a cumulative record of the quotient of the two. That is, miles per hour divided by gallons per hour would give the figure for the miles the automobile is traveling per gallon of gasoline. The students even came up with a way to filter and smooth out instantaneous fluctuations in either signal to ensure time-averaged data. Finally, they devised a bench-top experiment to prove the feasibility of their concept. The only thing missing was a flow meter that would measure the flow of gasoline to the engine in gallons per hour and produce a proportional voltage signal.

Nowadays, customers can order this feature as an option on some automobiles, but at the time the design was remarkably innovative. The professor directing the project was so impressed that he found a source of funds to buy the flow meter. He also encouraged the three students to draft an article describing their design for a technical journal.

Several weeks later the professor was surprised to receive a letter from the editor of a prominent journal, accepting for publication the "excellent article" that, according to the letter, he had "co-authored" with his three senior design students. The professor knew that the flow meter had not yet arrived, nor had he seen any draft version of the paper, so he asked the three students for an explanation. They explained that they had followed the professor's advice and prepared an article about their design. They had put the professor's name on the paper as senior author because, after all, it was his idea to write the paper and he was the faculty advisor. They did not want to bother the professor with the early draft. Further, they really could not wait for the flow-measuring instrument to arrive, because they were all graduating in a few weeks and planned to begin new jobs.

Finally, because they were sure the data would give the predicted results, they simulated some time-varying voltages on a power supply unit to replicate what they thought the flow-measuring voltages would be. They had every intention, they said, of checking the flow voltage and the overall system behavior after the flow meter arrived and, if necessary, making minor modifications in the paper.

As a matter of fact, the students incorrectly assumed that the flow and voltages would be related linearly. They also made some false assumptions about the response of the professor to their actions. The result was that the paper was withdrawn from the journal, and the students sent letters of apology to the journal. Copies of the letter were placed in their files, the students received an "F" in the senior design course, and their graduation was delayed six months. Despite this, one of them requested that the professor write a letter of recommendation for a summer job he was seeking!

It is possible that students are just more honest about their cheating than students in earlier generations. Whatever the reason, a survey by Donald McCabe suggests that there has been a substantial increase in the number of students who report incidents of the most serious forms of cheating on examinations. "For example, students admitting to copying from another student on an examination doubled from 26% to 52% between 1963 and 1993. Instances of helping someone else cheat on an examination and the use of crib notes each increased more than 50%."[5] There has also been an increase from 11% to 49% in the number of students who admitted they had collaborated on assignments when the instructor had specifically asked for individual work. The highest level of cheating is reported in the more vocationally oriented majors of business and engineering, the highest level being among business majors. Self-reported cheating among natural science majors is generally comparable to students majoring in the social sciences and humanities.[6] There was a significantly lower level of cheating by engineering students at schools with honor codes. Although they reported higher levels of cheating on written work than natural science, social science, and other majors, they reported the lowest levels on examinations.[7]

A student's experience in engineering school is a training period for his or her professional career. If dishonesty is as detrimental to engineering professionalism as we have suggested, part of this training should be in professional honesty. Furthermore, the pressures that students experience in the academic setting are not that different from (and perhaps less than) those they will experience in their jobs. If it is morally permissible to cheat on exams and misrepresent data on laboratory reports and design projects, why isn't it permissible to misrepresent data to please the boss, get a promotion, or keep a job?

As we shall see in the next section, there are exact counterparts in the scientific and engineering communities to the types of dishonesty exhibited by students. Smoothing data points on the graph of a freshman physics laboratory report to get an "A" on the report, selecting the research data that support the desired conclusion, entirely inventing the data, and plagiarism of the words and ideas of others all have obvious parallels in nonacademic settings.

6.5   Integrity in Engineering Research and Testing

Dishonesty in science and engineering takes several forms: trimming, cooking, forging, and plagiarism.[8]

Trimming is "the smoothing of irregularities to make the data look extremely accurate and precise." This is a temptation to which not only engineering students but engineering researchers as well are susceptible. As one person guilty of this form of dishonesty put it, "I smoothed out the data. I took the curves and smoothed them out."[9] If we assume that the data points indicated by asterisks in Figure 6.1 have been moved to justify the straight line, the figure illustrates trimming.

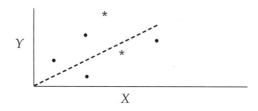

Figure 6.1
Trimming

Cooking is "retaining only those results that fit the theory and discarding others."[10] In a famous case of alleged cooking, physicist Robert A. Millikan, who later received the Nobel prize, was accused of selecting the data he reported in his famous paper on the electronic charge. The paper was based on a series of experiments on liquid droplets. It contained an explicit statement that his findings were based on "a selected group of drops" but not "all the drops experimented upon during 60 consecutive days."[11] Evidently, Millikan had enough data to make a sound case without selecting the data, but he was accused of misrepresenting the data anyhow. If we assume that the data points indicated by asterisks in Figure 6.2 will be thrown away to justify the straight line, the figure illustrates cooking.

Forging is "inventing some or all of the research data that are reported, and even reporting experiments to obtain those data that were never performed."[12] John Darsee was a medical school graduate doing research. He published papers based on his research there that were subsequently withdrawn due to falsified data.[13] He gave the following justification for his dishonesty:

> I had too much to do, too little time to do it in, and was greatly fatigued mentally and almost childlike emotionally. I had not taken a vacation, sick day, or even a day off from work for six years. I had put myself on a track that I hoped would allow me to have a wonderful academic job and I knew I had to work very hard for it.[14]

Darsee's research was in medicine. The disastrous effects that inaccurate data could have had on medical practice are frightening. Equally disastrous effects could occur in engineering. Imagine the consequence of using a published theory on a new lightweight bridge design that was based on falsified data.

The difficulty in determining the full import of apparent forging and cooking of the data is illustrated by research on the so-called Goodrich A-7 brake case. The case, involving brake data falsification for the A-7 military aircraft at B. F. Goodrich, has long been a standard item in engineering ethics.[15] Later research, however, raises some serious questions as to what really was at stake.[16]

In 1968 the B. F. Goodrich Corporation won the competition for a subcontract to LTV, Inc., to design and build the brakes for the Navy A-7 aircraft. They won the contract because they entered the lowest bid and their design was the most innovative. They were anxious to win this contract because they had lost some

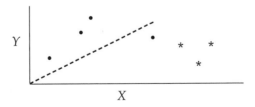

Figure 6.2
Cooking

aircraft business years before, due to a faulty component design, and wanted to reestablish their reputation. The bid promised a lighter four-rotor brake. John Warren, an experienced design engineer, had designed the four-rotor brake for the proposal.

When the contract was awarded, Goodrich assigned Searle Lawson, a young, recently graduated engineer, to take the laboratory data that would prove that the prototype four-rotor brake met all military standards, such as the required stopping time and maximum allowable temperature. Kermit Vandivier, a technical writer, was assigned to help write the reports based on the data Lawson was taking. Unfortunately, the data consistently showed that the four-rotor brakes did not meet military test standards, which had been established years earlier with the five-rotor brake performance in mind.

After a year of negative test results, none of which were reported to LTV, the brakes were flight-tested. On one landing test (out of many uneventful tests) the brakes overheated. The pilot was never in danger, and he had plenty of extra runway to let the aircraft coast to a stop. Nevertheless, the overheating was further evidence of the inadequacy of the four-rotor brake. Lawson represented Goodrich at the flight tests.

Unknown to Lawson and Vandivier, Goodrich higher management had written off the four-rotor brake design as a failure and had started a parallel development program to design and test a five-rotor brake at Goodrich's expense. At a lower level, the Goodrich engineering management team decided to present the four-rotor brake test results in the best possible light. To keep the LTV contract, they directed that laboratory tests be modified. They specified that the brakes should be allowed to coast longer between applications than allowed by military specifications, be cooled by fans between and during test runs, and be remachined between test runs. When this cooking of the data still did not yield the desired test results, they decided that the data should be forged.

At this point Lawson and Vandivier informed the FBI, which in turn alerted the Government Auditing Office (GAO). The GAO's investigation resulted in a hearing in the U.S. Senate, chaired by Senator William Proxmire. The press coverage portrayed Vandivier and Lawson as heroes who voluntarily blew the whistle to protect the public safety. Vandivier was dismissed by Goodrich and took a job as a reporter for a local newspaper for which he had been writing part time. Lawson resigned and went to work for another company.

Lawson and Vandivier knew nothing of the intentions of higher management. All they knew was what they observed. Although the distortion of the data at Goodrich cannot be excused, the ignorance of Lawson and Vandivier regarding the ultimate intentions of higher management made it impossible for them to correctly interpret the significance of this data falsification. Thus, the Goodrich case illustrates both the existence of data falsification and the need for lower-level employees to be informed about the actions of higher management that may put their work in a different perspective. Not having this information, Lawson and Vandiver were forced to jeopardize their careers or compromise their integrity. It is also important to remember that Goodrich did deceive the customer to keep the contract.

Plagiarism is the use of the intellectual property of others without proper permission or credit. It takes many different forms. Plagiarism is really a type of theft. Drawing the line between legitimate and illegitimate use of the intellectual property of others is often difficult, and the method of line-drawing is useful in helping us to discriminate between the two. Some cases are undeniable examples of plagiarism—as when the extended passages involving the exact words or the data of another are used without proper permission or attribution. On the other side of the spectrum, the quotation of short statements by others with proper attribution is clearly permissible. Between these two extremes are many cases where drawing the line is more difficult.

Multiple authorship of papers can often raise particularly vexing issues with regard to honesty in scientific and technological work.[17] Sometimes as many as forty or fifty researchers are listed as the authors of a scientific paper. One can think of several justifications for this practice. First, often a large number of scientists participate in some forms of research, and, furthermore, they all make genuine contributions. For example, large numbers of people are sometimes involved in medical research or research with a particle accelerator. Second, the distinction between whether someone is the author of a paper or merely deserves to be cited may indeed be tenuous in some circumstances. The fairest or at least the most generous thing to do in such circumstances is to cite such people as authors.

There are, however, less honest motives for the practice, the most obvious one being the desire of most scientists for as many publications as possible. This is true both of academic and nonacademic scientists. In addition, many graduate and postdoctoral students need to be published to secure jobs. Sometimes more senior scientists are tempted to list graduate students as authors, even though their contribution to the publication was minimal, to make the student's research record look as impressive as possible.

From a moral standpoint, there are at least two potential problems with multiple authorship. First, it is fraudulent to claim significant credit for scientific research when in fact a contribution is relatively insignificant. If claims to authorship are indeed fraudulent, those evaluating the scientist or engineer are not able to make informed decisions in their evaluations. Second, fraudulent claims to authorship give one an unfair advantage in the competition for jobs, promotions, and recognition in the scientific community. From the standpoint of fairness alone, unsubstantiated claims to authorship should be avoided.

6.6   Integrity in the Use of Intellectual Property

Intellectual property is property that results from mental labor. It can be protected in several ways, including trade secrets, patents, trademarks, and copyrights.

Trade secrets are formulas, patterns, devices, or compilations of information, which are used in business to gain an advantage over competitors who do not possess the trade secret. The formula for Coca-Cola is an example of a trade secret. Trade secrets must not be in the public domain and the secrecy must be protected by the firm, because trade secrets are not protected by patents.

Patents are documents issued by the government that allow the owner of the patent to exclude others from making use of the patented information for twenty years from the date of filing. To obtain a patent, the invention must be new, useful, and nonobvious. As an example, the puncture-proof tire is patented.

Trademarks are words, phrases, designs, sounds, or symbols associated with goods or services. "Coca-Cola" is a registered trademark.

Copyrights are rights to creative products such as books, pictures, graphics, sculpture, music, movies, and computer programs. The author retains the copyright for fifty years after his or her death. Copyrights protect the expression of the ideas, but not the ideas themselves. The script of *Star Wars* is copyrighted.

Many companies require their employees to sign a patent assignment, whereby all patents and inventions of the employee become the property of the company, often in exchange for a token fee of $1. Sometimes employees find themselves caught between two employers with respect to such issues.

Consider the case of Bill, a senior engineering production manager of a tire manufacturing company, Roadrubber, Inc. Bill has been so successful in decreasing production costs for his company by developing innovative manufacturing techniques that he has captured the attention of the competition. One competing firm, Slippery Tire, Inc., offers Bill a senior management position at a greatly increased salary. Bill warns Slippery Tire that he has signed a standard agreement with Roadrubber not to use or divulge any of the ideas he developed or learned at Roadrubber for two years following any change of employment. Slippery Tire assures Bill that they understand and will not try to get him to reveal any secrets and that they want him as an employee because of his demonstrated managerial skills.

After a few months on the job at Slippery Tire, someone who was not a part of the earlier negotiations with Bill asks him to reveal some of the secret processes that he developed while at Roadrubber. When Bill refuses, he is told, "Come on, Bill, you know this is the reason you were hired at the inflated salary. If you don't tell us what we want to know, you're out of here."

This is a clear case of an attempt to steal information. If the managers who attracted Bill to Slippery Tire were engineers, they also violated the NSPE code. Under "Professional Obligations," item III.1.d of the NSPE code says, "Engineers shall not attempt to attract an engineer from another employer by false or misleading pretenses."

Some cases are not as clear. Sometimes an employee develops ideas at Company A and later finds that those same ideas can be useful—although perhaps in an entirely different application—to her new employer, Company B. Suppose Betty's new employer is not a competing tire company but one that manufactures rubber boats. A few months after being hired by Rubberboat, Betty comes up with a new process for Rubberboat. It is only later that she realizes that she probably thought of the idea because of her earlier work with Roadrubber. The processes are different in many ways, and Rubberboat is not a competitor of

Roadrubber, but she still wonders whether it is right to offer her idea to Rubberboat.

Let's examine what the NSPE Code of Ethics has to say about such situations. Under "Rules of Practice," item II.1.c states, "Engineers shall not reveal facts, data or information obtained in a professional capacity without the prior consent of the client or employer except as authorized or required by law or this Code." Item III.4 states,

> Engineers shall not disclose confidential information concerning the business affairs or technical processes of any present or former client or employer without his consent. (a) Engineers in the employ of others shall not without the consent of all interested parties enter promotional efforts or negotiations for work or make arrangements for other employment as a principal or to practice in connection with a specific project for which the engineer has gained particular and specialized knowledge. (b) Engineers shall not, without the consent of all interested parties, participate in or represent an adversary interest in connection with a specific project or proceedings in which the engineer has gained particular specialized knowledge on behalf of a former client or employer.

Similarly, the NCEES Model Rules of Professional Conduct require engineers to "not reveal facts, data, or information obtained in a professional capacity without the prior consent of the client or employer as authorized by law" (I.1.d).

These code statements strongly suggest that even in the second case Betty should tell the management at Rubberboat that they must enter into licensing negotiations with Roadrubber. In other words, she must be honest in fulfilling all of her still-existing obligations to Roadrubber.

Other cases can be even less clear, however. Suppose the ideas Betty developed while at Roadrubber were never used by Roadrubber. She realized they would be of no use and never even mentioned them to management at Roadrubber. Thus, they might not be considered a part of any agreement between her and Roadrubber. Still, the ideas were developed using Roadrubber's computers and laboratory facilities. Or suppose Betty's ideas occurred to her at home while she was still an employee of Roadrubber, although the ideas probably would never have occurred to her if she had not been working on somewhat related problems at Roadrubber.

We can best deal with these problems by employing the line-drawing method. As we have seen, the method involves pointing out similarities and dissimilarities between the cases whose moral status is clear and the cases whose moral status is less clear.

Here is a simple illustration of how such a line-drawing analysis might work. In the following tables, the Positive column refers to features which, if present, count in favor of the action's being morally acceptable. The Negative column refers to features which, if present, count against the action's being morally acceptable.[18] The "test case" follows.

> *Case 1.* Tom is a young engineering graduate who designs automobile brakes for Ford. While working for Ford, he learns a lot about heat transfer and materials.

After five years, Tom leaves Ford to take a job at General Motors. While at General Motors, Tom applies his knowledge of heat transfer and materials to design *engines.* Is Tom stealing Ford's intellectual property?

Table 6.1 (Case 1)

Feature	Positive	Test Case	Negative
Generic Information	Yes	X—————————————	No
Different Application	Yes	—X————————————	No
Information Protected as a Trade Secret	No	X—————————————	Yes

Case 2. Tom is a young engineering graduate who designs automobile brakes for Ford. While working for them, he learns a lot about heat transfer and materials. After five years, Tom leaves Ford to take a job at General Motors. While at General Motors, Tom applies his knowledge of heat transfer and materials to design *brakes.* Is Tom stealing Ford's intellectual property?

Table 6.2 (Case 2)

Feature	Positive	Test Case	Negative
Generic Information	Yes	X—————————————	No
Different Application	Yes	——————————————X	No
Information Protected as a Trade Secret	No	X—————————————	Yes

Case 3. Tom is a young engineering graduate who designs automobile brakes for Ford. While working for them, Tom helps develop a new brake lining that lasts twice as long as conventional brake linings. Ford decides to keep the formula for this brake lining as a trade secret. After five years, Tom leaves Ford to take a job at General Motors. While at General Motors, Tom tells them the formula for the new brake lining. Is Tom stealing Ford's intellectual property?

Table 6.3 (Case 3)

Feature	Positive	Test Case	Negative
Generic Information	Yes	——————————————X	No
Different Application	Yes	——————————————X	No
Information Protected as a Trade Secret	No	——————————————X	Yes

In Case 1 Tom has not stolen Ford's intellectual property. Although it is true that he used generic scientific knowledge acquired while he was at Ford, the information is available to anyone. The application of the generic scientific knowledge is very different at General Motors. But because General Motors and

Ford both compete in the same market sector and brakes and motors are both parts of automobiles, the "X" does appear at the extreme left of the spectrum. In Case 2 Tom applies his knowledge to the same area, brake design, but the knowledge is still generic scientific knowledge over which Ford has no claim, even if Tom acquired this knowledge while at Ford.

In Case 3 Tom applies his knowledge to the same area, brake design, and the knowledge is specific knowledge of brake design over which Ford has a rightful claim. Tom's action in Case 3 is wrong.

There may be additional features that come to light in analyzing a particular case. There can also be other intermediate cases between the ones we have presented here. The particular case of interest must be compared with the spectrum of cases to determine where the line between permissible and impermissible action should be drawn.

6.7   Integrity and Client-Professional Confidentiality

Most engineers are employees of large corporations, but some, especially civil engineers, subcontract for design firms that have clients. For these engineers, there is an obligation to protect the confidentiality of the client-professional relationship, just as with lawyers and physicians. Confidentiality would ordinarily cover both sensitive information given by the client and information gained by the professional in work paid for by the client.

An engineer can abuse client-professional confidentiality in two ways. First, an engineer may break confidentiality when it is not warranted. Second, an engineer may refuse to break confidentiality when the higher obligation to the public requires it.

Here is an example of the first type of abuse.[19] Jane, a civil engineer, is contracted to do a preliminary study for a new shopping mall for Greenville, California. The town already has a mall that is twenty years old. The owner of the existing mall is trying to decide whether to renovate the old mall, or close it. He has done a lot of business with Jane and asks her some detailed questions about the new mall. Jane answers the questions.

Here is another example in the first category. Suppose engineer A inspects a residence for a homeowner for a fee. He finds the residence in generally good condition, although in need of several minor repairs. Engineer A sends a copy of his one-page report to the homeowner, showing that a carbon copy was sent to the real estate firm handling the sale of the residence.

This case was considered by the NSPE Board of Ethical Review, which ruled that "Engineer A acted unethically in submitting a copy of the home inspection to the real estate firm representing the owners." It cites section II.1.c of the NSPE code, which states: "Engineers shall not reveal facts, data, or information obtained in a professional capacity without the prior consent of the client or employer except as authorized by law or this Code."[20]

This opinion seems correct. The clients paid for the information and therefore could lay claim to its exclusive possession. The residence was fundamentally sound, and there was no reason to believe that the welfare of the public was at stake. The case would have been more difficult if there had been a fundamental structural flaw. Even here, however, we can argue that there was no fundamental threat to life. Prospective buyers are always free to pay for an inspection themselves.

The following hypothetical case raises more serious difficulties. Suppose engineer James inspects a building for a client before the client puts the building up for sale. James discovers fundamental structural defects that could pose a threat to public safety. James informs the client of these defects in the building and recommends its evacuation and repair before it is put up for sale. The client replies,

> James, I am not going to evacuate the building, and I am certainly not going to spend a lot of money on the building before I put it up for sale. Furthermore, if you reveal the information to the authorities or to any potential buyer, I am going to take whatever legal action I can against you. Not only that, but I have a lot of friends. If I pass the word around, you will lose a lot of business. The information is mine. I paid for it, and you have no right to reveal it to anyone else without my permission.

James's obligation to his client is clearly at odds with his obligation to the public. Although he may have an obligation to potential buyers, his more immediate and pressing one is to protect the safety of the present occupants of the building. Note that the section of the NSPE code quoted above requires engineers to keep the confidentiality of their clients in all cases, except where exceptions are authorized "by law or this Code." This is probably a case where part of the code (specifically, the part emphasizing the higher obligation to the safety of the public) should override the requirement of confidentiality.

Even here, however, James should probably try to find a creative middle way that allows him to honor his obligations to his client, to the occupants of the building, and to potential buyers. He might attempt to persuade the client that his intention to refuse to correct the structural defects is morally wrong and probably not even in his long-term self-interest. He might argue that the client may find himself entangled in lawsuits, and that surely he would find it hard to live with himself if a catastrophe occurred.

Unfortunately, such an approach might not work. James's client might refuse to change his mind. Then, James must rank his competing obligations. Most engineering codes, including the NSPE code is clear that the engineer's first obligation is to the safety of the public, so James must make public the information about the structural defects of the building, at least according to the NSPE code as we interpret it.

The limits of client-professional confidentiality are controversial in most professions. In many states physicians must reveal cases of child abuse, even if it violates patient-physician confidentiality. The "Model Rules of Professional Conduct" of the American Bar Association says that lawyers "may" revel confidential information when there is a threat of "imminent death or substantial bodily harm" (Rule 1.6b).

One of the most famous legal cases involving professional confidentiality involves a psychologist whose client, Prosenjit Poddar, killed his girlfriend,

Tatiana Tarasoff, after informing his psychologist of his intentions. Neither Tatiana nor her parents were warned of the danger, and, after Tatiana's death, the parents sued the University of California, where the psychologist was employed. A California court ruled in favor of the parents. Excerpts from the court's opinion are directly relevant to the situation sometimes faced by engineers:

> When a therapist determines, or pursuant to the standards of his profession should determine, that his patient presents a serious danger of violence to another, he incurs an obligation to use reasonable care to protect the intended victim. . . . We conclude that the public policy favoring protection of the confidential character of patient-psychotherapist communications must yield to the extent to which disclosure is essential to avert danger to others. The protective privilege ends where the public peril begins.[21]

The California court agrees with engineering codes in placing the interests of the public above those of clients or employers. Still, not all cases involving confidentiality will be as clear-cut as the one James faced. In fact, his situation might serve as one extreme on a spectrum of cases. The other extreme might be a case in which an engineer breaks confidentiality to promote his own financial interests. Between these two extremes are many other possible situations where the decision might be difficult. Again, in such cases, it is appropriate to use the line-drawing method.

6.8   Integrity and Expert Testimony

Engineers are sometimes hired as expert witnesses in cases involving accidents, defective products, structural defects, patent infringements, and other areas where competent technical knowledge is required. Calling upon an expert witness is one of the most important moves a lawyer can make in such cases, and engineers are usually well compensated for their testimony. However, being an expert witness is time-consuming and often stressful. Thomas A. Hunter is an engineering consultant from Westport, Connecticut, who often serves as an expert witness. Speaking at the winter annual meeting of the American Society of Mechanical Engineers in November 1992, he remarked, "Engineers must be credible in court. This credibility depends on the engineer's knowledge of engineering, the particular case, and especially the court process."[22] With regard to cases involving defective products, Hunter warned,

> To make a credible presentation to the jury, it is simply not enough to merely point out that there is a design defect. At a minimum, the expert must show three things. First, that the defect was recognizable by the designer; second, that there were means available to correct the defect when the product was designed; and third, that the costs of corrective features would not price the product out of the market or interfere with the product's effectiveness.[23]

When confronted with these demands, the expert witness faces certain ethical pitfalls. The most obvious is perjury on the witness stand. A more likely temptation is to withhold information that would be unfavorable to the client's case. In addition to being ethically questionable, such withholding can be an embarrassment to the engineer, for cross-examination often exposes it.

To avoid problems of this sort, an expert should follow several rules.[24]

First, she should not take a case if she does not have adequate time for a thorough investigation. Rushed preparation can be disastrous for the reputation of the expert witness as well as for her client. Being prepared requires not only general technical knowledge but detailed knowledge of the particular case and the process of the court before which the witness will testify.

Second, she should not accept a case if she cannot do so with good conscience. This means that she should be able to testify honestly and not feel the need to withhold information to make an adequate case for her client.

Third, the engineer should consult extensively with the lawyer, so that the lawyer is as familiar as possible with the technical details of the case and can prepare the expert witness for cross-examination.

Fourth, the witness should maintain an objective and unbiased demeanor on the witness stand. This includes sticking to the questions asked and keeping an even temper, especially under cross-examination.

Fifth, the witness should always be open to new information, even during the course of the trial. The following example does not involve an expert witness, but it does show how important new information gained during a trial can be. During a trial of a recent accident case in Kansas, the defendant discovered in his basement an old document that conclusively showed that his company was culpable in the accident. He introduced this new evidence in court proceedings, even though it cost his company millions of dollars and resulted in the largest accident court judgment in the history of Kansas.[25]

One position a potential expert witness can take with respect to a client is to say something like the following:

> I will have only one opinion, not a "real" opinion and a story I will tell for you on the witness stand. My opinion will be as unbiased and objective as I can possibly make it. I will form my opinion after looking at the case, and you should pay me to investigate the facts of the case. I will tell the truth and the whole truth as I see it on the witness stand, and I will tell you what I will say beforehand. If you can use my testimony, I will serve as an expert witness for you. If not, you can dismiss me.

This approach may not solve all the problems. If an expert witness is dismissed by a lawyer because he has damaging evidence, is it ethically permissible to simply walk away, without revealing the evidence, even when public safety is involved? Should the witness testify for the other side, if asked?

6.9   Integrity and Failure to Inform the Public

Some types of professional irresponsibility in handling technical information may be best described as a failure to inform those whose decisions are impaired by the absence of the information. From the standpoint of the ethics of respect for persons, this is a serious impairment of moral agency. The failure of engineers to ensure that technical information is available to those who need it is especially wrong where disasters can be avoided.

Dan Applegate was Convair's senior engineer directing a subcontract with McDonnell Douglas in 1972.[26] The contract was for the designing and building of a cargo hatch door for the DC-10.[27] The design for the latch of the cargo door was known to be faulty. When the first DC-10 was pressure-tested on the assembly line, the cargo hatch door blew out and the passenger cabin floor buckled, resulting in the destruction of several hydraulic and electrical power lines. Modifications in the design did not solve the problem. Later, a DC-10 flight over Windsor, Ontario, had to make an emergency landing in Detroit after the cargo hatch door flew open and the cabin floor again buckled. Fortunately, no one was injured.

In the light of these problems, Applegate wrote a memo to the vice-president of Convair, itemizing the dangers of the design. However, Convair managers decided not to pass this information on to McDonnell Douglas because of the possibility of financial penalties and litigation if accidents occurred. Applegate's memorandum was prophetic. Two years later, in 1974, a fully loaded DC-10 crashed just outside Orly Field in Paris, killing all 346 passengers. The crash happened for the reasons that Applegate had outlined in his memorandum. There were genuine legal impediments to disclosing the dangers in the DC-10 design to the federal government or to the general public, but this story emphasizes the fact that failure to disclose information can have catastrophic consequences.

In this case most of us would probably say that Dan Applegate's professional responsibility to protect the safety of the public required that he do something to make his professional concerns about the DC-10 known. The NSPE code, in requiring engineers to notify employers "or such other authority as may be appropriate" if their "professional judgment is overruled under circumstances where the safety, health, property or welfare of the public are endangered," seems to imply this (II.1.a). Using almost identical language, the NCEES Model Rules of Professional Conduct require registrants to "notify their employer or client and such other authority as may be appropriate when their professional judgment is overruled under circumstances where the life, health, property, and welfare of the public is endangered" (I.c). Failing to do more to alert others to the danger resulted in massive expense and loss of life and denied passengers the ability to make an informed decision in accepting an unusual risk in flying in the aircraft.

Similar issues are raised in another well-known case involving the Ford Pinto gas tank case in the early 1970s. At the time the Pinto was introduced, Ford was making every effort to compete with the new compact Japanese imports by producing a car in less than two years that weighed less than 2,000 pounds and cost less than $2,000.[28] The project engineer, Lee Iacocca, and his management team believed that the American public wanted the product they were designing. They also believed that the American public would not be willing to pay the extra $11 to eliminate the risk of a rupturing gas tank.

The engineers who were responsible for the rear-end crash tests of early prototype models of the Pinto knew that the Pinto met the current regulations for safety requirements in rear-end collisions; however, they also knew that the car failed the new higher standards that were to go into effect in just two years. In fact, the car failed eleven of twelve rear-end collisions at the newly prescribed twenty-miles-per-hour crash tests. In the crashes the gas tanks ruptured and the vehicles caught fire. Thus, many engineers at Ford knew that the drivers of the Pinto were subject to unusual risks of which they were unaware. They also knew that management was not sympathetic to their safety concerns. One of the engineers working on the Pinto test program found that the ignorance of potential drivers about the car's dangers was unacceptable and decided to resign and make the information public. The engineer thus gave car buyers the knowledge they needed to purchase the Pinto with informed consent.

There is evidence that Ford management did not necessarily have a callous disregard for safety. Only a few years earlier Ford management voluntarily reported that some of their line employees, in a misguided show of company loyalty, had falsified EPA emissions data on new engines to bring Ford into compliance with EPA regulations on a new model. As a result of this honest disclosure, Ford was required to pay a very stiff fine and had to substitute an older model engine on the new car at even greater expense.

Still another such case involves the Chevrolet Corvair. Early prototype testing of the Corvair showed that it had a propensity to roll over in high-speed turns due to a flaw in the rear-end, roll-bar suspension design. The problem was compounded by the fact that the drivers of these cars were likely to be young people who tended to drive fast. Tragically, the daughter of a GM executive was killed while driving an early model of the car.

The obligation of engineers to protect the health and safety of the public requires more than refraining from telling lies, or simply refusing to withhold information. It sometimes requires that engineers aggressively do what they can to see to it that the consumers of technology are not forced to make uninformed decisions regarding the use of that technology. This is especially true when the use of technology involves unusual and unperceived risks. This obligation may require engineers to do what is necessary to either eliminate the unusual risks or at the very least inform those using the technology of the dangers. Otherwise, their moral agency is seriously eroded. Placing yourself in the position of the seven *Challenger* astronauts, you probably would have wanted to hear all of the relevant engineering facts about the risky effects of low temperatures on the rocket booster O-ring seals before giving permission for liftoff. Similar considerations apply to those who flew the DC-10, or drove Pintos or Corvairs.

6.10   Conflicts of Interest

John owns a small company that uses valves. He usually specifies valves made by a relative in his designs, even when valves made by other companies might be more appropriate. John's situation involves a conflict of interest. Is John's action wrong? If so, why?

What Is a Conflict of Interest?

Michael Davis has provided one of the most useful discussions of conflict of interest. Using a modified version of Davis's definition, we shall say that a *conflict of interest* exists for a professional when acting in a professional role, he or she is subject to "influences, loyalties, temptations, or other interests" that tend to make the professional's judgment less likely to benefit the customer or client than the customer or client is justified in expecting.[29] In the preceding example, John has allowed his ownership of the valve company to unduly influence his professional judgment. He has betrayed the trust that his client has placed in his professional judgment by serving his own private interests rather than the interests of the client, as he was paid to do.

Conflicts of interest can strike at the heart of professionalism. This is because professionals are paid for their expertise and unbiased professional judgment, and conflicts of interest threaten to undermine the trust that clients, employers, and the public place in that expertise or judgment. Cases involving conflict of interest are the most common kinds of cases brought before the NSPE's Board of Ethical Review. Engineering codes usually address conflicts of interest.

In section I.f, the NCEES Model Rules of Professional Conduct forbid registrants from issuing "statements, criticisms, or arguments on technical matters which are inspired or paid for by interested parties, unless they explicitly identify the interested parties on whose behalf they are speaking, and reveal any interests they have in the matters."

Fundamental canon 4 of the NSPE code addresses the ideas that engineers should act as "faithful agents or trustees" in performing their professional duties. The first entry under the heading is that engineers should disclose all "known" or "potential" conflicts of interest to their employers or clients. Section III on professional obligations specifies some specific prohibitions:

> 5. Engineers shall not be influenced in their professional duties by conflicting interests.
>   a. Engineers shall not accept financial or other considerations, including free engineering designs, from material or equipment suppliers for specifying their product.
>   b. Engineers shall not accept commissions or allowances, directly or indirectly, from contractors or other parties dealing with clients or employers for the Engineer in connection with work for which the Engineer is responsible.

In considering these prohibitions and conflicts of interests more generally, however, several important points must be kept in mind.

First, a conflict of interest is not just any set of conflicting interests. An engineer may like tennis and swimming and cannot decide which interest is more important to her. This is not a conflict of interest in the special sense this term is used in professional ethics, for it does not involve a conflict that is likely to influence professional judgment.

Second, the interests of the client, employer, or public that the engineer must protect are restricted to those that are morally legitimate. An employer or client might have an interest that can be served or protected only through illegal activity (for example, fraud, theft, embezzlement, and murder). An engineer has no professional duty to serve or protect such interests. On the contrary, the engineer may have a duty to expose such interests to external authorities.

Third, we must distinguish between three types of situations where the term *conflict of interest* is used: actual, potential, and apparent conflicts of interest. Here are examples of each:

> *Actual.* John is participating in a design that requires 100,000 bolts. For the past 100 years, John's family has owned a company, JayCo, that makes bolts. If the bolts are specified in such a way that the bolts must be purchased from JayCo, John's stock in JayCo will increase by 20%. John specifies the JayCo bolts, even though they are not the best for the design.[30]

> *Potential.* John is engaged to Veronica, whose family has owned JayCo, a bolt-manufacturing company, for 100 years. If John marries Veronica he will immediately become a major stockholder in JayCo. If he specifies bolts in his designs manufactured by JayCo, he will benefit financially.

> *Apparent.* John marries Veronica, but he and Veronica have a fight with her family and divest themselves of all holdings in JayCo. This divestiture is public knowledge, but Rachael does not know about it. Rachael employs John to design a building for her. John specifies bolts that can only be manufactured by JayCo, because he believes they are the best for the building, even though he prefers not to give the business to JayCo. Rachael accuses John of conflict of interest.

It is best to avoid all conflicts of interests, whether actual, potential, or apparent, if it is possible to do so. Actual conflicts of interest can corrupt professional judgment. Potential conflicts of interest may corrupt professional judgment in the future, if not in the present. Apparent conflicts of interest decrease the confidence of the public in the objectivity and trustworthiness of professional services and thus harm both the profession and the public, even if professional judgment is not actually corrupted. If a conflict of interest in any of these three senses is unavoidable, the professional should reveal its existence, rather than wait for the customer or the public to find out about it on their own.

Fourth, even though it is best to avoid conflicts of interest, they must in all cases be *disclosed* to the relevant parties. Because conflicts of interest threaten fulfillment of one's professional duties, most codes of ethics urge professionals to guard against getting into a conflict-of-interest situation. However, sometimes, through no fault of the professional, a conflict of interest arises. Then, the requirement is to disclose it.

Fundamental canon 4 of the NSPE code says: "a. Engineers shall disclose all known or potential conflicts of interest to their employers or clients by promptly informing them of any business association, interest, or other circumstances which could influence or appear to influence their judgment or the quality."

After disclosure, clients and employers can decide whether they are willing to risk the possible corruption of the professional's judgment that such a conflict of interest might cause. Thus, the free and informed consent of clients and employers is preserved.

Conflicts of Interest and Accepting Gifts

Perhaps the most common situations in which engineers find themselves in actual, potential, or apparent conflicts of interest are those involving accepting gifts. Here, as so often in problems involving honesty and integrity, the situations are best analyzed as line-drawing problems.

Consider this example. Tom has been named the manager of a large new chemical plant, which is to be designed and constructed. Tom's responsibilities are to form the design staff; supervise the design staff; ensure that the plant is safe, operable, and maintainable; and start up the plant after construction. Tom recommends that the design staff specify a new ValCo valve to replace traditional gate valves. Now consider the following series of cases.[31]

Case 1. ValCo valves are *superior* to traditional gate valves because they seal more tightly and more quickly. *After* a large number of ValCo valves have been ordered, Jim, the ValCo salesman and a former classmate of Tom's, visits Tom and gives Tom a pen with the company logo stamped in gold. The pen is worth $5. Should Tom accept the pen?

Table 6.4 (Case 1)

Feature	Positive	Test Case	Negative
Gift timing relative to procurement	After	X———————————	Before
Quality of product	High	X———————————	Low
Gift cost	Low	X———————————	High
Gift-giver is a friend	No	———————————X	Yes

Case 2. ValCo valves are *superior* to traditional gate valves because they seal more tightly and more quickly. *After* a large number of ValCo valves have been ordered, Jim, the ValCo salesman and a former classmate of Tom's, visits Tom and invites Tom to play golf at an exclusive country club. Should Tom accept the golf invitation?

Table 6.5 (Case 2)

Feature	Positive	Test Case	Negative
Gift timing relative to procurement	After	X———————————	Before
Quality of product	High	X———————————	Low
Gift cost	Low	——X ———————	High
Gift-giver is a friend	No	——————————— X	Yes

Case 3. ValCo valves are *superior* to traditional gate valves because they seal more tightly and more quickly. *After* a large number of ValCo valves have been ordered, Jim, the ValCo salesman, visits Tom. Although Tom has never met Jim before, Jim offers to sponsor Tom for membership in an exclusive country club. Should Tom accept the offer of sponsorship?

Table 6.6 (Case 3)

Feature	Positive	Test Case	Negative
Gift timing relative to procurement	After	X———————————	Before
Quality of product	High	X———————————	Low
Gift cost	Low	———X———————	High
Gift-giver is a friend	No	X———————————	Yes

Case 4. ValCo valves are *superior* to traditional gate valves because they seal more tightly and more quickly. *After* a large number of ValCo valves have been ordered, Jim, the ValCo salesman and former classmate of Tom's, visits Tom. Jim offers to sponsor Tom for membership in an exclusive country club. Should Tom accept the offer of sponsorship?

Table 6.7 (Case 4)

Feature	Positive	Test Case	Negative
Gift timing relative to procurement	After	X———————————	Before
Quality of product	High	X———————————	Low
Gift cost	Low	——— X———————	High
Gift-giver is a friend	No	———————————X	Yes

Case 5. ValCo valves are *superior* to traditional gate valves because they seal more tightly and more quickly. *Before* ValCo valves have been ordered, Jim, the ValCo salesman and a former classmate of Tom's, visits Tom. Jim offers to sponsor Tom for membership in an exclusive country club. Should Tom accept the offer of sponsorship?

Table 6.8 (Case 5)

Feature	Positive	Test Case	Negative
Gift timing relative to procurement	After	———————————X	Before
Quality of product	High	X———————————	Low
Gift cost	Low	———X———————	High
Gift-giver is a friend	No	———————————X	Yes

Case 6. ValCo valves are *inferior* traditional gate valves. *Before* ValCo valves have been ordered, Jim, the ValCo salesman and a former classmate of Tom's, visits Tom. Jim offers to sponsor Tom for membership in an exclusive country club. Should Tom accept the membership?

Table 6.9 (Case 6)

Feature	Positive	Test Case	Negative
Gift timing relative to procurement	After	————————————————————X	Before
Quality of product	High	————————————————————X	Low
Gift cost	Low	——X————————————	High
Gift-giver is a friend	No	————————————————————X	Yes

Case 7. ValCo valves are *inferior* to traditional gate valves. *Before* ValCo valves have been ordered, Jim, the ValCo salesman and a former classmate of Tom's, visits Tom. Jim says he will treat Tom to an all-expenses-paid trip to the Bahamas. Should Tom accept the trip?

Table 6.10 (Case 7)

Feature	Positive	Test Case	Negative
Gift timing relative to procurement	After	————————————————————X	Before
Quality of product	High	————————————————————X	Low
Gift cost	Low	——————————————X——	High
Gift-giver is a friend	No	————————————————————X	Yes

Most people would say that Case 1 describes a permissible action and Case 7 describes an impermissible action. You should ask yourself whether the intermediate cases represent permissible or impermissible actions. You might also find that you would want to introduce some other features, such as the relative cost of the valves, into the charts. In any event, the analysis illustrates one useful way of handling problems involving conflicts of interest.

6.11   Chapter Summary

Engineering codes require engineers to be honest and impartial in their professional judgments. There are various ways, however, in which engineers can misuse the truth and thus violate this requirement. In addition to lying and deliberate deception, engineers can withhold the truth, fail to adequately promote the dissemination of information, fail to seek out the truth, reveal confidential or proprietary information, and allow their judgment to be corrupted.

From the standpoint of the ethics of respect for persons, dishonesty is wrong because it violates the moral agency of individuals by causing them to make decisions without informed consent. From the utilitarian perspective, dishonesty is wrong because it can undermine the relations of trust on which a scientific community is founded, as well as informed decision making, thus impeding the development of technology.

Dishonesty on campus accustoms a student to dishonesty, which can carry over into his or her professional life. There are, in fact, exact counterparts in the scientific and engineering communities to the types of dishonesty exhibited by students: trimming data, cooking data, forging data, plagiarism, and multiple authorship.

Decisions as to proper use of intellectual property with regard to trade secrets, patents, and copyrighted material are often difficult to make, because they often involve varying degrees of use of intellectual property. The line-drawing method is useful in resolving these problems.

An engineer may also misuse the truth by abusing client-professional confidentiality. This may be done either by breaking confidentiality when it is not warranted or refusing to break confidentiality when the higher obligation to the public requires it. The limits of client/professional confidentiality are controversial and often difficult to determine in engineering as in most professions.

Integrity in expert testimony requires engineers to take cases only when they have adequate time for preparation, refuse to take cases when they cannot testify in good conscience on behalf of their client, consult extensively with the lawyer regarding the technical and legal details of the case, maintain an objective and unbiased demeanor, and always be open to new information. Engineers also misuse the truth when they fail to inform employers, clients, or the public of relevant information, especially when this information concerns the health, safety, and welfare of the public.

A conflict of interest exists for a professional when acting in a professional role, he or she is subject to influences, loyalties, temptations, or other interests that tend to make the professional's judgment less likely to benefit the customer or client than the customer or client is justified in expecting. Conflicts of interest can be actual, potential, or apparent. A special case of conflict of interest is accepting gifts from vendors and others. The line-drawing method is again a useful tool in deciding when accepting a gift is permissible.

  CASES TO CONSIDER

Case 17 Faulty Heart Valves
Case 25 Hydrolevel
Case 28 Last Resort
Case 35 Price Is Right?
Case 54 Window Safety
Case 55 Wonderful Development?
Case 56 Working Overtime

NOTES

1. We are indebted to our student Ray Flumerfelt Jr. for this case. Names have been changed to protect those involved.

2. Ruth R. Faden and Tom L. Beauchamp, *A History and Theory of Informed Consent* (New York: Oxford University Press, 1985), p. 238.

3. Ibid., p. 243.

4. This case comes from the experience of one of our co-authors, M. J. Rabins.

5. Donald L. McCabe, "Classroom Cheating Among Natural Science and Engineering Majors," *Science and Engineering Ethics, 3*, no. 4, 1997, p. 435.

6. Ibid., p. 439.

7. Ibid., p. 439.

8. Sigma Xi, *Honor in Science* (1986), pp. 11–18.

9. William Broad and Nicholas Wade, *Betrayers of the Truth* (New York: Simon & Schuster, 1982), p. 174. Cited in *Honor in Science*, p. 12.

10. *Honor in Science*, p. 11.

11. This statement is originally found in R. A. Millikan, "On the Elementary Electrical Charge and the Avogadro Constant," *Physical Review, 1* (1913), 109–143. Quoted in *Honor in Science*, p. 12 and taken from Gerald Holton, "Subelectrons, Presuppositions, and the Millikan-Ehrenhaft Dispute," *Historical Studies in the Physical Sciences, 9* (1978), 161–224. Recent correspondence from Sigma Xi suggests that Millikan may have been falsely accused of misrepresenting his data. Whether or not this is true, the case represents the *kind* of thing we mean by "cooking the data."

12. *Honor in Science*, p. 11.

13. Arnold Relman, "Lessons from the Darsee Affair," *The New England Journal of Medicine, 308* (1983), 1415–1417.

14. "Conduct Unbecoming," *Sunday New York Times Magazine* (October 29, 1989), 41.

15. See Kermit Vandivier, "What? Me Be a Martyr," *Harper's Magazine* (July 1975), 36–44.

16. John Fielder, "Tough Break for Goodrich," *Journal of Business and Professional Ethics, 19*, no. 3 (Spring 1986), 223–238.

17. See *Honor in Science*, pp. 23–28.

18. Although the tables are our own, the case was suggested by Mark Holtzapple.

19. We are indebted to Mark Holtzapple for this example.

20. *Opinions of the Board of Ethical Review, Vol. VI* (Alexandria, Va.: National Society of Professional Engineers, 1989), p. 15.

21. California Supreme Court, July 1, 1976. 1331 *California Reporter*, pp. 14–33, West Publishing Co. Cited in Joan C. Callahan, *Ethical Issues in Professional Life* (New York: Oxford University Press, 1988), pp. 239–244.

22. "Engineers Face Risks as Expert Witnesses," *The Rochester Engineer* (December 1992), 27.

23. Ibid., 27.

24. For several of these suggestions, see Ibid., 27 and 29.

25. See "Plaintiffs to Get $15.4 Million," *Miami County Republic* [Paola, Kans.] (April 27, 1992), 1.

26. Paul Eddy, *Destination Disaster: From the Tri-Motor to the DC-10* (New York: Quadrangle/The New York Times Book Co., 1976), pp. 175–188. Reprinted in Robert J. Baum, *Ethical Problems in Engineering, Vol. 2* (Troy, N.Y.: Center for the Study of the Human Dimensions of Science and Technology, 1980), pp. 175–185.

27. Paul Eddy, *Destination Disaster: From the Tri-Motor to the DC-10*, pp. 175–188.

28. *Grimshaw v. Ford Motor Co.*, App., 174 Cal. Rptr. 348, p. 360.

29. See Michael Davis, "Conflict of Interest" in Deborah G. Johnson, *Ethical Issues in Engineering* (Englewood Cliffs, N.J.: Prentice Hall, 1991), p. 324. The original version was printed in *Business and Professional Ethics Journal, 1*, no. 4 (1982), 17–27. Davis should not be held responsible for this version of the definition.

30. These three examples are modifications of ones constructed by Mark Holtzapple.

31. These cases, first suggested by a chemical engineering professor, were modified by C. E. Harris and Mark Holtzapple.

Chapter 7

Risk, Safety, and Liability in Engineering

Don Hayward is employed as a chemical engineer at ABC Manufacturing.[1] Although he does not work with hot metals himself, he supervises workers who are exposed to hot metals eight hours a day, five days a week. Don becomes concerned when several workers develop respiratory problems and complain about "those bad smelling fumes from the hot metals." When Don asks his superior, Cal Brundage, about air quality in the workplace, the reply is that the workplace is in full compliance with OSHA guidelines. Don also learns that OSHA guidelines do not apply to chemicals that have not been tested and that a relatively small percentage of chemicals in the workplace have actually been tested. This is also the case with the vast majority of chemicals that workers are exposed to at ABC.

Don goes to ABC's science library, talks to the reference librarian about his concerns, and does a literature search to see if he can find anything that might be helpful in determining why the workers have developed respiratory problems. He finds the title of an article that looks promising and asks the reference librarian to send for a copy. The librarian tells Don that the formal request must have the signed approval of Cal Brundage, so Don fills out the request form and sends it to Cal's office for approval.

One month later the article has still not arrived. Don asks Cal about the request. Cal replies that he doesn't recall ever seeing it. He tells Don that it must have gotten "lost in the shuffle." Don fills out another form and this time personally hands it to Cal. Cal says he will send it to the reference librarian right away.

Another month passes and the article has not arrived. Don mentions his frustration to the reference librarian, who replies that he never received a request from Cal to order the paper. What should Don do now?

7.1   Introduction

Don's concern for safety in the workplace is a common one for engineers. How should engineers deal with issues of risk and safety, especially when they involve possible liability for harm? In the ABC case, the risk arises from a manufacturing process. Other risks arise from products, structures, and substances created by engineers.

Engineering necessarily involves risk. Even if engineers did not innovate, but rather designed things in the same way year after year, the chance of producing harm would exist. New hazards could be found in products, processes, and chemicals that were once thought to be safe. But the element of risk is greatly increased because engineers are constantly involved in innovation. A bridge or building is constructed with new materials or with a new design. New machines are created and new compounds synthesized, always without full knowledge of their long-term effects on humans or the environment.

Dealing with risk poses many perils for the engineer. In this chapter, we shall consider some of these perils, especially as they relate to the engineer's ethical and professional responsibilities. First, we shall look at some reasons why accidents are hard to anticipate and risk is often difficult to estimate. Some studies of accidents in technology-related areas have even suggested that accidents are inevitable and that there is such a thing as the "normal accident."

Next, we shall examine some reasons why it is easy for engineers to accept incrementally increasing risk, almost without realizing it. Using the events leading up to the *Challenger* explosion as an illustration, we shall show how engineers can increase the chance of accidents by a process, which may not be fully realized until an accident occurs.

Then, we shall look at several different approaches to the definition of acceptable risk. Engineers should be aware of the fact that different social groups have different definitions of acceptable risk and different agendas regarding proper management of risk. One approach is that of the risk expert, who wants to balance risk and benefit in a way that optimizes overall public well-being. The layperson, on the other hand, wants to protect himself or herself from risk imposed unjustly or without free and informed consent, especially if the risk involves certain dreaded events, such as cancer or nuclear catastrophe. This approach leads to a definition of acceptable risk that differs from the risk expert's. The government regulator wants as much assurance as possible that the public is not being exposed to unexpected harm. This approach is different from either of the other two.

To manage risk responsibly, engineers should also be aware of some of the issues posed by legal liability for risk. One of these issues is that the standards of proof are very different in science and tort law. This fact poses ethical problems, because the standards of tort law give more protection to the victims of technologically imposed risk, and the standards of science give more protection to the creators of technologically imposed risk. Another issue is the legal liabilities incurred by engineers in attempting to protect the public from unnecessary risk.

Before discussing any of this, however, we should consider what the engineering codes have to say about risk and safety.

7.2   The Codes and Engineering Practice Regarding Risk and Safety

Virtually all engineering codes give a prominent place to safety, stating that engineers must hold paramount the safety, health, and welfare of the public. The relationship of risk to safety is very close. If products, structures, processes, and substances are unsafe, they subject humans and the environment to undue risk. Therefore, the statements in the codes having to do with safety are relevant to the topic of risk.

The NSPE code, in sections II.1.b and III.2.b, requires engineers to design safely, defining this in terms of "accepted engineering standards." For example, item III.2.b instructs engineers not to "complete, sign or seal plans and/or specifications that are not of a design safe to the public health and welfare and in conformity with accepted engineering standards." Item II.1.a instructs engineers that if their professional judgment is overruled in "circumstances where the safety, health, property or welfare of the public are endangered," they are obligated to "notify their employer or client and such other authority as may be appropriate."

Many other engineering codes give similar instructions to engineers. For example, the IEEE Code of Ethics emphasizes members' responsibility for the public's health and safety in three ways. First, electrical engineers agree "to accept responsibility in making engineering decisions consistent with the safety, health, and welfare of the public, and to disclose promptly factors that might endanger the public or the environment." Second, they agree "to improve the understanding of technology, its appropriate application, and potential consequences." Third, they agree "to maintain and improve our technical competence and to undertake technological tasks for others only if qualified by training or experience, or after full disclosure of pertinent limitations." These last two items emphasize the importance of informed consent.

Engineering practice is suffused with concern with safety. One of the most pervasive concepts in engineering practice is the notion of "factors of safety." If the largest load a walkway will have to carry at any one time is 1000 pounds, for example, a prudent engineer might design the walkway geometry to carry 3000 pounds. The walkway dimensions for normal usage would then be designed with a factor of safety of three.

Accepted engineering practice goes still further. In choosing materials to build the walkway, an engineer might begin with a material that has an advertised yield stress of a given number of pounds per square inch, and then treat this material as if it had only half of that capability in determining how much material to include in the walkway construction. This introduces an additional factor of safety of two. The final overall factor of safety at the walkway would be the product of the two separate factors, or six in this example.

Thus, a prudent engineer would design the walkway to be six times as strong as required for normal everyday use to account for unpredictably high loads or unaccountably weak construction material. This approach is taught to all engineers early in their training, and factors of safety of six or higher are the norm rather than the exception.

Accidents, however, are often difficult to predict, and so the degree of risk is often hard to estimate, as we shall see in the next section.

7.3   Difficulties in Estimating Risk

Estimating risk has been described by one writer as looking "through a glass darkly."[2] If we could accurately predict the harm resulting from engineering work, there would be no risk. We would know precisely the harm to expect. Instead, we can only estimate the magnitude and probability of harm. To make matters worse, often we cannot even make our estimate with accuracy. In actual practice, therefore, estimating risk (or "risk assessment") is an uncertain prediction of the probability of harm. In this section, we shall consider some of the methods of estimating risk, the uncertainties in these methods, and the value judgments that these uncertainties necessitate.

Detecting Failure Modes

With respect to new technologies, engineers and scientists must have some way of estimating the risks that they impose on those affected by it. One of the methods for assessing risk involves the use of a fault tree. A fault tree is a diagram of the possible ways in which a malfunction or accident can occur. Fault trees are most often used to anticipate hazards for which there is little or no direct experience, such as nuclear meltdowns. It enables an engineer to analyze in a systematic fashion the various failure modes attendant to an engineering project. A failure mode is a way in which a structure, mechanism, or process can malfunction. For example, a structure can rip apart in tension, crumble to pieces in compression, crack and break in bending, lose its integrity due to corrosion (rusting), explode due to excessive internal pressure, or burn due to excessive temperature. Figure 7.1 illustrates how a fault tree analysis can be used to discover why an automobile will not start.

Another approach to a systematic examination of failure modes is the event-tree analysis. In a fault-tree analysis we begin with an undesirable event, such as a car not starting or the loss of electrical power to a nuclear power plant safety system. Then, we reason backward to determine what might have led to the event. By contrast, in an event-tree analysis, we begin with an initial event and reason forward to the state of the system to which the event can lead. Figure 7.2 on page 148 illustrates in schematic form an event-tree analysis.

This simplified event tree for an accident involving a loss of coolant in a typical nuclear power plant begins with a failure and enumerates the various events to which this failure could lead. This event tree shows the logical relationships

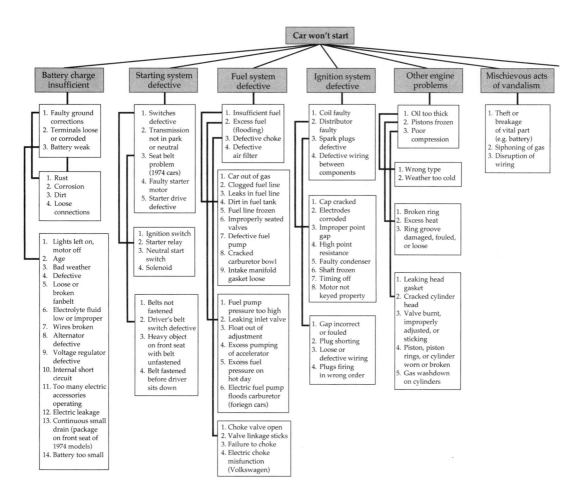

Source: This diagram is from B. Fischoff, P. Slovick, and S. Lichtenstein, "Fault Trees: Sensitivity and Estimated Failure Problem Representation," *Journal of Experimental Psychology: Human Perception and Performance*, 4 (1978): 330–344. Used with permission.

Figure 7.1
Fault-Tree Analysis of Failure of an Automobile to Start
The failure appears at the top of the fault tree, and the possible causes
of the failure appear as "branches" of the fault tree.

between the possible ways that a pipe break can affect the safety systems in a nuclear plant. If both a pipe and on-site power fail simultaneously, the outcome will be a very large release of radioactive coolant. If these two systems are independent, the probability of this happening is the product of the two probabilities taken separately. For example, if there is one chance in 10^{-4} ($P_1 = 0.0001$) that the pipe will break and one chance in 10^{-5} ($P_2 = 0.00001$) that the on-site power will fail, then the chance of a loss of a very large release is one in 10^{-9} ($P = P_1 P_2$).

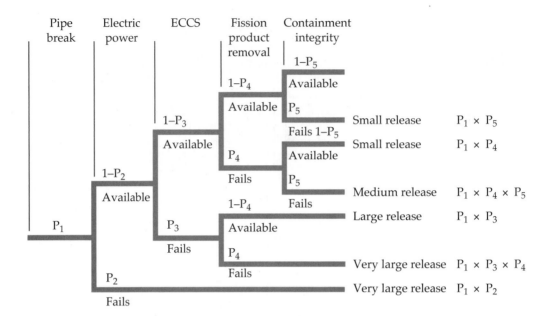

Reproduced, with permission, from the *Annual Review of Energy*, Volume 6, © 1981 by Annual Reviews, Inc. Courtesy N. C. Rasmussen.

Figure 7.2
An Event Tree Analysis of a Pipe Break in a Nuclear Plant

Although it is necessary to go through such analyses to ensure that we have taken into account as many failure modes as possible, they have severe limitations. First, we cannot anticipate all of the mechanical, physical, electrical, and chemical problems that might lead to failure. Second, we cannot anticipate all of the points of human error that could lead to failure. Third, the probabilities assigned to the failure modes are largely conjectural and based on analyses that cannot be corroborated by experimental testing. We are not, for example, going to melt down a nuclear reactor to determine the probability of such an occurrence leading to a chain reaction fission explosion. In many cases we do not know the probability of material behavior at extremely elevated temperatures. Fourth, we can never be sure we have all of the possible initiating events (even ones we know exist in different contexts) included on the event tree or placed in the right order.

Are There "Normal Accidents"?

Sociologist Charles Perrow confirms some of these problems by arguing that there are two characteristics of high-risk technologies that make them especially susceptible to accidents, so that we can speak of "normal accidents."[3] These two characteristics are the "tight coupling" and the "complex interactions" of the parts of a technological system. These two factors not only make accidents likely but also difficult to predict and control. This, in turn, makes risk difficult to estimate.

Processes are tightly coupled if they are connected in such a way that one process is known to affect another and will usually do so within a short time. In tight coupling there is usually little time to correct a failure and little likelihood of confining a failure to one part of the system, so that the whole system is damaged. A chemical plant is tightly coupled, because a failure in one part of the plant can quickly affect other parts of the plant. A university, by contrast, is loosely coupled, because if one department ceases to function, the operation of the whole university is usually not threatened.

Processes can also be complexly interactive, in that the parts of the system can interact in unanticipated ways. No one dreamed that when X failed, it would affect Y. Chemical plants are also complexly interactive, in that parts affect one another in feedback patterns that cannot always be anticipated. A post office, by contrast, is not so complexly interactive. The parts of the system are related to one another for the most part in a linear way and do not usually interact in unanticipated ways to cause the post office to cease functioning. If a post office ceases to function, it is usually because of a well-understood failure.

Examples of complexly interactive and tightly coupled technical systems include not only chemical plants but also nuclear power plants, space missions, and nuclear weapons systems. Being tightly coupled and complexly interactive, they can have unanticipated failures, and there is little time to correct the problems or keep them from affecting the entire system. This makes accidents difficult to predict and disasters difficult to avoid, once a malfunction appears.

Unfortunately, it is difficult to change tightly coupled and complexly interactive systems to make accidents less likely. To reduce complexity, decentralization is required, enabling operators to have the ability to react independently and creatively to unanticipated events. To deal with tight coupling, however, centralization is required, in which operators follow orders quickly and without question to avoid a failure or limit its effects. It may not be possible, furthermore, to make a system both loosely coupled and noncomplex. According to Perrow, therefore, accidents in complex, tightly coupled systems are inevitable and, in this sense, "normal." Engineers know that, to some extent, one can include localized and autonomous automatic controls to protect against complexity failures, coupled with manual overrides to protect against tight coupling failures.

Here is an example of an accident in a system that was complexly interactive and tightly coupled and that could have been prevented by the type of good engineering just described. In the summer of 1962 the New York Telephone Company completed heating system additions to a new accounting building in Yonkers, New York. The three-story, square-block building was a paradigm of safe design, using the latest technology.

In October 1962, after the building was occupied and the workers were in place, final adjustments were being made on the building's new, expanded heating system located in the basement. This system consisted of three side-by-side, oil-fired boilers. The boilers were designed for low pressures of less than 6.0 psi and so were not covered by ASME boiler and pressure vessel codes. Each boiler was equipped with a spring-loaded safety relief valve designed to open and release steam into the atmosphere if the boiler pressure got too high. Each boiler was also equipped with a pressure-actuated cutoff valve designed to cut off oil flow to the boiler burners in the event of excessive pressure. The steam pressure from the boilers was delivered to the steam radiators, each of which had its own local relief valve. Finally, in the event that all else failed, a one-foot diameter pressure gauge with a red danger zone painted on the face sat on the top of each boiler. If the pressure got too high, the gauge was supposed to alert a janitor who operated the boilers, so he could turn off the burners.

On October 2, 1962, the following events transpired.[4]

1. The building custodian decided to fire up boiler 1 in the heating system for the first time that fall. The electricians had just wired the control system for the new companion boiler (boiler 3) and successfully tested the electrical signal flows.

2. The custodian did not know that the electricians had left the fuel cutoff control system disconnected. The electricians had disconnected the system because they were planning to do additional work on boiler 3 the following week. They intended to wire the fuel cutoffs for the two boilers in series (that is, high pressure in either would stop both).

3. The custodian mechanically closed the header valve, because it was a warm, Indian Summer day, and he did not want to send steam into the radiators on the floors above. Thus, the boiler was delivering steam pressure against a blocked valve, and the individual steam radiator valves were thus out of the control loop.

4. As subsequent testing showed, the relief valve had rusted shut after some tests the previous spring in which the boilers had last been fired up. (Later, laws were enacted in New York state that require relief valves for low-pressure boiler systems to be operated by hand once every 24 hours to ensure that they are not rusted shut. At the time, low-pressure boiler systems were not subject to this requirement.)

5. This was on Thursday before payday, and the custodian made a short walk to his bank at the lunch hour to cash a check, shortly after turning on boiler 1.

6. The cafeteria was on the other side of the wall against which the boiler end abutted. Employees were in line against that wall awaiting their turn at the cafeteria serving tables. There were more people in line than there would have been on Friday, because on payday many workers went out to cash their paychecks and have lunch at local restaurants.

7. Boiler 1 exploded. The end of the boiler that was the most removed from the wall next to the cafeteria blew off, making the boiler into a rocketlike projectile. The boiler lifted off its stanchions and crashed into the cafeteria, after which it continued to rise at great velocity through all three stories of the building. Twenty-five people were killed and almost one hundred were seriously injured.

The events that led to this disaster were complexly interrelated. There is no possible way that fault-tree or event-tree analyses could have predicted this chain of events. If the outside temperature had been cooler, the custodian would not have closed the header valve and the individual steam radiator valves in each upstairs room would have opened. If the relief valve had been hand-operated every day, its malfunction would have been discovered and probably corrected. If the time had not been noon and the day before payday, the custodian might have stayed in the basement and seen the high pressure gauge reading and turned off the burners. If it had not been lunch time, the unfortunate victims would not have been in the cafeteria line on the other side of the wall from the boiler.

The events were also tightly coupled. There was not much time to correct the problem once the pressure started to rise and no way to isolate the boiler failure from a catastrophe in the rest of the building.

7.4   Normalizing Deviance

The complexity and tight coupling of technical systems are not the only factors that make accidents more likely. Engineers can also increase the risk to the public by allowing increasing numbers of deviancies from proper standards of safety and acceptable risk. Sociologist Diane Vaughn refers to this phenomenon as the *normalization of deviance*.[5]

Every design carries with it certain predictions about how the designed object should perform in use. Sometimes these predications are not fulfilled, producing what are commonly referred to as *anomalies*. Rather than correcting the design or the operating conditions that led to the anomalies, engineers or managers too often do something less desirable. They may simply accept the anomaly or even increase the boundaries of acceptable risk. Sometimes this process leads to disasters.

This process is dramatically and tragically illustrated by the events leading to the *Challenger* disaster. Neither the contractor, Morton Thiokol, nor NASA expected the rubber O-rings sealing the joints in the solid rocket booster (SRB) to be touched by the hot gases of motor ignition, much less to be partially burned. However, as flights confirmed damage to the sealing rings, the reaction by both NASA and Thiokol was to accept the anomalies without attempting to remedy the problems that caused the anomalies.[6]

Here are several examples of normalizing deviance:

1. In 1977, test results showed that the SRB joints would rotate open at ignition, creating a larger gap between the tang and clevis.[7] According to NASA engineers, the gap was large enough to prevent the secondary seal from sealing if the primary O-ring failed late in the ignition cycle. Nevertheless, after some modifications, such as adding sealing putty behind the O-rings, the joint was officially certified as an acceptable risk, even though the joint's behavior deviated from design predictions.

2. Another anomaly was discovered in November 1981 in flight STS-2, where there was "impingement erosion" of the primary O-ring in the right SRB's aft field joint.[8] The hot propellant gases had moved through the "blow holes" in the zinc chromate putty in the joints. The blowholes were caused by entrapped air introduced at the time the putty was installed. Even though this troubling phenomenon was not predicted, the joints were again certified as an acceptable risk.

3. A third anomaly occurred in 1984 with the launch of STS 41-B, when, for the first time, two primary O-rings on two different joints were eroded.[9] Again, the erosion on two joints was termed an acceptable risk.

4. Another anomaly occurred in 1985, when "blowby" of hot gases had reached the secondary seal on a nozzle joint.[10] The nozzle joints were considered safe because, unlike the field joints, they contained a different and very safe secondary seal, a "face seal." The problem was that a similar malfunction could happen with the field joint, where the danger was much more serious, and these problems were not dealt with.

5. Perhaps the most dramatic example of expanding the boundaries of acceptable risk was in the area of the acceptable temperature for launch. Prior to the *Challenger* launch, the lowest temperature of the seals at launch time was 53 degrees. (At that time, the ambient temperature was in the high 60s.) On the night before the launch of the *Challenger*, however, the temperature of the seals was expected to be 29 degrees. Thus, the boundaries for acceptable risk were expanded by 24 degrees.

The result of accepting these anomalies without making any adequate attempt to remedy the basic problem (poor seal design), and of lowering the temperature considered acceptable for launch, led to the tragic destruction of the *Challenger* and the loss of its crew.

Vaughn argues that these kinds of problems cannot be eliminated from technological systems and that, as a result, accidents are inevitable. Whether or not this is the case, there is no question that technology imposes risk on the public and that these risks are often difficult to detect, and eliminate. Now let us examine some of the controversies surrounding the concept of acceptable risk.

7.5   The Expert's Approach to Acceptable Risk: Identifying and Defining Acceptable Risk

Identifying Risk

To assess a risk, an engineer must first identify it. To identify a risk, an engineer must first know what a risk is. Most people would agree that the concept of risk involves the notion of adverse effect or harm. We might define a *harm* as an invasion or limitation of a person's freedom or well-being. Some of the most important types of well-being are physical well-being, psychological well-being, and economic well-being.

For the most part, engineering risks have to do with our physical and economic well-being. Engineering work can subject us to risks of health and accident or physical injury. This affects our physical well-being. Engineering work can also subject us to risks to our economic well-being. Faulty design of a building can cause it to collapse, resulting in economic loss to the owner and perhaps death for the inhabitants. Faulty design of a chemical plant can cause accidents and economic disaster.

This account of risk is in accord with the thought of many risk experts. William W. Lowrance, for example, defines risk as "a compound measure of the probability and magnitude of adverse effect."[11] Risk, according to Lowrance, is composed of two elements: the likelihood of an adverse effect or harm and the magnitude of that adverse effect or harm. By "compound," Lowrance means "the product." Risk, for the risk expert, is thus the product of the likelihood and the magnitude of the harm. A relatively slight harm that is highly likely might constitute a greater risk than a relatively large harm that is far less likely.

A 1992 National Public Radio story on the Environmental Protection Agency began with a quotation from EPA official Linda Fisher illustrating the risk expert's conception of risk:

> A lot of our priorities are set by public opinion, and the public quite often is more worried about things that they perceive to cause greater risks than things that really cause risks. Our priorities often times are set through Congress . . . and those [decisions] may or may not reflect real risk, they may reflect people's opinions of risk or the Congressmen's opinions of risk.[12]

Every time Fisher refers to "risk" or "real risk," we can substitute Lowrance's definition, or perhaps even a simpler one, such as "probability of death or injury." Fisher believes that, whereas both members of the U.S. Congress and ordinary laypeople may be confused about risk, the experts know what it is. Risk is something that can be objectively measured—namely, the product of the likelihood and the magnitude of harm.

Utilitarianism and Acceptable Risk

The risk expert's approach to risk is usually utilitarian. Utilitarianism holds that the answer to any moral question is to be found by determining the course of action that maximizes well-being. As we have seen, utilitarians often find cost/benefit analysis a useful tool in assessing risk. In applying this to risk, the technique is often called risk/benefit analysis, because the "cost" is measured in terms of the risk of deaths, injuries, or other harms associated with a given course of action. For simplicity, however, we shall continue to use the term "cost/benefit analysis."

Consider the case described at the beginning of this chapter from the cost/benefit standpoint. Is the risk to the workers from the fumes acceptable? Suppose Don, in conducting a more thorough literature search, discovers that the risk imposed by exposure to the fumes is greater than he originally thought. To determine whether this is an acceptable risk of death from the cost/benefit perspective, he would have to compare the cost of this rate of death with the cost of preventing or drastically reducing the risk.[13] To calculate the cost of preventing the deaths, we would have to include the costs of modifying the process that produces the fumes, the cost of providing protective masks, the cost of providing better ventilation systems, and the cost of any other safety measures necessary to prevent the deaths. Then, we must calculate the cost of not preventing the deaths due to the fumes. Here we must include such factors as the cost of additional health care, the cost of possible lawsuits due to the deaths, the cost of bad publicity, and the loss of income to the families of the workers. If the total cost of preventing the loss of life is greater than the total cost of not preventing the deaths, then the present level of risk is acceptable. If the total cost of not preventing the loss of life is greater than the total cost of preventing the loss, then the present level of risk is unacceptable. In determining the costs, one must be very careful not to overlook costs that are not immediately obvious and that could change the outcome of the analysis.

It might not be possible to give monetary evaluations for all of the various costs and benefits of the two options, so a strict numerical analysis of acceptable risk might not be possible. The engineer might have to be content with a more intuitive assessment of the various options in terms of their contribution to the overall utility.

Suppose Don is not able to find any conclusive evidence regarding the effects of the fumes. In the case of doubt, the utilitarian position might well favor placing the burden of proof on those who would want to restrict worker exposure to the fumes. The argument might well be that regulations on industry that are not necessitated by scientific studies impose an undue burden on the productive sector of the economy. This, in turn, leads to economic inefficiency, fewer jobs, and a lower standard of living for the whole society. The harm that might result to a few workers if exposure is not restricted would probably be outweighed by the benefits to the larger society of less restriction.

Risk as Maximizing Benefit

Given the earlier definition of risk as the product of the probability and the consequences of harm, we can state the risk expert's criterion of acceptable risk in the following way:

> An acceptable risk is one of where, given the options available, the risk of harm is at least equaled by the probability of producing benefit.

Regardless of the precise form of utilitarian analysis employed, however, an exclusive reliance on this method of determining acceptable risk suffers from the characteristic limitations of utilitarianism.

First, it might not be possible to anticipate all of the costs and benefits associated with each option. Insofar as this cannot be done, the cost/benefit method will yield an inconclusive result.

Second, it is not always possible to translate all of the risks and benefits into monetary terms. How do we assess the risks associated with a new technology, or with eliminating a wetland or with eliminating the unique species in a part of a Brazilian rain forest? Again, this would render the cost/benefit approach inconclusive.

The most controversial issue in this regard is, of course, the monetary value that should be placed on human life. But how are we to determine the value of other people's lives? One way is to estimate the value of future earnings, but this implies that the lives of retired people and others who do not work are worthless. So a more reasonable approach is to attempt to place the same value on people's lives that they place on it themselves. For example, people often demand a compensating wage to take a job that is more risky. By calculating the increased risk and the increased pay that people demand for more risky jobs, some economists say, we can come up with an estimate of the monetary value people place on their own lives.[14] Alternatively, we can calculate how much more people would pay for safety in an automobile or other things they use. The problem is that wealthy people pay more for safety than others, and women generally value their lives more than men in terms of dollar/risk trade-offs.

Using such calculations, economists have come up with widely different monetary evaluations of human lives, varying from a few hundred thousand to several million dollars.[15]

Third, the method in its usual applications makes no allowance for the distributions of costs and benefits. Consider the case at the beginning of this chapter again. If more overall utility were produced by exposing the workers in the plant to serious risk of sickness and death, the exposure would be justified. As long as the good of the majority outweighs costs associated with the suffering and death of the workers, the risk is justified. Yet most of us would probably find this an unacceptable account of acceptable risk.

Fourth, the method gives no place for informed consent to the risks imposed by technology. We shall see in our discussion of the lay approach to risk that most people think informed consent is one of the most important features of justified risk.

In spite of these limitations, cost/benefit analysis has a legitimate place in risk evaluation. When no serious threats to individual rights are involved, cost/benefit analysis may be decisive. In addition, cost/benefit analysis is systematic, offers a degree of objectivity, and provides a way of comparing risks, benefits, and costs by the use of a common measure—namely, monetary cost.

7.6   The Layperson's Approach to Acceptable Risk

Expert and Layperson

The approach to risk taken by the lay public can differ considerably from the expert approach. Here are two of the most important differences.

First, the public is sometimes mistaken in estimating the probability of death and injury from various activities or technologies. Risk expert Chauncey Starr notes that laypeople tend to overestimate the likelihood of low-probability risks associated with causes of death and to underestimate the likelihood of high-probability risks associated with causes of death. The latter tendency can lead to overconfident biasing, or *anchoring*. In anchoring an original estimate of risk is made, an estimate that may be substantially erroneous. Even though the estimate is corrected, it is not sufficiently modified from the original estimate. The original estimate "anchors" all future estimates and precludes sufficient adjustment in the face of new evidence.[16]

A study by Slovic, Fischhoff, and Lichtenstein shows that, although even experts can be mistaken in their estimations of various risks, they are not as seriously mistaken as laypeople. The study contrasts actual versus perceived deaths per year.[17] Experts and laypeople were asked their perception of the number of deaths per year for such activities as smoking, driving a car, driving a motorcycle, riding in a train, skiing, and so on. On a graph that plots perceived deaths against actual deaths for each of several different risks, if the perception (by either laypeople or experts) of deaths were accurate, the result would be a 45-degree line; that is, actual and perceived deaths would be the same. Instead, the experts were consistently about an order of magnitude (about 10 times) low in their perceptions of the perceived risk, and the lay public still another order of magnitude (about 100 times) too low.

A second reason for the different attitudes toward risk by risk experts and laypeople is that they perceive risk differently. Laypeople appear to often combine concepts of risk and acceptable risk, whereas experts clearly distinguish the two concepts. Experts, as we have seen, usually define risk as the product of the magnitude and the probability of harm and then define acceptable risk in utilitarian terms. Laypeople do not evaluate risk in strict actuarial terms, but consider other factors as well. According to Chauncey Starr, laypeople are generally willing to take voluntary risks that are 1000 times (three orders of magnitude) as uncertain as involuntary risks.[18] Thus, voluntarily assumed risks are more acceptable than risks not voluntarily assumed. The amount of risk people are willing to accept in the workplace is generally proportional to the cube of the increase in the wages offered in compensation for the additional risk. For example, doubling wages would tend to convince a worker to take eight times the risk. But laypeople may also separate by three orders of magnitude the risk perceived to be involved in involuntary exposure to danger (as when a corporation places a toxic waste dump next door to one's house) and the risk involved in voluntary activity (such as smoking). Here, voluntarily assumed risks are seen as inherently less risky, not simply more acceptable.

Laypeople also seem to be content with spending different amounts of money in different areas to save a life. In his study of 57 risk-abatement programs at five different government agencies in Washington (including the Environmental Protection Agency and the Occupational Safety and Health Administration), Starr shows that risk-abatement programs vary greatly in the amount of money they spend to save a life. Some programs spend $170,000 per life, whereas others spend $3 million per life.[19]

Another researcher, D. Litai, has separated risk into 26 risk factors, each having a dichotomous scale associated with it.[20] For example, a risk may have a natural or a human origin. If the risk has a human origin, Litai concludes from an analysis of statistical data from insurance companies that the perceived risk is 20 times as great as from having a natural origin. An involuntarily assumed risk (whether or natural or human origin) is perceived as being 100 times greater than a voluntarily assumed one. An immediate risk is perceived as being 30 times greater than a delayed one. A catastrophic risk is perceived as being 30 times greater than an ordinary one. By contrast, a regular risk is perceived as being just as great as an occasional one, and a necessary risk is just as great as a luxury-induced one. Here again there is evidence of the amalgamation of the concepts of risk and acceptable risk.

Informed Consent and Justice

Some of these differences may be attributable to factual errors laypersons make in estimating the probability or magnitude of harm, but they may also be attributable to differences between experts and laypeople in defining risk itself. For example, laypeople often seem to think of an involuntarily assumed risk as inherently more risky than one that is voluntarily assumed.

The following comments by Granger Morgan of Carnegie Mellon University (in contrast to those presented earlier by Linda Fisher on NPR) illustrate this lay conception of risk:

> For many years there has been an argument among some technical experts that the public is all mixed up, that they just don't have their risk priorities right. But experimental results in psychology in recent years have suggested that that's not true. If you give the public a list of hazards and say, "Sort these in terms of how many people die each year from each of them," they can do it. If instead you give them the same list and they are asked, "Sort them in terms of how risky they are," you get a very different order. The point is that to most people risk does not equal expected numbers of death. It involves a lot of other things, things like equity and whether you can control the hazard, whether you understand it. And so partly the arguments about priorities derive from this difference between making judgments just on the basis of expected numbers of deaths versus considering all these other factors.[21]

Whether or not one believes that the public is always able to accurately assess the magnitude and likelihood of harm, Morgan's conception of risk is fundamentally different from Fisher's. He believes that risk in the public's mind involves not only expectation of a certain number of deaths or injuries, but also other issues, like (1) whether you give free and informed consent to the hazard and (2) whether there is equity in the distribution of risk posed by the hazard.

These considerations suggest that the lay approach follows more closely the ethics of respect for persons than utilitarianism. According to this ethical perspective, it is wrong to deny the moral agency of individuals. Moral agents are beings capable of formulating and pursuing purposes of their own. We deny the moral agency of individuals when we deny their ability to formulate and pursue their own goals, or when we treat them in an inequitable fashion with respect to other moral agents. Let us examine each of these two concepts in more detail.

FREE AND INFORMED CONSENT AND COMPENSATION

To give free and informed consent to the risks imposed by technology, three things are necessary. First, a person must not be coerced. Second, a person must have the relevant information. Third, a person must be rational and competent enough to evaluate the information.

Unfortunately, meaningful informed consent is difficult to obtain for several reasons:

1. It is difficult to know when consent is free. Have workers given their free consent when they continue to work at a plant with known safety hazards? Perhaps they have no alternative form of employment.

2. People are often not adequately informed of dangers or do not evaluate them correctly. Sometimes, laypeople err in estimating risk. They underestimate the probability of events that have not occurred before or that do not get their attention, while overestimating the probability of events that are dramatic or catastrophic.

3. Often it is not possible to obtain any meaningful kind of informed consent from individuals who are subject to risks from technology. How would a plant manager obtain the consent of those who live near the plant for it to emit a substance into the atmosphere that causes mild respiratory problems in a small percentage of the population? Is the fact that the residents do not protest sufficient evidence that they have consented? What if they do not know about the substance, or do not know what it does, or do not understand its effects correctly, or are simply too distracted by other things?

In light of the problems in getting free and informed consent, we could compensate individuals after the fact for actual harms done to them through technology. For example, people could be compensated for harms due to defective design in an automobile or a release of a poisonous gas from a chemical plant. This approach has the advantage that consent does not have to be obtained, but it has some distinct disadvantages:

1. It does not tell us how to determine adequate compensation.

2. It limits the freedom of individuals, because some people would never have consented.

3. Sometimes there is no adequate compensation for a harm, as in the case of serious injury or death.

There are problems with both informed consent and compensation as ways of dealing with the ethical requirement to respect the moral agency of those exposed to risk due to technology. Nevertheless, some effort must be made to honor this requirement. Now let us return to the second requirement of respect for persons morality with regard to risk.

EQUITY OR JUSTICE

The ethics of respect for persons places great emphasis on respecting the moral agency of individuals, regardless of the cost to the larger society. John Rawls expresses this concern: "[E]ach member of society is thought to have an inviolability founded upon justice . . . which even the welfare of everyone else cannot override."[22] As an example of the requirement for justice derived from the ethics of respect for persons, consider the following statement by Mrs. Talbert whose husband's health was severely damaged by byssinosis, caused by cotton dust:

> My husband worked in the cotton mill since 1937 to 1973. His breath was so short he couldn't walk from the parking lot to the gate the last two weeks he worked. . . .
>
> He was a big man, liked fishing, hunting, swimming, playing ball, and loved to camp. We liked to go to the mountains and watch the bears. He got so he could not breathe and walk any distance, so we had to stop going anywhere. So we sold our camper, boat and his truck as his doctor, hospital and medicine bills were so high. We don't go anywhere now. The doctor said his lungs were as bad as they could get to still be alive. At first he used tank oxygen about two or three times a week, then it got so bad he used more and more. So now he has an oxygen concentrator, he has to stay on it 24 hours a day. When he goes to the doctor or hospital he has a little portable tank.
>
> He is bedridden now. It's a shame the mill company doesn't want to pay compensation for brown lung. If they would just come and see him as he is now, and only 61 years old.[23]

A utilitarian might be willing to trade off the very great harm to Mr. Talbert, resulting from failure to force cotton mills to protect their workers from the risk of byssinosis, for smaller advantages to a very large number of people. After all, such protection is often very expensive, and these expenses must eventually be passed on to consumers in the form of higher prices for cotton products. Higher prices would also make American cotton products more expensive and thus less competitive in world markets, thereby depriving American workers of jobs. Regulations protecting workers might even force many (perhaps all) American cotton mills to close. Such disutilities might well outweigh the disutilities to the Mr. Talberts of the world.

From the standpoint of the ethics of respect for persons, however, such considerations must not be allowed to obscure the fact that Mr. Talbert has been treated unjustly. While many enjoy the benefits of the plant, only Mr. Talbert and a few others suffer the consequences of unhealthy working conditions: the benefits and harms have been inequitably distributed. His rights to bodily integrity and life were unjustly violated. From the standpoint of the Golden Rule, probably few if any observers would want to be in the position of Mr. Talbert.

Of course, it is not possible to distribute all risks and benefits equally. Sometimes those who endure the risks imposed by technology may not share the benefits to the same degree. For example, several years ago a proposal was made to build a port for unloading liquefied natural gas in the Gulf of Mexico off the coast of Texas. The natural gas would be shipped to many parts of the United States, so that most citizens of the country would benefit from this project. Only those residents close to the port, however, would share the risk of the ships or storage facilities exploding.[24] Because there is no way to equalize the risk, informed consent and compensation should be important considerations in planning the project. Thus, informed consent, compensation, and equity are closely related considerations in moral evaluation.

Even though laypeople often combine the concept of risk with the concept of acceptable risk, we shall formulate a lay criterion of acceptable risk in the following way:

> An acceptable risk is one in which risk is freely assumed by free and informed consent, or properly compensated, and which is justly distributed.

We have seen that there are often great difficulties in implementing the requirements of free and informed consent, compensation, and justice. Nevertheless, they are crucial considerations from the layperson's—and from the moral—viewpoint.

7.7   The Government Regulator's Approach to Risk

According to William Ruckelshaus, former administrator of the Environmental Protection Agency, regulators face a dilemma regarding risk management.[25] On the one hand, regulators could decide to regulate only when there is a provable connection between a substance and some undesirable effect, such as cancer.

Given the element of uncertainty in many scientific estimations of risk and the difficulties in establishing the levels of exposure to toxic substances at which there is no danger, this option would expose the public to unacceptable risks. On the other hand, regulators could eliminate any possible risk, insofar as this is technologically possible. Choosing this option would result in the expenditure of large sums of money to eliminate minute amounts of any substance that might possibly pose risks to human beings. This would not be cost-effective. Funds might better be spent elsewhere to eliminate much greater threats to public health.

We can illustrate this conflict with the following example. Suppose Sue, a young engineer, is worried about a compound (call it Compound X) that her company is discharging into the air. Compound X is not regulated by the EPA, and she wonders whether its emission is a health hazard for the public. Her boss says he has looked at the epidemiological literature on Compound X, and it does not show any connection between Compound X and health problems.[26] Sue, however, is more sophisticated in her knowledge of the way such connections are established. How are the risks associated with such substances estimated?[27]

Assume that a scientist wants to investigate a causal link between a compound and cancer. In performing these studies (called cohort studies), the scientist would be especially concerned to avoid claiming that there is a link between Compound X and cancer when there is none. In fact, as a scientist, one is going to be more concerned about avoiding claiming there is a link between Compound X and cancer when there is none than in claiming that there is not a link between Compound X and cancer when there is. The reason for this is obvious: to make a claim about a causal relationship that is false is more damaging to one's reputation as a scientist than to fail to make a claim about a causal relationship that is true.

Unfortunately, as Sue is well aware, public-policy interests are not in agreement with scientific scruples at this point. From the standpoint of protecting the public from carcinogens, we are more interested in discovering a causal connection between Compound X and cancer if one in fact exists than in avoiding making a claim about a causal connection that does not exist. Only by adopting this policy can the public be adequately protected from carcinogens. Thus, whereas scientists have a bias against false positives (making a claim for a causal connection when there is not one), those whose highest priority is protecting the public have a bias against false negatives (claiming there is not a causal connection when there is one). Sue knows that there is another reason why scientists place primary emphasis on eliminating false positives. From a statistical standpoint, eliminating false negatives requires a larger sample than eliminating false positives, thus making the cohort studies more expensive. Thus, scientists avoid false positives for reasons based on economics, as well as one based on an interest in preserving their scientific reputations.

Sue is also aware of a third reason why some scientists might favor eliminating false positives: Some scientific studies are privately funded, and many scientists have vested interests in conclusions that give compounds a clean bill of health with regard to harm to the public. Many compounds have considerable value in the marketplace, and industrial firms are not anxious to have them declared a threat to the public health. Favoring the elimination of false positives tends to support the industry position.

Given these facts, Sue knows that scientific studies may not offer the public as much protection against carcinogens and other harmful substances as one might suppose. She is aware that there are value judgments involved in epidemiological estimates of risk, and these value judgments favor the discovery of scientific truth, economic efficiency, and perhaps even the interests of those who sponsor the research rather than protecting the public. She wonders why this should be true, especially if public funding is supporting the scientific investigations. Perhaps, as one writer suggests, there should be two kinds of studies: those devoted to pure science and those that will form the basis of public-policy decisions.[28]

Let us propose the following definition of acceptable risk from the standpoint of the government regulator:

> An acceptable risk is one in which protecting the public from harm has been weighted more heavily than benefiting the public.

7.8   The Engineer's Liability for Risk

We have seen that risk is difficult to estimate and that engineers are often tempted to allow anomalies to accumulate without taking remedial action, and even to expand the scope of acceptable risk to accommodate them. We have also seen that there are different and sometimes incompatible approaches to the definition of acceptable risk, as exhibited by risk experts, laypeople, and government regulators. Another issue that raises ethical and professional concerns for engineers has to do with legal liability for risk. There are at least two issues here. One is that the standards of proof in tort law and science are very different, and this produces an interesting ethical conflict. Another issue is that, in protecting the public from unnecessary risk, engineers may themselves incur legal liabilities. Let us consider each of these issues.

The Standards of Tort Law

Litigation seeking redress from harm most commonly appeals to the law of torts, which deals with injuries to one person caused by another, usually as a result of fault or negligence of the injuring party.[29] Many of the most famous legal cases involving claims of harm from technology have been brought under the law of torts. The litigation involving harm from asbestos is one example. In 1973 the estate of Clarence Borel, who began working as an industrial insulation worker in 1936, brought suit against Fiberboard Paper Products Corporation:

> During his career he was employed at numerous places usually in Texas, until disabled from the disease of asbestosis in 1969. Borel's employment necessarily exposed him to heavy concentrations of asbestos generated by insulation materials. In a pretrial deposition Borel testified that at the end of the day working with insu-

lation materials containing asbestos his clothes were usually so dusty that he could barely pick them up without shaking them. Borel stated, "You just move them a little bit and there is going to be dust, and I blowed this dust out of my nostrils by the handfuls by the end of the day. I even used Mentholatum in my nostrils to keep some of the dust from going down my throat, but it is impossible to get rid of all of it. Even your clothes just stay dusty continuously, unless you blow it off with an air hose." In 1964 doctors examined Borel in connection with an insurance policy and informed him that x-rays of his lungs were cloudy. The doctor told Borel that the cause could be his occupation as an installation worker and advised him to avoid asbestos dust as much as he possibly could. On January 19, 1969, Borel was hospitalized and a lung biopsy performed. Borel's condition was diagnosed as pulmonary asbestosis. Since the disease was considered irreversible Borel was sent home . . . [His] condition gradually worsened during the remainder of 1969. On February 11, 1970 [he] underwent surgery for the removal of his right lung. The examining doctors determined that Borel had a form of lung cancer known as mesothelioma, which had been caused by asbestos. As a result of these diseases, Borel later died before the district case reached the trial stage.[30]

The federal district court in Texas decided in favor of the estate of Mr. Borel, and the Fifth Circuit Court of Appeals upheld the decision.

The standard of proof in tort law is the preponderance of evidence, meaning that there is more and better evidence in favor of the plaintiff than the defendant. The plaintiff must show

(1) that the defendant violated a legal duty imposed by the tort law, (2) that the plaintiff suffered injuries compensable in the tort law, (3) that the defendant's violation of legal duty caused the plaintiff's injuries and (4) that the defendant's violation of legal duty was the proximate cause of the plaintiff's injuries.[31]

The standard of proof that a given substance was the proximate cause of a harm is less stringent than that which would be demanded by a scientist, who might well call for 95 percent certainty. It is also less stringent than the standard of evidence in criminal proceedings, which calls for proof beyond reasonable doubt.

As an illustration of this lower standard of evidence, consider the case of *Rubanick v. Witco Chemical Corporation and Monsanto Co.*[32] The plaintiff's sole expert witness, a retired cancer researcher at New York's Sloan-Kettering Cancer Center, testified that the deceased person's cancer was caused by exposure to polychlorinated biphenyls (PCBs). He based his opinion on:

(1) the low incidence of cancer in males under 30 (the deceased person was 29), (2) the decedent's good dietary and nonsmoking habits and the absence of familial genetic predisposition to cancer, (3) 5 of 105 other Witco workers who developed some kind of cancer during the same period, (4) a large body of evidence showing that PCB's cause cancer in laboratory animals, and (5) support in the scientific literature that PCB's cause cancer in human beings.[33]

The court did not require the expert to support his opinion by epidemiological studies, merely that he demonstrate   the appropriate education, knowledge, training, and experience in the specific field of science and an appropriate factual basis for his opinion.[34] Other better known cases, such as that of Richard Ferebee, who alleged that he suffered lung damage as a result of spraying the herbicide paraquat, also accepted standards of evidence for causal claims that would not have been acceptable for research purposes.[35]

Some courts, however, have begun to impose higher standards of evidence for recovery of damages through tort, standards that are similar to those used in science.[36] In the Agent Orange cases, Judge Jack B. Weinstein argued that epidemiological studies were the only useful studies having any bearing on causation, and that by this standard no plaintiff had been able to make a case. Bert Black, a legal commentator, has taken a similar view. He believes that the courts (that is, judges) should actively scrutinize the arguments of expert witnesses, demanding that they be supported by peer-reviewed scientific studies or at least have solid scientific backing. In some cases, he believes, they should even overrule juries who have made judgments not based on scientific standards of evidence.[37]

Even though this view represents a departure from the normal rules of evidence in tort law, it might in some cases be fairer to the defendants; for some decisions in favor of plaintiffs may not be based on valid proof of responsibility for harm. The disadvantage is also equally obvious. By requiring higher standards of proof, the courts place burdens of evidence on plaintiffs that they often cannot meet. In many cases, scientific knowledge is simply not adequate to determine causal relationships, and this would work to the disadvantage of the plaintiffs. There are also problems with encouraging judges to take such an activist role in legal proceedings.

The major ethical question, however, is whether we should be more concerned with protecting the rights of plaintiffs who may have been unjustly harmed or with promoting economic efficiency and protecting defendants against unjust charges of harm.

Protecting Engineers from Liability

The apparent ease with which proximate cause can be established in tort law may suggest that the courts impose a stringent standard of acceptable risk. But other aspects of the law afford the public less protection than it deserves. For example, the threat of legal liability can inhibit engineers from adequately protecting the public from risk. Engineers in private practice may face especially difficult considerations regarding liability and risk and in some cases, may need increased protection from liability.

Consider, for example, the safety issues in excavating for foundations, pipelines, and sewers.[38] A deep, steep-sided trench is inherently unstable. Sooner or later the sidewalls will collapse. The length of time that trench walls will stand before collapsing depends on a number of factors, including the length and width of the cut, weather conditions, moisture in the soil, composition of the soil, and how the trench was excavated. People who work in deep trenches are subjected to considerable risk, and hundreds of laborers are injured or killed each year when the walls collapse.

To reduce the risk, construction engineers can specify the use of trench boxes in their designs. A trench box is a long box with an upside-down-U-shaped cross section that is inserted inside the trench to protect the laborers. As long as workers remain inside the trench boxes, their risk of death or injury is greatly reduced. Unfortunately, the use of trench boxes considerably increases the expense and time involved in construction projects. The boxes must be purchased or rented, and then they must be moved as excavation proceeds, slowing construction work and adding further to the expense.

Engineers are placed in an awkward position with respect to the use of trench boxes, especially where the boxes are not required by building codes. If they do not specify the use of the boxes, they may be contributing to a situation that subjects workers to a very high risk of death and injury. If they do specify the use of boxes, they may be incurring liability in case of an accident. With situations such as this in mind, the National Society of Professional Engineers has been actively lobbying the U.S. Congress to pass a law that specifically excludes engineers from liability for accidents where construction safety measures are specified by engineers but then are either not used or used improperly by others. This would enable engineers to more effectively protect the safety of workers. Unfortunately, the proposals have never become law.

The problem with trench boxes illustrates a more general issue. If engineers were free to specify safety measures without being held liable for their neglect or improper use, they could more easily fulfill one aspect of their responsibility to protect the safety of the public.

7.9   Becoming a Responsible Engineer Regarding Risk

The development of new technology is intimately connected with risk. The obligation of engineers is to be ethically responsible with regard to risk. The first step in the process of becoming ethically responsible about risk is to be aware of the fact that risk is often difficult to estimate and can be increased in ways that may be subtle and treacherous. The second step is to be aware that there are different approaches to the determination of acceptable risk. In particular, engineers have a strong bias toward quantification in their approach to risk, which may make them insufficiently sensitive to the concerns of the lay public and even the government regulator. The third step is to be aware of the legal liabilities regarding risk.

We shall conclude with an attempt to formulate a Principle of Acceptable Risk. To formulate this principle, let us consider further some of the legal debate about risk.

The law seems to be of two minds about risk and benefit. On the one hand, some laws make no attempt to balance the two. The Chemical Food Additives Amendments to the Food, Drug and Cosmetics Act, enacted in 1958, require that a chemical "deemed to be unsafe" not be added to food unless it can be "safely used."[39] *Safe use* was defined by the Senate Committee on Labor and Public Welfare as meaning that "no harm will result" from its addition to food.[40] The well-known Delaney Amendment also prohibits the addition to food of any chemical known to cause cancer when ingested by animals.[41]

On the other hand, there is often an attempt to strike a balance between the welfare of the public and the rights of individuals. The Toxic Substances Control Act of 1976 (TOSCA) authorizes the EPA to regulate any chemical upon a finding of "unreasonable risk of injury to health or the environment."[42] But it is only "unreasonable risk" that triggers regulation, so some degree of risk is clearly tolerated. The report of the House Commerce Committee defines "unreasonable risk" for TOSCA purposes as:

> balancing the probabilities that harm will occur and the magnitude and severity of that harm against the effect of proposed regulatory action on the availability to society of the benefits of the substance or mixture, taking into account the availability of substitutes for the substance or mixture which do not require regulation, and other adverse effects which such proposed action may have on society.

Having said this, the report goes on to say that "a formal benefit-cost analysis under which monetary value is assigned to the risks . . . and to the costs of society" is not required.

The Atomic Energy Act of 1954 continually refers to the "health and safety of the public" but makes little attempt to define these terms.[43] The NRC rules, however, use the expression "without undue risk" and seem to suggest again a balancing of risks and benefits.[44] In the words of one legal commentator, in practice, especially in the earlier years, "the acceptability of risk was measured largely in terms of the extent to which industry was capable of reducing the risk without jeopardizing an economic and financial environment conducive to continuing development of the technology."[45] Again, we have an attempt to balance protection of individuals and promotion of the public welfare.

Sometimes the conflict between these two approaches is evident in a single debate. In the famous benzene case discussed in Chapter 2, for example, OSHA took an essentially respect for persons standpoint, arguing that the burden of proof should be on industry to prove that a given level of exposure to benzene was not carcinogenic. In its rebuke of OSHA, the Supreme Court argued that, in light of the evidence that present standards did not lead to harm to workers, risk must be balanced against benefits in evaluating more stringent standards and that the burden of proof was on OSHA to show that the more stringent standards were justified.[46]

Given these considerations, we can construct a more general Principle of Acceptable Risk, which may provide some guidance in determining when a risk is within the bounds of moral permissibility:

> People should be protected from the harmful effects of technology, especially when the harms are not consented to or when they are unjustly distributed, except that this protection must sometimes be balanced against (1) the need to preserve great and irreplaceable benefits and (2) the limitations on our ability to obtain informed consent.

The principle does not offer an algorithm that can be applied mechanically to situations involving risk. Many issues arise in its use; each use must be considered on its own merits. We can enumerate some of the issues that arise in applying the principle.

First, we must define what we mean by "protecting" people from harm. This cannot mean that people are assured that a form of technology is free from risk. At best, "protection" can only be formulated in terms of probabilities of harm, and we have seen that even these are subject to considerable error.

Second, many disputes can arise as to what constitutes a harm. Consider the case at the beginning of this chapter. Suppose the only effect of the fumes is the bad smell. Is having to breathe a foul odor all day long a harm? What about workers in a brewery or sewage disposal plant? Here the foul odors cannot be eliminated, so the question of what harms should be eliminated cannot be divorced from the question of whether the harms can be eliminated without at the same time eliminating other goods.

Third, the determination of what constitutes a great and irreplaceable benefit must be made in the context of particular situations. A food additive that makes the colors of frozen vegetables more intense is not a great and irreplaceable benefit. If an additive were found to be a powerful carcinogen, it should be eliminated. On the other hand, most people value automobiles highly, and they would probably not want them to be eliminated, despite the possibility of death and injury from automobile accidents.

Fourth, we have already pointed out the problems that arise in determining informed consent and the limitations in obtaining informed consent in many situations. From the standpoint of the ethics of respect for persons, informed consent is a consideration of first importance. It is often difficult to interpret and apply, however.

Fifth, the criterion of unjust distribution of harm is also difficult to apply. Some harms associated with risk are probably unjustly distributed. For example, the risks associated with proximity to a toxic waste disposal area that is not well constructed or monitored are unjustly distributed. The risks associated with coal mining might also be considered to be unjustly distributed, but coal may also be considered a great and irreplaceable benefit. So the requirement to reduce risk in the coal industry might be that the risks of coal mining should be reduced as much as possible without destroying the coal industry. This might require raising the price of coal enough to make coal mining safer and more economically rewarding.

Sixth, an acceptable risk at a given point in time may not be an acceptable risk at another point in time. Engineers' responsibility to protect the health and safety of the public requires them to reduce risk when this can be done as a result of technological innovation. As new risk-reducing technology becomes available, the responsibility of engineers to reduce risk changes.

7.10   Chapter Summary

Engineering codes require engineers to hold paramount the safety, health, and welfare of the public. This implies that engineers must protect the public from unacceptable risk. The implementation of this requirement, however, presents many problems for the engineer. It is not even easy to estimate risk, as the limitations of fault trees and event trees illustrate.

Students of risk sometimes argue that there are two characteristics of high-risk technologies that make them especially susceptible to accidents, so that we can speak of "normal accidents." These two features are the "tight coupling" and "complex interactions" of the parts of a technological system. Engineers can also expose the public to unnecessary risk by allowing increasing numbers of deviancies from proper standards of safety and acceptable risk. The *Challenger* disaster illustrates this departure from good engineering.

In assessing and managing risk with regard to technology, the engineer should be aware that there are at least three different approaches to risk. One approach is that of the risk expert. Experts define risk as the product of the probability and the magnitude of harm. They define an acceptable risk in broadly utilitarian terms, where the risk must at least equal the benefit.

Laypeople often do not distinguish between the definition of risk and the concept of acceptable risk. They are more apt to include such factors as the just distribution of risk, whether or not risk is voluntarily assumed, and whether or not risk could lead to a catastrophe in their conception of risk itself. In any case, their conception of acceptable risk includes these kinds of nonutilitarian considerations.

Government regulators are charged with protecting the public from unacceptable risk. Thus, they are more concerned with protecting the public from harm than in benefiting the public.

Engineers should also be aware of the ethical and professional issues regarding risk that are raised in the law. One of the issues is that the standards of proof in tort law are different from the standards of proof in science. The standard of proof in tort law is the preponderance of evidence, meaning that there is more and better evidence in favor of the plaintiff than the defendant. This is a much lower standard of proof than would be demanded in science. Some courts have begun to impose the higher standards of proof required in science. The lower standard gives the advantage to plaintiffs, the higher standard gives the advantage to defendants. This difference raises an important public-policy issue as to where the greater advantage should lie. Another issue raised by the law is the need of engineers to protect themselves from unfair liability, when they attempt to protect the public from undue risk.

Balancing the protection of individuals against the promotion of the public welfare poses one of the most difficult problems for those responsible for managing risk. A Principle of Acceptable Risk summarizes these considerations by requiring that people be protected from the harmful effects of technology, while considering the need to preserve great and irreplaceable benefits and the limitations on our ability to obtain informed consent.

 CASES TO CONSIDER

Case 5   Cadillac Chips
Case 7   Containers

Case 11	Dissent or Not Dissent?*
Case 30	Microwaves
Case 50	Walkway Disaster
Case 57	XYZ Hose

NOTES

1. See *Teaching Engineering Ethics: A Case Study Approach,* Michael S. Pritchard, ed., Center for the Study of Ethics in Society, Western Michigan University, NSF Report on Grant DIR-820837, June 15, 1992, pp. 190–198.

2. Carl F. Cranor, *Regulating Toxic Substances: A Philosophy of Science and the Law* (New York: Oxford University Press, 1993), p. 11.

3. Charles Perrow, *Normal Accidents: Living with High-Risk Technologies* (New York: Basic Books, 1984), p. 3.

4. See the *New York Times,* October 15, 1962 for an account of this tragic event. The engineering details are cited from an unpublished report by R. C. King, H. Margolin, and M. J. Rabins to the City of New York Building Commission on the causes of the accident.

5. Diane Vaughn, *The Challenger Launch Decision* (Chicago: The University of Chicago Press, 1996), pp. 409–422.

6. See the Presidential Commission on the Space Shuttle *Challenger* Accident, Report to the President by the Presidential Commission on the Space Shuttle *Challenger* Accident (Washington D.C.: Government Printing Office, 1986), 1:120. Quoted in Vaughn, p. 77.

7. See Vaughn, pp. 110–111. The following account is taken from Vaughn and from personal conversations with Roger Boisjoly. The account should be attributed to the authors, however, rather than to Diane Vaughn or Roger Boisjoly.

8. See Vaughn, pp. 121 ff.

9. Vaughn, pp. 141 ff.

10. Vaughn, pp. 153 ff.

11. William W. Lowrance, "The Nature of Risk," in Richard C. Schwing and Walter A. Albers, Jr., Eds., *Societal Risk Assessment: How Safe Is Safe Enough?* (New York: Plenum Press, 1980), p. 6.

12. The National Public Radio story was aired on "Morning Edition," December 3, 1992. This account is taken from the *Newsletter* of the Center for Biotechnology Policy and Ethics, Texas A&M University, 2, no. 1 (January 1, 1993), p. 1.

13. For a more extended treatment of this issue, see the discussion in Chapter 6.

14. The increased pay people will demand for more risky jobs is probably also a function of the availability of jobs. It seems reasonable to assume that if fewer jobs were available, people would be more likely to take more risky jobs, even if the pay were not higher. This consideration must be taken into account in these calculations.

15. For a discussion of the procedures used for placing a value on human life and the widely varying results, see Peter Dorman, *Markets and Morality* (Cambridge, England: Cambridge University Press, 1996), pp. 51–106.

16. Chauncey Starr, "Social Benefits Versus Technological Risk," *Science, 165* (September 19, 1969), 1232–1238. Reprinted in Theodore S. Glickman and Michael Gough, *Readings in Risk* (Washington, D.C.: Resources for the Future), pp. 183–193.

17. Paul Slovic, Baruch Fischhoff, and Sarah Lichtenstein, "Rating the Risks," *Environment, 21,* no. 3 (April 1969), 14–20, 36–39. Reprinted in Glickman, pp. 61–74.

18. Starr, 183–193.

19. Starr, 183–193.

20. D. Litai, "A Risk Comparison Methodology for the Assessment of Acceptable Risk," Ph.D. Dissertation, Massachusetts Institute of Technology, Cambridge, Mass., 1980.

---

* Includes an analysis of the case

21. *Newsletter* of the Center for Biotechnology Policy and Ethics, Texas A&M University, p. 1.

22. John Rawls, *A Theory of Justice* (Cambridge, Mass.: Harvard University Press, 1971), p. 3.

23. From the *Charlotte* (N.C.) *Observer*, February 10, 1980. Quoted in Carl F. Cranor, *Regulating Toxic Substances*, p. 152.

24. Ralph L. Keeney, Ram B. Kulkarni, and Keshavan Nair, "Assessing the Risks of an LGN Terminal" in Glickman pp. 207–217.

25. See William D. Ruckelshaus, "Risk, Science, and Democracy," *Issues in Science and Technology, 1*, no. 3 (Spring 1985), 19–38. Reprinted in Glickman, pp. 105–118.

26. Epidemiology is the study of the distribution of disease in human populations and the factors that causally influence this distribution.

27. See Carl F. Cranor, "Some Moral Issues in Risk Assessment," *Ethics, 101* (October 1990), 123–143. See also Cranor's *Regulating Toxic Substances*, pp. 12–48.

28. Cranor, *Regulating Toxic Substances*, pp. 139–143.

29. Harold P. Green, "The Role of Law in Determining Acceptability of Risk," in *Societal Risk Assessment: How Safe Is Safe Enough?* (New York: Plenum Press 1980), pp. 255–269.

30. *Boral v. Fiberboard Paper Products Corp. et al.*, 493 F.2d (1973) at 1076, 1083. Quoted in Cranor, p. 52.

31. Cranor, *Regulating Toxic Substances*, p. 58.

32. 576A.2d4 (N.J. Super. Ct. A.D. 1990) at 15 (concurring opinion).

33. Cranor, *Regulating Toxic Substances*, p. 81. Summarized from "New Jersey Supreme Court Applies Broader Test for Admitting Expert Testimony in Toxic Case," *Environmental Health Letter* 30 (August 27, 1991): 176.

34. Ibid., 176.

35. *Ferebee v. Chevron Chemical Co.*, 736 F.2d 11529 (D.C. Cir. 1984).

36. Bert Black, "Evolving Legal Standards for the Admissibility of Scientific Evidence," *Science, 239* (1987), 1510–1512.

37. Bert Black, "A Unified Theory of Scientific Evidence," *Fordham Law Review, 55*: 595–692.

38. See R. W. Flumerfelt, C. E. Harris, Jr., M. J. Rabins, and C. H. Samson, Jr., "Introducing Ethics Case Studies into Required Undergraduate Engineering Courses, Final Report to the NSF on Grant DIR-9012252," November 1992, pp. 262–285.

39. Public Law No. 85–929, 72 Stat. 784 (1958).

40. Senate Report No. 85–2422, 85th Congress, 2d Session (1958).

41. 21 United States Code, sect. 348 (A)(1976).

42. Public Law No. 94–469, 90 Stat. 2003 (1976). The same criterion of "unreasonable risk" is found in the Flammable Fabrics Act. See Public Law No. 90–189, Stat. 568 (1967).

43. Public Law No. 83–703, 68 Stat. 919 (1954), 42 United States Code 2011, et. seq. (1976).

44. 10 CFR 50.35 (a)(4).

45. Green, p. 265.

46. *Industrial Union Department, AFL-CIO v. American Petroleum Institute et al.*, 448 U.S. 607 (1980).

Part Three

Special Topics

Photo by Robert Adamenko

8   *Engineers as Employees*
9   *Engineers and the Environment*
10   *International Engineering Professionalism*
11   *Engineering Professionalism and Ethics: Issues Old and New*

Chapter 8

Engineers as Employees

In the mid-1970s the New York City Police Department had in operation an on-line computerized police car dispatching system called SPRINT. Upon receiving a telephoned request for police assistance, a dispatcher would enter the address into a computer, and the computer would respond within seconds by displaying the location of the nearest patrol car. By cutting the response time to emergency calls, the SPRINT system probably saved lives.

In 1977 another system, PROMIS, was being considered by the New York City prosecutors. It would use the same host computer as SPRINT. The PROMIS system would provide names and addresses of witnesses, hearing dates, the probation status of defendants, and other information that would assist the prosecutors or arresting officers who wanted to check on the current status of apprehended perpetrators. This project was being managed by the Criminal Justice Coordinating Council, or Circle Project, a committee of high-level city officials that included the deputy mayor for criminal justice, the police commissioner, and as chairman, Manhattan District Attorney Robert Morgenthau.

The committee employed a computer specialist as project director who in turn hired Virginia Edgerton, an experienced system analyst, as senior information scientist to work under his supervision. Soon after being employed, Edgerton expressed concern to the project director about the possible effect on the response time of SPRINT of loading the computer with an additional task, but he instructed her to drop the matter. Edgerton then sought advice from her professional society, the Institute of Electrical and Electronics Engineers (IEEE). After an electrical engineering professor at Columbia University agreed that her concerns merited further study, she sent a memorandum to the project director requesting a study of the overload problem. He rejected the memorandum out of hand, and Edgerton soon thereafter sent copies of the memorandum with a covering letter to the members of the Circle Committee. Immediately following this, Edgerton was discharged by the project director on the ground that she had, by communicating directly with the committee members, violated his orders. He also stated that the issues she had raised were in fact under continuing discussion with the police department computer staff, although he gave no documentation to support this claim.

The case was then investigated by the Working Group on Ethics and Employment Practices of the Committee on the Social Implications of Technology (CSIT) of the IEEE, and subsequently by the newly formed IEEE Member Conduct Committee. Both groups agreed that Virginia Edgerton's actions were fully justified. In 1979 she received the second IEEE-CSIT Award for Outstanding Service in the Public Interest. After her discharge, Edgerton formed a small company selling data processing services. [1]

8.1   Introduction

Virginia Edgerton's experience shows how a professional's concern for doing the right thing may place her in opposition to her employer. Because more than 90 percent of all engineers are employees, and the perspectives of engineers and managers sometimes differ, this case has many parallels in the engineering profession. It is by no means unique to engineering, however. More and more physicians are being employed by health maintenance organizations and other corporate entities, and many lawyers work for corporations and large legal firms. Many certified public accountants work for accounting firms and corporations, and the accounting profession also includes management accountants, who are usually employees of large corporations. Most architects are employees of architectural firms. The issue of professional employee rights is destined to become more common in all professional ranks.

We shall begin with a brief look at what the engineering codes say about employer-employee relationships. Then, we shall consider the changing legal status of employee rights. Next, we shall examine several facets of the engineer-manager relationship, a central issue in the debate over professional employee rights for engineers. Then, we shall develop some criteria for determining when decisions should be made by managers and when they should be made by ordinary engineers, applying the criteria to the decision to launch the *Challenger*. Because the appeal to loyalty to the organization is usually a part of the criticism of dissenting engineers, we shall examine the concept of organizational loyalty. Next, we shall consider the issue of professional employee dissent and how it can be exercised responsibly. Finally, we shall look at some ways that organizations can establish procedures for dealing with professional employee dissent in a positive and constructive way.

8.2   The Codes and Employer-Employee Relationships

The engineering codes provide some general guidelines for employer-employee relationships, but they also show that there are many possibilities for conflict and line-drawing issues in this area. We can use the code of the **National Society for**

Professional Engineers (NSPE) as an example. On the one hand, the code provides a clear basis for loyalty to the employer. Canon 4 states, "Engineers shall act in professional matters for each employer or client as faithful agents or trustees." On the other hand, the same code provides directives that could easily lead to conflict problems. Here are several examples.

Canon 1 requires engineers to "hold paramount the safety, health and welfare of the public in the performance of their professional duties." This can conflict with Canon 4, as it did in Virginia Edgerton's experience. The health, safety, and welfare of the public are to be placed first, but there are many situations in which it may not be clear whether the obligations to the public are weighty enough to override the obligations to the employer. Canon 2 requires engineers to "perform services only in the areas of their competence," but a manager can ask an engineer to take a job in an area where she believes her qualifications are marginal at best. Canon 3 requires engineers to "issue public statements only in an objective and truthful manner," but Roger Boisjoly reported that his boss reminded him that in his testimony before Congress after the *Challenger* disaster he should not unnecessarily malign the company. Company officials had reprimanded him for revealing that Morton Thiokol had not honored his requests for more tests on possible O-ring failures.[2]

Another source of conflict and line-drawing issues is the guidelines regarding confidentiality. In its "Professional Obligations" section, the NSPE code instructs engineers not to "disclose confidential information concerning the business affairs or technical processes of any present or former client or employer without his consent." Yet employers sometimes ask engineers to work on projects where information gained from a former employer can be used to good advantage. (This has already been discussed in Chapter 6, which addresses honesty and integrity in engineering practice.)

Conceptual issues related to employer-employee relationships are also produced by the codes. The NSPE code requires engineers to protect the "public," but it does not say who counts as the public. In the *Challenger* disaster a good case can be made for including the astronauts in the category of the "public," at least with respect to the O-ring problem. In any case, the terms must be defined. Engineers are also required to act as "faithful agents or trustees" for their employers, but these terms are undefined in the codes. Although they are defined in the law, the definitions may not always be adequate for ethical analysis. These terms are closely related to the concept of "loyalty" as it is commonly used, and we shall examine that term in more detail later.

Application issues also arise in interpreting the code. No matter how carefully we define such terms as "public" or "faithful agents or trustees," for example, their application to real-world examples will often be problematic. Even if we define "public" as anyone who is ignorant of the dangers to which they are subjected by engineering work, the question arises as to *how* ignorant people must be before engineers have a professional obligation to protect them. Even if we have defined the terms "faithful agent and trustee" as carefully as we can, we may still have problems determining whether a particular action conforms to the requirements of the code in this area.

This brief discussion is sufficient to show that the codes do not provide clear and easy answers to all of the issues that professional engineers face in relating to their employers, although they do provide clear answers to many questions. In this chapter, we shall attempt to interpret and extend the thinking embodied in the codes as it applies to employer-employee relationships. Legalities form an important background for this discussion, so it will be helpful to begin with a survey of the recent changes in the law and court decisions regarding employee rights.

8.3   The Changing Legal Status of Employee Rights

The legal status of employee rights is undergoing modification both in the courts and in statutory law. In the courts, the modification is primarily the result of the increasing importance of the so-called public-policy exception. In statutory law, the primary innovation is laws to protect whistle-blowers.

The Public-Policy Exception

Traditionally, American law has been governed by the common law doctrine of "employment at will." According to this doctrine, in the absence of a contract, an employer can discharge an employee at any time and for virtually any reason.[3] More recently, the courts have modified the at-will employment doctrine by what has come to be known as the public-policy exception. As several courts have pointed out, the public-policy exception to at-will employment is still in the process of evolution. In general, however, the public-policy exception allows a defense against employers when employees are acting to defend vital public interests or to claim uncontroversial rights as a citizen.[4]

Of the 47 jurisdictions that have ruled on the public-policy exception, 37 have recognized some form of legal cause of action for wrongful or retaliatory discharge, while only 9 have declined to recognize such a claim.[5] In general, however, most courts interpret the public-policy exception rather narrowly, confining it to such areas as an employee's refusing to break a law, performing an important public obligation (such as serving on a jury), and exercising a clear legal right (such as filing for unemployment compensation or exercising constitutional rights to free speech). Often, acting to protect the public from a clear threat to health or safety is also taken by the courts to be covered by the public-policy exception. The following limits on the public-policy exception as it is now interpreted by the courts are important.

First, there is still no clear distinction between dismissals that violate public policy and those that affect only the "private" interests of employees.[6] The courts, for example, have generally said that the public-policy exception should not be used to protect employees who have been asked to violate their conscience, arguing that the interests of the public must be involved for the public-policy exception to apply.

Second, the courts have usually declined to give the employee protection where there is a mere difference in judgment between employer and employee.

Third, many courts have distinguished between codes promulgated by "private" organizations, such as professional societies, and codes promulgated by administrative and judicial bodies, such as state regulatory boards.[7] Courts have in most cases declined to acknowledge "private" codes as sources of public policy. This is especially important to engineers, because it suggests that engineers who want to use the public-policy defense should appeal to the codes of their state regulatory boards, not the codes of their professional societies. It stands to reason that engineers' appeals to such codes would be more likely to be successful if they were registered professional engineers, because otherwise they would not be subject to those codes. This is one reason why engineers should obtain the P.E. license.

Fourth, most courts have appealed to the need to "balance" the interests of the public against those of the employer. This "balancing" often appears to be highly subjective, and greater weight usually seems to be given to the employer's interests, unless there has been a *clear* and *explicit* violation of whatever "source" of public policy the courts consider appropriate.

Statutory Protection

In addition to the judicial modification of at-will employment, dissenting employees have also received some statutory protection, primarily through whistle-blower laws. In April 1981, Michigan became the first state to pass a "Whistle Blowers Protection Act." According to the *Wall Street Journal*, the provisions were as follows:

> Any employee in private industry fired or disciplined for reporting alleged violations of federal, state or local law to public authorities can now bring an action in state court for unjust reprisal. If the employer cannot show that treatment of the employee was based on proper personnel standards or valid business reasons, the court can award back pay, reinstatement to the job, costs of litigation and attorney's fees. The employer can also be fined up to $500. . . . Every employer in Michigan must post a notice of this new law in the workplace.[8]

New Jersey's Conscientious Employee Protection Act (CEPA) forbids termination for conduct undertaken for the sake of compliance with "a clear mandate of public policy concerning the public health, safety or welfare."[9]

Protection of a somewhat different type is provided by the Illinois Right of Conscience Act, passed in 1985. The act provides that it is the public policy of the state "to respect and protect the right of conscience" of all persons or entities providing medical services or care and "to prohibit all forms of discrimination, disqualification, coercion, disability or imposition or liability upon such persons or entities by reason of their refusing to act contrary to their conscience or conscientious convictions in refusing to obtain, receive, accept or deliver medical services and medical care."[10] Note that this law protects only medical professionals.

The attempt to limit management autonomy will no doubt continue. Many people believe this is justified and that employees, particularly professional employees, must be granted more rights in the workplace. But there are arguments in favor of protecting management autonomy as well. We now begin an examination of the moral issues raised by the disagreements professionals can have with their employers.

8.4   The Manager-Engineer Relationship

Differences in Perspective Between Managers and Engineers

Many ethical and professional issues faced by engineers involve a conflict between themselves and managers. The most serious conflict is over decision-making prerogatives. What decisions are appropriately made by engineers, and what decisions are appropriately made by managers? Given their positions in the organizational structure, managers usually have the authority to overrule the decisions of engineers. The question we are raising here is an ethical question: when *should* managers (or at least management considerations) prevail and when *should* engineers (or at least engineering considerations) prevail in the decision-making process?

Management theorist Joseph Raelin, reflecting the position of many students of management, says, "There is a natural conflict between management and professionals because of their differences in educational background, socialization, values, vocational interests, work habits and outlook."[11] We can be somewhat more precise about the areas of conflict between engineers and managers.

First, although engineers may not always maintain as much identity with their wider professional community as some other professionals (such as research scientists), engineers do often experience a conflict in loyalties.[12] Like other professionals, they have obligations to both their profession and their employers. Most engineers want to be loyal employees who are concerned about the financial well-being of their firms and who carry out instructions from their superiors without protest. In the words of many engineering codes, they want to be "faithful agents" of their employers. At the same time, as engineers they are also obligated to hold paramount the health, safety, and welfare of the public. This obligation requires engineers to insist on high standards of quality and (especially) safety.[13]

Second, many managers are not engineers and do not have engineering expertise, so communication is often difficult. Engineers sometimes complain that they have to use oversimplified language in explaining technical matters to managers and that their managers do not really understand the engineering issues.

Third, many engineers who are not managers aspire to the management role in the future, where the financial rewards and prestige are perceived to be greater. Thus, many engineers who do not yet occupy the dual roles of engineer and manager probably expect to do so at some time in their careers.

This conflict can be internalized within the same person, because many engineers have roles as both engineers and managers. For example, Robert Lund, vice president for engineering at Morton Thiokol at the time of the *Challenger* disaster, was both an engineer and a manager. As we saw in Chapter 1, prior to the disaster, Lund was even directed by his superior to take the managerial rather than the engineering perspective.

Given the complexity of the relationship between engineers and managers and the likelihood of conflict, it would be helpful if we could find a way to distinguish the type of situation in which engineering considerations should predominate from the type of situation in which management considerations should prevail. Of course agreement and consensus between engineers and managers is always preferable to a more adversarial relationship. But it is still useful to know, when mutual agreement is impossible, which perspective should predominate. We can begin by isolating some characteristics of the engineering and management perspectives.

Two Empirical Studies

Investigators do not always agree about the nature of the engineer-manager relationship. Some investigators have found a yawning gap between the perspectives of managers and professionals, including engineers. According to Robert Jackall, this gap is especially prominent where ethical issues are concerned. In his study of managers in several large American corporations, Jackall found that large organizations place a premium on "functional rationality," which is a "pragmatic habit of mind that seeks specific goals."[14] Jackall found that the managers and firms he studied had several characteristics that were not conducive to respecting the moral commitments of conscientious professionals.

First, the organizational ethos does not allow genuine moral commitments to play a part in the decisions of corporate managers, especially highly placed ones. A person may have whatever private moral beliefs she chooses, as long as these beliefs do not influence behavior in the workplace. She must learn to separate individual conscience from corporate action. Managers, according to Jackall, prefer to think in terms of trade-offs between moral principles on the one hand and expediency on the other. What we might think of as genuine moral considerations play very little part in managerial decisions, according to Jackall. Faulty products are bad because they will ultimately harm the company's public image, and environmental spoilage is bad for business or will ultimately affect managers themselves, who are also consumers.

This attitude is in contrast to that of White, an employee who, according to Jackall, was concerned with a problem of excessive sound in his plant. White defined the issue of possible harm to employees as a moral concern instead of approaching it pragmatically. In another anecdote, Jackall recounted the story of Brady, an accountant who found financial irregularities that were traced to the CEO. Whereas Brady saw the issue as a moral one, managers did not. In discussing the case, they held that Brady should have kept his mouth shut and dropped the matter. After all, the violations were small relative to the size of the corporation.[15]

Second, loyalty to one's peers and superiors is the primary virtue for managers. The successful manager is the team player, the person who can accept a challenge and get the job done in a way that reflects favorably upon himself and others.[16]

Third, lines of responsibility are deliberately blurred to protect oneself, one's peers, and one's superiors. Details are pushed down and credit is pushed up. Actions are separated from consequences insofar as it is possible, so that responsibility can be avoided. In making difficult and controversial decisions, a successful manager will always get as many people involved as possible, so he can point his finger at others if things go wrong. He should also avoid putting things in writing to avoid being held responsible. Protecting and covering for one's boss, one's peers, and oneself supersedes all other considerations.

According to this account of managerial decision making, professionals' scruples have no place. In such an atmosphere a principled professional would often appear to have no alternative to organizational disobedience. Such was the case with Joe Wilson, an engineer who found a problem with a crane that he believed involved public health and safety. Wilson wrote a memo to his boss, who replied that he did not need such a memo from Wilson, and that the memo was not constructive. After Wilson was fired and went public, a *New York Times* investigation cited a corporate official's comment that Wilson was someone who "was not a team player."[17]

If engineers typically work in an organizational environment like the one Jackall described, their professional and ethical concerns will have little chance of being accorded respect. There is, however, a more constructive aspect to Jackall's study. He does suggest some characteristics of managerial decision making that are useful in analyzing the manager-engineer relationship.

1. Jackall's study implies that managers have a strong (probably overriding) concern for the well-being of the organization. Well-being is measured primarily in financial terms, but it also includes a good public image and relatively conflict-free operation.

2. Managers have few if any professional loyalties that transcend their perceived obligations to the organization.

3. The managerial decision-making process involves making trade-offs among the relevant considerations. Ethical considerations are only one type of consideration. Furthermore, if we are to believe Jackall, managers tend not to take ethical considerations seriously, unless they can be translated into factors affecting the well-being (for example, the public image) of the firm.

Another empirical study, funded by the Hitachi Foundation, examined the engineer-manager relationship in ten companies and arrived at a less discouraging picture.

First, the distinction between engineers and managers is not always clear in large organizations. Whereas employees in small companies could usually distinguish between engineers and managers, employees in large companies often could not do so easily. Two, three, or even four levels of organization might stand between employees regarded as "just bench engineers" and those regarded as "just managers." Sometimes some "group leaders" (those who supervise the work of 4 to 6 bench engineers) in an organization identified themselves as managers whereas others in the same organization identified themselves as "just engineers."[18]

Second, despite the fact that the interface between engineering and management is not always clear in the workplace, the report did find a difference in perspective between engineers and managers. The engineers and managers interviewed were "virtually unanimous in the way they distinguished the engineer's perspective from the manager's." They agreed that engineers had to change their perspective to become good managers. This change involved three elements:

1. Engineers must pay less attention to engineering details.
2. Engineers must develop a broader horizon to take account of nonengineering considerations.
3. Engineers must focus on people rather than things.[19]

A third finding of the Hitachi report is that most managers and engineers conceded that engineering considerations should have priority in matters of safety, and usually in matters of quality. Engineers were expected to "go to the mat," as one engineer put it, on fundamental considerations of safety and quality. On matters involving safety, they expressed little if any deference to management.[20] Even on questions of quality, customer satisfaction, and cost, engineers were willing to give managers the last word only after giving management what one engineer called an "ear full" first.[21]

We shall not attempt to make any final judgment about whether Jackall or the Hitachi Report provide the most accurate description of the engineer-manager relationship in large organizations. There seems to be some validity to both accounts. On the one hand, many engineers report experiences with managers who seem to fit Jackall's description. These managers are perceived by some engineers as being people who have little concern for morality and who do not respect the professional integrity of engineers. On the other hand, most engineers, like most professionals, report a high degree of job satisfaction. This would seem to imply that they find their relationship with managers satisfactory.

It is more important, however, to turn from the various *descriptive* accounts of how managers and engineers actually *do* relate to one another in the context of decision making to a *prescriptive* or normative account of how they *should* relate. We can put this issue in the form of a question: How should we establish the boundary between decisions that should be made by engineers and those that should be made by managers?

8.5   Paradigmatic Engineering and Management Decisions

Functions of Engineers and Managers

An answer to this question must begin with a delineation of the proper function of engineers and managers in an organization and of the contrasting points of view associated with these differing functions.

The primary function of engineers within an organization is to use their technical knowledge and training to create products and processes that are of value to the organization and its customers. But engineers are also professionals, and they must uphold the standards that their profession has decided should guide the use of their technical knowledge. Thus, engineers have a dual loyalty: to the organization and to their profession. Their professional loyalties go beyond their immediate employer.[22]

These obligations include meeting the standards usually associated with good design and accepted engineering practice. The criteria embedded in these standards include such considerations as efficiency and economy of design, the degree of invulnerability to improper manufacturing and operation, and the extent to which state-of-the-art technology is used.[23] We could summarize these considerations by saying that engineers have a special concern for quality.

Engineers also ascribe preeminent importance to safety. Moreover, they are inclined to be cautious in this regard, preferring to err on the conservative side in safety considerations. In the *Challenger* case, for example, the engineers did not have firm data on the behavior of the O-rings at low temperatures, even though their extrapolations indicated that there might be severe problems. So they recommended against the launch.

The function and consequent perspective of managers is different. Their function is to direct the activities of the organization, including the activities of engineers. Managers are not professionals in the strict sense. Rather than being oriented toward standards that transcend their organization, they are more likely to be governed by the standards that prevail within the organization, and in some cases perhaps by their own personal moral beliefs. Both Jackall and the Hitachi report imply that managers see themselves as custodians of the organization and are primarily concerned with its present and future well-being. This well-being is measured for the most part in economic terms, but it also includes such considerations as public image and employee morale.

This perspective differs from engineers'. Rather than thinking in terms of professional practices and standards, managers tend to enumerate all of the relevant considerations ("get everything on the table," as they sometimes put it) and then balance them against one another to come to a conclusion. Managers feel strong pressure to keep costs down and may believe engineers sometimes go too far in pursuing safety, to the detriment of such considerations as cost or marketability. By contrast, engineers tend to assign a serial ordering to the various considerations relevant to design, so that minimal standards of safety and quality must be met before any other considerations are relevant.[24] Although they may also be willing to balance safety and quality against other factors to some extent, engineers are more likely to believe that they have a special obligation to uphold safety and quality standards in negotiations with managers. They will usually insist that a product or process must never violate accepted engineering standards and that changes be made incrementally.

These considerations suggest a distinction between what we shall call a "proper engineering decision" (PED), a decision that should be made by engineers or from the engineering perspective, and what we shall call a "proper management decision" (PMD), a decision that should be made by managers or from the management perspective. While not claiming to give a full definition of either PED or PMD in the sense of necessary and sufficient conditions, we can formulate some of the features that should ordinarily characterize these two types of decision procedures. We shall refer to the following descriptions as "characterizations" of proper engineering and proper management decisions. They are as follows:

> *PED:* a decision that should be made by engineers or at least governed by professional engineering practice, because it either (1) involves technical matters that require engineering expertise or (2) falls within the ethical standards embodied in engineering codes, especially those requiring engineers to protect the health and safety of the public.

> *PMD:* a decision that should be made by managers or at least governed by management considerations, because (1) it involves factors relating to the well-being of the organization, such as cost, scheduling, marketing, and employee morale or welfare, and (2) the decision does not force engineers (or other professionals) to make unacceptable compromises with their own technical practices or ethical standards.

We shall make two preliminary remarks about these characterizations of engineering and management decisions. First, the characterizations of the PED and PMD show that the distinction between management and engineering decisions is made in terms of the standards and practices that should predominate in the decision-making process. Furthermore, the PMD makes it clear that management standards should never override engineering standards when the two are in substantial conflict, especially with regard to safety and perhaps even quality. However, what counts as a "substantial conflict" may often be controversial. If engineers want *much* more than *acceptable* safety or quality, it is not clear that the judgment of engineers should prevail.

Second, the PMD specifies that a legitimate management decision not only must not force engineers to violate their professional practices and standards but must not force other professionals to do so either. Even though the primary contrast here is the difference between engineering and management decisions, the specification of a legitimate management decision must include this wider prohibition against the violation of other professional standards. A complete characterization of a legitimate management decision should also include prohibitions against violating the rights of nonprofessional employees, but this would make the characterization even more complicated and is not relevant for our purposes.

Paradigmatic and Nonparadigmatic Examples

Several terms in both characterizations are purposely left undefined. The characterization of the PED does not define "technical matters," and it certainly does not define "health" and "safety." PMD does not fully specify the kinds of considerations that are typical management considerations, citing only "factors relating to the well-being of the company, such as cost, scheduling, marketing, and employee morale or welfare." The characterization of the PMD requires that management decisions not force engineers to make "unacceptable compromises with their own professional standards," but it does not define "unacceptable."

We do not believe that it is useful to attempt to give any general definition of these terms. The application of these terms will be relatively noncontroversial in some examples, and no attempts at definition can furnish a definitive clarification of all of the controversial cases. We shall refer to the relatively noncontroversial examples of PEDs and PMDs as *paradigmatic*.[25] The earlier-provided characterizations of PED and PMD are intended to describe such paradigms. These two paradigms can be thought of as marking the two ends in a spectrum of cases.

We can easily imagine a paradigmatic PED. Suppose engineer Jane is participating in the design of a chemical plant. She must choose between valve A and valve B. Valve B is sold by a friend of Jane's manager, but it fails to meet minimum specifications for the job. It has, in fact, been responsible for several disasters involving loss of life, and Jane is surprised that it is still on the market. Valve A, by contrast, is a state-of-the-art product. Among other things, it has a quicker shutoff mechanism and is also much less prone to malfunctions in emergencies. Although it is 5 percent more expensive, the expense is one that Jane's firm can well afford. Valve A, therefore, is the clear and unequivocal choice in terms of both quality and safety. Figure 8.1 illustrates this.

Here the decision should be made by Jane or other engineers, or at least in accordance with engineering considerations. This is because (1) the decision involves issues related to accepted technical standards and (2) the decision relates in important ways to the safety of the public, and therefore to the ethical standards of engineers. The choice between valves A and B is a paradigmatic PED.

We can modify the example to make it a paradigmatic PMD. Suppose valve A and valve B are equal in quality and safety, but valve B can be supplied much faster than valve A, is 15 percent cheaper, and is manufactured by a firm that is a potential customer for some of the products of Jane's firm. Valve A, however, is made by a firm that is potentially an even bigger customer for some of the products of Jane's firm, although cultivating the relationship with this firm will require a long-term commitment and will be more expensive. If there are no other relevant considerations, the decision as to whether to purchase valve A or valve B should be made by managers, or at least made in accordance with management considerations. Comparing the decision by the two criteria in the PMD, we can

Feature	PMD	Test	PED
Technical expertise	Not needed	——————X	Needed
Safety	Not important	——————X	Important
Cost	Important	——————X	Not important
Scheduling	Important	——————X	Not important
Marketing	Important	——————X	Not important

Figure 8.1
A Paradigmatic PED

Feature	PMD	Test	PED
Technical expertise	Not needed	X————————	Needed
Safety	Not important	X————————	Important
Cost	Important	X————————	Not important
Scheduling	Important	X————————	Not important
Marketing	Important	X————————	Not important

Figure 8.2
A Paradigmatic PMD

say that (1) management considerations (such as speed of delivery, cost, and the decision as to which customers should be cultivated) are important, and (2) no violation of engineering considerations would result from either decision. Figure 8.2 illustrates this case.

Many cases will lie between the two extremes of paradigmatic PEDs and paradigmatic PMDs. Some cases lie so near the center of the imaginary spectrum of cases that they might be classified as either a PED or PMD. Consider another version of the same case in which valve A has a slightly better record of long-term reliability (and is therefore somewhat safer), but valve B is 10 percent cheaper and can be delivered and also marketed more quickly. In this case, rational and responsible people might well differ on whether the final decision on which valve to buy should be made by engineers or managers. Considerations of reliability and safety are engineering considerations, but considerations of cost, scheduling, and marketing are typical management considerations. Figure 8.3 illustrates this situation.

Would ordering valve B be an "unacceptable" compromise of engineering standards of safety and quality? Are the cost, scheduling, and marketing problems significant enough to overbalance the engineering considerations? Here rational people of good will might differ in their judgments. In considering a case such as this, it is important to remember that, as in all line-drawing cases, *the importance or moral "weight" of the feature must be considered.* One cannot simply count the number of features that fall on the PMD or PED side, or the place of the "X" on the line.

Feature	PMD	Test	PED
Technical expertise	Not needed	————————X——	Needed
Safety	Not important	——————X————	Important
Cost	Important	——X————————	Not important
Scheduling	Important	———X———————	Not important
Marketing	Important	———X———————	Not important

Figure 8.3
PED/PMD: A Nonparadigmatic Case

Many issues having to do with pollution also illustrate the problematic situations that can arise in the interface between proper engineering and proper management decisions. Suppose process A is so much more costly than process B that the use of A might threaten the survival of the company. Suppose, furthermore, that B is more polluting, but it is not clear whether the pollution poses any substantial threat to human health. Here again, rational people of good will might differ on whether management or engineering considerations should prevail.

8.6 ✸ The *Challenger* Case

The *Challenger* case is another controversial example of the conflicting prerogatives of engineers and managers. In a teleconference on the evening before the fateful launch, Robert Lund, vice president of engineering at Morton Thiokol and both an engineer and a manager, had recommended against launch, in concert with the other engineers. The recommendation was based on a judgment that the primary and secondary O-rings might not seal properly at the low temperatures at which the vehicle would be launched. NASA officials expressed dismay at the no-launch recommendation, and Thiokol executives requested an interruption in the teleconference to reassess their decision. During the 30-minute interruption, Jerald Mason, senior vice president of Morton Thiokol, turned to Lund and told him to take off his engineering hat and put on his management hat. Lund reversed his no-launch recommendation.

In admonishing Lund to take off his engineering hat and put on his management hat, Mason was saying that this should be a managerial decision. Testifying before the commission that investigated the *Challenger* accident, usually referred to as the "Rogers Commission," Mason gave two reasons for this belief. First, the engineers were not unanimous: "[W]ell, at this point it was clear to me we were not going to get a unanimous decision."[26] If engineers disagreed, there was presumably not a clear violation of the technical or ethical standards of engineers; and, thus, it could be argued that neither requirement of the PMD was being violated.

There are reasons to doubt the factual accuracy of Mason's claim, however. In his account of the events surrounding the *Challenger* disaster given at MIT in 1987, Roger Boisjoly reported that Mason asked if he was "the only one who wanted to fly."[27] This would suggest that he did not have evidence at this point that other engineers wanted to fly. Whatever validity Mason could give to his argument that some engineers supported the launch (and therefore that the opposition of the engineers to the launch was not unanimous) was apparently based on conversations with individual engineers after the teleconference. So Mason probably had little justification at the time of the teleconference for believing that the nonmanagement engineers were not unanimously opposed to the launch.

Nevertheless, Mason may be correct in maintaining that there was some difference of opinion among those most qualified to render judgment, even if this information was not confirmed until after the event. If engineers disagreed about the technical issues, the engineering considerations were perhaps not as compelling as they would have been if the engineers had been unanimous. Thus, the first part of the PED criterion may not have been fully satisfied. Those who did not find a technical problem probably would not find an ethical problem either. So the second criterion of the PED may also not have been fully satisfied.

Mason's second reason was that no numbers could be assigned to the time required for the O-rings to seal at various temperatures:

Dr. Keel: Since Mr. Lund was your vice president of engineering and since he presented the charts and the recommendations not to launch outside of your experience base—that is, below a temperature of 53 degrees for the O-rings—in the previous 8:45 Eastern Standard Time teleconference, what did you have in mind when you asked him to take off his engineering hat and put on his management hat?

Mr. Mason: I had in mind the fact that we had identified that we could not quantify the movement of that, the time for movement of the primary [O-ring]. We didn't have the data to do that, and therefore it was going to take a judgment, rather than a precise engineering calculation, in order to conclude what we needed to conclude.[28]

This might also be a reason for holding that the decision to launch did not violate (2) of the PMD, and that it did not clearly satisfy (1) of the PED. The fact that no calculations could be made to determine the time it would take the O-rings to seal at various temperatures does not necessarily justify the conclusion that a management decision should be made. Surely the fact that failure of the O-rings to seal could destroy the *Challenger* implies that the engineering considerations were of paramount importance, even if they could not be adequately quantified. The engineer's concern for safety is still relevant.

Again, however, Mason's comment may make a valid observation. Given that engineers generally prefer to make judgments on the basis of quantitative calculations, they may well have been uncomfortable with the fact that there were no precise numbers for the degree of degradation of the O-rings at lower temperatures. As a result, the engineering judgment did not have the same degree of decisiveness that it would have had otherwise. All that Roger Boisjoly could argue was that the degree of degradation seemed to be correlated with temperature, and even the data he used to back up this claim was limited.

Mason's arguments, taken together, might be seen as an attempt to meet criterion (2) of the PMD. If the decision to recommend launch is not a clear violation of engineering practice, an engineer does not violate his technical practices by recommending launch. Thus, Mason's argument could be seen as a claim that the decision whether or not to launch was at the very least not a paradigm instance of a PED. A paradigm PED would be one where (among other things) the experts clearly agree and where there are quantitative measures that unambiguously point to one option rather than another. Thus the recommendation to launch was at the very least not a paradigm case of a violation of technical engineering practices.

Mason might also have argued that criterion (1) of the PMD was satisfied. A renewed contract with NASA was not assured, and failure to recommend launch might have been the decisive factor that persuaded NASA officials not to renew the contract with Morton Thiokol. Thus, the well-being of the company might have been substantially harmed by a no-launch recommendation.

Despite these arguments, we believe that the launch decision was properly an engineering decision, even though it perhaps was not a paradigm case of such a decision.

First, criterion (1) of the PMD was not as compelling a consideration as Mason might have supposed. There was no evidence that a no-launch decision would threaten the survival of Morton Thiokol, or even that it would in any fundamental way jeopardize Thiokol's financial wellbeing. In any case, engineering considerations should have had priority.

Second, criterion (2) of the PMD was not satisfied, because the decision to launch violated engineers' propensity to modify or change course only in small increments. The temperature was more than 20 degrees below any previous launch. This was an enormous change, which should have given an engineer good reason to object to the launch.

Third, criterion (1) of the PED was fulfilled. Even though the quantitative data were limited and certainly did not give conclusive evidence that there would be a disaster, the data did seem to point in that direction, so that the desire for quantitative measures was not wholly frustrated. Engineers, furthermore, are alert to the fact that composites, such as the ones the O-rings are made of, are temperature-sensitive and that one could reasonably expect substantially lower temperatures to produce substantially greater blowby problems.

Fourth, criterion (2) of the PED was met, because human life was at stake, and engineers are trained to be unusually cautious when there are serious issues of health and safety. This should be particularly important when those at risk do not give informed consent to special dangers. This was the case with the astronauts who did not have any knowledge of the problem with the O-rings.

The importance of the safety issue was further highlighted because the practice of requiring the burden of proof to be borne by anyone advocating a launch decision rather than a no-launch decision was violated. In testimony before the Rogers Commission, Robert Lund recounts this all-important shift in the locus of the burden of proof:

Chairman Rogers: How do you explain the fact that you seemed to change your mind when you changed your hat?

Mr. Lund: I guess we have got to go back a little further in the conversations than that. We have dealt with Marshall for a long time and have always been in the position of defending our position to make sure that we were ready to fly, and I guess I didn't realize until after that meeting and after several days that we had absolutely changed our position from what we had been before. But that evening I guess I had never had those kinds of things come from the people at Marshall that we had to prove to them that we weren't ready. . . . And so we got ourselves in the thought process that we were trying to find some way to prove to them it wouldn't work, and we were unable to do that. We couldn't prove absolutely that motor wouldn't work.

Chairman Rogers: In other words, you honestly believed that you had a duty to prove that it would not work?

Mr. Lund: Well that is kind of the mode we got ourselves into that evening. It seems like we have always been in the opposite mode. I should have detected that, but I did not, but the roles kind of switched.[29]

This last-minute reversal of a long-standing policy, requiring the burden of proof to rest with anyone recommending a no-launch rather than a launch decision, was a serious threat to the integrity of the engineering obligation to protect human life.

Although hindsight no doubt benefits our judgment, it does seem that the decision whether or not to recommend launch was properly an engineering decision rather than a management decision, even though it may not have been a paradigm case of a proper engineering decision. There is insufficient reason to believe that the case diverged so much from the paradigm engineering decision that management considerations should have been allowed to override the engineering constraints. Engineers, not managers, should have had the final say on whether or not to launch. Or, if the person wore both an engineering hat and a management hat—as Robert Lund did—he should have had his engineering hat on when he made the decision. The distinction between paradigmatic engineering and management decisions and the attendant methodology developed here help to confirm this conclusion.

8.7   Loyalty: Uncritical and Critical

Unfortunately managers and engineers are not always careful to restrict themselves to their proper roles. Although it is certainly possible for engineers to overstep their proper role and make decisions that should be made by managers, it is much more likely, given the authority structures in business and governmental organizations, that managers will overstep their management role and make decisions that should be made by engineers.

In justifying their demand for compliance on the part of engineers, one of the most common claims of managers is that engineers should show "loyalty" to the organization, that they should be "team players." For example, Kermit Vandivier, an employee of the B. F. Goodrich plant in Troy, Ohio, was uncomfortable with what he considered to be unwarranted test practices on a brake that Goodrich was designing for the Air Force. As a result of his concerns, he submitted a letter of resignation, which was to take effect in a few weeks, but the chief engineer informed Vandivier that his resignation was to be accepted immediately because of Vandivier's "disloyalty" to the company.[30]

The appeal to loyalty to an organization is not always illegitimate. We have seen that the NSPE code requires engineers to be "faithful agents or trustees" of their employers—that is, to be loyal. But because this appeal is frequently abused, it is important for responsible engineers to be able to think clearly about the concept of loyalty. Specifically, they must be able to distinguish between uncritical loyalty and critical loyalty.

Uncritical loyalty to an employer may be defined as placing the interests of the employer, as the employer defines those interests, above any other consideration.

Uncritical loyalty is sometimes espoused by business managers. In a 1973 CBS report on Phillips Petroleum, Inc., one of Phillips' top executives said that a loyal employee will buy only Phillips products and vote for those candidates who are most likely to support policies that are congenial to the interests of the company.[31] Only slightly more qualified claims are made by Herbert Simon in his classic text, *Administrative Behavior.* While admitting that all employees have limits to the direction they will accept from their employers, Simon holds that within these very broad limits an employee should accustom himself to "relaxing his own critical faculties" and permitting "his behavior to be guided by the decision of his superior, without independently examining the merits of that decision."[32] A subordinate accepts his superior's authority, according to Simon, when he "holds in abeyance his own critical faculties for choosing between alternatives and uses the formal criterion of the receipt of a command or signal as the basis for choices."[33] This means that professionals should accept their superior's suggestions and orders "without any critical review or consideration."[34] At most, their reasoning is aimed at anticipating commands by asking themselves how the superior would wish them to behave in given circumstances.[35]

What arguments can be made for this kind of uncritical, unquestioning—or "blind"—loyalty?[36]

1. We could argue that without uncritical loyalty organizational chaos would ensue. Ties of loyalty and discipline would dissolve, and blowing the whistle on one's superiors would become the norm instead of the last resort. This would decrease efficiency and productivity, which is clearly a loss in terms of the public good.

2. Any engineer whose loyalty to the public causes her to refuse to take an assignment from her employer will in many cases only pass the assignment along to a colleague of less refined sensibility. So her objections will not protect the public anyway. The faulty product will go on the market regardless of the objection of the supposedly conscientious professional, having been designed by someone else.

3. The engineer is not an expert in public policy. As a professional group, engineers, for example, have neither the ability nor the right to plan social change. They may contribute to debates on public policy as private citizens, but this is very different from subjecting their everyday professional work to the scrutiny of their own conscience. Should we risk oil spills and increase our reserves by offshore drilling? Should we accept the hazards of pesticides to feed hungry people? Should we stop building a dam and thereby preserve a wild river? These are political questions; the public should not abdicate its responsibility to decide these issues of public policy by expecting engineers to make the choices in the name of engineering ethics. It is better for an engineer to be loyal to his or her employer and leave ethical considerations to public policy.

Opposed to the notion of uncritical loyalty to the employer is *critical loyalty,* which we shall define as giving due regard to the interests of the employer, insofar as this is possible within the constraints of the employee's personal and professional ethics. The concept of critical loyalty is a creative middle way that seeks to honor both of these requirements: engineers should be loyal employees, but only as long as this does not conflict with fundamental personal or professional obligations. Rather than attempt to define the precise scope of such terms as "due regard," "personal ethics," or "professional ethics," we shall give some examples to illustrate the implications of the concept of critical loyalty.

By the standard of critical loyalty, the Phillips executive went too far in claiming that the concept of loyalty justified expecting Phillips employees to buy only Phillips products, and he also went too far when he appealed to loyalty to justify expecting Phillips employees to vote in a way that furthered the interests of the corporation. These expectations infringe on the rights of employees to exercise the prerogatives of citizenship and to shape the direction of their personal lives by making purchases according to their own inclinations. Engineers owe loyalty to their company, but this loyalty cannot justify violation of professional obligations to protect the health and safety of the public.

What arguments can be given to support the concept of critical loyalty? One type of argument is to show the weakness in the arguments for uncritical loyalty.

1. Uncritical loyalty can involve a serious abridgment of the autonomy and moral integrity of individuals. To be told that I do not have the right to protest obvious wrongs and that my only options are to continue working on a project that I consider immoral or to resign my job is to have my own freedom as a moral agent severely restricted. This is especially true when obtaining new employment involves considerable personal sacrifice.

2. Independent employees—and especially professional employees—can be very valuable to a firm. Companies do not usually want to engage in blatantly immoral or illegal actions. If nothing else, such activities often give the firm a bad public image and frequently embroil it in costly and time-consuming legal battles. Upper-level management may know nothing about the problems until they become public. The B.F. Goodrich aircraft brake case illustrates this: upper-level management at Goodrich evidently knew nothing of the problem until it became public.

3. Ethically aware professionals who are willing and able to protest, and in some cases refuse to participate in, morally questionable activities are a great resource for the public. It is not possible for the law to control all abuses in business.[37] Laws tend to be enacted only after serious abuses, many of which might have been avoided by ethically responsible employees. Furthermore, the law tends to be clumsy and inept at regulating activities that are potential sources of abuse.

4. The bad effects of occasional organizational disobedience can be exaggerated. Such actions are a relatively rare exception, not the rule. Further, a protest of an employer's action or a refusal to participate in a particular engineering project is not the same thing as guiding social policy in general.

Engineers must always keep in mind their professional obligations, while remaining loyal employees, insofar as this is possible. For engineers, critical loyalty implies that managers should never be allowed to make properly engineering decisions, nor should they be given jurisdiction over one's conscience. Nevertheless, organizational disobedience should always be a last resort. When it is unavoidable, it should be done in such a way as to minimize the negative consequences to both employer and employee. In the next section, we shall examine some ways in which responsible engineers can avoid the necessity of organizational disobedience and minimize its negative consequences when it is necessary. In the following section, we shall examine some ways in which managers can forestall the necessity of organizational disobedience by their employees.[38]

8.8   Responsible Organizational Disobedience

When we think of disagreements between employees and their employers, the term that most often comes to mind is *whistle-blowing*. But whistle-blowing in its most common usage refers to an employee's "going public" when she believes a company is guilty of serious wrongdoing. This may be the most dramatic instance of employee-employer disagreement, but it is not the most common one, especially for professionals. Jim Otten finds the expression "organizational disobedience" more appropriate as a generic term covering all types of actions taken by an employee that are contrary to the wishes of her employer. Given the similarities between this kind of action and civil disobedience, the term seems appropriate.[39] We shall not follow Otten's definition exactly, but we shall use his expression and define *organizational disobedience* as a protest of, or refusal to follow, an organization's policy or action.

It is helpful to keep the following two points about organizational disobedience in mind. First, the policy that a professional employee disobeys or protests may be either specific or general. It may be a specific directive of a superior or a general corporate policy, either a single act or a continuing series of actions. Second, the employer may not intend to do anything morally wrong. For example, when an engineer objects to the production of a faulty type of steel pipe, he is not necessarily claiming that his firm intends to manufacture a shoddy product. Rather, he is objecting to a series of actions that would probably result in unfortunate consequences, however unintended.

There are at least three distinct areas in which responsible engineers might be involved in organizational disobedience:

1. In engaging in activities contrary to the interests of the company, as perceived by management (Disobedience by Contrary Action)
2. In refusing to carry out an assignment because of moral or professional objections (Disobedience by Nonparticipation)
3. In protesting a policy or action of the company (Disobedience by Protest)

What guidelines should the responsible engineer use in deciding when to engage in organizational disobedience in these areas, and how should she carry out this disobedience? Let us consider each of these three areas.

Disobedience by Contrary Action

Engineers may sometimes find that their actions outside the workplace are objectionable to managers. Objections by managers are usually in one of two areas. First, managers may believe that a particular action or perhaps the general lifestyle of an employee reflects unfavorably on the organization. For example, an engineer might be a member of a political group that is generally held in low esteem by the community. Second, managers may believe that some activities of employees are contrary to the interests of the organization in a more direct way. For example, an engineer may be a member of a local environmental group that is pressuring his or her company to install anti-pollution equipment that is not required by law, or lobbying to keep the company from purchasing some wetland area that it intends to drain and use for plant expansion. How should an engineer handle such delicate situations?

Although we cannot investigate all of the issues fully here, a few observations are essential. Disobedience by Contrary Action is not a paradigm case of harm to the organization (as compared, for example, with theft or fraud), and its restriction by the organization is not a paradigm case of restriction of individual freedom (compared with a direction to do something the employee thinks is seriously immoral). Nevertheless, they are examples of these two concepts. Let us consider some of the arguments that might be offered to confirm this claim.

On the one hand, there is no doubt but that an organization can be harmed in some sense by the actions of employees outside the workplace. A company that has a reputation for hiring people whose lifestyles are offensive to the local community may not be able to hire some very desirable people, and it may lose business as well. The harm that an organization may suffer is even more obvious when employees engage in political activities that are directly contrary to the interests of the organization. A manager can argue with some persuasiveness that the simplistic assertion that nothing the employee does after 5 o'clock affects the organization does not do justice to the realities of business and community life. On these grounds, a manager might assert that the organization's right to the loyalty of its employees requires the employee not to harm the organization in these ways.

On the other hand, an employee's freedom suffers substantial curtailment if organizational restrictions force her to curtail activities to which she has a deep personal commitment. Nor can the manager persuasively argue that employees should simply resign if management finds their activities outside the workplace objectionable, for the same activities might harm other organizations in the same way. Thus, the consistent application of the argument that employees should never do anything that harms the organization results in the conclusion that employees should never engage in lifestyles or political activities that are controversial. This amounts to a substantial limitation of an employee's freedom.

In surveying these arguments, we believe a good case can be made that organizations should not punish employees for Disobedience by Contrary Action. Punishing employees for Disobedience by Contrary Action amounts to a considerable infringement on individual freedom. Moreover, employees may not be able to avoid this type of harm to organizations simply by changing jobs. Many organizations might be harmed by an engineer's political views or efforts on behalf of the environment. Thus, allowing this type of harm to count as justification for organizational control permits organizations to exert considerable influence over an employee's life outside the workplace. In a society that values individual freedom as much as ours does, such a substantial abridgment of individual freedom is difficult to justify.

Despite these considerations, however, many managers will act strenuously when they believe they or their organizations are threatened by actions of employees outside the workplace. Therefore two observations may be appropriate.

First, some actions by employees outside the workplace harm the organization in a much more direct fashion than others. An engineer's campaign for tighter restrictions on his or her own company's environmental pollution will probably have a more direct effect on her company than an engineer's private sexual life. Employees should be more careful in areas where the harm to their organization is more direct.

Second, there can be a major difference in the degree to which curtailment of an employee's activities outside the workplace encroaches on his freedom. Curtailment of activities closely associated with one's personal identity and with very strong moral or religious beliefs is more serious than limitation of activities that are connected with more peripheral beliefs. Therefore, employees should allow themselves more freedom in areas closely related to their basic personal commitments than in areas more peripheral to their most important concerns.

Disobedience by Nonparticipation

Engineers are most likely to engage in disobedience by nonparticipation in projects related to the military and in projects that may adversely affect the environment. Engineer James, a pacifist, may discover that an underwater detection system for which his company has received a contract has military applications and thereupon request to be relieved of an assignment to the project. Engineer Betty may request not to be asked to design a condominium to be built in a wetland area.

Disobedience by nonparticipation can be based on professional ethics or personal ethics. Engineers who refuse to design a product that they believe is unsafe can base their objections on their professional codes, which require engineers to give preeminence to considerations of public safety, health, and welfare. Engineers who refuse to design a product that has military applications because of their personal objections to the use of violence must base their refusal on personal morality, because the codes do not prohibit engineers from participating in military projects. The basis of objections to participating in projects that engineers believe are harmful to the environment is more controversial. As we shall see in the next chapter, only three professional engineering codes have any direct statements about the environment, and there are problems of interpretation in each case.

Several things should be kept in mind about disobedience by nonparticipation. First, it is possible (although perhaps unlikely) for an employee to abuse the appeal to conscience, using it as a means to avoid projects he finds boring or not challenging, or to avoid association with other employees with whom he has personal difficulties. An employee should be careful to avoid any appearance that would promote this interpretation of his action. Second, it is sometimes difficult for employers to honor a request for removal from a work assignment for several reasons. For example, there may be no alternative assignments, there may be no other engineer who is qualified to do the work, or the change may be disruptive to the organization. These problems are especially severe in small organizations.

Nevertheless, we believe an organization should honor most requests based on problems of conscience when it is possible to do so. Common morality holds that a violation of one's conscience is a serious moral matter. Employers should not force employees to make a choice between losing their job and violating their conscience. Of course, there are situations in which employers do not have any alternative work assignments, but many organizations have found ways to respect their employees' conscience without undue economic sacrifice.[40]

Disobedience by Protest

In some situations engineers find the actions of the employer to be so objectionable that they believe mere nonparticipation in the objectionable activity is insufficient. Rather, some form of public protest (or "whistle-blowing") is required. The protest may be either within or outside the organization. Such situations are best viewed as complex conflict situations in which engineers must balance obligations to their employers, their families, their careers, and the public.

According to the codes, the obligation to the health, safety, and welfare of the public must take priority over these other obligations, but this does not always make the choice an easy one. There are several reasons for the difficulties that sometimes occur in resolving these conflict situations. Sometimes it is not clear whether in the particular situation the interest is crucial enough to warrant the extreme personal sacrifice (such as loss of career) that is required. For example, the harm to the public may be minor, or whether or not the harm will occur may be questionable. Again, it may not be clear whether the protest will be successful in protecting the public.

Richard DeGeorge has provided a set of criteria that must be satisfied before whistle-blowing can be morally justified.[41] DeGeorge believes that whistle-blowing is morally *permissible* if:

1. the harm that "will be done by the product to the public is serious and considerable,"
2. the employees report their concern to their superiors, and
3. "getting no satisfaction from their immediate superiors, they exhaust the channels available" within the organization.

DeGeorge believes that whistle-blowing is morally *obligatory* if:

4. the employee has "documented evidence that would convince a responsible, impartial observer that his view of the situation is correct and the company policy is wrong," and
5. the employee has "strong evidence that making the information public will in fact prevent the threatened serious harm."

DeGeorge presents his five considerations as criteria for permissible and obligatory whistle-blowing for unsafe products. How he intends his criteria to apply to other contexts is not clear. Taken as general tests for justified or required whistle-blowing, however, they are subject to criticisms.[42] Let us consider each of these criteria in turn.

1. The first criterion appears too strong. DeGeorge seems to assume that the employee must *know* that harm will result and that the harm must be *great*. Perhaps just believing on the basis of the best evidence available is sufficient. Sometimes an employee is not in a position to gather evidence that is totally convincing.

2. It should not always be necessary for employees to report their criticisms to their superiors. Often one's immediate superiors are the cause of the problem and cannot be trusted to give an unbiased evaluation of the situation.

3. Nor is it always necessary to exhaust the organizational chain of command. Sometimes there is not time to do this before a disaster will occur. And sometimes employees have no effective way to make their protest known to higher management except by going public.

4. It is not always possible to get documented evidence of a problem. Often organizations deprive employees of access to vital information necessary to make a conclusive argument for their position. They deprive protesting employees of access to computers and other sources of information necessary to make their case.

5. Finally, it may not always be necessary to have strong evidence that a protest will be successful in preventing the harm to have an obligation to make the protest. Just giving those exposed to a harm the chance to give free and informed consent to the potential harm is often a sufficient justification of the protest.

The criteria offered by DeGeorge seem to have many exceptions, and it is probably not possible to construct a set of exceptionless criteria for justified or required employee protest. Rather than offering checklists of necessary conditions that must be met before protest is justified or required, it may be more useful to propose a series of considerations to be followed in protesting an employer's action. We shall assume that confrontation with an employer should usually be approached incrementally and that open protest should be a last resort. Given this assumption, let us consider the following considerations in responsible dissent by engineers.[43]

First, responsible engineers should exert every effort to assure themselves that their protest is justified. If possible, documented evidence should be sought. At the very least, employees should satisfy themselves that the best available evidence justifies their protest. They should attempt to consult others who might have relevant information and to check their own judgment that protest is justified against the judgment of others.

Second, if their organization has an ombudsman, an "ethics hotline" or some other in-house mechanism for raising ethical issues, responsible engineers should take advantage of these organizational resources. Failing this, professional societies or outside consultants might be able to offer some assistance, either in the form of advice, expert technical evaluation, financial support, or public support if protest external to the organization seems inevitable.

Third, responsible engineers should try to get other professional colleagues to stand with them. Responsible engineers should show others the documentation they have collected and ask for their support in approaching higher management. Again, the approach to higher management should not be done in a confrontational manner, but with the attitude of exhibiting professional responsibility and promoting the long-term interests of the organization.

Fourth, responsible engineers should make their objections known to their immediate supervisors if this is appropriate. Discussion should be as nonconfrontational as possible. Focus should be on the problem, not on personalities. The problem can be posed by saying "I have a problem" or "We have a problem," not "You have a problem."

Fifth, responsible engineers should make positive and concrete suggestions about how the problem they see might be resolved. Rather than simply pointing out what should not be done, they should show what should be done instead. When no criminal activity is involved and especially when the problem seems to have arisen inadvertently, responsible engineers can often propose solutions that allow individuals or the entire organization to find a face-saving way out of the situation. Providing an easy way out of the difficulty is often the key to preventing escalation of the problem.

Sixth, responsible engineers should attempt to find other sympathetic managers if their supervisor is unsympathetic. It is almost always better, however, to avoid the appearance of making an "end run" around one's own supervisor. This appearance can sometimes be avoided by strongly suggesting to other managers that any conversations with one's own manager be confidential and informal.

Seventh, if all else fails, responsible engineers may have to make the objectionable activity known to the public. This usually involves the press or governmental agencies in some form. Often the protest is most effective if one has already resigned from the organization; this minimizes the tendency of others to interpret one's actions as motivated by self-interest.

While few if any studies have been done that show the effects of whistle-blowing on organizations, studies of whistle-blowers themselves have shown that they usually suffer considerable harm. Even though most whistle-blowers say that they are proud of what they did and would do it again, they admit that both they and their families have often suffered considerable hardships.[44] In the next section, we shall consider some actions that organizations can take to avoid the need for whistle-blowing.

8.9   Implementing Professional Employee Rights

One of the most popular definitions of a right is that it is a "valid claim *to* something and *against* someone which is recognized by the principles of an enlightened conscience."[45] If we take an "enlightened conscience" to be one described by the concept of critical loyalty, employees should have the right to engage in justified and responsible forms of the three types of organizational disobedience discussed in the previous section without fear of dismissal or reprisals. Reprisals may include denial of raises and promotions, harassment, and assignment to unimportant, uninteresting, or demeaning tasks.

Managers should take positive steps to implement employee rights because employers and employees—even professional employees—are unevenly matched. An individual employee is no match for a powerful corporation or governmental bureaucracy and in many cases even for a small business. It is usually more difficult, and certainly more emotionally traumatic, for an employee to find a new job than for an employer to find a new employee. Employers and employees do not face one another as equals. The attitude of powerful corporations and bureaucracies toward their employees is sometimes like that of the proverbial elephant who exclaimed "Each for himself, and God for us all," as he danced among the chickens.

It is important that the policies implementing employee rights have several features.

1. They should focus on issues rather than on personalities. This helps to avoid excessive emotionalism and personality clashes, a prominent feature of many instances of organizational disobedience.

2. Written records should be kept on complaints. This is important if court proceedings are eventually involved. It also serves to "keep the record straight" about what was said and when it was said.

3. Generally, the complaints should be kept as confidential as possible for the protection of both the firm or governmental agency and the complainant.

4. There should be provisions for neutral participants from outside the firm or governmental agency when the dispute requires it. Sometimes employees within the organization are too emotionally involved in the dispute or have too many personal ties to make a dispassionate evaluation of the issues.

5. Explicit provision for protection from retaliation should be made, with mechanisms for complaint if an employee believes he has experienced retaliation. Next to the fear of immediate dismissal, probably the greatest fear of an employee contemplating organizational disobedience is that he or she will suffer discrimination in promotion and job assignment, even long after the controversy is resolved. Protection from this fear is one of the most important employee rights, although one of the most difficult to provide.

6. Finally, the procedure for handling organizational disobedience should proceed as quickly as possible. Delaying resolution of such issues can be a method of punishing dissent. Sufficient delay often allows management to perform the actions against which the protest was made. Prolonging the suspense and cloud of suspicion that accompanies an investigative process also serves to punish a protesting employee, even if his actions were completely justifiable.

During the past 20 years many proposals for improving corporate and governmental responsiveness to the demand for employee rights have been made; many of them have been instituted, with varying degrees of success. Corporate codes of conduct, corporate policy statements, "social audits," corporate (or shareholder) democracy, and the introduction of public and employee advocates on boards of directors are only some of these proposals. We shall focus on four proposals that seem especially important for professional employees.[46]

First, one of the simplest and most effective policies, especially suited to small firms and small governmental agencies, is the "open door" policy. Managers can make themselves available for hearing complaints on a regular basis and without prejudice to the complainants. This method is particularly appropriate where a single manager has the power to correct the problem. If the manager against whose action or policy the complaint is made has an open door policy, the issue can often be resolved in a way that produces least harm to the manager and the employee.

Second, in large organizations a formal procedure to handle complaints is essential. A procedure developed by the Nuclear Regulatory Commission (NRC) might be used by other organizations. The NRC has instituted a procedure for handling what it calls Differing Professional Opinions (DPOs). The process begins when an employee submits a concise written statement to her supervisor, summarizing both her own and the opposing views. If no accommodation is reached at this level, the DPO can be submitted to a competent, impartial peer review group for evaluation. If the originator is not satisfied with the disposition of the DPO by the review group, she may appeal the decision to any higher level within the NRC, including a commissioner or the commission as a whole. If the issue raised involves the public health or safety, the appeal can also be sent to the Advisory Committee on Reactor Safeguards (ACRSs) for their comments.

Safeguards have been instituted in an attempt to eliminate subversions and abuses of the process. A Special Review Panel consisting of two managers, two nonmanagers, and one person from outside the NRC monitors the operation of the system and recommends improvements. Written records are made of the entire proceedings and furnished to the originator of the DPO as soon as they are generated. There are also time limits attached to the proceeding so that managers cannot bury the DPOs by long delays. A potential problem with the procedure is that "national security" may be invoked to keep the complaint procedure secret, and managers might be able to use this loophole to protect themselves.[47]

Third, professional employee rights can receive protection through a corporate (or governmental) ombudsman. Registering employee complaints can often be done in a confidential and anonymous way. The ombudsman or advocate must operate independently of the corporate hierarchy and should have direct access to top management and (in corporations) to the board of directors. An ombudsman might not have sufficient expertise or power within a governmental or corporate bureaucracy to directly mediate a dispute between a professional and a manager, but he could facilitate a mediation. An employee should be able to have confidence that any complaint she submits will be treated fairly and honestly. Obviously, the ombudsman could be utilized by nonprofessionals, but his or her services would be available to professionals as well.

Fourth, some organizations have established an office, often at the vice-presidential level, whose primary concern is ethics and social responsibility. Such offices have as one of their duties the proper disposition of employee complaints. Any employee must have access to this office, which operates confidentially and in complete freedom from middle- and lower-level management.

Some corporate ethics offices also provide an "ethics hotline" that is accessible to employees and others, such as vendors, who may want to make inquiries about corporate ethics policies or to get advice on how to handle troublesome situations. For example, at Martin Marietta, the ethics hotline receives approximately 5000 anonymous calls each year. Many of the calls involve relatively minor problems—many of them being personal disagreements between employees or employees and managers. Resolving these problems has resulted in a substantial increase in employee retention. Some calls, however, have resulted in rectification of serious problems and even in criminal prosecutions.

A small business, such as an engineering, legal, or architectural firm, could not make use of some of the more elaborate mechanisms proposed here. But perhaps modified versions of the NRC's DPO procedure would not be beyond their means. In any event, the protection of professional employee rights is an issue of increasing importance in the workplace.

8.10   Chapter Summary

Engineering codes require engineers to be faithful agents of their employers, but they also require them to hold paramount the safety, health, and welfare of the public. These two obligations can, on occasion, conflict, producing difficult moral and professional problems for engineers. The common law doctrine of "employment at will" has traditionally given little protection to dissenting employees, but recent court decisions and whistle-blower protection laws have changed the situation to some extent. Employees may be able to expect some protection from the courts if they can show that their actions can be justified by considerations of the welfare of the public (public policy).

The engineer-manager relationship is at the center of most of the issues that engineers face as employed professionals. A study by Robert Jackall finds the engineer-manager relationship fundamentally adversarial; however, a study funded by the Hitachi Corporation comes to substantially different conclusions. In any case, it is useful to characterize the decisions that should be made by managers and those that should be made by engineers.

In general, decisions should be made by engineers if they involve engineering-related technical matters or if the ethical standards of engineers are at stake. Decisions should be made by managers if they involve factors relating to the well-being of the organization (cost, scheduling, marketing, employee morale, or welfare) and if the decision does not force engineers (or other professionals) to compromise their technical practices or ethical standards. Application of this distinction to the *Challenger* case shows that the decision was one in which engineers rather than managers should have had the decisive voice.

In justifying their claim to obedience from employees, managers usually appeal to the concept of loyalty. An analysis of the concept of loyalty shows that it is necessary to distinguish between "critical loyalty" and "uncritical loyalty" and that what employees owe managers is critical loyalty. Critical loyalty, however, cannot justify unquestioning obedience.

It is useful to develop some guidelines for the application of critical loyalty to three types of organizational disobedience. When engineers believe they must take actions contrary to the wishes of their employers, they should do so in a measured and responsible way, whether the dissenting actions are in the form of disobedience by contrary action, disobedience by nonparticipation, or disobedience by protest. With respect to the last category, which is often called "whistleblowing," it is difficult to construct strict criteria for the justification of employee protest of an employer's actions. The criteria suggested by Richard DeGeorge, for example, appear to have many exceptions. It is possible, however, to suggest some guidelines for responsible employee dissent.

Employers have used several methods to improve communication with employees and provide avenues within the organization through which employees can register their concerns. These methods include an open door policy, a mechanism for registering "Differing Professional Opinions," an ombudsman system, and an office devoted to ethical issues, which may contain an "ethics hotline."

 CASES TO CONSIDER

Case 15	An Excess?
Case 16	Failure
Case 19	Forced Sex
Case 21	Gilbane Gold
Case 33	Parkville
Case 38	Recommendation for a Friend
Case 46	Underground

NOTES

1. Stephen H. Unger, *Controlling Technology: Ethics and the Responsible Engineer* (New York: Holt, Rinehart & Winston, 1994), pp. 27–30.

2. These comments are available on videotapes of speeches given by Boisjoly at the University of New Mexico in Albuquerque and at Massachusetts Institute of Technology. Similar accounts are available in the transcripts of the Rogers Commission hearings.

3. Common law is the tradition of case law or "judge-made-law" that originated in England and is also fundamental in American law. It is based on a tradition in which a judicial decision establishes a precedent, which is then used by succeeding jurists as the basis for their decision on similar cases. Common law is to be distinguished from statutory law, or laws made by legislative bodies.

4. The first important case was *Peterman v. International Board of Teamsters Local Union 396,* 174 Cal. App. 2d 184 P.2d 25 (Cal. App. 1959). For this citation and a partial review of the public-policy exception, see *Martin Marietta Corporation, Petitioner v. Paul M. Lorenz, Respondent,* No. 90SC593, Supreme Court of Colorado, decided in 1992. The Lorenz case is an important recent case in the development of the public-policy exception, in which an engineer filed a tort claim against Martin Marietta for wrongful discharge on the grounds that he was fired for refusing to perform an illegal act.

Another important early case was *Geary v. United States Steel Corporation,* 456 Pa. 171, 319 A.2d 147 (1974). One of the most important cases was in 1982, *Pierce v. Ortho Pharmaceutical* 319 A.2d. at 178, in which the right of a professional to refuse an employer directive on the grounds that it violated professional ethics was first recognized, even though Dr. Pierce lost her case on technical grounds. This position was reaffirmed in *Kalman v. Grand Union Co.* 115 LRRM 4803 (NJ Super. Ct. 1982). In a 1996 case, *Colo-Rocky Mt. Hosp. & Medical Serv. v. Mariani,* 916 P.2d 519, 11 BNA IER Cas 1153, 52 ALR5th 857, the Colorado Supreme Court ruled in favor of a certified public accountant who claimed she had been fired for failing to violate her professional standards.

Although decisions in one state do not have any direct authority in another, they often establish precedents that are taken seriously in another jurisdiction.

5. See *Martin Marietta v. Paul M. Lorenz*.

6. See note (no author) "Protecting Employees at Will Against Wrongful Discharge: The Public Policy Exception," *The Harvard Law Review, 96*, no. 8 (June, 1983), 1931–1951.

7. See Genna H. Rosten, "Wrongful Discharge Based on Public Policy Derived from Professional Ethics Codes," *52 American Law Reports*, 5th 405.

8. *Wall Street Journal* (April 13, 1981).

9. NJ Stat Ann @ 34:19–1 to 19–8.

10. ILL Rev Stat ch11112, para5302(1985)

11. Joseph A. Raelin, *The Clash of Cultures: Managers and Professionals* (Boston: Harvard Business School Press, 1985), p. XIV.

12. Raelin, p. 12.

13. Raelin, p. 270.

14. Robert Jackall, *Moral Mazes: The World of Corporate Managers* (New York: Oxford University Press, 1988), p. 5. Jackall focuses only occasionally on the relationship between managers and professionals. But his occasional references to the relationship of managers to engineers and other professionals make it clear that he believes his general description of the manager/employee relationship also applies to the relationship of managers to professionals, including engineers.

15. Jackall, pp. 105–107.

16. Jackall, p. 69.

17. Jackall, p. 112.

18. See the unpublished manuscript, "Technical Communications Between Engineers and Managers: Preventing Engineering Disasters." This is a report prepared under a grant from the Hitachi Foundation. The panel conducting the study was chaired by Vivian Weil. The other members of the panel were Michael Davis, Thomas Calero, David Krueger, Robert Growney, Lawrence Lavengood, Elliot Lehman, and Vivian Weil. Draft version, October 24, 1990, pp. 18–19. Citations are used with permission. Davis discusses this study further in his *Thinking Like an Engineer* (New York: Oxford University Press, 1998), pp. 119–156.

19. Hitachi Report, pp. 22–24.

20. Hitachi Report, pp. 64–65.

21. Hitachi Report, p. 65.

22. Raelin also points out the importance of professional loyalties that transcend the organization, contrasting the "local" orientation of managers with the "cosmopolitan" orientation of most professionals. While describing engineers as more locally oriented than most professionals, he does not deny that engineers have loyalties to professional norms that transcend loyalties to their own organization. See Raelin, pp. 15–18 for a description of the local/cosmopolitan distinction.

23. State-of-the-art technology may not always be appropriate. If an engineer is designing a plow for use in Third World countries, simplicity, ease of repair, and availability of repair parts may be more important than the use of the most advanced technology.

24. We are indebted for this insight, as well as several others in this section, to Michael Davis. Davis uses John Rawls' term *lexical ordering* to describe the assigning of priorities. Rawls, however, seems to equate serial ordering with lexical ordering. He defines a lexical order as "an order which requires us to satisfy the first principle in the ordering before we can move on to the second, the second before we consider the third, and so on. A principle does not come into play until those previous to it are either fully met or do not apply. A serial ordering avoids, then, having to balance principles at all; those earlier in the ordering have an absolute weight, so to speak, with respect to later ones, and hold without exception." See John Rawls, *A Theory of Justice* (Cambridge, Mass.: Harvard University Press, 1971), p. 43. See also Michael Davis, "Explaining Wrongdoing," *Journal of Social Philosophy, 20* (Spring/Fall, 1988), 74–90.

25. We are again appealing to the method of casuistry as a way of resolving the line-drawing problems involving engineering and management decisions. For purposes of this

analysis, we are assuming that all decisions are either PEDs or PMDs—that is, that they should be made by either managers or engineers, rather than by anyone else.

26. *Report of the Presidential Commission on the Space Shuttle Challenger Accident,* Vol. IV, (February 26, 1986 to May 2, 1986), p. 764.

27. Roger Boisjoly, "The *Challenger* Disaster: Moral Responsibility and the Working Engineer" in Deborah G. Johnson, *Ethical Issues in Engineering* (Englewood Cliffs, N.J.: Prentice Hall, 1991), p. 6.

28. *Report of the Presidential Commission on the Space Shuttle Challenger Accident,* Vol. IV, (February 26, 1986 to May 2, 1986), p. 772–773.

29. Ibid., p. 811.

30. Kermit Vandivier, "Why Should My Conscience Bother Me?" in Robert Heilbroner, ed. *In the Name of Profit* (Garden City, N.Y.: Doubleday and Co., 1972), p. 29. Cited in Marcia Baron, "The Moral Status of Loyalty" in Deborah G. Johnson, p. 226.

31. "The Corporation," *CBS Reports,* December 6, 1973. Cited in Marcia Baron, in Deborah G. Johnson, *Ethical Issues in Engineering* (Englewood Cliffs, N.J.: Prentice Hall, 1991), p. 225.

32. Herbert A. Simon, *Administrative Behavior,* 3rd ed. (New York: Free Press, 1976), pp. 11 and 151. The citations are taken from Mike W. Martin, "Professional Autonomy and Employers' Authority" in Albert Flores, ed., *Ethical Problems in Engineering* (Troy, N.Y.: Center for the Study of the Human Dimensions of Science and Technology, 1980), pp. 177–181.

33. Simon, pp. 126–127.

34. Simon, p. 22.

35. Simon, p. 129.

36. Samuel Florman, "Moral Blueprints," *Harper's* (October 1978), 30–33.

37. See Christopher D. Stone, *Where the Law Ends: The Social Control of Business Behavior* (Prospect Heights, Ill.: Waveland Press, 1975).

38. For further discussion of the issue of loyalty, see Marcia Baron.

39. Jim Otten, "Organizational Disobedience," in Albert Flores, ed., *Ethical Problems in Engineering,* Vol. 1 (Troy, N.Y.: Center for the Study of the Human Dimensions of Science and Technology, 1980), pp. 182–186.

40. In Chapter 9 we shall consider at greater length the issue of problems of conscience for engineers.

41. Richard T. DeGeorge, *Business Ethics* (New York: Macmillan, 1982), p. 161. This account is taken directly from Richard T. DeGeorge, "Ethical Responsibilities of Engineers in Large Organizations," *Business and Professional Ethics Journal, 1,* no. 1 (Fall 1981), 1–14.

42. Several of these criticisms are suggested by Gene G. James, "Whistle-Blowing: Its Moral Justification," copyrighted in 1990 by Gene G. James. Reprinted in Deborah G. Johnson, ed. *Ethical Issues in Engineering,* pp. 263–278.

43. Many of these suggestions are taken from several helpful essays on whistle-blowing. In addition to the essays by DeGeorge and James already mentioned, see the following: Michael Davis, "Avoiding the Tragedy of Whistleblowing," *Business and Professional Ethics Journal, 8,* no. 4, 3–19 and Ronald Duska, "Whistle-Blowing and Employee Loyalty" copyrighted in 1983 and reprinted in Deborah Johnson, pp. 241–247.

44. See Myron Glazer, "Ten Whistleblowers and How They Fared," *Hastings Center Report* 13:6 (1983), 33–41. See also the special section on whistle-blowing in *Science and Engineering Ethics, 4,* no. 1 (Jan. 1998).

45. See Joel Feinberg's discussion in "Duties, Rights and Claims," *American Philosophical Quarterly, 3* (1966), 337–44. See also Joel Feinberg, "The Nature and Value of Rights," *Journal of Value Inquiry, 4* (1970), 243–55.

46. See also Michael Davis, "Avoiding the Tragedy of Whistleblowing."

47. See Unger, pp. 122–123.

Chapter 9

Engineers and the Environment

The Aberdeen Proving Ground is a U.S. Army facility where, among other things, chemical weapons are developed. The U.S. Army has used the facility to develop, test, store, and dispose of chemical weapons since World War II. Periodic inspections between 1983 and 1986 revealed serious problems with a part of the facility known as the Pilot Plant. These problems included:

> flammable and cancer-causing substances left in the open; chemicals that become lethal if mixed were kept in the same room; drums of toxic substances were leaking. There were chemicals everywhere—misplaced, unlabeled or poorly contained. When part of the roof collapsed, smashing several chemical drums stored below, no one cleaned up or moved the spilled substance and broken containers for weeks.[1]

When an external sulfuric acid tank leaked 200 gallons of acid into a nearby river, state and federal investigators were summoned to investigate. They discovered that the chemical retaining dikes were in a state of disrepair and that the system designed to contain and treat hazardous chemicals was corroded, resulting in chemicals leaking into the ground.[2]

 On June 28, 1988, after two years of investigation, three chemical engineers, Carl Gepp, William Dee, and Robert Lentz, now known as the "**Aberdeen Three**," were criminally indicted for illegally handling, storing, and disposing of hazardous wastes in violation of the Resource Conservation and Recovery Act (RCRA). Although the three engineers did not actually handle the chemicals, they were the managers with the ultimate responsibility for the violations. Investigators for the Department of Justice concluded that no one above them was sufficiently aware of the problems at the Pilot Plant to be assigned responsibility for the violations. The three engineers were competent professionals who played important roles in the development of chemical weapons for the United States. William Dee, the developer of the binary chemical weapon, headed the chemical weapons development team. Robert Lentz was in charge of developing the processes that would be used to manufacture the weapons. Carl Gepp, manager of the Pilot Plant, reported to Dee and Lentz.

Six months after the indictment, the Department of Justice took the three defendants to court. Each defendant was charged with four counts of illegally storing and disposing of waste. William Dee was found guilty of one count, and Lentz and Gepp were found guilty on three counts each of violating RCRA. Although each faced up to 15 years in prison and $750,000 in fines, they received sentences of 1,000 hours of community service and three years' probation. The judge justified the relatively light sentences on the grounds of the high standing of the defendants in the community and the fact that they had already incurred enormous court costs. Because the three engineers were criminally indicted, the U.S. Army could not assist them in their legal defense. This was the first criminal conviction of federal employees under RCRA.

9.1   Introduction

Dee, Lentz, and Gepp were responsible for serious environmental pollution. Their case marks one of the few times that engineers have been criminally indicted and convicted for actions committed in their professional capacity. Their actions illustrate in a dramatic way the importance of environmental issues for the engineering profession.

If environmental issues are important for the engineering profession, engineering is even more important for environmental issues. On the one hand, projects designed by engineers produce toxic chemicals that pollute the land, air, and rivers. Engineers also design projects that flood farmlands, drain wetlands, and destroy forests. On the other hand, engineers design projects and processes that reduce or eliminate these same threats to environmental integrity. If engineers have contributed to our environmental problems (as have most of the rest of us), they are also an essential part of their solution.

What obligations should the engineering profession (as opposed to engineers as private citizens) assume regarding the environment? We can begin to answer this question by looking at the three engineering society codes that refer to the environment and considering the issues raised by the ASCE code's references to sustainable development. Then we shall examine some of the reasons for the controversy over including environmental provisions in engineering codes. After a brief survey of some environmental laws and court decisions, we shall offer a definition of "clean" as it applies to the environment. Then, we shall consider the animal liberation and environmental movements, as they raise the larger question of engineering obligations to the environment where human health is not an issue. Finally, we shall present a proposal that we believe would allow engineers more freedom to exercise their obligation to protect human health, while not violating the consciences of engineers who do not believe engineers have professional obligations to the environment where human health is not at stake.

9.2   Engineering Codes and the Environment

Code References to the Environment

Three U.S. engineering codes make direct reference to the environment: the codes of the **American Society of Civil Engineers (ASCE), the Institute of Electrical and Electronics Engineers (IEEE), and the American Society of Mechanical Engineers (ASME)**. The 1977 ASCE code included for the first time the statement that "Engineers should be committed to improving the environment to enhance the quality of life" (section 1.f). The code as revised in 1996, however, contains many more references to the environment. Canon 1 says:

> Engineers shall hold paramount the safety, health and welfare of the public and shall strive to comply with the principles of sustainable development in the performance of their professional duties.

Under this canon, four statements address engineers' responsibility to the environment:

> c. Engineers whose professional judgment is overruled under circumstances where the safety, health and welfare of the public are endangered, or the principles of sustainable development ignored, shall inform their clients or employers of the possible consequences.

> d. Engineers who have knowledge or reason to believe that another person or firm may be in violation of any of the provisions of Canon 1 shall present such information to the proper authority in writing and shall cooperate with the proper authority in furnishing such further information or assistance as may be required.

> e. Engineers should seek opportunities to be of constructive service in civic affairs and work for the advancement of the safety, health and well-being of their communities, and the protection of the environment through the practice of sustainable development.

> f. Engineers should be committed to improving the environment by adherence to the principles of sustainable development so as to enhance the quality of life of the general public.

The code's environmental statements fall into two categories, which we may refer to as *requirements* and *recommendations*. By using the expression "engineers shall," the code *requires* engineers to comply with the principles of sustainable development, to inform their clients or employers of the possible consequences of ignoring the principles of sustainable development, to present information regarding the failure to comply with the principles of sustainable development to the proper authority in writing, and to "cooperate with the proper authority in furnishing such further information or assistance as may be required."

By using the expression "engineers should," the code merely *recommends* that engineers seek opportunities to work for the "protection of the environment through the practice of sustainable development" and that they be "committed to improving the environment by adherence to the principles of sustainable development so as to enhance the quality of life of the general public."

In general, the code requires engineers to comply with the principles of sustainable development in their own work and to provide information about the consequences of violating the principles and about those who do. The code merely recommends that engineers actively seek opportunities to protect and improve the environment.

The code of the Institute of Electrical and Electronics Engineers (IEEE), as revised in 1990, also makes reference to the environment. The first canon of the code commits IEEE members

> to accept responsibility in making engineering decisions consistent with the safety, health and welfare of the public, and to disclose promptly factors that might endanger the public or the environment.

IEEE members are required only to "disclose" possible dangers to the public and the environment. Should such dangers be disclosed only to one's immediate superior? What if one's superior is part of the problem? Should an engineer disclose threats to the environment to those outside his or her organization if there appears to be no internal remedy? Does an engineer have any right as a professional to refuse to participate in projects to which she has strong objections from an environmental standpoint? These questions are not addressed.

In 1998 the American Society of Mechanical Engineers became the third of the major engineering societies to introduce a canon on the environment into its code. Canon 8 reads:

> Engineers shall consider environmental impact in the performance of their professional duties.

The canon does not *require* engineers to modify their designs or change their professional work due to environmental factors, only to "consider environmental impact." It certainly does not say that environmental considerations should override all others. Nevertheless, the implication is that mechanical engineers should allow environmental impact a place in their professional work.

Sustainable Development

The ASCE code frequently refers to *sustainable development*. The term is defined in another ASCE document, "The Role of the Engineer in Sustainable Development":

> Sustainable development is a process of change in which the direction of investment, the orientation of technology, the allocation of resources, and the development and functioning of institutions [is directed] to meet present needs and aspirations without endangering the capacity of natural systems to absorb the effects of human activities, and without compromising the ability of future generations to meet their own needs and aspirations.[3]

According to this definition, sustainable development contains two essential ideas. On the one hand, as the word *development* suggests, economic and technical activity must be directed "to meet present needs and aspirations." On the other hand, as the word *sustainable* indicates, this activity must operate under constraints: not jeopardizing the "capacity of natural systems to absorb the effects of human activities" and not "compromising the ability of future generations to meet their own needs and aspirations."

The wide-ranging nature of the concept of sustainable development seems to be reflected in ASCE's definition. It would seem, however, that the special responsibility of the civil engineer (and of engineers generally) should be to the development of technology that conserves natural resources and protects the environment. Engineers should, however, point out that sustainable development involves political, social, and moral dimensions that go beyond the creation of more environmentally friendly technology. Their professional contribution as engineers must be matched by contributions from other elements of society.

The ASCE code marks a distinct advance over the codes of other engineering societies with respect to the environment, because the reference to sustainable development gives additional content to the mandate for environmental responsibility. One might even argue that commitment to the principles of sustainable development is a necessary aspect of concern for the environment and that it is implicit even in the reference to the environment in the IEEE and ASME codes. Nevertheless, in the next section we shall begin to develop a more modest conception of *professional* engineering responsibilities, however much we may admire the ASCE stand.

9.3   Controversy over the Environment

Two Important Distinctions

Currently, only three of the major engineering society codes make explicit reference to the environment. What kind of commitment to the environment do these codes make? Do the other codes make any commitment to the environment at all, even implicitly? Why is concern for the environment such a controversial matter for engineers? To begin to answer these questions, we must make two distinctions: between health- or non–health-related concerns and intrinsic or instrumental values.

First, there are two types of concern for the environment. Engineers can be concerned for the environment when environmental pollution poses a direct and clear threat to human health. We can call this a *health-related concern* for the environment. Engineers can also be concerned for the environment even when human health is not directly affected. We can call this a *non–health-related concern* for the environment.

When engineers are concerned for environmental protection because polluting the air or water introduces carcinogens, this is an example of a health-related concern. Engineering projects often have an impact on the environment, however, even when human health is not directly affected. An engineer may be asked to design a dam that will destroy a wild river or flood thousands of acres of farmland. Or she may be asked to design a sawmill that will be located in the middle of an old-growth forest or to design a condominium that will be built on wetlands. If an engineer objects to these projects for reasons having to do with the environment, the objection is based on a non–health-related concern.[4]

A second distinction is between the intrinsic and instrumental value of nature. Some people believe that trees, rivers, animals, mountains, and other natural objects have *intrinsic value*—that is, value in themselves—apart from human use or appreciation of them. Another way to make the same point is to say that natural objects (or at least some natural objects) are morally considerable. Others believe that natural objects have only *instrumental value*—that is, value insofar as they are used or appreciated by human beings. To these people natural objects are not morally considerable.

If we do not believe that forests or lakes or mountains—or even animals—have value in themselves, we can still justify their having instrumental value, even if they are not directly related to human health. Destruction of forests can affect the supply of wood and the availability of recreational opportunities. Destruction of plant and animal species can damage the ecosystem and limit recreational opportunities. Flooding farmlands can reduce the supply of food for present and future generations. Draining wetlands can damage the ecosystem in ways that ultimately affect human beings.

Now we are in a position to examine the codes with respect to environmental commitments. First, most engineering codes already implicitly commit engineers to health-related environmental concerns, whether or not they use the word *environment*. Most codes commit engineers to holding paramount the safety, health, and welfare of the public. Insofar as protecting the environment is necessary to protecting human health and safety, commitment to the environment is already present by implication.

Second, any commitments to non–health-related concerns and to the intrinsic value of the environment can only be sought in the three codes that explicitly refer to the environment, and even here the precise interpretation is controversial. The IEEE code requires members to disclose factors that could endanger "the public or the environment." Concern for "the public" probably refers to health-related issues, but concern for the environment could refer to non–health-related issues. These non–health-related issues could be based on the intrinsic value of the environment. The ASCE code's commitment to sustainable development is justified as a way to "enhance the quality of life of the general public." Therefore, it does not appear to contain a commitment to the intrinsic value of the environment. On the other hand, sustainable development does involve more than health-related concerns. The ASME canon, referring to "environmental impact," could suggest both health-related and non–health-related concerns, and these concerns might be based on the intrinsic value of the environment. These interpretations, however, are speculative.

One could perhaps make an argument that, just as there is an implicit commitment in all of the codes to health-related environmental concerns by way of the obligation to promote human health, so there is an implicit commitment to non–health-related environmental concerns by way of the obligation to promote human welfare. After all, ample recreational opportunities, a stable ecosystem, an adequate supply of renewable natural resources, wild rivers, and sufficient farmland are important aspects of human welfare. But this may be too wide an interpretation of the term *welfare* as it appears in the codes. It is difficult to understand the uneasiness that some engineering societies have shown about expanding the codes to cover non–health-related environmental concerns if this obligation is already implicit in the codes. At any rate, there is no evidence that engineering codes (with the possible exception of the three that refer to the environment) require any concern for the environment on any grounds other than its relation to human health.

Why the Reluctance to Be Concerned with the Environment?

The reticence of the codes to use the word *environment,* or to require concern for it that does not relate to human health, is reflected in the attitudes of many business managers and many members of the public at large. In a 1982 interview, David Roderick, chairman of U.S. Steel, said, "the primary role and duty of management really is to make money."[5] Economist Milton Friedman supported this view in a famous article in the *New York Times Magazine* when he said that it is the responsibility of business managers to "make as much money as possible while conforming to the basic rules of the society, both those embodied in law and those embodied in ethical custom."[6] He specifically mentions "avoiding pollution" as one of the items for which stockholder money should not be spent.

These sentiments reflect what one survey refers to as "crisis-oriented environmental management." Industries in this group often have no full-time personnel assigned to environmental concerns, devote as few financial resources as possible to environmental matters, and fight environmental regulations. As one representative of this group put it, "Why the hell should we cooperate with government or anyone else who takes us away from our primary goal (of making money)?"[7] He went on to say that it is cheaper to pay the fines and lobby than to devote resources to environmental matters.

Some industries have adopted a different philosophy, which we might call "cost-oriented environmental management." Firms with this orientation accept governmental regulation as a cost of doing business, but they often do so without enthusiasm or commitment. There is often a great deal of skepticism about the value of environmental regulation. Nevertheless, these firms usually have established company policies regulating environmental matters and separate units devoted to them.

A third group has adopted what can be called "enlightened environmental management." In these companies, being responsive to environmental concerns has the complete support of the CEO. The companies have well-staffed environmental divisions, use state-of-the-art equipment, and generally have good relationships with governmental regulators. One manager in this group said that people in his company saw themselves as good neighbors in the community. "Anyhow," he concluded, "in the long run it's in our own interest, to keep us from lawsuits and generate some good will."[8]

At least two arguments might be given for the "enlightened environmental management" position. First, business should be a good citizen of the community. One might argue that business has an implied contract with the larger society, according to which it must be a responsible citizen of the community in return for enjoying the advantages of being a profitable business enterprise. A second argument, suggested by the preceding manager, is the self-interested one that a positive attitude of cooperation with the law will be good for business in the long run, by generating goodwill and avoiding lawsuits.

The number of industries in this third group seems to be increasing. In some cases, an entire industry group has developed a program to increase environmental responsibility. One example is an initiative by the Chemical Manufacturers Association (CMA). For a number of years, the chemical industry had received a considerable amount of public criticism about such issues as safety and pollution. In response to these criticisms, the CMA established a program called "Responsible Care: A Public Commitment." On April 11, 1990, more than 170 member firms of CMA published a set of guiding principles in the *New York Times* and the *Wall Street Journal.*

The principles commit the industry to such policies as promoting the safe manufacture, transportation, use, and disposal of chemicals; promptly giving notice of safety and environmental hazards to the public and others potentially affected; operating plants in an environmentally safe manner; promoting research to improve chemicals with regard to their effects on health, safety, and the environment; participating with government in creating responsible laws regulating chemicals; and sharing with others information useful in promoting these goals.

To meet one major objective of the Responsible Care initiative, to respond to public concerns, the CMA established a Public Advisory Panel (PAP), consisting of fifteen nonindustry representatives of the public. The CMA has also made commitment to Responsible Care a condition of membership.

Minnesota Mining and Manufacturing (3M) has not only subscribed to the Responsible Care guidelines, but adopted policies that go beyond their requirements. In the past, 3M was one of the nation's major emitters of air pollutants. In the early 1990s, 3M initiated a vigorous environmental program to reduce their emissions at levels below those allowed by environmental regulations. For example, it installed $26 million worth of equipment to burn off solvents, even though the plants were already meeting EPA standards for air emissions, resulting in reducing their twenty-five million pounds of volatile organic solvents by 98 percent.

Further, 3M has now built its environment strategy into all layers of management and production. It wants to cut all emissions by 90 percent from the 1990 levels by the year 2000. It also helps customers reduce their waste problems by recycling some of its packaging. According to 3M, its more than 4,600 3P (Preventing Pollution Pays) projects have saved the company $800 million since 1975.[9]

Although it appears that more industries are moving toward the "enlightened environmental management" attitude, many have not yet embraced it. So it seems fair to say that not all leaders of business and nonbusiness organizations are sympathetic with environmental concerns.

Searching for a Criterion for "Clean"

Another reason for the controversy over including environmental statements in the codes may be that it is difficult to define the goal of environmental purity. Environmental pollution, however, is often a threat to human health; and as engineers are obligated to protect human health, they are obligated to promote a clean environment. But how do we determine what is clean? Engineers often ask, "How clean is clean?" What is an appropriate working criterion or definition of "clean" that can guide responsible engineers in thinking about health-related environmental pollution? Should the environment be "perfectly" clean? What would it be like to have an environment that is perfectly clean? If the environment cannot be perfectly clean (or if this concept does not even make any sense), how clean should it be? Table 10.1 lists some inadequate definitions of clean, with the reasons for their inadequacy.

Table 10.1
Inadequate Definitions of "Clean"

Criterion	Objections
1. *Comparative criterion:* The environment is clean if it imposes no greater threat to human life or health than other risks.	The levels of pollution presently accepted may be too high.
Application: Workers should not expect working conditions to be safer than the drive to and from work.	
2. *Normalcy criterion:* The environment is clean if the pollutants present in it are normally present in nature to the same degree.	The levels of pollution in nature vary and may sometimes be accepted only because they are unavoidable.
Application: Radiation as high as the level of ultraviolet radiation in Denver is acceptable.	
3. *Optimal-pollution reduction criterion:* The environment is clean if funds required to reduce pollution further could be used in other ways that would produce more overall human well-being.	Cost and benefits may be unfairly distributed.
Application: The funds required to reduce a pollutant further would save more lives if used elsewhere.	
4. *Maximum protection criterion:* The environment is clean only if any identifiable risk from pollution that poses a possible threat to human health has been eliminated, up to the capacity of available technology and legal enforcement to do so.	This criterion would require the elimination of many substances whose toxicity is doubtful or extremely limited.
Application: A new chemical is assumed to be harmful unless shown to be harmless.	
5. *Demonstrable harm criterion:* The environment is clean if every pollutant that is demonstrably harmful to human health has been eliminated.	It is often difficult to prove a substance is harmful, even when it is. Also, eliminating a pollutant completely may be too costly, as well as unnecessary if the pollutant is harmless at low levels.
Application: Eliminate anything that can be proven to be a pollutant; leave everything else as it is.	

As the objections indicate, all of these criteria are inadequate. It is no wonder that legislators and the courts have found it difficult to establish an adequate criterion for a clean environment, even where human health is concerned. These problems may also help to explain why engineers are reluctant to introduce environmental provisions into the codes. Yet legislative bodies and the courts realize that we must have environmental laws, and that they must be as plausible and rational as possible. So, even though moral criteria cannot be taken uncritically from the law, it may be instructive to survey some legislation and court decisions on the environment and public health. These laws and court decisions may serve as a basis for constructing a guideline for answering the question, "How clean is clean?"

9.4   What Does the Law Say?

Environmental degradation was not the subject of serious federal regulation until the late 1960s.[10] Until that time, an individual who wanted to combat pollution was usually forced to appeal to the common law. If no single individual was sufficiently harmed by pollution to be motivated to bring suit against a polluter, no action was taken. The states were equally ineffective in controlling pollution. This situation opened the way for federal intervention.

Federal Laws on the Environment

In 1969 Congress passed the National Environmental Policy Act, which declared "a national policy which will encourage productive and enjoyable harmony between man and his environment. . . ." The act attempts to "assure for all Americans safe, healthful, productive and aesthetically and culturally pleasing surroundings."[11] One of its best-known mandates is the environmental impact statement, now required of federal agencies when their decisions affect the environment. Congress then created the Environmental Protection Agency (EPA) to enforce its mandates.

Although directly concerned with worker health, the Occupational Safety and Health Act (1970) has important implications for the more general control of toxic substances. It authorizes the secretary of labor to set standards for "toxic materials or harmful physical agents." The standard for a given substance must be one that

> most adequately assures, to the extent feasible, on the basis of the best available evidence, that no employee will suffer material impairment of health or functional capacity even if such employee has regular exposure to the hazard dealt with by such standards for the period of his working life.[12]

The act seems to impose a strict standard: the employee must be protected from "material impairment of health or functional capacity" for his entire working life. But it also allows that the feasibility of the protection must be considered and that it need last only for the "working life" of the employee.

In 1970 Congress passed the Clean Air Act, amending it in 1977 and 1990. The act places health considerations ahead of balancing costs and benefits when dealing with hazardous pollutants.[13] It set a goal of a 90 percent reduction in auto emissions. It also permitted the EPA to consider economic and technological feasibility in deciding when the goals were to be met, but not in setting the goals themselves.

In 1972 Congress enacted the Clean Water Act and amended it in 1972, 1977, 1986, and 1987. The act, designed to "restore and maintain the chemical, physical, and biological integrity of the Nation's waters," makes it unlawful for any person, business, or governmental body to discharge any pollutant into navigable waters without a permit. The act mandated pollution control measures in two stages: (1) by 1977 all plants were to have installed water pollution control devices that represented the best practicable pollution control technology, and (2) by 1989 all plants were to have installed equipment that met more stringent standards. Plants discharging conventional pollutants must apply the best conventional pollutant control technology. Plants discharging toxic or unconventional pollutants must apply the best available technology economically achievable. The act requires polluters to do their very best to stop polluting, regardless of the cost.[14]

In 1976 Congress enacted the Resource Conservation and Recovery Act, designed to control the transportation, storage, treatment, and disposal of hazardous wastes. The act requires the producer of a hazardous waste to complete a "manifest," a form that describes the nature of the hazardous waste and its method of disposal. The transporter and the operator of the disposal site both must sign the manifest and return it to the producer of the waste. This procedure is supposed to provide a complete record of the disposal of the waste. The EPA is also required to regulate the disposal sites. The act requires that standards regulating hazardous waste be based solely on the protection of public health and the environment.[15]

The Pollution Prevention Act of 1990 establishes pollution prevention as a national objective. The act requires the EPA to develop and implement a strategy to promote reduction at the pollutant's source. This policy is in sharp contrast to most environmental protection, which simply attempts to manage pollutants. The act establishes pollution prevention as the most desirable practice, followed by recycling, treatment, and disposal, in a descending order of preference.

There are many other important pieces of environmental legislation. The Federal Insecticide, Fungicide and Rodenticide Act took its contemporary form in 1972 and has had five amendments. The Safe Drinking Water Act was passed in 1974 and was substantially amended in 1996. The Toxic Substances Control Act was passed in 1976 and amended three times. The act commonly referred to as "Superfund" was passed in 1980. In 1990, in response to the Exxon *Valdez* accident, the oil-spill provisions of the Clean Water Act were amended to form what is usually called the Oil Pollution Act. The Residential Lead-Based Paint Hazard Reduction Act was passed in 1992, and the Mercury-Containing and Rechargeable Battery Management Act was passed in 1996.

This short list by no means enumerates all of the environmental and health-related legislation passed by Congress in the past twenty-five years. It does illustrate, however, the range of positions taken on the proper criterion for a clean environment: all the way from the refusal to allow cost to play any part in the determination to the clear acceptance of cost considerations. None of these acts mandates cost/benefit analysis, although some allow cost to be considered in their implementation.

The Courts on the Environment

Critics still maintain, however, that congressional legislation is often unrealistic in the extent to which it ignores cost considerations. The courts, they argue, must face even more directly both the costs of pollution control to industry and governmental agencies and the technological limits to our ability to control pollution. In the process, they might provide a more useful guide to a criterion for a clean environment.

In *International Harvester v. Ruckelshaus,* the District of Columbia Circuit Court ruled in 1973 that EPA regulations might have been congruent with the Clean Air Act but were defective in their rulings because they failed to consider the feasibility and practicality of the technology required.[16] The District of Columbia Court of Appeals rendered a decision in 1973 with similar import. It interpreted a relevant section of the Clean Air Act as permitting the EPA to consider costs but not to impose a cost/benefit test.[17] In the famous "Benzene" decision of 1980, a plurality of justices on the U.S. Supreme Court found that "safe" does not entail "risk free." Justice Stevens argued that OSHA could not regulate a chemical simply because it posed *some* risk; OSHA would also have to show that the risk was "significant."[18]

In 1986 a tribunal for the Circuit Court in the District of Columbia reviewed a decision by the EPA to set a standard for vinyl chloride emissions at levels less strict than industry could have satisfied at the time if it had devoted great effort and expense to the task. The court ruled that when the EPA cannot determine a "safe" threshold for a pollutant, it may take not only health but also technological and economic factors into account in establishing emission standards that industry can achieve without paying costs "grossly disproportionate" to the level of safety achieved.[19]

In an earlier decision on asbestos, the District of Columbia Circuit Court of Appeals noted that Congress recognized that "employees would not be protected if their employers were put out of business." It also called attention, however, to the fact that "standards do not become infeasible simply because they may impose substantial costs on an industry, force the development of new technology, or even force some employers out of business."[20]

Carl Cranor summarizes the implications of the Circuit Court's decisions in the following way:

> The implicit principles embodied in the D.C. Circuit Court's decisions suggest the following. On the one hand, OSHA may set standards more stringent than existing ones in pursuit of better health for workers, unless they threaten the economic viability of an entire industry; that is too steep a price to pay for improved health. On the other hand, even the court interprets Congress as being willing to tolerate the loss of some jobs, and even some firms in an industry, if failure to impose health

regulations would materially impair the health or functional capacity for workers in that industry.[21]

So, How Clean Is Clean?

Any rational criterion for a clean environment must take into account both the need to protect the health of workers and the general public and the need to protect the financial viability of industries on which workers and the general public depend. Yet the balance suggested by Cranor's summary may not be the correct one, for it appears to allow serious violations of the health of individuals if this is necessary to protect a whole "industry." According to Cranor's summary, we may impose stricter health regulations, even if the result is the closing of some firms; but we may not impose regulations that force the closing of a whole "industry."

There are also conceptual issues having to do with how we determine what constitutes an "industry." As Cranor asks, "Are plastic container and metal container manufacturers part of the same industry, or are they two different industries?"[22] Suppose that protecting human health requires that we impose regulation on plastic production that would put all plastic container manufacturers out of business. If plastic container manufacturers are considered an "industry" in themselves, we may not impose these severe regulations, because it would eliminate an "industry." If, however, plastic container manufacturers and metal container manufacturers are considered a part of the same industry, the regulations may be imposed, because an entire industry will not be eliminated. This limitation on our ability to protect human health would presumably apply, regardless of the severity of the health risks to workers or the public.

Mark Sagoff has proposed a more stringent criterion for determining an acceptable level of cleanness, which he also believes has a basis in some of the same court decisions. According to Sagoff, we need an environmental policy that "might permit governmental agencies to take technological and economic factors into account, on a case-by-case basis, as long as they act in good faith to make progress toward reducing and, it is hoped, eventually eliminating damage to the environment and risks to human safety and health."[23] This criterion, however, seems excessively stringent. Like the Maximum Protection Criterion discussed in Table 10.1, it appears to justify enormous expenditures of money for very small increases in environmental purity. It argues that we must continue to "make progress" in the reduction of pollution, even if the small gains in environmental purity are enormously expensive and produce no appreciable improvement in human health.

Attempts by Congress and especially the courts to balance economic considerations against the need to protect human health have been only partially successful. They do suggest, however, the overall form of the balance; we must balance considerations of cost and technical feasibility against considerations of human health. Succinctly, we must balance considerations of wealth against considerations of health. A more direct analysis of the issues in terms of this familiar moral contrast may be helpful in constructing a criterion for determining when the environment is "clean."

9.5   Balancing Wealth and Health: A Criterion for "Clean"

In coming to grips with the issues with which the courts are struggling, we must begin with the assumption that we are trying to balance the goals of increasing job opportunities and income on the one hand with protecting the health of individuals on the other. Let us begin with the utilitarian approach to this issue.[24]

From the utilitarian standpoint, we want to increase income, job opportunities, and even overall public health. An increase in income produces utility, whether it is the income of workers or owners. Similarly, an increase in the number and the desirability of jobs also increases utility. Finally, good health is a precondition for achieving most other goods, and so is desirable also from a utilitarian standpoint. Utilitarians, however, permit trade-offs between any of these goods, if the trade-off will produce a net increase in overall utility. Because utilitarians consider the well-being of individuals only insofar as it affects overall utility, minor benefits to many might outweigh severe harms to a few. Thus, we might be justified in reducing health protection for some, in exchange for a net increase in overall utility.

Some environmental laws and (especially) some recent court decisions have attempted to guard against this unfortunate tendency of utilitarianism to forget the individual in the effort to promote greater overall utility; this often involves an appeal to considerations more compatible with respect for persons' morality. The ethics of respect for persons' attempts to take account of the distribution of goods and harm and of the special weight that some goods (such as health) have. From the respect for persons standpoint, an individual's health should not be sacrificed, even to increase the general welfare of everyone.[25]

A Degree-of-Harm Criterion

We believe that the engineer's obligation to hold paramount the health of the public should not be interpreted in purely utilitarian terms. However, the need to consider the economic effects of regulations protecting human health must not be forgotten. The proper criterion for evaluating what is clean must cover a spectrum of cases, with two extremes.

This spectrum is delineated in the following criterion, which we shall call the Degree-of-Harm Criterion:

> When pollutants pose a clear and pressing threat to human health, they must be reduced below any reasonable threshold of harm. Cost should not be considered a significant factor. Insofar as substances pose an uncertain (but possible) risk to health or when the threshold of danger cannot be determined, economic factors may be considered. If a harm is irreversible, it should be given higher priority.

According to this criterion, the task of protecting the environment where human health is concerned oscillates between two extremes. At one extreme, where the risk of causing harm to people is grave, the imperative of protecting human health must be primary. In some cases, this imperative might require the elimination of virtually all pollution, even if this involves great expense or shutting down the source of the pollution. At the other extreme, where the risk to human health appears to be small or is indeterminate, cost/benefit considerations are more appropriate. Although cost/benefit analysis cannot be used to determine to what extent serious threats to health must be eliminated, it may be used—within limits that cannot be precisely specified—to determine the extent to which suspected but undetermined threats must be eliminated.

We believe that this policy should guide the engineer's interpretation of the requirement in most engineering codes to protect the health of the public. If there are statements requiring engineers to protect the environment, we believe this criterion should be a guide in interpreting this obligation where human health is affected.

Let us consider some cases to illustrate how the criterion might serve as a guide in line-drawing problems. We can begin with a case in which the criterion has been violated. Suppose engineer Vivian is employed by Shady Chemical, a firm that follows the policies described as "crisis-oriented environmental management." The firm has a long history of producing pesticides that not only damage the environment, but also pose a threat to the workers who manufacture them, the farmers who apply them, and the consumers who eat the food to which they are applied. When one of its products is banned by the government, the usual procedure of Shady Chemical is to slightly modify its chemical formula, so that it no longer falls under the ban. By the time the new product is also banned, a new chemical is usually ready.

Vivian has been asked to participate in the development of an alternative to one of Shady Chemical's most successful products. The firm has learned on good authority that the product will shortly be banned because it has been found to be a virulent carcinogen. Following its usual policy, Shady wants to find a substitute for the active ingredient in the pesticide that is as close to the old product as possible.

Although one can never be sure that the modified product has similar toxic properties to the old one until extensive testing has been done, Vivian has good reason to believe that the proposed substitute may even be worse. Shady Chemical has violated the Degree-of-Harm Criterion.

Consider another example. The plant that employs engineer Bob has just discovered that its discharge into the atmosphere includes a new chemical that comes from one of their new product lines. The chemical is structurally similar to a class of chemicals that has been declared safe by the governmental regulatory agency. There is no reason to suspect the chemical is dangerous, although its effects on humans has not been extensively tested. The management at Bob's plant follows the policy described as "enlightened environmental management," and its Environmental Affairs Department is monitoring the new chemical. The department is prepared to take action to eliminate it from the discharge if any reason to suspect it is found, even if it is not banned by the government. In this case Bob's firm is probably showing sufficient regard for human health.

Many intermediate cases are more difficult to decide. Suppose engineer Melinda is employed by a plant whose management follows the policies described as "cost-oriented environmental management." A new chemical has been identified in the plant's discharge into the local river. The chemical is not a regulated substance, although it is structurally similar to substances that have been found to be carcinogenic in large concentrations. Elimination of the substance would be expensive, but its elimination would be economically feasible. In this situation the Degree-of-Harm Criterion would probably require that the plant begin making preparations to eliminate the substance from its discharge. Melinda would have to have more information, however, before she could be sure about the implications of the Degree-of-Harm Criterion. The importance of a thorough analysis of the facts, especially in non-paradigmatic line-drawing cases, cannot be overemphasized.

What should the codes say with regard to health-related environmental issues? We have maintained that the codes already implicitly commit engineers to protecting the environment where human health is concerned. From this perspective, there is no need for any additional statement. Nevertheless, we believe that the importance of environmental cases, together with the fact that many engineers do not recognize the implicit commitments in the codes regarding health-related issues, requires that there be an explicit reference to the environment. We suggest that, *as a minimum,* engineering codes should contain a statement such as the following:

> Engineers shall hold paramount the health, safety, and welfare of the public and the integrity of the environment, at least insofar as it affects human health.

9.6   The Anthropocentric Approach to Environmental Ethics

We have noted that at most only three codes commit engineers to non–health-related environmental concerns, and that there is not much evidence that the codes attribute intrinsic value to natural objects. The contemporary environmental movement challenges both of these positions. During the past two decades many objections have been raised to such activities as using animals in testing consumer products and in scientific laboratories; raising chickens and other animals in cages and similar confining conditions; killing whales, dolphins, and other higher mammals; destroying the natural habitats of animal and plant species; draining wetlands; cutting virgin forests; and flooding farmlands and wild areas. These objections go far beyond a concern for human health. Sometimes they go beyond a concern for human welfare of any type. And although environmentalists sometimes base these objections upon a view that natural objects (including animals) have only instrumental value, they sometimes hold that natural objects have intrinsic value.

It is useful to divide the movement to protect the nonhuman world into two parts: the animal liberation movement and the environmental movement. Increasingly, these two movements have gone their separate ways, and they sometimes can work at cross purposes. For example, forest fires are often caused by natural means and sometimes may produce beneficial results for plant life, but they may be highly destructive to animal life. In such situations, animal liberationists may find themselves in an adversarial relationship with other environmental groups. The environmental movement is considerably more pertinent to engineering ethics than the animal liberation movement. Nevertheless, it will be helpful to consider the common elements in the two movements, as well as some of the differences between them.

The common element in both the animal liberation and environmental movements is a rejection of the strong anthropocentric orientation prominent in Western ethics. An *anthropocentric* ethics holds that only human beings are "morally considerable"—that is, have intrinsic value. Nonhuman natural objects have value only as they contribute to human well-being. A *non-anthropocentric* ethics holds that at least some natural objects other than human beings (animals, plants, and perhaps even inanimate things such as rivers and mountains) have intrinsic value.

Animal Liberation and Engineering Ethics

Most Western moral philosophies focus primarily—or even exclusively—on human beings. Nonhuman animals, plants, and the nonliving world are to be considered only insofar as they are necessary means for promoting the utility of humans or the respect due to human persons. William Baxter stated this anthropocentric position in the following way:

> Penguins are important because people enjoy seeing them walk about rocks. . . . I have no interest in preserving penguins for their own sake.[26]

Notice that the penguins are not asked about their view of the matter! Human beings are the measure of the good.

The animal liberation movement challenges this account of the value of penguins and other forms of animal life. One of the most important challenges to such anthropocentrism as it applies to animals is based on some forms of utilitarianism, and it is easy to see how a concern for at least some nonhuman animals can be extracted from the utilitarian way of thinking. For utilitarians, happiness or well-being includes, among other things, the experience of pleasure and the avoidance of pain. Few people would deny that animals are able to experience pleasure and pain. Why, then, should only the pleasure and pain of humans be morally considerable? Can we give any reason, other than the anthropocentric position itself, for this limitation? If we cannot, then limiting ethical concern exclusively to the human species is arbitrary and unfounded, from a utilitarian point of view.

Peter Singer, a utilitarian advocate of protecting the welfare of animals, has referred to the anthropocentrism of Western ethics as *speciesism,* a viewpoint that excludes nonhuman animals from the ranks of the morally considerable.[27] Like racism and sexism, speciesism is arbitrary and morally unjustifiable, Singer believes. Racism excludes some human beings from full moral consideration on the basis of skin color or other racial characteristics, and sexism excludes some human beings from full moral consideration on the basis of their sex; speciesism excludes some living beings from full moral consideration on the basis of the species to which they belong. Singer does not deny that human interests may often justifiably outweigh the interests of nonhuman animals. Humans may, after all, have the capacity for more intense suffering because of their greater self-consciousness and ability to anticipate the future. But if the suffering of a human being and an animal is really equal in intensity, the suffering of the human does not deserve any more consideration than the suffering of the animal.

The animal liberation movement does have some relevance to engineering ethics. Engineering projects sometimes destroy the habitats and the lives of animals, and products developed by engineers are sometimes tested on animals in inhumane ways. In such situations engineers may be forced to make moral decisions about the proper attitude toward nonhuman animals.

The Environmental Movement and Engineering Ethics

The environmental movement, however, is much more relevant to the engineering profession. In its broadest aspects, the environmental movement is concerned with the living and the nonliving aspects of the natural world that form what Aldo Leopold, an important figure in the contemporary environmental movement, calls the "biotic community." According to many proponents of environmentalism, contemporary technologically advanced civilization is guilty of massive assaults on the biotic community. Western society in particular has tended to conceive of nature as passive, and thus, as the fit object of human manipulation and control.

This view of nature as passive is amply reflected in our language about the natural world. Land is to be "developed." "Raw" land is to be "improved." Natural resources are to be "exploited" and "consumed." Trees are to be "harvested." The rivers are to be "harnessed" to produce electrical power. The wilderness must be "managed." Nature, like the rest of the nonhuman world, is to be subservient to human purposes.

Aldo Leopold wrote in *A Sand County Almanac*:

> We abuse land because we regard it as a commodity belonging to us. When we see land as a community to which we belong, we may begin to use it with love and respect. . . . Perhaps such a shift in values can be achieved by reappraising things unnatural, tame, and confined in terms of things natural, wild, and free.[28]

For many proponents of the environmental movement, we must replace the traditional distinctions between things and moral agents with a wider view, according to which it is wrong to treat nature, or "the land," as a mere commodity that can be used in any way humans see fit. Leopold's view interprets nature as something to which we belong rather than something that belongs to us. It is something "wild" and "free" rather than a passive object on which we work our purposes. Nature is "a fountain of energy flowing through a circuit of soils, plants, and animals."[29]

Viewing nature as an interdependent biotic community, Leopold believed that nature elicits an ethical response. He called this ethical response the "land ethic" and stated its moral standard in these words: "A thing is right when it tends to preserve the integrity, stability, and beauty of the biotic community. It is wrong when it tends otherwise."[30]

In the light of this wider moral vision, some environmentalists have found that the importance of human beings must be reassessed. A dramatic and extreme statement of this idea is given by philosopher Paul Taylor:

> Every last man, woman, and child could disappear from the face of the Earth without any significant detrimental consequence for the good of wild animals and plants. On the contrary, many of them would be greatly benefited . . . If then, the total, final absolute extermination of our species should take place and if we should not carry all the others with us into oblivion, not only would the Earth's community of life continue to exist, but in all probability its well being would be enhanced. Our presence, in short, is not needed. If we were to take the standpoint of the community and give voice to its true interest, the ending of our . . . epoch would most likely be greeted with a healthy "Good riddance."[31]

Although a widespread belief that beings other than humans have intrinsic value has emerged from recent environmental thought, there is disagreement about how far the class of morally considerable beings should be extended. But we do not need to settle the question of precisely what parts of the natural world have intrinsic value. It is sufficient to point out that non–health-related environmental concerns can be justified by way of their connection with human welfare.

One way in which non–health-related concerns can be related to human welfare is through what some environmentalists call the experience of "the wild." Political theorist John Rodman expresses the need for this experience in the following way:

> The need for wilderness grows more acute every moment because it is, among other things, the need to experience a realm of reality beyond the manipulations of commodity production and technology . . . the need for realities that function as symbols of otherness that can arouse a response from the suppressed potentialities of human nature.[32]

If human welfare includes the need to experience a part of the natural world that is wholly beyond human life, which is characterized by mystery and "otherness," then there is a basis for concern for nature that goes beyond a consideration of human health. From this standpoint we can say that human welfare is adversely affected by the elimination of wilderness areas and other environmental assets, even if such elimination does not directly affect human health.

If one does not accept this argument, a concern for the nonhuman world can be related to human welfare in an even more direct and obvious way. Activities that reduce available farmland or drain underground water supplies can vitally affect the ability of human beings to support themselves. A healthy natural environment is important to human survival in the long run and is thus related to human welfare in the most fundamental sense of the term, namely human survival.

The integrity of the environment is vitally important for human welfare, but the issue is whether the codes should require engineers to promote environmental integrity even when human health is not at stake. It is doubtful that the framers of the codes had non–health-related environmental concerns in mind when they referred to human "welfare." The engineering community could, of course, decide to extend the term welfare to include non–health-related environmental issues regardless of what the framers of the code had in mind. Or it could impose such obligations on engineers, independently of an appeal to the reference to human welfare in many professional codes. What should engineering *professional* ethics require of engineers with regard to non–health-related environmental issues?

9.7 The Scope of Professional Engineering Obligations to the Environment

We can begin by considering some of the arguments of those who believe that professional engineering obligations to the environment should be extended beyond a concern for factors that endanger human health.

First, because engineers are usually the creators of technology that contributes to environmental degradation as well as environmental improvement, they should have a professional obligation to protect the environment. Let us say that people are morally responsible for something when they knowingly bring it about or cause it to exist or happen. If I turn out the lights while friends are walking up the stairs, knowing full well that they may fall, then I am responsible if they fall; that is, I can be blamed for their fall. If I did not know that anyone was on the stairs and had no reason to believe that they were, then I am not responsible; that is, I cannot be blamed.

According to this argument, engineers should share in the responsibility for environmental concerns, because they are often causal agents in projects and activities that affect the environment for good or ill. Engineers design dams that flood farmlands and wild rivers. They design chemical plants that pollute the air and water. They also design solar energy systems that make hydroelectric projects unnecessary and pollution control systems that eliminate the discharge of pollutants into the air and water. Furthermore, they usually are (or should be) aware of the effects of their work on the environment.

Many people believe that if engineers are morally responsible agents in issues affecting the environment, they should also be required as professionals to promote environmental integrity, even where human health is not at stake. If this is the case, this requirement should be a part of the codes.

Second, the engineering profession might well have a salutary impact on our attitudes and actions with respect to the environment. Engineers are, after all, major participants in virtually all of the projects that affect the environment. If even a small but substantial number of concerned engineers refused to contribute their professional skills to some of the most environmentally destructive projects, the result might well be the cancellation of the projects or at least a modification of them so they would produce less environmental devastation.

There are also three main arguments that engineers should not be assigned professional obligations where human health is not at stake:[33]

1. Many of the judgments that would have to be made in this area fall outside the area of professional engineering expertise. When engineers make such judgments, critics might accuse them of violating their professional responsibility by speaking outside their area of expertise. The **NSPE code**, for example, requires

engineers to "perform services only in the areas of their competence" (I.,II.2). Another section says:

> Engineers may express publicly a professional opinion on technical subjects only when that opinion is founded upon adequate knowledge of the facts and competence in the subject matter. (I.,II.3.b)

Many objections that government or private industry actions harm the environment find their bases in the biological sciences, not in engineering. Lacking this scientific background, perhaps most engineers should make their objections on the grounds of personal moral beliefs, not on the basis of professional ethics.

Suppose engineer Mary is asked to participate in the design of a condominium that will be built on a wetland. She objects because she believes that the wetland is especially important for the ecology of the area. This judgment is not a professional engineering judgment, but rather one more appropriately made by a biologist. Although an engineer may object to participating in the project on the grounds of her personal moral beliefs, it might not be proper to object on professional grounds.

The same problem exists in many other areas related to the environment. An engineer may object to a dam that will destroy a wild river or flood hundreds of acres of farmland. Or he may object to designing a sawmill that is to be built in the midst of an ancient forest. In all of these cases the judgments involve values or knowledge outside most engineers' professional expertise. An engineer may well object to these projects, but the question is whether he should object *as an engineer.* To do so, the critic will argue, is to invite public disrespect for the engineering profession.

We can summarize this argument in more concrete terms. Suppose the NSPE code contained a provision such as this: "Engineers will not participate in projects that are unnecessarily destructive to the environment, even if they do not endanger human life or health." Given the nature of present engineering education, the judgments necessary to comply with such a provision would often not be typically professional engineering judgments, because engineering education does not always cover these areas. Thus, incorporating such a provision into the NSPE code might well involve violating section II.3.b of the same code. So most engineers would have to rely on the judgment of others who do have expertise on such environmental issues.

2. Extending professional responsibility for the environment into areas not clearly related to public health or safety might cause considerable problems for engineering societies. Engineers disagree among themselves over environmental issues, especially where human health is not directly involved. Forcing members of professional societies to take policy stands on such issues would introduce a new source of divisiveness into the societies.

Another aspect of this same objection is that such issues would be especially troublesome for engineering managers who are members of engineering societies. Managers cannot always be expected to lend a sympathetic ear to policies that will inevitably result in greater expense for their organizations. The effect of introducing these issues into the societies may serve to weaken management support for the societies themselves.

Furthermore, extending the provisions of the codes into controversial areas might further weaken the influence of the codes on the engineering profession.

Many engineers have never seen a copy of their professional code, and relatively few have any detailed knowledge of their code's provisions, even though most engineers seem committed to protecting public health and safety. Some engineers may already view some aspects of the codes as unrealistic. Engineers might cite strong environmental provisions as a reason for regarding the codes as radical and politically biased and thus as a reason for ignoring them.

3. Requiring engineers to protect the environment even where human health is not an issue would produce problems of conscience for some engineers. Although there are probably few engineers who disagree with the provisions of engineering codes regarding such issues as conflict of interest, performing duties only in areas in which they are competent, and the necessity of avoiding deception, there are probably many engineers who would disagree with strong provisions requiring engineers to protect the environment where human health is not an issue. Requiring them to take a position contrary to their personal beliefs could force them into a situation with no desirable options. They would have to either act contrary to their personal beliefs, withdraw from their engineering society, or simply disobey their professional code. Engineering societies should avoid forcing their members to make such choices.

We believe there is considerable validity in arguments on both sides of this issue, but we will comment on the first of the three arguments. *As a professional,* one can call on the work of other professionals, but engineers should not, of course, imply that they have professional expertise when they do not. Engineers can avail themselves of the well-established conclusions of biologists and other environmental specialists in making judgments about the environment without violating their professional standards. Nevertheless, we believe a way should be found to accommodate as many of the conflicting arguments about engineers' responsibility for the environment as possible. In the next section, we shall present a proposal for achieving this end.

9.8   Two Modest Proposals

We believe that professional engineering obligations regarding non–health-related issues can best be handled in terms of two proposals:

• Although engineers should be required to hold paramount human health in the performance of their engineering work (including health issues that are environmentally related), they should not be required as professionals (that is, required by the codes) to inject non–health-related environmental concerns into their engineering work.

• Engineers should have the right to organizational disobedience with regard to environmental issues, as this is required by their own *personal* beliefs or their own individual interpretations of what professional obligation requires.

The first proposal embodies the idea that a minimal conception of professional obligation to safeguarding the environment should be incorporated into professional codes. The second proposal assumes that it is possible for individual engineers to have a conception of what it is for them to act as professionals that is not a consensus view, or that they may have personal beliefs about the environment they do not connect with professional obligation at all. It further holds that these views should be respected.

With regard to the second proposal, an engineer could say, "I know that all engineers do not agree with me here, but I believe it is unprofessional to participate in a project involving draining a wetland." Here, the engineer would be holding a view about what professional obligation to the environment entails. An engineer could also say, "I know that all engineers do not agree with me here, but, as a matter of personal conscience, I find it unacceptable to drain wetlands."

In Chapter 8 we considered three types of "organizational disobedience"; all three are relevant to our second proposal:

1. Engineers should have the right to disobedience by contrary action with regard to environmental issues; that is, they should have the right to promote their personal beliefs or their own individual interpretations of what professional obligation requires, including their beliefs about the environment, outside the workplace. For example, an engineer should be able to join an environmental group devoted to saving wetlands, even when her employer wants to drain a wetland to build a new plant. An engineer should be able to speak out against the building of a dam that will destroy a wild river, even when his firm may profit from construction of the dam.

2. Engineers should have the right to disobedience by nonparticipation with regard to environmental issues; that is, they should have the right to refuse to carry out assignments they believe are wrong, including environmentally related assignments. An engineer should be able to refuse to participate in the design of a plant that will adversely affect human health or that will be built on a reclaimed wetland. Similarly, she should have the right to refuse to design a dam that will destroy a wild river.

3. Engineers should have the right to disobedience by protest with regard to environmental issues; that is, they should have the right to protest employer actions they believe to be wrong, including actions that they believe are harmful to human health or the environment. Within the bounds of discretion and due regard for the employer, an engineer should be able to protest an employer's plan to design or build a dam that will destroy a wild river or a project that will involve draining a wetland.

To make these rights clear, we believe the following provision regarding the rights of engineers should be incorporated into engineering codes:

> Where organizational constraints permit, engineers shall not be required to participate in projects that violate their professional obligations as determined by the codes, their professional obligations as determined by their individual interpretations of professional responsibility, or personal beliefs. Engineers shall also have the right to voice responsible objections to engineering projects that they believe are wrong, without fear of reprisal. Engineers shall have the right to support programs and causes of their own choosing outside the workplace.

We can offer the following arguments in support of this provision:

1. There are precedents for such provisions as this one, which asserts a right of engineers rather than imposes an obligation on them. The unusual nature of this provision deserves emphasis. Most engineering codes are composed of a set of obligations that engineers impose on themselves; however, this provision asserts a right of engineers against their employers. There are precedents for the assertion of rights of professionals.

The code of the American Medical Association protects physicians from having to perform medical procedures to which they have personal moral objections. Article VI of the "Principles of Medical Ethics" of the American Medical Association says:

> A physician shall, in the provision of appropriate patient care, except in emergencies, be free to choose whom to serve, with whom to associate, and the environment in which to provide medical services.[34]

Suppose a physician objects to performing abortions or to prescribing contraceptives to unmarried people.[35] This provision of the AMA code allows physicians to refrain from performing these procedures, and still remain in compliance with their professional code. We believe engineers deserve similar protection.

There is even some precedent in engineering for similar assertions. In the next chapter we shall discuss a case examined by the Board of Ethical Review (BER) of the National Society of Professional Engineers. In case 82–5 (case 5 in 1982), the board defended the right of an engineer to protest what he believed were excessive costs and time delays in a defense contract. The BER concluded that, although the engineer did not have an ethical obligation to continue to protest his employer's tactics, he had "a right to do so as a matter of personal conscience." The proposed addition to professional engineering codes would serve a similar function of protecting engineers who have personal objections to projects they believe are harmful to the environment.

In his "model code" of engineering ethics, Stephen Unger also proposes a provision that gives similar protection to engineers. According to his proposal, engineers shall "endeavor to direct their professional skills toward conscientiously chosen ends they deem, on balance, to be of positive value to humanity; declining to pursue those skills for purposes they consider, on balance, to conflict with their moral values."[36] He points out that individual attorneys and physicians are not required to accept every client that asks for their services. The claim that even a guilty person deserves a lawyer and that every person desiring medical services deserves a physician has its limitations when applied to engineering. Some engineering projects may not deserve to be built at all, such as the gas chambers in the Nazi extermination camps. Even if an engineering project is legitimate, it does not follow that an engineer who has moral objections to it should design it.[37]

2. The proposal recognizes the limitations of organizations to honor the right of an engineer to refuse to participate in a project to which she has personal moral objections. Some organizations may have such limited resources that they cannot afford to reassign an engineer who objects to a project. This limitation is recognized in the opening phrase, "Where organizational constraints permit. . . ." Even though an employer can abuse this qualification, we believe that it is necessary to accommodate the legitimate limitations of employers.

3. This provision has the additional advantage of providing a means for non-management engineers to fulfill their professional obligations in a wide variety of issues. Engineers who are not managers often do not have a way to fulfill even their code-mandated obligations. For example, how are engineers who do not have decision-making powers to fulfill their obligations to protect the health of the public? Suppose engineer Jane believes that her plant's discharge into the local river violates the Degree-of-Harm Criterion, but management has decided to do nothing about it. In the absence of decision-making powers, how is she to carry out her responsibility to the public? The proposed code provision says that she may protest her plant's decision, or even refuse to work on projects that contribute to this unjustified pollution.

4. The provision would protect the conscience of engineers who do have strong personal objections to actions that perpetrate non–health-related harms on the environment, or who have a broader understanding of engineers' professional obligations to the environment. Suppose engineer Joe has been asked by his manager to be a part of a team that will design a dam that will flood several thousand acres of rich farmland. Joe believes the dam should not be built but is not in a position to make the decision. Our proposed provision would allow Joe to protest the building of the dam and even to request not to be assigned the task of helping in the design of the dam.

5. The provision would allow engineers who do not share the concern for environmental issues where human health is not at stake to follow their own beliefs as well. Suppose engineer Rhonda's firm also has a contract to design a dam that will flood thousands of acres of farmland. Rhonda has no objection to the dam and in fact thinks it should be built. This provision would allow her to follow that belief.

The question of the nature and extent of the rights and obligations of engineers regarding environmental issues is still highly controversial. The discussion of this question is in a very early stage. The proposals offered in this chapter are intended to contribute to the discussion of this question, as it takes place both within the engineering community and in the larger public arena.

9.9   Chapter Summary

 The codes of **three professional societies**—the IEEE, ASCE, and ASME—make explicit reference to the engineer's obligation to protect the environment. Further, the ASCE code breaks new ground by endorsing commitment to "the principles of sustainable development." A requirement to protect the health and safety of the public, however, which is a part of virtually all engineering codes, implies that engineers have an obligation to promote an environment that protects human health.

There are several reasons why including environmental provisions in the codes is controversial for engineers. One is that many managers are not sympathetic to environmental concerns. Another is that it is difficult to provide an acceptable criterion for a "clean"environment. However, the law suggests that an acceptable criterion must contain a balance between considerations of cost and technical feasibility on the one hand and the need to protect human health on the other. This may provide the basis for a criterion for identifying a clean environment.

The environmental movement has focused public attention on non–health-related environmental concerns. Many environmentalists believe that the environment should be protected for its own sake, but we can also justify attention to the environment on the grounds that it is essential to protecting human welfare in such areas as recreation and renewable natural resources.

It may not be advisable at the present time to require engineers to have obligations to protect the environment where human health is not at stake. The codes should, however, protect the rights of engineers to engage in public efforts to protect the environment, to protest employer actions that they believe are environmentally destructive, and to refuse to engage in projects they believe are environmentally destructive.

 CASES TO CONSIDER

Case 15	An Excess?
Case 21	Gilbane Gold
Case 29	Mere "Technicality"?
Case 33	Parkville*
Case 44	Trees
Case 51	Waste Disposal

NOTES

1. Steven Weisskoph, "The Aberdeen Mess," *Washington Post Magazine* (January 15, 1989).

2. *The Aberdeen Three,* a case prepared under National Science Foundation grant number DIR-9012252. The principal investigators were Michael J. Rabins, Charles E. Harris, Jr., Charles Samson, and Raymond W. Flumerfelt.

3. This document is most easily accessible on the ASCE website, www. asce.org. It was adopted by the ASCE Board of Direction on October 24, 1993.

4. Of course, all issues will not fit neatly into these two categories. And if we interpret "health" broadly enough, all environmental issues may affect human health, either physical or psychological. Nevertheless, we believe the distinction is useful.

5. From a 1982 documentary film, *The Business of America* (News Reel, San Francisco). See Joseph M. Petulla, "Environmental Management in Industry" in Albert Flores, Ed., *Ethics and Risk Management in Engineering* (Lanham, Md.: University Press of America, 1989), p. 143.

6. Milton Friedman, "The Social Responsibility of Business Is to Increase Its Profits," *New York Times Magazine* (September 13, 1970).

7. Petulla, p. 146. For a fuller discussion of the ethical aspects of this issue, see Charles E. Harris, Jr., "Manufacturers and the Environment: Three Alternative Views" in Mo Jamshidi, Mo Shahinpoor, and J. H. Mullins, Eds., *Environmentally Conscious Manufacturing: Recent Advances* (Albuquerque, N.M.: ECM Press, 1991), pp. 195–203.

---

* Includes an analysis of the case.

8. Petulla, p. 151.

9. This information was supplied by Mr. Tom Zosel of 3M.

10. This section utilizes several sources, both for legal citations and ideas. See Mark Sagoff, "Where Ickes Went Right, or Reason and Rationality in Environmental Law," *Ecology Law Quarterly,* 1987, pp. 265–323. See also Al H. Ringleb, Roger E. Meiners, and Frances L. Edwards, *Managing in the Legal Environment* (St. Paul: West, 1990), pp. 553–583. See also Carl F. Cranor, *Regulating Toxic Substances: A Philosophy of Science and the Law* (New York: Oxford University Press, 1993), especially pp. 160–163.

11. 42 U.S.C. sect. 4331 (1982) [note 20].

12. 29 U.S.C., sect. 655 (b)(5)(1976).

13. 42 U.S.C., sect. 7412(b)(1)(B)(1982) [note 21].

14. See Thomas F. P. Sullivan, ed., *Environmental Law Handbook* (Rockdale, Md.: Government Institutes, Inc., 1997) and Vicki R. Patton-Hulce, *Environment and the Law: A Dictionary* (Santa Barbara, Calif.: ABC-Clio, 1995).

15. 42 U.S.C., sections 6901–6986 (1982 & Sup. 1985) [note 21].

16. 478 F.2d 615 (D.C. Cir. 1973).

17. *Portland Cement Association v. Ruckelshaus,* 486 F.2d 375, 387 (D.C. Cir. 1973) [n. 197].

18. *Industrial Union Dept. AFL-CIO v. American Petroleum Institute,* 448 U.S. 607, 642 (1980).

19. *Natural Resources Defense Council v. EPA,* 804 F.2d 710 (D.C. Cir. 1986).

20. *Industrial Union Dept., AFL-CIO v. Hodgson,* 162 U.S. App. D.C. at 342, 499 F. 2d at 467, 477–78 (D.C. Cir. 1974)

21. Cranor, p. 161.

22. Cranor, pp. 161–162.

23. Sagoff, p. 314.

24. For suggestions for this utilitarian argument, see Cranor, pp. 163–168.

25. Recall Mrs. Steve Talbert's description, quoted in section 8.5, of the tragic effects on her husband of brown lung disease.

26. W. F. Baxter, *People or Penguins: The Case for Optimal Pollution* (New York: Columbia University Press, 1974), p. 5.

27. For a discussion of speciesism, see Peter Singer, *Practical Ethics* (Cambridge, England: Cambridge University Press, 1979), Chapter 3.

28. Aldo Leopold, *A Sand County Almanac* (New York: Oxford University Press, 1949), pp. viii, ix. Quoted in Edward Johnson, "Treating the Dirt: Environmental Ethics and Moral Theory," in Tom Regan, ed., *Earthbound: New Introductory Essays in Environmental Ethics* (New York: Random House, 1984), p. 352.

29. Leopold, p. 216. Quoted in Johnson, p. 352.

30. Leopold, pp. 224–225. Quoted in Johnson, p. 352.

31. Paul W. Taylor, "The Ethics of Respect for Nature," *Environmental Ethics, 3,* no. 3 (Fall 1981), 208–209. Quoted in William Aiken, "Ethical Issues in Agriculture" in Tom Regan, ed., p. 269.

32. John Rodman, "The Liberation of Nature?" *Inquiry, 20* (1977), 126. Quoted in Johnson in Regan, pp. 355–356.

33. In listing these criticisms, we are not necessarily agreeing with them. In particular, we believe the first argument has serious limitations. *As a professional,* an engineer can call on the work of other professionals. A professional judgment is not invalid merely because it relies on knowledge that is within the professional expertise of other professionals.

34. "Principles of Medical Ethics" (1995–1998). Available at the American Medical Association's website: http://www.ama-assn.org/ethic/pome.htm.

35. The right not to perform an abortion is explicitly asserted in AMA Opinion 2.01. However, the code provision has wider implications.

36. Stephen H. Unger, *Controlling Technology: Ethics and the Responsible Engineer* (New York: Holt, Rinehart & Winston, 1994) p. 36.

37. See Unger, pp. 37–38.

Chapter 10

International Engineering Professionalism

The clothing industry is perhaps the most competitive in the world.[1] Clothing manufacturing has been the first level of industrialization in most countries: in Hong Kong, South Korea, Taiwan, China, Myanmar, Bangladesh, Sri Lanka, the Maldives, Laos, Vietnam, Bahrain, Indonesia, El Salvador, Honduras, and the Dominican Republic. Many factories in these countries employ young women in sweatshop conditions. Yet, some argue that sweatshop conditions (and even perhaps child labor) are a necessary part of economic development. David Lindauer, Wellesley economist and World Bank consultant, remarks:

> We know of no case where a nation developed a modern manufacturing sector without first going through a "sweatshop" phase. How long ago was it that children could be found working in the textile factories of Lowell, Massachusetts; or Manchester, England; or of Osaka, Japan?[2]

Similarly, a workers' rights advocate in Bangladesh argues that throwing children out of work and onto the streets "would be a serious violation of their human rights."[3]

Harwell & James (H&J) is a small clothing manufacturer, with sales that equal only 1.5 percent of Levi Strauss's, the industry leader. It owns and operates a plant in Country X whose employees are mostly young women from the countryside. The young women live in company dormitories and work for $.80 per day, producing garments that are at the low end of the price spectrum. They work twelve-hour days in a clean, safe, well-lit factory. The young women describe the work as hard, but say that they still prefer it to village life. Some of the young women are probably the sole wage earners in their families and, without these jobs, might well be forced into begging or prostitution. H&J does not employ children under the age of 14, and there are no serious health or safety problems at the plant. Some critics have argued, however, that H&J should leave Country X. A manager for H&J responds that if his firm left

Country X another firm would take its place. "The message from business," he maintains, "is to follow the dollar and learn to effect changes from within."[4]

Hanna is an engineer whose company has been asked to design and supervise the manufacture of some new equipment for the H&J plant in Country X. Hanna will be asked to spend a year in Country X, supervising the installation of the equipment and training plant personnel in its use. The new equipment should improve efficiency and safety in the plant. Nevertheless, some of Hanna's engineering colleagues argue that she should not take the assignment, because it makes her a party to the exploitation of the young women.

10.1   Introduction

Increasing numbers of engineers are becoming involved in other countries, either working in other countries or designing or manufacturing products for other countries. Yet, as this case shows, this arena poses special ethical problems for engineers. The need for ethical and professional standards that apply worldwide is becoming increasingly evident.

Other countries are increasingly adopting standards for licensure that are similar in some respects to those in the United States. In the United States, all Professional Engineer (PE) licensing is based on three requirements: education, experience, and examination. Education and experience requirements are standard in licensure around the world, but examination requirements are much less universal.

For example, in the European Union (EU), the major voice of engineering is the *Federation European d'Associations Nationales d'Ingenieurs* (European Federation of National Associations of Engineers), formed in 1951. This organization (FEANI) represents more than eighty national engineering associations from twenty-seven European countries and about 1.5 million engineers. Engineers who meet FEANI's standards and code of professional conduct can earn the professional title EurIng, which is recognized throughout the European community. Requirements for this title include at least three years of university engineering education from a university approved by FEANI, two years of sanctioned professional experience, a recommendation from the applicant's national association, and acceptance by the European control committee. In January 1997, there were 19,919 engineers with the EurIng title: 11,546 from the United Kingdom, 2040 from France, 1837 from Germany, 1236 from Spain, and 744 from Ireland.[5]

There are some differences in the way professional engineers are regulated in Europe and the United States. In the United Kingdom, for example, engineers are regulated by their own societies, whereas in the United States the regulation is by state boards. In France, only the title *ingenieur diplome* (degreed engineer) is protected by law; otherwise, the engineering profession is neither controlled nor regulated by French law.

One of the most striking changes in world engineering professionalism is the increasing interest in mutual recognition of engineering licenses. A group of engineering organizations known as the Washington Accord, whose member countries include Australia, Canada, Ireland, New Zealand, South Africa, the United Kingdom, the United States, and Hong Kong, met in San Diego, California, in January 1997. The purpose of the meeting was to eliminate obstacles to mutual recognition of licenses.

Here are some other examples of the worldwide movement toward more stringent professional standards in engineering:

• *Australia:* There are few statutory requirements for registration and the title "engineer" is not protected. But registration is required in certain localities.

• *Brazil:* The government recently established a national test for all engineering students, but engineers are not restricted if they fail the test. All construction and engineering designs must be performed by registered engineers.

• *China:* In December 1996, China's National Administration Board for Architectural and Engineering Registration gave its first Fundamentals of Engineering (FE) and Structural Principles and Practice (PP) exams. The board gave the pilot FE exam to 1,500 candidates and the PP exam to 2,500 candidates. The board plans to give the structural PP exam to 70,000 engineers in 1998. The Chinese have worked closely with the National Council of Examiners for Engineers and Surveyors (NCEES) in developing the exams.

• *Japan:* Engineers gained registered status in 1957 with the enactment of the Registered Engineer Act. A registered engineer license is required for most government engineering projects but not always for private projects. From 1958 to May 1995, almost 36,000 engineers were licensed. The number of engineers applying for registration is increasing.[6]

The number of licensed engineers around the world will certainly increase, and the standards for licensure (including the ethical standards) will probably become increasingly uniform. Although this will be enormously helpful, it will not eliminate the difficult problems of interpreting the codes in the international context.

10.2   Problems in International Professionalism

Let us first look at some of the factors that cause problems in interpreting the codes in the international environment. We shall call the country in which the engineer is a citizen the "home" country, whether this country is the United States or some other country. We shall call the country in which the engineer is working, or for whose market the engineer is designing, the "host" country. If the engineer is a citizen of the United States, the "host" country would be any country other than the United States. If the engineer is a citizen of some country other than the United States, the "host" country could be the United States.

In considering these factors, we shall be especially—but by no means exclusively—concerned with the issues faced by the engineer from an industrialized country (IC) working in a less industrialized country (LIC).[7] Although few engineers from LICs will be working in ICs, engineers from ICs often work in other ICs. For example, American engineers may work in Europe or Japan, European engineers may work in the United States or Japan, or Japanese engineers may work in Europe. Now let us look at some of the cultural differences that can produce issues for engineers from an IC working in an LIC.

Values and Practices

Host countries can have different values and practices that may prove troubling to home-country engineers.

> James is an engineer working for an American company in Morotavia (an LIC). He has the responsibility for procuring certain parts for his plant that are manufactured in Morotavia. The Morotavian supplier's representative has told James that to get the materials on time, he should pay a "customary fee" to the representative. James believes that the representative is engaging in extortion and decides not to pay the fee. But his colleague, Ronald, says, "Everybody does it over here; you just have to get used to it."

In other cases, differing values may call into question the appropriateness of practices that are generally accepted in the United States. Whereas most Americans may find nothing wrong with serving alcoholic beverages at executive dinners, Muslims may consider it morally offensive. An engineer must decide in such cases whether it is appropriate to follow local customs.

In looking at cases that appear to illustrate differing values in different cultures, two things should be kept in mind. First, there are some core values that people in most—if not all—cultures share. These include courage, loyalty, devotion to family, honesty, compassion, the prohibition of murder and theft, adherence to contracts, and the need for protection from physical violence. Second, we should distinguish between what is sometimes or even often *practiced* in a foreign country and what is *accepted* as proper or right in that country. These are not always the same. Bribery might be frequently practiced in a given country, but it might not be considered morally acceptable. When it is brought to public attention, it can sometimes result in severe consequences to those exposed as having taken bribes. A few years ago, for example, Japanese Prime Minister Tanaka had to resign after being exposed as a bribe-taker, even though American businesspeople claimed they were told that giving bribes was common business practice in Japan.

Nevertheless, some norms differ. One of these areas is the relationship of individuals to the group. Some cultures, for example, regard nepotism as a virtue, because it is a way of fulfilling one's obligations to his or her extended family. Nepotism is generally frowned upon in the United States, however.

> Wanda works at a plant in India where one of the employee benefits is the guarantee of a job to at least one of the employee's family members. The policy is in agreement with the cultural values of the country, but Wanda is uncomfortable going along with it.

Another area where there are differences is in the fact that many people believe a business relationship can be established only on the basis of a prior personal relationship. Westerners believe that business can be carried on in the absence of personal relationships and that, in any event, personal relationships should not affect business relationships. In many cultures, however, personal relationships must precede and provide the foundation for business relationships. Furthermore, personal relationships must be cemented by the giving and receiving of gifts. The "abstract" nature of the Western view of business relationships is viewed as inhuman and offensive. Thus, what looks like a bribe to Westerners may be seen by people in other cultures as a token of friendship.

> James buys material from a local supplier in Country X. The local supplier is a friendly man who invites James to family functions and often offers him gifts and is clearly offended when James refuses them. For James the gifts are "kickbacks" and pose conflict-of-interest problems, but James's colleagues tell him that in Country X, business relationships are built on personal relationships, and personal relationships are cemented with gifts. James likes the man and thinks the way of doing business in Country X is more human and certainly more enjoyable. Yet he wonders if the relationship involves violations of his code of ethics.

The roles of women and men may also vary from culture to culture. Many cultures assign different roles to men and women, and these roles may be sanctioned by long religious and cultural traditions. In some cultures women do the farming. In some cultures men are offended to have to deal with a woman in a position of authority, and women are severely restricted in their ability to travel without the accompaniment of a man.

Economic Conditions

Economic conditions in host countries can be very different from conditions in the home country. Differences in wages paid to workers in host countries may seem appropriate if there is a lower level of economic development.

> One of Jane's nonprofessional supervisees in a Mexican plant complains about being paid $3.00 per hour, when U.S. factory workers employed at home by Jane's company for an equivalent job are paid $10.00 per hour. Yet $3.00 per hour is higher than the going wage for the same work in Mexico. Should Jane object to, or at least be troubled by, the wage?

Differing levels of economic development may go a long way to explain the lower health and safety standards in some host countries (noted in the next section). Sometimes there may be strong arguments for these lower standards, given the need for economic development, but they produce problems for home-country citizens.

Background Institutions

Often LICs do not have the laws and regulatory agencies under which businesses operate in ICs. Richard DeGeorge refers to these laws and regulatory agencies as "background institutions."[8] The absence of these background institutions may produce a very different business environment from the one in an IC.

> Diane faces a dilemma. To compete with other companies, she must allow health and safety standards in her plant that she knows are unsafe. Yet the standards are perfectly legal under host-country laws.

The absence of the background institutions in many ICs may affect business and professional activity in other ways as well. Financial institutions may not have the same regulations. Disclosure of health and safety hazards on products may not be required. Requirements for disclosure of toxic chemicals may be much looser, or even nonexistent. A common scenario is that the regulations are present but haphazardly or ineffectively enforced. Then IC engineers face the decision whether to follow the unenforced host-country standards (and place themselves at a competitive disadvantage with respect to those firms that disregard the standards), or to disregard the standards and damage the environment or human safety or health.

Corruption

Corruption is present in all countries, but we are concerned here with the corruption encountered by a home-country engineer in a host country, whether the host country is an IC or an LIC. Sometimes a host country may have widespread corruption, either in the government or on the part of syndicates and other groups. An engineer may wonder how he should relate to such corruption.

> Roger knows that the best parts obtainable in a host country come from a supplier controlled by organized crime. He wonders whether he should specify parts from another source, even though they are inferior.

Noncitizen Status

Home-country citizens are not citizens of the host countries and thus do not have either the same obligations or the same prerogatives as host-country citizens. As noncitizens of a host country, home-country citizens may wonder whether and to what extent it is inappropriate to lobby for some changes in the law in host countries, or to speak out on some public issues, even when they believe these changes are for the good of host-country citizens.

Vulnerability

Citizens of host countries, especially LICs, are often in a position of considerably greater vulnerability than most citizens in home countries, especially ICs. Many believe that, just as the greater vulnerability of children generates special moral obligations, so vulnerability of any type imposes moral obligations on the less vulnerable to protect and not to exploit the vulnerable.[9]

Vulnerability takes different forms. One type of vulnerability is the lack of education and knowledge. Citizens of host countries may be less educated and technologically sophisticated than citizens in the home countries. This may have a bearing on the appropriateness of certain kinds of advertising or sales tactics in host countries. In a famous controversy over the advertising and selling of infant formula in Africa and Latin America, a few years ago, certain companies were criticized for portraying the use of infant formula as the "modern" way to feed babies.[10] Many mothers in LICs were persuaded to use infant formula, even though they were not aware that diluting the formula could lead to malnutrition in their babies and that the use of contaminated water to dilute the formula could produce infections.

Similar problems can arise in the use and advertising of other products. Advertising and selling a pesticide presupposes a general knowledge of the dangers inherent in pesticide use. This knowledge may not be available to citizens of the host country. Host-country citizens may not be familiar with the safety hazards of operating agricultural machinery or plant machinery. Precautions that are common knowledge to people raised in a more technologically sophisticated society may be absent. This raises problems for engineers in designing and selling such products.

Another type of vulnerability is the lack of political and economic power. Citizens in some countries have little ability to influence events that affect their lives. Governments may not be democratic, or they may be controlled by groups that are only minimally responsive to the needs of the poor and economically deprived. This may create responsibilities for engineers that are different from those that would exist with regard to home-country citizens.

These differences between home and host countries can produce problems in interpreting professional responsibilities. Let us look at some provisions of the codes that are especially difficult to apply in the international context.

10.3 ❋ Problems in Interpreting and Applying the Codes in the International Context

In trying to decide what to do in ethically troubling situations, engineers naturally turn to their professional codes of ethics. One of the major engineering societies, the Institute of Electrical and Electronics Engineers (IEEE), is explicitly an international organization. Accordingly, its code opens with an acknowledgment of "the importance of our technologies in affecting the quality of life throughout the world. . . ." Without question, the IEEE code applies in the international environment. Recent changes in the code of the American Society of Mechanical Engineers (recently changed to "ASME International") make similar references to the international environment.

 A 1996 decision by the NSPE's Board of Ethical Review makes it clear that the NSPE code is intended to apply to the international environment. In **case 96-5**, the board considered an engineer (Engineer A) who was asked to submit a proposal on a major water project in Country A. Engineer A was encouraged to retain a local engineer in Country A, who would give substantial gifts to local officials responsible for awarding the contract for the water project. The board ruled that Engineer A was still bound by the NSPE code and must not participate in the practice, however customary it might be in the host country.

Most other U.S. engineering societies have members who are not citizens of the United States, and many societies appear to assume that their codes apply to member engineers in host countries. Therefore, we shall assume that they do. Many code requirements, however, can lead to troublesome problems in the international context. We shall consider a few of them.

The Welfare Requirement

Most engineering codes require engineers, in the words of the National Society of Professional Engineer's (NSPE) code, to "hold paramount the safety, health and welfare of the public in the performance of their professional duties" (I.1). Some codes amplify this general requirement and make it even more emphatic. For example, section III.2.a of the NSPE code requires engineers to "seek opportunities to be of constructive service in civic affairs and work for the advancement of the safety, health and well-being of their community." Here the requirement is not simply to "hold paramount the safety, health and welfare of the public," but to actively "work for the advancement" of these goals. The term "well-being" is probably intended to be synonymous with "welfare."

The requirement to hold paramount public safety, health, and welfare (or well-being) appears in most engineering codes. We shall refer to it as the *paramountcy requirement*.[11] We have already seen that the obligation to hold paramount the safety and health of host-country citizens can produce problems in countries where values, practices, and economic conditions are different. In this section, however, we shall focus on the specific requirement to hold paramount the welfare or well-being of the public, which we shall refer to as the *welfare requirement*. Sometimes the welfare requirement is stated independently of the more general paramountcy requirement. For example, the first Fundamental Principle of the ASCE code requires engineers to use "their knowledge and skill for the enhancement of human welfare." Section I.e of the "Guidelines" to the same code uses the expression "safety, health and well-being" instead of "safety, health and welfare."

The welfare requirement is rarely referred to in the decisions of the Board of Ethical Review. In **case 85-2**, however, the board argued that promoting public "welfare" justified an engineer's protesting employer policies that resulted in excessive costs and time delays in defense contracts. Thus, public welfare included the efficient use of tax funds. By similar reasoning, promoting public welfare in an LIC country might include promoting economic development and perhaps even such things as actively cooperating with policies designed to eliminate corruption and raise the standards of business and professional conduct.

But there are special complications in applying these ideas in host countries. On the one hand, the obligation to be concerned for public welfare may be greater than in the home country, due to the lower level of economic development or the greater vulnerability of host-country citizens. On the other hand, the welfare requirement may lead to unjustified paternalism. *Paternalism* may be defined as substituting one's own judgment for that of another (the recipient) to promote the recipient's benefit. As we have already seen, however, host-country values may not be the same as home-country values. Our definition of "welfare" or "well-being" may not be the same as theirs. (We shall return to the problem of paternalism.)

Another issue in applying the welfare requirement is what is meant by the *public*, the other important term in the welfare requirement. A useful definition of the "public" for which engineers are responsible is given by Michael Davis:

> I would suggest that what makes people a public is their relative innocence, help-lessness, or passivity. On this interpretation, "public" would refer to those persons whose lack of information, technical knowledge, or time for deliberation renders them more or less vulnerable to the powers an engineer wields on behalf of his client or employer. An engineer should hold paramount the public safety, health, and welfare to assure that engineers will not be forced to give too little regard to the welfare of those "innocents."[12]

The theme of Davis's definition is that the public is any group vulnerable to the work of the engineer. The second sentence, which contains his definition of public, omits a crucial element contained in the first sentence, namely that vulnerability can include not only a lack of information, knowledge, or time for deliberation but also a lack of power to defend oneself against the effects of technology on one's life. This powerlessness can be either political or financial, or both. It is this sense of vulnerability (that is, lack of power) that is especially characteristic of some host-country residents, especially those in lesser developed nations (LICs). So we shall amend Davis's definition to say that the *public* is any person or group vulnerable to the effects of technology, *through lack of political* or *financial power*, information, technical training, or time for deliberation.

The requirement to hold paramount the safety, health, and welfare of the public has important implications for professional conduct in the international arena. Interpreting the requirement—especially the requirement to hold paramount public welfare or well-being—raises many questions that must be addressed by the conscientious professional.

Bribery and Conflicts of Interest

We have already seen in Chapter 6, Honesty, Integrity, and Reliability, that most engineering codes contain strong prohibitions against undisclosed conflicts of interest and bribery. To cite a prominent example, section II.5.b of the NSPE code says:

> Engineers shall not offer, give, solicit or receive, either directly or indirectly, any political contribution in an amount intended to influence the award of a contract by public authority, or which may be reasonably construed by the public of having the effect or intent to influence the award of a contract. They shall not offer any gift, or other valuable consideration in order to secure work. They shall not pay a commission, percentage or brokerage fee in order to secure work except to a bona fide employee or bona fide established commercial or marketing agencies retained by them.

In the light of this statement, consider the following case:

Walter's company is constantly faced with the problem of getting equipment into Country X through customs. Company officials are often told that the equipment does not meet Country X's standards and that it can only be admitted if a "fee" is paid. The standards are so confusing that the company does not know whether it is being asked to pay a bribe to admit nonqualifying equipment or whether the "fee" is better described as a "grease" payment or perhaps simply an extortion payment. Walter does not know whether he should make the payment.

What, in your opinion, should Walter do?

The Environment

We have seen that some engineering codes require members to give due regard to the environment. Yet countries differ in the importance they attach to environmental concerns, or how environmental concerns should be balanced against the need for economic development. What should an engineer's obligations be in such circumstances?

Joyce is a civil engineer employed at a fertilizer plant in Country X. Her plant emits sulfur-dioxide pollution at a level far higher than would be allowed in her country. The plant is working overtime to produce fertilizer in a country with a malnourished population. Imposing stricter standards would drastically curtail production.

How, in your opinion, should Joyce balance the obligation to promote welfare against her code-mandated obligation to improve the environment?

Nondiscrimination

Some engineering codes require members to practice nondiscrimination. Canon 6 of the American Institute of Chemical Engineers (AIChE) code requires members to "treat fairly all colleagues and co-workers, recognizing their unique contributions and capabilities." Canon 8 of the IEEE code requires members to "treat fairly all persons regardless of such factors as race, religion, gender, disability, age, or national origin." Yet in some countries there are strong, even institutionalized, roles assigned to certain groups. For example, women have assigned roles in many cultures that prevent their full and equal participation in business and professional life. Is it a violation of an engineer's professional ethics to participate in or acquiesce in discriminatory practices? If an engineer's company does not practice discrimination within the company, either in hiring or promoting employees, does the firm have any obligation to promote nondiscriminatory policies in the larger society?

John, an electrical engineer, has a young engineer, Linda, working under his supervision in Country X. Linda volunteers to represent the firm in negotiations with a host-country firm that could become a very good customer. John knows that the assignment would be a professional advancement for Linda and that she is capable of handling the job. John also knows, however, that the executives of the host-country firm are insulted if they are asked to do business with a woman, and that designating Linda as his representative will pose a substantial impediment to the negotiations.

What, in your opinion, should John do?

The Reputation of the Profession

Some engineering codes require members to uphold the reputation of the engineering profession and not to associate with those engaged in unethical activity. Section II.1.d of the NSPE code requires engineers not to "associate in business ventures with any person or firm which they have reason to believe is engaging in fraudulent or dishonest business or professional practices." Section III.9.b says engineers must "not use association with a non-engineer, a corporation, or partnership as a 'cloak' for unethical acts, but must accept personal responsibility for all professional acts." Section 6.a of the ASCE code says engineers should "not knowingly act in a manner which will be derogatory to the honor, integrity, or dignity of the engineering profession or knowingly engage in business or professional practices of a fraudulent, dishonest or unethical nature."

Canon 6 of the American Society of Mechanical Engineers (ASME) requires engineers to "associate only with reputable persons or organizations." Section 6.a of the same code says engineers must not "knowingly associate with or permit the use of their names or firm names in business ventures by any person or firm which they know, or have reason to believe, are engaging in business or professional practices of a fraudulent or dishonest nature."

> Ed works in Country X, where government officials require "fees" before they will even consider bids for government work. The "fees" are more like extortion than bribes, because payment of the fees does not guarantee that a bid will be accepted—only that it will be considered. Yet Ed wonders whether paying the fees is a violation of the preceding code provisions.

Should Ed, in your opinion, pay the fees?

Promoting Knowledge and Avoiding Deception

Several codes require engineers to promote the knowledge of technology and to refrain from activities that deceive the public. In section III.3, the NSPE code requires engineers to "avoid all conduct or practice which is likely to discredit the profession or deceive the public." Section III.3.a expands this:

> Engineers shall avoid the use of statements containing a material misrepresentation of fact or omitting a material fact necessary to keep statements from being misleading or intended or likely to create an unjustified expectation, or statements containing prediction of future success.

Canon 5 of the IEEE code requires members "to improve the understanding of technology, its appropriate application, and potential consequences. . . ." Section 3.a of the ASCE code says engineers must "endeavor to extend the public knowledge of engineering, and shall not participate in the dissemination of untrue, unfair or exaggerated statements regarding engineering." Section 7.a of the ASME's "Criteria for Interpretation of the Canons" requires engineers to "endeavor to extend public knowledge, and to prevent misunderstandings of the achievements of engineering." In the light of these requirements, what should Jim do in the following case?

Jim is employed by a multinational in Country X. He is familiar with the loading and unloading practices in the harbor areas of Country X. Every day he sees workers in shorts and sandals handling toxic chemicals, and he knows they are inadequately protected. The workers are not direct employees of his company, and he wonders how much responsibility he has for their welfare. His company also produces products that he knows are inappropriately used by many of the citizens in Country X because of the citizens' low level of technological sophistication and lack of sensitivity to health and safety issues. Yet the company issues the same instructions and precautions used on the products in Jim's country, and the instructions are written in Country X's official language. Again, he wonders how much responsibility he or his company has for these abuses.

What, in your opinion, should Jim do?

10.4   Striking a Balance

The problems posed in the previous sections show that the codes are often insufficient to guide engineers in the area of international professionalism. In the next three sections we shall propose some additional guidelines for applying the codes in the international context. Before doing this, however, let us consider some of the problems that one encounters in applying moral concepts in this area. We can formulate these problems in terms of the need to strike a balance between various extremes.

1. *Between the extremes of moral absolutism and moral relativism:* One set of extremes is to succumb either to moral absolutism or moral relativism. In resolving ethical and professional problems, one approach engineers could take is to ignore the unique features of business in host countries and act as they would in the home country. This absolutist approach assumes that our values and practices are the only correct ones and that we must follow them without compromise in every situation. It does not take much thought to see, however, that this option is often not advisable, for at least two reasons.

First, the requisite technology, knowledge, economic resources, and social structures are not always available in host countries. For example, corruption may be so pervasive that it is impossible to do all of one's business with vendors or customers or government officials who are free of corruption. Grease payments (payments to hasten certain actions) may be necessary to do some kinds of business. It may not be possible to get government officials and other manufacturers to follow home-country standards of health, safety, and environmental protection. In some situations, the requisite economic resources to do so may simply not be available.

Second, it may be incorrect to assume that home-country standards and values should apply everywhere. Sometimes standards in other countries may not be either better or worse but just different. Whether Western individualism is superior to the group orientation predominant in many cultures (and once predominant in ours) is certainly debatable. Whether it is best to separate business and personal friendship as is often done in the West may also be a matter worthy of debate. In any case, home-country citizens who work abroad should be open to the values present in other cultures and not as clearly manifested in our own. This attitude is not only morally desirable, but it will also make their stay in another culture more enjoyable, more of an occasion for personal growth, and probably also more successful. People in other cultures generally respond more favorably to those who appreciate the values in their culture, just as we respond more favorably to those who appreciate the values in ours.

The other extreme is to adopt the guideline, "When in Rome, do as the Romans do"; that is, home-country engineers would simply follow local customs and laws and act as if they were citizens of the host country. This option is often associated with *moral relativism*, the view that the truth of our moral beliefs is determined by (or "relative" to) the culture in which we are living. Like the previous option, there are several problems with it.

First, it may lead to illegal actions. For example, the Foreign Corrupt Practices Act, passed by the U.S. Congress in 1977, makes it illegal for U.S. citizens to engage in practices, such as paying bribes and some types of extortion, that may be common in a host country.

Second, an action might be so clearly harmful or so morally repugnant that it would be difficult to justify. Following such practices would in some cases, moreover, severely compromise the conscience of a home-country professional. To take an extreme example, slavery is still practiced in some parts of the world, but few engineers would want to work in factories employing slave labor. To take a less extreme example, safety and health standards in a host country may allow practices that are so harmful to employees, the surrounding population, or the long-term well-being of the host country or the environment of the host country that following them would be a severe violation of both the consciences and the professional codes of U.S. professionals.

2. *Between the extremes of too little and too much personal responsibility:* A second set of extremes that engineers should avoid is taking too much or too little responsibility for their firms' actions in the international arena.

On the one hand, engineers need not take responsibility for decisions over which they have little or no control. Engineers do not ordinarily make corporate decisions. Engineers do not, for example, ordinarily make decisions on where to locate plants, what products to manufacture, how to interact with the local government, whether to install new pollution equipment even if it is not required by local laws, whether to provide company housing for employees, what kind of health benefits to provide for employees, and whether to contribute to local charitable enterprises. Their responsibility should not go beyond what they have the power to influence. Engineers as engineers are not managers, and they need not take full responsibility for management decisions.

On the other hand, engineers may often be asked to give advice in these areas, or they may have the opportunity to express an opinion. In some instances, they may find policies and practices of their firms in a host country so morally troublesome that they should refuse to carry them out, refuse to be a part of the firm's international operations, or even resign from the firm. Furthermore, engineers are responsible for the design, production, and implementation of technology. They have a responsibility to design this technology in accordance with standards of professional responsibility and in a way that is responsive to the needs of host countries. For example, if an engineer knows that agricultural work in a host country is done mostly by women, the engineer should design in the light of the requirements of women.

3. *Between the extremes of moral laxism and moral rigorism:* Many situations in the international sphere are not amenable to an ideal solution. In such situations, it is tempting to act in one of two ways, both of which are unsatisfactory from a moral standpoint.

One response is to become morally lax and perhaps even cynical. This is akin to the position in ethical thinking known as *moral laxism*. According to this position, as we shall interpret it, when a moral principle does not or cannot be strictly applied to a situation, we may do what we want, regardless of how far the action may depart from traditional morality.[13] The reasoning here might be, "Since there is no option in this situation that allows me to act in an ideal moral way, I will simply abandon any moral considerations and act in a way that is most compatible with my self-interest, or the self-interest of my firm." This option involves a rejection of ethical and professional considerations and may in some cases lead an engineer to embrace choices that are even illegal.

Another response is to be so concerned with doing the right thing that one may become excessively moralistic and adopt a kind of *moral rigorism*. According to this view, as we shall interpret it, moral principles must be strictly applied in every situation, no matter what the circumstances.[14] The moral rigorist is unwilling to accept the fact that although a given course of action is not the ideal, it may be the best that one can do in the situation, morally speaking. For example, we shall see that, although paternalistic action may be undesirable in a situation, it may be unavoidable. Even participation in actions that involve a degree of exploitation may be preferable, all things considered, to extracting oneself from the international environment altogether. To take another example, suppose social and economic conditions are such that a plant cannot be operated in the host country without damaging the environment. When all considerations are taken into account, including the effect on the host country of losing the plant, building and operating the plant may still be justified.

10.5   Guidelines for Interpreting the Codes: (1) Human Rights

The Internationalization of Rights

The ideal guidelines for interpreting the codes in differing cultural settings would be ethical norms that are universally accepted. Given such norms, it would be easy to decide whether to use the norms of the host country or the home country: the same norms would be applicable in both places.

Perhaps the most likely source of such universally accepted ethical standards is the doctrine of human rights. People in many cultures—including many non-Western cultures—now appeal to human rights in making their case for everything from minimal standards of living to protection from torture or political oppression. "Rights talk" has become a near-universal vocabulary for ethical discourse and can be justified by both utilitarian and respect for persons morality, although in different ways.

One measure of the cross-cultural nature of "rights talk" is the existence of the United Nation's International Bill of Human Rights. This document consists of the Universal Declaration of Human Rights, adopted by the UN in 1948, and two documents adopted later: the International Covenant on Economic, Social and Cultural Rights and the International Covenant on Civil and Political Rights.[15] These documents ascribe to all human beings the rights:

- to life

- to liberty

- to security of person

- not to be held in slavery

- not to be tortured or subjected to inhuman or degrading punishment

- to recognition before the law

- to impartial trial and protection from arbitrary arrest

- to freedom of movement

- to marriage

- not to marry without free consent

- to property ownership

- to freedom of thought

- to peaceful assembly and participation in government

- to social security and work

- to education

- to participate in and form trade unions

- to nondiscrimination

- to a minimal standard of living

This is a long list, and some might argue that it is simply a "wish list," given the conditions that actually prevail in many countries. Notice also that some of the rights (see the Chapter 4 "Rights" discussion) are what we called "positive" rights; that is, they are not simply rights to noninterference from others, such as the rights not to be held in slavery or tortured, but rights to certain advantages, such as education, social security, and work. These require from others not only a negative duty to noninterference but a positive duty to help others achieve these rights.

On the other hand, most of us would consider all of these rights highly desirable. The question is whether they should be considered *rights*, rather than simply desirable things to have. For example, should we say that one has a *right* to a minimal standard of living? Which of these rights do professionals in the international arena have an obligation to respect?

James Nickel helps to answer this question by setting up several conditions for accepting what we shall call an "international right." An *international right* is a specific right that every country should, if resources and conditions permit, grant to its citizens. In terms of generality and abstraction, an international right falls between the very abstract rights given in Chapter 4 and the more specific rights guaranteed by laws and constitutions by individual governments. Here are the conditions Nickel suggests that are most relevant for our purposes:

1. The right must protect something of very great importance.
2. The right must be subject to substantial and recurrent threats.
3. The obligations or burdens imposed by the right must be affordable in relation to the resources of the country, the other obligations the country must fulfill, and fairness in the distribution of burdens among citizens.[16]

If we judge the United Nations' list of rights by Nickel's criteria, we might have reason to question several of the rights. Some countries may not have the economic resources to support the claims to a minimal education and subsistence, however desirable these may be. Perhaps we should say that these rights are valid, insofar as a country can afford to provide them.

Another way of determining what rights people have is to look at the more abstract list of rights given in Chapter 4. Gewirth has derived his list of rights from a consideration of what is necessary for a person to exercise her moral agency. Gewirth lists a hierarchy of rights not provided by the UN documents, but there is a great deal of agreement between the two documents. In general, Gewirth's list of rights is either the same as the UN's list (as in the right to own property), or Gewirth's rights imply the more specific rights in the list (as the right to physical integrity implies the right not to be tortured). It is an interesting exercise to see how the other rights proposed by the UN documents can be derived from Gewirth's hierarchy. Given that utilitarians can also justify belief in rights by arguing that they are necessary to promote human happiness or well-being, it is also an interesting exercise to see how many of these rights a utilitarian would justify.

Agreement among several accounts of rights does not, of course, guarantee truth; but it does show that there is a high degree of consensus on what rights human beings should have, whether or not the rights are honored in practice. Furthermore, a utilitarian or respect for persons list of rights is derived from a fundamental ethical source—namely, from what is necessary to promote human well-being or human moral agency. This being the case, a policy that violates a human right is probably not in accord with the welfare requirement in most engineering codes. This is because "welfare" surely includes the promotion of human well-being and the protection of human moral agency.

Are Rights a Western Invention?

Some object to rights as a foundation for international morality on the grounds that the doctrine of rights is too closely associated with recent Western civilization. One argument is that, even in the West, rights are a recent invention. Prior to the eighteenth century, rights were not an important part of Western moral discourse. Why should such a recent innovation in morality in Western society be thought to have universal import?

Alan Gewirth has argued that rights have a longer pedigree in Western and other moral traditions than many suspect. Although the term *right* may be a recent invention, premodern societies had a concept of people having entitlements connected with property, the fulfillment of contracts, protection from physical assault, and so forth.[17] The doctrines of hierarchical political order in Plato and Aristotle, he argues, can be interpreted as implying the natural right of the wiser to rule those who are less wise. The doctrine of what we today might call "equality before the law" can be interpreted as implying a right to equality before the law. Many precepts in Roman law can be explained in terms of rights. And in the feudal era, the agreements between lords and vassals generated what we would today call rights and duties on both sides.

Another argument against rights is that the doctrine of rights implies a Western individualism that is contrary to the values of many non-Western cultures, where the group is more important than the individual. For some critics, embracing the doctrine of rights makes individuals more important than social groups, such as the family, clan, tribe, or larger society. Even if most governments officially endorse the UN human rights documents, they do so at the cost of denying their own cultural and ethical traditions. For example, in many cultures marriages are arranged by families rather than based on individual consent, and nondemocratic traditions of government emphasize the subservience of individual views to those of a single leader or the group.

The easy answer to this objection is that Western individualism is spreading around the world, just as Western technology is spreading around the world. Even if Western values are sometimes destructive of traditional cultures (just as Western technology sometimes is), the fact is that Western ways are sweeping the planet. The universally accepted values will tend more and more to be Western values.

Another answer, however, is that a doctrine of human rights need not lead to an unacceptable form of individualism, because rights usually imply correlative duties on the part of others. Although, as we have seen, some of the duties implied by rights are "negative," others are "positive." It is especially these positive duties that bind members of a community to one another. Being a member of a community is more than merely refraining from interfering with others. Each member of the community owes something to other members of the community in a positive way.

Let us see how these positive duties arise. Some believe that even many of the so-called negative rights imply positive and not merely negative duties on the part of others. The right to physical security is, to be sure, first and foremost a negative right, implying the negative duty of others to refrain from physically harming us. Some believe, however, that it also implies the positive duty of the state or community to provide protection. The rights to a minimal education and a minimal standard of living are positive rights and even more clearly imply certain positive duties on the part of the community. The right to political participation implies positive duties on the part of the community to guarantee these rights, as well as negative duties to noninterference in their free exercise.[18]

There does, however, seem to be some opposition between a doctrine of rights and the norms in some societies. The right not to enter into arranged marriages is much more in accord with Western individualism than with the group orientation of many societies. The right to ownership of property conflicts with the views of many cultures, where private ownership is not the norm. The right to nondiscriminatory treatment conflicts with the gender roles prescribed in many societies. The right to participation in government conflicts with the nondemocratic traditions of many societies. There are many other examples.

So we may conclude that the rights listed by the UN documents are an important guide in applying the codes, especially the welfare requirement. Nevertheless, the doctrine of rights, although often providing a useful guideline for applying the codes—especially the welfare requirement—is not completely free of a Western orientation.

10.6   Guidelines for Interpreting the Codes: (2) Avoiding Paternalism and Exploitation

Even apart from the problem of the Western bias, the appeal to rights is not a sufficient guideline for interpreting the codes, even the welfare requirement. An action might not violate any of the rights cited in the UN documents and still be unjustifiably exploitative or paternalistic. The concepts of paternalism and exploitation are especially useful in setting the outer limits on the interpretation of the welfare requirement. Paternalistic action exhibits an excessive—or at least misplaced—concern for the welfare of the public, and exploitation exhibits too little concern. The proper concern for public welfare should generally avoid both paternalism and exploitation, although there may be occasions when paternalistic and even mildly exploitative behavior may be justifiable in the light of some overriding consideration. We should avoid both an overly lax and overly rigorous application of these concepts.

First, consider exploitation. Here is a paradigm case of exploitation:

> Joe's firm, Coppergiant, is the most powerful copper-mining and copper-smelting company in the world. It controls world prices and keeps competitors away from some of the most lucrative sources of copper. Joe works for Coppergiant in Country X, the firm's most lucrative source of copper. In Country X, Coppergiant buys copper at prices considerably below the world market and pays its workers the lowest wages for mining and smelting work in the world. As a result, Coppergiant makes enormous profits. Because the company pays off government officials and has so much control over the world market in copper, no other mining and smelting company is allowed into the country. Country X is desperately poor, and copper is virtually its only source of foreign currency.

According to Robert E. Goodin, the risk of exploitation arises when the following five conditions are present:[19]

1. An asymmetrical balance of power.

2. The subordinate party needs the resources provided by the exploitative relationship to protect his vital interests.

3. For the subordinate party, the exploitative relationship is the only source of such resources.

4. The dominant party in the relationship exercises discretionary control over the needed resources.

5. The resources of the subordinate party (natural resources, labor, and so on) are used without adequate compensation.

The paradigm case meets all five of these conditions. There is an asymmetrical balance of power between Country X and Jim's firm. Country X desperately needs the foreign currency provided by Jim's firm. The revenues through Jim's firm are the only source of the currency. Jim's firm, through its control of the market, exercises discretionary control over these revenues. Finally, the natural and labor resources of Country X are used without adequate compensation.

Exploitation is usually wrong, because it violates the moral agency of individuals in an unacceptable way. As the characteristics of exploitation show, exploiting individuals or groups involves overriding their own goals and purposes without their free and informed consent. Nevertheless, there may be times when some degree of exploitation is justified because of some greater good. For example, paying low prices for an LIC's natural resources such as copper ore might be justified, if these prices represent the market value, even though the price is exploitatively low. An LIC government might rationally consent to these prices, as the only way to promote economic development, hoping that in the future prices will rise.

Next, consider paternalism, which we have already defined as substituting one's own judgment powers for that of another (the recipient) to promote the recipient's benefit. If exploitation of the public expresses too little concern for the public's well-being, paternalism expresses too much, or at least expresses it in the wrong way. Here is a paradigm case of paternalism:

> Robin's firm operates a large pineapple plantation in Country X. The firm has required the workers to leave their traditional villages and to live in company villages, consisting of small, uniform houses on uniformly laid-out streets. The firm's managers provide complete health care for the workers and believe (correctly) that they can provide sanitary living conditions and control disease more effectively in the company villages than in the traditional villages. The workers, however, prefer the older villages, where they can preserve much more of their traditional way of life. The managers refuse to relent, saying that the workers will be healthier and happier in the new environment.

Some ethicists argue that the paramountcy requirement in professional engineering codes is too paternalistic and that engineers can be too paternalistic in following it.[20] This claim is especially plausible with respect to the welfare requirement, because, to hold paramount the welfare of the public, one must know what welfare is. Yet deciding what constitutes someone else's welfare, especially where values differ, can be highly paternalistic and may appear patronizing and even insulting to the other person.

Paternalism, like exploitation, can violate the moral agency of individuals. It does this when it overrides the free and informed consent of individuals to actions and policies that affect them. We should, therefore, avoid it in most cases. Yet there may be cases when paternalistic action can be justified. To discuss these cases, we need to make a distinction between weak paternalism and strong paternalism. In *weak paternalism*, the paternalist substitutes her judgment for the recipient's when there is reason to believe the recipient may not be exercising his or her moral agency effectively. Weak paternalistic action thus *protects* the moral agency of the recipient.

There are several types of situations in which we might justifiably exercise weak paternalism. The presence of any one of these conditions is sufficient to justify weak paternalism:

- A person may be under undue emotional pressure.

- A person may be ignorant of the consequences of her action.

- A person may be too young to fully comprehend the factors relevant to her decision.

- Time may be necessary for the paternalist to determine whether a person is making a free and informed decision.

In *strong paternalism,* the paternalist substitutes her judgment for the recipient's, even when there is no reason to believe the recipient is not exercising his moral agency effectively. The paternalist's justification for doing this is the potential harm to the recipient that can be avoided or the benefit that can be produced by the paternalistic action. Whereas weak paternalism seems especially close to the respect for persons viewpoint, strong paternalism reflects more directly the ethics of utilitarianism.

The paradigm involving Robin's firm is an instance of strong paternalism. The managers believe that the value *to the employees* of more sanitary working conditions and more effective control of disease is so great that it justifies overriding the expressed wishes of the employees.

Citizens of LICs are particularly likely to experience the conditions that might justify weak and perhaps even strong paternalism. Corruption may be present, although it is often present in ICs as well. The lack of background institutions, the absence of democratic institutions, and a lower level of education and technological sophistication, however, can render LIC citizens less able to make responsible decisions affecting their well-being. In such circumstances, engineers may sometimes be justified in exercising weak paternalism in promoting the welfare of host-country citizens. Sometimes—although much more rarely—conditions may even justify strong paternalism. Here is a case where paternalistic action is probably justified.

> John is employed by a pharmaceutical firm in Country X. The firm markets a dietary supplement in Country X that must be mixed with water before it is ingested. John has good reason to believe that the citizens of the country where he works will not read or follow the instructions carefully. As a result of a failure to follow directions, as well as their general ignorance about nutrition, many consumers of the product in

Country X will mix the supplement with contaminated water and will also dilute the supplement to make it longer. These variations from the instructions will cause health problems. In addition, he believes the supplement is too expensive and that the citizens of Country X could spend their food budget in more profitable ways. So he gets the company to withdraw the product from the local market.

At least one of the conditions justifying weak paternalism (ignorance of the consequences of action) is satisfied, and one condition is sufficient. In addition, John's belief that citizens of Country X could spend their food budget in better ways might justify withdrawing the product on the basis of strong paternalism.[21]

Paternalism and exploitation are in general undesirable, but it may not always be the case that they should be avoided. They should nevertheless be the poles between which interpretation of the welfare requirement oscillates.

10.7 Guidelines for Interpreting the Codes: (3) Applying the Golden Rule

One of the most useful guides in the international context is the Golden Rule. One can ask herself, "How would I want foreign engineers and businesspeople to act in my country if I were a host-country citizen?" This question is not always easy to answer, however, because it may be difficult to put yourself in the position of a host-country citizen. This is especially true if the host-country citizen lives in very different economic and social circumstances, has a much lower level of education and technological sophistication, or has very different values and practices.

To help overcome these problems and apply the Golden Rule more effectively, the following three tests may be useful:

1. Refuse to engage in engineering activities that do intentional and avoidable harm.
2. Attempt to promote the overall well-being of host-country citizens.
3. Refuse to engage in engineering activities that fail to respect host-country norms, as long as these norms do not violate the guidelines set out in sections 10.5 and 10.6, one's own conscience, or relevant home-country and host-country laws.

Let us consider each of these tests.

1. *Refusing to engage in intentional and avoidable harm:* If we attempt to place ourselves in the position of host-country citizens, we could be certain that we would not want foreign engineers and businesspeople to engage in intentional and avoidable harm. The norm requiring foreigners to refrain from causing intentional harm may be obvious and relatively easy to follow. Engineers have an obligation to promote human well-being and so have an obligation to refrain from participating in the design, production, and implementation of technology that harms humankind.

The requirement to refrain from avoidable harm may be more difficult to interpret in some situations. Many—perhaps most—technological innovations produce some harm. A new dam may provide power, flood control, and recreation, but it may also uproot people from their homes and flood valuable farmland. The requirement is rather that the harm not be intentional (that is, malicious and intended to do harm for its own sake) and that it not be avoidable in producing the good. Even if a harm is overbalanced by a good, it should still be avoided if possible.

One way to determine whether all avoidable harm has been eliminated is to ask, "Is there anything more that can reasonably be done to eliminate the harmful features of a situation?" Consider the case presented at the beginning of this chapter. One of the questions that H&J managers should ask is, "Is there anything more that we can do, within economic and other limits, to eliminate any harmful aspects of the working condition of the employees in our plant?" Levi Strauss, for example, has "ethical sourcing" guidelines that require environmental protection, safe and healthy working conditions, wages and benefits that are in accord with the law or local practices, reasonable working hours, and appropriate training for young people. Children must not be employed if they are under the legal compulsory age to be in school.[22] H&J managers should ask whether they have adopted similar or even more stringent policies. If they have not done so and are able to do so, it will be difficult for them to argue that they are doing all they can to avoid harm.

2. *Promoting the overall well-being of host-country citizens:* If we were host-country citizens, we would probably conclude that we want foreign engineers and businesspeople in our country only if their activity promotes our overall well-being, all things considered. Holding paramount the welfare of the public also implies that engineers must engage in projects whose good outweighs the harm. One way to determine whether an action would promote the overall well-being of host-country citizens is to ask whether we, if host-country citizens, would consent to the action. As an illustration of this guideline, consider the following case:

> Your company produces a drug to treat a potentially fatal form of dysentery that affects many people in Country X. The drug, however, has some serious side effects and can produce death in some who take it. The drug is not sold in the United States because of these potentially fatal side effects, and your supervisor asks you whether you think your firm should remove the drug from the market in Country X. You know that although the drug results in some deaths, it will save ten thousand lives for every life lost as a result of the side effects.

In asking yourself whether you would want to have the drug available if you were a citizen of Country X, you might well decide that you would prefer to have it available. This consideration, along with the facts about lives saved and lost, would help you decide how to respond to your supervisor's request for advice.

3. *Avoiding (if possible) the violation of host-country norms:* As host-country citizens, we would not usually want foreigners to violate our own values and practices. However, the Golden Rule also applies to us; so, we do not want to violate our own conscience. It would be difficult for engineers, for example, to honor cultural norms that sanction human slavery or the use of torture. Another complicating factor is that in some cases many host-country citizens may themselves want to change their traditional norms, especially where they interfere with eco-

nomic development. In other cases, however, host-country citizens may want to preserve their norms and ways of life, even at the cost of less economic development. Economic development is not, after all, the only or the supreme human good.

Decisions on whether to comply with host-country norms can be difficult. Consider the following case, which is also modeled on an actual one:[23]

> You work for a steel company in India, which has the policy of partially compensating its employees with a promise to hire one of the employee's children. This policy is very popular with the employees in a country where there is a tradition of providing jobs for one's children and the members of one's extended family. But to you, the policy is nepotism and in conflict with the more desirable policy of hiring the most qualified applicant. What should you do?

Given the requirement of the Golden Rule, we should start with the presumption that it is better to comply with a host-country practice unless there is good reason to reject it. To determine whether there is good reason to reject it, however, it will often be useful to apply all of the guidelines and tests we set out. This will also serve as a brief review of moral considerations set out in this chapter:

a. The practice does not seem to constitute a serious violation of human rights, although it does mean that some people may not be given equal consideration for some of the jobs available.

b. The practice does not involve unacceptable paternalism or exploitation.

c. The practice does not involve any intentional or avoidable harm, other than the fact that a person who was most qualified for the job may not get it.

d. Complying with the practice probably promotes the overall well-being of the country, because rejecting the practice would be disruptive, not only to lives of the employees involved, but also to the system of family loyalties of which it is a part. On the other hand, the practice may not contribute to the greatest overall economic efficiency, because the best person may not always get the job.

e. Complying with the norm would probably not produce any severe violation of your conscience. In this regard, you might note that the practice has some features in common with our practice of allowing a father to pass on an inheritance to his son.

f. Finally, the practice does not involve you in any violation of home-country or host-country laws.

Although the practice may not contribute maximally to economic development because it allows a less qualified person to take some jobs and it may involve some injustice to some applicants for a job, we must balance these considerations against the fact that the practice is connected with a much larger cultural tradition of family loyalties and that there are somewhat analogous practices in our own culture. Given these considerations, there is probably nothing wrong—or at least nothing seriously wrong—with complying with the practice, although it might be better if the country eliminated it.This conclusion also illustrates the need not to be overly rigorist in resolving moral problems in the international context. Complying with the custom of nepotism may make most American engineers uncomfortable. But given the presumption in favor of respecting host-country norms—a presumption that seems to follow from the Golden Rule—and the fact that the violations of the guidelines seem to be minimal, it is probably better to comply with the norms.

10.8   Bribery, Extortion, Grease Payments, and Gifts

So far we have focused primarily on the implications of the welfare requirement of the codes. But we have seen that there are other provisions of the codes that are relevant to the international context. One of these is the prohibition of paying or accepting bribes.

Probably the single most important issue faced by U.S. engineers in the international environment is bribery and related phenomena. For example, many cases commonly described as illustrating bribery turn out to be better understood as examples of extortion. There are also *grease payments,* which are payments to hasten or facilitate the performance of certain functions, such as the passage of goods through customs, the installation of a telephone, or the processing of a legal document. Finally, many cultures encourage the giving and receiving of gifts as the proper way to cement a friendship. In many cultures it is also believed that friendships should be the basis of business relationships. Let us consider each of these practices.

Bribery

In 1977 the U.S. Congress passed the Foreign Corrupt Practices Act, specifically prohibiting bribery of government officials. Typically, a bribe is made to a government official in exchange for violating some official duty or responsibility. The payment might result, for example, in an official's not making a decision to buy a product on the merits of the product. Here is a typical or paradigm case of bribery:

> An executive of Company A hopes to sell twenty-five airplanes to the national airline of Country X. The deal requires the approval of the head of the Ministry of Transportation in Country X. The executive knows that the official, who has a reputation for honesty, can make a better deal elsewhere, but that he also is experiencing personal financial difficulties. So the executive offers the official $300,000 to authorize purchase of the planes from Company A. The official accepts the bribe and orders the planes to be purchased.[24]

On the basis of this paradigm case, we can give the following more complete definition of a bribe than the one offered in Chapter 2:

> A bribe is a payment of money (or something of value) to another person *in exchange for* his giving one special consideration that is incompatible with the duties of his office, position, or role.[25]

It is important to keep in mind that bribes presuppose an *agreement* that the bribe must be in exchange for a certain type of conduct. If this agreement is not present, it is hard to distinguish bribes from gifts or rewards.

Giving and receiving bribes are forbidden by professional engineering codes. There is good reason for this:

1. If an engineer takes a bribe, she is creating a situation that will most likely corrupt her professional judgment and tarnish the reputation of the engineering profession.

2. If she offers a bribe, she engages in activity that will also tarnish the reputation of her profession, if it is discovered, and probably violate her obligation to promote the well-being of the public.

3. Bribery induces the person taking the bribe to act immorally by violating the obligation to act on behalf of the interests of his client or employer. For example, it can induce a government official to break the obligation to act on behalf of the best interests of the citizenry.

4. Bribery can also undermine the efficiency of the market by inducing one to buy products that are not the best for the price.

5. Bribery can give one an unfair advantage over one's competitors, thus violating the standards of justice and fair play.

John T. Noonan, jurist and authority on the history of morality, argues that the opposition to bribery is becoming stronger throughout the world.[26] There is massive popular discontent with bribery in Japan, Italy, and other countries. The antibribery ethic is increasingly embodied in the law. Even campaign contributions, which have many similarities with bribery, are becoming increasingly suspect. Although there are many points of dissimilarity between bribery and slavery, there is some basis for saying that, just as slavery was once accepted and is now universally condemned, so bribery is—although not universally condemned—increasingly held to be morally unacceptable.

Extortion

Many cases that might look like bribery are actually cases of extortion. Suppose the same executive knows that he is offering the best deal on airplanes to the official in Country X, who has the authority to authorize purchases for his national airlines. The executive knows, however, that the official will not deal with him unless he offers the official a large cash payment. The executive offers the payment to the official, and the official authorizes the purchase of the airplanes. This is extortion, rather than bribery.

It is more difficult to offer a definition of extortion; for example, here is a proposed (but inadequate) definition:

> Extortion is the act of threatening someone with harm (that the extorter is not entitled to inflict) to obtain benefits to which the extorter has no prior right.[27]

This definition is inadequate because some actions not covered by the definition are still extortion. For example, my threatening to expose the official misconduct of a government official unless he pays me a large sum of money would be extortion, even though exposing the official would be both morally and legally permissible. We find it impossible, however, to give a completely adequate definition of extortion. All we can say is that this definition gives a *sufficient* (though not a necessary) condition of extortion.

Sometimes it is difficult to know whether one is paying bribery or extortion. An inspector who demands a payoff to authorize a shipment of a product may claim that the product does not meet standards. It may be difficult to know whether he is lying and too expensive to find out. In this case, a company may decide to pay off without knowing whether it is paying a bribe or extortion. Of course it may be irresponsible not to find out.[28]

Many of the most famous cases of corruption seem to lie near the border between bribery and extortion. Between 1966 and 1970 the Gulf Oil Corporation paid $4 million to the ruling Democratic Republican Party of South Korea. Gulf was led to believe that its continued flourishing in South Korea depended on these payments. Some believe that Lockheed's payments to Korean officials may have been extortion payments rather than bribery payments. If the payments gave Gulf special advantages over Boeing and McDonnell Douglas, it was bribery. If the Korean officials would have requested and received payments from either of the other two firms if Lockheed had refused, then the payments might better be classified as extortion payments.[29]

The moral status of paying extortion is different from the moral status of paying and accepting bribes, as a consideration of the five arguments against bribery shows:

1. Paying extortion will not usually corrupt professional judgment.

2. Although paying extortion can tarnish one's professional reputation, it will probably not do so as much as paying a bribe.

3. Paying extortion will not cause one to act contrary to the best interests of one's employer or client by, for example, selecting an inferior product, but it does involve the use of a client's or employer's money.

4. Paying extortion does not undermine the efficiency of the market by promoting the selection of inferior or more expensive products, but it does divert funds from their most efficient use.

5. Finally, paying extortion does not give one an unfair advantage over others, except insofar as others do not or cannot pay the extortion. The main problem with paying extortion is that it perpetuates a practice that is a type of theft.

Grease Payments

These are offered to facilitate routine bureaucratic decisions, such as hastening the passage of goods through customs. They do not give one an unfair advantage over others, assuming that others make the payments too, and they are often tacitly condoned by governments. Unlike bribes, grease payments aren't made to get someone to violate their duties. They are a form of petty extortion, or even perhaps fees for services to be rendered. For example, in many countries, customs officials may not be paid an adequate salary, and the government may assume that officials will receive grease payments to supplement their salary, just as employers assume waiters will receive tips. Still, grease payments would be better eliminated and replaced with higher fees, which could then be passed on to officials in the form of more adequate salaries. In this way, the payments would not have to be kept secret.

There is a slippery slope, furthermore, leading from grease payments to payments intended to gain special consideration over others. As was earlier noted, sometimes the grease payment may allow the passage of inferior goods through customs, thus giving one an advantage over those who do not make the payment. A fee to get telephone service in three weeks rather than six months or to get a permit expedited through a government bureaucracy, by putting a person at the front of the cue, clearly gives him an advantage over others.

Gifts

In some cultures an exchange of gifts is a way to cement personal relationships. Business relationships, in turn, are built on personal relationships. Further, in some cultures, one is expected to show favoritism toward "friends," even when one acts in an official capacity. Many societies find the impersonal nature of Western business transactions, separated as they are from personal friendships and family ties, to be unnatural and even offensive. Sometimes these payments may be illegal in the country, even though the laws may not be enforced. Geoffrey Fadiman suggests that one answer to this dilemma is to give gifts to the community rather than to individuals.[30]

10.9   Sweatshops in Asia

Now let us return to the case presented at the beginning of this chapter. We can begin by considering an argument the H&J manager made: "If we pulled out, someone else would take our place." The argument, which we can call the No Difference Argument (NDA), seems to go something like this:

Premise A: I am only doing something wrong if my action makes the world a worse place than it would be otherwise.

Premise B: My action in buying clothes from the Myanmar plant does not make the world a worse place than it would be otherwise, because someone else would perform the action if I didn't.

Conclusion C: So my action is not wrong.

There are at least three problems with this argument. First, it is not possible to know with certainty that the assumption of premise B that someone else will perform the action if I do not is true. If H&J withdraws, the plant might not be able to find another customer. In the case of Hanna, other engineers might have the same objection that she has. Second, premise B's assumption (that the only way the world will not be worse off is if nobody performs the action in question) is false. The example of some refusing to perform the action might have a long-term beneficial consequence, even if it did not prevent the action in question. Third, the claim of premise A that making the world a worse place than it would be otherwise is the only way that I can be doing something wrong is controversial. The action could also be wrong because it violates a moral rule, such as, "Do not harm others, even if they will be harmed anyhow."

Furthermore, Hanna will be responsible for the harm (if there is one) only if she participates in it. So, from the standpoint of personal moral responsibility, there is good reason to avoid participating in the harm, if there is one. To determine whether there is harm, however, we must look at the three guidelines proposed in this chapter.

1. The UN's Universal Declaration of Human Rights asserts that all human beings have a right to a minimal standard of living. Its International Covenant on Economic, Social and Cultural Rights makes a similar assertion. Is this right violated in the present case? Indonesian experts estimate that the wage paid to seamstresses in that country ($0.91/day) is only 67 percent of what is necessary to supply "minimum physical needs," and conditions in Country X are probably not that different.[31] One might dispute this claim, however. The seamstresses are given living quarters and a free lunch, and many of them apparently prefer the work to village life. Finally, there is the consideration that the right to subsistence must be limited, according to Nickel, by the ability of the society (or perhaps the market) to provide that right. According to the H&J manager, the workers are paid the "prevailing wage"; that is, their wage is the market wage in the area. The human rights issue may not be clear enough to decide whether Hanna should refuse the project.

2. Do the guidelines to avoid exploitation and paternalism help? The position of the young women seems to fit the first four conditions for exploitation. There is an asymmetrical balance of power; the young women need the wages to protect their vital interests; the exploitative relationship is the only (or virtually the only) source of the wages; and the owners of the factory and H&J exercise at least some discretionary control over the wages, within the limits of the market. The question is whether the labor of the young women is provided without adequate compensation. This is the same as the question considered earlier, and we shall again defer it. There is, however, some evidence for exploitation.

Now let us turn to paternalism. There is an argument that refusing to do business in the country is paternalistic. The young women have taken the jobs willingly, although few other alternatives for work are available. One young woman is reported to have said of similar working conditions: "Some days it's hard. But I'm just happy to have a job."[32] Furthermore, many LIC governments resent the paternalistic imposition of American standards on their economy. Developing countries, for example, succeeded in excluding the prohibition of child labor from the General Agreement on Tariffs and Trade.[33] There is, then, a prima facie case that refusing to participate in the project involves Hanna in paternalism. The requirement to avoid both exploitation and paternalism may be difficult to satisfy. We need further guidance.

3. How should the Golden Rule be applied to this situation? We shall use all three tests for applying the Golden Rule.

The first test is that there should be no intentional or avoidable harm. We shall assume that no intentional harm is being produced. If we consider the low wages and long working hours (which result from the low wages) to be a type of harm, the argument that the harm is unavoidable might go as follows. Although the wages paid the young women are shockingly low, and the working hours are shockingly long, other facts must be taken into account. There will, after all, always be a lowest wage, and an industry with the longest working hours. These conditions are, furthermore, likely to prevail in the clothing industry. Even if wages were raised substantially—say, to $1.50 per day—the wages would still be shockingly low. And if wages are raised too much, the garments will be priced out of the highly competitive clothing market and the young women will be out of a job. By one estimate, $0.04 per garment at wholesale is the maximum variation in the price of a garment that the market will tolerate.[34] This leaves little room for wage increases, although perhaps some.

The crucial question here seems to be whether H&J is doing all it can to improve the condition of the workers. Some firms have done more; for example, Levi Strauss has "ethical sourcing" guidelines (discussed earlier). However, creative solutions must often be found to suit local conditions. Levi Strauss, which does not employ children if they are under the legal compulsory age to be in school, found that in Bangladesh underage female employees were often the sole wage earners in their families and had few alternatives other than begging or prostitution. So the firm arranged for on-site schooling and funded the tuition, uniforms, and books for the children. We shall conclude that H&J probably could take some additional steps to (slightly) increase the wages of the young women and to improve the condition of the workers to some degree. So some avoidable harm is probably not being eliminated, although the extent to which this is the case is not entirely clear.

The second test is that the action must promote the overall well-being of host-country residents. The argument that Hanna's designing the new equipment contributes to the overall well-being of the host country might go as follows. First, because the clothing industry is usually the entry-level industry in the process of industrial development, it certainly contributes to the economic development of the host country. Second, the fact that many young women prefer these jobs to life in their villages—to say nothing of begging and prostitution—indicates that they think the plant produces more good than harm. At the very least, it is not clear that the harm outweighs the good.

The third test is that host-country norms must be respected, as long as they do not violate the other guidelines, the conscience of home-country residents, or relevant laws. There is no reason to believe that the plant violates host-country norms or any laws. Although we cannot be sure what Hanna's conscience requires, we shall assume that her conscience is not being violated if the first two guidelines (the proscriptions against engaging in unacceptable violations of human rights and the proscriptions against exploitation and paternalism) are met.

We have seen that the first two guidelines are met, unless H&J is not doing all it can to improve the condition of the workers. We have concluded that H&J probably could take some additional steps to improve the wages and working conditions of the young women, but that may not be substantial. Because we want to avoid excessive moral rigorism in the international environment, we shall conclude that the problem is probably not serious enough to warrant Hanna's refusing the assignment, at least not without further information.

10.10   Chapter Summary

Professional standards similar to those in the United States are increasingly being adopted worldwide. Engineers in many countries are increasingly asked to work in countries other than their own. This internationalization of professionalism presents many problems, because values, economic conditions, and institutions in other countries may not be like those in an engineer's home country. Citizens in some less industrialized countries may also be more vulnerable to exploitation than citizens in the more industrialized countries.

Certain parts of U.S. professional engineering codes are especially difficult to apply in the international setting. These include the requirement to hold paramount the safety, health, and welfare of the public; to avoid bribery and conflicts of interest; to respect the environment and not to discriminate; to uphold the reputation of the engineering profession; and to promote knowledge and avoid deception. Additional guidelines are needed for applying the codes in the international context. In applying the guidelines, engineers should avoid three sets of extremes: moral absolutism and moral relativism, assuming too much or too little personal responsibility for the firm's actions, and being excessively lax or rigorous in the application of moral principles.

The three guidelines useful in applying the codes are respecting human rights, avoiding paternalism and exploitation, and following the Golden Rule.

Although originating in the West, there is considerable evidence that the belief that all human beings possess certain rights is increasingly being adopted worldwide. Because of the special vulnerability of many host-country citizens, paternalism and exploitation are especially tempting and should generally be avoided. The ethical imperative of the Golden Rule requires us to place ourselves in the situation of host-country citizens and ask how we would want foreign engineers and businesspeople to behave in our country.

In applying the Golden Rule, three tests are useful. We should refuse to engage in engineering activities that do intentional and avoidable harm. We should attempt to promote the overall well-being of host-country citizens. And we should refuse to engage in engineering activities that fail to respect host-country norms, as long as these norms do not violate the guidelines we have set out, one's own conscience, or relevant home-country and host-country laws.

Bribery, extortion, grease payments, and gifts are especially common issues faced by engineers in host countries. Bribery is virtually always wrong, whereas paying extortion may sometimes be justified. Making grease payments and giving gifts, although often problematic, may often be justified.

CASES TO CONSIDER

Case 1	Aftermath of Chernobyl
Case 13	Disaster Relief
Case 20	Ghost of an Executed Engineer
Case 41	"Smoking System" (Apply this in an international setting.)
Case 47	Unlicensed Engineer
Case 57	XYZ Hose Co. (Apply this in an international setting.)

NOTES

1. This case is a modified version of an actual case presented in Lee A. Tavis, *Power and Responsibility: Multinational Managers and Developing Country Concerns* (Notre Dame, Ind.: University of Notre Dame Press, 1997), pp. 315–338.

2. Quoted in Tavis, p. 322.

3. Tavis, p. 322.

4. Tavis, p. 334.

5. "In Europe, Vive La Feani," *Engineering Times* (February 1997).

6. These facts are gleaned from various articles in the January 1977 issue of *Engineering Times*.

7. We have used the term Less Industrialized Country (LIC) or Less Industrialized Countries (LICs) rather than the more common Lesser Developed Nation (LDN), because the latter term seems unnecessarily prejudicial. Although many Less Industrialized Countries may not be as developed as some nations industrially and economically, they may be highly developed in other ways. For example, they may have highly developed and sophisticated religious, philosophical, or artistic cultures.

8. Richard DeGeorge, *Competing with Integrity in International Business* (New York: Oxford University Press, 1993), p. vi.

9. See Robert E. Goodin, *Protecting the Vulnerable: A Reanalysis of Our Social Responsibilities* (Chicago: University of Chicago Press, 1985).

10. This case is discussed in various places; for example, see "Abbot Laboratories Puts Restraints on Marketing Infant Formula in the Third World," in *Responsive Capitalism*, ed. Earl A. Molander (New York: McGraw-Hill, Inc. 1980), pp. 264–276.

11. For an interesting discussion of this requirement, see Robert. J. Baum, "Engineers and the Public: Sharing Responsibilities," in Daniel E. Wueste, ed., *Professional Ethics and Social Responsibility* (Lanham, Md.: Rowman and Littlefield, 1994).

12. Michael Davis, "Thinking Like an Engineer," *Philosophy and Public Affairs*, 20, no. 2 (Spring 1991), 150–167. (See pp. 164–165.)

13. See James F. Childress and John Macquarrie, Eds., *The Westminster Dictionary of the Christian Church* (Philadelphia, Pa.: The Westminster Press, 1986), p. 499.

14. Ibid., p. 633.

15. See *The International Bill of Human Rights,* with forward by Jimmy Carter (Glen Ellen, Calif.: Entwhistle Books, 1981). No author.

16. James W. Nickel, *Making Sense of Human Rights: Philosophical Reflections on the Universal Declaration of Human Rights* (Berkeley: University of California Press, 1987), pp. 108–109.

17. For an expanded version of this argument, see Alan Gewirth, *Reason and Morality* (Chicago: University of Chicago Press, 1978), pp. 98–102.

18. These ideas are modified versions of ones suggested by Alan Gewirth in *The Community of Rights* (Chicago: University of Chicago Press, 1966).

19. Goodin, *Protecting the Vulnerable,* pp. 195–196. Another recent treatment of exploitation can be found in Alan Wertheimer, *Exploitation* (Princeton: Princeton University Press, 1996).

20. For the criticism of professional codes as too paternalistic, see Baum, "Engineers and the Public" in Wueste. For the expression of concern about excessive paternalism on the part of engineers in host countries, see Eugene Schlossberger, "The Responsibility of Engineers, Appropriate Technology, and Lesser Developed Nations" in *Science and Engineering Ethics,* 3, no. 3 (July 1997), 317–325.

21. See *Responsive Capitalism*, pp. 264–276.

22. Tavis, p. 331.

23. For this case and related discussion, see Thomas Donaldson and Thomas W. Dunfee, "Toward a Unified Conception of Business Ethics: Integrative Social Contract Theory," *Academy of Management Review, 19*, no. 2 (1994), 152–284.

24. This scenario is a modification of one presented by Michael Philips, "Bribery" in Patricia Werhane and Kendall D'Andrade, *Profit and Responsibility* (New York and Toronto: Edwin Mellon Press, 1985), pp. 197–220.

25. For this definition and an excellent discussion of bribery and extortion, see Thomas L. Carson, "Bribery, Extortion, and the 'Foreign Corrupt Practices Act,'" *Philosophy and Public Affairs, 14*, no. 1 (1985), 66–90.

26. John T. Noonan, *Bribery* (New York: Macmillan, 1984).

27. Carson, 73.

28. Carson, 79.

29. Carson, 75.

30. See some of Fadiman's suggestions in the discussion of creative middle way solutions in J. A. Fadiman, "A Traveler's Guide to Gifts and Bribes," *Harvard Business Review* (July/August1986), 122–126; 130–136.

31. Tavis, p. 317.

32. Tavis, p. 317.

33. Tavis, p. 322.

34. Tavis, p. 327.

Chapter 11

Engineering Professionalism and Ethics: Issues Old and New

Brad graduated from Engineering Tech two years ago. Since then he has been employed by Brian and Associates, a small civil engineering firm.[1] He has been assigned to design schools, overhead walkways between buildings, and other projects. For some time he has been concerned that he may not have the experience required for such assignments, and he has conveyed this concern to his employer/supervisor, Charles Brian. Charles replied that he has always checked Brad's work and has found it satisfactory.

Later Brad learns that in fact Charles does not always check his work, but simply places his seal on it and sends the designs to his clients. He further learns that Charles places his seal on many designs that he has not checked and even allows other engineers to use his seal and forge his signature.

Brad becomes increasingly concerned about his employment situation and finally decides to look for another job. He tells his prospective employer why he is leaving Brian and Associates, and the employer hires him at once. Brad is encouraged by his new employer to report his former employer to the state registration board, which initiates action against Brian and Associates.

11.1   Introduction

This fictionalized version of an actual case illustrates the importance of ethical and professional issues in the experience of one young engineer. As a beginning engineer, Brad was forced to avail himself of some of the mechanisms for enforcing professional standards. These mechanisms have long been in place. But new issues for engineering professionalism and ethics are also emerging. In this chapter we shall discuss both some of the in-place standards and structures for promoting and enforcing ethics and also some of the emerging issues in the engineering profession.

To function properly, any community must have rules, along with ways of promoting and enforcing them. The same thing holds for a professional community. In the engineering community the responsibility for promoting high standards of ethical and professional conduct falls on several groups. Educational institutions clearly have an obligation to teach professional ethics. Engineering instructors should raise ethical considerations in the classroom, and engineering schools should offer courses in professional ethics. Business organizations should also support engineering ethics and professionalism and, unlike Brian and Associates, refrain from placing their employees in situations where they must resign to maintain their professional integrity.

We also believe that a special responsibility for promoting ethics lies with professional engineering societies. Professional societies are the proper forum for debating the controversial ethical issues that face the engineering profession. By promulgating ethical codes and recognizing and supporting members who uphold professional standards, they can do much to promote professionalism among their members. We begin by examining some of the ways that professional engineering societies already promote ethical conduct and some of the ways in which they might do so in the future.

The primary responsibility for enforcing ethical standards in the engineering community should rest with state boards of registration. State boards have the power to investigate violations of their own codes of ethics, to administer penalties, and, in extreme cases, to revoke the Professional Engineer (PE) license. We therefore describe the activities of state boards of registration and of a national organization for state boards.

New issues in ethics and professionalism are constantly arising. One of these issues is the question of universal licensure and the industry exemption. Engineers are not required to have a PE license to engage in all types of engineering work. This weakens the powers of state boards of engineering registration to enforce ethical standards in the engineering profession, because their chief power is the right to revoke the PE license. Therefore, we also consider some of the arguments for and against mandatory registration of engineers, as well as arguments for and against the so-called industry exemption from registration.

Finally, issues regarding gender and minorities are increasingly important for the engineering profession, as they are for our society in general. In the last section, we shall consider some of the problems these issues raise.

11.2   Professional Engineering Societies: Promoting Rather Than Enforcing Ethics

Limitations in Enforcing Ethics

Professional societies occupy a special place in the engineering community. Undoubtedly, the major function of most engineering societies is to promote the discovery and dissemination of technical knowledge. Most societies recognize, however, that they also have responsibilities for promoting professional ethics. Precisely what these functions are is open to discussion.

Engineering societies may have some obligations to enforce ethics. They do engage in investigations of ethical misconduct, much of it in an unobtrusive way. Such investigation may be especially appropriate when members are not registered professional engineers and therefore do not come under the authority of state registration boards. In these cases the only kind of discipline for ethical violations is censure, suspension, or expulsion from their professional societies.

The professional societies, however, should probably not be expected to be extensively involved in disciplining wayward members. One reason is that the most severe penalty that a professional society can impose is expulsion from the society, and membership in a professional society is rarely if ever a requirement for performing engineering work. Another reason is that disciplining wayward members might involve expenses that would impose heavy and perhaps intolerable financial burdens on professional societies. The expenses involved in investigating wayward members could be considerable, and there might also be legal fees.

A 1979 legal case, involving the American Institute of Architects (AIA), illustrates the problems that professional societies could encounter in attempting to enforce their own codes.[2] Keep in mind that the AIA is not the registration agency that grants licenses to architects but a professional society of architects. The greatest punishment that the AIA can administer is the revocation of society membership, and society membership is not required to pursue a career in architecture.

Mardirosian was hired by the city of Washington, D.C., to review the work of another architect who had designed the alteration and reconditioning of Union Station and its new National Visitor Center. The earlier architect's contract contained a provision that allowed the city government to terminate his services at its discretion. The city decided to take advantage of this provision and to employ Mardirosian to complete the architectural services for the visitor center. Mardirosian was charged with supplanting another architect in violation of AIA Standard.

> An architect shall not attempt to obtain, offer to undertake or accept a commission for which the architect knows another legally qualified individual or firm has been selected or employed, until the architect gives the latter written notice that the architect is so doing.

The AIA's National Judicial Board agreed with the charge against Mardirosian and recommended his expulsion from the AIA. After an appeal by Mardirosian, the discipline was modified to a one-year suspension of his membership.

The architect sued the AIA in the U.S. District Court for the District of Columbia, alleging that the ethics standards constituted unreasonable restraint of trade in violation of the Sherman Antitrust Act. The district court granted Mardirosian's motion for summary judgment as to liability. The amount of fines, including triple damages, was to be determined in a jury trial. In June 1980 the AIA voted to make compliance with its ethical standards voluntary rather than mandatory. In late 1981 the case was settled when the AIA paid Mardirosian $700,000 in damages. It also incurred approximately $500,000 in legal expenses.

The Mardirosian case is only a single example, and there are questions about whether the AIA applied its own standards correctly. In this particular case, many might be inclined to agree with Mardirosian. Nevertheless, the case shows why professional societies should probably not be expected to be the primary vehicle for enforcing professional ethics.

Promoting Ethics

Professional societies can, however, promote ethics. The promotion of ethics involves activities that support, reward, and encourage ethical conduct rather than punish members who act in an unethical manner. Here are some of the more specific ways in which professional societies can promote ethics.

1. Professional societies are the proper forum for debating what should be in a professional code of ethics. Should engineering codes have more to say about the environment? Should they have more to say about the professional rights of engineers in the workplace? Should they have stronger statements about conflicts of interest? Should codes of ethics have more specific statements about the professional responsibilities of engineers in the international arena? Should professional standards apply in the international arena in the same way they apply in the United States?

Such questions should be (and are) debated in professional engineering societies. The most likely alternative forum for such debate would be state engineering registration boards. Although state registration boards do carry on ethical debates regarding the proper content of their own codes of ethics, they have several limitations. The boards are made up of only a handful of engineers and probably cannot represent the entire profession. Furthermore, because their codes of ethics have the force of law, it is probably not proper that they be on the "cutting edge" of ethical change in the profession. Many believe that the law should represent a consensus that has already developed, rather than attempt to form that consensus. Another reason is that most engineers are not registered, so the deliberations of state boards would not apply to them. The unregistered engineers might be members of professional societies, however.

2. Promoting ethics might also involve establishing awards for engineers who exhibit exemplary ethical conduct. At the present time, two of the best-known awards for exemplary ethical conduct are the Award for Outstanding Service in the Public Interest of the IEEE's Committee on Social Implications of Technology and a similar award given by the American Association for the Advancement of Science (AAAS). The IEEE has given its award to the three Bay Area Rapid Transit engineers in San Francisco who protested what they considered to be faulty design in the system. The AAAS has given its award to Roger Boisjoly who protested the *Challenger* launch. A good argument can be made that every major engineering society should have such an award and give it a place of prominence in its meetings and in its literature.

There is no reason to limit such awards to employees. Employers often exhibit outstanding records in the area of ethics and professionalism, and they should also be rewarded. Many employers have strong traditions of adhering to ethical principles in their relationships with clients or customers and employees; they deserve to be honored and recognized as much as ethical employees.

3. Professional societies could also assist engineers who have been discharged because they adhered to high ethical standards. Often such engineers have trouble finding new jobs even though their dismissal was unjustified and was a result of conduct in the public interest. Stephen Unger has pointed out that an ethics committee could ascertain the facts of the case and then, if a member warranted support, help in finding new employment. A society might even compile a list of employers who would be particularly sympathetic to ethical employees who have been dismissed without just cause.[3] This kind of support would require investigation by a committee and could be controversial, time consuming, and expensive, but it would be of enormous help to ethical professionals.

4. Professional societies could establish "ethics helplines" (a better term, in our opinion, than "ethics hotlines") or other services whereby engineers could seek advice on difficult ethical issues. The helplines could also be a source of information about what assistance an engineer might expect from his or her professional society. Many organizations already have such helplines, and they often have been effective ways of resolving problems, usually before they reach crisis proportions. Although it later discontinued the service, the IEEE experimented with a helpline to assist engineers who encountered difficulties related to professional ethics.

5. Promoting ethics might also involve helping to educate the public about new technologies. Educating the public to the risks and benefits involved in new technologies and helping the public to avoid unnecessary fears of technology would be an invaluable service, provided it was not perceived as merely self-serving.

6. Professional societies should probably continue to investigate charges of wrongdoing by members, whether or not they use such investigations as a prelude to possible expulsion from the society. Such investigations are now usually conducted in a situation of relative privacy, and probably should continue to be conducted in this way. This approach protects innocent engineers who have been accused of wrongdoing because of malice or false information. Those who are guilty of wrongdoing are also probably more likely to cooperate and to reform when they do not have to defend themselves from public criticism.

7. Engineering societies could also promote the discussion and understanding of engineering ethics by rendering decisions on the application of their codes in disputed cases, thus helping engineers and the public to understand the practical implications of their codes.

There are other things that professional societies might do to support ethics, but many societies are probably reluctant to endorse even these proposals for promoting ethics. They may fear being embroiled in controversy, litigation, and expense that could limit their ability to achieve their primary mission: encouraging the discovery and dissemination of technical knowledge.

Steven Unger believes these fears are exaggerated.[4] Engineering societies can protect themselves from legal action by making an honest effort to find the truth in the cases they investigate and by displaying a consistent record of commitment to the public welfare rather than the self-interest of engineers. It is useful to keep in mind, he believes, that truth is an absolute defense against libel or slander in the American legal system, and evidence of a sincere attempt to find the truth is a strong defense.

At least two organizations have, according to Unger, been successful in escaping significant legal action because of their commitment to objectivity. For over half a century the American Association of University Professors (AAUP) has been investigating universities that violate the academic freedom of professors, and it has never been successfully sued for damages. The Consumers Union (CU) has also been publishing its reports on consumer products for about fifty years and has had only one judgment against it. This judgment (for less than $16,000) was overturned on appeal. These organizations have a strong reputation for investigating issues objectively and for acting in the public interest rather than in their self-interest. If professional societies act in a similar fashion, they should be reasonably successful in protecting themselves from litigation.

Many societies may be reluctant to actively support their members for fear of losing industry support. Unger believes this fear is also unfounded. Industry needs access to the technical information disseminated by technical societies. It also benefits from the participation of its employees in standards committees and its access to advertising space in society publications. Furthermore, as Unger has pointed out, "an organization that acquired a reputation for being hostile to engineering societies on the grounds of the latter's support for ethical engineers would thereby incur resentment on the part of many in the profession."[5]

Unger may have underestimated the difficulties professional societies could encounter in promoting ethics. Large organizations could attempt a boycott of engineering societies, and such boycotts might be more successful than Unger believes. Historian of engineering Edward Layton points out that many firms contribute directly to professional engineering societies and that many employers pay the dues of their employees.[6] These organizations might join with others in withdrawing support from the professional societies if they thought the societies acted contrary to their interests. This might include forbidding their employees to attend meetings or serve as officers, discontinuing any financial support of the societies, and perhaps withdrawing advertising from society publications. Under certain conditions, such actions might deal a severe blow to the continued viability of the societies themselves. Unger may also underestimate the divisiveness that a more activist promotion of ethics would cause among society members.

On the other side of the argument, many employers hold ethics in high regard. They would no doubt welcome increased support and recognition of their own efforts on behalf of ethics that the societies could give. Furthermore, from the standpoint of the professional societies, the very nature of the professions as communities with moral ideals requires that professional societies do as much as they can to promote professional ideals. It is not consistent to promulgate an ethical code and then fail to honor and support those who adhere to it. The evidence of the past decade indicates that engineers are increasingly recognizing this.

11.3   American Engineering Societies

Engineers in the United States have no single professional society that clearly represents the entire profession in the way that the American Medical Association represents the medical profession and the American Bar Association represents the legal profession. Engineers with a strong professional orientation often favor a single society. Those with a strong industry orientation often want a smaller society that focuses on their specialized interests. The actual situation in the United States is an intermediate position between these two extremes: a group of more than eighty professional organizations that fall into three general categories.

One category consists of so-called umbrella organizations to which all engineers—or all engineering societies—may belong. The two most prominent follow:

• The American Association of Engineering Societies (AAES), founded in 1980, has seventeen member societies (including the major organizations in chemical, electrical, mechanical, and civil engineering), eight associate societies, and three regional societies.[7]

• The National Society of Professional Engineers (NSPE), founded in 1934, is especially concerned with the professional development of engineers and promotes engineering registration and other causes associated with engineering professionalism.

There have been several attempts to form umbrella organizations in the history of American engineering, the AAES being only the most recent. The NSPE's members are individual engineers, not societies. Thus, it is an "umbrella" organization only in the sense that its membership is open to all engineers interested in professional development, although civil engineers, especially those in private practice, constitute the majority of its members. A code for the society was proposed in 1935, but none was adopted until 1946.[8]

The second category of engineering societies is composed of those engineering societies that represent the major engineering disciplines. Representatives of this category include the following organizations:

• The American Society of Civil Engineers (ASCE), founded in 1852, has more than 110,000 members, including students.

• The American Society of Mechanical Engineers (ASME), founded in 1880, has more than 140,000 members, including students.

• The Institute of Electrical and Electronics Engineers (IEEE), founded in 1884 and consolidated in 1963 from the American Institute of Electrical Engineers and the Institute of Radio Engineers, has more than 300,000 members, including students.

• The American Institute of Chemical Engineers (AIChE), founded in 1908, has more than 150,000 members, including students.

The third category consists of more specialized societies, usually with much smaller memberships. Whereas the societies in the second category tend to be somewhat academic and research-oriented and are primarily concerned with the advancement of technical knowledge in their respective branches of engineering, the societies in the third group are more likely to be oriented toward the application of engineering knowledge to business or manufacturing. Examples of societies in the third group include:

• The American Academy of Environmental Engineers (AAEE), founded in 1913, has approximately 2,500 members.

• The American Congress on Surveying and Mapping (ASCM), founded in 1941, has approximately 7,500 members.

• The American Society of Heating, Refrigerating and Air-Conditioning Engineers, Inc. (ASHRAE), consolidated in 1959 from the American Society of Heating and Air-Conditioning Engineers (founded in 1894 as the American Society of Heating and Ventilating Engineers) and the American Society of Refrigerating Engineers (founded in 1904), has approximately 45,000 members, including students.

• The Society of Automotive Engineers (SAE), founded in 1905, has a membership of approximately 75,000, including students.[9]

The organization of engineering professionalism often has a different structure in other countries. (In Chapter 10 we discussed professional societies in other countries.)

11.4   State Registration Boards

In 1907 Wyoming passed the first act in the United States that defined the standards that engineers must meet to be licensed (or registered) as a Professional Engineer (PE). Since that time, every state has enacted similar laws. State engineering registration boards are charged with the administration of the law. The state boards are in turn members of the National Council of Examiners for Engineering and Surveying (NCEES).

The organizations best equipped to enforce ethical and professional standards are the state boards of engineering registration. Even though the boards only have authority over those engineers who are registered with the board (that is, who have the PE license), they still have several advantages in enforcing professional standards over voluntary professional societies.

First, state boards do not have to rely on voluntary contributions. They depend on such sources as state funding and the fees charged for the PE license.

Second, state boards have legal powers that are not available to voluntary societies. Professional societies can only expel engineers from their membership, but state boards can revoke PE licenses and even initiate prosecution for violations of the law. Although it is true that engineers are not required to hold the PE license to practice engineering, they must have it to sign off on certain engineering documents. Thus, the loss of a PE license can be a severe handicap for some engineers.

Third, state boards usually have an in-house apparatus for investigating complaints of unprofessional conduct, whereas professional societies may have more limited investigative capabilities.

State registration boards not only supervise the process of registration or licensing, but they also provide directions for the engineer's work after licensing. For example, they have rules describing the manner in which an engineering drawing must be made and rules for the procedure by which a licensed professional engineer approves them. The drawings must be sealed with the PE's own numbered seal and signed by the engineer.

The boards have the responsibility for enforcing their own rules. Penalties for violating the state laws governing engineering practice or the rules promulgated by the boards have increasing degrees of severity, usually following this order:

1. Informal reprimand
2. Formal reprimand
3. Suspension of the license for a short period of time, with a longer probation
4. Longer suspension of the license
5. Revocation of the license
6. Fines

Unfortunately, state boards also face limitations on their enforcement powers. First, they may have inadequate staff and funding. A registration board probably needs at least one full-time investigator, but many do not meet this minimum requirement. In many states, registration boards must rely on district attorneys or the state attorney general's office. State law enforcement agencies often have time and resources for pursuing only the most serious violations.

Second, the fact that most engineers are not registered and many types of engineering can be practiced without a license limits the ability of state boards to enforce professional standards across the entire profession.

Third, board members may sometimes be excessively reluctant to use their enforcement powers against wayward engineers. One board investigative officer has maintained that this is because board members are successful, ethical professionals who do not like to deal with the unethical activities of their fellow professionals. One remedy for this would be to have nonengineer representatives of the public on all registration boards.

Despite these problems, we believe that the state boards are the best means for enforcing professional standards in the engineering profession.

11.5   The National Council of Examiners for Engineering and Surveying (NCEES)

The NCEES is a national organization of state registration boards which, among other functions, (1) has developed a model ethical code for state boards of registration and a model law governing engineering registration, (2) keeps records of disciplinary actions by state boards, and (3) constructs the examinations for licensure administered by state boards. We shall consider all three of these functions.

     1. *The model code and the model law:* The **NCEES Model Rules** is suggested as a template for state registration boards to follow in constructing their own codes. The Model Rules has no legal force, but tends to ensure some uniformity among state codes.

The NCEES has also developed a model law that sets forth the criteria for licensing engineers to practice and for regulating their practice after they are licensed. Most state laws regulating the practice of engineering follow the broad outlines of the model law. The model law sets several criteria for engineering licensure. The criteria require that a licensed engineer have a degree from a school with an engineering program accredited by the Accreditation Board for Engineering and Technology (ABET).

The link with ABET requirements provides an important connection of the NCEES with engineering ethics. The ABET *Engineering Criteria 2000* criterion 3 for evaluating engineering programs includes the requirement that engineering programs demonstrate that their graduates have "an understanding of professional and ethical responsibility," "the broad education necessary to understand the impact of engineering solutions in a global and societal context," and "a knowledge of contemporary issues." Criterion 4 requires that students have "a major design experience" that includes consideration of the impact on design of such factors as economics, sustainability, manufacturability, ethics, health, safety, and social and political issues.[10]

The model law also requires that an applicant must have four years of "credible" engineering work experience under the supervision of a registered professional engineer before the "professional practice" examination may be taken. Most boards define "credible" experience as work involving increasing levels of difficulty and responsibility. An application for a PE license also must include a detailed description of the work experience as well as information sufficient to verify the other requirements. The model law also requires the applicant to be of good moral character. Most states have reciprocity agreements, allowing engineers to practice in one state with a license from another state.

2. *Keeping records of disciplinary actions by state boards:* The following lists examples from the records of the NCEES of disciplinary actions taken by various state boards:

• A land surveyor was ordered to resurvey and pay restitution for negligence in improperly locating boundary lines.

• A professional engineer's license was suspended for one year for failure to comply with a board order to have work reviewed by a peer reviewer prior to submitting the work for construction.

• A professional engineer was reprimanded and ordered to have an architect make a building-code check for negligence because he accepted an architectural assignment outside his area of engineering registration.

• A professional engineer's license was revoked for violating the terms and conditions of probation. A board ordered a nonregistrant to stop practicing engineering without a license.

• A professional engineer's license was probated for two years due to the improper design of a roof. The engineer was required to submit quarterly reports of work performed.

• A professional engineer was publicly reprimanded for signing and sealing work not prepared by the engineer or under the engineer's supervision.

- A professional engineer was ordered to complete a technical competence seminar and the engineer's license was probated as a result of sealing work done by another engineer not under the engineer's supervision and for violating other board rules.

- A professional engineer's license was revoked after the engineer was convicted of a felony. The engineer's license was restored after he served time on probation, made a personal appearance before the state board, submitted a recommendation by his supervising parole officer, and took a three-hour college-credit course on professionalism and ethics.

- A professional engineer's license was restricted because of errors in the engineer's calculations and the absence of a detailed drawing.

- A professional engineer was placed on four years' probation, required to give 400 hours of community service, and required to complete an ethics correspondence course after being convicted of two felonies and the violation of board rules. The convictions and rules violations had to do with embezzlement.

3. *Constructing examinations for engineering licensure:* To be licensed, an engineer must also pass two written examinations. The "fundamentals" examination covers basic science, mathematics, and engineering science. This examination is usually taken while the applicant is in the senior year of the B.S. program. The "professional practice" examination requires applicants to give engineering solutions to problems that might arise in practice.

The NCEES conducts workshops in which experts from various branches of engineering construct questions for the licensing examinations. These questions are then placed in a question bank, from which examination questions are taken. The examinations are given twice a year. The "fundamentals" examination now includes questions on engineering ethics—one indication of the increased concern for ethics in the engineering profession. The ethics questions, constructed according to the same general guidelines as the technical questions, usually focus on the NCEES Model Rules.

11.6 Universal Engineering Licensure and the Industry Exemption

One issue facing the engineering profession is whether all engineers should be required to have the PE license to practice engineering. The power of state registration boards would be greatly increased if states required engineers to have a PE license to perform any (or at least most) engineering work. In contrast to Canada, where most engineers have the PE license, most engineers in the United States are not registered. This severely restricts state boards of engineering registration in their ability to punish unethical conduct. Although a high percentage of academic engineers are registered, most engineers who work for large corporations, for example, are not. If an engineer's license is suspended, the engineer can still engage in many forms of engineering, and his or her ability to earn a livelihood is not destroyed.

If all engineers were required to have a license to engage in engineering work, however, the ethical codes of state registration boards would then be legally binding on all engineers. Combined with sufficient resources for investigation and prosecution, state boards would be in a position to enforce ethical standards for all engineers.

The same enforcement procedures could also strengthen the position of the ethical engineer. Suppose a client or employer is attempting to persuade an engineer to engage in unethical conduct. If a PE license were required to engage in engineering work, an engineer could then say to such a client or employer, "I am sorry, but I cannot do what you ask. My state professional code does not permit such conduct, and I might lose my license if I comply with your request. The same code applies to all engineers in the state, so I do not think you are going to get another engineer to do what you ask either."

Registered engineers can also appeal to their state professional codes in legal proceedings. There is some evidence that the courts are more sympathetic to an appeal to a state professional code than to the code of a professional society. In contrast to the state codes, which are legal documents approved by governmental bodies, professional society codes are sometimes described by the courts as "private" codes, because they are promulgated by voluntary organizations and are not legally binding. It stands to reason that an engineer's appeal to a state board's code in defense of his or her conduct in a legal proceeding would be more convincing if the engineer were licensed by the state board and therefore legally subject to the board's code.

There are also some general arguments against requiring all engineers to be registered. First, it might be difficult in some cases to decide whether an activity requires the services of a registered engineer. Second, the prices of products and services might also increase because they would now require the services of licensed engineers. Third, the cost to states of policing the vastly increased numbers of professional engineers would be greatly increased.

The argument over engineering registration, however, usually focuses on the so-called industry exemption. The exemption is probably a major reason that many engineers do not seek registration as professional engineers. Under the industry exemption, most states now allow corporate employees to practice engineering without a license, whether or not their work affects public safety, health, and welfare, as long as some licensed engineer places his or her PE seal on the finished work. And even some finished work does not require a seal.

Various arguments have been put forth for retaining the industry exemption:

1. The evidence that requiring the licensing of all engineers who in any way work on projects that affect the public would improve the safety of those products is not convincing to everyone.

2. The license fee might be a financial burden for some engineers.

3. Removing the industry exemption might raise the price of engineering services because engineers would have a monopoly on some types of services, which could otherwise be performed more cheaply by nonengineers. This would increase the cost to the public.

4. To comply with such a law, it might be necessary to break up teams of engineers and nonengineers (including scientists). This might be the only effective

way to separate engineering work and nonengineering work. Such teams might have been important in technological advance, and their loss could hinder the progress of technology.

There are also arguments in favor of eliminating the exemption:[11]

1. The industry exemption seems inconsistent with the engineering commitment to public health and safety. Industrial products can affect public health and safety as much as structures. If the public needs the protection of the licensure requirement for those who design structures, it also needs it for those who design products.

2. The industry exemption requires that the "person in responsible charge" be licensed, but often this person is hard to identify and the determination is made arbitrarily. When products are designed by teams, the team leader of one of the teams may be designated as the "person in responsible charge." But this person may be no more responsible than the leader of another team or someone who is not a team leader at all.

3. Eliminating the industry exemption would increase the ability of engineers to enforce professional standards because more engineers would have to become registered engineers and thus meet registration standards. It would in fact move engineering closer to the position of law and medicine, where all practitioners must be licensed.

Eliminating the industry exemption would not require all engineers to be registered. The requirement for registration might be stated so that engineers involved in projects that clearly have no relation to public health and safety could avoid registration. It might be stated in such a way that those engineering managers not engaged in design could avoid registration. Nevertheless, eliminating the requirement would have a significant impact on both industry and the engineering profession.

For a number of years the NSPE has held a policy in favor of eliminating the industry exemption, but many engineers and engineering societies have not affirmed this policy. Many engineers are not sympathetic with the arguments for elimination, to say nothing of a policy requiring all engineers to be registered.

The question of universal licensure and the industry exemption is still a controversial issue in the professional engineering community. As with other issues, the engineering community must keep in mind that it must set ethical standards for itself in dialogue with the larger society it serves. The guiding principle has been established: Engineers must hold paramount the safety, health, and welfare of the public. The interpretation and application of this guideline is a continuing process.

11.7   Gender and Minority Issues

The engineering profession will continue to face new issues in professionalism and ethics in the future. One issue that is assuming increasing importance is gender and minority discrimination.

Jim Grimaldi, projects manager in the Sunnyvale Division of Universal Corporation, has just learned that in two weeks the headquarters in Los Angeles will be sending him a project engineer, Joan Dreer. Her job will be to supervise small groups of engineers involved in automotive brake design. Joan Dreer will be the first woman engineer at Sunnyvale. On learning that their new supervisor will be a woman, several of the engineers inform Jim Grimaldi that they don't like the idea of a woman supervising their work. After a few months, Grimaldi notices that the groups under Dreer's supervision have failed to meet several deadlines. Grimaldi wonders what he should do.[12]

This case exemplifies the problems that women (and minority groups) often have in employment in engineering and science. According to the National Science Foundation, women and underrepresented minority scientists and engineers have lower levels of employment in business and industry. In 1993 more than 3.2 million people were employed in science and engineering, including almost three-quarters of a million women. Just under 500,000 were members of minority racial or ethnic groups and 200,000 were so-called underrepresented minorities. Approximately 175,000 people in the science and engineering labor force in 1993 had disabilities.[13]

The responsibilities of the engineering profession in this area probably fall primarily on the engineering societies. There are at least three areas in which the societies might make further contributions.

First, the societies could introduce clear statements about nondiscrimination into their codes. The Institute of Electrical and Electronics Engineers (IEEE) already has a clear statement. Section 8 enjoins its members "to treat fairly all persons regardless of such factors as race, religion, gender, disability, age, or national origin." Section 6 of the code of the American Institute of Chemical Engineers enjoins its members to "treat fairly all colleagues and co-workers, recognizing their unique contributions and capabilities," implying nondiscrimination. The codes of other societies might well follow these examples, especially that of the IEEE.

Second, the societies could find other ways to promote nondiscrimination. They could, for example, promote nondiscriminatory practices in their literature, promote seminars on nondiscrimination, and provide special assistance to members who have had job-related problems due to discrimination.

Third, the engineering societies representing the major branches of engineering could attempt to be as supportive as possible of the societies promoting the interests of specialized groups. As long as there is discrimination, societies representing women engineers, African American engineers, and Hispanic engineers will continue to serve a useful function.

11.8   Chapter Summary

Professional societies are not well suited to enforce professional standards, because enforcement can be expensive and because an engineer does not have to be a member of a professional society to practice engineering or even to have the

PE license. Nevertheless, professional societies should promote ethics by providing a forum for debating professional ethics issues, rewarding ethical engineers and employers, assisting engineers who have been discharged, providing advice to engineers facing ethical problems, educating the public about new technologies, providing some investigative services, and helping engineers to understand how to apply ethical codes.

U.S. engineering societies may be divided into "umbrella organizations," societies representing the major engineering disciplines, and more specialized societies, often with an industry rather than academic orientation.

State registration boards are more able than professional societies to enforce ethical standards in the engineering profession. They also have limitations, however, such as inadequate staff and funding, the ability of engineers to practice many types of engineering without a license, and the reluctance of some board members to penalize other engineers. All regulatory boards are members of the National Council of Examiners for Engineering and Surveying, which provides a model code for state boards, keeps records of disciplinary actions by state boards, and constructs examinations for engineering licensure.

There are arguments for and against the thesis that a license should be required to practice engineering. Favoring universal licensure is the fact that it would give much greater enforcement powers to state boards and strengthen the position of ethical engineers. Some arguments against universal licensure are (1) it might be difficult to decide whether an activity requires the services of a registered engineer, (2) the prices of services of licensed engineers might increase, and (3) the cost of enforcing professional standards would increase. Many arguments against universal licensure center around the industry exemption, which allows many engineers employed by industry to forego licensure.

Women and underrepresented minorities have lower levels of employment in business and industry. To help remedy this situation, professional engineering societies should have clear nondiscrimination policies in their codes. They could also promote nondiscrimination in their literature and in seminars and provide special assistance to members with job-related problems due to discrimination. Finally, the societies representing the major branches of engineering could support the specialized societies representing women and minorities.

✳ CASES TO CONSIDER

Case 14	Employment Opportunity*
Case 22	Glass Ceiling
Case 26	Innocent Comment
Case 31	Moral Beliefs in the Workplace
Case 36	Promotion
Case 42	Sunnyvale

---

* Includes an analysis of the case.

NOTES

1. This case was suggested by an actual case brought to our attention by a student of Professor Lee Lowery. We have slightly modified the facts and changed the names.

2. *Mardirosian v. The American Institute of Architects (AIA)*, 474 F. Supp. 628 (1979).

3. Stephen H. Unger, *Controlling Technology: Ethics and the Responsible Engineer*, 2nd ed. (New York: Holt, Rinehart & Winston, 1994), p. 153.

4. Stephen H. Unger, "Would Helping Ethical Professionals Get Professional Societies into Trouble?" *IEEE Technology and Society Magazine*, 6, no. 3 (September 1987), 17–21. Reprinted in Johnson (1991), pp. 368–375.

5. Ibid., Johnson, p. 374.

6. Edwin T. Layton, Jr., *The Revolt of the Engineers* (Cleveland: The Press of Western Reserve University, 1971), p. 18.

7. See "AAES Strives Toward Being Unified Voice of Engineering," *Engineering Times*, 15, no. 11 (November 1993), 1; "U.S. Engineer Unity Elusive," *Engineering Times, 15*, no. 11 (November 1993), 15.

8. Ibid., 32.

9. These figures, taken from the *Engineering Times* articles cited in note 7, are approximate numbers for 1993.

10. Accreditation Board for Engineering and Technology. *Engineering Criteria 2000*, 3rd ed. (Baltimore: ABET, 1997). See also http://www.abet.org/EAC/eac2000.html.

11. Many of these arguments are taken from G. J. Kettler, "Against the Industry Exemption" in James H. Schaub and Karl Pavlovic, Eds., *Engineering Professionalism and Ethics* (New York: Wiley-Interscience, 1983), pp. 531–534.

12. Michael S. Pritchard, *Teaching Engineering Ethics: A Case Study Approach*, National Science Foundation, Grant No. DIR-8820837, pp. 391–404.

13. See "Women, Minorities, and Persons with Disabilities in Science and Engineering: 1996" at <http://www.nsf.gov/sbe/srs/nsf96311/foreword.html>.

Cases

List of Cases

Case 1   Aftermath of Chernobyl 287
Case 2   Air Bags 287
Case 3   Auditory Visual Tracker
          (AVIT)* 288
Case 4   Borrowed Tools 289
Case 5   Cadillac Chips 289
Case 6   Catalyst* 290
Case 7   Containers 294
Case 8   The Co-Op Student* 295
Case 9   Cost-Cutting 297
Case 10   The Deadline 297
Case 11   To Dissent or Not to Dissent?* 298
Case 12   Drinking in the Workplace 302
Case 13   Disaster Relief 303
Case 14   Employment Opportunity* 306
Case 15   An Excess? 309
Case 16   Failure 310
Case 17   Faulty Valves 310
Case 18   Fire Detectors 311
Case 19   Forced-Sex Accusation 312
Case 20   Ghost of an Executed
          Engineer 313
Case 21   Gilbane Gold 313
Case 22   Glass Ceiling 315
Case 23   Golfing 316
Case 24   Highway Safety
          Improvements 317
Case 25   Hydrolevel 318
Case 26   Innocent Comment? 321
Case 27   Inside Tool & Die 321
Case 28   Last Resort 322

Case 29   Mere "Technicality"? 323
Case 30   Microwaves 324
Case 31   Moral Beliefs in the
          Workplace 325
Case 32   Oil Spill? 325
Case 33   Parkville* 326
Case 34   Pinto 330
Case 35   Price Is Right? 331
Case 36   Promotion 332
Case 37   Pulverizer 332
Case 38   Recommendation for a Friend 333
Case 39   Renewable Energy 335
Case 40   Side-Saddle Gas Tanks 335
Case 41   "Smoking System" 339
Case 42   Sunnyvale 340
Case 43   Training Firefighters 342
Case 44   Trees 342
Case 45   TV Antenna 343
Case 46   "Underground" Project 344
Case 47   Unlicensed Engineer 345
Case 48   USAWAY 346
Case 49   Vacation 346
Case 50   Walkway Disaster 347
Case 51   Waste Disposal 348
Case 52   Whose Property? 349
Case 53   Why Won't They Read? 350
Case 54   Window Safety 351
Case 55   Wonderful Development? 352
Case 56   Working Overtime 353
Case 57   XYZ Hose Co. 354

* Includes an analysis of the case.

Taxonomy of Cases

Acknowledging Mistakes

Cadillac Chips 289
Catalyst* 290
Failure 310
Faulty Valves 310
Oil Spill? 325
Recommendation for a Friend 333
XYZ Hose Co. 354
USAWAY 346
Why Won't They Read? 350
Wonderful Development? 352

Careers

Aftermath of Chernobyl 287
Auditory Visual Tracker (AVIT) 288
Disaster Relief 303
Drinking in the Workplace 302
Employment Opportunity 306
Ghost of an Executed Engineer 313
Glass Ceiling 315
Innocent Comment? 321
Moral Beliefs in the Workplace 325
Recommendation for a Friend 333
Renewable Energy 335
"Smoking System" 339
Sunnyvale 340
Window Safety 351

Competence

Catalyst* 290
The Co-Op Student 295
Containers 294

Drinking in the Workplace 302
Promotion 332
Sunnyvale 340
Unlicensed Engineer 345
Vacation 346
Why Won't They Read? 350

Confidentiality and Trade Secrets

Drinking in the Workplace 302
Inside Tool & Die 321
Oil Spill? 325
Parkville 326
Promotion 332
Whose Property? 349

Conflicts of Interest

Golfing 316
Hydrolevel 318
Last Resort 322
Working Overtime 353

Dissent and/or Whistle-blowing

Borrowed Tools 289
Catalyst* 290
To Dissent or Not to Dissent? 298
An Excess? 309
Forced-Sex Accusation 312
Ghost of an Executed Engineer 313
Gilbane Gold 313
Last Resort 322
Moral Beliefs in the Workplace 325
Oil Spill? 325

Parkville 326
Pinto 330
Side-Saddle Gas Tanks 335
Training Firefighters 342
Waste Disposal 348
Whose Property? 349
Window Safety 351

Environmental Concerns

Aftermath of Chernobyl 287
Containers 294
To Dissent or Not to Dissent? 298
Employment Opportunity 306
An Excess? 309
Ghost of an Executed Engineer 313
Gilbane Gold 313
Mere "Technicality"? 323
Microwaves 324
Oil Spill? 325
Parkville 326
Renewable Energy 335
Trees 342
Unlicensed Engineer 345
Waste Disposal 348
XYZ Hose Co. 354

Exemplary Practice

Aftermath of Chernobyl 287
Air Bags 287
Auditory Visual Tracker (AVIT) 288
Disaster Relief 303
Ghost of an Executed Engineer 313
Moral Beliefs in the Workplace 325
Renewable Energy 335
Training Firefighters 342
Window Safety 351

Honesty

Borrowed Tools 289
Catalyst* 290
Containers 294
The Co-Op Student 295

The Deadline 297
Drinking in the Workplace 302
Employment Opportunity 306
An Excess? 309
Failure 310
Faulty Valves 310
Gilbane Gold 313
Golfing 316
Inside Tool & Die 321
Mere "Technicality"? 323
Oil Spill? 325
Parkville 326
Price Is Right? 331
Recommendation for a Friend 333
Unlicensed Engineer 345
USAWAY 346
Vacation 346
Wonderful Development? 352
Working Overtime 353
XYZ Hose Co. 354

Loyalty

Catalyst* 290
Containers 294
To Dissent or Not to Dissent? 298
Drinking in the Workplace 302
Employment Opportunity 306
Failure 310
Ghost of an Executed Engineer 313
Golfing 316
Inside Tool & Die 321
Oil Spill? 325
Parkville 326
Recommendation for a Friend 333
Sunnyvale 340
"Underground" Project 344
Whose Property? 349

Organizational Communication

Borrowed Tools 289
Catalyst* 290
Containers 294
The Co-Op Student 295

The Deadline 297
To Dissent or Not to Dissent? 298
Drinking in the Workplace 302
An Excess? 309
Gilbane Gold 313
Glass Ceiling 315
Hydrolevel 318
Inside Tool & Die 321
Last Resort 322
Parkville 326
Promotion 332
Recommendation for a Friend 333
Side-Saddle Gas Tanks 335
Sunnyvale 340
Vacation 346
Walkway Disaster 347
Waste Disposal 348

Quality Control

Containers 294
The Co-Op Student 295
Cost-Cutting 297
The Deadline 297
To Dissent or Not to Dissent? 298
Drinking in the Workplace 302
Failure 310
Faulty Valves 310
Inside Tool & Die 321
Microwaves 324
Price Is Right? 331
USAWAY 346
Wonderful Development? 352
Working Overtime 353

Product Liability

Cadillac Chips 289
Containers 294
Cost-Cutting 297
Failure 310
Faulty Valves 310
Fire Detectors 311
Gilbane Gold 313
Microwaves 324

Pinto 330
Pulverizer 332
Side-Saddle Gas Tanks 335
Training Firefighters 342
TV Antenna 343
USAWAY 346
Vacation 346
Walkway Disaster 347
XYZ Hose Co. 354

Public Service

Aftermath of Chernobyl 287
Air Bags 287
Auditory Visual Tracker (AVIT) 288
Disaster Relief 303
Ghost of an Executed Engineer 313
Last Resort 322
Moral Beliefs in the Workplace 325
Parkville 326
Renewable Energy 335
Window Safety 351

Responsibilities for Others' Actions

Aftermath of Chernobyl 287
Borrowed Tools 289
Containers 294
The Co-Op Student 295
Disaster Relief 303
Drinking in the Workplace 302
Ghost of an Executed Engineer 313
Gilbane Gold 313
Last Resort 322
Microwaves 324
Training Firefighters 342
TV Antenna 343
Window Safety 351
Working Overtime 353

Safety and Health

Aftermath of Chernobyl 287
Air Bags 287
Cadillac Chips 289

Containers 294
Cost-Cutting 297
Disaster Relief 303
To Dissent or Not to Dissent? 298
An Excess? 309
Faulty Valves 310
Fire Detectors 311
Gilbane Gold 313
Highway Safety Improvements 317
Hydrolevel 318
Mere "Technicality"? 323
Microwaves 324
Oil Spill? 325
Pinto 330
Pulverizer 332
Side-Saddle Gas Tanks 335
"Smoking System" 339
Sunnyvale 340
Training Firefighters 342

Trees 342
TV Antenna 343
Unlicensed Engineer 345
Vacation 346
Walkway Disaster 347
Waste Disposal 348
Why Won't They Read? 350
Window Safety 351
XYZ Hose Co. 354

Women in Engineering

To Dissent or Not to Dissent? 298
Forced-Sex Accusation 312
Glass Ceiling 315
Innocent Comment? 321
Promotion 332
Sunnyvale 340

✳ Cases

Case 1   Aftermath of Chernobyl

The 1986 Chernobyl nuclear accident in the Ukraine exposed thousands to excessive radiation and put all of Western Europe on alert. For more than a decade a team of scientists and engineers has been working at the facility to figure out how to contain the huge amount of nuclear fuel that makes it impossible for anyone ever again to live within a 20-mile radius of the facility and that threatens a much larger population unless the containment problem can be resolved.

The scientists and engineers are exposed to radiation levels far in excess of what is regarded as acceptable in the United States (some more than 60,000 times greater). Featured on CBS's *60 Minutes* (December 18, 1994), one of the team members said he turns in an "official" record of his level of exposure that is substantially below the actual exposure so that he will be allowed to continue on the project. Asked why he wants to stay, he replied, "Someone has to do this. Who else will go instead of me?" His two sons would like to join the team, but he does not want them to. Commenting on the team's efforts, a Ukrainian spokesperson characterized the volunteers as heroic and brave (if a bit "eccentric" and in some instances "foolish").

Identify and discuss the ethical dimensions of this situation.

Case 2   Air Bags[1]

More than thirty-five years after helping develop air bags for automobiles, retired scientist Carl Clark, well into his seventies, is still doing whatever he can to promote their appropriate use and improvement.[2] Recent warnings about the dangers air bags pose for young children riding in front seats lags more than thirty years behind the warnings Clark issued in the 1960s. He is now advocating air bags on bumpers, and he has even invented wearable air bags for the elderly to prevent broken hips. He does not expect his ideas to make him wealthy. (The bumper air bags were patented by someone else.) He says, "I get paid for about a quarter of my time—the other three-quarters is thinking about the future." In 1971 Clark patented a retrorocket braking system that (theoretically) prevents car crashes by shooting a rocket in front of the car before it goes into its skid. Acknowledging that there still are unsolved problems with this device, he nevertheless believes it is worth pursuing further. "At the beginning of the auto safety business," he comments, "we all said to run the tests to higher speeds as quickly as possible. And the government has not done that; the industry is too powerful." What motivates Carl Clark's continued efforts? Noting that many of his relatives were missionaries, he says that he grew up with the belief that he should leave the world in better shape than he found it.

Discuss Carl Clark's attitude toward his work (even in retirement). Compare it with yours.

Case 3　Auditory Visual Tracker (AVIT)

Students in Tom Talley's senior design course in electrical engineering at Texas A&M are required to develop a project design.[3] This usually involves building a working prototype. Among the kinds of projects Talley suggests students might undertake are some that qualify as volunteer service projects in the community. Students are not paid for such work; in fact, they may have to pay for needed materials themselves. Because these projects are undertaken as a service to others, it is expected that every effort will be made to bring them to successful completion. Given that this might involve more work and time (perhaps even beyond the current semester) than other possible projects, what reasons might a team have for selecting a volunteer service project?

Analysis

This is a situation that presents opportunities for what we have called *good works* (Chapter 5). Despite the common complaint that today's youths are a "me-generation," student volunteer work is on the rise. Many campuses have an office that provides students with a list of volunteer opportunities in the community. However, for most students, volunteer work bears no special relation to their academic work or professional preparation. Tom Talley's class provides ways of making the connection.

One project in particular illustrates the value of such opportunities. Undecided about what project to undertake, one team decided to work with the Brazos Valley Rehabilitation Center after Tom Talley showed them a letter from teacher Ellen Wood that indicated some of the center's needs. The specific task the team undertook was to design and build an Auditory Visual Tracker (AVIT). An AVIT is used to evaluate the training of visual skills in children with disabilities. On learning about the project, Ellen Wood commented that the center had wanted an AVIT for years but had been unable to afford purchasing one, adding: "This is a tremendous boost in working with children with disabilities ages 0 to 3. The opportunity of obtaining the AVIT is a dream come true."

The team successfully completed the project, but only by continuing to work on it after the end of the semester. Another design team did a follow-up project for the center during the next semester. In addition to helping the Brazos Center, team members seem to have gained much from the experience. Team member Robert Siller commented, "We liked that it was a project that was going to be genuinely used. It wasn't going to just end up in a closet. It's actually helping someone." Team member Myron Moodie added, "When we presented the AVIT to the center we got to see some of the kids use it. It was worth it watching the way children like it."

Tom Talley suggests that a key was team members' meeting some of the children: "The students met the children who were going to be using the project and fell in love. They worked day and night. Money couldn't buy you that kind of effort." He concludes, "They clearly went above and beyond—that's Aggie spirit. Someone is going to get some fine engineers."

Most engineers do not have the opportunity to interact in this way with those who ultimately benefit from their work. For those who benefit, their benefactors are anonymous. Nevertheless, knowing that one's work benefits others one will never meet can be quite satisfying, even without special recognition.

Tom Talley by no means stands alone in encouraging engineering students to undertake volunteer work related to their academic work. The Worcester Polytechnic Institute and Case Western Reserve University, for example, have well-established programs to encourage this. Dwayne Breger, Civil and Environmental Engineer at Lafayette College, has organized a team of students from engineering, biology, and environmental science to design a project that would provide renewable energy sources for the college. Steven Silliman, Civil Engineer at Notre Dame University, involves students in service projects in Latin America. No doubt there are many other equally impressive examples.

Case 4   Borrowed Tools[4]

Entil Corporation permits its employees to borrow company tools. Engineer Al House took full advantage of this privilege. He went one step further and ordered tools for his unit that would be useful for his home building projects even though they were of no significant use to his unit at Entil. Engineer Michael Green had suspected for some time that Al was ordering tools for personal rather than company use, but he had no

unambiguous evidence until he overheard a revealing conversation between Al and Bob Deal, a contract salesman from whom Al frequently purchased tools.

Michael was reluctant to directly confront Al. They had never gotten along well, and Al was a senior engineer who wielded a great deal of power over Michael in their unit. Michael was also reluctant to discuss the matter with the chief engineer of their unit, in whom he had little confidence or trust.

Eventually, Michael decided to talk with the contract procurement agent, whose immediate response was, "This really stinks." The contract procurement agent agreed not to reveal that Michael had talked with him. He then called the chief engineer, indicating only that a reliable source had informed him about Al House's inappropriate purchases. In turn, the chief engineer confronted Al. Finally, Al House directly confronted each of the engineers in his unit he thought might have "ratted" on him. When Al questioned Michael, Michael denied any knowledge of what took place.

Later Michael explained to his wife, "I was forced to lie. I told Al, 'I don't know anything about this.'"

Discuss the ethical issues this case raises.

Case 5   Cadillac Chips[5]

Charged with installing computer chips that resulted in emitting excessive amounts of carbon dioxide from their Cadillacs, General Motors agreed in December 1995 to recall nearly 500,000 late-model Cadillacs and pay nearly $45 million in fines and recall costs. Lawyers for the Environ-mental Protection Agency and the Justice Department contended that GM knew that the design change would result in pollution problems. Rejecting this claim, GM released a statement saying that the case was "a matter of interpretation" of complex regulations, but that it had "worked extremely hard to resolve the matter and avoid litigation."

According to EPA and Justice Department officials, the $11 million civil penalty was the third largest in a pollution case, the second largest under the Clean Air Act, and the largest involving motor vehicle pollution. This was also the first case of a court ordering an automobile recall to reduce pollution rather than to improve safety or dependability.

Government officials said that in 1990 a new computer chip was designed for the engine controls of Cadillac Seville and Deville models. This was in response to car owners' complaints that these cars tended to stall when the climate control system was running. The chips injected additional fuel into the engine whenever this system was running. But this resulted in tailpipe emissions of carbon dioxide well in excess of the regulations.

Although the cars are usually driven with the climate control system running, tests used for certifying the meeting of emission standards were conducted when the system was not running. This was standard practice for emission tests throughout the automotive industry.

However, EPA officials argued that, under the Clean Air Act, GM should have informed them that the Cadillac's design was changed in a way that would result in violating pollution standards under normal driving conditions. In 1970, the officials said, automobile manufacturers were directed not to slip around testing rules by designing cars that technically pass the tests but that, nevertheless, cause avoidable pollution. GM's com-

petitors, the officials contended, complied with that directive.

A GM spokesperson said that testing emissions with the climate control running was not required because, "It was not in the rules, not in the regulations; it's not in the Clean Air Act." However, claiming that GM discovered the problem in 1991, Justice Department environmental lawyer Thomas P. Carroll objected to GM's continued inclusion of the chip in the 1992–95 models, "They should have gone back and re-engineered it to improve the emissions."

In agreeing to recall the vehicles, GM said it now had a way of controlling the stalling problem without increasing pollution. This involves "new fueling calibrations," GM said, and it "should have no adverse effect on the driveability of the vehicles involved."

What responsibilities did GM engineers have in regard to either causing or resolving the problems with the Cadillac Seville and Deville models?

Case 6   Catalyst[6]

I

A recent graduate of Engineering Tech, Bernie Reston has been employed in Research and Development of Larom Chemical for the past several months. Bernie was recommended to Larom as the top Engineering Tech graduate in chemical engineering.

Alex Smith, the head of Bernie's unit, showed immediate interest in Bernie's research on processes using a particular catalyst (call it B). However, until last week, his primary research assignments at Larom were in other areas.

A meeting of engineers in Bernie's unit is called by Alex. He announces that the unit must make a recommendation within the next two days on what catalyst should be used by Larom in processing a major product. It is clear to everyone that Alex is anticipating a brief, decisive meeting. One of the senior engineers volunteers, "We've been working on projects like this for years, and catalyst A seems to be the obvious choice." Several others immediately concur. Alex looks around the room and, hearing no further comments, says, "Well, it looks like we're in accord on this. Do we have consensus?"

So far Bernie has said nothing. He is not sure what further testing will show, but the testing he has been doing for the past week provides preliminary evidence that catalyst B may actually be best for this process. This is also in line with what his research at Engineering Tech suggested with somewhat similar processes. If catalyst B should turn out to be preferable, a great deal of money will be saved; and, in the long run, a fair amount of time will be saved as well. Bernie wonders if he should mention his findings at this time or simply defer to the senior engineers, who seem as determined as Alex to bring matters to closure.

What would you advise Bernie to do? Identify and discuss any ethical questions this case raises.

II

Bernie somewhat hesitantly raises his hand. He briefly explains his test results and the advantages catalyst B might provide. Then he suggests that the unit might want to delay its recommendation for another two weeks so that he can conduct further tests.

Alex replies, "We don't have two weeks. We have two days." He then asks Bernie to write up the report, leaving out the preliminary data he has gathered about catalyst B. He says, "It would be nice to do some more testing, but we just don't have the time. Besides, I doubt if anything would show up

in the next two weeks to change our minds. This is one of those times we have to be decisive—and we have to *look* decisive and quit beating around the bush. They're really getting impatient on this one. Anyway, we've had a lot of experience in this area."

Bernie replies that, even if the data on B is left out, the data on A is hardly conclusive. Alex replies, "Look, you're a bright guy. You can make the numbers look good without much difficulty—do the math backward if you have to. Just get the report done in the next two days!"

Bernie likes working for Larom, and he feels lucky to have landed such a good job right out of Engineering Tech. He is also due for a significant pay raise soon if he plays his cards right.

What do you think Bernie should do? Should he write up the report as Alex says? Should he refuse to write up the report, saying he will have no part in falsifying a report? Or is there something else he might do? Explain your choice.

III

Bernie decides to write up the report. When he is finished, Alex asks him to sign it. Bernie now has second thoughts. He wonders if he should sign his name to a report that omits his preliminary research on catalyst B and that is based, in part, on "doing the math backward." What options does Bernie have at this point? Which one would you advise him to take? Explain.

IV

After reluctantly signing the report, Bernie continues to have second thoughts about what his unit has recommended. He now has an opportunity to do more research on catalyst B. After several weeks his research quite decisively indicates that, contrary to the earlier report, catalyst B really would have been, far and away, the better choice. What should Bernie do now? Keep the data to himself and not make trouble? Tell Alex and let him decide what, if anything, to do? Something else?

Analysis

We will now offer some commentary on the challenges Bernie Reston faced. Although convinced there may be reason to prefer catalyst B to A, Bernie may also be convinced that deferring to the judgment of the more experienced engineers is the best course of action—especially in this kind of situation. He may actually be persuaded that the others are probably right. His is a minority view, and he is considerably less experienced. The recommendation apparently cannot wait for further testing. Besides, Alex is Bernie's division head, and Bernie may believe that his job is to do as he is told. So, he may conclude, it is best to support his colleagues' recommendation—both from the standpoint of Larom and his own self-interest.

However, four cautions should be noted. First, although Bernie may have a general obligation to do what he is told by his superiors, blind or unthinking obedience is not obligatory. He has no obligation to do anything illegal or unethical, even if ordered to by his supervisor. (We discuss obedience and the limits of authority in Chapter 9.) In this case, it is not at all clear that Alex's superiors at Larom would approve of his effort to falsify the report, or that they would fault Bernie for refusing to comply with Alex's request. After all, the report is for them. Why would they willingly agree to be duped—especially since approving the wrong catalyst could turn out to be very costly to Larom?

Second, Bernie should be alert to the possibility of *groupthink* (discussed in Chapter 5). Several groupthink symptoms seem to be present at the initial meeting. There is evidence that at least some of the senior members of the group share the *illusion of invulnerability* ("We've been working on projects like this for years. . . .") *Rationalizations* for not having done more research on catalyst B follow on the heels of this illusion. Given the shared purpose of recommending the best catalyst for the job, the members may believe in the *inherent morality* of the group ("We know we're on the right side"). Silence in response to Alex's final look around the room for further comments may be the result of *self-censorship* (especially if Bernie fails to speak up). This, in turn, feeds an *illusion of unanimity*. Finally, Alex's evident desire to orchestrate the group to a quick and decisive resolution indicates a readiness to apply *direct pressure* on any dissenters. Much may be at stake for Larom in this situation, so Bernie is well advised to be alert to such group dynamics rather than simply deferring to his more senior colleagues.

Third, Bernie seems to be the only one with evidence that catalyst B might be preferable, and his previous work with catalyst B has already impressed Alex. If he does not speak up, who will? It is unfortunate that Alex did not assign Bernie to work on catalyst B earlier. Perhaps sometime earlier Bernie should have made a special point of discussing with his colleagues some of his previous work with catalyst B. But why didn't Alex take the lead? It seems that an opportunity for significant research was lost when Bernie first joined Larom. However, shifting responsibility to Alex for lacking foresight (a minimalist move) does not relieve Bernie of responsibility for speaking up now.

Fourth, Bernie is asked not only to suppress data about catalyst B but also to alter the other data; that is, he is asked to lie. Alex no doubt sees this as a lie intended to "protect the truth" (that A is preferable). However, as Sissela Bok convincingly argues, even lies of this sort are ethically question-able.[7] She points out that we have a tendency to overestimate the good that comes from lying and to underestimate the harm that comes from lying. Individually and collectively, lies do much to undermine trust. Also, by deceiving others, lies often lead people to make decisions they would not make if they had more reliable information, thus undermining their autonomy. Bok concludes that we should lie only after looking carefully to see if any alternatives preferable to lying are available; that is, we should seek a *creative middle way*.

One alternative that might work is for Bernie to suggest that they include all the available data but still recommend catalyst A. The data have not discouraged them from recommending A, so why should they fear being forthright with others? This seems ethically preferable to submitting a falsified report—signed or unsigned. No option guarantees there will be no complications. But why not do what seems right and let the "chips fall" where they will?

Although it might seem to Bernie that it would be prudent not to "rock the boat," it is not at all clear that this would be a good assessment on his part. There are too many ways in which things can go wrong for him to be sure what a prudent course of action would be. However, prudential and ethical considerations are not the same, and it seems that we can be more certain about what it would be ethical for Bernie to do.

Three basic lines of thought might help Bernie sort out what is at stake ethically when he is facing the initial question of whether to falsify data. One has already been discussed—thinking through the possible *consequences* of doing as Alex says and comparing this with other alternatives. In doing this, Bernie needs to consider his basic responsibilities to Larom. (How Larom's customers and the general public might be affected is perhaps too speculative here to be of much relevance.) Although in the "heat of the moment" Bernie may find it difficult to think of little else than Alex and the others pressing for closure, his responsibilities are not exhausted by relationships to his divisional colleagues.

A second line of thought rests on the idea of *universalizability*: Whatever is right for Bernie in this situation is right for similar persons in similar circumstances. It may not be easy to determine just what should count as relevantly similar circumstances, but any serious thinking about this will conclude that Bernie's situation is hardly unique—and this thinking should not be confined just to engineers who are deciding whether to falsify data. Bernie needs to think about the more general phenomenon of lying.

Just how sweeping must his acceptance of lying be for him to conclude, in good faith, that falsifying data in this case is justifiable? To say that the sweep should be very wide is not to predict that doing what Alex requests will result in widespread lying. Rather, it is to point to the *principle* of action that Bernie must implicitly accept if he does falsify the data. Once Bernie looks at his situation in terms of this broader principle, he will very likely find it much more difficult to conclude that falsifying the data is acceptable than if he asks only what the likely consequences are of doing what Alex requests.

Part IV of this case presents Bernie with a new set of problems. He has falsified the data, as requested. But his further research shows that his initial suspicion that catalyst B is superior to A is right. What should he do now? Although it may be too late to switch to catalyst B for this project, his findings may prove very useful for future projects. So, at the very least, he should share his findings with his unit. What if Alex, concerned that Bernie's further research will raise questions about the initial report recommending A, wants to suppress his findings? At this point Bernie may discover that he does not stand alone in his unit, and he may have allies to mount opposition to Alex. At the same time, hindsight might convince Bernie and his supporters that it would have been best not to "make the numbers look good" in the initial report. As noted, they all were convinced that A was superior despite Bernie's preliminary research, so a good faith recommendation of A could have been made without suppressing his findings. Instead, Bernie's unit still faces the question of whether to acknowledge falsifying its earlier report. Whatever decision is made now, the unit's credibility is potentially on the line—an unfortunate, but somewhat predictable, consequence of Bernie's original compliance with Alex's request.

Case 7   Containers[8]

Axtell, Inc. designs, manufactures, and installs large containers for storing highly active chemicals. These containers require strong, reliable safety seals to prevent spills and leakage, precision temperature control units, and an automated valve system to control inflow and outflow.

For several years Axtell only manufactured the containers. Its major customers installed them without supervision from Axtell. However, recent automated design innovations require intricate installation procedures. Mistakes can be very costly, ranging from damaged machinery and interrupted workflow to serious injury to workers. So, Axtell now sends engineers to each site to supervise installation.

As chief engineer of Axtell's Installation Division, Howard Hanson manages the installation supervisors. He is proud of his division's record during his five years on the

job. There have been only two reported incidents of serious accidents involving Axtell containers. Both were determined to have resulted from negligence on the part of chemical companies rather than any flaws in the containers.

Axtell's good record is in no small way attributable to the work of Howard's division. Although the supervisory work is tedious, Howard insists that his engineers carefully supervise each phase of the installation. There are times when the workload is so heavy that it is difficult for the engineers to meet installation deadlines; and occasionally customers apply pressure on Axtell to be allowed to install containers without Axtell supervision. However, Howard realizes that quality, and perhaps even safety, may be compromised without proper supervision. Furthermore, he is concerned to minimize Axtell's legal liabilities. So, he has a motto on his office wall: "Better late than sorry!"

Normally, only one Axtell engineer is sent to an installation site. But because the installations require several complex procedures, Howard has the work of new engineers double-checked by veteran engineers for the first month on the job. The veteran supervisor's job is to coach and monitor the newcomer's supervision as they oversee the installation together. Each container is given a dated inspection number that can be traced to the engineer. Those that are double-checked are given two numbers, one traceable to the new engineer, the other to the veteran engineer. Axtell's requirement that new engineers have a one-month training period was Howard's idea. Although he realized that it was not required by law, Howard convinced Axtell management that having such a requirement would enhance quality and safety.

Tom Banks was in the last week of his one-month trial period. He had been working with veteran engineer Charles Yost during the entire trial period. It was clear to Charles from the very first week that Tom had a real knack for thorough, efficient supervision. It seemed apparent to both of them by the end of the third week that Tom was more than ready to "go it alone." But, they reminded themselves that "rules are rules"; the training period is a full month. So they would have to stick it out for the full trial period.

At the beginning of the final week Tom noticed that Charles seemed somewhat lethargic and inattentive. When he asked Charles if he was all right, Charles replied, "I'm just a little tired. I've been under a lot of pressure lately, and it's been cutting into my sleep." Tom suggested that Charles take a couple of days of sick leave to get rested. "We can ask Howard to assign someone else to me for these last couple of days." Charles replied that he had exhausted his sick and vacation leave time for the year, and that he was too financially strapped to lose any pay. "Besides," he said, "Howard doesn't have anyone available to replace me this week, and this job can't wait. These guys are already champing at the bit." By Friday Charles was too ill to concentrate on his work.

Tom suggested that Charles go home for the day. But Charles replied, "I thought about staying home today, but I just can't afford it—and we have to get the job done this week anyway. I'll get some rest this weekend, and I'll be fine next week. We can get through today all right. Look, next week you're on your own anyway. I've been checking your work for three weeks. You're the best supervisor I've ever seen around here. Don't worry, you can handle it. Give 'em a good look and I'll just put my tag on."

What should Tom do? He could try to protect Charles and carry out the supervision by himself. He could stop the inspections and tell Charles that they need to talk to Howard. No doubt other options are available. Identify and discuss the ethical issues this case raises.

Case 8   The Co-Op Student[9]

Project leader Bruce Barton was being sorely pressed to complete the development of several engineering prototypes for a field test of a new appliance model for the XYZ Company. One particular plastic component of the new model had given difficulty in laboratory tests as it failed repeatedly before reaching the stress level necessary for successful operation. Bruce had directed a redesign of the component using a tough new engineering plastic recommended by the Research Laboratory's Material Science Department. Stress tests needed to be run on the redesigned component, but Bruce was running short of time and needed to get on with building the prototype.

Bruce sought out the manager of the Material Science Department for help in running stress tests on samples of the new component. With this assistance he could go ahead with prototype building and conduct the tests concurrently. The prototypes, of course, would not be released to field test until the stress tests on the redesigned component proved its design to be satisfactory.

Tom Mason, manager of the Material Science Department, was willing to assist because he knew how critical completion of the development was to XYZ's future appliance plans. However, this was also a busy time for Tom's department. So, Tom suggested to Bruce that he could assign the test work to one of the engineering co-op students. Tom was also coordinator of engineering co-op students, and he liked to use the co-op students in demanding situations to give them practical experience.

Tom assigned the test work to Jack Jacobs, an engineering co-op student from the State University who was completing his second work session at XYZ. Jack was familiar with the test equipment and previously had done similar test work. Jack was a good student and his co-op work had been usually well done. Tom commented to Jack that he would need to work diligently to complete the tests before he had to return to State University.

Jack completed the tests on schedule and turned in a report to Tom indicating the component had successfully passed the stress tests. Upon completion of the test report Jack returned to the university for his next school session. Tom gave Bruce the good news. The prototypes were completed and the field test of these prototypes got underway on schedule.

A few weeks later, Bruce rushed into Tom's office to tell him that most of the prototypes were out of operation because of a catastrophic failure of the component that had been tested in Tom's lab. Bruce wanted to discuss the test immediately with Jack, but Jack had already returned to the university, so he and Tom settled for studying Jack's lab notebook in detail.

After review Tom said, "Bruce, I hate to say it but these data look *too good*. I know the equipment and there should be more scatter in the measurements Jack took. I think some, if not all, these measurements are in error or they have been faked! At best, Jack probably took a few points and 'extrapolated' the rest!"

What ethical issues does this scenario raise?

Analysis

What ethical issues did Jack face? He had an obligation both to do the job well and to do it fast. Or, if he made the tests and found that the component failed, his problem may have been that he wanted both to please his superiors and to do the tests right, and he could not do both. But the first problem is probably the more plausible one.

The important factual questions are the following:

1. What happened in the testing? Did Jack fake the results or just make an error of some type?

2. The basic conflict was between doing the job right and doing it on time; did Jack, in fact, have enough time to do the job right?

3. If Jack could not do the job (either because he lacked competence or time), was it possible to get other people involved who could help him with his time problem or show him how to do the job right?

4. Was it standard practice to let a co-op student do a job this important? If so, this is relevant to the question of who is *responsible* for the errors. This is not central to how Jack should resolve his problem, but it is central to another issue, responsibility. We will not consider this further here, but a key consideration in this case is Tom's responsibility as Jack's immediate supervisor.

Note that there are many other factual questions that can be raised, but only those that are important in resolving the ethical issues in the case should be.

Now let us turn to conceptual questions of both meaning and application. First, we will consider questions about the meanings of some key concepts.

1. If one of the issues in understanding what Jack should do involves whether there was fakery or error, there is an obvious problem here. What do we mean by "fake"? Think of some ways to define fake. For example, the basic idea of fakery is a deliberate misrepresentation of facts.

2. Another question of meaning is, "What makes a 'satisfactory' design?" What are the criteria for satisfactorily passing the stress test? Here we do not know enough to state these criteria, but this does not seem like a question that is likely to be controversial.

Probably the criteria were clearly laid out and agreed on by all involved. Maybe we could say the design is "satisfactory" if it passes tests that are generally agreed on by the participants.

3. There is a possibility that Jack simply made an error; so what do we mean by "error"? This again does not seem like a question that is likely to be controversial, and it is also a term that we would find hard to define without much more detailed knowledge of the case. Perhaps we could say that "error" is a failure to get or record accurate measurements.

The application questions are as follows:

1. Did Jack fake the tests? Given that we do not know precisely what Jack did, we cannot say, "Here's what Jack did. Was it faking?" All we can do is suggest some things he *might* have done. For the purposes of this analysis, we do not even have to say which ones we would consider faking—we need only list some possibilities. Jack might simply have smoothed out a curve after taking a number of data points. He might have taken a single measure and filled in the rest. He might have taken two or three measures and guessed at the rest. Which, if any, would we count as faking?

2. If we know more of the facts of the case, we might have a major application question trying to decide whether the component was "satisfactory" in terms of the tests; that is, did the design pass the stress test in a way that could be called satisfactory? If the test numbers were just barely under minimal criteria, would the tests show the component is satisfactory?

3. What would count as "error" on Jack's part? Would something count as Jack's error, if unknown to Jack, the test equipment was faulty?

Case 9   Cost-Cutting

DuPont Automotive released a survey at the 1998 Society of Automotive Engineers (SAE) International Congress and Expo indicating that the number one concern of automotive engineers is staying within budget targets while meeting consumer demand for technological improvements.[10] At the SAE meeting, interior trim design engineer Paul Steele said that at Chivas Products Ltd. when they are given a new project, they are also given a target price, and "we meet the target or else." Esma Elmaz, an engineer in Ford's Power Train Quality Department, said that many engineers pin lists of quality and cost goals on their office walls: "We ask, 'What's the minimum we can spend on a car that people will want to buy?'"

What special ethical challenges does having to keep costs within tight budget targets pose for automotive engineers?

Case 10   The Deadline[11]

Ruskin Manufacturing has guaranteed Parker Products that it will deliver the complete order of small machines by the tenth of the month, a Friday. Parker had already extended its deadline once. This time, it insists, the date must be met. Tim Vinson, head of quality control, had been confident the deadline would be met. But on the eighth he learns that a new component of the machines is in short supply.

Tim realizes that he must decide whether to try to meet the deadline by using the old component (or by some other means) or to inform Parker Products that Ruskin will not be able to deliver the product on time. Before making a decision, Tim decides to consult with Chuck Davidson, the chief design engineer for this product. Chuck says, "I don't have a good answer for you. There's no time to come up with a completely satisfactory alternative. You could regrind, but given the time frame you might get a lot of impurities. Or you could just use the old components. But I'm not going to advise either of those. I don't want this hanging over my head. Maybe you should call Arnold."

Arnold Peterson is vice president of Product Engineering. Years ago, like Tim Vinson, Arnold served as head of quality control. Tim is somewhat uneasy about calling Arnold for two reasons. First, Tim feels responsible for not seeing the problem earlier, and he is reluctant to admit failure to the vice president. Second, he wonders if Arnold would really want to be bothered by something like this. He might simply tell Tim that the problem is his to solve — somehow. Still, Tim is not comfortable with the idea of just resolving the problem by himself, yet he decides to do so. How should he resolve it?

Case 11   To Dissent or Not to Dissent?[12]

I

Alison Turner is a department manager at a large commercial nuclear generating plant. She is also a member of the Plant Nuclear Safety Review Committee (PNSRC). The committee's responsibilities include reviewing and approving design changes, making procedural changes, and submitting information to the Nuclear Regulatory Commission (NRC).

Today, Alison finds herself in a difficult situation. PNSRC is meeting to decide what to do about a heat exchanger problem. Routine testing on the previous morning revealed

degraded cooling water flow and high differential pressure in one of the containment spray heat exchangers of one of the two generating units. This unit has just returned to service after two months of repairs. Test results on the second heat exchanger were similar. Although the other generating unit has been in continuous service, testing reveals that its two heat exchangers are operating at less than full capacity. The most likely cause of the problem is sand blockage on the lake water side of the four heat exchangers.

After extensive analysis by engineers in the Mechanical Engineering and Nuclear Safety and Licensing Departments, it has been concluded that the cooling water flow falls slightly below the minimum requirement set by the technical specifications under which the plant is licensed. Nevertheless, based on Mechanical Engineering's analysis, Nuclear Safety and Licensing has prepared a Justification for Continued Operation (JCO) for submission to the NRC. PNSRC is now meeting to decide whether to approve the JCO and forward it to the NRC.

As Alison reviews the JCO she is uncomfortable with one assumption made in the analysis. The analysis assumes that the heat exchangers still have 95 percent of their original heat transfer capability. It is concluded that this would be satisfactory. However, in anticipating possible accidents, Single Failure Criteria require the plant to assume the loss of one heat exchanger. Alison wonders if, under those conditions, the heat transfer problem would be manageable. The JCO does not discuss what might happen under that contingency.

Seven members of PNSRC are present, enough for a quorum. Alison is the least senior member present. From the outset of the meeting, committee chair Rich Robinson has made it clear that it is important to act quickly, because any shutdown will cost the company, and ultimately the rate payers, a lot of money in additional fuel costs. "Repairs," he says, "might take a couple of weeks. If we don't approve this, we may be facing a multimillion dollar proposition. Fortunately, the JCO seems fine. What do you think?" Brad Louks and Joe Carpello immediately concur. Rich then says, "Well, if no one sees any problems here, let's go with it." There is a moment of silence. Should Alison express her reservations?

II

Alison Turner expresses her reservations. Brad Louks replies, "We're talking about containment heat exchangers. It's an Accident Mitigation System, and it's never had to be used here—or at any other commercial nuclear plant that we know of, for that matter. In fact, lots of plants don't even have containment spray systems." "Right," adds Joe Carpello, "we're ahead of the game on this one. I don't see any problem here. Nothing's totally risk-free, but we've always been leaders in safety. Let's not get carried away with 'possibilities.'"

"I don't think Alison meant to have us get carried away with anything," Mark Reynolds interjects. "She's just wondering if the JCO should address the question of how things would look if we lost one of the heat exchangers. How much time would it take the Nuclear Safety and Licensing Department to make a calculation for us—another three hours? It's only 1:30 P.M., you know." "What's the point, Mark?" asks Joe. "Our track record is excellent, and the system is *optional*. It's not as though we're taking any extraordinary risks."

Nothing further is said, and Rich Robinson calls for the vote. Though not a committee requirement, PNSRC has always acted unanimously. It often rejects, sometimes approves, but always unanimously. As the call goes around the room, each member approves.

The last member called on to vote is Alison. She still has serious reservations about approving the JCO without the Nuclear Safety and Licensing Department making further calculations. How should she vote?

III

Suppose Alison casts a negative vote and subsequent calculations show that her worries were unfounded — in the event of an accident, a single heat exchanger would be adequate to manage any likely heat transfer problems. Would it follow that it was wrong for her to cast a dissenting vote? [Recall that a single dissenting vote would not defeat approval. It would only set a precedent of proceeding without unanimity.]

Analysis

This case raises two primary questions: (1) How should Alison vote? and (2) Did the atmosphere in the committee promote responsible professional judgment?

A number of factual considerations are important to Alison's decision. The most obvious consideration is whether a single heat exchanger would be able to handle the heat transfer load in an emergency. The refusal of the committee to ask the Nuclear Safety and Licensing Department to examine this issue means that Alison will not have an authoritative answer to the question before she votes.

Another question she should ask herself is, "Has the PNSRC been conscientious in carrying out its oversight responsibilities?" On the one hand, the fact that the plant has a good safety record and that the committee "often rejects" documents suggests that it has been. On the other hand, the insistence on unanimity suggests that the expression of professional disagreement may have been inhibited.

Yet another question is whether the plant is either already or potentially in violation of the law or NRC regulations. We are told that "the cooling water flow falls slightly below the minimum requirement set by the technical specifications under which the plant is licensed." This appears to mean that the plant is already violating the law or NRC regulations. Further, the Single Failure Criteria *require* that one assume the loss of one heat exchanger. If these criteria are set by law or the NRC, then the committee's willingness to ignore them means that it intends to further violate legal requirements. If these are in-house criteria, the committee is still derelict in its duty.

Another question is how the NRC will look on the plant's actions. Will they notice the committee's not fulfilling regulations? Evidently, the NRC has looked favorably on the plant until now, but this attitude may be about to change.

We need to know how great is the risk of an accident due to the failure of proper heat exchange. Joe Carpello says that the committee should not get carried away with "possibilities," but the committee is supposed to look at failure modes, which are "mere possibilities."

We also need to ask why the heat exchangers are not functioning properly. Is the problem really sand blockage? If so, why is this a problem on a unit that has just undergone two months of repairs? Will the heat exchange problem continue to deteriorate? If so, how fast will this deterioration progress, and what are the likely consequences? Finally, will the shutdown for repairs on the heat exchanger be costly enough to endanger the financial well-being of the company?

A number of conceptual questions need to be raised. First, we will take up several questions about the meanings of important concepts. Then, we will examine the applications of these concepts to this case.

There is a division of opinion on the committee over what we might call "responsible professional judgment." Rich Robinson, Joe Carpello, and Brad Louks think Alison's worries are trivial and irresponsible. Mark Reynolds is not so sure. What is meant by the term "responsible professional judgment"? We can give several criteria for responsible professional judgment in engineering:

1. It must be made in the light of professional knowledge and skill.
2. It must be made in light of all information relevant to the particular case.
3. It should be made in accordance with appropriate professional "technical" standards, which include such considerations as the use of state-of-the-art technology and quality.
4. It should be made in accordance with the appropriate professional ethical criteria, which include in particular a responsibility for the health and safety of the public.

A closely related issue is raised by the manner in which Rich Robinson, chair of the committee, conducted the meeting. What is the proper "professional climate" for the formation and expression of responsible professional opinions? A useful analogy is the working of the U.S. Supreme Court.[13] The justices of the Court rarely all agree on an opinion, but the atmosphere in their discussions is presumably one in which disagreement is respected. The justice who writes the majority opinion must circulate his or her draft opinion to all members of the Court, who respond with suggestions for changes and arguments for differing opinions. As they argue the issues in the case, some justices may change their minds, and the challenge to each justice to defend his or her position is a valuable part of the formation of responsible legal judgments. Using the Supreme Court example, we can say that the principal criteria for a "professional climate" are (1) that differing professional opinions should be encouraged and respected, and (2) that differing opinions should be subjected to as much criticism and evaluation by professional peers as possible.

Most of the committee members appear to be making the decision from a management standpoint at least as much as from an engineering one. Robinson, for example, is concerned about the time and expense if a shutdown is required. So another question is whether the decision to approve the JCO is properly a management or an engineering decision. This necessitates a prior decision: What do we mean by a proper management and a proper engineering decision?

Now let us turn to questions about the application of these key concepts to this case. First, in regard to "responsible professional judgment," we have no reason to doubt the professional expertise of the committee members. But responsible professional judgment about a particular case must be made in the light of all of the facts relevant to the case. Here we have problems. Most of the members of the committee were willing to approve the JCO without the information about how the plant would function if one of the heat exchangers were lost. So, we must say that the actions of the committee (with the exception of Alison) did not meet this criterion. Responsible professional judgment should be made in accordance with appropriate professional technical standards. In this case, some of the technical standards are provided by NRC regulations, which the committee was willing to violate in at least two respects. It was willing to overlook the fact that the plant was already not meeting the minimum cooling water flow standards. It was also willing to overlook the requirement to furnish data on the ability of the plant to operate properly with only one heat exchanger.

Responsible professional judgment should be made in accordance with the appropriate professional ethical standards. The most important ethical standard here is the responsibility of the engineer to be concerned with the health and safety of the public. There was a difference of opinion. On the one hand, Brad Louks pointed out that the heat exchangers were a part of an accident mitigation system and they had never been used at this or any other commercial plant. Joe Carpello also insisted that nothing can be completely safe. On the other hand, Mark Reynolds and Alison Turner pointed out that one of the possible failure modes, a failure of one of the heat exchangers, had not been thoroughly investigated. If a refusal to investigate a known but somewhat unlikely failure mode is a failure to look out for the health and safety of the public, this criterion for responsible professional judgment has not been met.

The full answer to this question involves the investigation of another conceptual issue ("What do we mean by looking out for the health and safety of the public?") and an application question ("Does the failure to investigate a possible but unlikely failure mode violate this criterion?"). But we shall assume that the criterion is not fulfilled by the committee's failure to investigate the heat exchange issue. The committee did not exhibit responsible professional judgment with respect to the approval of the JCO.

The second application issue is whether a "professional climate" has been preserved in the committee. One criterion for a "professional climate" is that differing professional opinions must be encouraged and respected. The atmosphere set in the committee did not fulfill this criterion. There was an atmosphere of intimidation and a pressure for unanimity that were not conducive to the expression of differing professional opinions. A second criterion is that professional opinions should be subjected to as much criticism and evaluation as possible. This criterion also was not fulfilled. Although criticism of Alison's opinion was encouraged (as it should have been), criticism of opposing views was strongly discouraged by the chairman of the committee, as well as several of its members. A professional climate was not preserved in the committee. (One wonders whether part of the explanation for this failure to preserve a professional climate relates to Alison being the first female engineer to serve on the PNSRC.)

The third application issue is whether the decision to approve the JCO is an engineering decision or a management decision. Our previous discussion has shown that there are good grounds for classifying the decision on the JCO as properly an engineering decision. The decision involved both technical engineering considerations and an application of standards from the codes, especially those requiring engineers to protect the health and safety of the public. The arguments of Louks, Carpello, and Robinson, however, can be grounds for maintaining the decision was also properly a management decision. They argued that the heat exchangers were not required and that the possibility of a catastrophe due to their malfunction was remote. They also argued that the decision involved substantial management considerations. That the approval of the JCO would involve a violation of regulations governing plant operation gives the edge to the argument that the decision was primarily an engineering one. Perhaps even more decisive is the observation that the committee's responsibility was apparently to make an engineering decision. Therefore, the committee should have made its decision on the basis of engineering considerations.

Finally, we must look to the apparent conflict Alison faced between her obligation to be a responsible employee and to make a responsible engineering decision. In this case, however, there does not appear to be a genuine conflict, because her true responsibility as an employee was to make a responsible engineering decision. Presumably, she was placed on the committee because her professional judgment was valued. The committee was supposed to render a competent and responsible engineering judgment. Whether or not she was ultimately right, her responsibility was to render the best professional judgment of which she was capable. She attempted to do this. Our analysis of the issues leads us to conclude that (1) she should vote against the approval of the JCO and (2) the atmosphere in the committee did not promote responsible professional judgment.[14]

Case 12   Drinking in the Workplace[15]

I

Branch Oil, Inc. has been losing ground to its competitors in recent years. Concerned that substance abuse may be responsible for much of Branch's decline, the company has just adopted a policy that imposes sanctions on those employees found to be working under the influence of alcohol or illegal drugs.

Karen and Andy have worked together in one of the engineering divisions of Branch for several years. Frequently, Karen has detected alcohol on Andy's breath when they were beginning work in the morning and after work breaks during the day. But, until the new policy was announced it never occurred to Karen that she should say anything to Andy about it, let alone tell anyone else about it. Andy's work always has been first rate, and Karen is not the kind of person who feels comfortable discussing such matters with others.

Two days before the announcement of the new alcohol and drug policy, Andy tells Karen that he is being considered for the position of chief safety inspector. Although pleased at the prospect of Andy's promotion, Karen wonders if Andy's drinking will get in the way of meeting his responsibilities. She worries that, with additional job pressures, Andy's drinking problem will worsen. Should she discuss her concerns with Andy?

Harvey Hillman, plant manager at Branch, knows that Andy and Karen have worked together for three years. He has narrowed his choice for head of safety inspection to Andy and one other person. He invites Karen out for lunch to see if he can learn something more about Andy from her. Should she volunteer information about Andy's drinking? Suppose Harvey says, "This is a really important decision. We need a top person for the chief safety inspector job. We've had some real problems the last few years with shoddy production and safety, probably because of alcohol and drug abuse in the workplace. I had to move Jack Curtis out of head of quality control because *he* was drunk on the job. We have to get this under control. The new policy might help. But quality control and safety will still have to keep a really close eye on things."

Discuss whether Karen should say anything to Harvey Hillman about Andy's drinking.

II

Branch's policy on the use of alcohol and drugs has been in effect for a year. It does not seem to have made a significant difference. Absenteeism is still high. Shoddy workmanship continues. There are still too many safety problems. And Branch's profit margins are still declining. Management is now proposing mandatory random drug testing for its nonprofessional workforce, and mandatory drug testing for all new workers. The labor union protests that such a policy is undesirable in two respects. First, it is an unwarranted invasion of the privacy of workers. Second, exempting professionals from the testing is discriminatory and, therefore, unjust. Karen knows you have a longstanding, serious interest in ethics, so she asks you what you think about the two concerns of the union.

Case 13   Disaster Relief[16]

We opened this book with a discussion of three engineers (William LeMessurier, Roger Boisjoly, and Frederick C. Cuny) whose work is regarded by many as ethically exemplary. Here we will discuss the remarkable story of Frederick C. Cuny in greater detail.

Among the twenty-four recipients of the John D. and Catherine T. MacArthur Foundation Fellowships for 1995 was Frederick C. Cuny, a disaster relief specialist. The fellowship program is commonly referred to as a "genius program," but it is characterized by MacArthur executives as a program that rewards "hard-working experts who often push the boundaries of their fields in ways that others will follow."[17] The program, says Catherine Simpson, director of the awards program, is meant to serve as "a reminder of the importance of seeing as broadly as possible, of being willing to live outside of a comfort zone and of keeping your nerve endings open."[18]

Cuny's award was unusual in two respects. First, at the time the award was announced, his whereabouts were unknown, and it was feared that he had been executed in Chechnya. Second, he was an engineer. Most MacArthur awards go to writers, artists, and university professors.

The first major engineering project Cuny worked on was the Dallas-Ft. Worth airport.

However, attracted to humanitarian work, he undertook disaster relief work in Biafra in 1969. Two years later, at age 27, he founded the INTERTECT Relief and Reconstruction Corporation in Dallas. INTERTECT describes itself as

> a professional firm providing specialized services and technical assistance in all aspects of natural disaster and refugee emergency management—mitigation, preparedness, relief, recovery, reconstruction, resettlement—including program design and implementation, camp planning and administration, logistics, vulnerability analysis, training and professional development, technology transfer, assessment, evaluation, networking and information dissemination.[19]

INTERTECT also prides itself on its "multi-disciplinary, flexible, innovative, and culturally appropriate approach to problem-solving."[20] Obviously, such an enterprise requires the expertise of engineers. But it also must draw from social services, health and medical care professionals, sociology, anthropology, and other areas.

Although trained as an engineer, Fred Cuny was apparently comfortable working across disciplines. As an undergraduate he also studied African history. So, it is understandable that he would take a special interest in the course of the conflict between the Nigerian and Biafran governments in the late 1960s. In 1969 he announced to the Nigerian minister of the interior, "I'm from Texas. I'm here to study the war and try to suggest what can be done to get in humanitarian aid when it's over."[21] Rebuffed by the minister, Cuny then flew to Biafra and helped organize an airlift that provided short-term assistance to the starving Biafrans.

Cuny learned two important lessons from his Biafran work. First, food distribution in disaster relief often pulls people from their homes and working areas to distribution centers in towns and airports. Cuny commented, "The first thing I recognized was that we had to turn the system around and get people back into the countryside away from the airfield." Second, Cuny realized that public health is a major problem, one that can effectively be addressed only through careful planning. This requires engineering efforts to, for example, build better drains, roads, dwellings, and so on. At the same time, Cuny realized that relatively few engineers were in relief agencies: hence, the founding of INTERTECT. Concerned to share his ideas with others, in 1983 Cuny published *Disasters and Development* (Oxford University Press), which provides a detailed set of guidelines for planning and providing disaster relief. A major theme of his book is that truly helpful relief requires careful study of local conditions to provide long-term assistance.

Despite its small size, since its founding in 1971, INTERTECT has become involved in relief projects in nearly seventy different countries. An especially daring project was the restoration of water and heat to a besieged section of Sarajevo in 1993.[22] Modules for a water filtration system were especially designed to fit into a C-130 airplane, which was flown from Zagreb (Croatia's capital) into Sarajevo. (Cuny commented that there were only three inches to spare on each side of the storage area.) To get the modules unnoticed through Serbian checkpoints, they had to be unloaded in less than 10 minutes.

Clearly, the preparation and delivery of the modules required careful planning and courage in execution. However, prior to that someone had to determine that such a system could be adapted to the circumstances in Sarajevo. When Cuny and his associates arrived in Sarajevo, for many the only source of water was from a polluted river. The river could be reached only by exposing oneself to sniper fire, which had already injured thousands and killed hundreds. So, residents risked their lives to bring back containers of water whose contaminated contents posed additional risks. Noting that Sarajevo had expanded downhill in recent years, and that the newer water system had to pump water uphill to Old Town Sarajevo, the Cuny team concluded that there must have been an earlier system for Old Town.[23] They located a network of old cisterns and channels still in good working order, thus providing them with a basis for designing and installing a new water filtration plant. This $2.5 million project was funded by the Soro Foundation, which also provided $2.7 million to restore heat for more than 20,000 citizens of Sarajevo.

Asked about his basic approach to disaster relief, Cuny commented: "In any large-scale disaster, if you can isolate a part that you can understand you will usually end up understanding the whole system."[24] In the case of Sarajevo, the main problems seemed to center around water and heat. So, this is what Cuny and his associates set out to address. In preparing for disaster relief work, Cuny was from the outset struck by the fact that medical professionals and materials are routinely flown into international disasters, but engineers and engineering equipment and supplies are not. His recurrent thought was, "Why don't you officials give first priority to, say, fixing the sewage system, instead of merely stanching the inevitable results of a breakdown in sanitary conditions?"[25]

It is unusual for engineers to receive the sort of public attention Fred Cuny has. We tend to take for granted the good work that engineers do. Insofar as engineers "make the news," more likely than not this is when an engineering disaster has occurred, a product is subjected to vigorous criticism, or an engineer has blown the whistle. Fred Cuny's stories are, largely, stories of successful humanitarian ventures.

Fred Cuny's untimely, violent death was tragic. In April 1995, while organizing a field hospital for victims in the conflict in Chechnya, Fred Cuny, two Russian Red Cross doctors, and a Russian interpreter disappeared. After a prolonged search, it was concluded that all four had been executed. Speculation is that Chechens may have been deliberately misinformed that the four were Russian spies. Cuny's recent *New York Review of Books* article, "Killing Chechnya," was quite critical of the Russian treatment of Chechnya, and it gives some indication of why his views might have well antagonized Russians.[26] Already featured in the *New York Times*, the *New Yorker Magazine*, and the *New York Review of Books*, Cuny had attained sufficient national recognition that his disappearance received widespread attention and immediate response from President Clinton and government officials. Reports on the search for Cuny and his colleagues regularly appeared in the press from early April until August 18, 1995, when his family finally announced that he was now assumed dead.

Many tributes have been made to the work of Fred Cuny. Pat Reed, a colleague at INTERTECT, was quoted shortly after Cuny's disappearance: "He's one of the few visionaries in the emergency management field. He really knows what he's doing. He's not just some cowboy."[27] At the Moscow press conference calling an end to the search, Cuny's son Chris said, "Let it be known to all nations and humanitarian organizations that Russia was responsible for the death of one of the world's great humanitarians."[28] William Shawcross fittingly concludes his article, "A Hero for Our Time":

> At the memorial meeting in Washington celebrating Fred's life it was clear that he had touched people in a remarkable way. He certainly touched me; I think he was a great man.

The most enduring memorials to Fred are the hundreds of thousands of people he has helped—and the effect he has had, and will have, on the ways governments and other organizations try to relieve the suffering caused by disasters throughout the world.

An Afterword

It is certainly appropriate to single out extraordinary individuals such as Frederick C. Cuny for special praise. His life does seem heroic. However, we would do well to remember that even heroes have helpers. Cuny worked with others, both at INTERTECT and at the various other agencies with whom INTERTECT collaborated. There are unnamed engineers in Sarajevo with whom he worked. For example, his Sarajevo team was able to locate the old cisterns and channels through the assistance of local engineers (and historians).[29] Local engineers assisted in installing the water filtration system.

Furthermore, once the system was installed, the water had to be tested for purity. Here a conflict developed between local engineers (as well as Cuny and specialists from the International Rescue Committee) and local water safety inspectors who demanded further testing. Convinced that they had adequately tested the water, the local engineers, Cuny, and the International Rescue Committee were understandably impatient. However, the cautious attitude of the water safety experts is understandable as well. Muhamed Zlatar, deputy head of Sarajevo's Institute for Water, commented: "The consequences of letting in polluted water could be catastrophic. They could be worse than the shelling. We could have 30,000 people come down with stomach diseases, and some of them could die."[30] Without presuming who might have been right, we might do well to

remember Fran Kelsey, the FDA official who, in 1962, refused to approve Thalidomide until further testing was done. In our rush to do good, caution should not be thrown to the winds.

Case 14   Employment Opportunity[31]

Part I: A Dilemma

Gerald Wahr was not prepared for such a sudden turn of events. He was scheduled to complete his degree in chemical engineering in June. He planned to return to help his parents run the family farm right after graduation. However, in early May his father became seriously ill, and it was evident he would have an extended, expensive stay in the hospital. Gerald's mother and his older brother could continue to operate the farm as long as they could manage the bills. But without an additional source of income, the family would soon begin defaulting on the farm's mortgage payments. The best hope for saving the farm would be for Gerald to find employment as an engineer.

Because Gerald had expected to return to the farm, he had foregone many opportunities to do job interviews. He would have to work quickly. After an intensive search, only one solid opportunity surfaced. Pro-Growth Pesticides, Inc. would be on campus next week to interview candidates for a supervisory job requiring a degree in chemical engineering.

Gerald certainly is academically well qualified for the job. However, there is a hitch. The Wahr farm uses strictly organic methods; Gerald's family has always opposed the use of pesticides. Gerald's father is noted in the area for his outspoken views about this; and Gerald admires this in his father. As a young child he often proudly announced that he wanted to grow up to be just like his father. Harold Wahr, however, had different ideas about this. A high school dropout, Harold had advised young Gerald to further his education. "Without a college degree you'll be as ineffective as I am. You have to fight fire with fire. If you really want to show those pesticide folks a thing or two, you've got to be able to talk their language." So, Gerald decided he would go to college and study chemical engineering.

Gerald's studies have done nothing to shake his conviction that organic farming is best. Quite the contrary. He is now more convinced than ever that the pesticide industry is not only harming the environment generally but farm products in particular. Despite this, should he go for the interview with Pro-Growth?

Analysis

Gerald Wahr's situation poses a number of ethical problems. First, there is the problem of his own *integrity*. Can he accept a job with a company whose primary business is to market products he adamantly opposes? Would this compromise his principles, and therefore himself? Or in difficult circumstances such as his, could he compromise his position without compromising his integrity?[32]

Second, Gerald has responsibilities to his family. Clearly, his parents and brother depend on him for support, if not survival. That they share his opposition to pesticides further complicates things. Even if Gerald can work out the problem of preserving his own integrity, his family may not find his resolution acceptable. He needs to convince not only himself but his family that taking a job with a pesticide firm is all right. What if his father, for example, rejects the thought of compromise? ("We don't *want* your money if that's where it's coming from!")

So far we have noted only what might be called problems of *personal ethics*. They are personal in the sense that they focus on Gerald's concerns about personal integrity and on personal relationships with others. In contrast, Gerald might focus primarily on matters that are more broadly matters of *social ethics*—for example, social, political, and legal issues concerning the environment. No doubt in Gerald's case personal and social ethics strongly overlap, because his personal concerns about the use of pesticides also relate to social, political, and legal issues. Nevertheless, the personal and social aspects of his concerns can be roughly distinguished.

There is another complicating ethical dimension: *professional ethics*. Although Gerald is not yet a professional engineer, he is now seriously contemplating becoming one. How does this alter the picture? What is a profession, and what does becoming a professional engineer entail? These are questions Gerald should seriously consider before he decides to go for an interview.

Part II. Conversations with Friends

At first Gerald rejects the idea of going for the interview. He thinks of it as a matter of integrity. How can he work for a company that researches, produces, and markets the very products he and his family have so long opposed? However, his friends counsel him otherwise. Here are some of their arguments. How might Gerald respond to them?

Ellen: Look, if you don't go for the job, someone else will. The job won't go away just because you stay away. So, the work's going to be done anyway. Your refusing the job won't change things.

Bob: Right! Furthermore, you need to look at this from a utilitarian point of view—the greatest good for the greatest number. If you don't go for the job, someone else who really believes in pesticides will—and that's going to make things even worse! If you take the job and aren't gung ho, that might just slow things down a little.

Dan: Besides, you might be able to introduce a few reforms from the inside. That won't kill the pesticide industry, but it might make it a little bit better—certainly better than if some zealous pesticide nut takes the job.

Ellen: So, it's pretty clear what to do. All things considered, you *ought* to go for the job. It's your only real chance to save the farm; and if someone else gets the job, Pro-Growth will cause even more harm. You can't be a purist about these things. It's not a perfect world, you know.

Analysis

Each of these urgings may initially seem somewhat attractive to Gerald Wahr. But he should look at them with some care. Ellen's first comment is especially troubling if taken alone. Although undoubtedly not intended to include such instances, it could be construed to endorse virtually *any* unethical act (for example, theft, murder) as long as one is assured that someone else will do it anyway. For example, suppose Gerald knew that if he did not steal a valuable laptop computer sitting in an unlocked office, two thieves would make their way into the office and steal it. Does this really give Gerald a reason to steal the computer? At the very least, Gerald needs some assurance that what he is contemplating is not clearly unethical (or illegal). But this is precisely the question he is trying to resolve in deciding whether he should work for a pesticide company.

Bob's appeal to the greater good may impress Gerald, but there are two features of this appeal that might give him pause. First, if Gerald really wants to serve the greater good,

he needs to ask whether he might do more good doing something else (for example, holding out until an opportunity to fight the pesticide industry comes along). After all, there are probably many other kinds of job (perhaps less well-paying) of which he could say, "If I take that job, I'll do less harm (or more good) than the person who will get it if I don't." Why should Gerald accept such an argument about *this* job—especially if this might damage his credibility as an opponent of pesticides? Unless he is very careful, Gerald is in danger of rationalizing the acceptance of a job that will address his short-run economic needs, but possibly at the expense of his long-run aims and his own integrity.

The second reason Gerald should worry about Bob's seeming utilitarian appeal also applies to Dan's comment. Is it professionally responsible to accept a job with the intent of disappointing the expectations of one's employer and fellow workers? This is what Bob is recommending. Dan's reasoning is more subtle; he suggests working for reforms. But Gerald must ask how he might go about this. Can he be up front about his aims and expect the respect and support of his employer and fellow workers? Or will this risk alienating them, perhaps resulting in the loss of his job? Is it professionally acceptable for him to be secretive about his real attitude about the pesticide industry?

Ellen's final observation is certainly worth noting. This is not a perfect world, and purist approaches to professional work are likely to result in disappointment if one's standards are exceptionally high. At the same time, Gerald needs to be concerned about whether compromising his standards may come at the cost of compromising himself. The fact that one can have unrealistically high standards does not mean that one can have no standards at all. *Where* to draw the line should be Gerald's problem, not *whether* a line should be drawn at all. Once he accepts the job,

Gerald's professional responsibilities (at least as seen by his employer and fellow workers) may require him to draw the line even farther from his original ideals than he anticipated. He must give these matters very careful thought before taking that first step.

Part III. The Interview

Gerald Wahr decides to go for the interview. He is quite uncomfortable during the interview, but it seems to be going rather well. However, the interviewer then asks: "There are a lot of people who disapprove of the use of pesticides in farming. Of course, Pro-Growth disagrees. What are your thoughts about the use of pesticides?" How should Gerald answer this question?

Part IV. Selecting Employment

Gerald Wahr's situation may seem extreme. However, it does raise important questions about job choices. To what extent should we be concerned about whether there is a good match between our basic ethical commitments and job selection? What kinds of engineering-related jobs, if any, would you decline because of ethical concerns?

Case 15   An Excess?[33]

I

Stephanie Simon knew environmental manager Adam Baines would not be pleased with her report on the chemical spill. The data clearly indicated that the spill was large enough that regulations required it to be reported to the state. Stephanie perceived Adam to be someone who thinks industry is overregulated, especially in the environmental area. At the same time, he prided himself on being a major player in maintaining LPC Chemical's public reputation as an environmental leader in the chemical industry. "We do a terrific job," he often said. "And we don't need a bunch of hard-to-read, difficult-to-interpret, easily misunderstood state regulations to do it. We got along just fine before the regulators ran wild, and we're doing fine now."

When Stephanie presents her report to Adam, he loses his temper. "This is ridiculous! We're not going to send anything like this to the state. A few gallons over the limit isn't worth the time it's going to take to fill out those damned forms. I can't believe you'd submit a report like this. Stephanie, go back to your desk and rework those numbers until it comes out right. I don't want to see any more garbage like this."

What should Stephanie do?

II

Stephanie refuses to rework the report. Instead she goes back to her desk, signs the report, writes a memo about her conversation with Adam, and then returns to Adam's office. She hands him the report and says, "You don't want to see any more garbage like this? Neither do I. Here's my original report—signed, sealed, and delivered. I've had it here. I'm not fudging data for anyone." As she turns to leave, she adds, "By the way, Adam, before you get any ideas about making it hard for me to get another job, I have a nice little memo about our earlier conversation. I won't hesitate to send it right upstairs at the slightest provocation."

Discuss Stephanie's way of handling this problem.

III

Bruce Bennett was pleased to have the job vacated by Stephanie Simon. It was an advancement in both responsibility and pay. He knew about the circumstances of Stephanie's angry departure. All went well for the first several months. Then there was another spill. Bruce's preliminary calculations indicated that the spill exceeded the specified limit requiring a report to the state. He also knew how Adam would react to the "bad news."

Bruce had worked hard to get his present position, and he looked forward to "moving up the ladder" at LPC. He certainly did not want to go job hunting at this time in his career. He thought, "These numbers are so close to falling below the limit that a little 'rounding off' here or there might save us all a lot of grief."

What should Bruce do?

IV

Imagine how these situations would be evaluated from the following perspectives:

1. A member of the state's environmental protection agency.
2. The CEO of LPC Chemical.
3. Attorneys at LPC who handle environmental affairs.
4. Other industries faced with similar environmental problems.
5. Members of the community whose health may be adversely affected if LPC and other industries do not responsibly handle environmental problems.

To what extent do you think Stephanie, Bruce, and Adam should take into consideration these perspectives in determining what their responsibilities are?

Case 16   Failure[34]

R&M Machinery had for years provided EXES with sophisticated equipment and reliable repair service. EXES returned a failed piece of equipment. A meeting was held that included Archie Hunter, a representative from EXES;

Norm Nash, R&M's returned goods area representative, and, Walt Winters, an R&M engineer intimately acquainted with the kind of equipment EXES had returned.

Norm Nash represented R&M's "official position": the piece of equipment is all right. However, during the course of the meeting it becomes apparent to Walt Winters that the problem has to be R&M's. He suspects that the equipment was not properly tested by R&M, and that it failed because of an internal problem.

Walt keeps silent during the meeting. After the meeting he talks with Norm about his diagnosis. He suggests they tell EXES that the problem is R&M's fault, and that R&M will replace the defective equipment. Norm replies, "I don't think it's wise to acknowledge that it's our fault. There's no need to hang out our wash and lessen EXES's confidence in the quality of our work. A 'goodwill' gesture to replace the equipment should suffice."

R&M management decides to tell EXES that they will adjust to the customer's needs "because you have been such a good customer all these years." Although R&M replaces the equipment at its own expense, it does not tell EXES the real nature of the problem.

Discuss R&M's resolution of the problem. Should R&M's way of handling the problem be of any concern to Walt Winters at this point, or is it basically a "management problem"? Discuss what you think Walt should do.

Case 17   Faulty Valves[35]

Shiley, Inc., a Pfizer subsidiary, was a pioneer in artificial heart valves. From 1965 to the late 1970s, Shiley manufactured and sold artificial heart valves that never had a fracturing problem. In the 1970s it came up with a new model, the C-C, that allowed better blood flow than other models, thereby reducing the risk of blood clots. The new valve consisted of a metal ring through which blood flows, with two wire struts protruding from the ring that hold a small disk in place. The disk tilts up and down within the struts, opening and closing the valve according to the natural flow of blood. About 86,000 C-C valves have been implanted in patients.

Unfortunately, about 450 fractured C-C valves have been reported so far, with nearly 300 resulting deaths. Investigators have come up with disturbing findings. Because fractures can be fatal, Shiley inspectors were told to look very carefully (through microscopes) for any evidence of cracks. Each valve was hand-built, with one strut welded to the valve's metal ring at a much sharper angle than in earlier models. Then the wire strut was bent up and down, often several times, to insert the disk. Scratches had to be polished off to let blood flow through smoothly. If any cracks were discovered, the valve was to be rewelded or discarded. Each valve was accompanied by a card recording dates and the manufacturing operations performed. What investigators discovered was that many cards indicating rewelding were falsified. Many cards were signed off by Inspector No. 2832, an employee who had left Shiley six months before the valve was first manufactured.

Investigators learned that some cracks were simply polished over rather than rewelded. Further investigation revealed skepticism about the notion that rewelding was an acceptable practice. Nancy Wilcox, a Shiley employee, testified in a Houston court case that she had talked with Cabot Corp., supplier of the metal alloy Shiley used with its struts. She reported that a Cabot official said they do not normally recommend rewelding.

Shortly after this conversation, Shiley stopped rewelding, and it disposed of any valves observed to have cracks. Shiley also reduced the angle of the outlet strut, thereby making the initial weld of strut to ring easier.

A 1984 internal memo written by a member of Shiley's task force on valve fractures expressed concern about pressure on quality control inspectors to inspect valves at a rate that causes eye fatigue, increasing the probability of not noticing some defects.

Pfizer apparently takes a different view. It is reported as holding that the major reason for fractures was an abnormal closure of the disk, causing it to hit the tip of one strut with too much force. Repeated striking can produce metal fatigue, ultimately resulting in a broken strut. In addressing this problem, Pfizer says that, in early 1984, it made design changes that avoided the abnormal disk closure—and that no valves with the new design have fractured.

The Federal Drug Administration's position is that no specific cause of fractures has been proven.

Identify and discuss the ethical issues this case raises. Discuss the safety issues this case should raise for engineers.

Case 18   Fire Detectors

Residential fires cause many deaths each year. Several companies manufacture fire detectors in a highly competitive market. Jim is a senior engineer at one of these companies. He has been invited to discuss with management the directions his company should take in manufacturing and marketing fire detectors.

Jim knows that there are two basic types of fire detectors. Type A is very good for certain types of fires, but for smoldering fires the detector will delay the alarm too long or fail to detect the fire at all, sometimes resulting in the loss of life. Most companies still manufacture type A because it is cheap to build and generally performs well. Type A sells for $6 to $15.

Type B detectors combine type A fire detecting abilities with a device for detecting smoldering fires, which constitute about 5 percent of all fires. Type B detectors sell for $15 to $30, but they could be sold for almost the price of type A detectors if they were manufactured in large quantities. To bring this about (short of government intervention prohibiting the sale of type A detectors), many companies would have to decide that, in the interest of greater public safety, they will sell only type B fire detectors.

There is little evidence that this is going to happen. As things stand, most companies either manufacture only type A detectors, or at least depend on type A detectors for the vast majority of their profit. Relatively few type B detectors will sell under present market conditions. However, we do not know for sure what the actual effect of a company's example of selling only type B detectors would be. It might stimulate other firms to follow the example, or it might cause the government to outlaw type A detectors.

Jim's company could still stay in business if it manufactured only type B detectors, because there is some market for them and fire detectors are only one of the products manufactured by Jim's company. Jim takes seriously the engineer's responsibility to hold paramount the safety and welfare of the public. He wonders what this obligation implies in this situation. As he sees it, he faces two options:

Option 1
He can make no attempt to change his firm's policy, which is to manufacture mostly type A detectors and sell a few type B detectors (3 percent of the firm's fire detector sales). Type A detectors, of course, are safety devices with a known deficiency, one of which can be corrected in type B detectors. However, type A detectors do work well 95 percent of the time. Also, far more people will buy type A detectors than B under present market conditions.

Option 2
He can urge his company to go out of the business of making type A detectors and make only type B detectors, arguing that this is the only ethically responsible thing to do. In the long run, if other companies did the same thing, more lives would be saved and people would not be exposed to a danger of which they are generally not aware. (People generally do not know of the differences between type A and type B detectors.)

Which of these two options do you think is preferable? Can you think of any other options that Jim should consider?

Note: The factual assumption you make about the effect the company's decision to stop manufacturing type A detectors would have on the rest of the market (or other effects it might have) is crucial in this case. State your assumption and stay with it throughout the analysis. One assumption, of course, is that you just don't have any idea what the effect would be. You could ask what conclusions you would get if you started with this. To complicate the situation, the assumption you make here may itself be in part governed by ethical considerations, even though it is about the facts; that is, when you don't know what the case will be in the future, what assumption is it most ethically justifiable to make? After all, a lot rides on this assumption.

Case 19   Forced-Sex Accusation

The New York Times (November 16, 1993, p. A12) reported that an engineer filed a lawsuit against her employer, claiming that her superiors "forced her to have sex with a Pentagon official so that the company could get millions of dollars in government financing." She said her bosses told her she would lose her job unless she maintained a sexual relationship with a key Pentagon official. She contended that "in an act of desperation" she went to bed with the official and that talks between her company and the official began the very next day. Adding that she "refused to continue the relationship," the engineer said that one of her superiors "retaliated by abusing her and degrading and humiliating her."

Discuss the ethical issues this set of circumstances raises.

Case 20 Ghost of an Executed Engineer

Loren Graham's *Ghost of an Executed Engineer* features engineer Peter Palchinksy, severe critic of the former Soviet Union's projects and policies in the 1920s.[36] Graham portrays Palchinsky as a visionary and prophetic engineer. The "ghost" of Palchinsky, Graham suggests, can be seen in the Soviet Union's continued technological mistakes in the sixty years following Palchinsky's execution in 1930, culminating in the 1986 Chernobyl nuclear disaster and the dissolution of the Soviet Union in 1991.

Ironically, although praising Palchinsky for his integrity, forthrightness, and vision, Graham ends his book with a mixed verdict: "It is quite probable that Palchinsky's execution resulted from his refusal, even under torture, to confess to crimes he did not commit. Palchinsky always prided himself on being a rational engineer. One can question whether his final act was rational, but one cannot question its bravery."[37]

Discuss the question of whether it can be rational to be willing to die rather than confess to crimes to which one has not committed. (Those familiar with Plato's *Crito* might compare Palchinsky's situation with Socrates, who also gave up his life rather than compromise his integrity.) How much personal sacri-

fice should one be willing to make to maintain one's professional integrity?

Case 21 Gilbane Gold

Below we include some of the transcript of the NSPE's video *Gilbane Gold*, a fictional story of the possible contamination of sludge used for fertilizer ("Gilbane Gold").[38] After viewing the video, examine and discuss the various attitudes toward responsibility expressed by the characters. (We discuss different possible attitudes in Chapter 3.)

Characters: Phil Port, manager in charge of environmental affairs; David Jackson, engineer working under Phil Port; Tom Richards, environmental engineering consultant fired by ZCORP; Winslow Massin, retired professor of engineering; Diane Collins, vice president of the local ZCORP plant.

Phil Port: We here at ZCORP hold the environment as a top priority. It's the only way I would take the job. We do business strictly according to the law. . . .

David Jackson: I'm getting higher levels from the discharge tests than ever before, levels that are consistently, if only a little, above what the city allows. . . . Why hasn't the city gotten on our case?

Phil Port: These data are right on the line. We're probably not over the limit at all.

David Jackson: I need to run more tests, I guess.

Phil Port: We can't afford to spend a lot of time and a lot of money double-checking everything. This isn't college, David. This is business.

David Jackson: But I'm the one that's ultimately responsible to the city, and I need to know that the data I'm signing off on are accurate. Now I suspect that at peak production we are releasing a lot more arsenic and lead than they can handle downstream.

Phil Port: But you don't know that. The data don't tell us anything about what's going on downstream. Look, if we were causing a problem, we would have heard about it from the water people, right? It's their responsibility, you know. They tell us what they want coming out of our pipes and then it's their job. . . .

Tom Richards: You've got a serious problem here. This plant is dumping heavy metals into a water treatment system that simply can't handle them.

Phil Port: I don't think we are, Tom. I mean data from the test system the city requires shows we're within acceptable limits.

Tom Richards: The test is flawed and you know it. The test isn't sensitive enough to accurately reflect the levels. . . .

[It is announced that ZCORP has signed a contract that will increase production fivefold.]

David Jackson: We may have a serious problem here, Phil. We're going to have to invest some serious dollars into water treatment.

Phil Port: It's real simple, David. Just do some calculations on how much more filtration we need with increased flow so that we don't pass the concentrations allowed by discharge.

David Jackson: But we'll still be putting out a lot of poison, Phil, and you know it. A lot more than they can handle downstream. Now, why can't we just go to the city and talk to them and alert them to the situation?

Phil Port: If you can solve this problem without spending a lot of extra money, people are going to view you in a completely different light. This may be your opportunity to shine. . . .

Diane Collins: Are we still in compliance with city regulations?

Phil Port: Technically, yes. But with the increased production anticipated—

Diane Collins: Have we heard from the Gilbane water treatment people? No. Are we in the sludge business? No. You don't even know if the sludge will be unsafe. The problem as I see it is not with the city but with my environmental affairs department. Now I want solutions. And that does not mean spending money we can't afford.

David Jackson: You just don't get it, do you, Diane? We are dumping poison into the city sewer system. Now, whether the law allows it or not, that poison is going to collect in substantial amounts in sludge, and that'll be passed on to the farmers.

Diane Collins: Look, Dave, I eat vegetables, too. I would not intentionally poison anyone any more than you would. But you don't have the data to substantiate your concerns. We are within city regs now, and will continue to be until the city council changes the law.

David Jackson: I think we have a broader responsibility to the public.

Diane Collins: You are exactly right. We provide this city with thousands of jobs and a substantial tax base. We are in the computer business. They are in the sludge business. They can stop selling it if they think it's dangerous. . . .

David Jackson: Winslow, what are we talking about here? Forcing ZCORP to upgrade their water treatment system, that's not going to break their back.

Winslow Maslin: Who are we to make the decision for them?

David Jackson: Is it the company's fault the law allows this much poison?

Tom Richards: The law is flawed.

Winslow Massin: It's not our responsibility. It's the city's.

Tom Richards: You've got to go with your conscience on this. I mean people might get hurt and you're going to have to live with it.

Winslow Massin: If you go public, you'll most certainly lose your job. Tom, we go back a long way, but I don't agree with you. I don't think David should go public.

Case 22   Glass Ceiling[39]

Brenda Jones, a chemistry laboratory technician at XYZ, returned to her laboratory frustrated and angry after her meeting with her department manager, Mike Richards. She had asked for the meeting to discuss a job posting for a process chemist in one of XYZ's factories. She regarded this job as a real opportunity to match her skills and abilities with her responsibilities.

Brenda had been a brilliant college student, excelling in chemistry and chemical engineering. However, when she sought employment the state of the economy made it very difficult for her to find an appropriate position. She took the only job related to her field that she could find—a chemistry laboratory technician in the research laboratories at XYZ. It soon became obvious to XYZ's research management that Brenda was capable of handling a much more demanding position. After a short time she was promoted to a chemist's position in XYZ's technical service organization. She regarded becoming a process chemist as a good next step in her career.

What frustrated and angered Brenda at her meeting with Mike was his flat refusal to place her name in application for the process chemist position. "Brenda," he said, "you would find the atmosphere in a factory too demanding for you as a woman. That's a very high-pressure job. What would you do if your kids got sick again? The factory has got to run, and they wouldn't wait for you while you stayed home to play nursemaid!"

This was not the first time Mike had indicated doubts about what she could handle. Shortly after her transfer into the technical service department, Mike told Brenda that, as the only woman in the department, she would not be invited to the department's annual off-site planning and recreational meeting. "You'd be the only woman there and I think you'd be very uncomfortable," he said, adding that "besides, the language in the discussions sometimes gets a little rough and we wouldn't want to subject you to that. OK?" Although too stunned to do anything but nod her assent, Brenda was very upset at Mike's attitude, which she considered to be quite unprofessional.

Even more upsetting to Brenda was Mike's first performance appraisal of her work. During her first year in the department, Brenda had to take several consecutive days off when one of her children became seriously ill. She had done her best not to let her work assignments fall behind and had worked many extra hours after her child's health was restored. However, during her annual appraisal, Mike had criticized her severely because of her "poor attendance record."

When she first considered whether to transfer into the technical service department, Brenda was warned by some of her co-workers that Mike Richards did not particularly like to have women working for him. But she decided to adopt a wait-and-see attitude. She was now convinced that her co-workers were right, but she was also faced with the question of what to do. She could take a grievance to XYZ's human resource manager. But he was also male and had a reputation for giving women who complained to him a hard time. She might ask for a lateral transfer to another department in the research laboratories. She might try to stick it out and make the best of a frustrating situation, while keeping her eyes open for opportunities with another company. Or perhaps she could confide in someone she trusts and ask for advice.

What advice might such a person give Brenda? What ethical questions does this case raise?

Case 23   Golfing[40]

I

Paul Ledbetter is employed at Bluestone Ltd. as a manufacturing engineer. He regularly meets with vendors who offer to supply Bluestone with needed services and parts. Paul discovers that one of the vendors, Duncan Mackey, like Paul, is an avid golfer. They begin comparing notes about their favorite golf courses. Paul says he's always wanted to play at the Cherry Orchard Country Club, but because it is a private club, he's never had the opportunity. Duncan says he's been a member there for several years and that he's sure he can arrange a guest visit for Paul. Should Paul accept the invitation?

II

Paul accepts the invitation. He, Duncan, and two other members have a very competitive, but friendly, eighteen-hole match. Paul is teamed up with one of the other members, Harvey. Although Paul does not normally bet money in matches, Duncan and the others persuade him to play for $3.00 a hole ("Just to keep things interesting"), along with the losers buying drinks for the winners. Paul and his partner win five holes to their opponents' two, thus winning $9.00 each. While they are having drinks Duncan says, "I think it's only fair that Bob and I get a rematch. What do you say, Paul? You can be Harvey's guest on Guest Day next month." Should Paul accept the invitation?

III

Paul accepts the invitation. The match is closer this time, but Paul and Harvey win $3.00 each. Soon Duncan and Harvey nominate Paul for membership at Cherry Orchard. The membership committee approves, and Paul is invited to join the country club. Paul accepts, thus beginning a long golfing relationship with Duncan.

Gradually, Paul overcomes his resistance to betting on the golf course, and the stakes eventually grow somewhat larger. Although Duncan occasionally bests Paul, the upper hand is clearly Paul's. In the subsequent years Paul does not keep close track of his overall winnings, but he realizes that, all told, he has won several hundred dollars from Duncan. Meanwhile, Duncan is still one of the vendors with whom Paul interacts. Does this pose any ethical problems?

IV

Bluestone's vice president of manufacturing calls a special meeting for engineers in her division who deal with vendors. She announces: "I've been told by the president that we have to make some cutbacks in the vending area. We're going to be in real trouble if we don't get more cost effective. So, I want each of you to do a review—your targeted cutback is 20 percent. If your unit deals with ten vendors now, cut it back to eight, and so on. Give me your recommendations—with a brief rationale by the first of next week."

Paul next discusses the problem with the two other engineers in his unit who deal with vendors. They have to recommend the elimination of two vendors. Should Paul bring up his golfing relationship with Duncan?

V

Paul mentions his golfing relationship with Duncan. He raises the question of whether this compromises his objectivity. The other engineers reassure him, pointing out that they, too, have formed friendships with some of the vendors and that each of them will just have to do the best they can at objectively assessing the situation. As the discussion continues, it becomes more and more worrisome to Paul that, if he were to be objective about it, he would have to recommend Duncan's elimination. Should he tell the others that this is what he is thinking, or should he let them take the initiative? (This way, either they would recommend two others for elimination—thus sparing Duncan—or perhaps both would recommend Duncan and it would not be necessary for Paul to recommend against his friend.)

VI

Paul lets the other two engineers take the initiative. They both recommend that Duncan be eliminated. Paul says nothing in opposition to their recommendation. The group decides to think about it overnight and make its final recommendation the next day.

Paul and Duncan are scheduled for a golf match later that same afternoon. Because Paul and Duncan are good friends, Paul decides he should tell Duncan about the bad news he is likely to receive soon. Duncan is understandably upset. He points out that he has done his best for Bluestone all these years, and he has always been pleased with what he thought was a good working relationship—especially with Paul. Finally, he asks Paul what he said to the other engineers. What should Paul say?

VII

Paul tells Duncan that he did not oppose the recommendations of the other two engineers. He reminds Duncan that he had to try to be objective about this: "We all talked about how hard it is to deal with this given that

friendships are involved. But we agreed that our basic obligation has to be to do what is best for Bluestone. Friendship should not be allowed to overturn good business. So, hard as it was, when I tried to be objective about it, I couldn't really disagree with their recommendations."

As Paul painfully explains his position, Duncan's face reddens. Finally, Duncan furiously explodes, "I don't believe this! What kind of friend are you, anyway? Didn't I get you into Cherry Orchard? And how good a golfer do you think you are, anyway? How do you think you've won all that money from me over the years? You don't really think you're *that* much better at golf than I am do you?"

Discuss the ethical issues that you now think this case raises. Would you now like to reconsider any of your earlier answers?

Case 24   Highway Safety Improvements[41]

David Weber, age 23, is a civil engineer in charge of safety improvements for District 7 (an eight-county area within a midwestern state). Near the end of the fiscal year, the district engineer informs David that delivery of a new snow plow has been delayed, and as a consequence the district has $50,000 in uncommitted funds. He asks David to suggest a safety project (or projects) that can be put under contract within the current fiscal year.

After a careful consideration of potential projects, David narrows his choice to two possible safety improvements. Site A is the intersection of Main and Oak streets in the major city within the district. Site B is the intersection of Grape and Fir roads in a rural area.

Pertinent data for the two intersections are as follows:

	Site A	Site B
Main road traffic (vehicles/day)	20,000	5,000
Minor road traffic (vehicles/day)	4,000	1,000
Fatalities per year (3-yr average)	2	1
Injuries per year (3-yr average)	6	2
PD* (3-yr average)	40	12
Proposed improvement	New signals	New signals
Improvement cost	$50,000	$50,000

*PD refers to property damage only accidents.

A highway engineering textbook includes a table of average reductions in accidents resulting from the installation of the types of signal improvements David proposes. The tables are based on studies of intersections in urban and rural areas throughout the United States, over the past twenty years.

	Urban	Rural
% reduction in fatalities	50	50
% reduction in injuries	50	60
% reduction in PD	25	−25*

*Property damage only accidents are expected to increase because of the increase in rear-end accidents due to the stopping of high-speed traffic in rural areas.

David recognizes that these reduction factors represent averages from intersections with a wide range of physical characteristics (number of approach lanes, angle of intersection); in all climates; with various mixes of trucks and passenger vehicles, various approach speeds, various driving habits; and so on. However, he has no special data about sites A and B that suggest relying on these tables is likely to misrepresent the circumstances at these sites.

Finally, here is some additional information that David knows about:

1. In 1975, the National Safety Council and the National Highway Traffic Safety Administration both published dollar scales for comparing accident outcomes, as shown next:

	NSC	NHSTA
Fatality	$52,000	$235,000
Injury	3,000	11,200
PD	440	500

A neighboring state uses the following weighting scheme:

Fatality   9.5 PD
Injury   3.5 PD

2. Individuals within the two groups pay roughly the same transportation taxes (licenses, gasoline taxes).

Which of the two site improvements do you think David should recommend? What is your rationale for this recommendation?

Case 25   Hydrolevel[42]

"A conflict of interest is like dirt in a sensitive gauge," one that can not only soil one person's career but can also taint an entire profession.[43] Thus, as professionals, engineers must be ever alert to signs of conflict of interest. The case of the *American Society of Mechanical Engineers (ASME) v. Hydrolevel Corporation* shows how easily individuals, companies, and professional societies can find themselves embroiled in expensive legal battles that tarnish the reputation of the engineering profession as a whole.

In 1971, Eugene Mitchell, vice president of sales at McDonnell and Miller, Inc., located in Chicago, was concerned about his company's continued dominance in the heating boiler low-water fuel cutoff market. The product ensures that boilers cannot be fired without sufficient water in them; insufficient water could cause an explosion.

Hydrolevel Corporation entered the market with an electronic low-water fuel supply cutoff that included a time delay on some of its models. With the time-delay devices the normal turbulence of the water level at the electronic probe would not cause inappropriate and repeated fuel supply turn-on and turn-off. Hydrolevel's valve had won important approval for use from Brooklyn Gas Company, one of the largest installers of heating boilers. Mitchell felt that McDonnell and Miller's sales could be protected if he could secure an interpretation stating that the Hydrolevel time delay on the cutoff violated the ASME B-PV Code. He referred to this section of the ASME code: "Each automatically fired steam or vapor system boiler shall have an automatic low-water fuel cutoff, so located as to automatically cut off the fuel supply when the surface of the water falls to the lowest visible part of the water-gauge glass."[44] Mitchell asked for an ASME interpretation of the mechanism for operation of the Hydrolevel device as it pertained to this section of the code. He did not, however, specifically mention the Hydrolevel device in his request.

Mitchell discussed his idea several times with John James, McDonnell and Miller's vice president of research. In addition to his role at McDonnell and Miller, James was on the ASME subcommittee responsible for heating boilers and had played a leading role in writing the part of the boiler code that Mitchell was asking about.

James recommended that he and Mitchell approach the chairman of the ASME Heating Boiler Subcommittee, T. R. Hardin. Hardin was also vice president of the Hartford Steam Boiler Inspection and Insurance Company. When Hardin arrived in Chicago in early April on other business, the three men went to dinner at the Drake Hotel. During dinner, Hardin agreed with Mitchell and James that their interpretation of the code was correct.

Shortly after the meeting with Hardin, James sent ASME a draft letter of inquiry and sent Hardin a copy. Hardin made some suggestions, and James incorporated them into a final draft letter. James's finalized draft letter of inquiry was then addressed to W. Bradford Hoyt, secretary of the B-PV Boiler and Pressure Vessel Committee.

Hoyt received thousands of similar inquiries every year. Hoyt could not answer James's inquiry with a routine, prefabricated response, so he directed the letter to the appropriate subcommittee chairman, T. R. Hardin. Hardin drafted a response without consulting the whole subcommittee, a task he had authorization for if the response was treated as an "unofficial communication."

Hardin's response, dated April 29, 1971, stated that a low-water fuel cutoff must operate immediately. Although this response did not say that Hydrolevel's time-delayed cutoff was dangerous, McDonnell and Miller's salespeople used Hardin's conclusion to argue against using the Hydrolevel product. This was done at Mitchell's direction.

In early 1972, Hydrolevel learned of the ASME letter through one of their former customers who had a copy of the letter. Hydrolevel then requested an official copy of the letter from ASME. On March 23, 1972, Hydrolevel requested an ASME review and ruling correction.

ASME's Heating and Boiler Subcommittee had a full meeting to discuss Hydrolevel's request and confirmed part of the original Hardin interpretation. James, who had replaced Hardin as chairman of the subcommittee, refrained from participating in the discussion but subsequently helped draft a critical part of the subcommittee's response to Hydrolevel. The ASME response was dated June 9, 1972.

In 1975, Hydrolevel filed suit against McDonnell and Miller, Inc., ASME, and the Hartford Steam Boiler Inspection and

Insurance Company, charging them with conspiracy to restrain trade under the Sherman Antitrust Act.

Hydrolevel reached an out-of-court settlement with McDonnell and Miller and Hartford for $750,000 and $75,000, respectively. ASME took the case to trial. ASME officials believed that, as a society, ASME had done nothing wrong and should not be liable for the misguided actions of individual volunteer members acting on their own behalf. After all, ASME gained nothing from such practices. ASME officials also believed that a pretrial settlement would set a dangerous precedent that would encourage other nuisance suits.

Despite ASME arguments, however, the jury decided against ASME, awarding Hydrolevel $3.3 million in damages. The trial judge deducted $800,000 in prior settlements and tripled the remainder in accordance with the Clayton Act. This resulted in a decision of $7,500,000 for Hydrolevel.

On May 17, 1982, ASME's liability was upheld by the second circuit. The Supreme Court, in a controversial 6 to 3 vote, found ASME guilty of antitrust violations. The majority opinion, delivered by Justice Blackmun, read as follows:

> ASME wields great power in the nation's economy. Its codes and standards influence the policies of numerous states and cities, and as has been said about "so-called voluntary standards" generally, its interpretation of guidelines "may result in economic prosperity or economic failure, for a number of businesses of all sizes throughout the country," as well as entire segments of an industry. . . . ASME can be said to be "in reality an extragovernmental agency, which prescribes rules for the regulation and restraint of interstate commerce." When it cloaks its subcommittee officials with the authority of its reputation, ASME permits those

> agents to affect the destinies of businesses and thus gives them power to frustrate competition in the marketplace.[45]

The issue of damages was retried in a trial lasting for approximately one month. In June, the jury returned a verdict of $1.1 million, which was tripled to $3.3 million. Parties involved were claiming attorney's fees in excess of $4 million, and a final settlement of $4,750,000 was decreed.

Following the decision, ASME revised its procedures as follows:

> In the wake of the Hydrolevel ruling, the Society has changed the way it handles codes and standards interpretations, beefed up its enforcement and conflict-of-interest rules, and adopted new "sunset" review procedures for its working bodies.
>
> The most striking changes affect the Society's handling of codes and standards interpretations. All such interpretations must now be reviewed by at least five persons before release; before, the review of two people was necessary. Interpretations are available to the public, with replies to nonstandard inquiries published each month in the codes and standards section of ME or other ASME publications. Previously, such responses were kept between the inquirer and the involved committee or subcommittee. Lastly, ASME incorporates printed disclaimers on the letterhead used for code interpretations spelling out their limitations: that they are subject to change should additional information become available and that individuals have the right to appeal interpretations they consider unfair.
>
> Regarding conflict-of-interest, ASME now requires all staff and volunteer committee members to sign statements pledging their adherence to a comprehensive and well-defined set of guidelines regarding potential conflicts. Additionally, the Society now provides all staff and volunteers with copies of the

engineering code of ethics along with a publication outlining the legal implications of standards activities.

Finally, the Society now requires each of its councils, committees and subcommittees to conduct a "sunset" review of their operations every two years. The criteria include whether their activities have served the public interest and whether they have acted cost-effectively, in accordance with Society procedures.[46]

Conflict of interest cases quickly become complicated, as the following questions illustrate:

• How could McDonnell and Miller have avoided the appearance of a conflict of interest? This applies to both Mitchell and James.

• What was T. R. Hardin's responsibility as chair of the B-PV Boiler code subcommittee? How could he have handled things differently to protect the interests of ASME?

• What can engineering societies do to protect their interests once a conflict of interest is revealed?

• Was the final judgment against ASME fair? Why or why not?

• Have ASME's revised conflict-of-interest procedures addressed the problems fully? Why or why not?

Case 26   Innocent Comment?

Jack Strong is seated between Tom Evans and Judy Hanson at a dinner meeting of a local industrial engineering society. Jack and Judy have an extended discussion on a variety of concerns, many of which are related to their common engineering interest. At the conclusion of the dinner, Jack turns to Tom, smiles and says, "I'm sorry not to have talked with you more tonight, Tom, but Judy's better looking than you."

Judy is taken aback by Jack's comment. A recent graduate from a school in which more than 20 percent of her classmates were women, she had been led to believe that finally the stereotypical view that women are not as well suited for engineering as men was finally going away. However, matters quickly changed on her first job. She found that she was the only woman engineer in her division. Now, even after nearly a year on the job, she has to struggle to get others to take her ideas seriously. She wants to be recognized first and foremost as a good engineer. So, she had enjoyed "talking shop" with Jack. But she was stunned by his remark to Tom, however innocently it might have been intended. Suddenly, she saw the conversation in a very different light. Once again she sensed that she was not being taken seriously enough as an engineer.

How should Judy respond to Jack's remark? Should she say anything? Assuming Tom understands her perspective, what, if anything, should Tom say or do? Do Tom and other male engineers have special responsibilities to help women engineers feel they are as well qualified as men for engineering?

Case 27   Inside Tool & Die[47]

At T&D Manufacturing, the procedure to obtain needed tooling is to have the tools designed in house by company tool engineers. When the design is approved, part prints and specifications are mailed to at least three approved outside vendors. The outside shop supplying the best price and delivery date is usually awarded a contract to produce the tool.

T&D also has an internal tool and die department. In the past this department has been used primarily to resharpen and repair the tools that are purchased outside. However, now the head of the department has requested management to allow them to offer a price to produce the tooling internally. This request is approved. Next the department head places a call to the Purchasing Department and asks for the prices obtained from the outside vendors before he submits his quote. "Look," he says, "we are all part of the same company. We should be working together." Is this an ethically acceptable procedure?

Case 28   Last Resort[48]

I

The New Wyoming State Board of Professional Engineers performs regulatory functions (for example, licensing of engineers) for the state. Members of the board are appointed by the state governor. Most of the board members are also members of the New Wyoming Society of Professional Engineers (NWSPE), a voluntary umbrella organization of professional engineers in New Wyoming. Membership in NWSPE is controlled by its own board and is not subject to approval by the state board.

NWSPE holds annual meetings at a pleasant resort area in New Wyoming. This year the NWSPE meeting will begin the day after one of the state board meetings. Because they share many common concerns about the engineering profession, the executive committee of NWSPE has recently expressed a strong interest in improving communication between NWSPE and the state board. Ordinarily, the state board meets in the state capitol building. Because the NWSPE annual meeting and the state board meeting will occur so close together—and most of the board members will be attending the NWSPE meeting anyway—the NWSPE Executive Committee extends an invitation to the state board to hold its meeting at the resort area. The board is invited to stay on for the NWSPE meeting, and an NWSPE session is planned for the board to conduct a roundtable discussion of state board activities and concerns. NWSPE offers to pay the travel and lodging expenses of state board members.

Should the state board accept the invitation?

II

Suppose the state board accepts the invitation, agreeing that this would be a good opportunity to improve communication with NWSPE. Several days later Brian Simpson begins to have second thoughts. A new appointee to the board, and the only board member who does not belong to NWSPE, Brian wonders if the board has set itself up for a conflict of interest. Although he knows of no instances in which the board has directly ruled on any NWSPE activities, it occurs to him that NWSPE and its members come within the purview of the board's regulatory functions. Finally, Brian writes to Harold Brock, chair of the state board:

Dear Mr. Brock:
I have some serious reservations regarding our acceptance of the hospitality offered by NWSPE to hold our August meeting at the Lakeshore Resort. Although I agree about the desirability for communication between the board and NWSPE, it is inappropriate for us as a regulatory body to accept anything of substantial value from the organization representing those whose profession we regulate. Acceptance of hospitality in the form of lodging and meals creates the appearance of a conflict of interest. Therefore, it is my intention to

pay any expenses not otherwise covered by the State of New Wyoming.

Sincerely,

Brian Simpson, P.E.

Before sending the letter, Brian shows it to you. He discusses his concerns with you and asks your advice about the letter. What is your advice to Brian?

III

Suppose Brian sends the letter as is. When Harold Brock receives the letter, he must decide what to do next. Should Harold:

1. Share the letter with other board members, inviting each to decide for himself or herself whether to follow Brian's example.
2. Call a special board meeting to discuss the matter.
3. Decide, on behalf of the board, to withdraw acceptance of the hospitality.
4. Other.

Discuss your choice.

IV

Suppose Harold sends the letter to the other board members, inviting them to decide for themselves whether to follow Brian's example. One other member, Ellen Price, agrees with Brian and indicates that she, too, will pay her own expenses. None of the others, including Harold Brock, think the issue raised by Brian warrants refusal of the hospitality. Should Brian and Ellen do anything further, or should they simply quietly continue their rejection of the offer of hospitality?

V

Suppose Brian and Ellen do not press the issue further but continue to insist that they will pay their own expenses. While the annual NWSPE meeting is taking place, a resort area reporter learns (not through Brian or Ellen) that NWSPE is hosting the state board. Like Brian and Ellen, the reporter thinks this might create a conflict of interest. She attempts to interview members of the board about how they see the situation. She approaches Brian and Ellen. What should they say?

Case 29   Mere "Technicality"?[49]

I

You have been assigned the position of environmental engineer for one of several local plants whose water discharges flow into a lake in a flourishing tourist area. Although all the plants are marginally profitable, they compete for the same customers. Included in your responsibilities is the monitoring of water and air discharges at your plant and the periodic preparation of reports to be submitted to the Department of Natural Resources. You have just prepared a report that indicates that the level of pollution in the plant's water discharges slightly exceeds the legal limitations. Your supervisor, the plant manager, says you should regard the excess as a mere "technicality," and he asks you to "adjust" the data so that the plant appears to be in compliance. He says that the slight excess is not going to endanger human or fish life any more than if the plant were actually in compliance. However, he says, solving the problem would require a very heavy investment in new equipment. He explains, "We can't afford new equipment. It might even cost a few jobs. It will set us behind our competitors. Besides the bad publicity we'd get, it might scare off some of the tourist industry, making it worse for everybody."

What are your basic responsibilities as an environmental engineer in this plant? How do you think you should respond to your supervisor's requests? What ethical questions does this case raise?

II

Consider the same scenario but from different perspectives. Look at the situation from the standpoint of:

- the plant manager of the company
- the chief executive officer of the company
- environmental engineers from the competing companies
- plant managers from the competing companies
- the Department of Natural Resources
- local merchants
- parents of children who swim in the lake
- those who fish in the lake (or eat fish from it)

Do your ideas about how an environmental engineer ought to deal with a situation like this change as you take into account these different perspectives? Now, looking at the case from an "all things considered" perspective, go back to Part I and discuss what you, as an environmental engineer, should do (and why).

Case 30   Microwaves

Your first job after completing your undergraduate engineering degree is with the Kitchen Shortcuts Company. Shortcuts manufactures microwave ovens and other time-saving kitchen equipment. You are hired into a low-level engineering position. Your first task is to test a series of microwave ovens to determine their defrosting capabilities. You proceed to your lab where you find a few dozen microwave ovens in their boxes waiting for you to start your testing. You notice that virtually every brand of microwave oven is here, including all of Shortcuts' competitors' brands.

You unpack all the microwave ovens and begin your tests. The process is rather slow. So while you are waiting for test items to defrost, you begin to dig through the cabinets in your lab to see what is there. You discover that this used to be the lab where they tested microwave oven doors for radiation permeability (the amount of radiation that could escape through the glass door of microwave ovens). You also find an intriguing little piece of hand-held equipment that apparently was used to measure radiation levels. Because you are an engineer, you cannot resist trying it out.

You switch on the meter and point it around the room and out the window. You notice that when you point the meter at some of the microwave ovens, it gives a very high reading. You turn off all the other microwave ovens and discover that the reading is not a fluke. The ovens you are standing in front of are emitting much higher-than-average levels of radiation. You discover that one of the ovens is from Shortcuts and the other is from Home Helpers, Shortcuts' archrival. These microwave ovens are currently the two best-selling ovens on the market, primarily because they are the least expensive. It seems that these bargain ovens may not be as safe as they seem.

You decide to look around a little more. You find the test report that discusses the radiation emissions from all of Shortcuts' models of microwaves. You learn that only the top of the line and the midlevel microwaves were thoroughly tested. The bargain ovens' results apparently were extrapolated from the test results from the other ovens.

Discuss at least two possibly conflicting obligations you have as an engineer in this case. Can you think of any ways in which you might be able to meet both of these conflicting obligations? Explain how each obligation is met. (Be sure to consider whether there are any other conflicting obligations that these solutions leave unresolved.)

Case 31   Moral Beliefs in the Workplace[50]

The heading of Don Shakow's obituary reads, "Don Shakow's moral beliefs put to test in the workplace."[51] Although an economist rather than an engineer, Shakow's commitments and expertise certainly overlapped those of some engineers. Among other things, he served as an expert witness on the economics of rapid-transit and public energy proposals. In the mid-70s he joined Mathematical Sciences Northwest to evaluate proposed power projects for Seattle City Light. His finding that regional energy needs were seriously overestimated resulted in Seattle City Light withdrawing its support for two Washington Public Power supply system nuclear plants. Shakow's former colleague Frank Miller commented that their eventual construction "resulted in the largest utility-bond default in U.S. history." Shakow supported organic farming, home-grown food, and food cooperatives. He protested the Vietnam War, co-founding the Little Bread Co., which carried messages on its reader board such as, "We Can't Support One Gov't—Let Alone Thieu." No doubt a somewhat controversial figure throughout his activist life, he was characterized by reporter Carole Beers as "that rare individual: He fully integrated his moral beliefs into his work life."

Discuss the difficulties of fully integrating one's moral beliefs into one's work life. Is it desirable to try to do this? Can this ever conflict with moral or ethical obligations that one has as a professional engineer or employee? If so, how should such a conflict be resolved?

Case 32   Oil Spill?[52]

Peter has been working with the Bigness Oil Company's local affiliate for several years, and he has established a strong, trusting relationship with Jesse, manager of the local facility.

The facility, on Peter's recommendations, has followed all of the environmental regulations to the letter, and it has a solid reputation with the state regulatory agency. The local facility receives various petrochemical products via pipelines and tank trucks, and it blends them for resale to the private sector.

Jesse has been so pleased with Peter's work that he has recommended that Peter be retained as the corporate consulting engineer. This would be a significant advancement for Peter and his consulting firm, cementing Peter's steady and impressive rise in the firm. There is talk of a vice presidency in a few years.

One day, over coffee, Jesse starts telling Peter a story about a mysterious loss in one of the raw petrochemicals he receives by pipeline. Sometime during the 1950s, when operations were more lax, a loss of one of the process chemicals was discovered when the books were audited. There were apparently 10,000 gallons of the chemical missing. After running pressure tests on the pipelines, the plant manager found that one of the pipes had corroded and had been leaking the chemical into the ground. After stopping the leak, the company sank observation and sampling wells and found that the product was sitting in a vertical plume, slowly diffusing into a deep aquifer. Because there was no surface or groundwater pollution off the plant property, the plant manager decided to do nothing. Jesse believes that somewhere under the plant there still sits this plume, although the last tests from the sampling wells showed that the concentration of the chemical in the groundwater within 400 feet of the surface was essentially zero. The wells were capped, and the story never appeared in the press.

Peter is taken aback by this apparently innocent revelation. He recognizes that state law requires him to report all spills, but what about spills that occurred years ago, where the effects of the spill seem to have dissipated? He frowns and says to Jesse, "We have to report this spill to the state, you know."

Jesse is incredulous. "But there *is* no spill. If the state made us look for it, we probably could not find it; and even if we did, it makes no sense whatever to pump it out or contain it in any way."

"But the law says that we have to report . . . ," replies Peter.

"Hey, look. I told you this in confidence. Your own engineering code of ethics requires client confidentiality. And what would be the good of going to the state? There is nothing to be done. The only thing that would happen is that the company would get into trouble and have to spend useless dollars to correct a situation that cannot be corrected and does not need remediation."

"But . . ."

"Peter, let me be frank. If you go to the state with this, you will not be doing anyone any good—not the company, not the environment, and certainly not your own career. I cannot have a consulting engineer who does not value client loyalty."

What are the ethical issues in this case? What factual and conceptual questions need to be addressed? How do you think Peter should deal with this situation?

Case 33   Parkville[53]

Elizabeth Dorsey is an engineer at CDC, Inc., a large corporation in a crowded metropolitan area. Elizabeth prefers living in a smaller community. So she commutes 30 miles daily from her home in Parkville, a community of fewer than 5,000 people.

Noted for her environmental concerns, Elizabeth is on Parkville's Committee for Environmental Quality, a small but active citizen's group. Last year the committee successfully spearheaded opposition to rezoning a Parkville recreational and wildlife area for commercial purposes. Acknowledging that commercial development would aid the local economy, the committee still convinced the city council that economic progress should not come at the expense of the environment.

However, now Elizabeth is facing a difficult problem. She has learned that CDC has its eyes on developing a new facility. But the immediate area has little to offer. In surveying surrounding areas, CDC's planning committee has determined that the most desirable location for its new facility would be in nearby Parkville's recreational and wildlife area. The planning committee is now authorized by CDC to approach Parkville's city council.

CDC makes what it considers to be a very generous offer to the city council. Presenting itself as an environmentally conscious corporation, CDC says it will need only 25 percent of the wildlife and recreational area; it will carefully monitor and control emissions into the air and water, using "beyond the state of the art" equipment and standards; and it will annually contribute funds for the preservation and maintenance of the remaining 75 percent of the wildlife and recreational area. In addition, CDC points out how its presence will increase the tax base of Parkville, create new jobs, and enhance the local economy.

A member of CDC's planning committee learns that one of CDC's engineers, Elizabeth Dorsey, lives in Parkville. He suggests to committee chair, Jim Bartlett, that someone talk to her to see if she might be able to "soften up" Parkville city council members. Jim thinks this is a good idea and calls David Jensen, chief engineer of Elizabeth's unit. "David," Jim says, "I'd like you to talk with one of your engineers, Elizabeth Dorsey, about our efforts to secure some land near Parkville." Jim goes on to detail CDC's plans and what he would like Elizabeth to be asked to do.

Shortly after his conversation with Jim Bartlett, David Jensen calls Elizabeth Dorsey into his office and relays to her Jim's message. Unaware of Elizabeth's participation on Parkville's Committee for Environmental Quality, David asks, "Is there anyone on the city council you know well enough to talk to about this?"

David Jensen reports to Jim Bartlett that he is not sure that Elizabeth Dorsey will be much help. "She said she doesn't know any council members well enough to talk to them," David says.

Much to David's surprise, Jim replies, "Guess what I learned just half an hour ago? I had a phone conversation with an old friend who moved away from Parkville last fall. He says Elizabeth Dorsey is on an environmental concerns committee in Parkville. She knows city council members all right—she and her committee members took on the council last year and blocked the council's effort to open up commercially the area we want! We're going to have to keep an eye on her. Tell her she'd better "cool it" on this one."

Over the next two weeks Elizabeth Dorsey keeps CDC's plans to herself. Then she receives a phone message indicating that the Committee for Environmental Quality is having an urgent meeting. At the outset of the meeting the committee chair announces that he has just learned of CDC's intentions. "We

have to act quickly to mobilize against this," he concludes.

Did Elizabeth misrepresent to her supervisors her relationship to the city council? Did she engage in withholding information about CDC's plans from the Committee for Environmental Quality? Should she now join with her fellow committee members in mobilizing against CDC's intentions?

Analysis

A number of unclear factual issues are important in the resolution of this case. What would be the effects on the wildlife and recreational area of selling 25 percent of it to CDC? Will Parkville be able to pay for the upkeep of the wildlife and recreational area without the contributions from CDC? Does CDC have other viable options for expansion? How much less desirable are they than the land in the wildlife and recreational area? What kind of environmental record does CDC have? How important is Elizabeth's participation in the fight to preserve the wildlife and recreational area? Is her participation essential, or does she want to participate primarily as a matter of conscience? Does she in fact know any members of the Parkville city council well enough to be of benefit to CDC?

One of the major conceptual issues is "deception." Elizabeth may be guilty of something akin to deception or dishonesty by telling her employer that she does not know any city council members well enough to influence them and by not alerting the Committee for Environmental Quality to CDC's plans. Without attempting to give a complete definition, we can say that deception is (1) affirming what we know to be false or denying what we know to be true or (2) failing to reveal information in a situation in which most would expect one to be forthcoming.

Another conceptual issue is "conflict of interest." Two principal points about conflicts of interest should be borne in mind: (1) Occupying a certain role justifies another person's relying on our judgment to be objective, and (2) we are (or might be) subject to influences that would make our judgment less objective and disinterested than others who rely on our judgment might expect.

Now let us turn to application problems. There are two instances where Elizabeth might be accused of deception. First, she can be accused of deception in not being more forthright with her employers about her relationship with the city council members. She has already been successful in exerting influence on the council members, so she must know them well enough to exert such influence. Although it may be true that she cannot influence them to reverse their position, the reason is not that she does not know them well enough. Rather, it might be that the council members would no longer respect her integrity if she reversed her position. She also has failed to reveal information her employers might have expected her to reveal, her involvement in the local environmental movement. Her action almost certainly has involved deception with respect to her employer.

The second instance of deception is in not revealing CDC's plans to the Committee for Environmental Quality. This seems to be a clear case of not revealing information where she would have been expected to reveal it. Information about CDC's plans would have been helpful to the members of the committee, giving them more time to prepare their response, and committee members might expect her to reveal such information. At the same time, CDC might regard its plans as confidential information at this time, thus placing Elizabeth in a conflict situation.

Whether Elizabeth's continued activity on the Committee for Environmental Quality represents a conflict of interest is a complex question. On the one hand, people probably rely on her judgment on environmental matters to be objective and in the interests of the general public, and her employment by CDC calls this judgment into question. On the other hand, if Elizabeth continues to oppose CDC's attempt to buy a portion of the recreational and wildlife area, most of the members of the community may conclude that she has resisted the influence of her employer and her continued presence on the committee is not objectionable. Nevertheless, there is always the danger that her views will be tempered in some way because of the actions of CDC. So it is not unreasonable to hold that there is still at least a potential conflict of interest from the committee's perspective.

It is also possible that CDC regards Elizabeth's serving on the Committee for Environmental Quality as a conflict of interest because she might join the committee in opposition to CDC. Still, because she is not on CDC's planning committee, it is not clear that Elizabeth has any special responsibility to recommend or otherwise advocate CDC's Parkville plan. In this respect, CDC should not fault her for her unwillingness to seek to influence Parkville's city council.

Nevertheless, CDC might believe that company loyalty requires, at least, that Elizabeth not join forces with the opposition. This would place her in a difficult position, because she is also an environmentally concerned citizen in the community into which CDC wishes to move. Engineering codes of ethics typically insist that an engineer's paramount obligation is to protect public health and safety. There is no indication that this obligation is meant to be restricted to the context of employment. Engineers are encouraged to take on broader responsibilities for the good of society. This is precisely what she took her involvement with the Committee for Environmental Quality to be.

So, Elizabeth faces several conflict issues. She faces a conflict in deciding whether to engage in deception with regard to CDC. On the one hand, she has strong reason to protect her job if possible. On the other hand, she has an obligation to tell the truth to her employer. She resolves the conflict by slightly misrepresenting the truth. She also faces a conflict in deciding whether to withhold information about CDC's plans from the Committee for Environmental Quality.

Elizabeth has already decided to engage in a certain amount of deception. Her more immediate problem is whether to join with the other members of the Committee for the Environmental Quality in opposing CDC's plan to acquire a portion of the recreational and wildlife area. If Elizabeth's employer respects the rights of its employees to follow their own conscience, especially in activities outside the workplace, Elizabeth would not have a problem. It is clear, however that Elizabeth's supervisors expect her either to support the CDC position or at the very least to remain neutral. Therefore, she faces a conflict—this time between a certain loyalty to her employer and to herself (because her job may be in jeopardy) and an obligation to the committee. How can she resolve the conflict?

The first possible resolution is to try to persuade CDC managers to consider purchasing another location for expansion that is not so environmentally sensitive. She can argue that the attempt to purchase the land will result in a bruising public fight that will damage CDC's reputation, whether the company wins or loses. Because of Elizabeth's position in the company and the evident determination of CDC managers to secure the land near Parkville, this option may not offer much promise, but it would have the advantage of preserving Elizabeth's integrity as an environmentalist and preserving her job.

The second possible resolution is to resign from the committee on the grounds of conflict of interest and then to remain neutral with respect to the controversy. Her claim that she has a conflict of interest has some justification, and the action might be enough to satisfy her supervisors. The problem with this is that it would require her standing by idly without taking sides on an issue about which she cares very deeply, and that it would probably tarnish her reputation in the community by making her look like a person who does not stand up for her convictions.

A third option is to resign from the committee but continue publicly to oppose the purchase of the wildlife area. This would no doubt anger her employer, but it might be the best way to preserve her integrity in the community, for it would remove any problem of conflict of interest and preserve her reputation as a staunch environmentalist.

The fourth possibility is to resign from the committee and take the side of her employer. This solution would please her supervisors the most, but it would severely damage both Elizabeth's reputation in the community and her own self-esteem; and it might result in environmental degradation in the Parkville area. This seems to be her least attractive option.

To make a responsible decision, Elizabeth must have some knowledge of her chances of getting another job. If they are good, she should risk losing her job by choosing the first or third option. Clearly, the first option is the most desirable, for if it is successful it will not only resolve the environmental crisis but also probably preserve her job. The third option would endanger her job but preserve her integrity in the community and her own self-esteem.

If losing her job would cause severe problems for her and the first option is not possible, Elizabeth faces a very serious conflict issue, and there may be no creative middle way out of it. She should certainly examine very carefully the arguments for and against selling 25 percent of the wildlife and recreational area to CDC. But if she decides to sup-

Is this a Cost Benefit Approach

port the CDC position, she will find it difficult to preserve her reputation in the community, or at least with the Committee on Environmental Quality. If she finds the arguments are against selling the land to CDC, she may have to choose the second option.

Case 34   Pinto[54]

In the late 1960s Ford designed a subcompact, the Pinto, weighing less than 2,000 pounds and selling for less than $2,000. Anxious to compete with foreign-made subcompacts, Ford brought the car into production in a little more than two years (compared with the usual three and one-half years). Given this shorter time frame, styling preceded much of the engineering, thus restricting engineering design more than usual. As a result, it was decided that the best place for the gas tank was between the rear axle and the bumper. The differential housing had exposed bolt heads that could puncture the gas tank if the tank were driven forward against them upon rear impact.

In court the crash tests were described in this way:

> These prototypes as well as two production Pintos were crash tested by Ford to determine, among other things, the integrity of the fuel system in rear-end accidents. . . . Prototypes struck from the rear with a moving barrier at 21-miles-per-hour caused the fuel tank to be driven forward and to be punctured, causing fuel leakage. . . . A production Pinto crash tested at 21-miles-per-hour into a fixed barrier caused the fuel tank to be torn from the gas tank and the tank to be punctured by a bolt head on the differential housing. In at least one test, spilled fuel entered the driver's compartment. . . .[55]

Ford also tested rear impact when rubber bladders were installed in the tank, as well as when the tank was located above rather than behind the rear axle. Both passed the twenty-mile-per-hour rear impact tests.

Although the federal government was pressing to stiffen regulations on gas tank designs, Ford contended that the Pinto met all applicable federal safety standards at the time. J. C. Echold, director of automotive safety for Ford, issued a study entitled "Fatalities Associated with Crash Induced Fuel Leakage and Fires."[56] This study claimed that the costs of improving the design ($11 per vehicle) outweighed its social benefits. A memorandum attached to the report described the costs and benefits in this way:

Benefits

Savings	180 burn deaths, 180 serious burn injuries, 2,100 burned vehicles
Unit cost	$200,000 per death, $67,000 per injury, $700 per vehicle
Total benefits	180 × $200,000 plus 180 × $67,000 plus 2100 × $700 = $49.15 million

Costs

Sales	11 million cars, 1.5 million light trucks
Unit cost	$11 per car, $11 per truck
Total costs	11,000,000 × $11 plus 1,500,000 × $11 = $137 million

The estimate of the number of deaths, injuries, and damage to vehicles was based on statistical studies. The $200,000 for the loss of a human life was based on a National Highway Traffic Safety administration study, which estimated social costs of a death in this way:[57]

Component	1971 Costs
Future productivity losses	
Direct	$132,000
Indirect	41,300
Medical costs	
Hospital	700
Other	425
Property damage	1,500
Insurance administration	4,700
Legal and court	3,000
Employer losses	1,000
Victim's pain and suffering	10,000
Funeral	900
Assets (lost consumption)	5,000
Miscellaneous accident cost	200
Total per fatality	$200,725

Discuss the appropriateness of Ford's using figures like these to decide whether or not to make a safety improvement in its engineering design. If you believe this is not appropriate, what would you suggest as an alternative? What responsibilities do you think engineers have in situations like this?

Case 35   Price Is Right?[58]

XYZ orders 5,000 custom-made parts from ABC for one of its products. When the order is originally made ABC indicates it will charge $75 per part. The contract states that ABC will use the "highest quality materials in manufacture."

After the agreement is completed, but before production of the part begins, ABC engineer Christine Carsten decides to do a little reading in the literature to find out whether there is any other material that can be used to manufacture the product. To her surprise and delight, she finds that a new and much less expensive metal alloy (M-2) can be used instead of M-1, which is cus-

tomarily used to manufacture the part. The use of M-2 will cut ABC's costs by $18 per part.

Christine fills out a Value Engineering Change Proposal (VECP) for the proposed material substitution. The VECP comes to the attention of ABC's Vernon Waller, the manager who authorized the sales agreement with XYZ. In discussing the substitution of M-2 for M-1, Vernon asks, "How would anyone know the difference?" Christine replies, "Probably no one would unless they were looking for a difference and did a fair amount of testing." He also asks whether there will be any difference in the quality of the final product for XYZ. "As far as we can tell," Christine replies, "there is no difference: the product will be no better, but no worse. Of course, the new material doesn't have the track record in actual use that the old material does. So we can't be completely sure about long-term reliability."

"Great, Christine," Vernon replies, "you've just made a bundle for ABC." Puzzled, Christine asks, "But shouldn't you tell XYZ about the change?" "Why?" Vernon asks, "The basic idea is to satisfy the customer with good quality parts, and you've just said we will. So what's the problem?"

The problem, Christine thinks to herself, is that the customer might not be getting a product with the same long-term reliability, although she admits that she does not know this is the case. Further, even if XYZ would be satisfied with the different part, shouldn't it be given the opportunity to decide if it finds the change acceptable—and to benefit from lowered cost?

Christine shares her further thoughts with Vernon. He replies, "I just don't agree, Christine. This is a management decision, not an engineering decision. XYZ will be a satisfied customer, and we'll be a satisfied supplier. We're not in the business of giving away money, you know. Besides, it cost us some time and money to find the new material."

The less expensive part is produced. As the shipment is prepared to be sent to XYZ, Christine is asked to sign a report verifying that the specifications for the part have been met. She is not sure whether Vernon's action involves any explicit violation of the contract. She wonders whether she would be violating her professional integrity by signing the document. What do you think?

Case 36   Promotion[59]

On the face of it, Darnell, Inc. has a strong commitment to affirmative action. Five years ago less than 1 percent of its professional and managerial staff were women. Now 8 percent are women. However, few of the women are in senior positions. Partly this is because most of the women have less seniority than the vast majority of men. But it is also because, until recently, there has been widespread skepticism at Darnell that women are well suited for the responsibilities that attach to the more senior positions. This may now be changing. Catherine Morris is one of the leading candidates for promotion to chief engineer in quality control at Darnell.

Although they work in different areas of Darnell, Judy Hanson and Catherine Morris have gotten to know one another rather well in the few months Judy has been with Darnell. Judy likes Catherine very much, but she has serious doubts that Catherine is the right person for the promotion. She does not think that Catherine has strong leadership qualities or the kinds of organizational skills that will be needed. Furthermore, she is worried that if Catherine fails at the job, this will only reinforce the prevailing skepticism at Darnell about women's ability to handle senior position responsibilities. Rather than

being a mark of women's progress at Darnell, it will be, Judy fears, a setback—one that will take its toll on other women at Darnell.

What, if anything, should Judy do? Suppose Judy overhears several male engineers talking about Catherine's possible promotion. They remark that she will never be able to handle the job—and that this will show once and for all how foolish, and potentially harmful, affirmative action in the workplace is. What should she do? Suppose it is Tom Evans, not Judy, who overhears the conversation? What should he do? Suppose Tom and Judy overhear the conversation together. What should each do?

Case 37   Pulverizer

Fred is a mechanical engineer who works for Super Mulcher Corporation. It manufactures the Model 1 Pulverizer, a 10-hp chipper/shredder that grinds yard waste into small particles that can be composted and blended into the soil. The device is particularly popular with homeowners who are interested in reducing the amount of garden waste deposited in landfills.

The chipper/shredder has a powerful engine and a rapidly rotating blade that can easily injure operators if they are not careful. During the five years the Model 1 Pulverizer has been sold, there have been 300 reported accidents with operators. The most common accident occurs when the discharge chute gets plugged with shredded yard waste, prompting the operator to reach into the chute to unplug it. When operators reach in too far, the rotating blades can cut off or badly injure their fingers.

Charlie Burns, president of Super Mulcher, calls a meeting of the engineers and legal staff to discuss ways to reduce legal liability associated with the sale of the Model 1 Pulverizer.

The legal staff suggest several ways of reducing legal liability:

- Put bright yellow warning signs on the Model 1 Pulverizer that say, "Danger! Rapidly rotating blades. Keep hands out when machine is running!"
- Include the following warning in the owner's manual: "Operators must keep hands away from the rotating blades when machine is in operation."
- State in the owner's manual that safe operation of the Model 1 Pulverizer requires a debris collection bag placed over the discharge chute. State that operators are not to remove the debris collection bag while the Model 1 Pulverizer is running. If the discharge chute plugs, the owner is instructed to turn off the Model 1 Pulverizer, remove the debris collection bag, replace the debris collection bag, and restart the engine. .

From operating the Model 1 Pulverizer, Fred knows the discharge chute has a tendency to plug. Because the machine is hard to restart, there is a great temptation to run the unit without the debris collection bag—and to unplug the discharge chute while the unit is still running.

In each of the following scenarios discuss the various ways Fred attempts to resolve the problem.

Scenario 1: Fred suggests to his engineering colleagues that the Model 1 Pulverizer should be redesigned so it does not plug. His colleagues reply that the company probably cannot afford the expense of re-engineering the Model 1, and they conclude that the legal staff's recommendations should be sufficient. Dissatisfied, in his spare time Fred redesigns the Model 1 Pulverizer and solves the plugging problem in an affordable way.

Scenario 2: Fred says nothing to his colleagues about the impracticality of

requiring the machine to be run with the debris collection bag. He accepts the legal staff's advice and adds the warning signs and owner's manual instructions. No changes are made in the design of the Model 1 Pulverizer.

Scenario 3: Fred suggests to his engineering colleagues that they try to convince management that the Model 1 Pulverizer should be redesigned so that it does not plug. They agree and prepare a redesign plan that will cost $50,000 to implement. Then they take their plan to management.

Case 38   Recommendation for a Friend[60]

I

Mike Hubbard sat in his study composing a work of fiction on his word processor. His efforts were not supposed to be fiction; he was actually writing a letter of recommendation for a friend from college days, engineer Tom Fellows.

Roommates at State University, both had majored in mechanical engineering. Mike was a superior student and continued on to get a Ph.D. Tom struggled with his studies, received a lot of help from Mike, spent much time on extracurricular activities, and frequently borrowed money from Mike because of irresponsible spending habits. Tom went to work in industry as soon as he got his bachelor's degree. Mike and Tom remained lifelong friends and kept in reasonably close touch over the years.

After graduate school Mike went to work for XYZ in its research laboratory. Now, ten years later, he was manager of mechanical engineering research. Tom held a series of jobs at which he had not been particularly successful and, three years ago, with Mike's help, landed a job in XYZ's computer-aided design department.

Two weeks earlier Tom had informed Mike that he had lost his XYZ job in a departmental budget reduction effort. At Tom's request, Mike went to Tom's supervisor to ask if his job could be salvaged. "Tom is a great guy and not a bad engineer," his supervisor replied, "but he doesn't concentrate on getting work out; he's more interested in the golf league, office gossip, the stock market, and a lot of other things. Also, he's turned in some very high expense accounts for trips and, although I can't prove it, I think he's padding some of them—maybe all of them. Given all this, I think he's one of the obvious choices for my reduction-in-force."

Mike discussed these comments frankly with Tom, at which point Tom asked if Mike would prepare a general letter of recommendation to help him find another job. "You know I won't get much of a recommendation from my supervisor," said Tom, "and, Mike, you've known me for years and know my abilities. If you help me get another job I'll really buckle down and show you how good an engineer I can be!"

So Mike sat at his word processor trying to put together a reasonably positive letter of recommendation for his friend. The letter contained a series of positive statements about Tom's ability and enthusiasm, was addressed "To Whom It May Concern," and given to Tom. Tom's weaknesses were not included. Although he did not state it explicitly, Mike implied that Tom had worked directly for him.

Several weeks had passed when Mike received a telephone call from the director of engineering of a small company that purchased components from XYZ. The director had interviewed Tom, was given Mike's letter, and was calling to discuss Tom's ability in regard to a specific project management assignment. Mike was as enthusiastic as pos-

sible because he felt the assignment would probably be one in which Tom would work well if he applied himself.

A few days later Tom telephoned Mike to tell him he had the job. Mike offered Tom serious advice about giving his all to this new job, and Tom assured Mike he had learned the "error of my ways."

Identify and discuss the ethical issues Mike Hubbard faced. How do you think he should have handled Tom's request to write a letter of recommendation for him? Assuming Tom works out well at his new job, do you think Mike acted appropriately?

II

A couple of months passed, during which Mike Hubbard and Tom Fellows played golf a couple of times; Tom told Mike that he had "everything under control" and that the job was working out well. Mike breathed a sigh of relief and felt he had really done the right thing in writing the letter of recommendation.

Mike's peace of mind was soon rudely shattered. One day he received a call asking him to come to the office of Pat Berry, Mike's boss and XYZ's director of research. When Mike entered Pat Berry's office, he found XYZ's director of human resources, Pete Gettings, also present.

"Mike, we've got a serious situation to discuss with you," Pat opened immediately. "A couple of days ago I got a telephone call from a long-time acquaintance of mine. He's vice president of engineering at the company Tom Fellows has joined. He said that recommending our 'dead wood' was not a very desirable way to treat a customer and wondered if they should continue to do business with us. He told me that Fellows had made an absolute mess of the management of a project assigned to him and had probably cost them a major government contract. When I questioned Pete about why we recommended Fellows, he had no record of making any recommendation at all. So I called my friend back. He said the individual in question had a letter of recommendation from you, Mike, which you further backed up in a telephone conversation with their director of engineering. What do you know about all of this?"

How should Mike answer Pat Berry's question? What action, if any should Pat Berry take against Mike?

Case 39   Renewable Energy[61]

Dwayne Breger, a civil and environmental engineer at Lafayette College, invited junior and senior engineering, biology, and environmental science students to apply to be on an interdisciplinary team to design a project that would use farmland owned by Lafayette College in a way that supports the college mission. Twelve students were selected for the project: two each from civil and environmental engineering, mechanical engineering, chemical engineering, and Bachelor of Arts in engineering, plus three biology majors and one in geology and environmental geosciences. These students had minors in such areas as economics and business, environmental science, chemistry, government, and law. The result of the project was a promising design for a biomass farm that could provide an alternative, renewable resource for the campus steam plant.[62]

This can be described as a service-learning project. Duane Breger regards projects such as this as providing important opportunities for students to involve themselves in work that contributes to restructuring our energy use toward sustainable resources. Of course, there are many other kinds of useful collaborative projects that students could undertake.[63] Discuss how such collaborative projects might contribute to students learning

about the ethical dimensions of engineering practice.

Case 40   Side-Saddle Gas Tanks

From mid-November 1992 through mid-February 1993, media coverage of the 1973 to 1987 Chevrolet and GMC pickup trucks was intense. In mid-November, two *New York Times* articles discussed a controversy about the models' fuel tank systems. These models placed a gas tank on each side of the vehicle, both outside the truck frame. The articles raised several important ethical questions about safety and responsibility. Although much that is contained in the articles is basically informational, the headlines make it clear that the primary intent is to prompt readers to focus on these ethical issues: "Data Show GM Knew for Years of Risk in Pickup Trucks' Design"; and "Despite Report that U.S. Standard Wasn't Cutting Fatal Car Fires, Little Was Done."[64]

Although the articles are bylined (with Barry Meier listed as author), they are not offered as editorial opinions. Readers are accustomed to informative pieces that may, nonetheless, slant information in one direction or another. The question here is whether these articles provide readers with the sorts of relevant information they need to adequately address the ethical questions.

The first headline suggests to readers that GM may have been negligent. Why, readers, may ask, did GM delay changing the location of the fuel tanks? Internal memos indicate that GM was trying to improve fuel tank safety as early as 1982. Yet, commenting on the change made in 1988, GM officials are quoted as saying it was made for reasons of design rather than safety.

Although the articles indicate that the issues are very complex, several matters are not in dispute. It is clear to all that the GM vehicles were in compliance with existing safety regulations. It is also clear to all that the redesigned models (beginning in 1988) render the gas tanks less vulnerable to damage in collisions. Although GM considered plans to relocate the gas tanks as early as 1982, the article notes that any significant change would require a "long lead time." The November 17 article cites a December 1983 internal GM document indicating GM's intention to change the fuel tank's position in 1987: "The fuel tank will be relocated inside the frame rails, ahead of the rear axle—a much less vulnerable location than today's tanks."[65]

According to the articles, one of GM's aims was to come up with a plan that would enable the vehicles to withstand collisions from the side without significant fuel leakage at speeds up to 50 mph—thus, far exceeding the 20-mph regulation in force since 1977. In 1984 a plastic shield for the tanks was introduced, successfully, according to GM director of engineering analysis, Robert A. Sinke, Jr.— but unsuccessfully, according to Clarence Ditlow, executive director of the Center for Auto Safety, who refers to this as a "Band-Aid fix." Despite introducing a redesign in 1988 that does seem to fulfill GM's aim to withstand 50-mph collisions, GM explained that the relocation of the gas tank was made for reasons of design, not safety.

Aside from questions about whether GM bore any special responsibility for past harms or deaths associated with the 1973 to 1987 model fuel tanks, at issue were two related questions about the present. First, should GM pickups manufactured during this period be recalled? Second, how safe or unsafe were these vehicles?

The National Highway Safety and Traffic Administration (NHSTA) was reportedly contemplating ordering a recall of the vehicles. One problem with this was that the vehicles were in compliance with existing regula-

tions; so, NHSTA would be questioning the adequacy of its own regulations. GM indicated it would resist any such recall as illegal. Further, when interviewed, a GM attorney, Chilton Varner, said that she believed the existing 20-mph standard was adequate to protect public safety. NHSTA, however, indicated that it might consider the question of whether the 20-mph standard was adequate. It might also consider whether the testing procedure itself should be changed. (The fuel tanks were presently tested by being struck with wide barriers at a 90-degree angle rather than with a narrower barrier at an oblique angle.)

This summary gives some idea of the complexity of the controversy. Meanwhile, the millions of owners of the vehicles in question wondered how safe their pickups were. Did the two articles help them determine this? Various data were provided (by different sources in the article). Thomas Carr, vice president of the Motor Vehicles Manufacturers Association (a trade group in Detroit) claimed that 66 percent of all fatal car crashes involving fires were at speeds exceeding 50 mph. (What Carr did not mention is that, apparently, fully 1/3 were not.) A 1990 study indicated that car fires have been reduced by 14 percent since the introduction of standards on fire safety, but that there was no observed reduction in the rate of fire-related deaths. (The report pointed out that the number of fires could decline without affecting the death rate if the fire deaths occurred at speeds above the standard.)

Failure Analysis Associates (a Houston consulting firm working with the auto industry) found that, from 1973 to 1989, GM pickups were involved in about 155 fatal side-impact collisions involving fires. Ford had 61 such accidents. However, the two companies had roughly the same number of pickups on the road. Federal investigators were still reviewing the fatal GM pickup accidents to see if the fires were actually caused by fuel tank leaks.

According to Sinke, to determine the safety of a vehicle, one must consider the overall picture. "Any time you look at a small slice of the whole apple, one manufacturer's vehicles will not look as good as others. You have to look at the whole apple, and our overall safety record is as good or better than anyone's."

According to Brian O'Neill, director of the Insurance Institute for Highway Safety, it is possible for a vehicle to have a fire problem and still have a good overall safety record, because fire deaths are only 4 percent of the highway fatalities. "Fires can get very easily lost in overall pool data, but the fire statistics suggest that they have a problem. It has been well known for a long time that fuel tanks near the perimeter of the vehicle are not a good idea."

NHSTA estimated that about 5,200 pickups and other light trucks catch fire every year. Older vehicles are more likely to catch fire than newer ones because of corrosion and other factors that could lead to fuel line and tank leakage.

Several days after the two *New York Times* articles were published, *Newsweek's* full-page account appeared. Entitled "Was GM Reckless?" the subtitle read, "The troubled automaker is accused of ignoring an unsafe gas-tank design."[66] Complete with a color photo of a GM pickup truck in flames flanked by diagrams of the pre-1988 tank locations and the current model, the article recounted much of the information provided in the *New York Times'* articles. But it made one significant addition. It cited a September 7, 1970, internal memo from GM safety engineer George Carvil that warned of possible fuel leaks resulting from side collisions: "Moving these side tanks inboard might eliminate most of these potential dangers."

A later Barry Meier *New York Times* article carried the headline, "Courtroom Drama Pits GM Against a Former Engineer."[67] Meier reported that former GM safety engineer Ronald E. Elwell had testified in an Atlanta jury trial that GM altered documents, conducted secret tests, and ordered employees not to criticize its vehicles in writing. Meier wrote:[68]

> In his testimony, Mr. Elwell contended that company officials knew in the early 1980's that the side-saddle fuel tank design was "indefensible." Furthermore, he said, the company a decade ago was developing a steel plate to protect the tanks against punctures in collisions.
>
> But development of the steel plate was dropped because officials feared it would alert the public to the tank's hazards, he testified. "It would produce the wrong image to the public," Mr. Elwell said.

Working against the credibility of Elwell's testimony was the fact that, in 1971, GM put him in charge of fuel safety for pickups, and he worked on the side-saddle design and later defended it. However, Meier reported:[69]

> Mr. Elwell has previously testified that he approved the tank's side location because the company, for marketing purposes, wanted to equip the pickups with large-capacity fuel tanks. But he said his views about the vehicle's safety changed in 1983, when he learned from his superior about company tests run from 1981 to 1983 that showed the tanks splitting open when a pickup was hit in the side by a car moving at 50 miles an hour.
>
> Mr. Elwell said he was outraged because G.M. had not made the tests available to him before he had testified in a San Francisco pickup case that year, leading him to feel he had perjured himself. "The tanks were split open like watermelons," he said.

Although GM officials and attorneys in the Atlanta case were not allowed to comment publicly on the case, Meier indicated that other lawyers not involved in the case predicted that GM would try to discredit Elwell's testimony, depicting him as a disgruntled former employee. Elwell reportedly complained that GM began easing him out of serving as an expert witness shortly after the 1983 San Francisco case. Some suggested that Elwell might be seeking revenge for being pushed into taking early retirement in 1986 after a thirty-year career at GM. (Elwell was 56 in early 1993.)

Meier concluded his article:[70]

> Though Mr. Elwell's motivations may never be fully clear, consumer advocates believe in him. "He could be out selling his testimony against General Motors, but he isn't doing that," said Clarence M. Ditlow, director of the Center for Auto Safety, a Washington Consumer group.
>
> G.M. lawyers also indicated in pre-trial dispositions that they might assert that Mr. Elwell threatened the company, for not hiring him as a private consultant after he retired.

On February 5, 1993, the verdict in the Atlanta jury trial was announced.[71] The court ruled that GM must pay $101 million to the parents of Shannon Moseley, a 17-year-old boy who burned to death in a 1989 crash in his GMC pickup. This was the first punitive award among the many court cases involving GM's side-saddle vehicles. The court also awarded $4.2 million in compensatory damages to Shannon Moseley's parents. GM objected to the $105.2 million verdict and indicated its intent to appeal.

Only three days later, on February 8, 1993, GM launched a vigorous attack against NBC for its November 1992 *Dateline NBC* portrayal of GM pickups.[72] *Dateline NBC* had presented footage to demonstrate what could happen to a GM pickup in a side-impact crash, showing a 1977 Chevrolet pickup erupting into flames. The NBC corre-

spondent explicitly stated that the demonstration was "unscientific" and that it was presented as a random experiment to see what might happen. However, she failed to mention that the private testing company in Indiana had attached tiny toy rockets to the underside of the truck and ignited them by remote control to make sure sparks would be present when a Chevrolet Citation struck the side of the pickup. Although NBC initially defended its actions, it soon issued a public apology. Public attention was suddenly shifted from safety issues to questions of media responsibility.

Press coverage of the GM controversy also made a decided shift. The May 10, 1993, issue of *Newsweek* carried a full-page article entitled, "Just as Safe at Any Speed: The Feds asked GM to recall its trucks, but has the pickup-fire flap unfairly tainted the automaker?"[73] The article reported that GM was challenging NHTSA's request for a "voluntary" recall of GM pickups, claiming that NHTSA's own data showed that GM trucks were safer to drive than most other vehicles. NHTSA's data indicated that drivers of GM pickups had a 1 in 6,605 chance of dying in an accident. Odds for Ford pickup drivers were only slightly better (1 in 6,916). For Dodge it was 1 in 8,606, whereas for Nissan's light, compact model it was 1 in 4,521. For all passenger cars it was 1 in 6,053.

However, *Newsweek* pointed out, these data were about fatalities in general, not fatalities related to fires. William Boehly, the NHTSA enforcement director who had asked for the "voluntary" recall, conceded that the GM pickups did well in *overall* safety—but not in regard to fatalities resulting from fire. *Newsweek* reported:[74]

> The NHTSA's investigators, relying in part on information compiled in 120 lawsuits filed against GM by personal-injury lawyers, detected a tendency for GM trucks to catch fire in fatal crashes

more often than big Ford or Dodge trucks. Fires rarely happen—only 6 percent of all big-pickup fatalities involve fires. Unfortunately for GM, federal regulators have targeted fires that are caused by side-impact collisions for special concern. The chances of an individual owner dying from this subset of fires is infinitesimal: a driver could spend 31,673 lifetimes before meeting such a fate, assuming he kept the truck for 15 years. Still, the NHTSA calculates that this tiny risk is 50 percent greater than the chance of a fatal fire in a Ford pickup during a similar accident. Those numbers are too high for safety advocates like Clarence Ditlow, who called the GM trucks "rolling firebombs." And it is this small risk—in a truck basically as safe as Ford's—that has led the NHTSA to ask GM for a recall.

According to *Newsweek*, Boehly claimed that NHTSA tests indicated that six lives a year might be saved if the pickups were fixed. GM's reply was that, to support this, NHTSA tests had to be highly selective for certain kinds of side-impact crashes—such as impacts against telephone poles at the point where cab and truck bed meet. GM's Ed Lechtzin is quoted as saying, "Our truck's safe. It's as if we get A-minus but still flunk the test."

Newsweek pointed out that the Highway Safety Act requires that NHTSA focus its attention on flaws that pose "an unreasonable risk to safety"; but, it concluded:[75]

> In the GM case, the NHTSA seems to be asserting that any vehicle below average in even one tiny aspect of its design is unreasonably risky. Applied systematically, the NHTSA would be establishing a rule that recalls Garrison Keillor's community of Lake Wobegon—"where all the children are above average." But Keillor was joking. The problem for GM is that the NHTSA watchdogs are not.

Identify the ethical issues surrounding the controversy over the GM side-saddle tanks. What are the relevant facts? What factual, conceptual, and application issues are there? Some more specific issues you might address are, Given that motor vehicles will always place us at some risk, how are we to understand "safe"? If NHSTA is questioning its own standards, what kinds of criteria do (and should) they use? Can a product be unacceptably risky even though it satisfies current safety regulations? What does it mean to say that a redesign improves safety but it was made for reasons of design rather than safety? Is this acceptable engineering practice? If a vehicle has an *overall* safety rating as good as its competitors, does it follow that it should not be required to improve any *particular* safety features?

Case 41   "Smoking System"[76]

Philip Morris has been testing a micro-electronic cigarette holder that eliminates all smoke except that exhaled by the smoker. Battery-powered, it is expected to cost about $50. The result of years of research, it cost approximately $200 million to develop.

Tentatively called the Accord, the device uses cigarettes that are 62 millimeters long (compared with the standard 85 millimeters). Users will have to remember to recharge the Accord's battery (a 30-minute process, but extra batteries can be purchased). A cigarette is inserted into the 4-inch long, 1 1/2-inch wide device. A microchip senses when the cigarette is puffed and transmits power to eight heating blades. A display shows the remaining battery charge and indicates how many puffs are left in the eight-puff cigarette. The device also contains a catalytic converter that burns off residues.

Supporters of this product say it will be welcomed by smokers who currently refrain from smoking in their homes or cars for the sake of nonsmoking family members, guests, and passengers. Although smokers will inhale the same amount of tar and nicotine as from conventional "ultralight" cigarettes, 90 percent of secondhand smoke will be eliminated. Furthermore, the same smoking restriction rules in public places will apply to the device.

Critics claim that the Accord will simply reinforce addiction to cigarettes. Richard A. Daynard, chair of the Tobacco Products Liability Project at Boston's Northeastern University School of Law, an antitobacco organization, asks: "Who would use an expensive and cumbersome thing like this if they weren't hooked? There is something grim and desperate about it. This is hardly the Marlboro Man, getting on his horse and checking the battery." He also expresses concern that children might be encouraged to smoke, because the Accord would enable them to hide smoking from their parents. However, Philip Morris replies that the device has a locking device for parents.

Consider the following questions:

- Imagine that it is several years ago and you have just received your engineering degree. You are in search of your first job. You are invited to interview with a research division of Philip Morris that is about to begin research to develop the Accord. Would you have any reservations about accepting such a position? Discuss.
- If you would have some reservations, would the fact that this job pays $10,000 more a year than any other offer you have convince you to take the Philip Morris offer?
- Assuming you took the job, what kinds of ethical concerns might you have about how the device should be designed? (For example, would you agree that it should have a locking device?)

Case 42   Sunnyvale[77]

I

Jim Grimaldi, projects manager in the Sunnyvale Division of Universal Corporation, has just learned that in two weeks the headquarters in Los Angeles will be sending him a project engineer, Joan Dreer. Her job will be to supervise small groups of engineers involved in automotive brake design. The Los Angeles headquarters is anxious to move women into all company levels, and it has targeted Grimaldi's engineering division at Sunnyvale as a good place for Joan Dreer.

Joan Dreer will be the first woman engineer at Sunnyvale. On learning that their new supervisor will be a woman, several of the engineers inform Jim Grimaldi that they don't like the idea of a woman supervising their work.

What, if anything, should Jim Grimaldi do to prepare for Joan Dreer's arrival?

II

Joan Dreer has been with the Sunnyvale Division for several months now. The contracts her groups have been working on have tight deadlines and allow only extremely narrow margins for error. So, the engineering groups have had to work at maximum speed and under a great deal of pressure. Jim Grimaldi has become increasingly concerned about the work of the groups under Joan Dreer's supervision. He comments:

A couple of months ago I was sent a new engineer from our plant in Los Angeles, Joan Dreer, and told to put her to work right away as a project engineer. The company was making a push to move women into all company levels but had apparently run into a lot of problems with their engineers down in Los Angeles. They had decided that our place would have the fewest problems adjusting to women, and they were pretty insistent that we find a way to work things out. When I first took Joan around our plant so she could get to know the men and the kind of work we do, several of the engineers took me aside and let me know in no uncertain terms that they didn't want a woman to supervise their work. To make matters worse, Joan came on as a pushy and somewhat aggressive feminist. When one of the young engineers asked her if she was a "Miss" or a "Mrs.," she retorted that her private life was her own affair and that he should get used to calling her "Ms."

Jim Grimaldi has not found any of the groups under Joan Dreer's supervision outrightly refusing to work. But they do seem to have been dragging their feet in small ways so that sometimes they miss their deadlines, and the other groups have also been showing some reluctance to cooperate with the groups under her supervision. So, Jim Grimaldi has become increasingly concerned about the impact Joan Dreer's presence seems to be having on his ability to meet deadlines, and he is concerned about how this might affect his own career. He is also worried about the safety factors involved in the brake design. He concludes:

> I agree that it's important to move women into supervisory positions in the company, but I don't know whether we can really afford to do it just yet. Women aren't really suited for this kind of work. I don't want to fire any of my engineers. That would be unfair because they have worked hard in the past under a lot of pressure. What should I do?

What do you think Jim Grimaldi should do? Explain. What ethical questions about this situation need to be raised?

III

Parts I and II provide little information about Joan Dreer and how she happened to come to Sunnyvale. Consider the following possible background information:

> Joan Dreer was excited about her transfer to Sunnyvale. But she was also apprehensive. Although she received very high marks for her work at the Los Angeles headquarters of Universal, she had just gone through an extremely unpleasant experience. Her immediate supervisor in Los Angeles made it very clear that, in return for a recent promotion, he expected sexual favors. When she resisted, he became verbally abusive and tried his best to make life miserable for her at Universal. His derisive remarks about women engineers did not go unnoticed by others—several of whom found them quite amusing. Fortunately, her complaints to the corporate ombudsperson were taken seriously. Disciplinary action was taken against the supervisor. Joan Dreer requested a transfer to a division that would be more receptive to women engineers. So, she hoped the Sunnyvale Division would give her a fresh start.
>
> Unfortunately, Joan Dreer's first day at Sunnyvale proved quite challenging. She took a small group of engineers by surprise when she entered the Sunnyvale lounge. A young engineer with his back to the door was commenting that he didn't like the idea of being told how to do his work by a woman, but that he would figure out how to handle the situation once he found out whether she was a "Miss" or a "Mrs." Another added, "Right, Johnson, what are you going to say to her, 'Should we call you Miss Honey or Mrs. Honey?'"
>
> The laughter ended abruptly when Joan Dreer's entrance was noticed. Realizing that she was facing her first challenge, she tersely announced, "Mr. Johnson, my private life is my own affair. You'd better get used to calling me 'Ms.'"

> How, if at all, does this background information change your understanding of the situation described in Part II? What do you now think are the major ethical concerns? How would you suggest they be approached?

Case 43   Training Firefighters[78]

Donald J. Giffels, civil engineer and president of a large engineering consulting firm, was puzzled by the design of a government facility to train firefighters who deal with fire crashes of airplanes. His firm was under contract to do the civil engineering work for installing equipment at the facility. Because it contaminates the soil, jet fuel had recently been replaced by liquid propane for simulating crash fires. However, Giffels was concerned about a lack of design specificity in a number of areas crucial to safety (for example, sprinkler systems, safeguards against flashbacks, fuel quantity, fuel controls). Furthermore, no design analysis was submitted. Giffels concluded that none existed. However, none of this fell within the direct responsibility of Giffels's firm, whose contract was simply to do the civil engineering work required for installation.

Nevertheless, Giffels concluded that his firm could not simply let this go. He contacted the designers and asked them how they could justify putting their professional seal of approval on the design. They replied, "We don't need to. We're the government." Giffels agreed, but he persisted (to the point, he suspects, of making a pest of himself). Noting that it is easy to be a minimalist (for example, stay within the law), Giffels worried that one might nevertheless fail to fulfill a responsibility to society. He contacted another engineering firm that had installed a similar design at ten sites. They, too, had been concerned about safety when looking at the designs. The firm had contacted a mechanical engineering firm, asking it to do a design study. This request was turned down because of liability fears. So, the civil engineering firm had asked the government agency to write a letter absolving it of any responsibility in case of mishaps due to the inadequate design.

Although not contesting the legality of this firm's way of dealing with the problem, Giffels insisted that this was not the right way to proceed. His company refused to proceed with the installation until the safety issues were adequately addressed. The government agency agreed to bring in three other firms to deal with the concerns. The contract Giffels's firm had was modified to provide assurances that the safety issues would be addressed. Giffels stresses the importance of being able to communicate effectively about these matters—a communication responsibility. Good communication, he says, is essential to getting others on board.

Although successful in its efforts to ensure safety, Giffels says that this is not a story that would receive press notice. However, *not* resisting, he insists, might well have resulted in press coverage—for example, if deaths of firefighters going through their simulations had resulted.

Discuss the ethical challenges facing Giffels and his strategy in dealing with them.

Case 44   Trees[79]

Kevin Clearing is the engineering manager for the Verdant County Road Commission (VCRC). VCRC has primary responsibility for maintaining the safety of county roads. Verdant County's population has increased by 30 percent in the past ten years. This has resulted in increased traffic flow on many secondary roads in the area. Forest Drive, still a two-lane road, has more than doubled its traffic flow during this period. It is now one of the main arteries leading into Verdant City, an industrial and commercial center of more than 60,000 people.

For each of the past seven years at least one person has suffered a fatal automobile accident by crashing into trees closely aligned along a three-mile stretch of Forest Drive. Many other accidents have also occurred, causing serious injuries, wrecked cars, and damaged trees. Some of the trees are quite close to the pavement. Two law suits have been filed against the road commission for not maintaining sufficient road safety along this three-mile stretch. Both were dismissed because the drivers were going well in excess of the 45-mph speed limit.

Other members of VCRC have been pressing Kevin Clearing to come up with a solution to the traffic problem on Forest Drive. They are concerned about safety, as well as lawsuits that may some day go against VCRC. Clearing now has a plan—widen the road. Unfortunately, this will require cutting down about thirty healthy, longstanding trees along the road.

Clearing's plan is accepted by VCRC and announced to the public. Immediately, a citizen environmental group forms and registers a protest. Pat Northington, spokesperson for the group, complains, "These accidents are the fault of careless drivers. Cutting down trees to protect drivers from their own carelessness symbolizes the destruction of our natural environment for the sake of human 'progress.' It's time to turn things around. Sue the drivers if they don't drive sensibly. Let's preserve the natural beauty and ecological integrity around us while we can."

Many letters on both sides of the issue appear in the Verdant Press, the issue is heatedly discussed on local TV, and Tom Richards presents VCRC with a petition to save the trees signed by 150 local citizen.

Discuss how Kevin Clearing should proceed at this point.

Case 45   TV Antenna[80]

Several years ago, a TV station in Houston decided to strengthen its signal by erecting a new, taller (1,000-foot) transmission antenna in Missouri City, Texas. The station contracted with a TV antenna design firm to design the tower. The resulting design employed twenty 50-foot segments that would have to be lifted up into place sequentially by a jib crane that moved up with the tower. Each segment required a lifting lug to permit that segment to be hoisted off the flatbed delivery truck and then lifted into place by the crane. The actual construction of the tower was done by a separate rigging firm that specialized in such tasks.

When the rigging company received the twentieth and last tower segment, it faced a new problem. Although the lifting lug was satisfactory for lifting the segment horizontally off the delivery truck, it would not enable the segment to be lifted vertically. The jib crane cable interfered with the antenna baskets at the top of the segment. The riggers asked permission from the design company to temporarily remove the antenna baskets and were refused. Officials at the design firm said that the last time they gave permission to make similar changes, they had to pay tens of thousands of dollars to repair the antenna baskets (which had been damaged on removal) and to remount and realign them correctly.

The riggers devised a solution that was seriously flawed. They bolted an extension arm to the tower section and calculated the size of the required bolts based on a mistaken analysis. A sophomore-level engineering student who had taken a course in statics could have detected the flaw, but the riggers had no engineers on their staff. The riggers, knowing they lacked engineering expertise, asked the antenna design company engineers to review their proposed solution. The engineers again refused, having been ordered by company management not only not to look at the drawings but also not to visit the construction site during the lifting of the last segment. Management of the design firm feared that they would be held liable if there were an accident. The designers also failed to suggest to the riggers that they should hire an engineering consultant to look over their lifting plans.

When the riggers attempted to lift the top section of the tower with the microwave baskets, the tower fell, killing seven men. The TV company was taping the lift of the last segment for future TV promotions, and the videotape shows the riggers falling to their death.

Consider how you would react to watching that tape if you were the design engineer who refused to look at the lifting plans, or if you were the company executive who ordered the design engineer not to examine the plans.

To make an analogy, consider a physician who examines a patient and finds something suspicious in an area outside her specialty. When asking advice from a specialist, the physician is rebuffed, on the grounds that the specialist might incur a liability. Furthermore, the specialist does not suggest that the patient should see a specialist.

What conceptions of responsibility seemed most prevalent in this case? Can you suggest other conceptions that might have helped avoid this tragedy?

Case 46 "Underground" Project[81]

Joe Hall walked out of Tom Evers's office feeling "on top of the world." A young and relatively inexperienced development engineer with XYZ Appliance, Joe had just been given the green light to develop an idea he had for a modular water purification device for the home. Not only had director of New Product Development Tom Evers liked the idea, he asked Joe to form and head a project team to develop a prototype of the device.

Joe found the task to be more challenging than he had expected. To keep costs down, Joe had to select team members with less experience than he wanted. Because of the inexperience of the team, some of Joe's design ideas and materials choices had to be corrected, and he soon realized that the cost of the prototype (and the ultimate selling price of the appliance) would be higher than he originally estimated.

However, finally the day came when the project team ran a successful series of tests on an operating prototype. Joe set up a review and demonstration with Tom. Tom then agreed to arrange a review with XYZ's vice president of marketing to ascertain marketing's interest in the water purification device. Unfortunately, the meeting with marketing did not go well. The marketing vice president interrupted Joe's presentation of product cost, saying "I wish you guys in development would ask for marketing input *before* you begin to work on a new product. I can tell you our department is not interested in any type of a water appliance! I think you've wasted company money and created an albatross. From my viewpoint, you can shut off the project and put your prototype 'on the shelf.' I'll get back to you if we ever develop interest in this area but don't expect that to be soon!"

Tom instructed Joe to write a final report and consign the prototype to the development "morgue." All team members were assigned to other projects.

Upset that his first project team leader assignment failed, Joe decided he could not give up so easily. XYZ had a policy of permitting R&D employees to use 10 percent of their time to pursue new ideas without any further authorization. So, Joe continued to work on his project during this time.

Although Joe had every intention of confining his time on the project to 10 percent, he soon got so absorbed that he spent more and more time. He made some additional vendor contacts to get improved materials, "conned" a friend in Electronics Research to work on the control system, and had the machine shop do some additional work on the prototype (charging the shop time to another project of his).

Although progress on Joe's other assignments suffered, he was able to make substantial improvements in the water purification appliance. He debated with himself about when, and how, to confess to Tom that he had not really closed out the project. He wished that he could somehow get market research data that would convince Tom it had been the right move to continue on the project, and to get him to push for a marketing go-ahead.

Joe often discussed the project with his wife, and one day she gave him an idea about how to get some quick market data. She had seen a food products exhibitor in a local shopping mall get passers-by to answer questionnaires about the products displayed. Joe arranged for members of his wife's garden club to demonstrate the water purification appliance at the local mall and ask viewers to fill out a questionnaire determining their interest in the appliance and the price they would pay if it were for sale. Joe was careful not to show any XYZ identification on the prototype, particularly because he had no authorization to remove it from the XYZ laboratory.

Despite an amateurish approach, a considerable amount of data was collected. Reviewing the data, Joe was more convinced than ever that he had developed a marketable product and was anxious to convince Tom of this. He was sure he could make a very persuasive argument about the potential market,

and that Tom would overlook the fact that Joe had overridden his orders to cease work on the appliance. Joe resolved to see Tom as soon as possible.

If you were Tom, how would you respond to Joe when he makes his presentation? Does the fact that Joe has a possible success on his hands justify what he did?

Case 47 Unlicensed Engineer [82]

Charles Landers, former Anchorage assemblyman and unlicensed engineer for Constructing Engineers, was found guilty of forging partner Henry Wilson's signature and using his professional seal on at least forty documents. The falsification of the documents was done without Wilson's knowledge, who was away from his office when they were signed. Constructing Engineers designs and tests septic systems. The signed and sealed documents certified to the Anchorage city health department that local septic systems met city wastewater disposal regulations. Circuit Judge Michael Wolverton banned Landers for one year from practicing as an engineer's, architect's, or land surveyor's assistant. He also sentenced him to 20 days in jail, 160 hours of community service, $4,000 in fines, and one year of probation. Finally, Landers was ordered to inform property owners about the problems with the documents; explain how he would rectify the problem; and pay for a professional engineer to review, sign, and seal the documents.

Assistant Attorney General Dan Cooper had requested the maximum penalty: a four-year suspended sentence and $40,000 in fines. Cooper argued that "the 40 repeated incidents make his offense the most serious within the misuse of an engineer's seal." This may have been the first time a case like this was litigated in Alaska. The attorney general's office took on the case after seeking advice from several professional engineers in the Anchorage area.

According to Cooper, Landers said he signed and sealed the documents because "his clients needed something done right away." (The documents were needed before going ahead with property transactions.) Landers's attorney, Bill Oberly, argued that his client should be sentenced as a least offender because public health and safety weren't really jeopardized—subsequent review of the documents by a professional engineer found no violations of standards (other than forgery and the misuse of the seal themselves). The documents were resubmitted without needing changes.

However, Judge Wolverton contended that Landers's actions constituted a serious breach of public trust. The public, he said, relies on the word of those, like professional engineers, who are entrusted with special responsibilities: "Our system would break down completely if the word of individuals could not be relied upon."

The judge also cited a letter from Richard Armstrong, chairman of the Architects, Engineers, and Land Surveyors Board of Registration for Alaska's Department of Commerce and Economic Development. Armstrong wrote:

> Some of the reasons for requiring professional engineers to seal their work are to protect the public from unqualified practitioners; to assure some minimum level of competency in the profession; to make practicing architects, engineers, and land surveyors responsible for their work; and to promote a level of ethics in the profession. The discovery of this case will cast a shadow of doubt on other engineering designed by properly licensed individuals.

Identify and discuss the ethically important elements in this case. How relevant is it that subsequent review showed that none of the falsified documents needed to be changed? (Although Judge Wolverton did not impose the maximum penalty, he did not treat Landers as a least offender.)

Case 48   USAWAY[83]

John Budinski, a quality control engineer at Clarke Engineering, has a problem. Clarke contracted with USAWAY to supply a product subject to the requirement that *all* parts are made in the United States. Although the original design clearly specifies that all parts must satisfy this requirement, one of Clarke's suppliers failed to note that one of the components has two special bolts that are made only in another country. There is not time to design a new bolt if the terms of the contract are to be met. USAWAY is a major customer, and John fears that not meeting the deadline can result in unfortunate consequences for Clarke.

John realizes that the chances of USAWAY discovering the problem on its own are slim. The bolts in question are not visible on the surface of the product. Furthermore, it is highly unlikely that those who work on repairs will notice that the bolts are foreign-made. In any case, Clarke is under contract to do any needed repairs. Meanwhile, it can work on a bolt design so that it will be ready with U.S.–made bolts when, and if, replacements are needed.

What possible courses of action are available to John Budinski? What do you think he should do?

Case 49   Vacation[84]

I

Dan Dorset had been looking forward to this trip for weeks. Once he was assigned to help

Rancott install its equipment for Boulding, Inc. he arranged his vacation at a nearby ski resort. The installation would be completed on the twelfth, and his vacation would begin on the thirteenth, leaving a full week of skiing with three of his old college buddies.

Unfortunately, not all of Rancott's equipment arrived on time. Only eight of the ten identical units were installed by mid-morning on the twelfth. Even if the remaining two units had arrived that morning, it would have taken another full day to install them. However, Dan was informed that it might take as long as two more days for the units to arrive.

"Terrific," Dan sighed, "there goes my vacation—and all the money I put down for the condo."

"No problem," replied Boulding engineer, Jerry Taft. Jerry had worked side by side with Dan as each of the first eight units was installed. "I can handle this for you. We did the first eight together. It's silly for you to have to hang around and blow your vacation." Jerry knew why Rancott had sent Dan to supervise the installation of his firm's new equipment. Rancott's equipment had to be properly installed to avoid risking serious injuries to those who use the equipment. For years Rancott had trusted its clients to follow the carefully stated directions for installation. But several recent accidents were directly traceable to failure to follow proper installation procedures. So, it was now Rancott's policy to send one of its engineers to supervise all installations.

Dan was confident that Jerry was as fully capable as he to supervise the installation of the remaining two units. What should Dan do?

II

Tempting as it is to leave early, Dan decides to stay until the job is completed. He loses all but the last two days of his vacation, but he feels he has done the right thing. Some time later Dan and his unit's chief of engineering, Ed Addison, are having a drink after work. Eventually, the conversation turns to Dan's vacation.

Dan: What would you have done if you found out I left before all the units were installed?

Ed: Honestly? Probably nothing. It sounds like Jerry Taft had everything under control.

Dan: So if I had called, you would have told me it was okay to leave before the job was completed?

Ed: I didn't say that. I don't think it would be wise for me to *officially* approve something like that. Then it would be my neck, too, if anything went wrong.

Dan: Meaning it would have been on my neck if anything had gone wrong?

Ed: Sure. My only point is that I probably wouldn't have done anything about your leaving early—unless something went wrong. That's a chance you would have been taking. But it sounds like it wouldn't have been a very big risk.

Dan: Would you have taken it?

Ed: That depends on how badly I wanted to ski. Actually, I never have cared for skiing—it's too risky.

What do you think of Ed's position on this matter? If Dan had known Ed's position when he was at Boulding, would it have been all right for Dan to leave early?

Case 50   Walkway Disaster

The tragic 1981 Kansas City Hyatt Regency walkway collapse received extensive coverage in the *New York Times* some four years after its occurrence. Here is how a November 16, 1985, article begins:

> KANSAS CITY Mo., Nov. 15—A state
> judge today found the structural engineers

for the Hyatt Regency Hotel guilty of "gross negligence" in the 1981 collapse of two suspended walkways in the hotel lobby that killed 114 people.

Many of those killed were dancing on the 32-ton walkways July 17, 1981, when an arrangement of rods and box beams suspending them from the ceiling failed. Others of the dead and 200 injured were crushed under the structures.

Judge James B. Deutsch, an administrative law judge for Missouri's Administrative hearing commission, in a 442-page ruling, found the structural engineers guilty of gross negligence, misconduct and unprofessional conduct.

One day before the judge's decision, the American Society of Civil Engineers (ASCE) announced a policy of holding structural engineers responsible for all aspects of structural safety in their building designs. This policy resulted from the deliberations of an ASCE committee named in 1983 to address questions raised by the disaster.

Judge Deutsch found the project manger guilty of "a conscious indifference to his professional duties as the Hyatt project engineer who was primarily responsible for the preparation of design drawings and review of shop drawings for that project." He also concluded that the chief engineer's failure to closely monitor the project manager's work betrayed "a conscious indifference to his professional duties as an engineer of record." Responsibility for the collapse, it was decided, lay in the engineering design for the suspended walkways. Expert testimony claimed that even the original beam design fell short of minimum safety standards. Substantially less safe, however, was the design that actually was used.

This court case shows that engineers can be held responsible, not only for their own conduct, but also for the conduct of others under their supervision. It also holds that engineers have special *professional* responsibilities, and it seems to acknowledge the importance of engineering societies in articulating and supporting those responsibilities. Discuss the extent to which you think engineering societies should play the sort of role ASCE did in this case. To what extent do you think practicing engineers should support (for example, by becoming members) professional engineering societies' attempts to articulate and interpret the ethical responsibilities of engineers.

Case 51   Waste Disposal[85]

I

ABC's chemical waste is stored in a warehouse at an off-site location. While inspecting the warehouse, engineer Scott Lewis notices several leaking drums. He calls Tom Treehorn, head of ABC's Division of Chemical Waste. Tom responds, "I'll be right over with a crew to bring the leaking drums over here." Scott points out that the law forbids returning chemical waste to the "home" site. Tom replies, "I know, but I don't have any confidence in the off-site folks handling this. We know how to handle this best. It might not be the letter of the law, but our handling it captures its spirit."

Scott believes that Tom Treehorn is serious about preventing environmental problems—especially those that might be caused by ABC. Still, he knows that the Environmental Protection Agency will be upset if it finds out about Tom's way of dealing with the problem; and if anything goes wrong, ABC could get into serious legal difficulties. After all, he thinks, ABC is not a waste disposal facility.

What should Scott do at this point?

1. Tell Tom that he will inform Tom's superior if Tom goes ahead with his plan.

2. Tell Tom that he will not interfere with Tom's plan, but he will not help him with it either.

3. Advise Tom not to go ahead with his plan but not interfere if Tom insists on going ahead anyway.

4. Say nothing and help Tom with his plan.

5. Other.

II

Although he isn't sure they are doing the right thing, Scott says nothing further to Tom and helps him load the leaking drums onto the truck for their return to ABC. The chemical waste is disposed of on the ABC site, with no apparent complications.

In further justification of his actions Tom points out to Scott that ABC also saved a lot of money by taking care of the problem themselves rather than having to pay someone else to dispose of the chemicals.

Do you agree that they chose the proper course of action?

III

It might well turn out that, for all practical purposes, this is the end of the matter—that no further complications ever arise. However, there is a "worst case" possible scenario. Consider the following:

It is now several years later. Tom Treehorn has retired and moved to Florida. Scott Lewis left ABC shortly after he discovered the chemical leaks in the warehouse. He is now a senior engineer in a company in a nearby city. One day, he is startled by a front-page story in the press. ABC is being charged with contaminating the groundwater in the community surrounding ABC. The paper claims there is substantial evidence that ABC had for years violated the law by dumping waste materials on site. Tom Treehorn is mentioned as the

main person who was in charge of overseeing the handling of chemical waste during the years of most flagrant violation. Those years included the short time Scott spent at ABC. A local group of citizens has started a class action suit against ABC.

Three weeks later Scott Lewis receives a letter requesting his appearance at a court hearing concerning the charges against ABC. What should Scott say in his testimony if asked if he was aware of any violations on the part of ABC?

Case 52   Whose Property?[86]

I

Derek Evans used to work for a small computer firm that specializes in developing software for management tasks. Derek was a primary contributor in designing an innovative software system for customer services. This software system is essentially the "lifeblood" of the firm. The small computer firm never asked Derek to sign an agreement that software designed during his employment there would become the property of the company. However, his new employer did.

Derek is now working for a much larger computer firm. Derek's job is in the customer service area, and he spends most of his time on the telephone talking with customers having systems problems. This requires him to cross-reference large amounts of information. It now occurs to him that by making a few minor alterations in the innovative software system he helped design at the small computer firm the task of cross-referencing can be greatly simplified.

On Friday Derek decides he will come in early Monday morning to make the adaptation. However, on Saturday evening he attends a party with two of his old friends, you and Horace Jones. It has been some time since you have seen each other, so you spend some time discussing what you have been doing recently. Derek mentions his plan to adapt the software system on Monday. Horace asks, "Isn't that unethical? That system is really the property of your previous employer."

"But," Derek replies, "I'm just trying to make my work more efficient. I'm not selling the system to anyone, or anything like that. It's just for my use—and, after all, I did help design it. Besides, it's not exactly the same system—I've made a few changes."

This leads to a discussion among the three of you. What is your contribution?

II

Derek installs the software Monday morning. Soon everyone is impressed with his efficiency. Others are asking about the "secret" of his success. Derek begins to realize that the software system might well have companywide adaptability. This does not go unnoticed by his superiors. So, he is offered an opportunity to introduce the system into other parts of the company.

Now Derek recalls the conversation at the party, and he begins to wonder if Horace was right after all. He suggests that his previous employer be contacted and that the more extended use of the software system be negotiated with the small computer firm. This move is firmly resisted by his superiors, who insist that the software system is now the property of the larger firm. Derek balks at the idea of going ahead without talking with the smaller firm. If Derek doesn't want the new job, they reply, someone else can be invited to do it; in any case, the adaptation will be made.

What should Derek do now?

III

Does Horace have any responsibility to alert the smaller firm about Derek's plans? Do you? What if Horace is friends with people who work at the smaller firm? What if you are?

Case 53   Why Won't They Read?[87]

Sid Fisher was fuming. The manager of mechanical engineering research for XYZ had spent most of the morning in a research project review. He had listened patiently at first, then impatiently, to two young engineers review their research efforts on the development of a more efficient heat transfer surface. Realizing they were reporting efforts that had been unsuccessful, he finally interrupted and exclaimed, "Do you men realize that you have gone down the same blind path that Edwards and O'Malley did about five years ago? Their detailed research report is in our technical library. Did you read it before you began your work?"

The two engineers admitted they had not heard of Edwards and O'Malley's previous work, had not read the report covering it, and had made no effort to check the current technical literature for related publications.

Sid thought about these wasted efforts and the money the unproductive research had cost his company. He remembered, painfully, at least two other recent efforts where inadequate literature research had cost XYZ the expense of wasted research and development activities. In one case a team of XYZ engineers worked hard for two years on a project only to discover that one of XYZ's competitors had a four-year-old patent covering almost precisely the same innovation they were developing. Until one of XYZ's patent attorneys called attention to the competitive patent after reading a monthly research report mentioning the engineers' project, none of the engineers on the development team had made any effort to review the patent literature.

In the second case, there had been a long, tedious research effort to modify the properties of a material for use in a new component of one of XYZ's products. No progress at all was made until one of XYZ's scientists got a clue at a technical society meeting that it might be useful to check an article in a foreign technical journal. The article provided major help in accelerating the materials development significantly.

Sid thought to himself, "Why won't my engineers read?" Certainly XYZ provided the wherewithal—a modern technical library adequately supplied with current and past engineering and scientific journals, facilities for computerized literature searching, and a staff to assist engineers and scientists in using literature resources. Most of his engineers seemed to lack the incentive to read the literature, Sid thought. At best they seemed to confine their reading to a current trade journal or two.

Looking for clues to cure the "won't read" syndrome, Sid called an old friend who was head of the mechanical engineering department at a nearby university. He asked him what sort of reading requirements were part of an engineer's course of study at present. The department head explained that engineering students, because of demanding course loads, did well to read the assigned textbooks and related technical handbooks and computer manuals. Significant outside reading began only in the M.S. or Ph.D. thesis research program. Not overly encouraged by this response, Sid began to think about what he could do to encourage greater use of available technical literature on the part of his engineers.

Discuss the responsibilities XYZ engineers have to keep up with readings relevant to

their research. What responsibilities does Sid Fisher have in this regard? What might Sid Fisher do to deal effectively with this problem? Do university engineering programs have any special responsibility to help companies like XYZ with this problem?

Case 54   Window Safety[88]

W. Lynn Beason is an engineer who often serves as a consultant or expert witness in his area of specialization, window safety. He became interested in this as an area of research as a graduate student when the area in which he lived was hit by a tornado. He saw that there were design problems with windows, and he decided to try to clear them up. Now he regards himself as a public safety advocate. Eschewing the label of "crusader," he says that he simply uses the public interest as a guidepost when undertaking his work, especially as an expert witness. Noting that some engineers he knows operate as "guns for hire" when serving as expert witnesses, Beason is very uncomfortable with this. Instead he says to a potential client: "I will look at your case, and I will do my best to understand the truth of your case, and I will tell you what I think; and if you want me, that's great, and if you don't, just pay me what you owe me and I'm gone. And I tell that to everybody, you know, because that's very comfortable."

This does not mean that Lynn Beason's life as an expert witness is easy. What he says on the witness stand is not necessarily welcomed by all sides.[89] Threatened with being sued for over a million dollars for allegedly making false statements in questioning someone's window safety testing methods posed his greatest challenge. But instead of backing off, he filed a countersuit and continued his campaign. Eventually, his adversary withdrew its suit against him. Undaunted by the unpleasantness (and potential costliness) of all this, Beason remains dedicated to his cause. He describes himself as a very stubborn, persistent person.

Reflecting on his approach to his work, Beason says, "I would like to feel good about what I do, okay, and you know, you can do lots of things and not feel bad about what you do, but I would like to feel good about what I do."

Discuss Lynn Beason's way of handling expert witnessing, including his rationale.

Case 55   Wonderful Development?[90]

Philip Harding is an engineer at a small family business called Wonder Products, Inc. (WPI). The majority of WPI's work involves designing and producing parts for larger products that are sold by other companies. WPI is under contract to design and produce a complex component for General Farm's (GF) farm harvesting equipment.

Despite a nagging, though small, problem that does not find a "perfect" solution, WPI designs the part to GF's satisfaction. The price is set at $200 for each component. GF orders 1,000 components, with the understanding that because things have gone so well, they will be talking to WPI and Philip about other contracts.

WPI begins production and ships a sample of the order to GF on time. GF at this point is very happy with the component and wants WPI to ship the remainder of the order as soon as feasible. As Philip is working on the component, he thinks of an apparent solution to the "nagging problem" that bothered him through design. It would be a small change in the production process while incurring four dollars more per part. The improvement in

the part would be significant, but it would not be considered revolutionary in its design.

Because he is in a rush to complete the order, Philip does not have much time to work on anything other than the order. He wonders if he should investigate this new idea immediately or wait until he has more time to test it. He decides to work over the weekend and check out his new idea.

Philip confirms the fact that the new design solves the problem. But he has gotten slightly behind in the order. He brings the development to the attention of others at WPI. He says that although they can fulfill the contract and be safe from legal reproach if they say nothing to GF, they have an ethical obligation to offer the new design to GF immediately, whether or not WPI ends up picking up some of the costs for making changes. He contends that the flaw in the initial design was an oversight on WPI's part. "We contracted with GF with the understanding that we would provide them with the best design we could come up with," Philip says. "So we ought to tell them about the improvement."

The financial leader of the company, Connie, expresses her concern about the four dollar per part addition to production cost. She says that they are working on a narrow profit margin now; and although this represents only a 2 percent increase in cost, this really adds up to a fair amount of money as well as further production delays. She thinks that WPI would be better off introducing the improvement if and when GF makes another order.

Tim, in charge of sales and public relations, suggests a compromise. He suggests that they offer to share the cost of the improvement. Concerned with the image WPI projects, Tim worries about GF later complaining about WPI not coming to them with the development during the first order. Although WPI could insist that the design change was not conceived of until after the first order was made, there would always remain the doubt, indeed a correct doubt, that WPI held out on GF by not offering them the best product they could come up with. In the long run this could mean distrust and, in the worst scenario, a reducing or even severing of business ties between the two. "Granted," Tim acknowledges, "the withholding of this information would mean an increase in our short-term income. But it could mean a disaster to our future with GF—and a setback in our standing in the business community! Besides, we are behind as it is."

What do you think of Philip's position in this case? What options does WPI have? What do you think WPI should do?

Case 56   Working Overtime[91]

I

Ryan Redgrave was young, inexperienced in industry, and naive about industry methods of operating. He did, however, possess superb qualifications in statistics and in computer programming and applications. He was hired by XYZ to improve quality control in plastic parts.

Ryan began implementing elements of statistical process control, and steady improvement in the quality of plastic parts was observed. Ryan noted that one vendor, IMP, a small company, produced a high-quality raw material that gave a superior part except that frequently, when color was involved, their batch-to-batch color consistency was not good. He called this to the attention of IMP's sales representative, Mark, a personable young man about Ryan's age. Mark asked for Ryan's help in solving the inconsistency problem, and over dinner one evening Ryan outlined a series of experiments to get to the root cause of the color inconsistency.

Mark agreed that IMP would supply the necessary material samples, and Ryan worked late several nights to conduct the experiments he had devised. As a result of these experiments, Ryan was able to suggest some formulation changes to Mark to improve the color consistency of their raw material. To show his gratitude, Mark took Ryan and his wife to an expensive restaurant for dinner. "This will make up for some of the late hours you worked trying to solve our mutual quality problem," Mark exclaimed.

The formulation changes Ryan suggested did work and the color consistency of the IMP material improved markedly. Mark continued to check its performance on frequent sales calls at XYZ. The friendship between Mark and Ryan grew, with Mark frequently taking Ryan to lunch. On several of these occasions, Mark urged Ryan to recommend that XYZ buy more of its plastic from IMP.

Ryan did recommend to his procurement department that, because of the improved quality of the material, XYZ buy more from IMP. A small increase was put into effect, although procurement told Ryan that IMP's price was the highest of any of the plastics vendors with which XYZ dealt.

Identify and discuss any ethical issues this case raises. Has Ryan done anything wrong? Mark? Ryan worked extra hours, without pay, to improve IMP's color consistency; so, is this an instance of "good works" on his part?

II

Shortly after IMP was granted a larger order, Mark stopped by Ryan's office at XYZ to invite him to accompany several other IMP customers on a short ski trip to Colorado. Although only a beginning skier, the thrill of skiing the Colorado slopes was so appealing that Ryan accepted the invitation.

XYZ policy prohibited accepting favors from vendors, but this had never been communicated to Ryan and he saw nothing wrong with accepting the invitation. He did not know that two members of XYZ's procurement department had also been invited on the trip but declined because of the company's policy.

When Ryan mentioned the ski trip to a fellow employee in quality control, he was told he was violating a company policy. But Ryan decided he had earned the trip, would go anyway, and told his fellow employee to say nothing. Ryan advised his supervisor he was going to take a couple of days vacation "to catch up on some repairs on the house."

Ryan enjoyed the skiing trip immensely—especially as its cost was beyond anything he could have managed on his own budget. Unfortunately, he was not as expert a skier as he should have been. On the last day he took a bad fall, strained his shoulder, and returned home with his arm in a sling. At work the following Monday he explained that he had fallen off a ladder while cleaning ice from the eaves of his house.

Secrets are difficult to keep, even in industrial plants. Word reached Ryan's supervisor about the ski trip, and he called Ryan in to discuss the policy violation. Ryan pleaded ignorance of the policy, and the supervisor let him off with a verbal reprimand and the instruction that he contact IMP and repay the cost of the trip.

Ryan telephoned Mark, asked how much the trip cost, and told him why he needed to know. Mark laughed. "Forget it, Ryan, you earned that trip for what you did in helping us with our quality. If anyone asks us, we'll tell them you paid for your share. We may need your help again!" Ryan was greatly relieved because there was no room in his family budget to repay such a trip.

Identify and discuss the ethical issues in this case. Should Ryan have accepted Mark's final offer? Why would XYZ have a policy prohibiting free ski trips? Did Ryan's coworker have any special responsibility to more aggressively discourage Ryan from taking the trip? Do you think Ryan's supervisor handled the situation well?

Case 57   XYZ Hose Co.[92]

Farmers use anhydrous ammonia to fertilize their fields. The anhydrous ammonia reacts violently with water, so care must be exercised in disbursing it. Farmers' cooperatives rent anhydrous ammonia in pressurized tanks equipped with wheels, so the tanks can be pulled by tractors. The farmers also rent or purchase hoses that connect the tanks to perforated hollow blades that can be knifed through the soil to spread the ammonia. Leaks from the hose are potentially catastrophic.

For years the industry standard hose was one made of steel-meshed reinforced rubber, which was similar in construction to steel-reinforced automobile tires. Two separate trade associations had established these industrywide standards.

About twenty years ago a new, heavy-duty plastic became available that could replace the steel in the hoses. The plastic-reinforced hoses were less expensive, lighter, and easier to process than the steel-braided rubber. The new hose met the industry standards. One company, the XYZ Hose Company, began marketing the plastic-reinforced hose to farmers. Officials of XYZ knew, as a result of tests run by a consultant at a nearby state agricultural college, that the plastic did not react immediately to the anhydrous ammonia; however, over the years the plastic did degrade and lose some of its mechanical properties. Accordingly, they put warnings on all the hoses they manufactured, indicating that they should be replaced periodically.

After the product had been on the market a few years, several accidents occurred in which the XYZ hoses ruptured during use and blinded and severely injured the farmers using them. Litigation followed, and XYZ argued in its defense that the farmers had misused the hoses and not heeded the replacement warnings. This defense was unsuccessful, and XYZ made substantial out-of-court settlements.

XYZ has since dropped this product line and placed advertisements in farmers' trade journals and producers' cooperatives newsletters asking farmers to turn in their XYZ hoses for full refunds. The advertisements stated that the hoses are "obsolete," not that they are unsafe.

Identify and discuss the ethical issues this case raises, paying special attention to relevant, key ideas presented in Chapter 7. What are the relevant facts? What factual, conceptual, and application issues are there? What methods for resolving these issues might be used?

Notes

1. From Michael S. Pritchard, "Professional Responsibility: Focusing on the Exemplary," *Science and Engineering Ethics*, 4 (1998), 222.

2. This account is based on Linell Smith, "Air Bags Are His Bag," *Baltimore Sun* (July 7, 1997), sect. d1, d8.

3. This case is based on a personal interview with Tom Talley, as well as on Dave Wylie's, "AVIT Team Helps Disabled Children," *Currents, Electrical Engineering*, Texas A&M University (Summer 1993), 7.

4. From NSF Grant No. DIR-8820837, in Michael S. Pritchard, ed., *Teaching Engineering Ethics: A Case Study Approach*, June 1992. The case and accompanying commentaries are on pp. 25–36.

5. This account is based on John H. Cushman, Jr., "G.M. Agrees to Cadillac Recall in Federal Pollution Complaint," *New York Times* (December 1, 1995), A1, A12.

6. The following set of case studies is inspired by two short fictional cases presented by Philip M. Cohn and Roy V. Hughson in *Chemical Engineer* (May 5, 1980). "The Falsified Data" and "The Falsified Data Strike Back" are just two of several fictional cases they present in this issue. They appear on pp. 100–107.

7. Sissela Bok, *Lying: Moral Choice in Public and Private Life* (New York: Random House, 1978), pp. 32–33.

8. Case and commentaries from Pritchard, *Teaching Engineering Ethics*, pp. 61–76.

9. This fictional case is an adaptation of W. Gale Cutler, "Did Jack 'Fake' It?," *Research.Technology. Management* (May/June 1988), 50. This adaptation and accompanying commentaries are in Pritchard, *Teaching Engineering Ethics*, pp. 37–47.

10. This account is based on Rachel Konrad, "Engineers Find Cost-Cutting Takes Top Priority on Projects," *Detroit Free Press* (February 25, 1998), sect. E1.

11. Case and commentaries from Pritchard, *Teaching Engineering Ethics*, pp. 77–91.

12. Pritchard, *Teaching Engineering Ethics*, pp. 92–113.

13. See the commentary on this case by Wade Robison in Pritchard, *Teaching Engineering Ethics*, pp. 105–108.

14. For a discussion of the shortcomings of the committee from the standpoint of organizational communication and Irving Janis's theory of "groupthink," see Lea Stewart's commentary on this case in Pritchard, *Teaching Engineering Ethics*, pp. 92–113. Janis's theory of "groupthink" is discussed in Chapter 5 in this book.

15. Case and commentaries from Pritchard, *Teaching Engineering Ethics*, pp. 114–131.

16. From Michael S. Pritchard, "Professional Responsibility: Focusing on the Exemplary," *Science and Engineering Ethics*, 4 (1998), 230–233. In addition to sources cited below, there is an excellent PBS *Frontline* documentary on Cuny, "The Lost American." This is available at PBS Video, P.O. Box 791, Alexandria,

VA 22313-0791. There is a wealth of additional information on Cuny on website http://www.pbs.org/wgbh/pages/frontline/shows/cuny/bio/chron.html. Also, Cuny is featured as a Moral Leader on the WWW website Ethics Center for Science and Engineering: http://ethics.cwru.edu.

17. Karen W. Arenson, "Missing Relief Expert Gets MacArthur Grant," *New York Times* (June 13, 1995), A12.

18. Ibid.

19. From INTERTECT's corporate brochure.

20. Ibid.

21. Quoted in William Shawcross, "A Hero of Our Time," *New York Review of Books* (November 30, 1995), 35. The next paragraph is based on Shawcross's article.

22. The following is based on Chuck Sudetic, "Small Miracle in a Siege: Safe Water for Sarajevo," *New York Times* (January 10, 1994), A1, A7.

23. This account is based on "The Talk of the Town," *New Yorker, 69,* no. 39 (November 22, 1993), 45–46.

24. Ibid.

25. Ibid. This expresses a thought attributed to Cuny.

26. Frederick C. Cuny, "Killing Chechnya," *New York Review of Books* (April 6, 1995), 15–17.

27. Marilyn Greene, "Texas Disaster Relief 'Visionary' Vanishes on Chechnya Mission," *USA Today* (May 10, 1995), A10.

28. Shawcross, 39.

29. "Talk of the Town," p. 46.

30. Sudetic, A7.

31. Case and commentaries from Pritchard, *Teaching Engineering Ethics,* pp. 245–263.

32. For an insightful discussion of under what kinds of circumstances one can compromise without thereby compromising one's integrity, see Martin Benjamin, *Splitting the Difference* (Lawrence: University Press of Kansas, 1990).

33. Case and commentaries from Pritchard, *Teaching Engineering Ethics,* pp. 132–147.

34. Case and commentaries from Pritchard, *Teaching Engineering Ethics,* pp. 148–171.

35. The information for this case is drawn from William M. Carley, "Fatal Flaws: Artificial Heart Valves That Fail Are Linked to Falsified Records," *Wall Street Journal* (November 7, 1991), A6. For a discussion of ethical issues in this case, see John H. Fielder, "Ethical Issues in Biomedical Engineering: The Bjork-Shiley Heart Valve," *IEEE Engineering in Medicine and Biology* (March 1991), 76–78.

36. Loren Graham, *The Ghost of an Executed Engineer* (Cambridge, Mass.: Harvard University Press, 1993).

37. Ibid., p. 106.

38. This video, produced in 1989, is available from NSPE in Alexandria, Va.

39. This is an adaptation of W. Gale Cutler's fictional case, "Brenda Hits the Ceiling," *Research. Technology.Management* (January/February 1989), 51–52.

40. Case and commentaries from Pritchard, *Teaching Engineering Ethics,* pp. 172–189.

41. This is an adaptation of a case developed by James Taylor, Department of Civil Engineering, Notre Dame University.

42. This account is drawn from R. W. Flumerfelt, C. E. Harris, M. J. Rabins, and C. H. Samson, Eds., *Introducing Ethics Case Studies into Required Undergraduate Engineering Courses,* NSF Grant No. DIR-9012252, November 1992. The full version is on our CD-ROM.

43. Paula Wells, Hardy Jones, and Michael Davis, *Conflicts of Interest in Engineering,* Module Series in Applied Ethics, Center for the Study of Ethics in the Professions, Illinois Institute of Technology (Dubuque, Iowa: Kendall/Hunt, 1986), p. 20.

44. American Society of Mechanical Engineers, Boiler and Pressure Vessel Code, section IV, paragraph HG-605a.

45. Charles W. Beardsley, "The Hydrolevel Case—a Retrospective," *Mechanical Engineering* (June 1984), 66.

46. Ibid., 73.

47. Case and commentaries from Pritchard, *Teaching Engineering Ethics,* pp. 199–213.

48. Case and commentaries from Pritchard, *Engineering Ethics,* pp. 368–382.

49. This case is an adaptation of "Cover-up Temptation," one of several fictional vignettes appearing in Roger Ricklefs, "Executives Apply Stiffer Standards Than Public to Ethical Dilemmas," *Wall Street Journal* (November 3, 1983).

50. From Michael S. Pritchard, "Professional Responsibility: Focusing on the Exemplary," *Science and Engineering Ethics*, 4 (1998), 222.

51. Carole Beers, "Don Shakow's Moral Beliefs Put to Test in the Workplace," *Seattle Times* (February 16, 1997), B4.

52. This case was developed by P. Aarne Vesilind, Department of Civil and Environmental Engineering at Duke University.

53. Case and commentaries from Pritchard, *Teaching Engineering Ethics*, pp. 284–309.

54. Information for this case is based on a case study prepared by Manuel Velasquez, "The Ford Motor Car," in Manuel Velasquez, *Business Ethics: Concepts and Cases*, 3rd ed. (Englewood Cliffs, N.J.: Prentice Hall, 1992), pp. 110–113.

55. *Grimshaw v. Ford Motor Co.*, app., 174 Cal. Rptr. 348, p. 360.

56. This is reported in Ralph Drayton, "One Manufacturer's Approach to Automobile Safety Standards," *CTLA News*, VIII, no. 2 (February 1968), 11.

57. Mark Dowie, "Pinto Madness," *Mother Jones* (September/October 1977), 28.

58. Case and commentaries from Pritchard, *Teaching Engineering Ethics*, pp. 310–324.

59. Case and commentaries from Pritchard, *Teaching Engineering Ethics*, pp. 325–335.

60. This is an adaptation of W. Gale Cutler's fictitious case, "Tom Asks for a Letter of Reference," *Research.Technology.Management* (November/December 1990), 47–48.

61. From Michael S. Pritchard, "Professional Responsibility: Focusing on the Exemplary," *Science and Engineering Ethics*, 4 (1998), 224.

62. See the May 1997 report by the Biomass Energy Design Project Team, "Design and Feasibility Study of a Biomass Energy Farm at Lafayette College as a Fuel Source for the Campus Steam Plant."

63. See the analysis of the Texas A&M AVIT project.

64. Barry Meier, "Data Show G.M. Knew for Years of Risk in Pickup Trucks' Design," *New York Times* (November 17, 1992), A1, A10. Barry Meier, "Despite Report That U.S. Standard Wasn't Cutting Fatal Car Fires, Little Was Done," *New York Times* (November 21, 1992), A6.

65. Meier, "G.M. Knew," A10.

66. *Newsweek* (November 30, 1992), 61. The article is written by Thomas McCarroll.

67. Barry Meier, "Courtroom Drama Pits G.M. Against a Former Engineer," *New York Times* (January 19, 1993), C1, C14.

68. Ibid., C14.

69. Ibid.

70. Ibid.

71. Michael J. McCarthy and Douglas Lavin, "GM Ordered by Jury to Pay $105.2 Million over Death," *Wall Street Journal* (February 5, 1993), A3.

72. Elizabeth Kolbert, "In TV 'Crash,' News and Law Collide," *New York Times* (February 10, 1993), A16.

73. Rich Thomas, with Frank Washington and Myron Stokes, "Just as Safe at Any Speed," *Newsweek* (May 10, 1993), 52.

74. Ibid.

75. Ibid.

76. This case is based on Glenn Collins, "What Smoke? New Device Keeps Cigarettes in a 'Box,'" *New York Times* (October 23, 1997), A1, C8.

77. Parts I and II of this case study adapted from Manuel Velasquez, *Business Ethics*, 1st ed. (Englewood Cliffs, N.J.: Prentice Hall, 1981), p. 6.

78. From Michael S. Pritchard, "Professional Responsibility: Focusing on the Exemplary," *Science and Professional Ethics*, 4 (1998), 225–226. This is based on Donald J. Giffels's commentary on Pritchard's talk, "Education for Responsibility: A Challenge to Engineers and Other Professionals," at the Third Annual Lecture in Ethics in Engineering, Center for Academic Ethics, Wayne State University, April 19, 1995.

79. Cases and commentaries from Pritchard, *Teaching Engineering Ethics*, pp. 418–430.

80. This case is presented in greater detail, complete with an instructor's guide and student handouts, in R. W. Flumerfelt, C. E. Harris, M. J. Rabins, and C. H. Samson, Eds., *Introducing Ethics Case Studies into Required Undergraduate Engineering Courses*, final report to NSF on Grant No. DIR-9012252, November 1992, pp. 231–261. This report is on our accompanying CD-ROM.

81. This fictional case study is an adaptation of W. Gale Cutler's case study, "Joe Takes His Project 'Underground,'" in *Research.Technology.Management*, pp. 51–52.

82. This case is based on Molly Galvin, "Unlicensed Engineer Receives Stiff Sentence," *Engineering Times 16*, no.10 (October 1994), 1, 6.

83. Case and commentaries from Pritchard, *Teaching Engineering Ethics*, pp. 431–444.

84. Pritchard, pp. 445–461.

85. Pritchard, pp. 462–475.

86. Pritchard, pp. 336–346.

87. This is based on W. Gale Cutler's fictional case, "When 'Johnny' Won't Read," *Research.Technology. Management* (September/October 1988), 53.

88. This is from Michael S. Pritchard, "Professional Responsibility: Focusing on the Exemplary," *Science and Engineering Ethics*, 4 (1998), 226.

89. For an illustration of Beason's involvement in areas of considerable controversy, see his articles, "The New SBCCI Impact Standard," *Glass Magazine* (February 1996), 35–41; and "Impact Resistance Testing," *Glass Magazine* (February 1996), 42–43.

90. Case and commentaries from Pritchard, *Teaching Engineering Ethics*, pp. 476–484.

91. This is an adaptation of W. Gale Cutler's fictional case, "Ryan Goes Skiing," *Research.Technology. Management* [n.d.], 48–49.

92. This case is supplied by an engineering colleague who was an expert witness in the case. We have given the company the fictitious name of "XYZ." See R. W. Flumerfelt, C. E. Harris, M. J. Rabins, and C. H. Samson, *Introducing Ethics Case Studies into Required Undergraduate Engineering Courses*, pp. 287–312 for a fuller account.

Bibliography

Books and Monographs

Alger, P. L., Christensen, N. A., and Olmstead, S. P. *Ethical Problems in Engineering*. New York: Wiley, 1965.

Alpern, K. D. "Moral Responsibilities for Engineers," *Business and Professional Ethics Journal*, Vol. 2, No. 2, 1983, 39–48.

Anderson, R M., Perrucci, R., Schendel, D. E., and Trachtman, L. E. *Divided Loyalties: Whistle-Blowing at BART*. West Lafayette, IN: Purdue Research Foundation, 1980.

Bailey, M. J. *Reducing Risks to Life: Measurement of the Benefits*. Washington DC: American Enterprise Institute for Public Policy Research, 1980.

Baier, K. *The Moral Point of View*. Ithaca, NY: Cornell University Press, 1958.

Baker, D. "Social Mechanics for Controlling Engineers' Performance." In Albert Flores, Ed., *Designing for Safety: Engineering Ethics in Organizational Contexts*. Troy, New York: Rensselaer Polytechnic Institute, 1982.

Baram, M. S. "Regulation of Environmental Carcinogens: Why Cost-Benefit Analysis May Be Harmful to Your Health," *Technology Review*, Vol. 78 (July-August) 1976.

Baron, M. *The Moral Status of Loyalty*. Dubuque, Iowa: Center for the Study of Ethics in the Professions, Kendall/Hunt, 1984.

Baum, R. J. "Engineers and the Public: Sharing Responsibilities," in Wueste, D. E., Ed. *Professional Ethics and Social Responsibility* Lanham, MD: Rowman and Littlefield, 1994.

Baum, R. J., and Flores, A., Eds. *Ethical Problems in Engineering*. Vols. 1 and 2. Troy, NY: Center for the Study of the Human Dimensions of Science and Technology, Rensselaer Polytechnic Institute, 1978.

Baum, R. J. *Ethics and Engineering*. Hastings-on-Hudson, NY: The Hastings Center, 1980.

Baxter, W. F. People or Penguins: *The Case for Optimal Pollution*. New York: Columbia University Press, 1974.

Bayles, M. D. *Professional Ethics*. 2nd ed. Belmont CA: Wadsworth, 1989.

Bazelon, D. L. "Risk and Responsibility," *Science*, Vol. 205 (July 20) 1979, 277–280.

Beauchamp, T. L. *Case Studies in Business, Society and Ethics*. 2nd ed. Englewood Cliffs, NJ: Prentice Hall, 1989.

Bellah, R., et al. *Habits of the Heart: Individualism and Commitment in American Life*. New York: Harper and Row, 1985.

Belmont Report: Ethical Principles and Guidelines for Protection of Human Subjects of Biomedical and Behavioral Research. Publication No. OS 78-00f12. Washington, D.C.: DHEW, 1978.

Benham, L. "The Effects of Advertising on the Price of Eyeglasses," *The Journal of Law and Economics*, Vol. 15, 1972, 337–352.

Benjamin, M. *Splitting the Difference: Compromise in Ethics and Politics*. Lawrence: University Press of Kansas, 1990.

Black, B. "Evolving Legal Standards for the Admissibility of Scientific Evidence," *Science*, Vol. 239, 1987, 1510–1512.

Blackstone, W. T. "On Rights and Responsibilities Pertaining to Toxic Substances and Trade Secrecy," *The Southern Journal of Philosophy*, Vol. 16, 1978, 589–603.

Blinn, K. W. *Legal and Ethical Concepts in Engineering*. Englewood Cliffs, NJ: Prentice-Hall, 1989.

Board of Ethical Review, NSPE, Opinions of the Board of Ethical Review, Vols. I-VII. Arlington, VA: NSPE Publications, National Society of Professional Engineers. Various dates.

Boeyink, D. "Casuistry: A Case-Based Method for Journalists." *Journal of Mass Media Ethics*. Summer 1992, 107–120.

Bok, S. *Common Values*. Columbia, MO: University of Missouri Press, 1995.

Bok, S. *Lying: Moral Choice in Public and Private Life*. New York: Vintage Books, 1979.

Broad, W., and Wade, N. *Betrayers of the Truth*. New York: Simon & Schuster, 1982.

Buchanan, R. A. *The Engineers: A History of the Engineering Profession in Britain, 1750–1914*. London: Jessica Kingsley Publishers, 1989.

Cady, J. F. *Restricted Advertising and Competition: The Case of Retail Drugs*. Washington DC: American Enterprise Institute, 1976.

Callahan, D. and Bok, S. *Ethics Teaching in Higher Education*. New York: Plenum Press, 1980.

Callahan, J. C., Ed. *Ethical Issues in Professional Life*. New York: Oxford University Press, 1988.

Cameron, R., and Millard, A. J. *Technology Assessment: A Historical Approach*. Dubuque, IA: Center for the Study of Ethics in the Professions, Kendall/ Hunt, 1985.

Carson, T. L. "Bribery, Extortion, and the 'Foreign Corrupt practices Act,'" *Philosophy and Public Affairs*, Vol. 14, No. 1, 1985, 66–90.

Chalk, R., Frankel, M., and Chafer, S. B. *AAAS Professional Ethics Project: Professional Ethics Activities of the Scientific and Engineering Societies*. Washington DC: American Association for the Advancement of Science, 1980.

Childress, J. F. and Macquarrie, J., Eds. *The Westminster Dictionary of the Christian Church*. Philadelphia: The Westminster Press, 1986.

Cohen, R. M., and Witcover, J. *A Heartbeat Away: The Investigation and Resignation of Vice President Spiro T. Agnew*. New York: Viking Press, 1974.

Cranor, C. F. "The Problem of Joint Causes for Workplace Health Protections [1]," *IEEE Technology and Society Magazine* (September) 1986, 10–12.

Cranor, C. F. *Regulating Toxic Substances: A Philosophy of Science and the Law*. New York: Oxford University Press, 1993.

Curd, M., and May, L. *Professional Responsibility for Harmful Actions*. Dubuque, IA: Center for the Study of Ethics in the Professions, Kendall/ Hunt, 1984.

Davis, M. "Avoiding the Tragedy of Whistleblowing," *Business and Professional Ethics Journal*, Vol. 8, No. 4, 1989, 3–19.

Davis, M. "Conflict of Interest," *Business and Professional Ethics Journal*, (Summer) 1982, 17– 27.

Davis, M. "Explaining Wrongdoing," *Journal of Social Philosophy*, Vol. 20 (Spring-Fall) 1988, 74–90.

Davis, M. "Thinking Like an Engineer: The Place of a Code of Ethics in the Practice of a Profession," *Philosophy and Public Affairs*, Vol. 20, No. 2 (Spring) 1991, 150–167.

Davis, M. *Thinking Like an Engineer*. New York: Oxford University Press, 1998.

De George, R. T. "Ethical Responsibilities of Engineers in Large Organizations: The Pinto Case," *Business and Professional Ethics Journal*, Vol. 1, No. 1 (Fall) 1981.

Donaldson, T. and Dunfee, T. W. "Toward Unified conception of Business Ethics: Integrative Social Contract Theory," *Academy of Management Review*, Vol. 19, No. 2, 152–184.

Douglas, M., and Wildavsky, A. *Risk and Culture*. Berkeley and Los Angeles: University of California Press, 1982.

Eddy, E., Potter E., and Page, B. *Destination Disaster: From the Tri-Motor to the DC-10*. New York: Quadrangle Press, 1976.

Elbaz, S. W. *Professional Ethics and Engineering: A Resource Guide*. Arlington, VA: National Institute for Engineering Ethics, 1990.

Ethics Resource Center and Behavior Resource Center. *Ethics Policies and Programs in American Business*. Washington, DC.: The Ethics Resource Center, 1990.

Faden, R. R., and Beauchamp, T. L. *A History and Theory of Informed Consent*. New York: Oxford University Press, 1986.

Fadiman, J. A. "A Traveler's Guide to Gifts and Bribes." *Harvard Business Review*, (July-August) 1986, 122–126 and 130–136.

Feinberg, J. "Duties, Rights and Claims," *American Philosophical Quarterly*, Vol. 3, No. 2, 1966, 137–144.

Feliv, A. G. "The Role of the Law in Protecting Scientific and Technical Dissent," *IEEE Technology and Society Magazine* (June) 1985, 3–9.

Fielder, J. "Tough Break for Goodrich," *Journal of Business and Professional Ethics*, Vol. 19, No. 3, 1986.

Fielder, J. "Organizational Loyalty," *Business and Professional Ethics Journal*, Vol. 11, No. 1, 1991, 71–90.

Fielder, J., and Birsch, Douglass, Eds. *The DC 10*. New York: State of New York Press, 1992.

Firmage, D. A. *Modern Engineering Practice: Ethical, Professional and Legal Aspects*. New York: Garland STPM, 1980.

Flores, A., Ed. *Designing for Safety*. Troy, NY: Rensselaer Polytechnic Institute, 1982.

Flores, A. *Ethics and Risk Management in Engineering*. Boulder, CO: Westview Press, 1988.

Flores, A., Ed. *Professional Ideals*. Belmont, CA: Wadsworth, 1988.

Flores, A., and Johnson, D. G. "Collective Responsibility and Professional Roles," *Ethics*, Vol. 93 (April) 1983, 537–545.

Florman, S. C. "Moral Blueprints," *Harper's Magazine*, Vol. 257, No. 1541 (October) 1978, 30– 33.

Florman, S. C. *The Existential Pleasures of Engineering*. New York: St. Martin's Press, 1976.

Florman, S. C. *Blaming Technology: The Irrational Search for Scapegoats*. New York: St. Martin's Press, 1981.

Florman, S. C. *The Civilized Engineer*. New York: St. Martin's Press, 1987.

Flumerfelt, R. W., Harris, C. E., Jr., Rabins, M. J., and Samson, C. H., Jr. *Introducing Ethics Case Studies Into Required Undergraduate Engineering Courses*. Report on NSF Grant DIR- 9012252, November 1992.

Ford, D. F. *Three Mile Island: Thirty Minutes to Meltdown*. New York: Viking Press, 1982.

Frankel, M., Ed. *Science, Engineering, and Ethics: State of the Art and Future Directions*. Report of an American Association for the Advancement of Science Workshop and Symposium, February 1988, AAAS.

Fredrich, A. J. *Sons of Martha: Civil Engineering Readings in Modern Literature*. New York: American Society of Civil Engineers, 1989.

French, P. A. *Collective and Corporate Responsibility*. New York: Columbia University Press, 1984.

Friedman, M. "The Social Responsibility of Business Is to Increase Its Profits," *The New York Times Magazine* (September 13) 1970.

Garrett, T. M. et al. *Cases in Business Ethics*. New York: Appleton Century Crofts, 1968.

General Dynamics Corporation. *The General Dynamics Ethics Program Update*. St. Louis, MO: General Dynamics Corporation, 1988.

Gert, B. "Moral Theory, and Applied and Professional Ethics," *Professional Ethics*, Vol. 1, Nos. 1 and 2, (Spring/ Summer), 1992, 1–25.

Gert, B. *Morality*. New York: Oxford University Press, 1998.

Gewirth, A. *Reason and Morality*. Chicago: University of Chicago Press, 1978.

Glazer, M. "Ten Whistleblowers and How They Fared," *Hastings Center Report*, Vol. 13, No. 6, 1983, 33–41.

Glazer, M. *The Whistleblowers: Exposing Corruption in Government and Industry*. New York: Basic Books, 1989.

Glickman, T. S., and Gough, R. *Readings in Risk*. Washington, DC: Resources for the Future, 1990.

Goldman, A. H. *The Moral Foundations of Professional Ethics*. Totowa, NJ: Rowman and Littlefield, 1979.

Goodin, R. E. *Protecting the Vulnerable*. Chicago: University of Chicago Press, 1989.

Gorlin, R. A., Ed. *Codes of Professional Responsibility*. 2nd ed. Washington, DC: Bureau of National Affairs, 1990.

Graham, L. *The Ghost of an Executed Engineer*. Cambridge, MA: Harvard University Press, 1993.

Gray, M., and Rosen, I. *The Warning: Accident at Three Mile Island*. New York: W. W. Norton, 1982.

Greenwood, E. "Attributes of a Profession," *Social Work* (July) 1957, 45–55.

Gunn, A. S. and Vesilind, P. A. *Environmental Ethics for Engineers*. Chelsea, MI: Lewis Publishers, 1986.

Harris, C. E. *Applying Moral Theories*. 3rd ed. Belmont, CA: Wadsworth, 1997.

Harris, C. E. "Engineering Responsibilities in Lesser-Developed Nations: the Welfare Requirement," *Science and Engineering Ethics*, Vol. 4, No. 3, July 1998, 321–331.

Harris, C. E., Pritchard, M. S., and Rabins, M. J. *Practicing Engineering Ethics*. New York: Institute of Electrical and Electronic Engineers, 1997.

Heilbroner, Robert, Ed. *In the Name of Profit*. Garden City: Doubleday, 1972.

Hick, J. *Disputed Questions in Theology and the Philosophy of Religion*. New Haven, CT: Yale University Press, 1986.

Howard, J. L. "Currents Developments in Whistleblower Protection," *Labor Law Journal*, Vol. 39, No. 2 (February) 1988, 67–80.

Hunter, Thomas. "Engineers Face Risks as Expert Witnesses," *The Rochester Engineer* (December) 1992.

Hynes, H. P. "Women Working: A Field Report," *Technology Review* (November-December) 1984.

Jackall, R. "The Bureaucratic Ethos and Dissent," *IEEE Technology and Society Magazine* (June) 1985, 21–30.

Jackall, R. *Moral Mazes: The World of Corporate Managers*. New York: Oxford University Press, 1988.

Jackson, I. *Honor in Science*. New Haven, CT: Sigma Xi, 1986.

Jaksa, J. A., and Pritchard, M. S. *Communication Ethics: Methods of Analysis*. 2nd ed. Belmont, CA: Wadsworth, 1994.

James, G. G. "In Defense of Whistle Blowing." In W. Michael Hoffman and Jennifer Mills Moore,

Eds., *Business Ethics*. New York: McGraw-Hill, 1984.

Jamshidi, Mo, Shahinpoor, Mo, and Mullins, J. H., Eds. *Environmentally Conscious Manufacturing: Recent Advances*. Albuquerque, MN: ECM Press, 1991.

Janis, I. *Groupthink*. 2nd ed. Boston: Houghton Mifflin, 1982.

Johnson, D. G. *Ethical Issues in Engineering*. Englewood Cliffs, NJ: Prentice-Hall, 1991.

Johnson, D. G. *Computer Ethics*. 2nd ed. Englewood Cliffs, NJ: Prentice-Hall, 1993.

Johnson, D. G., and Snapper, J. W., Eds. *Ethical Issues in the Use of Computers*. Belmont, CA: Wadsworth, 1985.

Johnson, E. "Treating Dirt: Environmental Ethics and Moral Theory," In Tom Regan, *Earthbound: New Introductory Essays in Environmental Ethics*. New York: Random House, 1984.

Jonsen, A. L., and Toulmin, S. *The Abuse of Casuistry*. Berkeley, University of California Press, 1988.

Jurmu, J. L., and Pinodo, A. "The OSHA-Benzene Case." In T.L. Beauchamp, *Case Studies in Business, Society, and Ethics*. 2nd ed. Englewood Cliffs, NJ: Prentice-Hall, Inc. 1989, 203–211.

Kahn, S. "Economic Estimates of the Value of Life," *IEEE Technology and Society Magazine* (June) 1986, 24–31.

Kant, I. *Foundations of the Metaphysics of Morals, with Critical Essays*. Robert Paul Wolff, Ed., Indianapolis, IN: Bobbs-Merrill, 1969.

Kemper, J. D. *Engineers and Their Profession*. 3rd ed. New York: Holt, Rinehart & Winston, 1982.

Kettler, G. J. "Against the Industry Exemption." In James H. Shaub and Karl Pavlovic, Eds. *Engineering Professionalism and Ethics*. New York: Wiley-Interscience, 1983.

Kipnis, K. "Engineers Who Kill: Professional Ethics and the Paramountcy of Public Safety," *Business and Professional Ethics Journal*, Vol. 1, No. 1, 1981.

Kolhoff, M. J. "For the Industry Exemption..." In James H. Shaub and Karl Pavlovic, Eds. *Engineering Professionalism and Ethics*. New York: Wiley-Interscience, 1983.

Kultgen, J. "Evaluating Codes of Professional Ethics," In Wade L. Robison, Michael S. Pritchard, and Joseph Ellin, Eds. *Profits and Professions*. Clifton, NJ: Humana Press, 1983. 225–264.

Kultgen, J. *Ethics and Professionalism*. Philadelphia: The University of Pennsylvania Press, 1988.

Ladd, J. "Bhopal: An Essay on Moral Responsibility and Civic Virtue," *Journal of Social Philosophy*, Vol. XXII, No. 1 (Spring) 1991.

Ladd, J. "The Quest for a Code of Professional Ethics," In Rosemary Chalk, Mark S. Frankel, and Sollie B. Chafer, Eds. *AAAS Professional Ethics Project: Professional Ethics Activities of the Scientific and Engineering Societies*. Washington DC: American Association for the Advancement of Science, 1980.

Ladenson, R. F., Choromokos, J., d'Anjou, E., Pimsler, M., and Rosen, H. *A Selected Annotated Bibliography of Professional Ethics and Social Responsibility in Engineering*. Chicago: Center for the Study of Ethics in the Professions, Illinois Institute of Technology, 1980.

Ladenson, R. F. "The Social Responsibilities of Engineers and Scientists: A Philosophical Approach." In D. L. Babcock and C. A. Smith, Eds. *Values and the Public Works Professional*. Rolla: University of Missouri–Rolla, 1980.

Ladenson, R. F. "Freedom of Expression in the Corporate Workplace: A Philosophical Inquiry." In Wade L. Robison, Michael S. Pritchard, and Joseph Ellin, Eds. *Profits and Professions*. Clifton, NJ: Humana Press, 1983, 275–285.

Larson, M. S. *The Rise of Professionalism*. Berkeley, University of California Press, 1977.

Layton, E. T., Jr. *The Revolt of the Engineers: Social Responsibility and the American Engineering Profession*. Baltimore, MD: John Hopkins University Press, 1971, 1986.

Leopold, A. *A Sand County Almanac*. New York: Oxford University Press, 1966.

Lichtenberg, J. "What are Codes of Ethics for?" In M. Coady and S. Bloch, *Codes of Ethics and the Professions*. Melbourne, Australia: Melbourne University Press, 1995, 13–27.

Litai, D. "A Risk Comparison Methodology for the Assessment of Acceptable Risk." Ph.D. Dissertation, Massachusetts Institute of Technology, Cambridge, MA, 1980.

Lockhart, T. W. "Safety Engineering and the Value of Life," *Technology and Society (IEEE)*, Vol. 9 (March) 1981, 3–5.

Lowrance, W. W. *Of Acceptable Risk*. Los Altos, CA: William Kaufman, 1976.

Luebke, Neil R. "Conflict of Interest as a Moral Category," *Business and Professional Ethics Journal*, Vol. 6, No. 1, 1987, 66–81.

Luegenbiehl, H. C. "Codes of Ethics and the Moral Education of Engineers," *Business and Professional Ethics Journal*, Vol. 2, No. 4, 1983, 41–61.

Lunch, M. F. "Supreme Court Rules on Advertising for Professions," *Professional Engineer*, Vol. 1, No. 8 (August) 1977, 41–42.

MacIntyre, A. *A Short History of Ethics*. New York: Macmillan, 1966.

MacIntyre, A. "Regulation: A Substitute for Morality," *Hastings Center Report* (February) 1980, 31–41.

Magsdick, H. H. "Some Engineering Aspects of Headlighting," *Illuminating Engineering* (June) 1940, 533.

Malin, M. H. "Protecting the Whistleblower from Retaliatory Discharge," *Journal of Law Reform*, Vol. 16 (Winter) 1983, 277–318.

Mantell, M. I. *Ethics and Professionalism in Engineering*. New York: Macmillan, 1964.

Margolis, J. "Conflict of Interest and Conflicting Interests." In T. Beauchamp, and N. Bowie, Eds., *Ethical Theory and Business*, 1st ed. Englewood Cliffs, NJ: Prentice-Hall, 1979, 361–372.

Marshall, E. "Feynman Issues His Own Shuttle Report Attacking NASA Risk Estimates," *Science*, Vol. 232 (June 27) 1986, 1596.

Martin, D. *Three Mile Island: Prologue or Epilogue?* Cambridge, MA: Ballinger, 1980.

Martin, M. W. *Everyday Morals*. Belmont, CA: Wadsworth, 1989.

Martin, M. W., and Schinzinger, R. *Engineering Ethics*. 3rd ed. New York: McGraw-Hill 1996.

Martin, M. W. "Rights and the Meta-Ethics of Professional Morality," and "Professional and Ordinary Morality: A Reply to Freedom," *Ethics*, Vol. 91, July 1981, 619–625 and 631–622.

Martin, M. W. "Professional Autonomy and Employers' Authority." In A. Flores, *Ethical Problems in Engineering*. Vol. 1. Troy, NY: Rensselaer Polytechnic Institute, 1982, 177–181.

Martin, M. W. *Self-Deception and Morality*. Lawrence: University Press of Kansas, 1986.

Mason, J. F. "The Technical Blow-by-Blow: An Account of the Three Mile Island Accident," *IEEE Spectrum*, Vol. 16, No. 11 (November) 1979, 33–42.

May, W. F. "Professional Virtue and Self-Regulation." In J. L. Callahan, Ed., *Ethical Issues in Professional Life*. New York: Oxford, 1988, 408–411.

McCabe, D. "Classroom Cheating Among Natural Science and Engineering Majors." *Science and Engineering Ethics*, Vol. 3, No. 4, 1997, 433–445.

McIlwee, J. S., and Robinson, J. G. *Women in Engineering: Gender, Power, and Workplace Culture*. Albany: State University of New York Press, 1992.

Meese, G. P. E. "The Sealed Beam Case," *Business and Professional Ethics Journal*, Vol. 1, No. 3 (Spring) 1982, 1–20.

Milgram, S. *Obedience to Authority*. New York: Harper and Row, 1974.

Mill, J. S. *Utilitarianism, with Critical Essays*. Samuel Gorovitz, Ed. Indianapolis, IN: Bobbs-Merrill, 1971.

Mill, J. S. *Utilitarianism*. G. Sher, Ed. Indianapolis, IN: Hackett, 1979.

Millikan, R. A. "On the Elementary Electrical Charge and the Avogadro Constant," *Physical Review*, Vol. 2. 1913, 109–143.

Morgenstern, J. "The Fifty-Nine Story Crisis," *New Yorker Magazine*, May 29, 1995, 45–53.

Morrison, C., and Hughes, P. *Professional Engineering Practice: Ethical Aspects*. 2nd ed. Toronto, CA: McGraw-Hill Ryerson, 1988.

Murdough Center for Engineering Professionalism, *Independent Study and Research Program in Engineering Ethics and Professionalism*. Lubbock: College of Engineering, Texas Technological University, October, 1990.

Nader, R. "Responsibility and the Professional Society," *Professional Engineer*, Vol. 41, (May) 1971, 14–17.

Nader, R., Petkas, Peter J., Blackwell, Kate. *Whistle Blowing*. New York: Grossman, 1972.

National Academy of Science, Committee on the Conduct of Science. *On Being a Scientist*. Washington DC: National Academy Press, 1989.

Okrent, David, and Whipple, Chris. *An Approach to Societal Risk Assessment Criteria and Risk Management*. Report, UCLA-Eng-7746. Los Angeles, UCLA School of Engineering and Applied Sciences, 1977.

Oldenquist, A. "Commentary on Alpern's 'Moral Responsibility for Engineers,'" *Business and Professional Ethics Journal*, Vol. 2, No. 2 (Winter) 1983.

Otten, J. "Organizational Disobedience." In A. Flores, *Ethical Problems in Engineering*. Vol. 1, Troy, NY: Center for the Study of the Human Dimensions of Science and Technology, Rensselaer Polytechnic Institute, 1978, 182–186.

Peterson, J. C., and Farrell, D. *Whistleblowing: Ethical and Legal Issues in Expressing Dissent*. Dubuque, IA: Center for the Study of Ethics in the Professions, Kendall/ Hunt, 1986.

Petroski, H. *To Engineer is Human: The Role of Failure in Successful Design*. New York: St. Martin's, 1982.

Petroski, H. *Beyond Engineering: Essays and Other Attempts to Figure Without Equations.* New York: St. Martin's, 1985.

Philips, M. "Bribery," in Werhane, P. and D'Andrade, K., Eds. *Profit and Responsibility.* New York: Edwin Mellon Press, 1985, 197–220.

Pinkus, R. L. D, Shuman, L. J., Hummon, N. P., and Wolfe, H. *Engineering Ethics.* New York: Cambridge University Press, 1997.

Pletta, D. H. *The Engineering Profession: Its Heritage and Its Emerging Public Purpose.* Washington DC: University Press of America, 1984.

Pritchard, M. S. "Beyond Disaster Ethics," *The Centennial Review*, Vol. XXXIV, No. 2, (Spring) 1990, 295–318.

Pritchard, M. S. "Bribery: The Concept," *Science and Engineering Ethics*, Vol. 4, No. 3, 1998, 281–286.

Pritchard, M. S. "Good Works," *Professional Ethics*, Vol. 1, Nos. 1 and 2 (Spring/Summer) 1992, 155–177.

Pritchard, M. S. "Professional Responsibility: Focusing on the Exemplary." *Science and Engineering Ethics*, Vol. 4, No. 2, 1998, 215–233.

Pritchard, M. S. and Holtzapple, M. "Responsible Engineering: *Gilbane Gold* Revisited." *Science and Engineering Ethics*, Vol. 3, No. 2, April 1997, 217–231.

Pritchard, M. S., Ed. *Teaching Engineering Ethics: A Case Study Approach*, National Science Foundation, Grant No. DIR-8820837, June 1992.

Rachels, J. *The Elements of Moral Philosophy.* 3rd ed. New York: Random House, 1999.

Rabins, M. J. "Teaching Engineering Ethics to Undergraduates: Why? What? How?" *Science and Engineering Ethics*, Vol. 4, No. 3, July 1998, 291–301.

Raelin, J. A. *The Clash of Cultures: Managers and Professionals.* Boston: Harvard Business School Press, 1985.

Rawls, John. *A Theory of Justice.* Cambridge, MA: Harvard University Press, 1971.

Relman, A. "Lessons from the Darsee Affair," *The New England Journal of Medicine*, Vol. 308, 1983, 1415–1417.

Richardson, "Specifying Norms," *Philosophy and Public Affairs*, Vol. 19, No. 4, 1990, 279–310.

Ringleb, Al H., Meiners, Roger E., and Edwards, Frances L. *Managing in the Legal Environment.* St. Paul, MN: West, 1990.

Rogers Commission, "Report to the President by the Presidential Commission on the Space Shuttle Challenger Accident," Washington DC, June 6, 1986.

Ross, W. D. *The Right and the Good.* Oxford, England: Oxford University Press, 1988.

Ruckelshaus, William D. "Risk, Science, and Democracy," *Issues in Science and Technology*, Vol. 1, No. 3 (Spring) 1985, 19–38.

Sagoff, Mark. "Where Ickes Went Right or Reason and Rationality in Environmental Law," *Ecology Law Quarterly*, Vol. 14, 1987, 265–323.

Schaub, J. H., and Pavlovic, K. *Engineering Professionalism and Ethics.* New York: Wiley-Interscience, 1983.

Schlossberger, E. *The Ethical Engineer.* Philadelphia, PA: Temple University Press, 1993.

Schlossberger, E. "The Responsibility of Engineers, Appropriate Technology, and Lesser Developed Nations" *Science and Engineering Ethics*, Vol. 3, No. 3, July 1997, 317–325.

Schwing, R. C., and Albers, W. A., Jr., Eds. *Societal Risk Assessment: How Safe is Safe Enough?* New York: Plenum Press, 1980.

Schrader-Frechette, K. S. *Risk and Rationality.* Berkeley, University of California Press, 1991.

Science and Engineering Ethics, Special Issue on Ethics for Science and engineering Based International Industries. Vol. 4, No. 3, July 1998, 257–392.

Simon, Herbert A. *Administrative Behavior.* 3rd ed. New York: Free Press, 1976.

Singer, M. G. *Generalization in Ethics.* New York: Knopf, 1961.

Singer, M. G., Ed. *Morals and Values.* New York: Charles Scribner's Sons, 1977.

Singer, Peter. *Practical Ethics.* Cambridge, England: Cambridge University Press, 1979.

Slovic, Paul, Fischoff, Baruch, and Lichtenstein, Sarah. "Rating the Risks," *Environment*, Vol. 21, No. 3 (April) 1969, 14–39.

Solomon, R. C., and Hanson, K. R. *Above the Bottom Line: An Introduction to Business Ethics.* New York: Harcourt Brace Jovanovich, 1983.

Starry, Chauncey. "Social Benefits Versus Technological Risk," *Science*, Vol. 165 (September 19) 1969, 1232–1238.

Stone, Christopher. *Where the Law Ends.* Prospect Heights, IL: Waveland Press, 1991.

Strand, P.N. and Golden, K. C. "Consulting Scientist and Engineer Liability." *Science and Engineering Ethics*, Vol. 3, No. 4, October 1997, 347–394.

Taeusch, C. F. *Professional and Business Ethics.* New York: Henry Holt & Co., 1926.

Tavis, L. A. *Power and Responsibility: Multinational Managers and Developing Country*

Concerns. Notre Dame, IN: University of Notre Dame Press, 1997.

Taylor, P. W. *Principles of Ethics: An Introduction*. Encino, CA: Dickenson, 1975.

Taylor, P. W. "The Ethics of Respect for Nature," *Environmental Ethics*, Vol. 3, No. 3 (Fall) 1981, 197–218.

Toffler, A. *Tough Choices: Managers Talk Ethics*. New York: Wiley, 1986.

Unger, S. H. *Controlling Technology: Ethics and the Responsible Engineer*. 2nd ed. New York: Holt, Rinehart & Winston, 1994.

Unger, S. H. "Would Helping Ethical Professionals Get Professional Societies into Trouble?" *IEEE Technology and Society Magazine*, Vol. 6, No. 3 (September) 1987, 17–21.

Urmson, J. O. "Saints and Heroes." In A. I. Meldon, Ed. *Essays in Moral Philosophy*. Seattle: University of Washington Press, 1958.

Urmson, J. O. "Hare on Intuitive Moral Thinking." In S. Douglass and N. Fotion, Eds., *Hare and Critics*. Oxford: Clarendon Press: 1988.

Vandivier, R. "What? Me Be a Martyr?" *Harper's Magazine* (July) 1975, 36–44.

Vaughn, R. C. *Legal Aspects of Engineering*. Dubuque, IA: Kendall/Hunt, 1977.

Vaugn, D. *The Challenger Launch Decision*. Chicago: The University of Chicago Press, 1996.

Velasquez, M. "Why Corporations Are Not Responsible for Anything They Do," *Business and Professional Ethics Journal*, Vol. 2, No. 3 (Spring) 1983, 1–18.

Velasquez, M. *Business Ethics*. 3rd ed. Englewood Cliffs, NJ: Prentice-Hall, 1992.

Vesilind, P. A. "Environmental Ethics and Civil Engineering," *The Environmental Professional*, Vol. 9, 1987, 336–342.

Vesilind, P. A. and Gunn, A. *Engineering, Ethics, and the Environment*. New York: Cambridge University Press, 1998.

Vogel, D. A. "A Survey of Ethical and Legal Issues in Engineering Curricula in the United States," Stanford Law School, Winter 1991.

Wall Street Journal, "Executives Apply Stiffer Standards Than Public to Ethical Dilemmas," (November 3) 1983.

Weil, V., Ed. *Beyond Whistleblowing: Defining Engineers Responsibilities*. Proceedings of the 2nd National Conference on Ethics in Engineering, March 1982.

Weil, Vivian, Ed. *Moral Issues in Engineering: Selected Readings*. Chicago: Illinois Institute of Technology, 1988.

Weisskoph, Michael. "The Aberdeen Mess," *The Washington Post Magazine*, (January 15) 1989.

Wells, P., Jones, H., and Davis, M. *Conflicts of Interest in Engineering*. Dubuque, IA: Center for the Study of Ethics in the Professions, Kendall/Hunt, 1986.

Westin, A. F. *Individual Rights in the Corporation: A Reader on Employee Rights*. New York: Random House, 1980.

Westin, A. F. *Whistle Blowing: Loyalty and Dissent in the Corporation*. New York: McGraw-Hill, 1981.

Whitbeck, C. *Ethics in Engineering Practice and Research*. New York: Cambridge University Press, 1998.

Whitbeck, Caroline. "The Trouble with Dilemmas: Rethinking Applied Ethics," *Professional Ethics*, Vol. 1, Nos. 1 and 2, (Spring/Summer) 1992, 119–142.

Williams, B., and Smart, J. J. C. *Utilitarianism: For and Against*. New York: Cambridge University Press, 1973.

Wills, Jocelyn. "Goodrich Revisited," *Journal of Business and Professional Ethics*, forthcoming.

Videotapes for Use in Engineering Ethics

Name/Subject	Source/Address/Telephone	Cost
"The Aberdeen Three Case" *A tape of the seminar presentation by the U.S. Justice Department lawyer who successfully prosecuted the three U.S. Army civilian employees developing chemical weaponry who violated the U.S. Resource Conservation & Recovery Act by dumping toxic wastes illegally. Approx. 40 min.*	Dr. Michael J. Rabins Texas A&M University Mechanical Engineering Department College Station, TX 77843-3123 (409) 845-2615	approx. $17.75
"Bridge to Academic Integrity" *Four 5-minute tapes based on four different academic integrity violations on the campus. Written & acted by students and faculty at Duke University. Covers cheating on exams, plagiarizing, falsifying lab data, etc. Excellent triggers for classroom discussions. Instructors guidelines provided.*	Program in Science Technology and Human Values School of Engineering Duke University PO Box 90287 Durham, NC 27708 (919) 660-5204	$50 (including shipping)

Name/Subject	Source/Address/Telephone	Cost
"The 59 Story Crisis: A Lesson in Professional Behavior" *A vivid description of the original mistake made in designing the NYC Citicorp Building Structural support, and the dramatic race against time to prevent a hurricane-caused disaster. A positive case with a happy ending due to the good work of the building engineer, LeMessurer. Approx. 20 min.*	World Wide Web Ethics Center for Engineering and Science wwwethics@po.cwru.edu (216) 368-0528 fax (216) 368-2216 (Attn: Jude)	$50.00 (plus $4.00 shipping and handling)
"Gilbane Gold" *A fictionalized account of one engineer's struggle to do the right thing about his company's dumping of toxic waste. Loosely based on several real-world cases. Covers such issues as falsifying reports, whistle-blowing, professional responsibility and engineering vs. management decision-making roles. Approx. 35 min.*	NSPE PO Box 1020 Sewickley, PA 15143 (703) 684-2882 (800) 417-0348	$65 + $7 (shipping & handling) for an institution; $95 + $7 (shipping & handling) for an individual
"The Story Behind the Space Shuttle *Challenger* Disaster" *This powerful instructional unit provides users with a full overview of the* Challenger *disaster, and reveals how it resulted from dynamic processes typical of most organizations. It can be customized for advanced high school students plus undergraduate and graduate courses plus leadership training and development.*	Dr. Mark Maier Founding Chair Organization Leadership Program 333 N. Glassell St. Orange, CA 92866 (714) 744-0943 fax (714) 744-3889	schools—$395 plus $25 shipping & handling corporations—$700 plus $25 shipping & handling

Name/Subject	Source/Address/Telephone	Cost
"To Engineer Is Human" *An excellent presentation loosely based on the book of the same title by Prof. Henry Petroski. Gives numerous graphical examples of how engineers learn to deal better with risk by carefully studying previous failures. Approx. 55 min.*	Films, Inc. Video Education Department 5547 N. Ravenswood Ave. Chicago, IL 60640-1199 (800) 323-4222 ext. 323	$149—product # 825758
"The Lost American" *A PBS Frontline exploration of the career of engineer Frederick C. Cuny. Cuny's 25 years of humanitarian relief work around the world is documented, right up to his apparent execution in Chechyna in 1995. A complete transcript of this video (plus many other things written about Cuny) is available at http://www.pbs.org/wgbh/pages/ frontline/shows/cuny/reports/trans form.html Approx. 60 min.*	PBS Video P.O. Box 791 Alexandria, VA 22313-0791 (800) 328-7271	Cost unknown
"Moral Development" *A simulation of the famous Milgram experiments on obedience, in which volunteers are led to believe that they are administering shocks to other volunteers in a learning and punishment experiment. Lawrence Kohlberg's theory of moral development is used to characterize the different kinds of responses volunteers have to instructions to administer shocks. Approx. 30 min.*	CRM Educational Films McGraw-Hill Films 1221 Avenue of the Americas New York, NY 10020 (800) 421-0833	Cost unknown

Name/Subject	Source/Address/Telephone	Cost
"Truesteel Affair" *A fictionalized version of the circumstances similar to those surrounding the Hyatt-Regency walkway collapse. Approx. 30 min.*	Fanlight Productions 47 Halifax St. Boston, MA 02130 (617) 524-0980	$195 + $9 shipping & handling
"Groupthink" *A dramatization of social psychologist Irving Janis's well known theory of "groupthink," featuring the Challenger disaster as a case study. Janis characterizes "groupthink" as a set of tendencies of cohesive groups to achieve consensus at the expense of critical thinking. Approx. 30 min.*	CRM films McGraw-Hill Films 1221 Avenue of the Americas New York, NY 10020 (800) 421-0833	Cost unknown
"Testing Water . . . and Ethics" *A young engineer facing his first professional dilemma attempts to solve the problem by treating it as analogous to a design problem in engineering. Approx. 30 min.*	Institute for Professional Practice 13 Lanning Road Verona, NJ 07044-2511 (888) 477-2723 email: Bridge2PE@aol.com	$150

Index

A

AAAS (American Association for the Advancement of Science), 268
AAEE (American Academy of Environmental Engineers), 271
AAES (American Association of Engineering Societies), 271
AAUP (American Association of University Professors), 270
ABA (American Bar Association), 270–271
Model Rules of Professional Conduct, 133
Aberdeen Proving Ground, 206
ABET (Accreditation Board for Engineering and Technology), 18–19, 53, 274
Acknowledging mistakes, 289–294, 310–311, 325–326, 333–335, 346, 350–351, 352–355
Affirmative action, 42–44
Aftermath of Chernobyl, 287
AIA (American Institute of Architects), 267–268
AIChE (American Institute of Chemical Engineers), 271
code of ethics, 242, 278
Air Bags, 287–288
AMA (American Medical Association) code of ethics, 229, 270–271
Animal liberation, 222–223
Animal rights, 221–222
Applegate, Dan, 136
Asbestosis, 163–164
ASCE (American Society of Civil Engineers), 271
Code of Ethics, 122, 207–211, 230, 240, 243
ASCM (American Congress on Surveying and Mapping), 272
ASHRAE (American Society of Heating, Refrigerating and Air-Conditioning Engineers, Inc.), 272

ASME, (American Society of Mechanical Engineers), 271
boiler and pressure vessel codes, 151–152
code of ethics, 208–210, 230
Aswan High Dam (Egypt), 81
Atomic Energy Act, 1954, 167
Auditory Visual Tracker (AVIT), 288–289

B

Bates v. State Bar of Arizona. See U.S. Supreme Court decisions
Baxter, William, 222
Belmont Report guidelines, 35–37
Benzene, 30–31, 41–42, 44, 46–47, 167
Biomedical research
human subjects, 35–37, 60–61, 93–94
Black, Bert, 165
Boisjoly, Roger, 5–6, 49, 72, 188, 268
Borel, Clarence, case, 163–164
Borrowed Tools, 289
Bribery, 50–52, 66, 241–242, 245, 256–257, 262. *See also* Extortion
Byssinosis, 160–161

C

Cadillac Chips, 289–290
Carcinogens, 162–168, 206–207, 210, 220–221
Case analysis, 22–26, 37–41. *See also* Paradigm cases
Forklifter, The, 24–26
Catalyst, 290–294
Challenger case, 4–6, 7, 72–73, 122–123, 137, 146, 153–154, 177, 180–181, 184, 188–202
Chemical additives, 166–167
Chemical weapon disposal, 206
Chernobyl, 287

Chevrolet Corvair, 137

Child labor, 233

Citicorp building, 3–4, 7, 109

Clean Air Act, 215, 289–290

Clothing industry, 233

CMA (Chemical Manufacturers Association), 213

Competence, 290–297, 302–303, 332–335, 340–342, 345–347, 350–351

Computerized police dispatching systems, 175–176

Confidential information, 121, 132–134, 177, 143

Confidentiality, 321–322, 325–330,

Conflict resolution. *See* Moral problems, resolution

Conflicts of interest, 137–143, 241–242, 318–323, 353–354

Conscientious Employee Protection Act, 179

Containers, 294–295

Convair, 136

"Cooking," 126

The Co-op Student, 295–297

Cost-Cutting, 297

Cranor, Carl, 217–218

Creative middle way techniques, 60–73, 75–76, 93–94

Crime and corruption problems, 238

CU (Consumers Union), 270

Cultural differences
   women's roles, 237, 242–243, 246

Cultural values and practices, 236–237
   women's roles, 237, 242–243, 246

D

Darsee, John, 126

Davis, Michael, 111, 138, 241

The Deadline, 297–298

Dee, William, 206–207

DeGeorge, Richard, 197–199, 237

Delaney Amendment, 167

Differing professional opinions (DPOs), 201–203

Disaster Relief, 303–306

Dishonesty, 121–123, 125–128. *See also* Honesty

Disobedience. *See* Organizational disobedience

To Dissent or Not to Dissent , 298–302

Drinking in the Workplace, 302–303

E

Economic conditions
   differing national standards, 233–234, 237

ECPD (Engineers' Council for Professional Development). *See* ABET

Edgerton, Patricia, case, 175–178

"Employment at will" doctrine, 178

Employment Opportunity, 306–309

Engineering codes, 14–16, 122, 147–148, 168–169, 202, 221, 224–231
   employer-employee guidelines, 176–178
   environmental provisions, 211–212
   international applications, 239–240, 242–259, 262. *See also* Ethical and professional standards; Professional engineering societies by name

Engineering disaster relief, 6–7

Engineering employment, 277–279

Engineering environmental obligations, 225–231

Engineering licenses,
   improper use, 265

Engineering profession
   gender and minority issues, 242, 277–279. *See also* Minority issues; Women engineers; Women's roles

Engineering profession
   reputation, 243

Engineering professional ethics
   enforcement, 265–270, 278
   ethical conduct awards, 268
   ethics "helplines," 269
   promotion of ethics, 268–277
   support for ethical engineers, 269

Engineering professional societies, 266–272. *See also* Engineering Professional ethics; Professional societies by name

Engineering professionalism
   international issues, 233–262

Engineering registration and licensure, 234–235, 272–279, 345–346. *See also* Engineering licenses, improper use
   universal engineering licensure, 275–277, 279
   Washington Accord, 234–235

Engineering/management decisions
   paradigmatic engineering/management decisions, 183–188, 191
   proper engineering decisions (PED), 184–190
   proper management decisions (MD), 184–190

Engineers
   competition and pricing, 53–55, 66–67, 78
   degree of personal responsibility, 245–246
   personal beliefs and professional responsibilities, 227–231

Engineers and the environment
  engineering codes, environmental provisions,
    211–212
  responsibility for the environment, 208–210
Engineers as employees, 175–203
  legal aspects, 178–180
  manager/engineer relationships, 180–188
  professional standards, 175–178, 182–185
  public-policy exception, 178–179
Engineers in private practice, 53–55
Environment
  government regulation, 212–213, 215–219
  intrinsic value, 210–212
Environmental controversies, 210–213, 230–231
Environmental court decisions, 217–219
Environmental ethics
  anthropocentric approach, 221–222
Environmental issues, 206–231, 242, 287, 294–295,
    298–302, 306–309, 313–315, 323–330, 335, 342,
    345–346, 348–349, 354–355. *See also*
    Environmental pollution; Public safety;
    Utilitarianism
Environmental management policies, 212–213
Environmental movement, 223–225
  differing ethical positions, 221–227
Environmental pollution, 66, 70–72, 78–81. *See also*
    Environmental issues; EPA; Exxon *Valdez* oil
    spill; Oil Pollution Act; Pollution Prevention
    Act; Safety and health; Solid waste management
Environmental standards, 213–221
EPA (Environmental Protection Agency), 137, 155,
    158, 161–163
Ethical and professional standards
  international application, 234–237
Ethics
  preventive, 17–22
  professional. *See* Professional employees, ethics
Ethics hotlines, 201, 203
Ethics offices, 201, 203
An Excess?, 309–310
Expert testimony, 134–135
Exploitation, 250–251
  paradigm cases, 250–253
Extortion, 257–258, 263. *See also* Bribery
Exxon *Valdez* oil spill, 216. *See also* Environmental
    pollution

F
Factual issues, 41–45

Failure, 310
Failure modes. *See* Risk, assessment of
Fault-tree analysis, 148–150. *See also* Risk
Faulty Valves, 310–311
FEANI (*Federation European d'Associations
    Nationales d'Ingenieurs*), 234
Federal Insecticide, Fungicide and Rodenticide
    Act, 216–217
Ferebee, Richard, 165
Fire Detectors, 311–312
Fischhoff, Baruch, 157
Forced-Sex Accusation, 312–313
Ford Pinto case, 136–137, 330–331
Foreign Corrupt Practices Act, 245
Forgery, 126–127, 265
Friedman, Milton, 212

G
Gepp, Carl, 206–207
Gewirth, Alan, 91, 248–250
Ghost of an Executed Engineer, 313
Gift-giving, 139–142, 237, 259, 263. *See also*
    Conflicts of interest
Gilbane Gold, 69–72, 313–315
Glass Ceiling, 315–316
Golden rule, 85–88, 253–256, 261
Golfing, 316–317
Good works, 104–107, 287–289, 303–306. *See also*
    Responsibility
Goodin, Robert E., 250–251
Goodrich A-7 brake case, 126–127
Grease payments, 258–259, 263
Gulf Oil Co., 258

H
Harm. *See also* Responsibility; Risk
  avoidable harm, 253–254, 261
  intentional harm, 100, 253–254, 261
  minimalist view, 101–104
  negligently causing harm, 100
  reasonable care, 103–104
  recklessly causing harm, 100
Health. *See* Safety and health
Highway Safety Improvements, 317–318
Hitachi report, 182–183, 202
Honesty, 38–41, 117–132, 142–143, 289–290, 298,
    310–311, 316–317, 321–330, 331–332, 345–347,
    352–355. *See also* Withholding information
Honesty on campus, 123–125, 143

Host country citizens
    overall well-being, 254, 261–262
Host-country norms
    respect for, 254–256
Human rights, 246–250
    history, 248–250
    internationalization, 246–248
Hunter, Thomas A., 134
Hydrolevel, 318–321

I

IEEE (Institute of Electrical and Electronic
    Engineers), 168, 268–269, 271, 278
    code of ethics, 122, 147, 208–211, 230, 239,
        242–243
    CSIT (Committee on the Social Implications of
        Technology), 175–176
Industrialized countries (IC) and less industrial-
    ized countries (LIC), 235–239
    safety and health, 237–238, 245
Informed consent, 122–123, 147, 158–160, 169
Innocent Comment?, 321
Inside Tool and Die, 321–322
Integrity, 125–137, 143
Intellectual property, 128–132. *See also*
    Confidential information

J

Jackall, Robert, 181, 183

K

King, Martin Luther, Jr., 65

L

Last Resort, 322–323
Lawson, Searle, 127
Layton, Edwin T., Jr., 270
LeMessurier, William, 3–4, 109
Lentz, Robert, 206–207
Leopold, Aldo, 223
Liability. *See* Risk and liability
Lichtenstein, Sarah, 157
Lindauer, David, 233
Line-drawing, 51, 59–64, 73, 75–76, 131–132,
    134, 140–142. *See also* Moral problems,
    resolution
Litai, D., 158
Lockheed Corporation, 258
Lowrance, William W., 154–155

Loyalty to the organization, 290–295, 298–303,
    316–317, 325–326, 333–335, 340–342, 344–345,
    349–350
    critical, 192–194, 202
    uncritical, 191–194, 202
Lund, Robert, 5, 72, 180–181, 188–191
Lying, 119–121, 289–290. *See also* Truth;
    Withholding information

M

Mardirosian, 267–268
Martin Marietta, 201–202
Mason, Jerald, 5, 72, 188–190
McAuliffe, Christa, 6
McDonnell Douglas DC-10, 136–137
Mercury-Containing and Rechargeable Battery
    Management Act, 216–217
Mere "Technicality"?, 323–324
Microwaves, 324–325
Milgram, Stanley, 111–112
Mill, John Stuart, 77
Millikan, Robert A., 126
Minnesota Mining and Manufacturing Company
    (3M), 213
Minority issues. *See* Engineering profession,
    gender and minority issues
Moral absolutism, 244–245
Moral Beliefs in the Workplace, 325
Moral Concepts, 36–37, 45–52, 177
    international context, 244–246, 262
Moral justification, 35–37
Moral laxism, 246
Moral problems,
    resolution, 31–32, 52–56, 59–73, 78–84. *See also*
        Creative middle way techniques
Moral relativism, 244–245
Morality,
    common, 13–14, 22–34
    respect for persons, 36–37, 76, 84–92, 159–161
    role, 9–11
Morgan, Granger, 159
Morton Thiokol, 4–6, 153, 177, 180–181,
    188–191
Multiple authorship issues, 128

N

NASA (National Aeronautics and Space
    Administration), 4–6, 72–73, 122–123, 146,
    153–154, 188–191

National Commission for the Protection of Human Subjects of Biomedical and Behavioral Research, 35–37, 60–61. *See also* Biomedical research

National Environmental Policy Act, 215

NCEES (National Council of Examiners for Engineering and Surveying), 8

Model Rules of Professional Conduct, 130, 136, 138, 273–275

Nepotism, 236–237

New York Telephone Company explosion, 151–153

Nickel, James, 248, 260

No Difference Argument (NDA), 259–260

Noncitizen status, 238–239

Nondescrimination, 242–243

Noonan, John T., 257

NRC (Nuclear Regulatory Commission), 201–202

NSPE (National Society of Professional Engineers), 8, 10–11, 54, 60, 271

BER (NSPE Board of Ethical Review), 16–17, 39–41, 105

code of ethics, 130, 132–133, 136, 138, 147, 176–178, 191, 225–226, 239–241, 243

O

Oil Pollution Act, 216–217. *See also* Environmental pollution

Oil Spill?, 325–326

Ombudsmen, 201, 203

Organizational communication, 289–295, 302–303, 309–310, 313–316, 318–322, 326–330, 333–342, 346–349

Organizational disobedience, 193–203, 227–231

by contrary action, 194–196

by nonparticipation, 196–197

by protest, 197–199

O-rings, 5–6, 122–123, 153–154, 177, 188–191

OSHA (Occupational Safety and Health Administration), 30–32, 41–42, 76, 145, 158, 167, 215

P

Paradigm cases, 50, 61–64. *See also* Case analysis; Engineering/Management decisions; Exploitation, paradigm cases

Parkville, 326–330

Paternalism, 240–241, 250–253, 255, 260

PE (professional engineer). *See* Engineering registration and licensure

PE licenses, 179

Perrow, Charles, 150–151

Phillips Petroleum, 192

Pinto, 330–331. *See also* Ford Pinto case

Plagiarism, 128

Pollution Prevention Act, 216. *See also* Environmental pollution

Pollution. *See* Environmental pollution

Price is Right?, 331–332

Problem analysis, 30–56

Product liability, 290–290, 294–295, 310–312, 330–333, 335–339, 342–344, 346–347, 354–355

Professional employees

ethics, 8–9, 13, 306–309

rights, 178–180, 199–202

Professional judgment, 121, 138–139

Professional opinions

differences, 201–203

Professional virtue, 107–108, 287–289, 303–306, 313, 325, 335, 342, 351–352. *See also* Good works

Professionalism, 11–13, 313, 315–317, 321, 325, 333–335, 340–342, 351–352. *See also* Engineering codes

autonomy, 13

obligations, 132–134

self-regulation, 13

workplace behavior, 302–303

Promotion, 332

Proprietary information, 59–63, 121

Public safety, 133, 135–137, 206–213, 218–221. *See also* Environmental issues

Public service, 287–289, 303–306, 322–323, 325–330, 335, 351–352.

Public welfare, 254

Pulverizer, 332–333

Q

Quality control, 294–295, 297–303, 310–311, 324–325, 330–332, 346, 349–350, 352–354

R

Raelin, Joseph, 180

RCRA (Resource Conservation and Recovery Act), 206–207

Recommendation for a Friend, 333–335

Renewable Energy, 335

Residential Lead-Based Paint Hazard Reduction Act, 216–217

Respect for persons morality. *See* Morality, respect for persons

Responsibility
legal and moral, 99–114. *See also* Good works; Professional virtue; Vulnerable populations, professional responsibilities toward

Responsibility for others' actions, 287, 289–291, 294–295, 303–306, 317–318, 324–325, 353–354.

Responsibility impediments
egocentric tendencies, 110
fear, 109
groupthink, 112–113
ignorance, 110
microscopic vision, 110–111
self-deception, 109–110
self-interest, 108–109
uncritical acceptance of authority, 111–112

Rights. *See also* Animal rights; Human rights; Professional employees, rights; UN human rights documents
hierarchy of rights, 91–92
individual rights and duties, 89–92

Risk. *See also* Harm; Informed consent; Responsibility
acceptable, 145–146, 153–161, 166–169
assessment of, 148–156
compensation for, 155–161, 163–169
complex interactions, 150–153, 169
engineering codes, 147–148
experts' assessment, 154–159
government regulation, 161–163
laypersons' perception, 157–161
normalizing deviance, 153–154

Risk and engineers' liability, 146, 163–168

Risk and tort law, 146, 163–166, 169

Risk of accidents, 146–148, 150–154, 165–166

Risk to health, 145, 154–169

Roderick, David, 212

Rubanick v. Witco Chemical Corp. and Monsanto Co., 164–165

Ruckelshaus, William, 161–162

S

SAE (Society of Automotive Engineers), 272

Safe Drinking Water Act, 216–217

Safety
factors of, 147–148
importance to engineers, 147–148

Safety and health, 11, 46–50, 67–69, 177, 180, 218–221, 225, 237–241, 245, 251–252, 262, 287, 289–290, 294–295, 297–306, 309–311, 313–315, 318–326, 330–333, 335–344, 346–352, 354–355. *See also* Benzine; Industrialized countries (IC) and less industrialized countries (LIC); OSHA; Solid waste management

Safety in the workplace, 145–146

Sagoff, Mark, 218

Side-Saddle Gas Tanks, 335–339

Simon, Herbert, 192

Singer, Peter, 222–223

Slovic, Paul, 157

"Smoking System," 339–340

Solid waste management, 75–76

South Korea
Democratic Republican Party, 258

Starr, Chauncey, 157–158

Sunnyvale, 340–342

"Superfund." *See* TOSCA

Sustainable development, 208–211

Sweatshop conditions, 233–234, 259–262

T

Taylor, Paul, 223

TOSCA (Toxic Substances Control Act, 1976), 167, 216–217

Toxic waste, 206–207. *See also* Carcinogens; Solid waste management; TOSCA

Training Firefighters, 342

Trees, 342–343

Trench boxes, 165–166

"Trimming," 125

Truth, 117–119. *See also* Honesty; Withholding information

TV Antenna, 343–344

U

U.S. Steel, 212

U.S. Supreme Court decisions
Bates v. State Bar of Arizona, 53–54
Goldfarb v. Virginia State Bar, 54

UN human rights documents, 247–248, 260

"Underground" Project, 344–345

Unger, Stephen, 229–230, 269–270

Universalizability principle, 37, 39, 85–89

Unlicensed Engineer, 345–346
USAWAY, 346
Utilitarianism, 76–84, 142–143, 159, 161
　act utilitarian approach, 81–82
　cost/benefit analysis, 79–81, 155–156, 167,
　　219–221
　environmental issues, 219–223, 242
　rule utilitarian approach, 82–84

V

Vacation, 346–347
Vandivier, Kermit, 127, 191
Vaughn, Diane, 153–154
Vulnerable populations
　professional responsibilities toward, 238–241,
　　243–244

W

Walkway Disaster, 347–348
Waste Disposal, 348–349
Whistle-blower laws, 179–180
Whistle-blowing, 109, 192, 197–199, 202–203,
　290–294, 298–302, 309–310, 312–315, 322–323,
　325–331, 335–339, 349–352

Whose Property?, 349–350
Why Won't They Read?, 350–351
Wilson, Joe, 182
Window Safety, 351–352
Withholding information, 117, 119–120, 135–137,
　142. *See also* Truth; Lying
Women engineers
　discrimination, 242, 315–317, 321, 332–335,
　　340–342 *See also* Cultural differences, women's
　　roles; Engineering profession, gender and
　　minority issues; Women's roles
Women engineers, sexual harassment, 312–313
Women's roles
　cultural differences, 237, 242–243, 246
Wonderful Development?, 352–353
Workers' rights, 233
Working Overtime, 353–354

X

XYZ Hose Co., 354–355